MEDICAL MALPRACTICE
LAW AND LITIGATION

WEST LEGAL STUDIES

Options.
Over 300 products in every area of the law: textbooks, CD-ROMs, reference books, test banks, online companions, and more – helping you succeed in the classroom and on the job.

Support.
We offer unparalleled, practical support: robust instructor and student supplements to ensure the best learning experience, custom publishing to meet your unique needs, and other benefits such as West's Student Achievement Award. And our sales representatives are always ready to provide you with dependable service.

Feedback.
As always, we want to hear from you! Your feedback is our best resource for improving the quality of our products. Contact your sales representative or write us at the address below if you have any comments about our materials or if you have a product proposal.

Accounting and Financials for the Law Office • Administrative Law • Alternative Dispute Resolution • Bankruptcy • Business Organizations/Corporations • Careers and Employment Civil Litigation and Procedure • CLA Exam Preparation • Computer Applications in the Law Office • Contract Law • Court Reporting • Criminal Law and Procedure • Document Preparation • Elder Law • Employment Law • Environmental Law • Ethics • Evidence Law • Family Law • Intellectual Property • Interviewing and Investigation • Introduction to Law Introduction to Paralegalism • Law Office Management Law Office Procedures Legal Nurse Consulting • Legal Research, Writing, and Analysis • Legal Terminology • Paralegal Internship • Product Liability • Real Estate Law • Reference Materials • Social Security Sports Law • Torts and Personal Injury Law • Wills, Trusts, and Estate Administration

---

West Legal Studies
5 Maxwell Drive
Clifton Park, New York 12065-2919

For additional information, find us online at:
www.westlegalstudies.com

THOMSON
DELMAR LEARNING

MEDICAL MALPRACTICE
LAW AND LITIGATION

Beth Walston-Dunham

THOMSON
DELMAR LEARNING

Australia Canada Mexico Singapore Spain United Kingdom United States

WEST LEGAL STUDIES

MEDICAL MALPRACTICE LAW AND LITIGATION
Beth Walston-Dunham

Career Education Strategic Business Unit:
Vice President:
Dawn Gerrain

Director of Editorial:
Sherry Gomoll

Editor:
Shelley Esposito

Editorial Assistant:
Brian Banks

Director of Production:
Wendy A. Troeger

Production Editor:
Betty L. Dickson

Technology Project Manager:
Sandy Charette

Director of Marketing:
Wendy Mapstone

Marketing Specialist:
Gerard McAvey

Cover Design:
Dutton and Sherman

COPYRIGHT © 2006 Thomson Delmar Learning, a part of the Thomson Corporation. Thomson, the Star Logo, and Delmar Learning are trademarks used herein under license.

Printed in the United States
1 2 3 4 5 XXX 08 07 06 05

For more information contact Delmar Learning, 5 Maxwell Drive, P.O. Box 8007, Clifton Park, New York 12065.

Or find us on the World Wide Web at http://www.westlegalstudies.com

ALL RIGHTS RESERVED. No part of this work covered by the copyright hereon may be reproduced or used in any form or by any means—graphic, electronic, or mechanical, including photocopying, recording, taping, Web distribution or information storage and retrieval systems—without written permission of the publisher.

For permission to use material from this text or product, contact us by
Tel   (800) 730-2214
Fax (800) 730-2215
www.thomsonrights.com

Library of Congress Cataloging-in-Publication Data

Walston-Dunham, Beth.
  Medical malpractice law and litigation / Beth Walston-Dunham.
    p. cm. -- (West Legal Studies)
  Includes index.
  ISBN 1-4018-5246-7 (pbk. : alk. paper)
  1. Physicians--Malpractice--United States. I. Title. II. Series.

KF2905.3.Z9W35 2006
344.7304'11--dc22
                                    2005041901

NOTICE TO THE READER

Publisher does not warrant or guarantee any of the products described herein or perform any independent analysis in connection with any of the product information contained herein. Publisher does not assume, and expressly disclaims, any obligation to obtain and include information other than that provided to it by the manufacturer.

The reader is notified that this text is an educational tool, not a practice book. Since the law is in constant change, no rule or statement of law in this book should be relied upon for any service to any client. The reader should always refer to standard legal sources for the current rule or law. If legal advice or other expert assistance is required, the services of the appropriate professional should be sought.

The Publisher makes no representation or warranties of any kind, including but not limited to, the warranties of fitness for particular purpose or merchantability, nor are any such representations implied with respect to the material set forth herein, and the publisher takes no responsibility with respect to such material. The publisher shall not be liable for any special, consequential, or exemplary damages resulting, in whole or part, from the readers' use of, or reliance upon, this material.

DEDICATION
For my boys Bobby, Sam & Ben

CONTENTS

Table of Cases ... xii

Preface ... xiii

Acknowledgments ... xiv

PART 1: ISSUES IN THE DEVELOPMENT OF THE LAW OF MEDICAL MALPRACTICE

Chapter 1: A Brief History of Civil Liability for Professional Malfeasance

Development of the Law of Negligence in the United States ... 2
    Negligence as a Concept ... 3
    Elements of Negligence ... 3
The Use of Res Ipsa Loquitur ... 9
Respondeat Superior in Cases of Negligence ... 11
Intentional Torts in Cases of Medical Malpractice ... 25
    Abandonment ... 28
    Assault ... 29
    Battery ... 29
    Miscellaneous Torts ... 30
Strict Liability ... 32
Contractual Liability ... 37
Chapter Summary ... 38

Chapter 2: The Development of Medical Malpractice Law

Early Cases	40
Refinement of Theories and Principles	51
The Legislative Movement	55
Licensure and Certification of Providers and Facilities	59
Chapter Summary	61

Chapter 3: Medical Malpractice Law and Litigation

Injuries Resulting Directly from Care/Treatment/Services	63
Injuries Resulting from Violation of Ethical Duties	64
Injuries Resulting from Professional Misconduct Which Is Also Criminal	79
Cases Against Physicians	84
Cases Involving Non-Physician Medical Professionals	93
Cases Involving Independent Pharmacists, Dentists, Chiropractors, Psychologists, and Optometrists and Other Independent Non-Physician Health Care Providers	95
Cases Against Health Care Facilities	99
Hospitals	100
Clinics Offering Outpatient Services	111
Long-Term Care Facilities	113
Cases Involving Non-Traditional and Alternative Care	120
Cases Resulting from Defective Products/Equipment	122
Chapter Summary	130

Chapter 4: Risk Management Issues In the Health Care Industry

Risk Management as Part of the Delivery of Health Care	132
Informed Consent	133

Confidentiality and Patient Privilege	138
Documentation	151
Provider Qualifications and Compliance with Standards	153
Good Samaritan Doctrine	155
Facility Safety	164
Chapter Summary	175

Chapter 5: The Role of Insurance in Medical Malpractice Claims

Professional Liability Insurance	177
Patient Insurance	187
Chapter Summary	206

PART 2: ANATOMY OF A LAWSUIT: THE MEDICAL MALPRACTICE CASE

Chapter 6: Discovery/Disclosure of the Injury

The Discovery Rule	210
Cases Involving Injury to Minors and Those Legally Incompetent	230
Chapter Summary	246

Chapter 7: Investigation of the Claim by the Potential Plaintiff

Establishing the Cause of the Injury	248
Identification of All Persons Connected to the Injury in a Professional Capacity	253
Interviewing Potential Witnesses	256
Obtaining Necessary Evidence	263

Evaluation of the Viability of the Claim 269
    Generally as an Act of Malfeasance 269
    Legislation That Might Affect Recovery 270
    As Affected by Comparative Negligence of the Plaintiff 271
Chapter Summary 272

Chapter 8: Investigation of the Potential Claim by the Defendant

Establishing the Cause of the Injury 273
Identification and Interview of All Persons Connected to the Injury 274
Documentary Evidence 280
Medical Devices and Equipment 283
Photographic and Tangible Evidence 284
Expert Opinions 285
Evaluation of the Viability of the Claim 285
Chapter Summary 290

Chapter 9: The Pretrial Stages of a Malpractice Claim

Statutory Considerations 291
Commencement of the Suit 293
Pleadings and Pretrial Motions 294
The Discovery Process Primary Objective: A Prima Facie Case or Not? 302
Arbitration, Mediation, and Settlement Considerations 318
Chapter Summary 320

Chapter 10: The Medical Malpractice Trial

Voir Dire—Selecting a Jury in a Medical Malpractice Case	321
Opening Statements—Don't Let Your Mouth Write a Check Your Evidence Can't Cash	333
The Presentation of Evidence	334
Case in Chief—The Prima Facie Case	334
The Defense	337
The Closing, Deliberation, and Verdict	337
Post-Trial Proceedings	338
Chapter Summary	340

Appendix A

Comprehensive Assignment	342
Facts	342
Assignments	343
Glossary	346
Index	349

TABLE OF CASES

Parker v. Mercy General Health Partners, 2004 WL 243359 (Mich.App.).	5
Estate of Hegarty, 249 Wis. 2d 142, 638 N.W.2d 355 (2002).	12
Wilkensen v. Duff, 575 S.E.2d. 335 (W Va. 2002).	33
Commonwealth v. Thompson, 6, Mass. 134 (Mass. 1809).	41
Monahan v. Devinny 223 A.D. 547, 229 N.Y.S. 60 (1928).	45
Smothers v. Hanks, 34 Iowa 286, 11 Am.Rep. 141 (1872).	47
Lewis v. Capalbo, 720 N.Y.S.2d 455, 280 A.D. 2d 257 (NY App. 1st Dept. 2001).	68
RW et al. v. Schrein, et al., 264 Neb. 818, 652 N.W. 2d 574 (2002).	72
Medical Mutual Liability Ins. Soc. of MD v. Azzato, 94 Md App. 632, 618 A.2d 274 (1993).	79
Zaverl v. Hanley, 64 P.3rd 809 (Alaska 2003).	84
Tempchin v. Sampson, 262 Md. 156, 277 A.2d 67 (1971).	97
Bing v. Thunig et al., 2 N.Y.2d 656, 143 N.E.2d 3, 163 N.Y.S.2d 3 (1957).	101
Gonzalez v. Paradise Valley Hospital, 3 Cal.Rptr. 3d 903 (App. 4th Dist. 2003).	106
Barker v. St. Barnabas Hospital, 305 A.D.2d 130, 759 N.Y.S.2d 65 (2003).	111
Advocat, Inc. v. Sauer, 111 S.W. 3d 346 (AR 2003).	114
Charrell v. Gonzalez, 673 N.Y.S.2d 685, (N.Y.App. 1st Div. 1998).	121
Estate of Chin, 711 A.2d. 352 (NJ App 1998).	123
Doe v. Chand, 335 Ill.App.3d 809, 781 N.E.2d 340, 269 Ill.Dec. 543 (Ill.App. 5th Dist. 2003).	143
Velazquez v. Jiminez et al., 172 N.J. 240, 798 A.2d 51 (NJ 2002).	155
Methodist Hospital of Indiana, Inc., 438 N.E.2d 315 (Ind. App. 4th Dist. 1982).	165
Winona Memorial Foundation of Indianapolis v. Lomax, 465 N.E.2d 731 (Ind.App. 4th Dist. 1984).	167
Saucedo v. Winger, 22 Kan. App.2d 259, 915 P.2d 129 (1996).	180
Burks v. St. Joseph's Hospital, 596 N.W.2d 391, 227 Wis.2d 811 (Wis 1999).	189
Aetna Health Care Inc. v. Davila et al., 124 S.Ct. 2488 (2004).	198
Fox v. Ethicon Endo-Surgical, Inc. , 6 Cal.Rptr 3d 300 (Cal.App.5 Dist. 2003).	211
Green v. Sacks, 56 S.W.3d 513 (Tenn.App. 2001).	223
Raley v. Wagner, 346 Ark. 234, 57 S.W.3d 683 (Ark. 2001).	231
Storm v. Legion Insurance Company, 265 Wis. 2d 169, 665 N.W.2d 353 (Wis. 2003).	235
Sills v. Oakland Gen. Hosp., 220 Mich.App.303, 559 N.W.2d 348 (1996).	286
McCarty v. Jaenicke, M.D., 2003 WL 3095693 (KYAPP. 2003).	322
Dempsey v. Phelps, 700 So.2d 1340 (Ala. 1997).	326

PREFACE

The goal of this text is to objectively address current medical malpractice principles from the perspective of both a plaintiff and defendant. The subject is particularly appropriate at this time, given the federal and state government attention focused on medical malpractice claims. This area of law continues to grow at an explosive rate. Legislative measures are being put in place to help control verdicts because these verdicts are often seen as the catalyst for increasing malpractice insurance rates. Technological advances, hopefully, will help eliminate medical mishaps leading to medical malpractice cases, but they do not rule out the risk of human error and, ultimately, litigation. The text explores the subject matter of medical malpractice law in theory and practice to provide insight into the background and practical approaches necessary for legal professionals. The text provides not only the traditional university approach of history and development of an area of law, but includes current issues and practices that are essential to thorough education and training as a legal professional.

The format of the text is a logical progression detailing the development of malpractice law in the United States from the time malpractice was considered criminal conduct to a highly complex area of civil law that, in many states, has resulted in specialty legislation limited to these types of civil cases. Following this are several chapters that detail how the medical malpractice case is developed by both the plaintiff and defense during the litigation process.

Features of the text include multiple applications, most of which are true-to-life examples of malpractice scenarios. Edited malpractice cases from a number of different jurisdictions, with wide-ranging views and rules, are included throughout the text to allow the reader insight as to how the courts have addressed the various legal issues of this area of law. Each chapter contains relevant assignments as well as a comprehensive assignment that addresses development of a continuing case throughout the text. Finally, numerous exhibits are included to show actual documents that are created and used in the arena of medical malpractice. Some examples included are the initial privacy policy statements given to patients, various medical and legal records, and pleadings used in litigation. After completing the text, the reader should have a clear and comprehensive view of the legal issues from the perspective of both a plaintiff and defendant as to how a medical malpractice case evolves.

Supplemental Teaching Materials

- **Online Companion™** - The Online Companion™ Web site can be found at http://www.westlegalstudies.com in the Resource section of the Web site. The Online Companion™ contains the following:
  - Relevant Web sites
  - Primary Organ Anatomical Terms
  - Medical Terminology Abbreviations
  - Medical Malpractice Statutory Reference Guide

  Instructor Note: Chapter Quizzes and the Quiz Answer Key are located in the Instructor's Center in the Online Companion™

- **Web page** - Visit our Web site at http://www.westlegalstudies.com where you will find valuable information specific to this book, such as hot links, sample materials to download, as well as other West Legal Studies products.
- **Westlaw®** - West's on-line computerized legal research system offers student "hands-on" experience with a system commonly used in law offices. Qualified adopters can receive ten free hours of Westlaw®. Westlaw® can be accessed with Macintosh and IBM PC and compatibles. A modem is required.

Acknowledgments

This text is for all those who brought this fascinating subject of malpractice to my life. First is Dick Shaikewitz, esq. of counsel, and the rest of the Wiseman Firm, Alton, Illinois. Dick, you were my first and most important mentor. You taught me two very important lessons about malpractice: 1) Don't ever risk the damage such a suit can do to an indivdual's career unless you are certain the allegations are well founded and the action is clearly meritorious enough to pursue on behalf of your client, and, just as important, 2) If professionals or their profession do not police themselves in terms of substandard professional conduct, then it is the obligation of the legal system and government to do it for them in order to protect an innocent and trusting public.

The text is also dedicated to those who showed me the other side of the coin and the seriousness with which the vast majority of health care professionals take their responsibilities with regard to their patients on a continuous basis quite literally day and night. Specifically, I thank and memorialize my late husband, Dr. M. George Dunham, and also offer great thanks to our longtime friend and partner Dr. Terry Wooldridge, Fremont Pediatrics and Adolescent Care, in Fremont, Nebraska.

I would also like to thank the following reviewers:

Stacey Barone, JD
Educational Consultant
Dix Hills, NY

Jeff Butterworth, MBA, BSN, RN
Legal Nurse Consultant/Nurse Paralegal
Robins, Kaplan, Miller & Ciresi L.L.P.
Atlanta, GA

Marilyn R. Cohen, BA, JD
Instructor
University of New Orleans Paralegal Institute
New Orleans, LA

Leslie (Les) Sturdivant Ennis, J.D., Ed.D.
Administration/Faculty, Education and Law
Samford University
Birmingham, AL

Lori A. Gray
Paralegal
Rockwell Automation, Inc.
Mayfield Heights, OH

Please note the Internet resources are of a time-sensitive nature and
URL addresses may often change or be deleted.

Contact us at westlegalstudies@delmar.com

PART 1
ISSUES IN THE DEVELOPMENT OF THE LAW OF MEDICAL MALPRACTICE

Part 1

Part 1 of the text examines the progression of medical malpractice action from the origins of civil tort law in the United States to the present-day sophisticated legislative and judicial standards. Two centuries ago, there was the initial issue of whether professional malpractice causing physical injury was a matter for criminal prosecution or for the civil courts. Once this was resolved as a civil matter due to the lack of criminal intent, standards for civil cases began to develop. Commensurate with the development of legal standards were the scientific and technological advancements in medicine throughout the nineteenth and twentieth centuries. Added to the equation were widespread educational opportunities, mass communication, insurance issues, and the population's general awareness of their legal rights.

This portion of the text examines how these various factors developed and came into play in the American legal system through legislation, regulation, and the development of common law standards. The second part of the text, Part 2, explores the modern day litigation process for a case of medical malpractice.

CHAPTER 1

A Brief History of Civil Liability for Professional Malfeasance

CHAPTER OBJECTIVES

When you complete this chapter, you should be able to:

- Define the concept of negligence
- Explain the role of the elements of an action based on negligence
- Discuss the purpose of the doctrine of res ipsa loquitur
- Define the theory of respondeat superior in negligence
- Distinguish the theories of negligence, intentional torts, and strict liability
- Describe how contractual liability is an issue in the field of medical malpractice law

DEVELOPMENT OF THE LAW OF NEGLIGENCE IN THE UNITED STATES

It is just as difficult to imagine the absence of medical malpractice in American society as to imagine a society without need for a judicial system to remedy issues that arise between parties. Allegations of malpractice date back to the very beginnings of this country. As the legal system has grown and developed, so has the science of medicine and the health care professions. The inevitable product of the two has been a continuing increase in medical malpractice litigation. From the viewpoint of health care providers and their insurers, litigation is often unwarranted and juries are far too generous with awards. These awards, in turn, are then blamed for the skyrocketing costs of insurance and health care. Conversely, as recently as 2001, the Robert Wood Johnson Foundation reported that fully 95 percent of doctors admit to having witnessed a major medical mistake, and that many errors included cancer diagnosis/treatment.[1] Additionally, legal analysts point out that the costs of health care and insurance company profits far outpace the costs associated with malpractice litigation. The purpose of this text is neither to take sides nor propose change. Rather, it is to examine the development of the law applicable to cases of medical malpractice and to present a functional approach to cases that arise. The result is that attorneys and paralegals have a challenging task to keep abreast of changes and to adapt methods of practice.

Negligence as a Concept

In the United States, medical malpractice evolved as part of the development of the American system of tort law. Throughout the 1800s, principles regarding **negligence** developed into a well-established legal theory. The underlying premise was that individuals should be accountable for less than prudent conduct if it resulted in injury to innocent parties. While principles of negligence had been loosely formed in England, it was greatly broadened and defined in application in American law. Today, it is a fundamental part of the American legal system and American society as well.

Although negligence was initially applied to ordinary situations, it was quickly adapted to accommodate the responsibility of professionals toward their clients. The basic theory advanced explained that if someone held themselves out as having special knowledge that others should rely on, then the more knowledgeable party also had a responsibility to use their skill in a reasonably careful manner so as not to cause injury as the result of the reliance of another. This was applied in virtually all professions including medicine.[2]

During the nineteenth century, as medical knowledge advanced and increased so did the responsibility for those using it to help others. Even though the practice of medicine was still largely a matter of judgment over skill, less knowledgeable and vulnerable individuals placed their trust in medical practitioners for the best available care and treatment. The population was largely illiterate and had little or no access to information regarding medical care for injuries, diseases, and infections. The failure to seek treatment of what today would be considered minor medical conditions could result in disability, disfigurement, and even death. Thus, individuals sought the care of any medical practitioner available and placed total trust in his or her knowledge.

Historically, there has been a reluctance by the courts, and society in general, to place any sort of responsibility on medical practitioners. A tremendous respect, dating back centuries has existed for those with the ability to heal others. Even today there is a perception in some circles that to hold physicians accountable for the injury/illness of others would discourage health care practitioners from offering assistance to those most in need. But, through the 1800s, knowledge about treatment of illness and injury developed more than it had at any time in history. It far surpassed the former common sense, religious, and sometimes magical principles and evolved into a more complex scientific process. As treatments developed and became more refined, the notion that people should be required to administer medical care with some degree of skill began to grow in popularity and acceptance. By the mid-1800s it was firmly established in the law of negligence that physicians were held accountable to a level of knowledge and skill comparable to that of their peers. This was to protect both the public and the profession from those who would engender the trust of the public and practice medicine negligently causing harm to the individual and damage to the integrity and trust in the profession. In remarking on an 1853 Pennsylvania case, an Iowa court, in 1872, made the following observation: "The question was not whether the doctor had skill enough to make the leg as straight and long as the other, but whether he had employed such reasonable skill and diligence as are ordinarily exercised in his profession. For less than this he is responsible in damages . . . " Smothers v. Hanks, 34 Iowa 286, (1872). From the time of this opinion, the law of medical malpractice—specifically claims in negligence—has grown in direct proportion to the knowledge and skill of medical practitioners in modern medicine.

Elements of Negligence

Negligence is a legal action used in a wide variety of circumstances. It does not matter that the case is based on alleged malfeasance by a medical professional, a truck driver, or any other circumstance. The elements that must be established to prevail are the same. Only the evidence that is used to prove them changes. These elements have been in place in the American legal system for more than 200 years and have seen little change other than refinement of definition. In any civil lawsuit, the plaintiff has the burden of a prima facie case. That is to say, they must produce at least some evidence in support of each and every element of the legal cause of action advanced against the defendant. To establish a prima facie case in a medical malpractice case based on negligence, the plaintiff must show that:

- the defendant owed a duty to care for the safety or rights of the plaintiff;
- the duty was somehow breached by the defendant by failing to exercise the proper standard of care in the delivery of professional care, services, or treatment;
- the breach in turn was the proximate cause of injury to the plaintiff;
- the injuries were significant enough to be considered compensable.[3]

The duty of care has been expanded somewhat in recent years but the basic premise has remained the same. Each individual is obligated to be aware of the effect of their actions on others. Consequently, all persons owe a duty or obligation to act or omit from acting in such a way that endangers those around them of whom they should be reasonably aware. Some jurisdictions apply a broader area than others with regard to whom the actor must take into consideration. But generally, the rule is that one must act, or refrain from acting, when the action could endanger others in a reasonably foreseeable area. Thus, foreseeability is a key element of the extent of one's duty. Essentially, the question must always be asked "was the danger to the injured person the reasonably foreseeable result of the defendant's action or omission?" If the answer is in the affirmative, it is likely a duty was owed by the defendant to the plaintiff.

The second fundamental element of negligence is the standard of care. That is to say that each person must act in a manner that is consistent with how a reasonable person would have acted under similar circumstances. The standard of care varies dramatically from case to case. The general premise is that one must act as a similarly situated reasonable person with similar skills and attributes would have acted. Consequently, if the actor were a person driving a car, then the reasonable person of comparison would be a prudent driver under the given circumstances taking into account all relevant factors such as weather, traffic, and road conditions. In the case of a medical professional accused of malfeasance, the professional would be held accountable to the level of knowledge and skill as one similarly situated within the profession.

One significant change that has occurred in the arena of medical malpractice in recent years has been the standard of care. Historically, one was held to a standard of other medical professionals in the same geographic area. The rationale was that medical professionals in small, rural communities did not have access to the advanced training available in large, urban areas. However, with technological advances and mass communication, the majority rule was changed in the late twentieth century. It is now considered reasonable in the vast majority of jurisdictions that all medical professionals have access to essentially the same level of training and knowledge and are thus held accountable to the same standard of care on a national scale. This places the burden on health care professionals to keep abreast of research and technological advances. It also indirectly provides the promise of comparable health care to all individuals regardless of their geographical location. This expansion of the standard of care is addressed in much greater detail in subsequent chapters.

Once it has been established that the defendant owed a duty toward the plaintiff, and that the defendant breached the required standard of care, there is still the element of proximate cause left to establish before damages or compensation can even be considered. In cases of medical malpractice this is often the most difficult hurdle to overcome. To establish proximate cause, both parts of a two-pronged test must be met. The test requires both factual and legal causal links to be established between the defendant's conduct and the plaintiff's injury. It should be clearly stated at the outset that, while something can be factually traced from an act or omission to an injury, the conclusion of a legal causation may or may not follow. Some events are so remotely connected or so profoundly affected by intervening factors as to prevent a finding of legal causation.

In the test to establish whether proximate cause is present, the cause in fact prong of the test is often the easiest to prove. The plaintiff needs only to trace a chain of events, short or long, that leads directly from the defendant's allegedly wrongful conduct to the plaintiff's injuries. This is influenced somewhat by the extent of the duty of the defendant to reasonably foresee the potential effects by his or her actions. In simple situations where there are no intervening forces or remote circumstances, cause in fact and legal cause may be established by the same evidence. If there is no access to the evidence, an alternative theory may be advanced known as "**res ipsa loquitur**." This will be defined more thoroughly in a subsequent section. However, for the purposes of this initial discussion, it will be assumed that the plaintiff is aware of exactly how the injury occurred. The second prong of the test is the legal causation. This requires the plaintiff to produce proof that the direct and legal cause of the injury was a breach of conduct by the defendant. Most often proximate cause is determined by one of two popularly accepted methods. The first is often referred to as the but-for test. In the jurisdictions that apply this method of establishing proximate cause, the judge or jury is asked to consider the facts of the case and answer the following questions: "But for the defendant's actions, would the plaintiff's injuries still have occurred?" This question within the context of medical malpractice is addressed in the following case of Parker v. Mercy General Health Partners, 2004 WL 243359 (Mich.App. 2004).

CASE

2004 WL 243359 (Mich.App.)

Court of Appeals of Michigan.

Ginger L. PARKER, Plaintiff-Appellant,
v.
MERCY GENERAL HEALTH PARTNERS and Elizabeth Tindall, Defendants-Appellees.

Feb. 10, 2004.

PER CURIAM.

Plaintiff arrived at Mercy General Health Partners' emergency room complaining of a skin rash. A physician started an intravenous line (IV) in her right hand. Plaintiff complained of nausea and Elizabeth Tindall, a licensed practical nurse, administered an intravenous dose of Phenergan, an anti-nausea medication. Plaintiff felt a burning sensation in her hand. She developed a superficial phlebitis, which resulted in a sclerotic vein in her hand. Subsequently, plaintiff underwent surgery to remove the vein.

Plaintiff filed suit alleging that Tindall breached the applicable standard of care in administering the Phenergan. She submitted an affidavit of merit from a registered nurse who opined that Tindall breached the applicable standard of care when administering Phenergan to plaintiff, and that Tindall's negligent actions proximately caused the superficial phlebitis which resulted in a sclerotic vein in plaintiff's right hand.

Defendants moved for summary disposition pursuant to MCR 2.116(C)(10) arguing that no evidence showed that plaintiff's sclerotic vein and subsequent pain were proximately caused by the negligent administration of Phenergan. The trial court granted defendants' motion, finding that plaintiff presented no medical evidence that created an issue of fact regarding whether her injury was proximately caused by the administration of Phenergan.

(continued)

We review a trial court's decision on a motion for summary disposition de novo. *Auto Club Group Ins Co v. Burchell,* 249 Mich.App 468, 479; 642 NW2d 406 (2001) "In a medical malpractice case the plaintiff bears the burden of proving: (1) the applicable standard of care, (2) breach of that standard by the defendant, (3) injury, and (4) proximate causation between the alleged breach and the injury."*Wischmeyer v. Schanz,* 449 Mich. 469, 484; 536 NW2d 760 (1995) "Expert testimony is required in medical malpractice cases to establish the applicable standard of care and to demonstrate that the defendant somehow breached that standard." *Birmingham v. Vance,* 204 Mich.App 418, 421; 516 NW2d 95 (1994) "Proof of causation requires both cause in fact and legal, or proximate, cause." *Haliw v. Sterling Heights,* 464 Mich. 297, 310; 627 NW2d 581 (2001) Cause in fact requires that the injury would not have occurred but for the negligent conduct. *Id.* Cause in fact may be established by circumstantial evidence, but such proof must be subject to reasonable inferences and cannot consist of mere speculation. *Skinner v. Square D Co,* 445 Mich. 153, 163-164; 516 NW2d 475 (1994) . An explanation that is consistent with known facts but not deducible from them constitutes impermissible conjecture. *Id.* at 164. Proximate cause is that which, in a natural and continuous sequence, unbroken by a new and independent cause, produces the injury. *McMillan v. Vliet,* 422 Mich. 570, 576; 374 NW2d 679 (1985)

Plaintiff argues that the trial court erred by granting defendants' motion for summary disposition. We disagree and affirm. Plaintiff's action depended on her ability to establish by medical testimony that her injury was more probably than not proximately caused by the errant administration of Phenergan. *Haliw, supra; Birmingham, supra.* Plaintiff's own expert witness acknowledged that her role was not to give an opinion regarding the nature or cause of plaintiff's injury. No physician who treated plaintiff opined that the administration of Phenergan proximately caused her injury. Her family physician stated that a sclerotic vein could result from the insertion of an IV needle itself and could be unrelated to the administration of medication. Her surgeon stated that a sclerotic vein could result from a number of things, including the insertion of an IV needle or the administration of medication. He could not opine that it was more probable than not that plaintiff's sclerotic vein resulted from the administration of Phenergan. Her pain management specialist acknowledged that it would be logical to question whether the administration of Phenergan resulted in the sclerotic vein, but he could not opine that it was more likely than not that plaintiff's injury resulted from the administration of Phenergan. No medical evidence showed that it was more probable than not that the administration of Phenergan resulted in plaintiff's sclerotic vein. That the administration of Phenergan resulted in plaintiff's sclerotic vein was an explanation consistent with the known facts; however, it was not deducible from those facts, and thus constituted only impermissible speculation. *Skinner, supra.* Plaintiff did not make out a prima facie case on each element of medical malpractice. MCL 600.2912a(2) ; *Wischmeyer, supra.* Therefore, summary disposition was correct.

Affirmed.

As society and technology become more complex, circumstances that lend themselves to such a black-and-white view of cause are fewer and fewer. Quite often someone's actions may impact another, but as a contributing factor rather than a sole producing cause. The view that one must be totally responsible or not at all in producing an injury is used less and less because it would permit too many to avoid responsibility for conduct that plays a significant role in producing an injury.

In place of the decreasing use of the but-for test has been the increased application of a more equitable test. This popular method of establishing proximate cause is commonly known as the "substantial factor analysis." Under this test, the defendant's conduct is considered in light of all relevant facts in the situation, and it is determined whether or not the defendant's conduct was a substantial factor in producing the plaintiff's injury. Irrespective of other factors that may have contributed to the injury, if the defendant's conduct was a substantially producing factor then cause in fact has been established.[4]

Sometimes an injury occurs and the cause is not easily foreseeable. In that situation, causation is much more difficult to prove. It may be easy to trace a chain of events from an action/nonaction to an injury. But in a case of negligence, the injury has to be traced backward to an action or omission that the defendant should have foreseen as a possible cause of injury to another (i.e., breach of duty). Proximate cause can be established in fairly remote situations, even when other forces come into play producing the injury. However, when these remote situations become so removed and convoluted with other facts that the occurrence is considered bizarre or a freak accident, the direct connection and significance of the defendant's conduct may be difficult to prove. Similarly, when an intervening force capable of producing the injury independently occurs between the moment of the conduct of the defendant and the moment of injury, the proximate cause is very difficult to prove in terms of the original defendant. Again, the courts often apply the but-for test or "substantial factor analysis" to determine legal causation. Application 1.1, which follows, demonstrates how a minor change in the facts of a case can move the legal analysis in an entirely different direction.

APPLICATION 1.1

Dr. B is an experienced anesthesiologist. He uses a disposable plastic two-way tube that is part of the assembly of regular equipment used when a patient is under anesthesia. Oxygen passes through one portion of the tube into the lungs of the patient. Exhaled carbon dioxide passes out through another portion of the tube. The tube is color-coded to denote various sizes for use with patients with different airway dimensions such as in children versus adults. On this particular occasion, the patient is a child and the appropriately sized plastic tube is colored a solid dark blue. During surgery the patient appears to not be receiving enough oxygen and the amount delivered is steadily increased. Suddenly, the patient dies. During autopsy it appears the patient's lungs literally exploded from overinflation. Dr. B is sued for medical malpractice. He did, in fact, continue to deliver increasing amounts of oxygen to the patient based on his instrument readings and patient symptoms. And it was, in fact, this delivery of oxygen at high levels that caused the patient's death. However, investigation of the equipment revealed that the particular tube had a manufacturing defect whereby a small piece of plastic leaked into the center portion of the tube during its fabrication. The additional bit of plastic prevented any carbon dioxide from being expelled from the patient's lungs and consequently severely limited the intake of additional oxygen. The dark color of the tube prevented Dr. B from seeing the blockage on examination and it was only discovered when the tube was cut apart. In this case, while there is a direct factual link, there is an intervening factor which Dr. B could not have reasonably foreseen.

(continued)

> Assume the following change of facts:
>
> A monitor to measure the amount of carbon dioxide being expelled from the lungs was available. However, Dr. B did not use the device as the surgery was a routine tonsillectomy that required only a minimal amount and time for anesthesia. In that event, it may be established that the failure to employ available safety precautions was a direct and proximate cause of the patient's death.

The final element in any action for negligence is damage. Damage is the legal term used to describe the injury. After the duty, standard, breach, and causal links are established, it remains necessary to establish damage. A defendant's conduct can be utterly reprehensible, but if no compensable damage has occurred there is no basis for an action at law in negligence. The plaintiff must prove that he or she suffered some type of compensable injury; that is, that something happened to the plaintiff or the plaintiff's property as the proximate result of the defendant's breach of standard of care that warrants compensation by the defendant to the plaintiff. Damage comes in many forms. It can be monetary, physical, mental, and emotional. It can affect a person or the person's property. However, in a negligence action it must be something that the courts recognize as compensable and must be significant enough under the circumstances to warrant a monetary award as compensation. See Application 1.2.

APPLICATION 1.2

Suzanne is 48 years old and works as a casino waitress. The majority of her income is based on tips from customers. She feels her physical appearance is a key element in her ability to generate income. Suzanne decides to have cosmetic surgery on her face. The physician informs her that the recovery time for sutures and incisions is about three weeks. After that, it will take approximately six months for the effects of the surgery to fully heal and reach maximum potential. After the surgery, Suzanne plans to return to work in three weeks. She did not have enough vacation time accumulated and, as a result, was required to take an unpaid leave of absence. At the time she returns to work there are still numerous red suture lines visible on her neck and eyes and her eyelids appear very tight and drawn. She is embarrassed about her appearance and works only the minimum hours required to keep her job, often asking for the shifts where casino traffic is light. At the end of six months the effects of the surgery have all but disappeared and Suzanne returns to her former work schedule. Her surgeon considers the procedure a total success. Suzanne, however, feels that she lost a significant portion of six months' income due to her appearance. She is able to prove that her income did, in fact, decrease. She sues the physician for medical malpractice claiming he did not fully disclose to her the effects on her appearance during the healing process. If the case were to go to trial, the jury would have to determine whether the physician gave Suzanne sufficient information to make an informed consent to the procedure. They would also have to determine if the lost income was the proximate result of the failure to provide sufficient information, and whether there were any other facts that contributed to Suzanne's decreased income during this period of time.

> **ASSIGNMENT 1.1**
>
> Consider the following situation and identify the specific facts that would represent each element of an action in negligence.
>
> Carlo is diagnosed with a brain tumor. This particular type of tumor is slow growing and often responds well to drug therapy. Carlo is given a prescription and takes it to a local pharmacist. Unknown to Carlo, the pharmacist makes an error in filling the prescription and gives Carlo a blood pressure medication. Carlo takes the prescription as directed and has it refilled over a period of several months. However, he continues to deteriorate. Ultimately, the physician admits Carlo to the hospital. When reviewing the medications that Carlo brought to the hospital with him, the doctor discovers the error. Unfortunately, the tumor had been left untreated for many months and had progressed to an irreversible stage. Carlo died soon after. With proper treatment, Carlo could have been expected to live another three to five years.

THE USE OF RES IPSA LOQUITUR

As mentioned previously, one of the key elements in a case of negligence is proximate cause. In cases of medical malpractice this can often be the most difficult element to establish. For example, if a patient is under anesthesia at the time of the alleged malfeasance, how can he or she know exactly what went wrong? Similarly, many of the bases for claims of malpractice in other related areas such as pharmaceutical and products liability occur outside the presence of the injured party. Thus, it may well be an insurmountable task to establish the traditional elements of negligence despite the validity of the claim.

A lack of access to causal evidence is not limited only to cases of medical malpractice. For hundreds of years there have been occurrences that are clearly the result of negligent acts or omissions, yet the injured do not have access to or control over the evidence to prove it. Consequently, the theory of res ipsa loquitur was established to supplement the law of negligence. The Latin term res ipsa loquitur is translated to "the thing speaks for itself."[5] Originally developed shortly after the formal acceptance of the negligence doctrine, res ipsa loquitur is used under very special circumstances in cases of negligence as a means to aid disadvantaged plaintiffs. A plaintiff claiming negligence may also seek to have the theory of res ipsa loquitur applied in certain cases where the defendant has an unfair advantage over the plaintiff in access to essential evidence. A plaintiff may only claim the doctrine under very special circumstances when the following elements can be proven.

- The occurrence was of a type that would not happen without negligence.
- The instrument/action/omission producing the injury during the occurrence was within the exclusive control of the defendant at all relevant times.
- The plaintiff in no way contributed to the injury.

Res ipsa loquitur was developed for cases in which a plaintiff was injured but unable to prove the chain of events required in proximate cause because the defendant controlled the evidence that depicted the details of the occurrence. An example of this situation might be a patient who was supposed to have surgery to replace her right hip and woke up only to discover her left hip had been replaced instead. To prevent unwarranted claims of negligence, however, the three aforementioned elements must be proven in place of proof of the exact way in which the duty was breached and in lieu of the missing elements of the proximate cause issue. As a result, res ipsa loquitur is no easier to establish than straight negligence and is applicable only in limited circumstances. Nevertheless, it does provide a much-needed remedy for plaintiffs who would otherwise be unable to prove a case successfully as the result of a defendant's ability to control or conceal the necessary evidence or prevent the plaintiff from gaining access to it.

In the latter part of the twentieth century a whole new arena for res ipsa loquitur opened up. Advancements in technology gave negligent defendants a distinct upper hand in the control of evidence. Mass production of medical equipment and devices included some defective products, and plaintiffs were injured by these products as a result of the negligent production. Plaintiffs often had no means of knowing or discovering the exact acts of negligence, but when all elements were present, res ipsa loquitur could provide an avenue of legal recourse for the injured plaintiffs. Similarly, great advancements in medicine created a higher incidence of medical procedures performed and an increase in manufactured medical devices and tools used. Often these procedures were performed while the patient was asleep, medicated, or otherwise incapacitated. The availability of the doctrine of res ipsa loquitur to plaintiffs injured during such procedures revolutionized the methods and conditions under which all medical procedures are performed. It placed the general safety of the patient on an equal level with the importance of the specific medical procedure performed. As a result, awareness of the broader duty toward patients has been recognized and safety-conscious practices and procedures have been identified as priorities. See Application 1.3.

APPLICATION 1.3

Connelly was a 19-year-old high school senior. He was injured during an athletic event and was admitted to the hospital for surgery to repair his injuries. Following surgery, he developed a serious infection that resulted in multiple additional surgeries and an extended hospital stay including eight days in intensive care. His recovery at home lasted for more than one month before he was able to return to school. As a result of the severity and length of his illness, he was unable to participate in competitive sports for the remainder of the school year. Connelly had previously been an All-State athlete and had been contacted by two universities regarding scholarships. But, as the result of the infection and multiple surgeries, his continued athletic ability came into question and the scholarship offers were rescinded. The original injuries were not considered serious and in ordinary conditions would have healed without permanent disability of any kind. Connelly and his parents believe that the infection was the result of inadequate care during the initial surgery and/or subsequent hospitalization. They have consulted three other physicians who have confirmed their suspicion that Connelly's recovery was not within the normal expected range of events and was likely due to substandard care. They feel this was the cause for his loss of financial scholarship valued at more than $100,000.

Under the theory of res ipsa loquitur, Connelly could plead that the required elements were met and account for the source of the infection. Obviously, he would need to establish the other elements of negligence and respond to any defenses such as the infection being a normal risk of the procedure. But, in the absence of res ipsa loquitur, he would have little chance of establishing proximate cause since he was under anesthesia and medicated during the surgeries and hospitalization, and was largely unaware of the critical elements of his medical care.

As can be seen from the application above, a key element in any case of res ipsa loquitur is the inaccessibility of actual evidence to the plaintiff that cannot be restored through legal procedures such as a court-ordered delivery of evidence. Often, there is no documentation of the negligent act and no witnesses who can or will testify to personal knowledge of the incident. Yet, the circumstances are clear that something occurred that would be considered unreasonable. Examples of these events in medical malpractice include, but are not limited to, situations such as when medical instruments or supplies are left within a patient's body during surgical procedures, a medical procedure is performed on the wrong part of the body (e.g., amputation of the wrong limb), and any variety of other circumstances. It should be noted, however, that the courts will not rely upon res ipsa loquitur as a basis for negligence when the foundation of the case is no more than an undesirable or unsuccessful result, or when the injury claimed was well within the range of the known and disclosed risks of the procedure.

RESPONDEAT SUPERIOR IN CASES OF NEGLIGENCE

All jurisdictions in the United States have long accepted and upheld the legal standard known as **respondeat superior**. The theory holds that when one is acting within the scope of their employment, the employer may be held accountable for the acts of the employee with respect to third parties.[6] Generally, an injured third party has the right to sue either the employer or the employee if it can be proven that the defendant who was responsible for the injury was an employee and not an independent contractor.

The independent contractor is one who works on a per-job basis and is not subject to the direct supervision and control of the employer with respect to how the work is carried out.[7] Respondeat superior requires it be shown that the employee was acting within the scope of employment and/or under the direction, supervision, or control of the employer. Simply stated, the employee must be acting subject to the ultimate supervision of the employer at the time of the alleged tortuous conduct. The employee does not need to be engaged in a regular job duty as long as he or she is engaged in a task that benefits the employer in some direct manner.

In the case of medical malpractice based on negligence, there has been much debate over the years and an infinite number of claims alleging respondeat superior. As a result, the law and practices in the health care field have evolved dramatically. As the field of medicine has developed so have the number and variety of professions associated with health care. From an economic standpoint, the once standard independent physician practice has been replaced largely by various types of clinics and multispeciality groups. Some physicians are the employees of hospitals or universities that operate hospitals. Some work for corporations that operate freestanding clinics, outpatient surgery centers, or are contracted out to other corporations. Some still practice independently or in small groups. And for each physician, there are literally dozens of related health care professionals including physician assistants, nurses, nurse practitioners, medical assistants, and various technicians.

The relationship of all these individuals to one another and to the organizations with whom they do business is of great significance with regard to the potential claims for malpractice. From a plaintiff's point of view, the more defendants that can be named increases the likelihood of recovery and adequate resources among defendants to actually pay any settlement or judgment. The defendant's perspective may take different approaches. One may be to have so many individuals involved that proximate cause by a specific defendant is virtually impossible to establish. Another approach is if each defendant, individual, or company can isolate itself from other health care providers, the less likely he or she is to be named in a lawsuit with respect to something someone else allegedly did in a negligent manner. Obviously, the approach taken is affected largely by the unique circumstances of the particular case. However, as a general rule, many who are in a supervisory role opt, whenever possible, for the approach to isolate and avoid liability for the acts of others who could be seen as subordinates. See Application 1.4.

APPLICATION 1.4

Dr. Zeway shares office space with three other physicians. Each has his or her own practice and only share the physical facility and clerical staff. Each physician maintains separate billing systems and nursing staff. The doctors do not share patients, responsibilities for hospital rounds, and do not actively refer patients to one another. Dr Zeway is named in a malpractice suit brought against one of the other physicians under the respondeat superior theory claiming the other physician was employed by a multiphysician practice. In this circumstance, Dr. Zeway would probably not be responsible under respondeat superior. However, if the facts changed only slightly, the outcome might be entirely different. Assume the physicians see each other's patients when one of them is absent, share hospital responsibilities and nursing staff, and refer to one another on various cases. In this situation, the arrangement appears to be much more of a collaborative effort which benefits the entire group and thus might subject them to the definition of a joint medical practice and, in turn, result in a viable claim under respondeat superior.

The point of Application 1.4 above demonstrates that respondeat superior can be a very gray area of the law. As a result, a series of factors must be considered when determining whether to apply the doctrine and ultimately hold those other than the alleged tortfeasor responsible. The case below, Estate of Hegarty, 249 Wis. 2d 142, 638 N.W.2d 355 (2002), demonstrates the complexity of the situation and the factors that must be considered when making a determination of whether third parties should be held accountable for the actions of another.

CASE

249 Wis. 2d 142, 638 N.W.2d 35 (2002).

ESTATE OF Sarah M. HEGARTY, deceased, by Jeremiah J. HEGARTY

Involuntary-Plaintiff,
v.
Angela BEAUCHAINE, M.D., Ernest Stremski, M.D., Children's Hospital of Wisconsin, Inc., a Wisconsin hospital corporation, OHIC Insurance Company, a foreign insurance corporation, and The Medical College of Wisconsin, Inc., a Wisconsin corporation, Defendants,
Medical College of Wisconsin Affiliated Hospitals, Inc., a Wisconsin corporation,† Defendant Respondent,
Physicians Insurance Company of Wisconsin, Inc., a Wisconsin insurance corporation, Defendant,
Mary Jo Zimmer, M.D., Fireman's Fund Insurance Company and Wisconsin Patients Compensation Fund, Defendants-Respondents.

(continued)

In 1992, Sarah Hegarty (Sarah), then age twelve, became a patient of pediatrician Mary Jo Zimmer, M.D. (Dr. Zimmer). When Sarah began developing abdominal pain in 1995, she consulted with Dr. Zimmer. Dr. Zimmer referred Sarah to a pediatric gastroenterologist at Children's Hospital, who diagnosed her with irritable bowel syndrome.

On March 20, 1996, Sarah developed severe abdominal pain, nausea and vomiting. She was rushed to Children's Hospital's emergency room at 4:30 p.m. Sarah was initially treated by Ernest Stremski, M.D., the emergency room physician, and later by Angela Beauchaine, M.D., a first-year medical resident. Dr. Stremski admitted Sarah at 8:00 p.m.

Sarah's condition rapidly deteriorated. Dr. Beauchaine, who took over Sarah's care after she was admitted, was a first-year resident, not yet licensed to practice medicine. Dr. Beauchaine was enrolled in a graduate medical training program through the Medical College of Wisconsin (Medical College) and the Medical College of Wisconsin Affiliated Hospitals (Affiliated Hospitals). From the time of Sarah's admission until Dr. Zimmer arrived at 7:30 a.m. on the morning of March 21, 1996, no licensed physician saw Sarah to evaluate her condition.

The medical records reflect that by 6:00 a.m. on March 21, 1996, Sarah's abdomen was distended, rigid and tender. Sarah's condition became critical at 11:45 a.m.; she was resuscitated and taken to surgery at approximately 1:45 p.m. However, by that time, Sarah was diagnosed with small bowel volvulus with complete bowel infarction, meaning her small bowel had been twisted and cut off from the blood supply.

On March 16, 1998, after more than fifty surgical procedures related to her intestinal difficulties, Sarah died. The cost of Sarah's medical care over this two-year period reached nearly $3,000,000. On December 18, 1998, the plaintiffs filed suit setting forth survival claims on behalf of Sarah's estate and wrongful death claims on behalf of Sarah's parents. The complaint was brought against Dr. Beauchaine, Dr. Stremski, Children's Hospital, the Medical College, Affiliated Hospitals, their respective liability insurers, and the Wisconsin Patients Compensation Fund.

As part of a discovery request, the plaintiffs received medical records from Children's Hospital in April of 1997, but it was not until September of 1999 that the plaintiffs took the depositions of Drs. Stremski, Beauchaine and Zimmer. In their depositions, Drs. Stremski and Beauchaine stated that Dr. Zimmer had been involved in Sarah's care before arriving at the hospital on the morning of March 21, 1996. They revealed that each had spoken with Dr. Zimmer over the telephone on March 20, 1996, and that Dr. Zimmer had directed Sarah's treatment throughout the evening and into the early morning. On December 20, 1999, based on information disclosed at these depositions, the plaintiffs filed an amended complaint adding Dr. Zimmer to the lawsuit.

The trial court dismissed the claims against Dr. Zimmer, determining that the action was barred by the medical malpractice statute of limitations, Wis. Stat. § 893.55 The court also dismissed the claims against Affiliated Hospitals, which were based on the doctrine of respondeat superior. The trial court ruled that Affiliated Hospitals could not be held vicariously liable for Dr. Beauchaine's negligence when it had no control over the details of her work.

... In reviewing a trial court's grant of summary judgment, we first consider which statute of limitations applies. *See Ritt v. Dental Care* 199 Wis.2d 48, 60, 543 N.W.2d 852 (Ct.App.1995) Determining which statute of limitations applies to an action is a question of law which we review *de novo*. *Webb,* 232 Wis.2d at 502, 606 N.W.2d 552

The trial court ruled that all claims brought by the Hegartys and Sarah's estate were subject to the medical malpractice statute of limitations, Wis. Stat. § 893.55(1) The Hegartys contend that the general statute

(continued)

of limitations concerning injury to the person, found in Wis. Stat. § 893.54 should be applied to their wrongful death claim. We disagree and conclude that wrongful death claims caused by medical malpractice are subject to the specific statute of limitations concerning medical malpractice, found in Wis. Stat. § 893.55(1)

Wisconsin Stat. § 893.55(1) provides:
Medical malpractice; limitation of actions; limitation of damages; itemization of damages.
(1) Except as provided by subs. (2) and (3), an action to recover damages for injury arising from any treatment or operation performed by, or from any omission by, a person who is a health care provider, regardless of the theory on which the action is based, shall be commenced within the later of:
(a) Three years from the date of the injury, or
(b) One year from the date the injury was discovered or, in the exercise of reasonable diligence should have been discovered, except that an action may not be commenced under this paragraph more than 5 years from the date of the act or omission.

Wisconsin Stat. § 893.54 provides:
Injury to the person. The following actions shall be commenced within 3 years or be barred:
(1) An action to recover damages for injuries to the person.
(2) An action brought to recover damages for death caused by the wrongful act, neglect or default of another.

...Whether the Hegartys' wrongful death action is time barred by the statute of limitations that governs medical malpractice actions is an issue of first impression involving statutory construction. See Paul v. Skemp, , 242 Wis.2d 507, 625 N.W.2d 860 "A court will not ordinarily engage in statutory construction unless a statute is ambiguous."*Czapinski v.St. Francis Hosp.*, 236Wis.2d316, 613N.W.2d 120
[T]he purpose of statutory construction is to ascertain and give effect to the intent of the legislature. In determining legislative intent, however, first resort must be to the language of the statute itself. .... A statute is ambiguous when it is capable of being understood by reasonably well-informed persons in two or more different senses. *State v. Martin*, 162 Wis.2d 883, 893-94, 470 N.W.2d 900 (1991)
Here, reasonable minds have understood the interplay of these statutes in different ways; therefore, we are required to interpret the statute to determine the intent of the legislature. While either statute considered independently could be applicable, only one will be applied. See *Clark v. Erdmann*, 161 Wis.2d 428, 436, 468 N.W.2d 18 (1991) Since Wis. Stat. § 893.55 is the more specific of the two statutes, we begin our analysis there to determine if its terms are met. *Id.* at 436-37, 468 N.W.2d 18
We first turn to the language of the statute itself. Wisconsin Stat. § 893.55 encompasses "damages for injury arising from any treatment or operation performed by .... a health care provider, *regardless of the theory on which the action is based*":...Section 893.55 clearly is the more specific of the two statutes. Unlike sec. 893.54 it concerns itself not only with injury to the person, but also with a particular way in which the injury arises, *i.e.*, resulting from an act or omission of a "health care provider." *Id.* at 436-37, 468 N.W.2d 18 Thus, it is apparent that the legislature intended that any claim alleging negligence against a health care provider would be controlled by § 893.55 even though the medical malpractice claim is based on a wrongful death theory of negligence.
Despite the existence of case law supporting our conclusion, the Hegartys argue that Wis. Stat. § 893.55(1) deals only with medical malpractice *injury* claims, not death. However, this distinction is of no consequence in a medical malpractice setting. In analyzing § 893.55 the supremecourt stated: "[T]here is no logical distinction between injury and death claims arising out of medical malpractice. Once medical

(continued)

malpractice produces a loss, a remedy exists regardless whether the consequence is injury or death." *Rineck v. Johnson,* 155 Wis.2d 659, 671, 456 N.W.2d 336 (1990) .

In *Rineck,* the supreme court examined the relationship between ch. 655, Stats., and § 893.55 *Id.* at 665, 456 N.W.2d 336The court stated: "Chapter 655, Stats., enacted by ch. 37, Laws of 1975, established an exclusive procedure for the prosecution of malpractice claims against a health care provider. .... Chapter 655 sets tort claims produced by medical malpractice apart from other tort claims, and parties are conclusively presumed to be bound by the provisions of the chapter regardless of injury or death." *Id.* . "[S]oon after the enactment of Chapter 655, the legislature passed Wis. Stat. § 893.55 in part, to limit the damages a claimant could recover under medical malpractice claims." *Czapinski,* , 236 Wis.2d 316, 613 N.W.2d 120; Section 893.55 is the exclusive statute of limitations for Chapter 655 claims and limits "[e]conomic damages recovered under ch. 655 for bodily injury *or death.*" Wis. Stat. § 893.55(4)(e) (emphasis added).

While *Rineck* and *Czapinski* dealt with the issue of damages in medical malpractice claims, they clearly stand for the proposition that "by singling out medical malpractice claims in such a manner, the legislature intended to set medical malpractice cases involving death apart from other death cases to which the general wrongful death statute applies." *Rineck,* 155 Wis.2d at 671, 456 N.W.2d 336Thus, we must conclude that § 893.55 unequivocally applies to both injury and death claims resulting from medical malpractice. Therefore, wrongful death claims that are the result of medical malpractice are subject to § 893.55.

The amended complaint against Dr. Zimmer was filed in December of 1999, more than three years from the date of Sarah's injury. The trial court ruled that the amended complaint was also filed more than one year from the date the Hegartys should have discovered Dr. Zimmer's role in Sarah's hospitalization and treatment. Accordingly, the trial court granted summary judgment in favor of Dr. Zimmer, concluding that the amended complaint was barred by the statute of limitations, § 893.55(1) …

The discovery rule was established in *Hansen v. A.H. Robins Inc.,* 113 Wis.2d 550, 335 N.W.2d 578 (1983) . Under the discovery rule, a cause of action accrues on the date the injury is discovered or with reasonable diligence should be discovered, whichever occurs first. *Id.* at 560, 335 N.W.2d 578

This rule was further developed in *Borello v. U.S. Oil Co.,* 130 Wis.2d 397, 388 N.W.2d 140 (1986) The plaintiff in *Borello* had a furnace installed in her basement and within a few weeks was suffering from headaches, dizziness and respiratory problems. *Id.* at 400, 388 N.W.2d 140 She saw a number of doctors and, despite her insistence to the contrary, they told her that her symptoms were probably not related to the furnace. *Id.* at 409, 388 N.W.2d 140 Two years after her initial symptoms began, a doctor diagnosed her with "metal fume fever" which was caused by the defective furnace. *Id.* She filed suit and a statute of limitations defense was advanced. *Id.* at 399, 388 N.W.2d 140 The supreme court concluded that the plaintiff had not discovered her injury until the doctor's diagnosis of "metal fume fever." *Id.* at 401, 388 N.W.2d 140 In concluding that discovery includes discovery of the probable cause of injury, the court stated that "a cause of action will not accrue until the plaintiff discovers, or in the exercise of reasonable diligence should have discovered, not only the fact of injury but also that the injury was probably caused by the defendant's conduct or product." *Id.* at 411, 388 N.W.2d 140

In the present case, the Hegartys claim they did not obtain knowledge of Dr. Zimmer's negligent conduct regarding Sarah's care until September of 1999 when the depositions of Drs. Beauchaine and Stremski were taken. However, "the question at this stage of the proceedings is not when [the Hegartys] actually learned [they] had a claim against [Dr. Zimmer], but when [they] should have known." *Groom,* 179 Wis.2d at 250 n. 3, 507 N.W.2d 121

Dr. Zimmer asserts that the Hegartys should have known the extent of her involvement after examining the medical records. Therefore, we must examine the medical records to determine whether the plaintiff exercised reasonable diligence in discovering not only the injury but also "the defendant[']s part in that cause." *Kolpin v.*

(continued)

Pioneer Power & Light Co., 162 Wis.2d 1, 24, 469 N.W.2d 595 (1991) Additionally, in our summary judgment analysis, we look to see whether any facts are disputed regarding discovery and, if undisputed, whether only one inference can be reasonably drawn from those facts. *See Ford Farms,* 145 Wis.2d at 654, 430 N.W.2d 94

The Hegartys maintain that by 6:00 a.m. on March 21, Sarah's condition had deteriorated so drastically that no medical attention could have saved her life. They argue that Sarah's abdomen would not have become distended and her small intestines would not have died, requiring further surgeries, but for the negligence of those attending to her the night of March 20 and into the early morning. They contend that based on the medical records provided by Children's Hospital, they reasonably concluded that Dr. Stremski and Dr. Beauchaine were primarily responsible for the negligence; not Dr. Zimmer, whose name did not appear in the medical records as attending to Sarah until after 8:00 a.m. March 21.

No one disputes that Dr. Zimmer's name was listed in several places in Sarah's Children's Hospital medical records received by the Hegartys: (1) The "History and Physical Examination" form, listing Dr. Zimmer as Sarah's primary physician, and her phone number at the top of the page (this form was eventually signed by Dr. Zimmer at 8:15 a.m. on March 21, 1996); 2) The "Emergency Service Admission Orders," a preprinted form, stating that Sarah was a private patient of Dr. Zimmer; (3) The "Patient Admission Information" form, a computer-generated data sheet, which, among other information, contains the writing, "ATT1 Zimmer, Mary Jo"; and (4) The "Progress Notes," containing medical entries by Dr. Zimmer, all entered after the early morning on March 21, 1996. These entries referencing Dr. Zimmer are simply administrative or pro forma entries, and the fact that Dr. Zimmer's name is listed as Sarah's primary pediatrician says nothing about whether Dr. Zimmer was involved in Sarah's care during the "critical time period" of the late afternoon on March 20 until early morning on March 21. Further, Dr. Zimmer's entries made on the morning of March 21, gave no indication that Dr. Zimmer was involved in Sarah's care during the "critical time."

Ultimately, these records provide very limited information regarding Dr. Zimmer's role in Sarah's treatment during the critical hours of her care. Certainly the Hegartys already knew that Dr. Zimmer was their daughter's primary physician and that she had arrived at the hospital at approximately 8:00 a.m. on March 21, but these records do not indicate in any way that Dr. Zimmer was called several times on March 20, nor do they clarify that Dr. Zimmer discussed Sarah's care with Drs. Beauchaine and Stremski and recommended the critical course of future treatment, over the phone, based on a first-year resident's observations, which would carry Sarah through the night.

The Hegartys submit that it was not until they deposed Drs. Stremski and Beauchaine in the Fall of 1999 that they discovered Dr. Zimmer's crucial role in the admission and care of their daughter during the evening of March 20, 1996, and the early morning of March 21, 1996. At the depositions, they discovered that Dr. Stremski called Dr. Zimmer before admitting Sarah at 8:00 p.m. on March 20. They also learned that during this phone conversation, Dr. Zimmer discussed Sarah's condition, accepted the admission and concurred with Dr. Stremski's course of treatment. They also were surprised to learn that Dr. Beauchaine spoke with Dr. Zimmer by telephone at approximately 8:00 p.m. on March 20 and that all of the orders that Dr. Beauchaine recommended throughout the night were based on Dr. Zimmer's recommended course of treatment. Moreover, the Hegartys assert they had no knowledge that at approximately 6:00 a.m. on March 21, Dr. Beauchaine again spoke with Dr. Zimmer and informed her of Sarah's deteriorating condition and only then did Dr. Zimmer tell her to request a gastrointestinal consultation.

This information simply is not attainable from the records alone. Based on the medical records provided to the Hegartys in April of 1997, in the exercise of reasonable diligence, they could not have suspected Dr. Zimmer's negligence. *See Groom,* 179 Wis.2d at 247-48, 507 N.W.2d 121 However, the trial court stated:

So that from the records that I have referenced here this morning, I conclude that Dr. Zimmer's supervision of Dr. Beauchaine .... could be inferred to be within the reach of the plaintiff from the documents....

(continued)

.... So that the conclusion is that I don't believe under the circumstances that the plaintiff is entitled to the date of the discovery rule. The information in the medical records is sufficient.

This author disagrees. The medical records do not yield an accurate account of the pertinent events that led to Sarah's injury. Nowhere in the medical records does it clearly reflect that Dr. Zimmer was involved in Sarah's care, nor do they refer to Dr. Zimmer's directions to Dr. Beauchaine in regards to Sarah's course of treatment. The circumstances present here are distinguishable from those in *Groom*, relied upon by the trial court.

In *Groom*, a woman brought a medical malpractice action against a doctor for the death of her husband. *Id.* at 245, 507 N.W.2d 121 She later amended her complaint to add another doctor and his medical group, but the trial court dismissed her amended complaint as barred by the medical malpractice statute of limitations, Wis. Stat. § 893.55 because the amended complaint was filed more than one year after she should have discovered her claims against the additional doctor. *Id.* The trial court ruled that the date of discovery was the day hospital records were sent to her containing "the identities of [her husband's] health care providers *and the nature of care provided to him.*" *Id.* at 248, 507 N.W.2d 121 (emphasis added).

In *Groom*, this court examined the medical records and concluded that "the only reasonable inference from them is that [the wife] had information to form the basis for an objective belief that [the doctor]'s treatment was a cause of her husband's death." *Id.* at 249-50, 507 N.W.2d 121 . The hospital records in *Groom* not only disclosed the identity of the physicians connected with her husband's care, but also contained information that the doctor in question took a cardiac history of her husband, knew her husband's course of treatment, and had knowledge that another doctor had prescribed the drug that caused her husband's death. *Id.* at 250, 507 N.W.2d 121 Finally, the records also revealed that this doctor had developed a clinical impression and a course of treatment. *Id.*

Unlike *Groom*, where the court determined that "the material facts are undisputed," and that there was "only [one] reasonable inference from these undisputed facts," *id.* at 249-50, 507 N.W.2d 121, the present case has a number of unresolved factual issues and any number of conflicting inferences which can be drawn from the medical records. With respect to Dr. Zimmer's allegations that the Hegartys should have known that she was called by examining the medical records, the trial court stated:

It is certainly true that the records don't contain everything that happened here. There were the telephone calls that took place. Not every telephone call is noted. ..

The Milwaukee Children's Hospital records are not complete in every respect. As I said before, they don't reflect every phone call between Dr. Zimmer and Dr. Beauchaine. There were evidently phone calls made.

First, no telephone calls are "noted" in the medical records. The medical records failed to note *any* phone calls between "Dr. Zimmer and Dr. Beauchaine." Second, during oral argument, the parties' own attorneys could not agree on the number of phone calls referenced in the medical records. However, in Dr. Zimmer's brief in support of dismissal, she argues that "[t]he medical records are clear as to who treated Sarah, when they treated her, and what the treatment consisted of. .... The Plaintiffs knew that Dr. Zimmer was involved in Sarah's treatment." Further, in argument to this court, Dr. Zimmer insisted that, "the emergency room records clearly reflect telephone calls on the evening of March 20, 1996 to the 'admitting physician,' Dr. Zimmer, which, at the very least would warrant counsel's immediate attention." Dr. Zimmer's contentions are incorrect.

A careful review of the medical records reveals no clear evidence of phone calls to Dr. Zimmer. Dr. Zimmer points to two documents in support of her conclusion: (1) the "Emergency Room [N]ursing [N]ote," and (2) the "History and Physical Examination" form. The "Emergency Room [N]ursing [N]ote," dated March 20, 1996, written before Sarah was admitted to the hospital, lists a number of notes and observations, and their times:

.... [T]oday, [no] diarrhea. Started [approximately] 1 hr. ago. Lips dry. To room 3—[Doctor] to examine. 1735--LR bolus started, [complained of] being cold, blankets given....

(continued)

> 1750--[Patient] states not feeling any better, feeling worse....
> 1850--To have x-ray .... x-ray done[.] *Admitting called.* (emphasis added)
> 1945--Fleets enema given .... Awaiting results.....
> 2000--Report to [nurse] ....
> ADM. CALLED @ 1940

Nothing in this note conclusively states that Dr. Zimmer was called. The Nursing Note only states that "Admitting" was called. Nothing indicates that "Admitting" is a doctor, let alone Dr. Zimmer. In fact, "Admitting" is more likely the admitting desk of the hospital. The second document, the "History and Physical Examination" form, is a four-page document that has Dr. Zimmer's name and phone number written on the top of the front page, but there is no reference in that document that Dr. Zimmer was ever actually called.

These documents simply do not substantiate that Dr. Zimmer was called on March 20, 1996. Thus, contrary to Dr. Zimmer's argument, the records do not "clearly reflect telephone calls" on the evening of March 20, 1996, to the " 'admitting physician,' Dr. Zimmer." Absent the information supplied by Drs. Beauchaine and Stremski in their depositions, no one could reasonably surmise from these minor references to "doctor" or "admitting" in the medical records that Drs. Beauchaine and Stremski actually spoke to Dr. Zimmer about Sarah's care on March 20, 1996, or the morning of March 21. From these pro forma references, one could conclude only that Dr. Zimmer was Sarah's pediatrician, but no one could reasonably suspect that Dr. Zimmer discussed Sarah's condition with the treating physicians, concurred with their course of treatment, and recommended all of Sarah's treatment orders throughout the night. While Dr. Zimmer's name is certainly listed on the medical records, the records do not reveal Dr. Zimmer's role in supervising Sarah's care.

While true that "[p]laintiffs may not close their eyes to means of information *reasonably accessible* to them and must in good faith apply their attention to those particulars which may be inferred *to be within their reach*," *Groom*, 179 Wis.2d at 251, 507 N.W.2d 121 > (emphasis added), without more in the medical records, it was impossible for the Hegartys to know of Dr. Zimmer's crucial role without the information later supplied by Drs. Beauchaine's and Stremski's deposition testimony regarding the phone calls. Unlike *Groom*, these records do not readily demonstrate Dr. Zimmer's involvement during the critical hours of Sarah's care. [FN5] Further, this factual dispute goes to the heart of whether the evidence contained in the medical records provided the Hegartys with sufficient information such that they should have known Dr. Zimmer's role in the cause of Sarah's injury. Accordingly, the number, clarity and presence of any reference in the hospital records to phone calls made by Dr. Stremski and Dr. Beauchaine to Dr. Zimmer on the dates in question is a material fact that remains in dispute.*Borello v. U.S. Oil Co.*, 130 Wis.2d 397, 388 N.W.2d 140 (1986) also makes clear that subjective beliefs, suspicions, or hunches will not be enough to establish a date of discovery. *Id.* at 411-16, 388 N.W.2d 140 This rationale becomes relevant in light of the present facts and the supreme court's recent decision in *Jandrt v. Jerome Foods, Inc.*, 227 Wis.2d 531, 597 N.W.2d 744 (1999) ≥, where the court concluded that a law firm unreasonably followed an expert/doctor's suggestion to continue a lawsuit in order to "take discovery" concerning a weak causal link. *Id.* at 565-66, 597 N.W.2d 744 In sanctioning the lawyers for continuing a frivolous lawsuit, the court explained that lawyers will not be allowed to claim "safe harbor" where they choose to file an action first and then sort out the underlying element of causation through discovery where an investigation could be completed without discovery. *Id.* at 567-69, 597 N.W.2d 744 The court concluded that the "file first and ask questions later" approach to litigation will not carry the day. *Id.* at 569, 597 N.W.2d 744

Additionally, Dr. Zimmer challenged, at trial and on appeal, whether the Hegartys had personal knowledge of the level of Dr. Zimmer's involvement. Both parents filed affidavits with the trial court stating that they had no knowledge of Dr. Zimmer's involvement in their daughter's care during the evening of March 20

(continued)

and the early morning of March 21 until after the depositions of the other doctors. However, in its decision granting summary judgment, the trial court, referencing the medical records, stated:

> "At the bottom of this form appears the signature of Sarah's mother. The signature and time is not indicated nor is the date. ..I certainly wouldn't expect that Mrs. Hegarty, in signing that last document that I mentioned, the consent form, would have immediately taken note of the paragraph that I read if for no other reason than that she was under considerable stress .... but it would be some disclosure to anybody looking over those records that there is a hierarchy here and that residents are under the supervision of attending physicians".

This dispute surrounding what the Hegartys knew and when they knew it becomes more apparent in light of Dr. Zimmer's attorney's oral argument immediately preceding the trial court's decision in which counsel stated: "They are claiming that even when [Dr. Zimmer] got there, she didn't do the right thing. They knew that. They have known that since the date this took place. Mrs. Hegarty was standing right there. They knew that when they went to an attorney. They had a suspicion." In her brief, Dr. Zimmer argued that "Sarah's mother was present at the time of injury" and "[p]laintiffs knew of all physicians rendering treatment." In her pleadings, Dr. Zimmer argued that the medical records "would only have confirmed what Sarah's mother already knew because she was present with Dr. Zimmer at Children's." Finally, Dr. Zimmer concluded that "[t]his time frame includes the 22 hour 'delay' which constitutes the basis of the Plaintiff's claim," *i.e.*, the critical time...

It is clear that the parties dispute whether Sarah's parents had actual knowledge of Dr. Zimmer's negligence. Moreover, the trial court implied that, at some point, the Hegartys attained personal knowledge of Dr. Zimmer's supervision, despite their affidavits to the contrary. As referenced above, the trial court relied on this fact in its summary judgment analysis.

"When the material facts are undisputed, and only one inference can reasonably be drawn from them, whether a plaintiff exercised reasonable diligence in discovering [the] injury is a question of law." *Id.* at 249, 507 N.W.2d 121 Moreover, if "only one reasonable inference may be drawn from the undisputed facts, then the drawing of that inference is a question of law, and an appellate court may draw it." *Id.* However, we will reverse a summary judgment if a review of the record reveals that disputed material facts exist or undisputed material facts exist from which reasonable alternative inferences may be drawn. *Grams v. Boss,* 97 Wis.2d 332, 338, 294 N.W.2d 473 (1980).

Here, a number of material facts remain in dispute. First, based on the arguments at trial and on appeal, it is clear that the parties disagree as to whether the Hegartys had personal knowledge of Dr. Zimmer's supervision before the fall of 1999. This dispute is material because without knowing of Dr. Zimmer's supervision of Sarah's care during the evening, the Hegartys were unaware of their daughter's "injury, its nature, its cause, *and the identity of the allegedly responsible defendant.*" *Spitler v. Dean,* 148 Wis.2d 630, 635, 436 N.W.2d 308 (1989).

Second, as noted, there is a factual dispute as to the number and nature of the phone calls between the hospital and Dr. Zimmer as reflected in the medical records. While the trial court correctly concluded that this does not affect whether the Hegartys *actually* knew, it does affect whether "there [wa]s information available to the claimant of .... the cause of her injury [ ] and the defendant's part in that cause." *Ford Farms Ltd. v. Wisconsin Elec. Power Co.,* 145 Wis.2d at 657, 430 N.W.2d 94

Finally, "whether a factual inference may be drawn, whether it is reasonable and whether it is the only reasonable inference are all questions of law for this court to decide." *Id.* at 249, 507 N.W.2d 121 The trial court concluded that Dr. Zimmer's supervision of Dr. Beauchaine could be inferred from the hospital records alone. After an independent review of the medical records, this is not the only reasonable inference.

One could just as easily infer that Dr. Zimmer had nothing to do with Sarah's medical treatment until the morning of March 21, 1996. The record is insufficiently developed to dispositively resolve these issues. Absent the information from Drs. Beauchaine's and Stremski's depositions, the Hegartys could not have

(continued)

known "the identities of [their daughter's] health care providers and the nature of care provided to [her]." *Groom,* 179 Wis.2d at 248, 507 N.W.2d 121 "We have often stated summary judgment is a drastic remedy and should not be granted unless the material facts are not in dispute, no competing inferences can arise, and the law that resolves the issue is clear." *Lecus v. American Mut. Ins. Co. of Boston,* 81 Wis.2d 183, 189, 260 N.W.2d 241 (1977) . "Summary judgment is not to be a trial on affidavits and depositions." *Id.* Unfortunately, this has become just that—a trial on affidavits, depositions and medical records—a task better left to the jury. A significant jury question exists as to when the Hegartys actually knew or should have known the extent of Dr. Zimmer's involvement in the care of their daughter on March 20, 1996, and the early morning of March 21, 1996. *See Ford Farms,* 145 Wis.2d at 659, 430 N.W.2d 94 . Accordingly, the trial court's grant of summary judgment was inappropriate.

In its grant of summary judgment, the trial court determined that Affiliated Hospitals had no vicarious liability with respect to Dr. Beauchaine. Under the doctrine of respondeat superior, the trial court concluded that even though Dr. Beauchaine was employed by Affiliated Hospitals, she was not Affiliated Hospital's "servant" because it lacked the right to control the details of her work.

It is undisputed that Dr. Beauchaine was an employee of Affiliated Hospitals. The Hegartys contend that the terms "employee" and "servant" are used interchangeably and, therefore, once there is an employment relationship, respondeat superior liability follows as a matter of law. We disagree.

Under the doctrine of respondeat superior, the master is subject to liability for the torts of the servant committed while acting in the scope of his or her employment. Restatement (Second) of Agency § 219(1) (1958) While the distinction between "employer" and "master," and "employee" and "servant," has become blurred, the distinction remains important. The supreme court has stated:

In more recent times the words "employer and employee" have nearly supplanted the older term of "master and servant." This shift has been due no doubt to the vast increase in the employment of skilled persons in industry. The word "servant" has certain connotations which are distasteful to many persons .... so that it has come about that the terms "servant," "employee" and "agent" are often used interchangeably without regard to their strict legal meaning.

Ryan v. Wisconsin Dep't of Taxation, <242 Wis. 491, 496-97, 8 N.W.2d 393 (1943) (citation omitted).

The legal significance is great. A servant is not only "one employed to perform a service for another," but also "is subject to the other's control or right of control." *Kashishian v. Port,* 167 Wis.2d 24, 33, 481 N.W.2d 277 (1992) (citations omitted). Wisconsin's civil jury instruction defining these terms adds further clarity to this distinction: "A 'servant' is one employed to perform service for another in his or her affairs and who, with respect to his or her physical conduct in the performance of the services, is subject to the other's control or right to control." WIS JI—CIVIL 4030. Therefore, the trial court applied the correct legal standard by distinguishing between an "employee" and a "servant."

Accordingly, since Affiliated Hospitals admits that Dr. Beauchaine was its employee, we must examine whether it had "the right to control the details of [her] work." *Madison Newspapers, Inc. v. Wisconsin Dep't of Revenue,* 228 Wis.2d 745, 764, 599 N.W.2d 51 (Ct.App.1999) "The right to control is the dominant test in determining whether an individual is a servant." *Pamperin v. Trinity Mem'l Hosp.,* 144 Wis.2d 188, 199, 423 N.W.2d 848 (1988) "However, other factors are considered, including the place of work, the time of the employment, the method of payment, the nature of the business or occupation, which party furnishes the instrumentalities or tools, the intent of the parties to the contract, and the right of summary discharge of employees." *Id.* at 199, 423 N.W.2d 848

Here, Affiliated Hospitals claims that it served primarily as "an administrative or bookkeeping function on behalf of hundreds of medical trainees." This statement ignores undisputed facts that suggest Affiliated

(continued)

Hospitals was more than an administrative entity: (1) Affiliated Hospitals employed Beauchaine under a written employment agreement; (2) Beauchaine received her paycheck and W2 from Affiliated Hospitals; (3) residents like Beauchaine were placed at hospitals through Affiliated Hospitals' graduate medical training program(4) Affiliated Hospitals provided Beauchaine with health, disability, life, and accidental death and dismemberment insurance; (5) Affiliated Hospitals set Beauchaine's vacation schedule; (6) Affiliated Hospitals had the right to unilaterally terminate Beauchaine's contract and to fire her (7) the program directors, who are responsible for the evaluation and advancement of residents like Beauchaine, were subject to Affiliated Hospitals' policies and procedures governing staff education and (8) Affiliated Hospitals agreed to provide Dr. Beauchaine with legal defense and to indemnify her for any medical malpractice occurring within the scope of her employment.

In its respondeat superior analysis, the trial court relied on *Kashishian*. In *Kashishian,* the supreme court held that a hospital and a doctor did not have a master/servant relationship where the hospital "did not exercise control over the manner in which Dr. Port's cardiological services were provided." *Id.* at 34, 481 N.W.2d 277 . Dr. Port was a cardiologist and the Director of Nuclear Cardiology within the Cardiovascular Disease Section of the Milwaukee Clinical Campus run by the University of Wisconsin Medical School. *Id.* at 29-30, 481 N.W.2d 277 Because of Dr. Port's "exercise of independent professional judgment" the court concluded that the hospital was not in a position to, and generally would not, exercise control over such an employee. *Id.* at 34, 481 N.W.2d 277

The respondeat superior analysis in the current case involves vicarious liability of the medical program rather than the hospital, but there are other important distinctions. In *Kashishian,* no one challenged that "Dr. Port was an employee/servant of the University Physicians Milwaukee Clinical Campus Practice Plan, Inc." *Id.* at 33, 481 N.W.2d 277 . However, in concluding that Dr. Port was not a servant of the hospital, the court noted:

Other factors also indicate that Dr. Port was not [the hospital's] servant at the time of the alleged malpractice. Dr. Port's paycheck came from the Milwaukee Practice Plan, a corporate entity controlled by the University. .... [T]he Associate Dean of the University of the University of Wisconsin Medical School, stated in an affidavit that .... he held the direct responsibility to supervise the activities of the University faculty. .... He further indicated that all final decisions on appointments and reappointments of the faculty .... were made by the Dean of the University Medical School. *Id.* at 34-35, 481 N.W.2d 277 " A number of undisputed facts establish that Affiliated Hospitals, a group similar to the corporate entity controlled by the university in *Kashishian,* had authority over Dr. Beauchaine's employment. First, "the method of payment of compensation, **375 and the presence .... of the right of the employer to summarily terminate the contract or hiring" establish that Affiliated Hospitals exercised control over Dr. Beauchaine. *See Scholz v. Indus. Comm'n,* 267 Wis. 31, 37, 64 N.W.2d 204 (1954) In addition, in an affidavit, the executive director of Affiliated Hospitals stated that Dr. Beauchaine would be "performing medical services under the supervision and control of the program director." Although the program director is not an employee, Affiliated Hospitals admits that Dr. Lewis was "an officer of [Affiliated Hospitals]." Finally, Dr. Beauchaine signed a "medical training agreement" with Affiliated Hospitals stating that she would "comply with the administrative and professional policies, procedures, rules and regulations of [Affiliated Hospitals], The Medical College of Wisconsin, and the affiliated institution to which he/she is assigned." This agreement further noted that, "[t]hese policies may change from time to time in [Affiliated Hospitals'] sole discretion." While Affiliated Hospitals may not have exercised exclusive or absolute control over her work, we note that the trial court failed to fully address a key relationship relevant to the control element—whether Dr. Beauchaine was a loaned or borrowed servant. *See Borneman v. Corwyn Transp., Ltd.* 212 Wis.2d 25, 43, 567 N.W.2d 887 (Ct.App.1997) In *Borneman,* we applied the *Seaman* test to determine whether an individual is a loaned employee...Those issues are not relevant here. This is not a "temporary help agency" case like *Gansch* involving the Worker's Compensation Act. In all other cases involving the loaned employee doctrine, the supreme

(continued)

court still utilizes the *Seaman* test and has declined to revise it. *See Borneman*, 219 Wis.2d at 355, 580 N.W.2d 253 . We thus apply the test originally enunciated in *Seaman*.

The relation of employer and employee exists as between a special employer to whom an employee is loaned whenever the following facts concur: (a) Consent on the part of the employee to work for a special employer; (b) Actual entry by the employee upon the work of and for the special employer pursuant to an express or implied contract so to do; (c) Power of the special employer to control the details of the work to be performed and to determine how the work shall be done and whether it shall stop or continue. *Id.* at 32, 567 N.W.2d 887 The focus of the overall inquiry is "to determine whether a new employment contract was created by the parties." *Id.* at 33, 567 N.W.2d 887

This determination is a key element in the present respondeat superior analysis because of "a well-established presumption relevant to the control element of the *Seaman* test." *Id.* at 43, 567 N.W.2d 887 This presumption states:

In the absence of evidence to the contrary, there is an inference that the actor remains in his [or her] general employment so long as, by the service rendered another, he [or she] is performing the business entrusted to [them] by the general employer. There is no inference that because the general employer has permitted a division of control, [the employer] has surrendered it.

Id. at 43-44, 567 N.W.2d 887 "This inference has risen to the level of a legal presumption." *Id.* at 44, 567 N.W.2d 887 Affiliated Hospitals argues that it is not required to prove it loaned Dr. Beauchaine to a particular institution, nor was the trial court required to make a finding in that regard. We disagree. Simply because Affiliated Hospitals allowed a division of this control, we cannot assume that it intended to relinquish it. *See generally Seaman Body Corp. v. Indus. Comm'n*, 204 Wis. 157, 235 N.W. 433 (1931) Where the trial court never fully considered the issue, the record is insufficient to overcome the presumption that Dr. Beauchaine remained in her general employment with Affiliated Hospitals. *See Borneman*, 212 Wis.2d at 44, 567 N.W.2d 887 . Affiliated Hospitals must overcome this presumption by showing that it relinquished full control of its servant. *See Edwards v. Cutler-Hammer*, 272 Wis. 54, 64, 74 N.W.2d 606 (1956)

The general employer may rebut the presumption by showing that it relinquished full control of its servant. *Id.* Therefore, once the plaintiffs have established a prima facie case that the general employer is the master, as the Hegartys have here, "the burden is on upon the general employer to establish not only that he loaned the servant but that he surrendered control and direction over the servant to the borrower." *Borneman*, 212 Wis.2d at 44, 567 N.W.2d 887 .

As the trial court stated, "if it is not [Affiliated Hospitals] and it is not Children's [Hospital], then who is it?" Someone was Dr. Beauchaine's "master." Unlike the doctor in *Kashishian*, Dr. Beauchaine was not given full discretion in the "exercise of independent professional judgment." She was a first-year, unlicensed medical resident. In her deposition, Dr. Beauchaine stated that she could not perform any procedures, she was not authorized to call for a surgical consult, and was otherwise limited in her ability to write prescriptions and order procedures. This is not the unfettered discretion of the independent cardiologist in *Kashishian*.

While the record is not adequately developed on this point, it appears from the pleadings and excerpts of depositions that the residents in the program rotate from hospital to hospital. Therefore, while at Children's Hospital, Dr. Beauchaine was under the supervision of a number of people. While on the floor admitting patients, Dr. Beauchaine was supervised by the attending physician and a senior resident. However, Dr. Beauchaine's day-to-day assignments, supervision and review were supervised by the Medical College through a pediatric faculty member. This faculty member, previously referred to as the program director, does not rotate from hospital to hospital, but is assigned to a specific hospital.

(continued)

In Dr. Beauchaine's residency at Children's Hospital, her program director was Dr. David Lewis. Dr. Lewis stated in his deposition:

The training program directors are a part of [Affiliated Hospitals'] committee of training program directors that administer or that oversees all the training programs, and that participates in the process of reaccreditation and evaluation of programs and evaluation of the overall well-being of residents in all of the [Affiliated Hospitals'] programs. Although Dr. Lewis was an employee of the Medical College, as a program director, he did oversee and enforce Affiliated Hospitals' policies and procedures governing staff education. Additionally, as "an officer" of Affiliated Hospitals, Dr. Lewis was also apparently subject to Affiliated Hospitals' policies and procedures while at Children's Hospital pursuant to the "INSTITUTION AGREEMENT."

The residents, like Dr. Beauchaine, rotate from hospital to hospital. While at a hospital, a number of individuals "control the details of their work." One of these individuals being the program director who, as previously stated, is a member of Affiliated Hospitals' committee that oversees the residency program and is subject to the policies and procedures of Affiliated Hospitals.

More importantly, before a resident is assigned to a specific hospital or while waiting for an assignment, it appears that Affiliated Hospitals is the sole employer and master. We conclude that the evidence, as set forth in the pleadings, was sufficient to create the presumption that Dr. Beauchaine was both an employee and a servant of Affiliated Hospitals. The trier of fact must determine whether Affiliated Hospitals intended to relinquish control to the hospital, attending physician, or someone else.

We conclude that reasonable persons might disagree as to whether Dr. Beauchaine was a servant of Affiliated Hospitals and, if so, whether Affiliated Hospitals intended to relinquish full control to another institution. Resolving any doubts regarding a factual issue against the party moving for summary judgment, here Affiliated Hospitals, *see L.L.N. v. Clauder,* 209 Wis.2d 674, 684, 563 N.W.2d 434 (1997) we conclude that summary judgment is inappropriate and a trial is necessary to resolve these issues, *see Preloznik,* 113 Wis.2d at 116, 334 N.W.2d 580 After examining the pleadings, affidavits, depositions, and other papers on file, we conclude that a genuine issue exists as to a number of material facts, and reasonable conflicting inferences may be drawn from the undisputed facts, therefore requiring a trial. *See Green Spring Farms,* 136 Wis.2d at 315, 401 N.W.2d 816. Two significant jury questions have been presented: (1) at any time, was Dr. Beauchaine a servant of Affiliated Hospitals, *i.e.,* was she employed by Affiliated Hospitals and was she subject to Affiliated Hospitals' control or right to control; and, if so (2) did Affiliated Hospitals loan Dr. Beauchaine to another and surrender the right to control Dr. Beauchaine to that other institution or person? Accordingly, we reverse the trial court's grant of summary judgment as to Affiliated Hospitals' vicarious liability.

Orders affirmed in part; reversed in part and cause remanded.

As seen in the case above, there are many considerations in the respondeat superior claims involving alleged medical malpractice. In the illustrated case, the defendant hospital was found to be vicariously liable. However, medical facilities and practitioners are becoming increasingly difficult to tie together. Part of the reason is economics. The more one can isolate oneself, the less likelihood of liability for the acts of others. Technological advances support this as well. As scientific methods in medicine develop, specialized knowledge increases the gap among various health care professionals. Less than 75 years ago, the majority of physicians were individual practitioners responsible for diagnosis and treatment of virtually all illnesses a patient might encounter. Many physicians were regular employees of relatively small hospitals. Now, a patient with even a fairly straightforward medical condition might be under the care of any number of specialized physicians and technicians while traveling to multiple health care facilities for the purposes of diagnosis, testing, and treatment.

The exhibit that follows lists relevant considerations that courts will utilize when making a determination of whether an employer/employee relationship occurred in such a manner that the employer should be held legally accountable for the actions of the employee. If many or all of these questions are answered in the affirmative, then it is likely that respondeat superior can be established and the alleged employer held legally and financially responsible for the actions of the alleged employee.

Exhibit 1.1   Factors to Determine Applicability of Respondeat Superior in a Medical Malpractice Action

1. Did the alleged employer have the right to control the details of the alleged employee's work?

2. Where was the work performed?

3. What was the time and method of payment for employment?

   a) Was it periodic or continuing;

   b) was payment on a per-case basis or at a regulated rate such as hourly;

   c) were taxes withheld from payment;

   d) were employer-related fees/taxes paid such as worker's compensation; social security and Medicare?

4. Which party furnished the tools necessary for the work to be accomplished?

5. What was the intent of the parties with respect to the employment arrangement?

6. Did one party have the right to summarily discharge the other party?

7. Were any employee benefits provided for the alleged employee such as group health, life or disability insurance?

8. Did the alleged employer provide professional liability insurance and/or legal defense for the professional conduct of the alleged employee?

9. Did the alleged employer have the right to loan the services of the alleged employee to others?

10. Did the actions of the employee constitute an intentional tort?

    a) if so, was the intentional tort encouraged or acquiesced by the employer?

(continued)

Exhibit 1.1, continued

> 11. Did the allegedly negligent act(s) involve the execution of highly specialized knowledge and judgment?
>
> 12. Did the allegedly negligent act involve conduct that involved the administration of a particular skill rather than independent judgment?
>
> 13. Did the alleged employee maintain a professional status such as a private practice independent of the alleged employer?
>
> 14. Did the patient independently select the alleged employee for care, treatment or services, or was the alleged employee selected by the hospital?
>
> 15. Did the patient have a prior professional relationship with the employee?
>
> 16. Was the alleged employer responsible for regular payment of wages, fees, or a salary to the alleged employee?
>
> 17. Did the alleged employer provide equipment, supplies, support personnel, office space, and patient billing for the services provided by the alleged employee?
>
> 18. Did the alleged employer set the schedule, and/or establish policies and procedures to be followed by the alleged employee?
>
> 19. Did the alleged employer represent to the patients or the public at large as a provider of medical services and that the alleged employee or individuals in that capacity were employees or under the general direction and control of the alleged employer?

INTENTIONAL TORTS IN CASES OF MEDICAL MALPRACTICE

As discussed above, negligence involves an action or omission that the actor should have reasonably foreseen as a potential danger to others. But what of the instance when the actor knows or should know with substantial certainty that an action or omission will cause injury to a party and the actor moves forward anyway? This type of conduct is addressed by the **intentional tort**. Because of the much greater knowledge and risk of specific injury, the intentional tort action requires more exact evidence but, it may produce much greater consequences for a defendant. In the case of medical malpractice, the intentional tort, like negligence, is fault based. However, intentional torts require more specific conduct which demonstrates a greater responsibility for knowledge of the near certainty of injury.

As in negligence, the knowledge of the actor in an intentional tort case is constructive. Thus, the question is not what the actor actually knew but rather what he or she should have known under the circumstances. In the case of medical malpractice, the reasonable defendant similarly situated and with appropriate education, training, and skill would be aware of all risks associated with a particular act or omission. The defendant's actual conduct is then compared to that standard. In the case of medical malpractice based on an alleged intentional tort, the question is this: Did the defendant have constructive knowledge that the act or omission was substantially certain to cause injury to the plaintiff?

A common misconception by those without knowledge of this area of law is that an intentional tort describes an action toward another with the intent to cause injury. This is not at all the case. Such conduct as described would likely be more appropriately addressed in a criminal action. Rather, an intentional tort does have an essential element of intent, but it is the intent to act without regard as opposed to the intent to injure. More specifically, the intentional tort requires proof that the defendant acted voluntarily, even with the knowledge that the act would almost certainly bring about the injury. Thus, unlike negligence where only an awareness or foreseeability of the possibility is needed, the intentional tort imposes much greater knowledge on the actor. An example of an intentional tort of battery might be a physician who fails to account for the instruments used during surgery and leaves a metal clamp within a patient's body.

Another distinguishing factor between negligence and intentional torts is specificity with respect to the factual situations. The elements of negligence remain the same regardless of how the case arose, whether it is a case involving an automobile accident or a case of negligent infliction of emotional distress or medical malpractice. In a case claiming intentional tort, there are specific types of intentional tort actions for specific types of occurrences. Each action has distinct elements that must be proven by the plaintiff and, typically, only established types of actions for intentional tort may be brought. Therefore, if a circumstance is not addressed by a recognized form of intentional tort it must be brought under a different legal theory such as negligence.

Intentional tort differs from the degree of duty concept in negligence because in an intentional tort the risk is so great that it can virtually be counted on to produce the injury. If the actor commits the action despite this knowledge, then the action may constitute an intentional tort against the injured party. A major distinction between gross negligence and an intentional tort is that mere knowledge and appreciation of a danger are insufficient in an intentional tort. As stated, there must be evidence of voluntary conduct in light of the knowledge and appreciation of the danger. In addition, the risk of harm must be a near certainty rather than a degree of probability.

There are many intentional torts and the elements of each tort are somewhat broadly stated to accommodate a variety of factual situations. Some of these are described in Exhibit 1.2 below. In the case of medical malpractice, an intentional tort may be committed by any number of different health care providers in an infinite number of circumstances. But if the conduct matches the elements of a specific type of tort, then an action may be brought. See Application 1.5.

Exhibit 1.2 Common Medical Malpractice Intentional Torts/Elements

INTENTIONAL TORT	**REQUIRED PROOF**
Abandonment	severance by the provider of the professional relationship with the patient at a time when continued care, treatment, or services are still necessary and without providing reasonable notice and opportunity to seek alternative professional services.

(continued)

Exhibit 1.2, continued

Assault	when relevant circumstances are such as to lead a person to reasonably apprehend injury from the unpermitted act of another.
Battery	when medical care, treatment or services performed are substantially different from that to which patient consents.
Breach of Confidentiality	when a health care provider establishes a professional relationship with the patient and discloses confidential patient information as the result of that professional relationship thereby causing damage to the patient.
Appropriation	when the health care provider makes use of the patient's likeness in a public forum, without consent and primarily for a commercial purpose.
False Light	a health care provider knowingly and recklessly makes a public disclosure of a false communication about a patient that would be highly offensive to a reasonable person.

APPLICATION 1.5

Thirty-one-year old Barbara is pregnant with her first child. A late term exam shows that the baby is in a transverse breech position and a cesarean section will be necessary to deliver the child. Prior to surgery, Barbara informs her physician that after an appendectomy as a teenager she discovered that she is allergic to the soluble suture generally used for internal sutures and that, unlike most people, her body does not dissolve them over time. The surgeon ignores this assuming that Barbara is incorrect because only one in 10,000 people reject soluble sutures and the appendectomy was more than a decade before. Different sutures were available but took longer to put in place and were not normally used in this situation. He performs the surgery and uses the soluble sutures for the internal layers of tissue. The sutures generally dissolve in 90 days and rarely last more than six months. One year later Barbara presents herself to the physician with an inflamed incision site that is severely infected. The physician notes that a number of the soluble sutures are not only present, they have worked their way to an area just below the skin surface and are the cause of the infection. Barbara is taken back to surgery. The entire incision must be reopened, the sutures removed, and a different type of suture put in their place. She is then treated for the infection. Her recovery lasts almost two months.

(continued)

> In the above case, an intentional tort probably occurred because the physician knew or should have known that individuals do, in fact, sometimes react to the particular type of suture. The patient informed him that she was one such person and had the reaction in the past. In spite of this information, he proceeded with the use of the soluble sutures and significant injuries occurred as a result.

In Application 1.5 above, the principle is demonstrated that the physician knew or should have known of the almost certain injury to his patient given the history she provided. Thus, there was constructive knowledge of the substantial certainty of injury and in spite of the knowledge, the physician acted in a manner that did, in fact, produce the injury. This is an example of an intentional tort. As stated in Exhibit 1.2, there are a number of specific types of intentional torts. If none of these fit the circumstance an alternative cause of action, such as negligence, must be considered. The discussion below describes some of the more common intentional torts used in medical malpractice actions.

Abandonment

In this type of intentional tort it is alleged that the provider of health care, treatment, or services did not complete the terms of the professional relationship with the patient and as a result caused injury. If a provider takes on the responsibility for a patient and then unilaterally and prematurely severs that relationship without assisting the patient, or at the very least providing reasonable opportunity to obtain appropriate alternative care, the provider can be deemed to have abandoned the patient. If injury occurs as a result, the patient may be able to recover under an intentional tort theory. It is essential that a health care provider continue the professional relationship with the patient until such time as the patient no longer requires care, treatment, or services, or the patient has access to suitable alternatives. These may include referrals to other competent providers or adequate notice of the intent to discontinue the professional relationship enabling the patient to seek other care. The amount of involvement by the health care provider depends on the condition of the patient and the degree of immediate and long-term care required. See Application 1.6.

APPLICATION 1.6

Maxine is involved in a car accident and suffers a broken jaw. She is seen in the emergency room and taken to surgery by a licensed oral surgeon. He performs repairs to Maxine's jaw that requires it to be wired shut for a period of six weeks. She is instructed (in accordance with standard routine) by a nurse to call the surgeon's office in five weeks to make an appointment to have her jaw released from the wires. Unknown to Maxine, the physician is planning to retire and move away in a period of five weeks. When Maxine calls, the office has been closed and phones disconnected. There are no referral numbers or other physicians' names given. This was the only oral surgeon in the community. After a period of several days, Maxine is able to obtain an appointment with an oral surgeon 100 miles away, but the surgeon is on vacation and Maxine cannot be seen for a period of two additional weeks beyond the original six. As a result, she is required to have her jaw remain wired shut for this additional time. The surgeon who operated had a responsibility to either care for Maxine through completion of her treatment or arrange for her proper care. The failure to do either constitutes patient abandonment.

Assault

In tort law, assault has a quite different meaning than the more commonly known criminal act of assault. In criminal law, assault is usually associated with a physical contact and injury. But in civil law, assault is the creation of a reasonable apprehension of immediate physical harm by another. It is not necessary that actual physical contact and/or injury follow. Rather, the injury is the creation of fear. While at first this may seem somewhat shallow as a basis for civil litigation and a potential award of damages. However, it has a particular application in the realm of medical malpractice. Quite often, patients find themselves in an already vulnerable position. One who acts in way that is substantially certain to produce fear of harm in an already vulnerable person is a particularly offensive act to most judges and juries. See Application 1.7.

APPLICATION 1.7

George is an elderly patient in a long-term care facility. He is confined to bed and in fragile health. A nursing assistant is assigned to feed George two of his three daily meals. However, the assistant eats these meals. He threatens George with various torturous acts if he attempts to inform anyone of what is going on and states that the worst that could happen to him, if caught, is that he would be reprimanded and, thus still able to carry out his punishment of George. Due to the decreased food intake, George is slowly deteriorating; this is blamed on his advanced age. The threats of harm to one who cannot protect himself constitutes a civil assault in this circumstance. The actual withholding of food is likely actionable as well.

Battery

In general terms, the intentional tort of battery is a relatively simple matter. By definition, the battery must consist of an unpermitted physical contact that causes harm. This may be something as simple as someone who strikes another individual during a fight, or as complicated as the cases found in the arena of medical malpractice. In the latter situation, there are a number of additional factors to be considered. For example, health care providers do not ordinarily go about randomly treating individuals on the street. Rather, the individuals typically present themselves to health care providers and seek care, treatment, and services. Thus, the question of whether the contact was permitted becomes significant.

In cases of alleged battery as the result of the conduct of a health care provider, most often the allegation is that the battery was somehow a deviation from that to which the patient had consented. The facts of these cases vary dramatically. Usually, the claim involves either an allegation that a procedure was performed in other than the usual manner or that a different procedure was performed. This may be a case involving surgery not specifically consented to previously by the patient, or some other scenario in which the patient, without knowledge and/or consent, is subjected to some intentional act by the provider that in turn causes injury. In the early 1990s there was an infamous case of a physician who sexually assaulted female patients and in some cases performed surgical alterations of the patients' genitalia during or just after delivery of babies. While not all battery cases involve intentional acts of a sexual nature, these do occur and tend to be covered more in the popular media. A sexual battery is any physical contact without consent that is reasonably perceived by the patient to be of a sexual nature. But many other types of battery occur as well. Again, the key element is that the act of the provider is one of an unpermitted physical contact.

The issue of consent is a major element in any case of alleged malpractice. As a result, most providers and health care facilities have detailed statements of consent to potential risks associated with procedures that patients must sign in advance. However, circumstances still occur that fall outside the boundaries of the signed consent. Additionally, the patient's condition at the time consent is given must be such that the defendant can establish, if needed, that the patient was fully aware of and understood the nature and terms of the consent. While battery can occur in a wide variety of circumstances, those discussed above are a few of the ways in which medical malpractice claims of alleged battery might arise. See Application 1.8.

APPLICATION 1.8

Colin was employed on a farm and was involved in an implement accident in which his right leg was nearly severed. He was rushed to the nearest community hospital and extensive narcotic pain medication was administered during transport. He was given a standard consent form to complete which permitted the amputation of his leg. When he came out of surgery and was no longer under the influence of the medications he was enraged. He distinctly recalled (as did a witness at the scene) that he wanted to be transported as quickly as possible by helicopter to a nearby city where there might be trained medical personnel and advanced technology to save his leg. In this case, the consent Colin signed was suspect because of the influence of narcotics on his ability to make an informed consent. This is further bolstered by the fact that his wishes were made clear prior to the administration of the narcotics.

Miscellaneous Torts

There are a number of other intentional torts that have been the subject of fewer instances of litigation in recent years. Nevertheless, if the circumstances are appropriate, there exist several viable causes of action and they should be mentioned. They include communication torts and other actions that relate to the personal nature of the relationship between a patient and health care provider.

For centuries, the doctor-patient relationship has been one based on absolute trust and confidentiality. As tort law has evolved, this relationship has continued to receive the utmost protection and has been widely expanded to include a variety of health care providers. The rule is quite basic. The information provided by a patient belongs to the patient and cannot be used, passed on, communicated, or implied in any way without the patient's direct, or in select cases implied, consent. Additionally, health care professionals are under an obligation to refrain from communicating negative personal opinions about a patient that are not clearly based on fact.

There are a variety of torts that can arise from communications about a patient by a health care provider to a third party. They include the following:

- Breach of confidentiality - Private information originally disclosed within the confines of the provider-patient relationship is disclosed to third parties. Disclosure may include a single instance of unpermitted communication or dissemination in a more public, widespread manner. The latter may be categorized as a tort of public disclosure of private facts.
- Defamation - when one knowingly communicates false information about another and that communication causes damage to the reputation of the person who is the subject of the communication.

- False Light - when one knowingly and publicly communicates information in a general fashion about another in such a way that an inappropriate/untrue and negative impression is created among third parties.

- Misappropriation - when one's likeness or name is used in an unauthorized manner to benefit another in a commercial or noncommercial way.

All of these torts claim, in one way or another that there has been an abuse of personal information accessed through the professional relationship. The following Application 1.9 demonstrates how each of the actions might occur in a medical setting.

APPLICATION 1.9

Elvin is a singer and current pop idol. He develops nodules in his throat that affect his voice. He seeks the treatment of a well-known surgeon who also happens to be a friend of Elvin's parents. As a favor to his parents, Elvin previously helped promote the surgeon's new book. The surgery is a success and after several months of rehabilitation at a private clinic, Elvin's voice is fully returned. When news of Elvin's condition first reached the media prior to surgery, the surgeon was sought out by a popular national morning television program. Unknown to Elvin until after the fact, the surgeon agrees to be interviewed and describes in detail the condition of Elvin's throat. He states that the progressive loss of voice quality has been going on for some time and will likely continue. He even goes so far as to say that Elvin's most current CD shows a clearly poorer voice quality than prior recordings. He further states that not always, but quite often, the condition is brought about by years of alcohol abuse, drug use, and heavy smoking. In truth, Elvin neither drinks nor smokes and has a large following of religious fans because of his past public protests against teen smoking, alcohol abuse, and drug use. The surgeon does not indicate that Elvin's case was brought on by other causes. Finally, the physician uses the opportunity on national television to promote the book he has written. The back cover of the book (which is broadcast on the show) shows the physician with his arm around Elvin as both stand smiling. Following the broadcast, Elvin's record sales and concert ticket sales plummet and never again reach their former levels.

ASSIGNMENT 1.2

Consider Application 1.9 above. Identify how each of the communication torts might be represented by the facts of the case.

As can be seen from the discussion above, there are countless scenarios that might create a viable claim for malfeasance by a health care provider. The discussion of possibilities within this text is not exhaustive. Rather, the intent is to demonstrate how some of the more common intentional torts are applied. There are many kinds of intentional torts and unlimited circumstances to support them. The key is to be aware of the various ways in which a case can be pursued and defended based on an analysis of the facts and necessary elements to prove a case.

STRICT LIABILITY

A final area of tort law that may apply in some situations of alleged medical malpractice is strict liability. Unlike negligence or intentional torts where a key element is the failure to consider the effects of one's actions on others, **strict liability** is not based in any kind of fault. Rather, it goes back to a narrow area of law that has expanded with technology regarding unreasonably dangerous or ultrahazardous activities. Specifically, the concept was originally limited to what were considered ultrahazardous activities of dealing with explosives and dangerous animals, but it was expanded in the mid-twentieth century to include certain product manufacturing defects. Since that time, it has been carried over into a variety of circumstances which present the underlying theories that caused creation of the tort of strict liability in the first place.

Strict liability was developed to address those situations where someone benefited from an activity that was, by its very nature, so dangerous that the public could not protect itself if the activity escaped control. As mentioned, this was originally applied to explosives and dangerous animals. The basis for the tort was that someone who benefits from something so dangerous must also bear responsibility for injuries caused to others by the activity regardless of how it happened. For more than a century in the United States, this was limited to the most extreme situations. The reasoning was simple. If someone was to be held responsible for injuries regardless of how much care they took, then liability should be limited to the most dangerous of circumstances. Otherwise, all incentive for careful conduct would be eliminated. On the other hand, if an innocent public was subject to significant dangers from which they could not reasonably protect themselves, there should be some accountability for those who benefited in some way from the danger.[8]

This theory began to expand in the early to mid-twentieth century as the dangers associated with mass production of products came to public light. Frequently, technological advancements were well ahead of adequate safety measures and the latter were all too often put into place only after the dangers were discovered in the form of injury or death. This carried easily into the realm of medical malpractice where technological advancements were greater in the twentieth century than at any time in history. An example is imaging. Prior to the twentieth century, most internal and skeletal injuries were discovered through observation of symptoms and physical manipulation. But, in the course of 100 years, medicine advanced from the most rudimentary X rays to Ultrasound, MRI, EEGs, EKGs, CAT Scans, and a battery of other electronic tests that can identify and isolate with a great degree of specificity the most minute occurrences inside the human body without ever entering through the skin. Historically, treatment included a handful of medicines, herbal products, and a few simple external devices such as plaster casts and splints. Today, treatments include any number of devices used externally and internally, traditional and nuclear medicine, radioactive materials, and electronically based strategies through the use of various machines, etc. As a result, there is a public largely uneducated about the inherent dangers of many treatments and realistically unable to protect themselves.

While not all treatments and medical products are subject to the theory of strict liability, it has been used for situations which warrant it. For example, if a sophisticated product is manufactured and there is some sort of defect which injures a patient when used, even if applied properly, there may be a case of strict liability against the manufacturer and even the health care provider that prescribes or utilizes the product with patients. The manufacturer benefits both monetarily from the sale and by use of the product. Patients cannot be expected to educate themselves thoroughly about every potential error in the design or manufacturing process of all medical products. Nor can patients be held accountable for knowledge of all dangers that might ultimately lead to injury if a manufacturing or design defect occurred with regard to a particular prescribed product for treatment. These principles are demonstrated in the following case, Wilkinson v. Duff, 575 S.E.2d 335 (W.Va. 2002), and in the subsequent Application 1.10.

CASE

575 S.E.2d 335 (W.Va. 2002)

Supreme Court of Appeals of
West Virginia.

Danny Scott WILKINSON, Administrator of the Estate of Teddi D. Wilkinson,
Plaintiff Below, Appellee,
v.
W. Rexford DUFF, M.D.; Bariatrics, Inc., of West Virginia, a West Virginia corporation; Defendants Below, Appellants David Life, M.D.; and Montgomery General Hospital, Inc., a West Virginia corporation, Defendants Below,
and
W. Rexford Duff, M.D., and Bariatrics, Inc. of West Virginia, Plaintiffs Below,
Appellants,
v.
Eon Laboratory Manufacturers, Inc., and Calvin Scott and Co., Inc., Third-Party Defendants Below, Appellees.

Decided Dec. 5, 2002.

On January 22, 1998--approximately seven weeks after giving birth to her third child--28-year-old Teddi Wilkinson visited a weight loss clinic in Charleston, West Virginia, that was owned and operated by appellant and defendant-below Bariatrics, Inc. At the clinic, Mrs. Wilkinson was attended to by a doctor, appellant and defendant-below W. Rexford Duff.

Dr. Duff asserts that he obtained a medical history from Mrs. Wilkinson, conducted an examination, discussed diet and exercise, and finally prescribed the drug phentermine to assist her in losing weight. One potential side effect associated with phentermine is elevated blood pressure. Dr. Duff's records suggest that Mrs. Wilkinson never told Dr. Duff that she was "postpartum"--that is, had recently given birth--or might be breast feeding her newborn child. However, Dr. Duff's records also suggest that he never asked Mrs. Wilkinson, either orally or in his medical history questionnaire, whether she was postpartum or breast feeding.

Four days later, Mrs. Wilkinson began experiencing severe chest pain, and thereafter went into cardiac arrest. Mrs. Wilkinson suffered irreversible brain damage from oxygen deprivation during her cardiac arrest, and later died. A post-mortem autopsy revealed that Mrs. Wilkinson had suffered a heart attack triggered by a spontaneous right coronary artery dissection. The inner lining of Mrs. Wilkinson's right coronary artery had separated from the outer lining, clogging the artery and depriving the heart muscle of oxygen.

Mrs. Wilkinson's husband, plaintiff below Danny Wilkinson, subsequently filed a medical malpractice action against Dr. Duff and Bariatrics, Inc Mr. Wilkinson asserted that his wife's use of the phentermine prescribed by Dr. Duff elevated her blood pressure which, in turn, caused her coronary artery to spontaneously dissect. Experts retained by Mr. Wilkinson suggested that women who are postpartum and breast feeding are at a heightened risk of experiencing adverse reactions to phentermine. These same experts

(continued)

concluded that Dr. Duff had performed an "unbelievably superficial" and "totally inadequate examination" of Mrs. Wilkinson, such that he did not notice she had recently given birth and was breast feeding.

The experts retained by Mr. Wilkinson also stated that various guidelines indicate that phentermine should only be used in "the treatment of exogenous obesity for patients with a body mass index (weight in kilograms divided by height in meters, squared) equal to or greater than 30[.]" Mrs. Wilkinson's body mass index, as calculated by Dr. Duff, was only 25.5. Accordingly, Mr. Wilkinson's experts concluded Dr. Duff was negligent in ignoring the guidelines and prescribing phentermine to Mrs. Wilkinson.

Dr. Duff has consistently denied that the phentermine played any role in the decedent's death, and steadfastly maintains there is nothing dangerous about the drug. However, Dr. Duff asserts that he fashioned his oral and written questions to his patients after the labeling and warning inserts provided by the manufacturer and distributor of the phentermine, third-party defendants below and appellees Eon Labs, Inc. and Calvin Scott & Company, respectively. Dr. Duff contends that those labels and warning inserts provided no warnings about the alleged heightened risk that phentermine poses to postpartum and breast feeding women. Accordingly, Dr. Duff contends that the phentermine was defective and unreasonably dangerous for its intended use because of the improper labeling and warning inserts.

Dr. Duff therefore suggests that, if the phentermine he prescribed to Mrs. Wilkinson caused or contributed to her death, then the manufacturer and distributor are partly liable under a products liability theory. Accordinglyto preserve his rights to contribution from the manufacturer and distributor, Dr. Duff filed the third-party complaint that is the subject of the instant appeal against the manufacturer and distributor of the phentermine used by Mrs. Wilkinson...

The crux of Dr. Duff's lawsuit against the manufacturer and distributor is that if he had received proper warnings about the hazards of prescribing phentermine to postpartum and breast feeding women, he would have presented those hazards to Mrs. Wilkinson in the oral and written information he provided, and would have altered the questions contained in his medical history so that Mrs. Wilkinson would have given this information to Dr. Duff. ...

However, during discovery, Dr. Duff introduced no evidence or witnesses regarding whether the product manufactured by the third-party defendants was unsafe for its intended use and/or failed to contain a required warning. Instead, Dr. Duff contended that he intended to rely upon Mr. Wilkinson's evidence that phentermine caused or contributed to Mrs. Wilkinson's death--in other words, if the plaintiff proved to a jury that Mrs. Wilkinson took phentermine in accordance with Dr. Duff's instructions, and that dosage caused or contributed to her death, then Dr. Duff would rely on the plaintiff's evidence to show that the manufacturer and distributor of the phentermine were also liable. However, none of Mr. Wilkinson's witnesses opined that the labels or warning inserts provided by the manufacturer and distributor were insufficient or otherwise defective.

Furthermore, during discovery Dr. Duff admitted that he does not accept patients who are less than three months postpartum, and admitted that it would be a violation of a doctor's standard of care to prescribe phentermine to a patient who was postpartum and/or breast feeding. He asserted that had Mrs. Wilkinson volunteered that she had given birth to a child approximately seven weeks previously, he would not have dispensed phentermine to her.

Appellees Eon Labs and Calvin Scott & Company subsequently filed motions for summary judgment as to the third-party complaint arguing, *inter alia,* that Dr. Duff had failed to establish a duty to warn of a heightened risk of an adverse effect from phentermine by women who were postpartum or breast feeding, and had failed to establish that the alleged failure to warn was a proximate cause of injury to the plaintiff's decedent.

On July 5, 2001, the circuit court entered an order granting both appellees' motions, finding that Dr. Duff had failed to present sufficient evidence to create a genuine issue of material fact that the appellees had a duty

(continued)

to warn under West Virginia law. Additionally, the circuit court concluded that Dr. Duff had failed to show that any alleged failure to warn was a cause of Mrs. Wilkinson's death, because Dr. Duff had admitted that even in the absence of a warning he never would have prescribed phentermine to a postpartum or breast feeding patient.

Dr. Duff now appeals the circuit court's order granting summary judgment to third-party defendants Eon Labs and Calvin Scott & Company.

We review a circuit court's order granting summary judgment *de novo.* Syllabus Point 1, *Painter v. Peavy,* 192 W.Va. 189, 451 S.E.2d 755 (1994)

In reviewing summary judgment, this Court will apply the same test that the circuit court should have used initially, and must determine whether "it is clear that there is no genuine issue of fact to be tried and inquiry concerning the facts is not desirable to clarify the application of the law." Syllabus Point 3, *Aetna Casualty & Surety Co. v. Federal Insurance Co. of New York,* 148 W.Va. 160, 133 S.E.2d 770 (1963) As with the circuit court, we "must draw any permissible inference from the underlying facts in the light most favorable to the party opposing the motion," that is, the appellant. *Painter v. Peavy,* 192 W.Va. at 192, 451 S.E.2d at 758 The appellant, Dr. Duff, contends that the circuit court erred in granting summary judgment because genuine issues of material fact exist regarding whether the phentermine was defective due to a lack of proper labels and warnings, and whether that lack of proper labels and warnings was a proximate cause of Mrs. Wilkinson's death.

We begin our analysis of these questions with an overview of our law regarding product liability actions. We first recognized a strict liability cause of action for defective products in *Morningstar v. Black and Decker Mfg. Co.,* 162 W.Va. 857, 253 S.E.2d 666 (1979) In a strict liability action, "the initial inquiry, in order to fix liability on the manufacturer, focuses on the nature of the defect and whether the defect was the proximate cause of plaintiff's injury." 162 W.Va. at 888, 253 S.E.2d at 682

We held in Syllabus Point 3 of *Morningstar* that a strict liability cause of action is "designed to relieve the plaintiff from proving that the manufacturer was negligent in some particular fashion during the manufacturing process and to permit proof of the defective condition of the product as the principal basis of liability." The general test of whether a product is defective was established in Syllabus Point 4, where we held:

> In this jurisdiction the general test for establishing strict liability in tort is whether the involved product is defective in the sense that it is not reasonably safe for its intended use. The standard of reasonable safeness is determined not by the particular manufacturer, but by what a reasonably prudent manufacturer's standards should have been at the time the product was made.

In Morningstar, we stated that "a defective product may fall into three broad, and not mutually exclusive, categories: design defectiveness; structural defectiveness; and use defectiveness arising out of the lack of, or the adequacy of, warnings, instructions, and labels." 162 W.Va. at 888, 253 S.E.2d at 682

The appellant, Dr. Duff, asserts that this is a "use defectiveness" or "failure to warn" case that implicates the adequacy of the instructions on the phentermine labels and warning inserts. We stated in *Morningstar* that in failure to warn cases, "the focus is not so much on a flawed physical condition of the product, as on its unsafeness arising out of the failure to adequately label, instruct or warn." 162 W.Va. at 888, 253 S.E.2d at 682. A failure to warn cause of action "covers situations when a product may be safe as designed and manufactured, but which becomes defective because of the failure to warn of dangers which may be present when the product is used in a particular manner." Syllabus Point 2, *Ilosky v. Michelin Tire Corp.,* 172 W.Va. 435, 307 S.E.2d 603 (1983)

In ascertaining whether a duty to warn exists, the fundamental inquiry is whether it was reasonably foreseeable that the product would be unreasonably dangerous if distributed without a particular warning. "For

(continued)

the duty to warn to exist, the use of the product must be foreseeable to the manufacturer or seller." Syllabus Point 3, *Ilosky v. Michelin Tire Corp., supra.*

Dr. Duff argues that the evidence of record raises a question of fact regarding whether the manufacturer and distributor of the phentermine adequately labeled the product or warned of potential hazards if the product were used by postpartum or breast feeding women. We disagree. In the instant case, Dr. Duff presented absolutely no evidence of whether it was foreseeable to Eon Labs or Calvin Scott & Company that use of phentermine by women such as Mrs. Wilkinson could cause spontaneous coronary artery dissection. Dr. Duff also did not present any evidence as to the adequacy or inadequacy of the labels and warning inserts provided by the manufacturer and distributor, and did not present any evidence of what a proper label or warning insert should contain.

Additionally, Mr. Wilkinson presented absolutely no evidence that Mrs. Wilkinson's use of phentermine was a hazard foreseeable to the manufacturer and distributor. The record suggests that Mr. Wilkinson intends to introduce evidence focused solely on the standard of care of a weight loss physician toward a postpartum or breast feeding patient. Mr. Wilkinson's evidence contains no suggestions as to the proper standard of care for a manufacturer or distributor of phentermine--hence, its lack of utility in supporting Dr. Duff's claims. Therefore, Dr. Duff cannot avoid his own failure to produce evidence and claim reliance upon Mr. Wilkinson's evidence to establish a duty to warn by the manufacturer and distributor.

Furthermore, Dr. Duff argues that the manufacturer's and distributor's failure to warn of the drug's hazards proximately caused Mrs. Wilkinson's death, because Dr. Duff patterned his oral and written warnings and the medical history form completed by Mrs. Wilkinson after the labels and warning inserts provided by the manufacturer and distributor Dr. Duff argues that, had the appellees warned of a heightened risk of adverse reactions by women in the postpartum or breast feeding periods, Dr. Duff would have tailored his medical history form to obtain that information and fashioned his oral and written warnings to warn his patients of the risk. However, the appellees point out that Dr. Duff admitted that--irrespective of any labels or warnings--he simply does not accept patients who are less than three months postpartum Dr. Duff admitted it would be a violation of the standard of care for a doctor to prescribe phentermine to a patient who was postpartum and/or breast feeding, as was Mrs. Wilkinson. Furthermore, Dr. Duff stated he would not have dispensed phentermine to Mrs. Wilkinson had he known, or had Mrs. Wilkinson informed him, that she was approximately seven weeks postpartum.

" 'Proximate cause' must be understood to be that cause which in actual sequence, unbroken by any independent cause, produced the wrong complained of, without which the wrong would not have occurred." Syllabus Point 3, *Webb v. Sessler,* 135 W.Va. 341, 63 S.E.2d 65 (1950) "The proximate cause of an injury is the last negligent act contributing to the injury and without which the injury would not have occurred." Syllabus Point 5, *Hartley v. Crede,* 140 W.Va. 133, 82 S.E.2d 672 (1954) *overruled on other grounds, State v. Kopa,* 173 W.Va. 43, 311 S.E.2d 412 (1983) .

Dr. Duff made plain in his own deposition testimony that the content and form of the labels provided by the manufacturer and distributor did not motivate his dispensing of phentermine to Mrs. Wilkinson. Irrespective of the actions of the manufacturer and distributor, Dr. Duff stated that he would not have prescribed the drug had he known Mrs. Wilkinson was only seven weeks postpartum. We therefore cannot, on this record, say that the alleged actions or inactions of Eon Labs and Calvin Scott & Company produced the wrong complained of, and were in any way a proximate cause of Mrs. Wilkinson's death.

To be clear, we believe that Dr. Duff raised novel issues of law by filing his third-party product defect complaint against the manufacturer and distributor of phentermine.. Dr. Duff, however, contending that there is nothing wrong with phentermine and that the drug did not contribute to Mrs. Wilkinson's death, chose to not introduce evidence regarding any alleged defect, but instead chose to rely upon the plaintiff-below's evidence.

(continued)

Unfortunately, the plaintiff-below's evidence focused on the duties, and alleged breach thereof, of Dr. Duff, and not on the dangerousness of phentermine due to inadequate labeling by the manufacturer and distributor.

After careful examination of the record, we find no genuine issue of fact that Eon Labs and Calvin Scott & Company had a duty to warn of any hazards regarding the use of phentermine by postpartum or breast feeding women. Furthermore, we find no genuine issue of fact that any failure by Eon Labs or Calvin Scott & Company to include warnings was a proximate cause of Mrs. Wilkinson's death. The circuit court was therefore correct in granting summary judgment to these third-party defendants.

Accordingly, the circuit court's July 5, 2001 order is affirmed.

Affirmed.

APPLICATION 1.10

Corey suffers chronic back pain. His physician prescribes a product worn much like a large bandage that releases heat directly into the affected area over a long period of time. The instructions are to use the adhesive tabs to hold the product in place. Because of a defect, the heat causes the adhesive to melt on Corey's skin and he suffers severe burns. In this situation, Corey is following the advice of his physician and trusts his judgment and the product. He has no way of knowing how much the product will heat up and its effect on the adhesive. The manufacturer, on the other hand, benefits from the product usage and places t in commerce for use by uneducated consumers.

CONTRACTUAL LIABILITY

Finally, one of the oldest forms of liability pursued in medical malpractice cases is based on the contractual relationship between the patient and the health care provider. In its most primitive definition, the patient **contracts** with the provider for the consideration (performance) of medical care, treatment, or services.[9] In exchange, the patient renders some form of contractual consideration, generally monetary, to the provider. As a rule, courts do not question the value, quality, or degree of consideration in allegations of **breach of contract**. Rather, they only consider whether each party had the opportunity to assess the value, quality, or degree of consideration and whether the other contractual elements are present. Essentially, this includes contractual capacity, more than two parties to the agreement, a legal purpose for the agreement, and a promise or performance in exchange for a promise or performance. Most health care providers have learned to emphasize the absence of guarantees in medical care since all cases and individuals are unique. Nevertheless, there are circumstances in which the patient is considered reasonable in expecting a certain outcome or result based on statements made. While most patients and providers consider their relationship more professional than contractual, the basic elements are present. And, if the conduct of the provider is more than tortuous in that a specific guaranteed result is reasonably perceived, a court may allow a breach of contract action to proceed. See Application 1.11.

APPLICATION 1.11

Dr. Crawford prescribes a medication for a patient. The patient is a woman suffering severe hair loss and Dr. Crawford tells her that the latest studies show a 99-percent success rate for hair growth with daily use of the medication. Based on this, he says he is certain that in a period of six to eight months her hair will be fully restored. He tells her to take the medicine daily and return in six months. There is no such study but he hopes to lift the spirits of the woman whose hair loss he attributes to stress. He feels as her life situation improves, the hair will come back naturally and the medication will only provide some assistance with the problem and, more importantly, emotional reassurance for his patient. After several months of the medication, which is very expensive, the woman is now completely bald and she has suffered through extensive physical side effects which ultimately resulted in the loss of her employment.

Dr. Crawford made specific guarantees to a patient and, based on those guarantees, she endured financial expense, physical side effects, and loss of employment. In this circumstance it is entirely possible a court may allow a breach of contract action against the physician.

Problem 1.1

Complete 1.1 of the Comprehensive Problem in Appendix A.

CHAPTER SUMMARY

In terms of dramatic growth, the law of medical malpractice has paralleled the development of civil law in the United States. The largest contributing factor has been the ever widening gap between the individual as a patient and the information and skill available to the great variety of health care providers. While the physician was always held in a position of esteem for specialized knowledge, the various types of health care providers and facilities have become so advanced, that a great deal more trust is required by the ordinary person seeking medical treatment. With this trust came increased responsibility to care for the patient in accordance with current medical knowledge, and to respect the various personal rights of the patient. The failure to do so by a medical provider or health care employee can have devastating results. The law of medical malpractice has expanded to include a variety of tort and contract actions to impose liability for any and all damage caused as the result of the violation of legal rights of the patient. Tort actions include cases of negligence that may include reliance on the theory of res ipsa loquitur when the patient does not have access to evidence regarding causation. But such reliance increases the elements the plaintiff must prove to win. In addition to negligence, tort cases may be predicated upon a claim of intentional tort when the defendant acts despite substantial certainty that it will produce injury. Also, strict liability may be applied if the conduct of the defendant is considered to be ultrahazardous and one from which the plaintiff cannot reasonably protect him or herself. Finally, breach of contract actions may be permitted if specific promises or guarantees are reasonably perceived by the plaintiff and not realized. This broadened scope of liability has had a chain-reaction effect on the costs of liability insurance, health care, and has ultimately resulted in legislation to better control the types of cases brought and number of verdicts permitted.

Key Terms

breach of contract	res ipsa loquitur
contract	respondeat superior
intentional tort	strict liability
negligence	

End Notes

[1] <http://www.rwjf.org/reports.html>

[2] Ardoin v. Hartford Acc. & Indem. Co., 360 So.2d 1331 (LA 1978).

[3] Gross v. Burt, 2004 WL 362445 (Tex.App. 2004).

[4] Scott-Neal ex rel Scott v. New Jersey, 2004 WL 305984 (NJ Super A.D.)

[5] Oran's Dictionary of the Law, 3rd ed., 1991, Thomson Learning.

[6] State ex rel Green v. Neal, 2004 WL 334387 (MO).

[7] Branson v. Community United Methodist Hospital Inc., 2004 WL 405932 (KyApp).

[8] Jansen Pharmeceutica v. Armond, 2004 WL 307449 (Miss.)

[9] Jacobs ex rel Jacobs v. Kirshenbaum, 2004 WL 377057 (Conn. Super.)

For additional resources, go to http://www.westlegalstudies.com.

CHAPTER 2

The Development of Medical Malpractice Law

CHAPTER OBJECTIVES

When you complete this chapter, you should be able to:

- Describe the progression of medical malpractice law through the nineteenth and twentieth centuries

- Explain the rationale and development of legislative law as it affects the medical profession

- Describe the process and reasoning for licensure and certification of health care providers

EARLY CASES

As discussed in Chapter 1, medical malpractice cases have been present in the American legal system since the early days of this country. However, it was not a clearly established area of civil law from the start. In fact, when the first allegations of malfeasance began to appear, it occurred within an entirely different context. One of the first reported judicial opinions to discuss malpractice at length was in 1809. The case of Commonwealth v. Thompson, 6 Mass. 134 (1809) is included on the next page. In that case, the physician allegedly responsible for the death of a patient as the result of medical treatment was charged with murder. Even though he was acquitted, the issue of whether a physician should be held liable under criminal charges for questionable medical practices was addressed. Ultimately, the court determined that if one acting as a physician honestly intended to help a patient, and through ignorance caused death, he or she could not be found to have the requisite intent for a criminal charge of murder. However, the court indicated that in some instances manslaughter might apply if the physician should have known that the method of treatment could be fatal. The court also implied that perhaps the legislature should get involved in the question of who the public should be able to trust for medical care. This reference to constructive knowledge (what the physician actually knew or should have known) and standards for public trust would be built upon as the civil law of medical malpractice took shape in the coming years.

6 Mass. 134, 1809 WL 1120 (Mass.)

Supreme Judicial Court of Massachusetts.

COMMONWEALTH
v.
SAMUEL THOMPSON.

FNd1. The reporter, not being present at this trial, was favored with a report of it by a highly-respected friend.

November Term, 1809.

If one, assuming the character of a physician, through ignorance administer medicine to his patient, with an honest intention and expectation of a cure, but which causes the death of the patient, he is not guilty of felonious homicide.

AT the beginning of the term, the prisoner *Thompson* was indicted for the wilful murder of *Ezra Lovett, Jun.*, by giving him a poison, called *lobelia,* on the ninth day of January last, of which he died on the next day. On the twentieth day of December, at an adjournment of this term, the prisoner was tried for this offence, before *the chief justice,* and the judges *Sewall* and *Parker.*

On the trial, it appeared in evidence, that the prisoner, some time in the preceding December, came into *Beverly,* where the deceased then lived, announced himself as a physician, and professed an ability to cure all fevers, whether black, gray, green, or yellow; declaring that the country was much imposed upon by physicians, who were all wrong, if he was right. He possessed several drugs, which he used as medicines, and to which he gave singular names. One he called *coffee;* another, *well-my-gristle;* and a third, *ramcats.* He had several patients in *Beverly* and in *Salem,* previous to Monday, the second of January, when the deceased, having been for several days confined to his house by a cold, requested that the prisoner might be sent for as a physician.

He accordingly came, and ordered a large fire to be kindled to neat the room. He then placed the feet of the deceased, with his shoes off, on a stove of hot coals, and wrapped him in a thick blanket, covering his head. In this situation he gave him a powder in water, which immediately puked him. Three minutes after, he repeated the dose, which in about two minutes operated violently. He again repeated the dose, which in a short time operated with more violence. These doses were all given within the space of half an hour, the patient in the mean time drinking copiously of a warm decoction, called by the prisoner his *coffee.* The deceased, after puking, in which he brought up phlegm, but no food, was ordered to a warm bed, where he lay in a profuse sweat all night. Tuesday morning the deceased left his bed, and appeared to be comfortable, complaining only of debility; and in the afternoon he was visited by the prisoner, who administered two more of his emetic powders in succession, which puked the deceased, who, during the operation, drank of the prisoner's *coffee,* and complained of much distress. On Wednesday morning, the prisoner came, and after causing the face and hands of the deceased

(continued)

to be washed with rum, ordered him to walk in the air, which he did for about fifteen minutes. In the afternoon, the prisoner gave him two more of his emetic powders, with draughts of his *coffee*. On Thursday, the deceased appeared to be comfortable, but complained of great debility. In the afternoon, the prisoner caused him to be again sweated, by placing him, with another patient, over an iron pan, with vinegar heated by hot stones put into the vinegar, covering them, at the same time, with blankets. On Friday and Saturday, the prisoner did not visit the deceased, who appeared to be comfortable, although complaining of increased debility. On Sunday morning, the debility increasing, the prisoner was sent for, and came in the afternoon, when he administered another of his emetic powders with his *coffee,* which puked the deceased, causing him much distress. On Monday, he appeared comfortable, but with increasing weakness, until the evening when the prisoner visited him, and administered another of his emetic powders, and in about twenty minutes repeated the dose. This last dose did not operate. The prisoner then administered pearlash mixed with water, and afterwards repeated his emetic potions. The deceased appeared to be in great distress, and said he was dying. The prisoner then asked him how far the medicine had got down. The deceased, laying his hand on his breast, answered *here;* on which the prisoner observed that the medicine would soon get down, and unscrew his navel; meaning, as was supposed by the hearers, that it would operate as a cathartic. Between nine and ten o'clock in the evening, the deceased lost his reason, and was seized with convulsion fits; two men being required to hold him in bed. After he was thus seized with convulsions, the prisoner got down his throat one or two doses more of his emetic powders; and remarked to the father of the deceased, that his son had got the *hyps* like the devil, but that his medicines would fetch him down; meaning, as the witness understood, would compose him. The next morning, the regular physicians of the town were sent for, but the patient was so completely exhausted, that no relief could be given. The convulsions and the loss of reason continued, with some intervals, until Tuesday evening, when the deceased expired.

From the evidence it appeared that the *coffee* administered was a decoction of *marsh-rosemary,* mixed with the bark of *bayberry-bush,* which was not supposed to have injured the deceased.--But the powder, which the prisoner said he chiefly relied upon in his practice, and which was the emetic so often administered by him to the deceased, was the pulverized plant, trivially called *Indian tobacco.* A Dr. *French,* of *Salisbury,* testified that this plant, with this name, was well known in his part of the country, where it was indigenous, for its emetic qualities; and that it was gathered and preserved by some families, to be used as an emetic, for which the roots, as well as the stalks and leaves, were administered; and that four grains of the powder was a powerful puke.-- But a more minute description of this plant was given by the Rev. Dr. *Cutler*. He testified that it was the *lobelia inflata* of Linnaeus; that many years ago, on a botanical ramble, he discovered it growing in a field not far from his house in *Hamilton;* that, not having *Linnoeus* then in his possession, he supposed it to be a non-descript species of the *lobelia;* that by chewing a leaf of it, he was puked two or three times; that he afterwards repeated the experiment with the same effect; that he inquired of his neighbor, on whose ground the plant was found, for its trivial name. He did not know of any, but was apprized of its emetic quality, and informed the doctor that the chewing of one of the capsules operated as an emetic, and that the chewing more would prove cathartic. In a paper soon after communicated by the doctor to the American Academy, he mentioned the plant, with the name of the *lobelia medica*. He did not know of its being applied to any medical use until the last September, when, being severely afflicted with the asthma, Doctor *Drury,* of *Marblehead,* informed him that a tincture of it had been found beneficial in asthmatic complaints. Dr. *C.* then made for himself a tincture, by filling a common porter bottle with the plant, pouring upon it as much spirit as the bottle would hold, and keeping the bottle in a sand heat for three or four days. Of this tincture he took a table-spoonful, which produced no nausea, and had a slight pungent taste. In ten minutes after, he repeated the potion, which produced some nausea, and appeared to stimulate the whole internal surface of the stomach. In ten minutes, he again repeated the potion, which puked him two or three times, and excited in his extremities a strong sensation, like irritation; but he was relieved from a paroxysm of the asthma, which had not since returned. He had since mentioned this tincture

(continued)

to some physicians, and has understood from them, that some patients have been violently puked by a teaspoonful of it; but whether this difference of effect arose from the state of the patients, or from the manner of preparing the tincture, he did not know.

The solicitor-general also stated that, before the deceased had applied to the prisoner, the latter had administered the like medicines with those given to the deceased, to several of his patients, who had died under his hands; and to prove this statement, he called several witnesses, of whom but one appeared. He, on the contrary, testified that he had been the prisoner's patient for an oppression at his stomach; that he took his emetic powders several times in three or four days, and was relieved from his complaint, which had not since returned. And there was no evidence in the cause, that the prisoner, in the course of his very novel practice, had experienced any fatal accident among his patients.

The defence stated by the prisoner's counsel was, that he had, for several years, and in different places, pursued his practice with much success; and that the death of the deceased was unexpected, and could not be imputed to him as a crime. But as the Court were satisfied that the evidence produced on the part of the commonwealth did not support the indictment, the prisoner was not put on his defence.

The chief justice charged the jury; and the substance of his direction, and of several observations, which fell from the Court during the trial, are, for greater convenience, here thrown together.   As the testimony of the witnesses was not contradicted, nor their credit impeached, that testimony might be considered as containing the necessary facts, on which the issue must be found.

That the deceased lost his life by the unskilful treatment of the prisoner, did not seem to admit of any reasonable doubt; but of this point the jury were to judge. Before the Monday evening preceding the death of *Lovett*, he had, by profuse sweats, and by often-repeated doses of the emetic powder, been reduced very low In this state, on that evening, other doses of this *Indian tobacco* were administered. When the second potion did not operate, probably because the tone of his stomach was destroyed, the repetition of them, that they might operate as a cathartic, was followed by convulsion fits, loss of reason, and death.

But whether this treatment, by which the deceased lost his life, is, or is not, a felonious homicide, was the great question before the jury.

To constitute the crime of murder, with which the prisoner is charged, the killing must have been with malice, either express or implied. There was no evidence to induce a belief that the prisoner, by this treatment, intended to kill or to injure the deceased; and the ground of express malice must fail. It has been said that implied malice may be inferred from the rash and presumptuous conduct of the prisoner, in administering such violent medicines. Before implied malice can be inferred, the jury must be satisfied that the prisoner, by his treatment of his patient, was wilfully regardless of his social duty, being determined on mischief. But there is no part of the evidence which proves that the prisoner intended by his practice any harm to the deceased. On the contrary, it appears that his intention was to cure him. The jury would consider whether the charge of murder was, on these principles, satisfactorily supported.

But though innocent of the crime of murder, the prisoner may, on this indictment, be convicted of manslaughter, if the evidence be sufficient. And the *solicitor-general* strongly urged that the prisoner was guilty of manslaughter, because he rashly and presumptuously administered to the deceased a deleterious medicine, which, in his hands, by reason of his gross ignorance, became a deadly poison.

The prisoner's ignorance is in this case very apparent. On any other ground consistent with his innocence, it is not easy to conceive that on the Monday evening before the death, when the second dose of his very powerful emetic had failed to operate, through the extreme weakness of the deceased, he could expect a repetition of these fatal poisons would prove a cathartic, and relieve the patient; or that he could mistake convulsion fits, symptomatic of approaching death, for a hypochondriac affection. But on considering this point, the Court were all of opinion, notwithstanding this ignorance, that if the prisoner acted with an

(continued)

honest intention and expectation of curing the deceased by this treatment, although death, unexpected by him, was the consequence, he was not guilty of manslaughter.

To constitute manslaughter, the killing must have been a consequence of some unlawful act. Now, there is no law which prohibits any man from prescribing for a sick person with his consent, if he honestly intends to cure him by his prescription And it is not felony, if, through his ignorance of the quality of the medicine prescribed, or of the nature of the disease, or of both, the patient, contrary to his expectation, should die. The death of a man, killed by voluntarily following a medical prescription, cannot be adjudged felony in the party prescribing, unless he, however ignorant of medical science in general, had so much knowledge, or probable information of the fatal tendency of the prescription, that it may be reasonably presumed by the jury to be the effect of obstinate, wilful rashness, at the least, and not of an honest intention and expectation to cure.

Our ancestors, in the year 1649, when physicians were few, and quacks were numerous, endeavoring to guard against the folly and presumption of ignorant practitioners, passed the following ordinance:--

"FORASMUCH as the law of God allows no man to impair the life or limbs of any other, but in a judicial way,--

It is therefore ordered, that no person or persons whatsoever, employed at any time about the bodies of men, women, and children, for the preservation of life or health, as surgeons, midwives, physicians, or others, presume to exercise or put forth any act contrary to the known, approved rules of the art in each mystery and occupation; nor exercise any force, violence, or cruelty upon or towards the body of any, whether young or old, (no, not in the most difficult and desperate cases,) without the advice and consent of such as are skilful in the same art, (if such may be had,) or at least of some of the wisest and gravest there present, and consent of the patient or patients, if they be *mentis compotes*, much less contrary to such advice and consent; upon such severe punishment, as the nature of the fact may deserve. Which law, nevertheless, is not intended to discourage any from all lawful use of their skill, but rather to encourage and direct them in the right use thereof; and inhibit and restrain the presumptuous arrogancy of such as through perfidence of their own skill, or any other sinister respects, dare boldly to attempt to exercise any violence upon or towards the bodies of young or old, one or other, to the prejudice or hazard of the life or limb of man, woman, or child."

Old Colony Laws, p. 28

In the present case, there is no evidence that the prisoner, either from his own experience, or from the information of others, had any knowledge of the fatal effects of the *Indian tobacco,* when injudiciously administered; but the only testimony produced to this point, proved that the patient found a cure from the medicine.

The law, thus stated, was conformable, not only to the general principles which governed in charges of felonious homicide, but also to the opinion of the learned and excellent Lord Chief Justice *Hale*. He expressly states that if a physician, whether licensed or not, gives a person a potion, without any intent of doing him any bodily hurt, but with intent to cure, or prevent a disease, and contrary to the expectation of the physician, it kills him, he is not guilty of murder or manslaughter.

If, in this case, it had appeared in evidence, as was stated by the *solicitor-general,* that the prisoner had previously, by administering this *Indian tobacco,* experienced its injurious effects in the death or bodily hurt of his patients, and that he afterwards administered it in the same form to the deceased, and he was killed by it, the Court would have left it to the serious consideration of the jury, whether they would presume that the prisoner administered it from an honest intention to cure, or from obstinate rashness and foolhardy presumption, although he might not have intended any bodily harm to his patient. If the jury should have been of this latter opinion, it would have been reasonable to convict the prisoner of manslaughter, at least. For it would not have been lawful for him again to administer a medicine of which he had such fatal experience.

(continued)

It is to be exceedingly lamented, that people are so easily persuaded to put confidence in these itinerant quacks, and to trust their lives to strangers without knowledge or experience. If this astonishing infatuation should continue, and men are found to yield to the impudent pretensions of ignorant empiricism, there seems to be no adequate remedy by a criminal prosecution, without the interference of the legislature, if the quack, however weak and presumptuous, should prescribe, with honest intentions and expectations of relieving his patients

[If death ensue from the *gross* ignorance, carelessness, negligence, or rashness of any one who undertakes to administer medicine, without any intent to do harm, the offence has often been held, by eminent judges, to amount to manslaughter.-- *Nancy Simpson's Case, Wilcock,* 227.--4 C. & P. 407.--*Lewin's C. C.* 172.--*Rex* vs. *Spiller,* 5 Car. & P. 335.-- *Fergusson's Case, Lewin,* 181.--*Senior's Case,* 1 Mood, C. C. 346.--*Rex* vs. *St. John Long,* 4 C. & P. 435, 398.-- *Webb's Case,* 1 M. & Rob 405.-- *Tessimond's Case, Lewin's C. C.* 169.--*Williamson's Case,* 3 Car. & P. 635.-- *Van Butchel's Case,* 3 Camp. 629.--And see *Britton's* Ch. 5.-- *Minor's* Ch. 4, § 16. And *Rae's Case, Allison's Cr. L.* 4.--And this not only seems to be sound, but wholesome doctrine.--ED.]

The prisoner was acquitted

Even with the insight of the early opinion of Commonwealth v. Thompson, it took nearly a century for the causes of action and negligence to fully develop as alternatives when alleged malpractice occurred. The 1928 case of Monahan v. Devinny, set out below, was one of the earliest cases to distinguish and enumerate the causes of action applicable to the majority of cases.

223 AD 547, 229 NYS 60 (1928)
CATHERINE MONAHAN, Appellant,
v.
GEORGE DEVINNY and Another, Doing Business under the Firm Name and Style of
DEVINNY & DEVINNY, Respondents. [FNa1]

Supreme Court of New York, Appellate Division, Third Department.

May 16, 1928.

The complaint states a cause of action for malpractice. The defendants were chiropractors who had undertaken to treat plaintiff for certain ailments. It appears that as a result of unskillful acts on their part the plaintiff became paralyzed.

The defendants moved to dismiss the complaint on the ground that the action had not been brought within two years from the time the cause of action accrued. (Civ. Prac. Act, § 50, subd. 1; Rules Civ. Prac. rule 107, subd. 6.) The plaintiff argues that the section cited has no application because the defendants were not physicians and were not legally practicing medicine.

(continued)

The practice of medicine is defined in section 1250, subdivision 7, of the Education Law (as added by Laws of 1927, chap. 85). Under that definition the defendants were practicing medicine, although their acts were illegal, for they were not qualified or licensed. (Education Law, § § 1251, 1256, 1259, 1260; People v. Allcutt, 117 App. Div. 546 affd., 189 N. Y. 517;Samuel, Inc., v. Hams, 187 id. 783.) In anaction of this kind they must be held to the same standards of skill and care as prevail amongst those who are licensed. (Brown v. Shyne, 242 N. Y. 176, 181; .) The allegation of unskillful treatment with injurious results indicates that the action is based on malpractice; and the limitation of the statute has run against the plaintiff's cause of action. (Horowitz v. Bogart, 218 App. Div. 158;

The action is one growing out of the breach of a consensual relation and is tortious in its nature. We think it would be possible for the plaintiff still to obtain partial relief by suing strictly on the contract, against which cause of action the statute has not run. (See Civ. Prac. Act, § 48.) Recovery of damages could not be had for the wrong involving unskillful treatment; but plaintiff might be entitled to recover sums paid to defendants, on the contract to furnish proper medical aid, and for sums paid out for nurses and medicines or other damages that flow naturally from the breach of whatever contract was made between the parties. (Frankel v. Wolper, 181 App. Div. 485

The order should be modified to grant leave to plaintiff at her election to amend the complaint within twenty days upon payment of ten dollars costs and disbursements of this appeal. If such election is not made, then the order should be affirmed, with ten dollars costs and disbursements.

An interesting element of the early law of malpractice associated with medical care is the wide variety of schools of study for those delivering health care. Today, the mainstream health care practitioner has a foundation in traditional medical science, training, and education. There are, of course, other fields such as homeopathic practitioners, but the extent of their practice is somewhat limited by licensing statutes. Such was not the case in nineteenth-century America. Physicians were trained in any number of what were known as "systems" based on different sciences. It was up to the patient to have reasonable expectations of the specific system which was the background of the particular physician. In the 1848 case of Bowman v. Woods, 1 Greene 441 (IA 1848), the court stated that the practitioner had an obligation to exercise ordinary care and skill in his practice according to his "professed and avowed" system. In that particular case, the doctor was trained as a botanic physician. The court held that no system of training was prohibited and none was held up as superior, not even traditional medicine which was known as "the regular system." This was, however, recognized as a problem because it placed a great deal of responsibility on the public regarding knowledge of the various systems and what should be expected of their respective practitioners. As a result, the court again indicated that legislation could greatly benefit the public with regard to whom they should trust for medical care. In fact, throughout the latter 1800s many states began passing legislation to regulate and establish minimum standards for those who professed to have knowledge, training, and ability to provide medical treatment to the public.

The civil law of medical malpractice developed rather quickly and by the middle to late 1800s it was firmly established that a physician could be held accountable for monetary damages to a plaintiff injured in a case where ordinary skill as a physician was not exercised. However, standards for licensure including a demonstration of knowledge and skill took many decades to appear in all the states. In 1858, a case was brought by a physician to collect his fees for the treatment of slaves. The defendant slave owner counterclaimed for malpractice alleging that the improper diagnosis of cholera rather than the true illnesses of typhoid fever and measles caused the death of some of the slaves. In that case, it was noted that the courts had abandoned application of the statute based on a history of failure by the state government to enforce it consistently. The court discussed at length and firmly established that even in the absence of enforced licensure statutes, one who represented to be a physician had an obligation to exercise ordinary care and skill of a fully qualified doctor. The court tempered its statement with an acknowledgment that a physician could not be held accountable for every patient lost or injured. Rather, liability would ensue only in the event a physician either had proper knowledge and skill, and did not employ it in the particular case, or when the requisite level of knowledge and skill others should expect did not exist. Graham v. Gautier, 21 Tex. 111 (1858). The Graham case established that the physician had a responsibility to act in a manner consistent with what a trained professional knew or should have known. Thus, constructive knowledge of a physician's level of skill was clearly placed as an essential element in meeting the standard of care required.

By the later decades of the 1800s, more detailed rules for the standard of care for physicians were fairly well established. The requirement of ordinary skill and care was discussed and settled as the predominant standard in the case of Smothers v. Hanks, 34 Iowa 286, 11 Am.Rep. 141 (IA 1872). This case was relied upon repeatedly by the courts of other jurisdictions as a definitive statement. Physicians had an obligation to exercise the degree of skill, knowledge, and care that would be expected of members of the profession as a whole. The failure to do so would be considered malpractice and cause the physician to be liable to the injured party for compensatory damages. Even though the primary question was answered, this obligation of skill and care in fact generated a great many more legal questions and, when combined with advancements in medical science, the issues became even more complex.

CASE

34 Iowa 286, 11 Am.Rep. 141 (1872).

Supreme Court of Iowa.
SMOTHERS
v.
HANKS.

Jun. 21, 1872.

ACTION to recover damages of the defendant, a practicing physician, for alleged negligent, ignorant and unskillful treatment, by him, of the plaintiff's arm, the bones of which had been fractured near the wrist. The cause was tried to a jury, and the evidence introduced tended to show that plaintiff's arm had been broken; that defendant, who held himself out as a surgeon, undertook the cure; that, by reason of defendant's negligence or ignorance, a perfect cure was not effected; that the arm, hand and fingers were crooked and stiff--perhaps permanently so, perhaps not. The jury found a verdict for plaintiff for $2,000, which, on a motion for a new trial, was reduced to $1,200, and judgment was rendered thereon, from which defendant appeals. The further facts are stated in the opinion.

(continued)

COLE, J.

I. The first error assigned is, that "the court, in the instructions, commented on the facts, and plainly indicated to the jury what facts had been proved."

The tenth instruction given by the court is, in part, the basis of this alleged error. It is as follows: "If you find for the plaintiff, he will be entitled to recover for the pain, anguish and suffering of the body and mind, which he has suffered by reason of the want of ordinary skill and care on the part of the defendant, together with a fair and reasonable compensation for the future pain, suffering and anguish which it is reasonably certain from the evidence that he will yet have to suffer; and the loss and damage which you believe, as reasonable men, he will necessarily suffer by reason of the permanent injury to his hand in its effects on his power to earn money and conduct business and improve his prospects for life." This instruction is one of a series, and follows others in which the questions of fact respecting the care and negligence of defendant, the injury to plaintiff, its causes and extent, are carefully and fairly referred to the jury for their consideration and finding. The tenth, as above set out, is then given as a rule whereby the jury should measure the damages to which the plaintiff might be entitled upon the different hypotheses of fact before referred to them for their finding. Having thus in view the whole series of instructions, it can hardly be fairly said that the court indicated to the jury what facts had been proved. When taken in connection with the other instructions given, we think the law is stated in the tenth "in such a manner as to enable a person of common understanding to know what is intended," and this is sufficient even in criminal law. Rev., § 4657. It may be true that the language of the instruction when subjected to the test of hypercriticism, may seem vulnerable to the objection made; but not so, when fairly construed and taken in its plain and ordinary meaning. There could be, of course, no objection to stating the substance of the instruction in more guarded and unmistakable language. The same, in substance, may be said of the other instructions, to which the same objection is made.

II. It is next assigned that the court erred in giving the seventh instruction, which is as follows: "If the defendant undertook, in the capacity of a surgeon, to treat the fractured arm of the plaintiff, he thereby contracted to possess and employ, in the treatment of the case, such reasonable skill and diligence as are ordinarily exercised in the profession by thoroughlyeducated surgeons, having regard to the improvements and advanced state of the profession at the time; and if he has failed in so doing, without any fault or neglect of the plaintiff, he is liable in damages therefor."

In our opinion this instruction does not give the true legal standard as to the skill and diligence required. The error consists in requiring the measure of skill and diligence ordinarily exercised by *thoroughly educated* surgeons; whereas, the true measure is that ordinarily exercised in the profession by the members thereof as a body. That is, the average of the reasonable skill and diligence ordinarily exercised by the profession as a whole. Not that exercised by the *thoroughly educated;* nor yet that exercised by the *moderately educated,* nor merely of the *well educated,* but the *average* of the thorough, the well, and the moderate--all, in education, skill, diligence, etc. We do not stop to discuss critically the meaning of the term, "thoroughly educated;" nor is it necessary to prove that it means "fully, completely and perfectly educated," or that it necessarily implies an entire and perfect knowledge. It is enough that it must mean that the standard of the skill and diligence was not the average of the whole body of the profession, or in other words, *ordinary skill,* but was that exercised by some defined or undefined portion of the profession, or in other words *more than* mere *ordinary skill.* Of course in determining this ordinary skill, "regard should be had to the improvements, and advanced state of the profession at the time" the case was treated, for such regard is necessary in order to correctly ascertain

(continued)

the true standard of ordinary skill. It is also doubtless true that the standard of ordinary skill may vary even in the same state, according to the greater or lesser opportunities afforded by the locality, for observation and practice, from which alone the highest degree of skill can be acquired. As to this last thought, see Shearm. & Redf. on Neg., § 436, p. 491. And as to skill and diligence generally as above stated, see Id., § § 431-443, and the cases cited in the notes. See, also, *Howard v. Grover,* 28 Me. 97; *Simonds v. Henry,* 39 Id. 155; *Patten v. Miggin,* 51 Id. 595; *Lawdon v. Humphrey,* 9 Conn. 209; *Reynolds v. Graves,* 3 Wis. 416; *Gallagher v. Thompson,* Wright's Rep. (Ohio) 466; *Bowman v. Woods,* 1 G. Greene, 441.

We are not disposed in any degree, not even in the very least, to let down or lower the true standard of professional skill or diligence, either in medicine, law, or other applied science. But we recognize the fact that this standard must be a practical and attainable one, and not one of mere theory or fancied perfection, the enforcement of which would cause much litigation, and necessarily drive from the profession a large portion of those from whose practice the largest measure of practical good is attained.

The case of *McCandless v. Mc Wha,* 22 Penn. St. 261, is so often cited, and parts of the opinion by WOODWARD, J., so often quoted in text-books and cases, that we deem it proper to give it here a somewhat extended analysis. The case arose in Pittsburg, Penn., and was decided by the supreme court, 1853. The plaintiff had in some way, suffered "*an oblique comminuted fracture of the tibia and fibula* of the leg, which fracture was nearly half way from the ankle to the knee." The defendant, a regular practicing physician and surgeon, was called to treat it. The plaintiff claimed that by the want of skill and attention by defendant, the leg had become shorter than the other. The defendant denied the want of skill, and alleged that the shortening came from the improper loosening by plaintiff of the bandages and extensions, and the previous intemperate habits of plaintiff. There was a jury trial in the court below, and the court instructed the jury "that the defendant was bound *to bring to his aid the skill necessary* for a surgeon to set the leg so as to make it straight, and of equal length with the other when healed, and if he did not, he was accountable in damages, just as a stone mason or bricklayer would be in building a wall of poor materials, and the wall fell down; or if they build a chimney, and it would smoke by reason of a want of skill in its construction, they could not only not recover pay for building, but would be accountable for damages; and, if suits were more frequently brought, we would perhaps have fewer practitioners of medicine and surgery not possessing the requisite professional skill and knowledge than we now have. But it is due to the defendant to state that, with the exception of the matter complained of in this suit, there is nothing in the evidence given to show that he is not respectable in his profession."

The opinion of a majority of the court was delivered by WOODWARD, J., and, in remarking upon the first instruction above, he says: "It is impossible to sustain this proposition. It is not true in the abstract, and if it were, it was inapplicable to the circumstances under investigation. The implied contract of a physician or surgeon is not to cure, to restore a fractured limb to its natural perfectness, but to treat the case with diligence and skill. The fracture may be so complicated that no skill vouchsafed to man can restore original straightness and length; or the patient may, by willful disregard of the surgeon's directions, impair the effect of the best conceived measures. He deals not with insensate matter like the stone mason or bricklayer, who choose their materials and adjust them according to mathematical lines, but he has a suffering human being to treat, a nervous system to tranquilize, and a *will* to regulate and control. The evidence before us makes this strong distinction between surgery and masonry, and shows how the judge's inapt illustration was calculated to lead away the jury from the true point of the cause.

(continued)

The question was not whether the doctor had brought to the case skill enough to make the leg as straight and long as the other, but *whether he had employed such reasonable skill and diligence, as are ordinarily exercised in his profession.* For less than this he is responsible in damages; but if he be held to the measure laid down by the court below, the implied contract amounts on his part to a warranty of cure, for which there is no authority in law. * * * The only remaining error assigned (upon the other instruction) is scarcely worthy of notice. The action depended so entirely on its own circumstances, that the observation of the court as to the policy of such suits was irrelevant, and we may fairly presume harmless. But, for misdirection on the other point, the judgment is reversed, and a *venire de novo* awarded."

The precise point decided by the case is, that physicians are not accountable in damages for a failure to make a perfect cure, just as a stone-mason or bricklayer is liable for a failure to make a perfect job. What is above quoted from the opinion, is substantially all that legitimately pertains to it. But the learned judge says very much more, and some of it is not entirely consistent with that we have quoted, while some of it is. To illustrate we quote further: "We have stated the rule to be reasonable skill and diligence; by which we mean such as thoroughly educated surgeons ordinarily employ. If more than this is expected, it must be expressly stipulated for; but this much every patient has a right to demand in virtue of the implied contract which results from intrusting his case to a person holding himself out to the world as qualified to practice this important profession." But afterward, he uses this language: "The law has no allowance for *quackery*. It demands *qualification* in the profession practiced--not extraordinary skill, such as belongs only to a few men of rare genius and endowments, but *that degree which ordinarily characterizes the profession.* And in judging of this degree of skill, in a given case, regard is to be had to the advanced state of the profession at the time." In our opinion, in this last quoted paragraph, the learned judge re-announced the correct rule of law, the same as he had in the body of the opinion as set out above. But in the preceding quotation, he announced a very different rule, to wit: "Such reasonable skill and diligence as *thoroughly educated* surgeons ordinarily employ."

The whole case of *McCandless v. Mc Wha* is a remarkable one. None of the evidence taken upon the trial in the court below was before the supreme court, except the deposition of one of the witnesses on the part of the defense, and yet, LEWIS, J., without dissenting from the opinion of WOODWARD, J., filed an extended opinion in which he discusses, the merits of the case upon the evidence in the light of a large number of medical treatises, from which he quotes and upon which he comments. But he sums up his discussion with a statement that the main question is, "Did the surgeon *exercise ordinary skill and care in his reatment of the patient?* If he did, he is not liable. If he did not, he is." While BLACK, Ch. J., delivered the following opinion: "We all concur in the law of this case. The judge in his charge fell into an error in stating the amount of skill required in the treatment of the case. We reverse for that reason. But when we decide the legal point we are done with it. We are not authority on questions of surgery. Our hands are abundantly full with questions that belong to our profession, without volunteering opinions on sciences which relate to others. I think it necessary to say this in order to prevent the court below, on a second trial, from supposing that we intend to give them any instructions on matters in which we have no jurisdiction."

The fact that we now have before us two cases in which the courts below have been led into error by quotations from Judge WOODWARD'S opinion, found in the notes in different text-books, has led us to give the case this extended notice. The point decided and the law actually ruled in the case, were right beyond question. But very much of the opinions of WOODWARD and LEWIS, JJ., are outside of the case, and their observations are well calculated to mislead. It may not be out of place to remark, that a majority of this court

(continued)

concur with Chief Justice BLACK in his observation that "our hands are abundantly full with questions that belong to our own profession without volunteering opinions on sciences which relate to others." For the error in the instruction as before noticed the judgment is

Reversed.

34 Iowa 286, 1872 WL 234 (Iowa), 11 Am.Rep. 141

REFINEMENT OF THEORIES AND PRINCIPLES

Prior to twentieth-century America, full-scale hospitals were found predominantely in large cities. Physicians in rural communities often had no particular office facility as many individuals who were considered ill enough to warrant a physician were often unable to travel the distance to where a physician was located. Additionally, a part of a physician's treatment depended on a thorough knowledge of how the patient actually lived as conditions were much less consistent than today in terms of access to clean water, heat, basic nutrition, and hygienic or sanitary conditions. Consequently, the physician frequently came to the patient. If there was an office, it often consisted of little more than a room with a bed and some rudimentary supplies. In some communities there were trained nurses who saw to many of the lesser ills of the population. Midwives were often trained on the job by a relative or friend and may have had no formal education. Nonetheless, they assisted in difficult deliveries of babies when a doctor was not available. Dentists were becoming more common as urban communities grew throughout the country. Until the early twentieth century, freestanding medical facilities other than hospitals and some physician or dentist offices were a rarity. Just before the turn of the twentieth century, medicine began to make rapid advancements. Chemists and researchers began to create more effective medicines that were more complex than the extract of a variety of individual herbs. X rays were developed as a diagnostic tool, and universities were becoming established throughout the entire United States to contribute not only formal training of various types of health care providers but research as well. With all of these advancements, new questions began to arise regarding the potential liability when things went wrong.

Some of the questions that arose for health care professionals included how the standard of care was determined. The basic premise at the time was that it seemed unfair to hold a physician who lived and worked in a community somewhere in rural America, with minimal access to training in medical advancements, to the same standard as a physician located in a large urban community near major universities. To do so would discourage medical practitioners from locating in rural areas and thus deprive a large segment of the population of medical care. Another question considered whether one who was not a licensed physician, but who provided medical care in the absence of a physician, was held to a legal standard. Yet another question developed regarding when the lawsuit must be brought. Unlike an event such as an accident when injuries were usually immediate and readily apparent, what determined treatment for events when effects did not instantly develop? Did the statute of limitations with regard to the time allowed to bring suit apply? If so, when did it commence and end? All of these, and more, were legal questions that needed to be addressed as medical care advanced and became more readily available to the general population.

As mentioned earlier, the effects of an alleged lack of a degree of skill required of a medical practitioner moved from the criminal courts to a vague standard in the civil courts. While licensing statutes were encouraged by the judiciary, and were passed, the courts also developed their own legal principles and decreed that physicians were to adhere to a standard of care, knowledge, and skills ordinarily possessed by members of their profession. These principles were a tremendous advancement in settling a major question of law. But the position of the courts also generated great controversy. The United States was still a relatively young country with a vast range of education and training available to members of nearly every profession, including those in health care. In some areas, physicians were highly trained, constantly learning and studying the most current theories. In others, they were virtually cut off from the rest of the world due to a lack of communication devices and adequate modes of transportation. In many instances these medical professionals' entire body of knowledge came from a handful of books and the wisdom passed down from older physicians. It hardly seemed appropriate that both types of professionals (urban and rural) be held to the same standard when it was not realistic for them to achieve similar education and training. Consequently, a legal standard known as the "**locality rule**" was developed. The example in Application 2.1 below demonstrates how, at the time, two physicians with similar backgrounds, but in different professional circumstances, would receive disparate treatment if a locality rule were not applied at the time.

APPLICATION 2.1

In 1892, Josiah and Frederick Kremer were brothers and physicians. Both were trained initially at the same university. Josiah was a professor at the University of New York School of Medicine and a renowned surgeon in New York City. Frederick became a local doctor in a small community in western Wyoming. Josiah employed the most current methods of treatment with the most innovative devices and medications available. He consulted frequently with other physicians who practiced and studied medicine on a regular basis. Frederick, on the other hand, had very limited accessibility and often created his own medical devices and medications from natural resources in the area. Mail delivery was sporadic and often unreliable depending on the time of the year and weather conditions in the mountains. Frederick had virtually no means of regular contact with other physicians and relied instead on a few books he had brought west with him some 15 years before. In this situation, if the same alleged malpractice was perpetrated by both brothers, it would be inherently unfair to hold both to the same standard of knowledge and skill.

By the later 1800s it was recognized by the courts that the degree of skill and knowledge of physicians varied widely by community. In 1886, a case much relied upon by subsequent courts issued the rule that a physician's standard of care was measured against other physicians and surgeons in the area where he practiced. Gates v. Fleischer, 67 Wis. 504, 30 N.W. 674 (Wis. 1886). This was one of the earliest applications of the locality rule. It was meant to place physicians in a fairer position with regard to what was expected of them. As time passed the rule became widely accepted. Physicians were held to a degree of knowledge and skill that would be found among other physicians in their own or a similar community. Considerations included population, medical facilities, availability of modern equipment for diagnosis, access to current literature and training, and the degree of knowledge and training of other physicians in the community. This locality rule seemed to be the fairest under the conditions that existed at the time. The locality rule remained in place for the better part of a century. However, as mass transit and communication technology advanced, the reasons for the locality rule began to disappear.

By the early 1970s a distinction was being made in malpractice cases against general practitioners and specialist physicians and other types of health care professionals. Those who held themselves out to the public to have specialized training were expected to maintain knowledge of the most current scientific advancements. Because the locality rule was initially developed to protect general practitioners who did not have access to the latest medical knowledge and training, the theory did not support those specialists who, by definition, claimed to have advanced training and skill. As a result, in a majority of jurisdictions specialists were no longer able to claim the benefits of the locality rule. Rather, they were required on a national level to meet the standard of knowledge and training of other specialists. This was the beginning of the decline of the locality rule.

Throughout the 1970s, a majority of jurisdictions undertook to modify the locality rule. First, specialists were placed under a stricter standard to keep abreast of the most current practices within the area of specialty as this was a reasonable expectation of those seeking out specialized care. The thought process was that those who specialized and benefited from the reliance by the public should be accountable to maintain knowledge of the prevailing medical practices regardless of the geographical location of the physician. At first, courts were reluctant to abandon the rule entirely and risk posing a deterrent to specialists otherwise willing to locate in rural areas. In those jurisdictions, a compromise was found by expanding the geographic definition of a "locality" rather than abandoning the rule. In some jurisdictions, the courts expanded the "locality" used to measure standards and practices of specialists to a statewide area.[1] In time, a majority of courts abandoned the locality and statewide rule for general practitioners and specialists alike.[2] Soon thereafter the courts followed with similar findings for all physicians. The availability of mass communications and rapid transit meant physicians outside urban areas were no longer considered isolated, and information was no longer inaccessible. Satellite and extensive fiberoptic and cable-supported communication systems made continuing education possible without ever leaving one's community or even their offices. National organizations and publications for virtually every area of medical science and every type of health care practitioner communicated research and advancements. Thus, by the 1980s the original rationale for the locality rule had largely disappeared and once again the majority of courts relied on a general standard of care based on the particular practitioner's area of practice. Today, health care providers of all types in most jurisdictions are required to exercise a reasonable degree of care, skill, knowledge, and training that would be expected of properly trained and educated members of that particular profession at a national level.

As mentioned above, throughout the 1800s the states individually enacted licensing statutes that set standards for physicians. Slowly these were refined and enforcement began to occur. At first, many were allowed to continue practice despite a lack of formal training if they could establish adequate experience and training attested to by other physicians. But, over time the restrictions became much more rigorous to ensure that all those representing themselves as medical doctors had a foundation of formal education and training. Today, the most basic requirements vary little among the states. Typically, one is required to have completed a degree in medicine from an accredited university (this is usually preceded by a bachelor's degree) and a minimum number of years of post-graduate training. Most physicians will elect an area of practice or specialty and the number of post-graduate training years required is determined by the area chosen. This post-graduate training is most commonly referred to as an **internship** and/or **residency**. In a number of jurisdictions doctors in internship or residency training are permitted to practice only subject to supervision of a fully licensed doctor. After completion of the internship/residency programs, physicians may complete additional specialty training through what are known as fellowships. Physicians may also seek specialist certification from professional organizations but these are voluntary and the doctors who achieve them are not required to obtain an additional statutory license to practice. However, one who represents him or herself as a "board-certified" specialist is also held to a higher standard of knowledge and skill than one who practices only as a licensed physician.

Another area of law that has developed largely within the twentieth century is about alleged malpractice by health care providers other than physicians. It is fairly unusual to have a case brought singly against a nurse, therapist, or technician employed by a physician or health care facility. Instead, these cases typically are brought against the physician and/or facility as well. Often these non-physician practitioners are employed by physicians or health care facilities.[3] But there have been cases wherein nurses have been found negligent for their actions independent of liability of a supervising physician or facility. These include cases where nurses acted regardless of constructive knowledge that their actions could be harmful or illegal; cases where nurses are employed without physician or facility supervision, such as in industrial settings; and cases where nurses undertook to provide care for patients whose physical conditions required skills clearly exceeding those of the nurse. Much the same approach has been taken toward pharmacists. The rationale is that they play an integral part in the delivery of health care services, but the degree of liability is directly related to the amount of independent conduct of the pharmacist in the particular case.

An interesting role is that of emergency medical personnel. For these individuals, a variety of views must be considered. First, the law encourages those who help others who are in trouble. Thus, the majority of jurisdictions have Good Samaritan laws that relieve persons from liability when, in good faith, they undertake to render assistance. This rule has been applied to emergency medical personnel. The **Good Samaritan rule** typically relieves these individuals from liability unless they are responsible for gross negligence or willful misconduct.[4] Secondly, many emergency medical personnel are employees of local government entities. And, in many states, there are immunity statutes that prohibit actions against government entities for ordinary negligence. So for some who are employed by local government, this is an additional shield from liability. However, the issue of gross negligence and intentional torts may eliminate that shield. Finally, most courts that have considered the issue have held that there is no immunity from suit for those emergency medical personnel involved in circumstances that do not involve delivery of emergency care. An example might be malpractice that occurs while a patient is being transferred from one facility to another in a nonemergency situation.

The more complicated malpractice issues have involved those who are not clearly within the confines of traditional medical care. The law is not yet definitive about who is included within the definition of a health care provider. In fact, it often varies by jurisdiction. In those states with medical malpractice statutes, there are numerous cases involving a variety of professionals and the issues arise of whether they are considered a health care provider and subject to the application of medical malpractice statutes in jurisdictions that have such laws. Typically medical laboratories and clinics are considered health care facilities and subject to malpractice laws. However, a distinction may be made if the clinic provides only basic counseling and referrals for more extensive care and no actual delivery of health-related services. Home health care professionals, even if certified or licensed as health care providers, are usually not considered subject to malpractice laws if the alleged injury occurred as the result of something that did not relate directly to diagnosing and treating a patient's medical complaints.[5]

While other independent service providers such as dentists, podiatrists, and chiropractors may well be subject to actions sounding in tort for alleged malfeasance, the courts are still divided on the issue of whether these individuals should be governed by medical malpractice statutes. The key question seems to lie in the language of the statutes themselves. It is important to note that not all jurisdictions have medical malpractice statutes. In those states without them, the question of whether a person or entity has committed malpractice is more a focus on the alleged act or omission. In jurisdictions where medical malpractice statutes have been enacted the courts have examined the statutory language in detail. If health care providers are referred to in general terms, it is more likely those other than licensed physicians and hospitals will be included. However, if the state legislature specifically includes others such as dentists, then those not mentioned are more likely to fall outside the medical malpractice statute. This does not mean they cannot be sued for malfeasance. Rather, it only means that the action will be treated as any other action for negligence, breach of contract, intentional tort, or whatever the case is based on. Malpractice states typically have specific procedures not common to the ordinary lawsuit and those also would not apply. The key to approaching an alleged case of malpractice is to identify the various parties who were involved and identify whether there are applicable medical malpractice statutes that might affect the statute of limitations and procedures in the case. Assignment 2.1 demonstrates how this might occur in a potential case of malpractice.

ASSIGNMENT 2.1

Examine the following situation. Identify each of the potential defendants and explain what conduct would be actionable and whether each defendant is likely to fall within the definition of the malpractice statute.

Mason alleges that his recent injuries and problems from a car accident were made worse by his subsequent medical care. Specifically, he claims that while he was trapped in the vehicle, he had no specific pain or disability in his back or neck. The car was smoking and there was a danger of fire as the attendants removed Mason. He claims the ambulance team, in removing him from the car, caused his back and neck to be twisted severely and it resulted in severe pain and a sensation of numbness in his lower body. Once at the hospital, he claims the lab work was conducted in error when a report was issued that he had a blood alcohol level twice that of the legal limit. After placing stitches in a fairly large laceration in Mason's face, the emergency room doctor pronounced Mason to be well enough to leave the hospital and he was discharged to the custody of the police who charged him with driving under the influence and placed him in a cell overnight. The next day, after his release from jail, he went to a chiropractor who manipulated his back and neck in such a way that made the pain much worse and caused him to lose all feeling in his legs. Until this time no X rays or diagnostic tests had been performed. Mason was taken to a hospital and it was confirmed that his back was broken and he would be a paraplegic for the rest of his life. He also claims that by not having a plastic surgeon put in the stitches, he is permanently disfigured. Mason's family physician confirmed that Mason had long been documented as severely allergic to alcohol and consumption in any quantity would cause a potentially fatal reaction. Therefore, it was impossible that he could have been intoxicated as the lab work indicated following the accident. The jurisdiction where all of this occurred, and where Mason lives, has a medical malpractice statute that applies to all "health care providers."

THE LEGISLATIVE MOVEMENT

From the earliest beginnings of the judicial system, legislative involvement in issues relating to medical malpractice was encouraged by the courts. Initially, the call was for licensing statutes. The purpose of statutes was protective. With clearly stated standards for qualification, the public could trust that there was at least some proof of knowledge and skill by the physicians who practiced in their communities. Throughout the 1800s and first half of the twentieth century, legislatures promulgated a wide variety of statutes designed to define the standards for licensure, practice, and discipline of all types of providers of services related to the public health. This included not only physicians and nurses, but hospitals, clinics, laboratories, and related professions such as dentists, chiropractors, podiatrists, pharmacists, optometrists, and a wide range of others. But, it was during the second half of the twentieth century that other issues came to the forefront as warranting legislative intervention. This period of time in the United States was frequently described in the media as a "litigation explosion."

A large number of variables contributed to the dramatic increase in civil lawsuits in the middle and late twentieth century, not the least of which was the notable increase in population, technology, and commerce following World War II. Like other areas of civil law, medical malpractice also saw a surge of growth in the number of cases filed. Practitioners were trying to keep up with rapid scientific developments and may not have discovered associated dangers until after the developments were placed into practice. An unsuspecting public was the recipient of these too-late discoveries. One example was a widely administered drug in the early 1960s, commonly known as Thalidomide, that proved to have an exceptionally high risk of causing major birth defects when the drug was given to pregnant women. Today, even with extensive studies prior to approval of a technique or product, many problems are still not evident until widespread use occurs. A consequence of the increased number of lawsuits was an increase in the cost of malpractice insurance. This, in turn, was passed along in the form of increased health care costs to the consumer. As the problem began to grow, there was concern that providers would leave their professions in light of the threat of increasing costs of insurance and large judgments against them. In fact, to some extent this has occurred. In some jurisdictions known for their generous jury verdicts, it is difficult to recruit or keep physicians in the area. There are even instances of providers changing professions or moving into related fields such as teaching, insurance, and consulting.

There are conflicting opinions regarding the effects of medical malpractice suits on the costs of health care. Associations of lawyers cite studies demonstrating that malpractice insurance and jury verdicts do not support the dramatic increases in the costs of health care. Insurance companies and health care provider groups claim that verdicts in malpractice cases are so inflated that they raise costs and intimidate health care providers in the delivery of services. The legislatures have reacted by passing a variety of laws to respond to the issues specific to cases of alleged medical malpractice. In a short five-year period during the 1970s and early 1980s, 43 states passed more than 300 laws related to medical malpractice litigation. Since that time, additional legislation in a vast majority of states has been considered and/or passed, laws have been refined, and there is currently a major push for more extensive federal legislation effecting malpractice cases and judgments. As noted above, medical malpractice statutes may or may not be extended to apply to those beyond the traditional health care providers such as hospitals and physicians depending on the statutory language and its interpretation by the courts of the jurisdiction. In some jurisdictions, certain types of cases, such as those based in contract, may not be considered within the confines of malpractice statutes aimed primarily at cases based in tort.

A key element seen in many medical malpractice statutes is that, as mentioned above, there are typically special rules of procedure for those cases of professional negligence that fall within the definition of the statute. For those outside the statute, the case is prosecuted as any other case of ordinary negligence and standard rules of civil procedure apply. But in the event a medical malpractice statute is considered applicable to the provider who is accused of negligence, there may be different statutes of limitation, discovery rules, even pretrial procedures. For example, some states require affidavits from other health care professionals that declare, in their professional opinion, malpractice has occurred. For example, Michigan Compiled Laws Annotated (2003) provides:

"1) Subject to subsection (2), the plaintiff in an action alleging medical malpractice or, if the plaintiff is represented by an attorney, the plaintiff's attorney shall file with the complaint an affidavit of merit signed by a health professional who the plaintiff's attorney reasonably believes meets the requirements for an expert witness under section 2169. The affidavit of merit shall certify that the health professional has reviewed the notice and all medical records supplied to him or her by the plaintiff's attorney concerning the allegations contained in the notice and shall contain a statement of each of the following:

(a) The applicable standard of practice or care.
(b) The health professional's opinion that the applicable standard of practice or care was breached by the health professional or health facility receiving the notice.
(c) The actions that should have been taken or omitted by the health professional or health facility in order to have complied with the applicable standard of practice or care.
(d) The manner in which the breach of the standard of practice or care was the proximate cause of the injury alleged in the notice."

Other common statutory provisions include a panel that must first evaluate the viability of the case and determine there is a real issue of malpractice. Consider the following New Mexico statutory language:

"New Mexico Statutes Annotated § **41-5-15. Commission decision required; application** 1A. No malpractice action may be filed in any court against a qualifying health care provider before application is made to the medical review commission and its decision is rendered.

3B. This application shall contain the following:

(1) a brief statement of the facts of the case, naming the persons involved, the dates and the circumstances, so far as they are known, of the alleged act or acts of malpractice; and
(2) a statement authorizing the panel to obtain access to all medical and hospital records and information pertaining to the matter giving rise to the application, and, for the purposes of its consideration of the matter only, waiving any claim of privilege as to the contents of those records. Nothing in that statement shall in any way be construed as waiving that privilege for any other purpose or in any other context, in or out of court."

It is very common to find language which establishes a rule for the time when an action must be commenced starting from the date when the plaintiff had constructive knowledge of the alleged malpractice. All of these are designed to allow only those cases that are soundly based in fact, and which provide both parties with a reasonable opportunity to present evidence in their behalf. Special rules also often apply in the case of minors who are the alleged victims of medical malpractice and the time they have for bringing suit.

Additionally, many states have placed limitations of varying kinds on the monetary recovery available to plaintiffs in medical malpractice cases. In some jurisdictions the limit or cap is placed on the entire amount recoverable, in others it limits recovery for damages that cannot be supported by factual documentation of value, medical bills, etc. A common example of limited damages are for conditions such as pain and suffering. These are often referred to as noneconomic damages. In 2003, a measure was introduced into the United States Congress to place a cap on noneconomic damages in medical malpractice cases but it failed to win the support needed to pass into legislation. The question of limitation on these damages is one that is extremely volatile. Consider the example below in Application 2.2.

APPLICATION 2.2

Troy is the 62-year-old victim of alleged malpractice. His injuries have resulted in a physical condition that will likely cause him regular pain and limited disability for the remainder of his life. In his suit, he is seeking a judgment that includes a request for pain and suffering in the amount of $15 million. A statutory cap on noneconomic damages limits his recovery to $500,000. Given all relevant factors, his life expectancy is approximately another five years.

Sam is an eight-year-old victim of alleged malpractice in the same jurisdiction as Troy. Sam's injuries have resulted in a physical condition that will likely cause him regular pain and suffering and disability for the remainder of his life as well. Sam's life expectancy is approximately another 70 years. Under the statutory cap on recovery, he is limited to the same $500,000 judgment as Troy. This is despite the fact that his noneconomic damages will be endured for an additional 65 years and may well affect career choices and employability.

As can be seen from the examples, there is an inherent unfairness in the noneconomic damage limits because they do not consider the individual circumstances of the case and all plaintiffs are treated exactly the same. However, from the defendant's perspective, a case left entirely to a jury's discretion could result in financial ruin for a single mistake by a provider and eliminate one more provider from the available pool. There is no doubt that statutory damage award limits are not the ideal response to the medical malpractice crisis. However, at this point, without an alternative acceptable to all sides, they are one of the most common responses by the legislatures.

Another issue regarding monetary damage limits are punitive damage awards. Punitive or exemplary damages are permitted in some jurisdictions when the conduct of the defendant was so blatant as to constitute a reckless disregard for the welfare of the patient. These damages are in addition to compensatory damages (both economic and noneconomic). And, in many jurisdictions, punitive damages are considered uninsurable. That is to say, one cannot purchase insurance to protect against an award of punitive damages as a matter of public policy. The rationale in these jurisdictions is that a party has little incentive to act with a basic level of regard to the welfare of others if they have nothing to lose personally. If a case is brought and a jury finds in favor of the plaintiff awarding both compensatory and punitive damages, and the jurisdiction prohibits insurability of punitives, the cost of the punitive damages is wholly borne by the plaintiff personally. Such an award, even if for a single act within the entire career of a defendant, can be financially devastating.

The reasons behind time and monetary limits are simple. The rapid increase in the number of cases and the often large judgments awarded created a perception of a medical malpractice crisis. Unlike other types of suits whose judgments varied widely, medical malpractice judgments were often very high. There are any number of speculations as to why juries gave large awards but, no doubt, the often serious and long-term effects of injuries and the idea that a sacred trust between health care provider and patient had been violated were contributing factors. Regardless of the reasons why they have increased in number, medical malpractice cases have a direct effect on the general public and the economy. As mentioned above, large judgments in numerous quantities led to higher insurance rates and ultimately these costs were passed on to the consumer. This occurred at the same time as scientific and technological advances were coming at an increasingly rapid rate and the costs of implementing the changes were significant. Additionally, certain geographical areas face continuing difficulty in retaining medical providers because of the risk of generous monetary judgments associated with the jury awards in that jurisdiction. The result of all these factors has been to focus national attention on the perceived crisis and create legislation to help bring these circumstances under control and ultimately contain costs while making health care professions appealing in all geographical areas.

ASSIGNMENT 2.2

Select a jurisdiction and locate a state medical malpractice statute as well as other relevant statutes, including those affecting contract actions based on malpractice, and answer the following questions about the statute:

1. Is there a different statute of limitations for cases based on medical malpractice, ordinary negligence, and breach of contract cases? If so, distinguish.

2. Are health care providers referred to generally or are specific professions identified (e.g., doctors, dentists, nurses)?

3. Is there a limitation on damages generally?

4. Is there a limitation on noneconomic damages?

5. Are there any prerequisites to filing suits in court such as affidavits, panels, arbitration, mediation, etc.?

LICENSURE AND CERTIFICATION OF PROVIDERS AND FACILITIES

It is already established that statutory intervention was requested and the legislatures responded with various measures to license health care providers, but it has been a long and arduous process. For example, nursing assistants who are often the primary caregivers for the most disabled members of our society in long-term care facilities were not even required to have minimum training and education in most states until the 1970s. Today, however, every state has extensive procedures and requirements for all providers of care in the health-related fields.

Physicians must establish minimum levels of education and training to obtain a license to practice medicine. American graduates take a national exam to test basic medical knowledge. If the education/training is obtained in a foreign country, the physician must pass an additional exam for foreign medical graduates that includes medical knowledge as well as a basic command of the English language and medical terminology. Once a national exam or foreign graduate medical exam is passed, licensure is applied for in the specific state of practice. However, many states require the graduate to be enrolled in post-graduate internship/residency for a limited license. Most states also require an applicant to have completed such training before unlimited licensure to practice is given. As part of the licensing process, states also typically require documented proof of education and training. Additional training and testing may also be pursued by the graduate as part of the foundation to obtain certification as a specialist in a particular field. This designation is provided by recognized professional organizations rather than government. Thus, the term "**board certified**" applied to a physician is issued from a group consisting of professionals and not any government agency.

For other health care professionals including, but not limited to, various therapists, nurses, dentists, podiatrists, chiropractors, and technicians, each state has a licensing procedure. Typically it includes successful completion of an approved educational program and exam that is administered either at the national or state level. Until the late twentieth century, it was also quite common for states to grant reciprocity. That is to say, if an individual was properly licensed in one state, another state may grant licensure based on the evidence of good standing in the state where licensed. The trend in all professions has been to require all the components of licensure be satisfied regardless of status in another state. Another beneficial development of licensing has been a national data bank. In the past, if a health care professional ran into difficulty with licensure due to malpractice, ethical issues, or other reasons, that person could simply move to another state and start over. However, it became apparent that some unscrupulous or even dangerous individuals were simply taking their show on the road and foisting themselves on unsuspecting citizens who were powerless to protect themselves. The result was a national data bank whereby states contribute information about certain disciplinary actions against health care providers. States also have become increasingly willing to share information about the status of their present or previously licensed health care professionals. Any state in which an individual seeks licensure can access the data bank and determine if the individual has a history that might cause him or her to be seen as a danger to the citizens of the jurisdiction. If so, licensure can be withheld, granted conditionally pending further investigation, or even denied.

In addition to initial licensure, most states now require providers of health care services to maintain their skills and knowledge through continuing education. As recently as 20 to 30 years ago, if someone was licensed or certified, the question was often resolved and the individual was free to go about his or her career. More recently, most states have passed legislation that requires a minimum amount of periodic continuing education in order to maintain licensure. This is also a common requirement by malpractice insurers to sustain coverage and adds one more step to protect the public from those who might otherwise allow their skills to become outdated or even obsolete.

APPLICATION 2.3

Dr. Bupkis was a psychologist practicing in State N. He was the subject of a complaint to the state for an inappropriate and intimate relationship with a patient. He denied the allegation. Because his "therapy" sessions were individual, it was his word against that of his patient. However, when word of the complaint leaked out to the media, several former patients came forward and filed similar complaints. Interestingly, the doctor decided he need a change of scenery and relocated to another state. At the time of his move and application for licensure in State H, no action had been taken against his license in State N. However, when State H contacted State N in regard to licensure status and discovered the action history, they discovered that five complaints were under investigation against Dr. Bupkis. Prior to licensure, State H required that he fully disclose the documents surrounding each investigation. The officials of State H further conditioned any licensure of Dr. Bupkis would first require a positive outcome without any significant disciplinary action in State N. The doctor withdrew his application for licensure.

In the past, a situation like this would likely result in the doctor moving from state to state without detection. However, with the advent of information sharing among jurisdictions, many individuals who would otherwise be predators are stopped early on.

Like individual practitioners, health care facilities undergo similar licensing requirements. The qualifying factors must be satisfied for most facilities before they can begin operations. A facility must meet all applicable local, state, and federal requirements for a public business and specific requirements for the particular type of business. For facilities, a variety of issues must be addressed. Often the requirements are driven by the type of facility in terms of the services delivered. For example, facilities with laboratory equipment that processes any type of fluid or tissue may be required to keep maintenance records of the equipment, certified operators, and often specific environmental conditions of equipment and/or specimens. Facilities in which any type of instruments are used and/or where specimens are collected or processed need proper equipment and procedures for disinfection and/or sterilization and containment of anything considered to be a potential biohazard. Facilities which are open to the public must meet the standards of the Americans with Disabilities Act and be handicap-accessible with proper entrances, exits, and lavatory access. Facilities must also comply with applicable building and fire codes. Local ordinances may also apply with regard to the number of exterior parking places required per square foot of building space, the proper placement and type of any signage, building capacity, zoning for use, etc.

In addition to all of the more general aspects of a commercial building, there are often accreditation issues that are equally important for a successful venture. In order to be approved to receive payment for services by insurance companies and government programs such as Medicare (government subsidized elder and some disabled health care) and Medicaid (government subsidized health care primarily for indigent children and some disabled individuals) a facility may be required to have appropriate accreditation by an independent organization. There are a variety of such organizations and they are often specific to the type of facility. Essentially, what these organizations do is visit a facility and evaluate all relevant factors ranging from fire codes to the qualifications of personnel. If all is satisfactory, the facility is issued a certificate of approval for a specified period of time. If there are problems, the certification may be limited or denied, or suspended while time is provided to correct any outstanding issues.

Periodically, the government agency in charge of licensure of a health care facility will conduct what is commonly referred to as a "survey" or "audit." At that time, all of the licensure requirements are reviewed for continuing compliance as well as any newly applicable laws, regulations or ordinances. A facility is obligated to maintain compliance on a continuing basis and notice is not always given that a survey/audit is going to be conducted. Failure to comply can result in a wide variety of penalties ranging from monetary fines to closure of the facility. Most minor violations result in citations with a specified period of time to correct the deficiencies.

An additional element that facilities providing health care services must address are private company audits. Frequently, insurance companies who pay for services provided to their clients will conduct such audits. These are very similar in nature to government audits. They examine compliance of the physical conditions of the facility with all applicable government laws, regulations, and ordinances. But they also consider the practice habits of the providers as well. It is usually necessary to show that all of the providers are in good standing with regard to personal licensure or certification. Additionally, the insurance company typically considers the number of patients seen in a given period of time, the types of diagnostic tests performed and the time for response, record keeping methods for patient charts, etc.

With regard to the issue of medical malpractice, licensure/certification of the provider and facility are extremely important. While most involved in litigation are concerned with the specific instance, the history of accreditation, licensure, or certification can have a tremendous impact by establishing a pattern of conduct that either supports or devastates the allegations of malpractice. For this reason, when involved in malpractice litigation, it is always important to examine the history of the individual and facilities involved.

ASSIGNMENT 2.3

Prepare a list of all of the specific items that might be examined during an audit of a health care facility such as a medical doctor's office that conducts its own basic blood lab work and X rays.

Problem 2.1

Complete 2.1 of the Comprehensive Problem in Appendix A.

CHAPTER SUMMARY

The development of the legislative impact on the health care professions is perhaps more dramatic than any other. Initially, there was no legislation whatsoever and the courts repeatedly voiced the need for control over those who would provide such services to a population largely ignorant of medical science. Ultimately, legislation was passed that established basic qualifications for those employed as health care practitioners. This legislation broadened as the various career paths within the area of health care developed. The courts oversaw issues of malpractice and required a standard of care that imposed a responsibility to act in a like manner with other similarly situated professionals in the same geographical area.

However, after a period of time, rapid advances in medical science, modes of transportation, and mass communication warranted modification of the standard. In the past 25 years it has become common for a provider to be held to a national standard of knowledge and skill because of the readily available resources. In correspondence with this, state governments and accrediting agencies also require much more extensive compliance with standards for knowledge, training, skill, and even facility management. Failure to comply and maintain a current status as changes occur can result in the loss of all applicable licensure, certification, and/or accreditation. Failure to comply can also impact any potential or pending litigation based on alleged malpractice.

Key Terms

board certified	locality rule
Good Samaritan rule	residency/internship

End Notes

[1] Bryant v. Rankin, 332 F.Supp. 319, (S.D. Iowa 1971); affd. 468 F2d 510 (8th Cir.App.).

[2] Logan v. Greenwich Hosp. Assoc., 191 Conn. 282, 465 A.2d 294 (Conn. 1983).

[3] Romine v. Fernandez, 124 S.W.3d 599 (Tenn App 2003).

[4] Malcolm v. East Detroit, 468 N.W.2d 479 (MI 1991).

[5] Headly v. Maxim Healthcare Serv. Inc., 100 Ohio Misc. 2d 19, 716 N.E.2d 1241 (C.P. 1999).

For additional resources, go to http://www.westlegalstudies.com.

3 CHAPTER

Medical Malpractice Law and Litigation

CHAPTER OBJECTIVES

When you complete this chapter, you should be able to:

- Discuss the various sources of medical malpractice actions
- Discuss the various potential individual defendants in medical malpractice actions
- Discuss and contrast the nature of medical malpractice actions that are brought against facilities and/or against individual providers
- Describe the unique characteristics of medical malpractice actions involving product liability issues

INJURIES RESULTING DIRECTLY FROM CARE/TREATMENT/SERVICES

Historically, and even today, the concept of medical malpractice usually causes thoughts of claims by patients against doctors. However, those cases represent only a percentage of the situations that result in claims of professional malfeasance resulting from health care, treatment, products, and services. This chapter explores the various circumstances that give rise to claims of malpractice to help the reader gain a broader perspective of this area of law and the potential plaintiffs and defendants involved.

Most claims grounded in allegations of medical malpractice arise from situations in which a patient received medical care and for some reason the result was unacceptable. The possible things to go wrong are as different and varied as the individuals involved in them. While some cases have received a certain notoriety in the media, the fact remains that the practice of medicine involves an infinite number of variables that can cause an equally limitless number of potential outcomes. The vast majority of treatments are successful; with constant technological advancements medicine is more science than art. Nevertheless, those occasions do arise in which the health care providers make an error in judgment or skill, or the patient perceives the outcome to be less than what was originally expected. When this happens, claims of malpractice are frequently alleged.

INJURIES RESULTING FROM VIOLATION OF ETHICAL DUTIES

Whatsoever things I see or hear concerning the life of men, in my attendance on the sick or even apart therefrom, which ought not be noised abroad, I will keep silence thereon, counting such things to be as sacred secrets.
- Oath of Hippocrates, 4th Century, B.C.E.

Like most professionals, those in the health care fields have certain codes of **ethics**. These individuals and entities are in a position of trust with those they serve and as such are bound to honor the elements of that trust. There was a time when an individual might have the same physician literally from the cradle to the grave. The physician was the individual's only source of medical care. The relationship was long term and both parties honored the trust that was a natural part of the physician–patient association. Ethical concerns were not often an issue. However, medical advancements brought specialists, technicians, and large-scale clinics and hospitals that, in turn, greatly diminished the personal doctor–patient relationship. While the ultimate boundaries of ethical behavior remained essentially the same, the face-to-face contact largely disappeared and with it much of the trust. The result has been that patients are less hesitant to sue a health care provider with whom they have no personal investment. Providers as well may not always be as cognizant of their ethical obligations to individuals as the delivery of services becomes increasingly impersonal. Also, with technological advancements, many new ethical questions have arisen that were never anticipated by prior generations. The example below in Application 3.1 demonstrates the manner in which the technological ability to obtain information about a patient's medical condition—through what have become ordinary tests—can have a tremendous impact on the patient's life if the information is not handled properly.

APPLICATION 3.1

Kate and Leon planned to be married. As part of the premarital blood tests required by state law, an HIV test was performed. Kate also had some routine blood tests done necessary for a drug screen at her new job. The drug screen was negative, but Kate's HIV test came back positive. A lab technician simply copied the entire report, including the HIV status, and faxed it to Kate's new employer. When the employer saw the information, he or she determined that Kate's condition could cause an increase in the premiums for the employee health insurance plan and a significant amount of work time to be lost if Kate's condition progressed. As a result, Kate was not kept beyond her 90-day probationary period on the job despite excellent job performance. The disclosure of information beyond that which Kate had authorized, specifically the drug screen, cost Kate her employment and potentially other employment if the information were passed along to future possible employers by the company that let her go. This release of confidential information invaded Kate's right to privacy and caused her significant damage.

The information within a patient file is presumed to be just as confidential as the communications between a patient and a provider. While the physical record is the property of the provider, the information contained within it is deemed the property of the patient. In the past, there have been a variety of circumstances in which a provider released the information to third parties and was then held liable for injury, and in some instances subject to disciplinary action, for the improper disclosure.

Not all disclosures of patient information are considered improper or legally actionable. Disclosure is usually considered acceptable and legal only if it is necessary for purposes of

- treatment,
- payment,
- consultation for the benefit of the patient's care,
- to obtain consent from a relative in an emergency situation when the patient cannot effectively provide consent,
- and to those identified by the patient as having the right to access the patient file.

In the absence of these situations, a patient must generally provide express consent as to the exact scope of information released and exact recipients for whom it is intended. And, even if one of the enumerated situations above exists, the provider still is obligated to first seek express consent whenever possible. Most health care providers now furnish patients with a written statement of the provider's privacy policy. Examples of such statements can be found in Chapter 4 which discusses in more detail the specific obligations of providers.

One exception to the rule of patient confidentiality involves litigation. If a patient files a lawsuit of any kind that places their health status, care, or treatment in issue, then they are presumed to waive any confidentiality of that information with respect to the parties and counsel involved in the litigation. The example below demonstrates how this occurs.

APPLICATION 3.2

Lance is involved in a car accident and sues the other driver. Any medical records that have a connection to Lance's injuries from the accident are required to be made available to the opposing side in the lawsuit. This might even include records prior to the accident if they disclose a pre-existing condition that was also alleged as connected in any way with the accident.

While privacy of records has always been protected by the courts and many statutes, federal regulations were issued in 2003 to allow even greater definition to the rights of patients and providers with respect to the confidential nature of medical records. These new regulations were designed to provide basic rules of a national scope since health care has become a very mobile industry with patients traveling to various jurisdictions for treatment and many health care providers who have practices and/or facilities in more than one jurisdiction.

The Health Insurance Portability and Accountability Act known as "**HIPAA**" (45 CFR Parts 160 and 164) is designed to protect the individual with regard to all that is considered to be private health information, often referred to as "PHI." With these new regulations issued by the Department of Health and Human Services, clear lines are drawn to protect individuals and guide providers regarding the disclosure of records that relate to past, present, and even anticipated health issues. Violation of the regulations can not only result in civil litigation by the patient, but also civil and criminal penalties imposed by the government.

The new regulations provide very specific rights for those with protected information. They include the following:

- Right to access, inspect, and copy PHI held by hospitals, clinics, health plans, and other "covered entities," with some exceptions
- Right to request amendments to PHI held by "covered entities"
- Right to request an accounting of disclosures that have been made without authorization to anyone other than the individual for purposes other than treatment, payment, and health care operations
- Right to receive a Notice of Privacy Practices from doctors, hospitals, health plans, and others in the health care system
- Right to request confidential communications of PHI, e.g., having PHI transmitted to a different address or a different telephone number
- Right to request restrictions on uses or disclosures, although the "covered entity" receiving the request is not obligated to accept it
- Right to complain about privacy practices to the "covered entity" and to the Secretary of Health and Human Services

Health care providers are also given clear rules for the use of patient information in the absence of express consent that include the following:

- providing treatment to the individual;
- payment activities, such as claims adjudication and premium setting, for operating their businesses;
- if required or permitted by other laws—e.g., laws related to reporting of child or elder abuse—public health oversight, and national security investigations.

Certain types of information are more closely protected because of the long-term and serious effects they might have on an individual's personal and professional life. Unlike a medical history that discusses something like an accidental broken bone or a routine surgery like an appendectomy, information with respect to issues such as substance abuse affect one's credibility, reputation, and perception of character. For that reason, there are special regulations that govern when this information may be disclosed. Section 543 of the Public Health Service Act requires that any disclosure of information related to substance abuse and chemical dependency treatment be accompanied by the individual's signed authorization. There are no exceptions for disclosures related to treatment, payment, or health care operations. The only exception relates to movement of information between different components of the Armed Services, including the Veterans Administration.

In addition to these regulations, many state and federal laws and regulations govern procedures for creating and maintaining records. There are also requirements for disclosure to law enforcement and health-related government agencies in very specific situations, such as those that might be associated with public health concerns or criminal activity. For example, most providers are required to report treatment of gunshot wounds. Also, certain highly communicable diseases must be reported to the appropriate state and/or federal agencies. One such agency is the Center for Disease Control (CDC). The HIPAA regulations enacted in 2003 are some of the most comprehensive legal standards ever created to protect an individual's private health information. In the past, many malpractice actions based on an improper disclosure consisted of a hodgepodge approach combining state and federal laws with judicially recognized common law standards. At the time of this publication, the laws are so new that there is insufficient data available to determine how this will affect future cases of malpractice. It can only be assumed that such clearly stated standards will benefit both providers and individuals by a reduced number of improper disclosures.

The disclosure of information is not the only ethical issue that faces providers today. Virtually any ethical violation can result in a civil suit, but the most common suits involve three basic areas: improper disclosure of information, patient abandonment, and inappropriate contact or communication between provider and patient. The issues surrounding improper disclosure of information have been addressed at length above, however, there is just as much controversy and litigation with regard to the second and third areas.

Essentially, any ethical violation that results in harm to a patient could potentially support a malpractice judgment. The term abandonment at first might invoke thoughts of someone being left alone in an area where they are unable to provide for their own needs. In more ordinary circumstances one might think of leaving a child unattended. The medical malpractice definition of patient abandonment is no different in theory. A cause of action for abandonment occurs when a provider is actively providing care, treatment, or services to a patient and ceases without proper notice and opportunity for the patient to make other arrangements and transfer records. The courts have long encouraged providers to give patients adequate time and opportunity to seek alternative sources of care as a matter of public interest. If not, providers could discharge patients at will and without notice, leaving them without care that, in some instances, could produce life-threatening circumstances. For an illustration of the potential problems, consider Application 3.3 below.

APPLICATION 3.3

Joe is in an accident and transported to an area hospital. He arrives under the influence of narcotics and is combative. During his examination, he assaults his longtime physician and breaks the doctor's nose and knocks out his two front teeth. Several months later, Joe is seriously burned over a large part of his body while at work. An ambulance brings him to the same hospital and the same physician is on duty. The physician recognizes Joe immediately and refuses to treat him. Instead, the doctor ordered the ambulance company to transport Joe to another hospital. During transport, Joe died. Even though Joe had been in an altercation with the doctor previously, there was still an obligation to provide care in a life-threatening situation such as this.

The obligation to furnish emergency care is not the only circumstance which obligates a provider to a patient. In fact, most documented cases of patient abandonment involve an established patient relationship that has been breached. In the case that follows, a patient of a large practice came to the hospital where she was examined by one of the associates of the practice. A number of unfortunate events occurred after admission, primarily the conduct of the examining physician, supporting a claim for patient abandonment.

720 NYS 2d 455, 280 AD 2d 257 (NYAPP 1st. Dept. 2001).

Satira C. Lewis et al., Appellants,
v.
Andrea Capalbo, M.D., Respondent, et al., Defendant.

Supreme Court, Appellate Division, First Department, New York

(February 1, 2001)

Plaintiff, Paulette S. Lewis, on behalf of her infant daughter Satira, and individually, brought this action alleging medical malpractice committed by defendant hospital and defendant Andrea Capalbo, M.D. during the birth of Satira. Dr. Capalbo was one of five obstetricians at the Manhattan Medical Group also known as the Yorkville HIP Center (HIP Center), which Ms. Lewis visited for prenatal care numerous times a few months near the end of her third trimester.

On the day of delivery, August 4, 1986, at 4:30 P.M., Dr. Capalbo, the HIP Center attending physician on call, examined Ms. Lewis, but left the hospital afterwards and had no further contact with her. Although Ms. Lewis was placed on a fetal monitor, according to her testimony she began the labor process on her own until the baby's head had partially traveled outside the birth canal and she was holding it on the palm of one of her hands. At this point, her husband ran out and called in an unidentified doctor standing in the hallway who, along with several nurses, completed the delivery.

Satira was delivered at 4:55 A.M. on August 5, 1986, weighing five pounds six ounces with an APGAR score of eight at one minute and an APGAR score of nine at five minutes (scores range from one to ten and a number above seven is normal). However, in the subcategory of respiratory effort, Satira received an APGAR score of one at one minute and two (changed from one) at five minutes, and in the category of skin color, an APGAR score of one both after one minute and after five minutes (scores for subcategories range from zero to two, and a score of one signifies an irregularity, while a score of two is normal).

Despite the APGAR score of two after five minutes for respiratory effort, it is undisputed that a short time after her birth Satira was admitted to the neonatal intensive care unit with serious respiratory difficulties where she remained for 12 days until her discharge, the first four of which she was in a ventilator. Satira's newborn medical records are incomplete. She currently suffers from seizure disorders and cognitive and developmental problems that will require lifelong medical care.

Dr. Capalbo moved for summary judgment dismissing the complaint against her, arguing that she had not delivered Satira and that Ms. Lewis's prenatal care was within acceptable standards of medical care. The IAS Court initially denied the motion because the medical expert's name and signature were redacted. On renewal and upon submission of an unredacted medical affidavit, the motion was granted on the grounds that Dr. Capalbo did not owe a duty to monitor Ms. Lewis personally during Satira's birth and that Satira's

(continued)

injuries were not the result of an independent act or omission by Dr. Capalbo. For the reasons stated below, we disagree.

As a preliminary matter, the IAS Court exercised its discretion appropriately in permitting Dr. Capalbo to renew her motion for summary judgment upon an unredacted medical expert affidavit in the interest of justice (*see generally, Petito v Verrazano Contr. Co.,*

It is well established that a doctor who undertakes to examine and treat a patient (thus creating a doctor-patient relationship) and then abandons the patient may be held liable for medical malpractice (*O'Neill v Montefiore Hosp., Heraud v Weissman,* In this case, there are triable issues of fact as to whether Dr. Capalbo was Ms. Lewis's doctor and whether she departed from good medical practice by allegedly abandoning Ms. Lewis after admitting her to the hospital during the early stages of labor.

Dr. Capalbo argues that there was no doctor-patient relationship between her and Ms. Lewis because she only saw Ms. Lewis once at the HIP Center and neither Ms. Lewis nor Ms. Lewis's husband attempted to contact her prior to Satira's delivery. However, Ms. Lewis testified in her deposition that she was told that Dr. Capalbo would be her attending physician and the one who would deliver her baby (*compare, Kleinert v Begum,* [no prior relationship between doctor and patient other than examination two hours prior to the baby's delivery]). Dr. Capalbo, in fact, was the attending physician who examined Ms. Lewis when she was admitted to Beth Israel in the early stages of labor. Although Dr. Capalbo was not in the hospital at Satira's delivery, she signed Ms. Lewis's labor and delivery chart as well as her discharge forms certifying that the matter of Ms. Lewis's treatment was "cleared for billing." Thus, a jury could reasonably conclude that Dr. Capalbo was Ms. Lewis's doctor.

Dr. Capalbo does not dispute that she left the hospital after examining Ms. Lewis and had no further contact with her. Instead, she argues that she did not have a duty to continually monitor Ms. Lewis and thus did not abandon her because the admission and medical authorization form Ms. Lewis signed stated that the delivery and related care could be provided by "associates or assistants" of Beth Israel Medical Center of Dr. Capalbo's choice. The record, however, contains nothing to indicate that Dr. Capalbo affirmatively transferred the care of Ms. Lewis to the two doctors whose names, in addition to Dr. Capalbo's, appear in the Labor and Delivery Summary form (even though neither of them participated in Satira's delivery according to the testimony of Ms. Lewis). Dr. Capalbo did not inform Ms. Lewis that the two doctors would be monitoring her after the initial examination took place. In addition, there is nothing in the record to indicate that the two doctors were associates or assistants of Dr. Capalbo.

As to proximate cause, the affidavit of plaintiffs' pediatric neurologist expert, Dr. Daniel G. Adler, stated that it was his impression that Satira suffered from, among other things, "newborn respiratory distress," "seizure disorder," and "language-based learning disability," which resulted from "a significantly abnormal newborn interval." Dr. Adler based his opinion, among other things, on a review of Satira's labor and delivery records, her billing records, and a personal examination. Dr. Adler's affirmation was, therefore, specific and based on the record (*see, Romano v Stanley,*

Plaintiffs' obstetrics expert reviewed Satira's labor and delivery records as well as Dr. Adler's report in concluding that Satira's condition was probably due to hypoxia (deficient oxygenation of the blood). According to the expert, had Dr. Capalbo monitored Ms. Lewis's progress, hypoxia could have been avoided or significantly minimized.

The experts' affidavits in conjunction with the lack of fetal monitoring from 3:00 A.M. to 5:00 A.M., along with Ms. Lewis's undisputed testimony that the baby was traveling down the birth canal, that the baby stopped and that she was holding the baby's head in her hand before any physician attended to the delivery,

(continued)

raise triable issues of fact regarding Dr. Capalbo's negligence in failing to attend the delivery of Satira and whether her absence caused Satira's injuries.

Concur--Rosenberger, J. P., Ellerin, Lerner and Friedman, JJ.
N.Y.A.D.,2001.

As can be seen from the case above, a long-term relationship need not be established between two individuals. Rather, if a patient has a reasonable expectation of care by a specific provider or member of an organization that employs or contracts services of providers, then the relationship has been created and any failure to meet the legal obligation supporting it can result in a claim of patient abandonment.

Last, in this rather limited discussion of ethical issues that can produce allegations of medical malpractice, is the question of inappropriate contact. Because of the general mores of society and importance placed on privacy of personal matters in nineteenth-century America, this is something that came to public light largely in the twentieth century and especially in later decades and in the early twenty-first century. An obvious target for media attention, such cases have been widely publicized and have led to extensive regulation and legislation for virtually all types of providers with regard to what type and the extent of relationships that are considered proper within the scope of the patient relationship.

Some of the most inflammatory cases reported from the courts by the media depict various types of health care providers who had relationships of a sexual nature with patients in unusual circumstances, such as when the patient was under anesthesia or as part of what the patient was told were routine or necessary procedures. To most people these situations are obviously inappropriate and a violation of the trust engendered by the patient–provider relationship. There are, of course, a number of cases in which the circumstances are much cloudier on the issue of ethical behavior and it is these which have prompted many of the cases and subsequent regulations and legislation. For example, in the majority of jurisdictions, all health care workers, who are certified or licensed to provide primary care at any level, are required to undergo a criminal background check prior to certification. This even applies to workers such as Certified Nurse Assistants whose total training and certification process may require fewer than 100 hours training time. The objective is to install safeguards against providers who might be disposed toward inappropriate conduct when faced with an opportunity to injure vulnerable individuals. However, the safeguards are not fail-safe and circumstances may occur that cause injury.

As discussed earlier, the doctor in the traditional patient–physician relationship was revered and respected. It was not unusual for patients to do whatever was asked of them by a provider in deference to the advanced skill and knowledge of the provider. This circumstance lasted for a long period of time, leaving the door open for a great deal of abuse which went undetected. However, as our society became more open and the media began reporting on subjects once considered off-limits, providers who abused their ethical obligations for personal gratification were exposed. In the past, patients and families were so embarrassed that they had been taken advantage of, they were reluctant to bring attention to the provider's conduct. But, there was also a strong sense of betrayal. As more patients came forward and these practices were exposed, condemnation by the courts, government agencies, legislatures, and professional disciplinary organizations followed.

This is an area where **respondeat superior** is also applied. If an employee engages in inappropriate conduct, it is possible that the employer will be held accountable if the conduct occurred within the scope of the individual's employment. Consider the following possible scenario in Application 3.4.

APPLICATION 3.4

Caesar is employed as a custodian at a nursing home. He generally works from midnight to 8 A.M. because there is less activity in the facility, thus making it easier to clean floors, bathrooms, etc. On one such night, Caesar is discovered by a co-worker as Caesar sexually assaults a comatose patient in the facility. In this situation, it is very possible that the family of the patient would have a viable action against the facility for the inappropriate actions of its employee.

The range of scenarios is broad, but the courts have been relatively consistent in initially finding that any contact of a sexual nature, occurring during or as the result of psychiatric or physical examination or treatment, is inappropriate. The jurisdictions are divided as to whether a romantic relationship that develops between a provider and patient after the conclusion of the professional relationship is appropriate. But those involving mental health providers largely discourage or prohibit such relationships at any time. Other situations in which providers have been disciplined and even sued include, but are not limited to, the following:

- physical contact of a suggestive nature such as massage by hand or instrument during examination;
- romantic touching or kissing;
- suggestive remarks, conversations, or stories with patients who are under hypnosis or medication that alters one's mental state;
- sexually explicit or suggestive content in phone calls;
- touching, examination or manipulation of physical areas unrelated to the reason for the exam (e.g., touching genital area during exam of an injured foot);
- physical examination of children or women without presence of another health care worker;
- being present while a patient disrobes.[1]

A more difficult point to resolve in cases of alleged sexual misconduct by a health care provider is the recovery of damages. While it may not be difficult to obtain the sympathy and even a favorable verdict by a judge or jury when a provider acts in a manner that is unethical and clearly takes unfair advantage of the patient trust, the malpractice insurance company, in many instances, is not required to represent the provider or cover any verdicts that may be rendered. Thus, while a verdict is one form of satisfaction, it in no way guarantees that one can actually recover an award of damages unless the provider has adequate resources.

The reason for this is discussed very thoroughly in the case that follows. Essentially, most policies, determination as to whether or not a malpractice carrier is responsible for coverage in a case such as this turns on whether the conduct occurred as an integral part of the delivery of professional services. If it is in addition to, or the result of, some further relationship that develops, then it is likely the policy will not be considered applicable.

CASE

246 Neb. 818, 652 N.W.2d 574 (2002).

Supreme Court of Nebraska.

R.W. et al., Appellants,
v.
Daniel B. SCHREIN, M.D., Appellee,
and
The Medical Protective Company of Fort Wayne, Indiana, Garnishee-Appellee.
Nov. 1, 2002.

ISSUES ON REHEARING

In our first opinion, we affirmed the judgment of the district court, relying in part on the affidavit of Harlan C. Schriner, Jr., M.D., a pediatrician who opined that Schrein's actions did not constitute or arise out of professional services and that Schrein's actions thus did not breach any applicable standard of care. Appellants filed timely motions for rehearing, arguing in part that this court erred in relying on Schriner's affidavit because the affidavit, although present in the record on appeal, had not been received into evidence by the district court. We granted appellants' motions for rehearing. We ordered that the issues on rehearing include all the issues originally briefed and offered the parties leave to file supplemental briefs addressing the following additional issues:

(1) Did the district court rule on appellants' objections to the affidavits of Schriner offered in each of these cases at the time the objections were made?

(2) If there were no rulings at the time of the objections, did appellants insist upon rulings prior to submission of the motions for summary judgment? If not, were the objections waived?

(3) Were the objections and/or the grounds upon which they were based addressed and resolved by the district court in its order of July 28, 2000, and if so, how were the issues resolved?

(4) Did the district court rule on appellants' alternative requests for a continuance pursuant to Neb.Rev.Stat. § 25-1335 > (Reissue 1995) at the time the requests were made?

(5) If not, did appellants insist upon such rulings prior to submission of the motions for summary judgment? If not, were the requests for continuance waived?

STANDARD OF REVIEW

Summary judgment is proper only when the pleadings, depositions, admissions, stipulations, and affidavits in the record disclose that there is no genuine issue as to any material fact or as to the ultimate inferences

(continued)

that may be drawn from those facts and that the moving party is entitled to judgment as a matter of law. *Pinkard v. Confederation Life Ins. Co.* 264 Neb. 312, 647 N.W.2d 85 (2002) In reviewing a summary judgment, an appellate court views the evidence in a light most favorable to the party against whom the judgment is granted and gives such party the benefit of all reasonable inferences deducible from the evidence. *Id.*

The meaning of an insurance policy is a question of law, in connection with which an appellate court has an obligation to reach its own conclusions independently of the determination made by the lower court. See *American Fam. Mut. Ins. Co. v. Hadley* 264 Neb. 435, 648 N.W.2d 769 (2002)

ANALYSIS
SCHRINER AFFIDAVIT

We turn first to the issues presented by the motion for rehearing. As set forth above, we granted rehearing on the issue whether Schriner's affidavit, on which our opinion relied, was properly received into evidence by the district court. We conclude that we are unable to resolve this issue on the record presented. The record does not show that the district court either explicitly ruled on appellants' objections to the affidavit or received the affidavit into evidence. This ambiguity in the record precludes us from relying on the affidavit or resolving any issues to which the affidavit might be relevant on appeal.

We note that the presentation of an adequate record for appellate review is primarily the responsibility of the parties. It is well established that a party who fails to insist upon a ruling to a proffered objection waives that objection. See, e.g., *State v. Harris,* 263 Neb. 331, 640 N.W.2d 24 (2002) *Jameson v. Liquid Controls Corp.,* <http260 Neb. 489, 618 N.W.2d 637 (2000) We have also stated:

" 'If when inadmissible evidence is offered the party against whom such evidence is offered consents to its introduction, or fails to object, *or to insist upon a ruling on an objection to the introduction of the evidence,* and otherwise fails to raise the question as to its admissibility, he is considered to have waived whatever objection he may have had thereto, *and the evidence is in the record for consideration the same as other evidence.*' "

(Emphasis in original.) *State v. Nowicki,* 239 Neb. 130, 134, 474 N.W.2d 478, 483 (1991) (quoting *In re Estate of Kaiser,* 150 Neb. 295, 34 N.W.2d 366 (1948) See, also, *State v. Fellman,* 236 Neb. 850, 464 N.W.2d 181 (1991) . That we have chosen, in this case, not to consider the disputed affidavit should not be taken to mean that we will not, in other cases, consider disputed evidence where an objection thereto has not been properly preserved by insistence upon a ruling on that objection. It is the responsibility of trial courts to rule on the objections presented to them. However, parties and counsel are cautioned that they must insist on such rulings in order to preserve those objections; they fail to do so at their own peril.

The fact that Schriner's affidavit is not available for our review, however, does not change our ultimate conclusion from *R.W. I.* There is no factual controversy regarding Schrein's underlying conduct, which for purposes of this proceeding is assumed to have been as alleged in appellants' petitions. Similarly, the interpretation of a contract is a question of law. See *Hadley, supra.* Thus, we are presented with an integrated question of law-- whether the allegations in the petitions set forth a claim for damages based on "professional services" within the meaning of the insurance policy. See, *Cluett v. Medical Protective Co.,* 829 S.W.2d 822 (Tex.App.1992) ; *Hirst v. St. Paul Fire & Marine Ins. Co.,* 106 Idaho 792, 683 P.2d 440 (Idaho App.1984).

(continued)

A medical professional such as Schriner can opine regarding a breach of the applicable standard of medical care, but cannot advise this court on a question of law, i.e., the meaning of a term in a contract. Our previous opinion erred in relying on Schriner's affidavit because the evidence was not relevant to the question presented to this court. After further consideration, we conclude that the dispositive question in this appeal is a question of law, on which expert testimony has no bearing. Therefore, we withdraw the section of *R.W. I* under the subheading "2. RENDERING OF 'PROFESSIONAL SERVICES,' " *id.* at 716, 642 N.W.2d at 512, and ends prior to the subheading "3. PUBLIC POLICY," *id.* at 721, 642 N.W.2d at 515. In its place, we substitute the following discussion of the issue:

RENDERING OF PROFESSIONAL SERVICES

The applicable language of the insurance policy issued to Schrein provides that Medical Protective will pay damages "based on professional services rendered or which should have been rendered … by the insured or any other person for whose acts or omissions the insured is legally responsible, in the practice of the insured's profession." An insurance contract is to be construed as any other contract to give effect to the parties' intentions at the time the contract was made. *American Fam. Mut. Ins. Co. v. Hadley*, 264 Neb. 435, 648 N.W.2d 769 (2002) . When the terms of a contract are clear, a court may not resort to rules of construction, and the terms are to be accorded their plain and ordinary meaning as the ordinary or reasonable person would understand them. *Id.* While an ambiguous insurance policy will be construed in favor of the insured, ambiguity will not be read into policy language which is plain and unambiguous in order to construe against the preparer of the contract. *Id.* We conclude that the language of the insuring agreement is unambiguous. The determinative question, then, is whether Schrein's actionable conduct constituted "professional services" within the meaning of the policy.

This court has previously defined the term "professional services" in the context of a liability policy for professional negligence. In *Marx v. Hartford Acc. & Indem. Co.* a physician's employee mistakenly poured benzine instead of water into a sterilization container, resulting in an explosion and a fire. The physician was insured by a policy covering damages arising out of " 'malpractice, error or mistake of the insured, or of a person for whose acts or omissions the insured is legally responsible … in rendering or failing to render professional services.' " (Emphasis omitted.) *Id.* at 13, 157 N.W.2d at 871. Noting that the precise question presented was whether the damages arose out of the rendering or failure to render professional services, we stated:

> The insurer's liability is thus limited to the performing or rendering of "professional" acts or services. Something more than an act flowing from mere employment or vocation is essential. The act or service must be such as exacts the use or application of special learning or attainments of some kind. The term "professional" in the context used in the policy provision means something more than mere proficiency in the performance of a task and implies intellectual skill as contrasted with that used in an occupation for production or sale of commodities. A "professional" act or service is one arising out of a vocation, calling, occupation, or employment involving specialized knowledge, labor, or skill, and the labor or skill involved is predominantly mental or intellectual, rather than physical or manual…. In determining whether a particular act is of a professional nature or a "professional service" we must look *824 not to the title or character of the party performing the act, but to the act itself.

(Citations omitted.) *Id.* at 13-14, 157 N.W.2d at 871-72. Finding that the boiling of water for sterilization was "not a part of any patient's treatment per se any more than any other routine cleaning or arranging procedure incidental to the proper general operations of the plaintiffs' offices," we concluded that the act was not a professional service covered by the language of the insurance policy. *Id.* at 14, 157 N.W.2d at 872

(continued)

In *Marx, supra,* the determinative question was whether the act performed was "professional" as distinguished from the act of a layperson. In this case, however, the critical issue is whether the act performed is "professional" as opposed to unprofessional. In other words, the fact that the actions occurred between a doctor and patient is pertinent only if the act itself is of a professional nature. See *St. Paul Ins. Co. of Illinois v. Cromeans,* 771 F.Supp. 349 (N.D.Ala.1991) .

We recently revisited the *Marx* holding in *Iwanski v. Gomes,* 259 Neb. 632, 640, 611 N.W.2d 607, 613 (2000) which presented the question whether "a doctor commits malpractice by engaging in sexual relations or having consensual sex with an individual with whom the doctor concurrently maintains a physician-patient relationship." After recognizing our holding in *Marx v. Hartford Acc. & Indem. Co.,* 183 Neb. 12, 157 N.W.2d 870 (1968) we concluded that in order to establish that conduct by a physician constitutes malpractice, the acts of the physician upon which the claim is based must " 'be such as exacts the use or application of special learning or attainments of some kind' " that would constitute the " 'performing or rendering of "professional" acts or services.' " *Iwanski,* 259 Neb. at 641, 611 N.W.2d at 614 (quoting *Marx, supra* > In addressing whether the acts of the physician fell within this definition, we referred to case law from other jurisdictions interpreting "professional services" coverage in insurance contracts. We then stated:

> We agree that the fact that sexual misconduct occurs in a medical professional's office "does not automatically transmute the act into a professional service [because the] location of an act's occurrence is not determinative of liability." *Lindheimer v. St. Paul Fire & Marine Ins.,* 643 So. 2d 636, 638 (Fla.App.1994) When the only connection between the sexual misconduct and treatment is that the activity occurred in the medical professional's office, such a connection is too remote from the actual rendering of proper services to impose liability upon the medical professional for malpractice. See *Roe v. Federal Ins. Co.,* 412 Mass. 43, 587 N.E.2d 214 (1992)
>
> We conclude, based on the foregoing rationale, that there must be a causal relationship between the alleged harm and the complained-of professional act or service. When there is a claim of medical malpractice based on unwanted sexual contact, the determination of liability should focus not solely on the locale of the alleged harm or the professional status of the actor, but, rather, on the context of the alleged medical service involved in the action. In other words, it is the physician's deviation from the recognized medical standard of care *during the course of treatment* that is the essence of a claim for medical malpractice, and *there must exist a causal relationship between the alleged harm and the complained-of deviation from that standard of care in order for liability to attach.*

(Emphasis in original.) (Emphasis supplied.) *Iwanski,* 259 Neb. at 642, 611 N.W.2d at 614. In applying this standard to the facts, we held that the relationship between the adult parties was consensual and that as to the only incident related to the direct provision of medical services, the evidence established that the sexual act between the patient and the physician took place well after the physician had completed a gynecological examination. We thus held that there was no actionable claim for "professional negligence." *Id.* at 643, 611 N.W.2d at 615

Relying on our decision in *Marx, supra,* > and consistent with our decision in *Iwanski, supra,* the clear majority rule among other jurisdictions is that outside the unique circumstance of mishandling the transference phenomenon in psychiatric counseling, sexual conduct is not a professional act or service for which medical malpractice insurance coverage is provided. See, e.g., *Snyder v. Major,* 789 F.Supp. 646 (S.D.N.Y.1992) *St. Paul Ins. Co. of Illinois v. Cromeans,* 771 F.Supp. 349 (N.D.Ala.1991) *Physicians Ins. Co. v. Pistone,* 555 Pa. 616, 726 A.2d 339 (1999) > 165 Mich.App. 719, 419 N.W.2d 60 (1988)

There is no dispute among appellate courts, even in those cases that find insurers to be liable for sexual contact, about the applicability of the holding in *Marx v. Hartford Acc. & Indem. Co.,* 183 Neb. 12, 157 N.W.2d

(continued)

870 (1968) Generally, cases that find sexual contact to be "professional services" do so by either (1) expanding the scope of the "act" to include the sexual **582 contact or (2) lowering the requirement for causation between the act and the damages. There is no dispute that when a court is determining the coverage of a professional liability insurance policy, it must examine the nature of the act performed, rather than the title or professional character of the actor. *Niedzielski, supra.*

Based on these standards, courts have generally refused to require insurers to provide coverage for sexual acts, based on professional liability insurance policies with medical care providers, because sexual activity with a patient is not a part of the delivery of professional services or part of medical treatment. See *Snyder, supra*. When the physician's sexual contact with his or her patient is not necessitated by the particular course of medical treatment, then the malpractice insurance policy does not provide coverage for the damages sustained by the victim. *Blakeslee, supra*. The most well-known statement of the minority rule is *St. Paul Fire & Marine Ins. Co. v. Asbury,* 149 Ariz. 565, 720 P.2d 540 (Ariz.App.1986) In that case, the Court of Appeals of Arizona articulated the following rationale for concluding that sexual assault was a "professional service":

> The claims of Dr. Asbury's patients that he manipulated their clitorises while performing routine gynecological examinations, if true, was tortious conduct committed while providing professional services and covered by his insurance policy. Most of the cases cited to us by St. Paul are distinguishable because the tortious sexual abuse of the patient was not intertwined with and inseparable from the services provided.

Id. ...*St. Paul Fire and Marine Ins. Co. v. Shernow,* 222 Conn. 823, 610 A.2d 1281 (1992) The *Asbury* court adopted the rationale of the trial court in that case, quoting the trial court's opinion:

> "The question of insurance coverage does not turn on whether the conduct was negligent or intentional, or whether or not there was an assault and battery. Regardless of the category in which the underlying complaints are placed, they clearly allege tortious conduct while treating the patients, and seek damages resulting from the providing of professional services. Furthermore, the tortious conduct, if it occurred, took place in the course of and as an inseparable part of the providing of professional services. Consequently, any damages would be those resulting from the providing of professional services by the insured."

Asbury, 149 Ariz. at 566, 720 P.2d at 541. Accord, *Torpoco, supra; Shernow, supra*. See, also, *Princeton Ins. Co. v. Chunmuang,* 151 N.J. 80, 698 A.2d 9 (1997) But see, e.g., *St. Paul Ins. Co. of Illinois v. Cromeans,* 771 F.Supp. 349, 353 (N.D.Ala.1991) (rejecting *Asbury* as "illogical"); *Physicians Ins. Co. v. Pistone,* 555 Pa. 616, 623, 726 A.2d 339, 343 (1999) (stating *Asbury* "has no basis in logic"); *N.M. Physicians Mut. Liability v. LaMure,* 116 N.M. 92, 97, 860 P.2d 734, 739 (1993) (uncertain of *Asbury* test's "workability or its support in public policy").

However, the *Asbury* rule has received significant criticism. First, it has been noted that in determining the scope of a liability insurance policy, the issue "is not whether the conduct in question is negligence, but whether a particular contract was intended to cover this conduct." *Snyder v. Major,* 789 F.Supp. 646, 650 (S.D.N.Y.1992) *modified* 818 F.Supp. 68 (S.D.N.Y.1993) See *Volquardson v. Hartford Ins. Co.* 264 Neb. 337, 647 N.W.2d 599 (2002) The minority rule would be more logical if presented in the context of a tort action, i.e., expanding the set of wrongs from which tort victims should be protected. See *Snyder, supra*. However, where the issue is the scope of coverage under an insurance policy, expanding the meaning of "professional services" is inconsistent with our responsibility to give effect to the intent of the parties at the time the contract was written. See *Volquardson, supra*. In light of the case law set out above supporting the majority rule, along with our own decisions in *Marx v. Hartford Acc. & Indem. Co.*, 183 Neb. 12, 157 N.W.2d 870 (1968) and *Iwanski v. Gomes,* 259 Neb. 632, 611 N.W.2d 607 (2000), it is unlikely that parties entering into medical malpractice insurance contracts are operating under the assumption that the sexual misconduct of physicians may be covered by the malpractice insurance. It would decrease the likelihood of capturing the parties' intent to hold otherwise. See *Snyder, supra*.

(continued)

Furthermore, the minority rule erodes the concept of legal causation until the requirement of proximate cause is essentially meaningless. As stated by one commentator:

> The decisions that find coverage for allegations of sexual abuse or molestation against physicians and dentists do so only through flawed reasoning. They appear to apply what amounts to a simple "but for" test: Because the assault occurred during an otherwise proper and necessary medical procedure, the injury arose out of the performance of that professional service. Of course, the "but for" test is virtually boundless, as almost no subsequent event would take place were it not for some antecedent event, and as all events are, at some level, interrelated. It is simply unreasonable to conclude that conduct such as sexual molestation of a patient, which must be known to be only harmful and not beneficial, and which also must be known by the doctor to further no preventive or corrective interest of the patient, is part of a professional medical procedure. It cannot, therefore, be part of the professional service that the doctor contracts with the patient to provide.

David S. Florig, *Insurance Coverage for Sexual Abuse or Molestation,* This analysis, with which we agree, echoes some of the most basic and familiar concepts of tort causation.

> "Proximate cause" ... is merely the limitation which the courts have placed upon the actor's responsibility for the consequences of the actor's conduct. In a philosophical sense, the consequences of an act go forward to eternity, and the causes of an event go back to the dawn of human events, and beyond. But any attempt to impose responsibility upon such a basis would result in infinite liability for all wrongful acts, and would "set society on edge and fill the courts with endless litigation." As a practical matter, legal responsibility must be limited to those causes which are so closely connected with the result and of such significance that the law is justified in imposing liability. Some boundary must be set to liability for the consequences of any act, upon the basis of some social idea of justice or policy.
>
> This limitation is to some extent associated with the nature and degree of the connection in fact between the defendant's acts and the events of which the plaintiff complains.

W. Page Keeton et al., Prosser and Keeton on the Law of Torts § 41 at 264 (5th ed. 1984 & Supp.1988).

The majority rule, then, expresses a difficult truth: that appellants' injuries, in the instant case and most others, are not caused by any act of medical treatment that would normally be associated with the provision of a "professional service." The common thread running throughout the majority rule cases is the necessity for, and lack of, a direct causal link between appellants' damages and any legitimate medical treatment. "[T]here must be a causal relationship between the alleged harm and the complained-of professional act or service, that is, it must be a medical ... act or service that causes the harm, not an act or service that requires no professional skill." *Roe v. Federal Ins. Co.,* 412 Mass. 43, 49, 587 N.E.2d 214, 217 (1992) Accord, *Lindheimer v. St. Paul Fire & Marine Ins.,* 643 So.2d 636 (Fla.App.1994); *Steven G. v. Herget,* 178 Wis.2d 674, 505 N.W.2d 422 (Wis.App.1993) . "[T]here must be a causal relationship between the treatment (*i.e.,* professional services) and the harm alleged by the victim." *Standard Fire Ins. v. Blakeslee,* 54 Wash.App. 1, 10, 771 P.2d 1172, 1177 (1989) (citing *Hirst v. St. Paul Fire & Marine Ins. Co.,* 106 Idaho 792, 683 P.2d 440 (Idaho App.1984) .

As most clearly stated by the Supreme Court of New Hampshire, "[t]he specified source out of which damages must arise, according to the terms of the insurance policy, is professional services rendered, or which should have been rendered." *Niedzielski v. St. Paul Fire & Marine Ins. Co.,* 134 N.H. 141, 146-47, 589 A.2d 130, 133 (1991) The minority rule abrogates this principle.

The court in *St. Paul Fire & Marine Ins. Co. v. Asbury,* 149 Ariz. 565, 720 P.2d 540 (Ariz.App.1986) , attempts to connect the plaintiffs' damages to professional services by asserting that the professional service "is intertwined

(continued)

with and inseparable from" the tortious conduct which was the actual direct cause of the plaintiffs' damages. However, the *Asbury* approach rests on the assertion that it is impossible to separate legitimate medical treatment from sexual assault. There may, in some cases, be a fact question presented as to whether the medical professional's conduct was, in fact, legitimate medical treatment. This does not mean, however, that we can conclude it is not possible for the trier of fact to separate legitimate medicine from a sexual assault, to determine which acts of the care provider were professional treatment and which were not, and then assess by which acts the plaintiffs' damages were caused. In any event, there is no fact question presented in the instant case as to which acts of Schrein caused appellants' damages, and none of those acts are within the scope of coverage of Schrein's liability insurance policy.

For the foregoing reasons, we reject appellants' contention that this court should follow the minority rule. Instead, we continue to adhere to the majority rule as indicated by our decisions in *Marx v. Hartford Acc. Indem. Co.,* 183 Neb. 12, 157 N.W.2d 870 (1968), and *Iwanski v. Gomes,* 259 Neb. 632, 611 N.W.2d 607 (2000). In the instant case, the substance of appellants' allegations is that Schrein's behavior went beyond the scope of legitimate medical treatment and that their damages result entirely from actions that were not legitimated by any appropriate medical purpose. Appellants did not establish any harm attributable to any failure to properly diagnose or treat a medical condition. Rather, their injuries and damages resulted solely from the affirmative acts of abuse and molestation committed by Schrein under the guise of medical examination and treatment. Consequently, the "act" that caused each of appellants' damages was not medical treatment and not a "professional service" within the meaning of the policy.

CONCLUSION

As previously indicated, the foregoing discussion is substituted for that section of our opinion in *R.W. I* in which we erred and which has been withdrawn. In all other respects, we continue to adhere to the reasoning and conclusions of *R.W. I,* as they pertain to appellants' remaining assignments of error on appeal and rehearing. For the reasons stated in *R.W. I* and this supplemental opinion, we affirm the judgment of the district court.

MOTIONS FOR REHEARING SUSTAINED. FORMER OPINION MODIFIED.

As can be seen from the discussion and cases above, ethical issues can be the basis for cases of medical malpractice and criminal charges (more fully discussed in the following section). However, as with any lawsuit, no matter how objectionable the conduct, it does not necessarily translate into a successful outcome for the plaintiff. All factors must be examined, including whether the conduct is considered a violation of professional duty, whether it occurs as part of the delivery of professional services, whether any violations of law have occurred, and whether recovery of a verdict is likely. While these are issues for any case of malpractice, in ethical matters, they each take on an increasing importance before it can be established that a viable case exists.

INJURIES RESULTING FROM PROFESSIONAL MISCONDUCT WHICH IS ALSO CRIMINAL

As with any career or profession, there are individuals whose conduct is less than exemplary and for a variety of reasons step over not only professional, but legal boundaries as well. When this occurs within the context of a relationship between a health care provider and a patient, there can be multiple results. The provider may receive professional discipline, ranging from reprimand to revocation of licensure. The patient or patients injured as a result of the conduct may file a civil suit for malpractice. And finally, in some instances, there may be a criminal prosecution of the provider for acts which are considered not only as injury to an individual, but conduct which, by its very nature, is deemed injurious to the welfare of the general public. One of the most notorious cases in recent years involved a Midwestern pharmacist who diluted chemotherapy drugs with placebos in order to increase his own profit. The pharmacist not only was the defendant in multiple malpractice actions, he was criminally prosecuted and sentenced to jail time as well.

Matters of professional discipline, alleged malpractice, and criminal prosecution are all dealt with independently in separate courts or forums. However, they often impact one another. For example, if a medical professional is convicted of **criminal conduct** that was committed while engaged in his or her licensed profession, then licensure may be at stake. Many states condition certain professional licensures on the absence of a felony conviction. Even if there is not a conviction, the allegations and evidence may be used in a licensure/disciplinary proceeding for conduct related to the profession. Cases of medical malpractice are slightly different. The rules of evidence in some cases may exclude evidence relating to allegations of criminal activity. But there is a more practical effect. Most policies of medical malpractice insurance expressly state that coverage does not apply for acts which are deemed criminal. Thus, even if one is liable for professional misconduct, collection of any damage award may be limited if no insurance coverage is available.

CASE

94 MdApp. 632, 618 A2d 274 (1993).
Court of Special Appeals of Maryland.

MEDICAL MUTUAL LIABILITY INSURANCE SOCIETY OF MARYLAND
v.
Nicholas M. AZZATO, et al.

Jan. 13, 1993.

. MOTZ, Judge.

This insurance coverage dispute arises out of a malpractice action filed against Dr. Nicholas M. Azzato, appellee, by his former patient, Regina Warsaw, and her husband, Lewis Warsaw. Dr. Azzato, a plastic

(continued)

surgeon, performed a number of surgical procedures on Mrs. Warsaw from 1984 through 1986. In 1984, he operated on her right nostril, and on January 21, 1986, he performed a similar operation on her left nostril. He testified that on each occasion he packed the affected nostril with a combination of Pontocaine and pharmaceutical cocaine to "anesthetize the nose and shrink the blood vessels down so there is less bleeding." Mrs. Warsaw claims he only packed her nose after the first operation; in any event, no one suggested that these procedures or medications were in any way inappropriate.

Shortly after her operation on the left nostril, however, Mrs. Warsaw heard Dr. Azzato and one of his nurses discuss some "pharmaceutical cocaine" that was in the office and she asked Dr. Azzato "a lot of questions" about it. According to Mrs. Warsaw, "[a]t that point, he pulled a vial out of his coat ... and he had this little ivory spoon" and he offered her some cocaine. From that time on, Mrs. Warsaw began coming to Dr. Azzato's office, and then to his home, on a routine basis to obtain drugs--first, just cocaine, and then a host of other drugs, including seconal and morphine. As she told him after a few weeks, she had been addicted to PCP, speed and other drugs from 1973 through 1977 but was detoxified in 1977 and drug free until 1986 when she was given cocaine by Dr. Azzato. Nevertheless, Dr. Azzato continued to provide Mrs. Warsaw with drugs. She testified that he indicated that the drugs might help premenstrual syndrome ("PMS") and other medical problems.

Within the next few months, Dr. Azzato and Mrs. Warsaw began a personal relationship, in which they, *inter alia,* engaged in frequent ("hundreds of times") recreational drug use together; on occasion Mrs. Warsaw used "bags of drugs" provided by Dr. Azzato. During this period, Mrs. Warsaw continued to be Dr. Azzato's patient; indeed, he performed a minor surgical procedure on her in August, 1986, and a breast augmentation in September, 1986. In November, 1986, Mrs. Warsaw was admitted to the Psychiatric Institute for her mental and drug related problems. After six weeks of treatment, she was discharged from that hospital; a week after discharge, she again obtained drugs from Dr. Azzato. In April, 1987, she was admitted to Suburban Hospital as psychotic and near death from drug abuse. Ultimately, she was discharged from Suburban and after one final episode of drug use with Dr. Azzato, in May, 1987, she has had no further drug use or contact with Dr. Azzato.

On April 21, 1987, Dr. Azzato was arrested for illegal possession and distribution of valium, seconal, and cocaine. He pled guilty to two counts of violation of the controlled substance statute with respect to distribution of valium. Dr. Azzato was sentenced to a short period of incarceration in the Montgomery County Prerelease Center and is presently on probation under the jurisdiction of the Montgomery County Department of Parole and Probation. He has been suspended from medical practice by the Commission on Medical Discipline.

On July 7, 1987, Mr. and Mrs. Warsaw filed a malpractice claim against Dr. Azzato with the Health Claims Arbitration Office. Dr. Azzato requested that his insurer, appellant, Medical Mutual Liability Insurance Society of Maryland ("Medical Mutual"), undertake his defense and provide coverage for this claim. Medical Mutual refused to do so. Dr. Azzato retained other counsel to represent him. After a two day hearing, on May 5, 1989, a Health Claims Arbitration panel issued a decision finding Dr. Azzato liable to Mrs. Warsaw for $31,000 in past medical expenses and $104,000 in noneconomic damages and liable to Mr. Warsaw for $25,000 for loss of consortium, for a total award of $160,000. On August 29, 1989, this award was confirmed by the Circuit Court for Montgomery County.

On March 21, 1992, Dr. Azzato, for the use of Mr. and Mrs. Warsaw and their attorney, filed the present coverage action, alleging breach of contract and negligence by Medical Mutual for failing to provide him coverage. Dr. Azzato asked that Medical Mutual be required to pay him $160,000, the amount of the judgment owed to the Warsaws, plus post-confirmation interest. The complaint did not seek reimbursement for Dr. Azzato's costs in defending the malpractice action. The parties filed cross motions for summary judgment. After hearing

(continued)

argument from counsel for both sides, on February 26, 1992, the circuit court granted summary judgment in favor of Dr. Azzato and against Medical Mutual in the amount of $160,000 and post-judgment interest. The court declined to award pre-judgment interest.

On appeal, Medical Mutual makes two arguments:

1. Medical Mutual's policy forbids recovery in this case, since it unambiguously excludes coverage for injuries arising out of criminal activities.

2. Medical Mutual is not precluded [by the arbitration award] from raising its policy defenses.

Dr. Azzato cross appeals, asserting that he is entitled to interest from August 29, 1989, the date of the confirmation of the arbitration award. Dr. Azzato was covered for liability arising out of medical malpractice under two professional liability insurance policies issued by Medical Mutual. Both policies provide that Medical Mutual "will pay ... all sums" that Dr. Azzato "shall become legally obligated to pay as damages" because of "injury arising out of a medical incident" or "due to personal injury." Both policies then specifically exclude from this coverage injuries arising out of criminal acts performed by the insured. The first policy, covering the period from July 31, 1985 to July 31, 1986, provides that coverage does not apply to injury arising out of any dishonest, fraudulent, criminal or malicious act or omission of any Insured. The second policy, covering the period from July 31, 1986 to July 31, 1987, provides that coverage does not apply to injury arising out of the performance by any named Insured of a criminal act.

The Court of Appeals has held similar language in a professional liability insurance policy to be unambiguous and to exclude coverage for losses resulting from criminal acts. *Aragona v. St. Paul Fire & Marine Ins. Co.*, 281 Md. 371, 378 A.2d 1346 (1977). In that case, the Aragonas sued a lawyer for vicarious liability because of his partner's misappropriation of their funds and for his own negligence in failing to uncover the misappropriation; they recovered on both grounds. The Aragonas then sought to recover the amount of their judgment from the lawyer's malpractice insurer. In its policy, the insurance carrier had promised to pay all sums which the Insured shall become legally obligated to pay as damages arising out of the performance of professional services for others in the Insured's capacity as a lawyer and caused by the Insured or any other person for whose acts the Insured is legally liable. 281 Md. at 372,. The policy, however, excluded coverage for "any dishonest, fraudulent, criminal or malicious act or omission of the Insured, any partner or employee." *Id.* The Aragonas argued *inter alia* that these policy provisions were "ambiguous" and so "must be strictly construed against the insurer, and ... in favor of the policyholder." 281 Md. at 374, 378 A.2d 1346. The Court of Appeals held the exclusion unambiguous: "[w]e see no ambiguity in this language." *Id.* at 375, 378 A.2d 1346. After rejecting the Aragona's remaining argument (an argument not made or applicable here) the Court concluded:

We think the parties intended, from the language used in the insurance contract construed as a whole, that any loss which resulted from any dishonest or criminal act ... was excluded from coverage, and that the exclusionary clause of the policy was all-encompassing in this respect. 281 Md. at 379.

In its very short oral remarks, the court below stated that "there is an ambiguity in the policy." In light of the Court of Appeals's clear holding in *Aragona,* Dr. Azzato disavows any argument that the policy is ambiguous. Instead, he claims that his case "is clearly distinguishable" from *Aragona* because "there is a significant factual difference," *i.e.,* "[h]ere, unlike *Aragona,* there was nothing 'criminal' in what Dr. Azzato was doing except for the false prescriptions for valium which he wrote in April of 1987, for which he was arrested and subsequently pled guilty." Thus, Dr. Azzato asserts that his distribution of drugs to Mrs. Warsaw on "hundreds" of occasions during the year prior to April, 1987, was not criminal activity. He is wrong. His admitted, frequent distribution to Mrs. Warsaw of drugs that were "controlled dangerous substances," as

(continued)

defined in Art. 27, § 277(f), for "recreational," rather than medicinal, purposes was clearly criminal activity in violation of several provisions of the Maryland Controlled Dangerous Substance Act. *See* Art. 27, § 287(a) and § 288(c). In sum, contrary to Dr. Azzato's assertions, it is just as clear here, as it was in *Aragona*, that the complained-of activity was criminal.

Nor do any of the cases upon which Dr. Azzato relies aid his cause. Many of them do not even involve a determination of insurance coverage. Instead, they simply hold that improper conduct by a health care provider, like Dr. Azzato, can constitute malpractice or professional negligence. *See e.g., Figueiredo-Torres v. Nickel,* 321 Md. 642, 584 A.2d 69 (1991); *Los Alamos Medical Center v. Coe,* 58 N.M. 686, 275 P.2d 175, 178 (1954); *McCarroll v. Reed,* 679 P.2d 851, 854 (Okla.App.1983); *Ballenger v. Crowell,* 38 N.C.App. 50, 247 S.E.2d 287, 291 (1978). Other cases involve insurance policies that contain *no* criminal act exclusion. *See e.g., Public Service Mut. Ins. Co. v. Goldfarb,* 53 N.Y.2d 392, 442 N.Y.S.2d 422, 425 N.E.2d 810, 814 (1981); *Vigilant Ins. Co. v. Kambly,* 114 Mich.App. 683, 319 N.W.2d 382, 384 (1982) (coverage of criminal acts not excluded, only coverage "for legal expense incurred due to alleged criminal act" excluded).

To the extent that the cases relied upon by Dr. Azzato are relevant they indicate that some courts, when confronted with similar, but not identical, situations, have concluded that an insurance policy was "ambiguous" because it was unclear whether "it was meant to cover acts ... which constitute ... malpractice but which also are defined as criminal." *See, L.L. v. Medical Protective Co.,* 122 Wis.2d 455, 362 N.W.2d 174, 179 (Wis.App.1984). (unclear whether policy, which covered "negligibly inflicted bodily injury" but excludes "criminal acts," covers injuries resulting from involuntary manslaughter). Although, as noted above, Dr. Azzato does not claim that this policy is similarly ambiguous, this seems to be "the ambiguity" that troubled the court below.

In *Aragona,* the Court of Appeals did not address this precise alleged ambiguity. Implicit in the *Aragona* holding, however, is the conclusion that acts can constitute both malpractice and criminal behavior and that a professional liability policy excluding coverage in language like that at issue in *Aragona*--and here-- excludes coverage for injuries arising from such acts. This is so because the criminal act in *Aragona,* a lawyer's misappropriation of his client's funds, clearly also constitutes legal malpractice. *See* Maryland Lawyers' Rules of Professional Conduct Rules 1.15 (and 8.4); *Attorney Grievance Comm'n v. White,* 328 Md. 412, 614 A.2d 955 (1992); *Attorney Grievance Comm'n v. Moore,* 301 Md. 169, 170-171, 482 A.2d 497 (1984). If the Court of Appeals had concluded that there was any ambiguity in the policy possibly permitting coverage because this misappropriation also constituted malpractice, its holding would have had to be different. Accordingly, the ambiguity seen by courts in other jurisdictions was *sub silentio* rejected by the *Aragona* court. That result is surely sound. All activity that is expressly excluded from coverage in this or any other insurance policy would, at least arguably, be covered if not so excluded. Thus, it would make no sense to interpret this policy to be ambiguous simply because the activity it excludes would, absent the exclusion, be covered.

Even if the criminal activities exclusion would otherwise bar coverage for the judgment obtained by the Warsaws against him, Dr. Azzato claims "Medical Mutual is estopped from raising the criminal activities exclusion." The basis for this argument is the Court of Appeals' recent holding in *Allstate Insurance Co. v. Atwood,* 319 Md. 247, 572 A.2d 154 (1990). There the Court carefully outlined how and when an insurer is to litigate whether acts are tortious and, therefore, covered acts or intentional and, therefore, excluded. It cautioned that declaratory judgment actions to determine this question in advance of the underlying tort trial "should be rare." 319 Md. at 254, 572 A.2d 154. *See Brohawn v. Transamerica Ins. Co.,* 276 Md. 396, 347 A.2d 842 (1975). Rather, the insurer is generally "bound by the finding in a tort action against its insured that the insured was liable due to negligence." 319 Md. at 260, 572 A.2d 154. The insurer, however, will be "bound by the tort action's resolution of the intentional/negligence issue if, but only if, that issue was fairly

(continued)

litigated in the tort trial." *Id.* at 261, 572 A.2d 154. In order to determine if this issue was "fairly litigated" in the underlying tort action, the *Atwood* court permitted the insurer in that case to bring a separate declaratory judgment action after the tort judgment became final and remanded so that the trial judge could "first determine whether the intentional/negligence issue was fairly litigated in the tort case." *Id.* at 263, 572 A.2d 154. The Court indicated, however, that in the future, "a separate declaratory judgment action" would not be allowed; rather, in order to determine this coverage issue, the insurer must move to intervene in the tort action "no later than ten days after entry of judgment" in that action. *Id.* at 264, 572 A.2d 154.

Dr. Azzato asserts that *Atwood* governs the coverage question at issue here. He argues that "the issues between Warsaw and Azzato were fully and fairly litigated by [the] Health Claims [arbitration panel]," that Medical Mutual, which was on notice of these claims, did not attempt to intervene in the Health Claims Arbitration hearing or file a declaratory judgment action and so should not "be permitted to relitigate" those issues now. The critical difficulty with this argument is that the procedure outlined in *Atwood* is simply inapplicable to the present question. The *Atwood* procedure only applies when the issue to be resolved in the coverage action is "the same as an issue in the tort action." *Id.* at 259-263, 572 A.2d 154. Judge Eldridge in *Atwood* carefully distinguished that situation from cases where questions of policy coverage "are independent and separable from the claims asserted in a pending suit by an injured third party." *Id.* quoting *Brohawn, supra,* 276 Md. at 405, 347 A.2d 842. In the latter situation, the Court of Appeals has approved the use of a separate action *prior* to a pending tort action, *see e.g., Northern Assurance Co., v. EDP Floors,* 311 Md. 217, 533 A.2d 682 (1987) or *after* resolution of the tort action, *e.g., Aragona, supra,* as generally appropriate means for determining coverage questions.

Here, as in *Northern Assurance* and *Aragona,* the coverage question, *i.e.,* whether the complained of acts were crimes, was clearly "independent and separable" from the claim asserted in the pending tort action, *i.e.,* whether the acts were medical malpractice. Thus, resolution of the tort action did not, and could not, resolve the coverage question. Acts can be held not to constitute malpractice and still be crimes. *See e.g., In Re Meyerson,* 190 Md. 671, 685, 59 A.2d 489 (1948). Acts can be held to constitute malpractice and not be crimes. *See e.g., Aetna Life & Casualty Co., v. McCabe,* 556 F.Supp. 1342, 1352 n. 7 (E.D.Pa.1983). And, as this case demonstrates, acts can be held to constitute both malpractice and crimes. Thus, determination of whether acts are malpractice simply does not resolve the question of whether they are crimes. Since the latter question is independent and separable from the former, the *Atwood* procedure is inapplicable here. Accordingly, Medical Mutual is not "estopped" from raising the criminal act exclusion because of the prior determination by the Health Claims Arbitration panel that the complained of conduct constituted malpractice. The fundamental principle, which has escaped Dr. Azzato, is that an insured's acts may be held to constitute malpractice making him liable to his patients for injuries resulting from those acts and yet the insured may, nevertheless, be unable to recover from his malpractice insurer because the policy does not cover injuries resulting from those acts. This is the distinction that Chief Judge Murphy pointed to in *Aragona* "between causes of loss for which liability may be imposed upon an insured by law, [all malpractice] and causes of loss for which the insurer may have contracted to be liable [here only non-criminal malpractice]." 281 Md. at 375-76, 378 A.2d 1346. As in *Aragona,* the insured, here Dr. Azzato, is legally liable for damages resulting from his acts but cannot obtain reimbursement from his insurer, because the insurer did not contract to provide coverage for the damages resulting from those acts In view of our holding here, the issue raised in the cross appeal is moot.
JUDGMENT REVERSED.

CASES AGAINST PHYSICIANS

Initially, in the United States, medical malpractice actions were brought against physicians. They were essentially the only health care providers who offered medical treatment to a large portion of the population.

As hospitals, medical facilities, and technology increased, so did the potential defendants. But the physicians have long been the most common and pervasive target in medical malpractice actions. The reason is the same as it has always been. In most cases, the physician is the ultimate authority and responsible party for directing care, treatment, and services provided to patients. They are also the individuals in whom patients place their trust. Thus, when something goes wrong, it is the physician to whom the patient most often looks for accountability.

The possible legal theories against physicians were discussed in earlier chapters. Most often, the case will involve a collection of alternative causes of action. Essentially, the plaintiff claims that if the actions of the physician are not successful under one legal theory, the same facts support an action under another. Very often, the complaint will include a cause of action sounding in negligence. This is the simplest legal theory and therefore the most readily supported by evidence. More complicated theories advanced include intentional torts, breach of contract, and, in some situations, even strict liability.

The facts of medical malpractice cases are infinitely varied. But they typically fall into one of several common categories. The plaintiff may allege a breach of an ethical obligation or criminal conduct. More often the complaint is based on the actual delivery of medical care, treatment, or services by the physician or someone under the physician's supervision. If the claim is based on the actual conduct of the physician, the issues are clearer. Specifically, it must be determined if the physician's conduct met the required standard of care based on what a similarly trained physician would do under similar circumstances, or if the elements of a particular tort, such as battery or abandonment, were established.

As introduced earlier in the text, a physician who holds him or herself out to the public as a **specialist** of any kind in medicine is presumed to have advanced knowledge and training over an ordinary licensed physician. It is not necessary for the physician to be actually certified in a specialty. The question is whether a reasonable conclusion was reached by the patient based on the representations of the physician. These representations may be made to the specific patient or to the general public, for example through advertising. It this is proven, then the physician is required to have practiced according to the standards and requirements of a specialist.

64 P3rd 809 (2003).

Supreme Court of Alaska.

William ZAVERL, Personal Representative of the Estate of Margaret M. Zaverl,
Appellant,
v.
Owen Q. HANLEY, M.D., and James B. Borden, M.D., Appellees.

Feb. 14, 2003.

(continued)

Before: FABE, Chief Justice, MATTHEWS, EASTAUGH, BRYNER, and CARPENETI, Justices.

Margaret Zaverl coughed up a significant quantity of blood on October 2, 1994. [FN1] She was taken to Fairbanks Memorial Hospital where Dr. Eric Stirling, an emergency medicine specialist, examined her. She reported that she had coughed up and vomited bright red blood and that she experienced shortness of breath and wheezing. Her medical history included regular cigarette smoking, a left thoracotomy for coarctation of the aorta at age seventeen, and removal of an anaerobic tumor of the abdomen in early 1970. Margaret was forty-five years old in 1994.

Dr. Stirling consulted with Dr. James Borden, a surgeon. Dr. Borden performed a bronchoscopy which "showed an apparent tumor in the bronchus to the right middle lobe and right lower lobe." Dr. Borden could not remove the tumor during the bronchoscopy. The fiberoptic bronchoscope showed marked inflammation of the tracheal wall and blood clots. The right side of the bronchial tree appeared to be more inflamed than the left--a condition which Dr. Borden found to be consistent with the presence of the suspected tumor.

Dr. Borden consulted with a Fairbanks internist, Dr. Kenneth Starks. Chest X-rays revealed that infiltrates obscured the lower bases of Margaret's lungs. Dr. Borden admitted Margaret to the hospital's intensive care unit, made arrangements for a follow-up bronchoscopy, and arranged for her to see Dr. Owen Hanley, a pulmonologist, when Dr. Hanley returned to Fairbanks. Margaret underwent a variety of tests to determine the cause of her illness. Dr. Hanley saw Margaret on October 6. Dr. Hanley was unable to ascertain immediately the cause of her massive hemoptysis, and he recommended another bronchoscopy. Margaret was discharged on October 8. Dr. Hanley made arrangements for a follow-up visit in ten days to perform a computerized axial tomography (CAT or CT) scan once the infiltrates had cleared from Margaret's lungs.

When the doctors told Margaret that they were uncertain what was causing her bleeding, she asked if the bleeding could be related to her aorta repair. There was evidence that the doctors assured Margaret that the bleeding was not related to her aorta repair.

Margaret began to cough up blood again on the evening of October 9. Her family took her to Fairbanks Memorial Hospital. Margaret lost consciousness en route and died at the hospital soon after. Autopsy revealed that sections of the graft on her aorta had adhered to the pulmonary parenchyma; some of the tissue had died, leaving marked accumulation of blood in the pulmonary parenchyma directly adjacent to the aortal graft. The autopsy summary concluded that this accumulation "most likely represents the origin of the patient's severe hemoptysis."

Margaret's husband, William Zaverl, as personal representative of her estate, filed a superior court complaint against Drs. Borden and Hanley in October 1996. The superior court appointed an expert advisory panel at the defendants' request. The case proceeded to trial beginning mid-May 1999. The estate offered evidence that Drs. Hanley and Borden failed to consider Margaret's prior aorta repair in diagnosing her condition, but the jury returned a verdict for both physicians.

Drs. Hanley and Borden moved for awards of costs and attorney's fees against William Zaverl as personal representative of Margaret's estate and against the individual statutory beneficiaries jointly and severally. The court granted the motion and awarded Dr. Hanley costs and fees of $57,824.52 and Dr. Borden costs and fees of $67,149.40. These joint and several awards were against the estate, Margaret's spouse, and her children. The caption on the final judgment names "WILLIAM ZAVERL, Personal Representative of the Estate of Margaret M. Zaverl." But the final judgment states that it is against the estate and the individually named statutory beneficiaries.

This appeal followed. William Zaverl is the named appellant, acting as personal representative of the estate.

(continued)

A. It Was an Abuse of Discretion To Permit Dr. Borden To Testify at Trial on Topics He Refused To Discuss at His Deposition.

The estate argues that it was an abuse of discretion to allow Dr. Borden's trial lawyer to question him at trial about topics his attorney instructed him not to discuss at his deposition. We agree, and remand to the superior court to determine the effect of this error.

1. Dr. Borden testified at trial about matters he refused to address at his deposition.

At Dr. Borden's pre-trial deposition, the estate's lawyer asked Dr. Borden, "Did Margaret Zaverl die because the connection between the massive hemoptysis and her history of prior aortic repair was not diagnosed?" Dr. Borden's attorney objected and instructed Dr. Borden not to answer:

> I object to the form of the question. He's not an expert in that area.... He's not going to testify as an expert in that area, and I won't allow him to testify on this--on the speculation of something nobody will ever know and he's not a cardiovascular surgeon, cardiac thoracic surgeon, so he's not going to answer that question.

When the estate's attorney asked Dr. Borden what treatment he would have provided if the aortobronchial fistula had been diagnosed, Dr. Borden's attorney stated:

> I'm going to instruct him not to answer. He's not going to speculate on something which he did not do.... He's not an expert. I'm not going to offer him as an expert in the area of cardiovascular treatment and handling of aortic breakdown, I mean breakdowns of coarctation repairs of the aorta.

Dr. Borden did not answer these questions at his deposition.

At trial, near the end of Dr. Borden's direct testimony, his trial attorney asked Dr. Borden if he had "a fairly good understanding of what's necessary to repair ... an aortobronchial fistula such as Margaret Zaverl had." The estate's attorney objected. He argued that when he asked Dr. Borden the same question at the deposition, Dr. Borden's deposition attorney instructed Dr. Borden not to answer and not to speculate about something he did not do and something that did not occur. When the trial court stated that a motion to compel would have been the way to deal with the attorney's instruction, the estate's attorney indicated that he had understood counsel's statement at the deposition to mean that Dr. Borden would not be offered as an expert on these topics.

The trial court overruled the estate's objections. The court reasoned that Dr. Borden was a general surgeon, not a cardiovascular surgeon who does such repairs or who is an expert in repairing such conditions. The court stated that Dr. Borden's knowledge in 1994 "is an important issue" and "to the extent he's a defendant in this case, as to the standard of care he gave, it appears to the court relevant and admissible for those issues to be discussed with him, by both sides." The court also noted that the estate would have an opportunity to cross-examine.

Dr. Borden then testified that he did have "a reasonably good understanding" of aortobronchial fistulae. He proceeded to testify at some length about particular nuances of diagnosing and treating this condition. Dr. Borden testified that he wished he had thought of "this particular kind of fistula," even though "these other smart guys wouldn't have thought about it." Nonetheless, he concluded that his treatment of Margaret, including his failure to detect the fistula which may have caused her hemoptysis, did not fall below the applicable standard of care.

2. Dr. Borden should not have been permitted to testify to matters he refused to discuss at his deposition.

The estate argues on appeal that it was error to permit Dr. Borden to testify at trial about matters he was instructed not to discuss at his deposition. The estate asserts that discovery was thwarted when Dr. Borden's attorney instructed him at his deposition not to respond to questions concerning detection and repair of aortobronchial fistulae, stated that he would not offer him as an expert on the detection and repair of aortobronchial fistulae, and then questioned him on precisely those areas at trial without giving advance notice of his changed intentions. The estate relies on *Yukon Equipment, Inc. v. Gordon,* which upheld a trial court's exclusion of testimony not described in interrogatory answers.

(continued)

Dr. Borden responds that he was not qualified to give testimony on aortobronchial fistulae when the estate took his deposition in August 1997, but was qualified to do so when he testified at trial in May 1999. Dr. Borden distinguishes *Yukon Equipment* on the theory that he did not fail to disclose information, as the witness did in *Yukon Equipment*. Dr. Borden asserts that he simply did not have the information to answer at his deposition but did at trial.

We conclude that the estate was affirmatively led to believe that Dr. Borden would not express opinions at trial on matters beyond the expertise of a general surgeon, and more specifically, that Dr. Borden would not testify about the treatment of aortobronchial fistulae. Dr. Borden never disclosed his intention to testify at trial about what he had learned since his deposition, about surgery a general surgeon would not perform, or in reliance on expertise he acquired after his lawyer disclaimed that expertise at Dr. Borden's deposition. Assuming that Dr. Borden's inconsistent positions were the result of an innocent misstep not meant to unfairly disadvantage the estate, we nonetheless agree with the estate that the purpose of discovery was thwarted. The opportunity to cross-examine at trial was no substitute for pretrial discovery in this case.

Dr. Borden asserts that the estate should have raised any objection to the deposition by filing a motion to compel. But no pretrial motion to compel was necessary to preserve the estate's trial objection that Dr. Borden could not testify about things he refused to discuss at his deposition. The estate was not obliged to anticipate that Dr. Borden might claim at trial that he now knew more than he did when he treated Margaret Zaverl or when he was deposed. Only if the estate had been given reason to think Dr. Borden intended to address the foreclosed topics at trial would it have been required to file a motion to compel. So far as we can determine, Dr. Borden apparently did not reveal that intention until his trial lawyer began asking him the disputed questions at trial. Having followed his lawyer's deposition instruction not to testify about certain topics, Dr. Borden had to live with that decision absent fair notice to the estate.

The issue is not whether Dr. Borden was eligible to express any opinions, but whether he could do so on topics he refused to discuss at his deposition. In *Miller v. Phillips*, a medical malpractice case, we thought it significant that the Millers had received Dr. Newton's affidavit setting out the substance of his opinions "well before trial." Here, the estate had no advance notice that Dr. Borden would offer the disputed testimony or rely on expertise he had disclaimed at his deposition. There is no reason in this situation to permit such undisclosed opinions.

Under the circumstances, it was error to permit Dr. Borden to testify at trial about relevant topics he declined to discuss at his deposition.

3. We remand to the trial court to determine whether the error was harmless.

The circumstances that convinced the trial court that the disputed evidence was relevant and not redundant or speculative preclude us from saying as a matter of law that the error of allowing the testimony was harmless. Dr. Borden's testimony was important evidence bearing on liability. It was offered by a treating physician who was also a defendant and whose credibility and candor may have been critical to the jury trying to decide whether he breached the applicable standard of care. He described the quality of his care favorably, apparently applying the knowledge he acquired after his deposition. This permitted him to address the medical issues in a light most favorable to himself and to increase his stature as a witness.

The effect of this error is not clear. We consequently asked the parties for supplemental briefing on how the testimony affected the case against each defendant physician.

The estate argues that the error was not harmless because the jury could have relied on Dr. Borden's testimony to decide that Dr. Borden's treatment was not negligent. The estate also contends that because Dr. Borden testified that Margaret Zaverl's overall treatment was not substandard, the jury could have relied on Dr. Borden's testimony to absolve Dr. Hanley of liability.

(continued)

Dr. Borden's supplemental response is two-fold: the jury was not misled, because he admitted that he did not have knowledge of these fistulae when he treated Margaret Zaverl; and his testimony about the standard of care only "echoed" the testimony of his expert witness, Dr. Joseph Stapleton Coselli. Dr. Borden implies that because the estate's attorney was prepared to cross-examine Dr. Coselli, the estate's attorney also must have been prepared to cross-examine Dr. Borden. Further, Dr. Borden asserts that the jury could have found and was encouraged to find an absence of negligence in reliance on Dr. Coselli's testimony, without considering Dr. Borden's testimony on the standard of care. Dr. Borden also contends that his own testimony was relevant because he was the only witness who could discuss what he knew when he treated Margaret Zaverl and that his testimony was not speculative because he spoke from his own knowledge.

He also argues that the estate was not prejudiced by the testimony because the estate's lawyer was given wide latitude to examine Dr. Borden on exactly when he acquired his knowledge and could easily emphasize to the jury that Dr. Borden did not have this knowledge when he treated Margaret Zaverl.

Finally, Dr. Borden concludes that the testimony only affected himself, not Dr. Hanley, and that even if the testimony had been excluded, there was more than enough evidence regarding the relevant standard of care to support the jury's verdict.

Dr. Hanley simply argues that he was not affected by Dr. Borden's testimony because the jury was instructed that Dr. Hanley was to be held to a distinct standard of care and because he had his own experts to establish that standard. He consequently asserts that he did not rely on Dr. Borden's testimony at all.

We cannot say, even after the supplemental briefing, that the error was harmless. We therefore remand to the trial court to determine the effect of admitting the disputed testimony. Having heard the evidence admitted at trial, the trial court is in the best position to consider the effect of Dr. Borden's disputed trial opinions in the context of the other evidence, those deposition passages submitted to the jury, the opinions of other experts, and other trial events, including the parties' arguments to the jury. Remand will give the parties the best opportunity to explore whether the error prejudiced the estate's claims against either defendant or was harmless. This may be a fact-intensive inquiry that requires more flexibility than the appellate forum permits. It may depend on the tactics the parties employed at trial.

B. The Court Did Not Err in Refusing To Admit Evidence and Instructing on the Standard of Care for Medical Specialists.

The estate argues that errors prevented the jury from holding Dr. Borden to the standard of care of a specialist in thoracic and vascular surgery, rather than the lower standard of care of a general surgeon. Thus, it asserts that it was error not to admit into evidence medical directories and Yellow Pages advertisements listing Dr. Borden as a vascular and thoracic surgeon. It further asserts that the jury should have been instructed that Dr. Borden held himself out as a specialist in thoracic and vascular surgery and that a specialist's failure to use the care and skill practiced in that specialty is negligence.

Dr. Borden responds that he is only a general surgeon and that he testified that he was board certified only in general surgery. He argues that he has only had some experience in thoracic and vascular surgery and that he should not be held to the standard of care of a specialist because he never represented to Margaret Zaverl that he was a specialist in those areas. He argues that his training, knowledge, and skill did not rise to the level of a specialist and that it would have been error to give the estate's proposed jury instruction or to admit the advertisements. He argues that his testimony on his experiences in those areas was sufficient to inform the jury of the standard by which he should be judged. Because the estate was allowed to cross-examine Dr. Borden at trial about his experiences and his listings and advertisements, Dr. Borden argues that the trial court did not err in determining that admitting the listings and advertisements into evidence would be irrelevant and cumulative.

Physicians who hold themselves out to the public as having specialized knowledge or skill must be held to the standard of care of specialists with those enhanced qualifications. It does not matter whether the

(continued)

physician led any specific patient to have an actual expectation that the physician would exercise a greater level of skill, so long as the physician has taken "affirmative steps" to present himself or herself to the public as a specialist.

But we discern no reversible error with respect to the evidence or the instructions. Dr. Borden defended on the theory that regardless of specialty, skill, training, or place of practice, no physician--even a specialist in cardiovascular surgery--would have correctly diagnosed and treated Margaret Zaverl's condition. Thus he relied on the opinions of Dr. Coselli, a prominent cardiovascular surgeon who practiced at a teaching hospital in Houston, Texas. Dr. Borden likewise relied on his own testimony, discussed above in Part III.A, expressing the same opinion based on his post-treatment research. Dr. Borden's closing argument did not attempt to defend on a theory that a general surgeon was not required to do what specialists could do.

We therefore conclude that it was not an abuse of discretion to exclude the listings and advertisements. We also conclude that, given the nature of Dr. Borden's defense, it was not error to reject the proposed instruction. The proposed instruction correctly stated the law. But it was unnecessary because, as seen above, Dr. Borden's defense did not rest on the proposition that, as a general surgeon, he should be held to a lower standard of care than thoracic, vascular, or cardiovascular surgeons.

Of course, should the trial court's resolution on remand of the Borden testimony issue require retrial, the case may be in a different posture, requiring the trial court to revisit these evidentiary and instructional issues.

C. The Court Did Not Err in Refusing To Strike the Expert Advisory Panel.

The estate argues that the members of the court-appointed three-member expert advisory panel were biased because they had social relationships with the defendants or had prior knowledge of the case or opinions about it. It consequently argues that rule, statute, or due process required the trial court to disqualify each member. It also argues that the panel violated the procedural requirements of AS 09.55.536 in producing its report

The estate sued Drs. Hanley and Borden in 1996. The defendants asked the court to appoint an expert advisory panel. Drs. Steven Kilkenny, Tim Coalwell, and Beth Baker were ultimately nominated. Dr. Borden notified the court and plaintiff in June 1997 that the law firm representing him was also representing Dr. Kilkenny in an unrelated matter. Dr. Baker disclosed in June 1997 that she may have previously discussed the case because she thought it had been "presented" at a 1994 meeting she attended. The estate did not object to these possible conflicts of interest, and in August 1997 the trial court entered an order appointing these three physicians to the panel. In June 1998 Dr. Borden notified the court and plaintiff that the law firm representing him was also representing Dr. Coalwell in an unrelated matter.

The panel never met in person, but the panelists each issued a report on November 20, 1997. Dr. Baker summarized the three reports. In February 1999 the estate moved to strike the entire panel and its report, alleging that all three panelists were biased and had failed to confer in person or submit a single report, in alleged violation of the requirements of AS 09.55.536. The trial court denied these motions in March 1999.

The estate argues on appeal that it was error not to order the panel and its reports struck. Drs. Borden and Hanley respond by contending, among other things, that the estate waived any challenge by waiting over a year to object to the panel.

We agree with Drs. Borden and Hanley that the objections to the panel and its opinions were raised too late and were therefore waived. The estate knew no later than June 1997 of possible conflicts as to two members and no later than June 1998 of a possible conflict as to the third member. Nonetheless, the estate did not take the depositions of panelists until early February 1999, about three months before trial was to begin. The estate filed its objections to the panel and its findings about eighteen months after the panel was appointed, about fourteen months after it issued its report, and about three months before trial. By then it was impossible to appoint a new panel and the delay potentially would have prejudiced the defendants. This likely would have meant submitting the case to the jury without any advisory report.

(continued)

Nothing about the grounds for objections under Alaska Civil Rule 72.1 or AS 09.55.536 precludes their rejection as untimely. And due process is not inconsistent with requiring litigants to raise timely procedural and substantive objections.

Given the patent untimeliness of the estate's motions to strike the panel and its reports, the court did not err by denying them. We consequently do not need to decide whether the estate's motions were meritorious.

D. The Court Did Not Err by Allowing Dr. Halvorsen To Testify About the Standard of Care.

The trial court accepted Dr. Robert Halvorsen as an expert in diagnostic radiology. *820 According to the estate, Dr. Halvorsen stated in his deposition that he was not capable of testifying to the standard of care of thoracic surgeons, general surgeons, or pulmonologists. The estate argues that it was error to permit Dr. Halvorsen to testify at trial that the care provided by Drs. Hanley and Borden "was well within acceptable medical standards."

Dr. Hanley argues that Dr. Halvorsen did not testify to the general standard of care provided by the defendants, as the estate contends. Dr. Hanley asserts that Dr. Halvorsen instead testified to the standard of care from the perspective of a radiologist.

Dr. Halvorsen testified:"I believe the care provided of Mrs. Zaverl by Drs. Hanley, Borden and Starks as well as the care provided by Fairbanks Memorial Hospital, was well within acceptable medical standards. The physicians used the appropriate radiographic modalities as well as bronchoscopy to exclude the diagnosable cause of hemoptysis. Unfortunately, she died of a rare condition that could not be diagnosed with the facilities available to those physicians. Think that there is information on these. The chest x-ray and on the CT that would have guided these physicians at the time they were involved in the care of this patient in 1994 away from a diagnosis that actually turned out to be a correct diagnosis that was proved on autopsy."

According to Dr. Hanley, the context of Dr. Halvorsen's remarks demonstrates that Dr. Halvorsen was only testifying about the standard of care for diagnosis based on radiological techniques. The estate's reply brief does not respond to these arguments.

The estate has not shown that the trial court abused its discretion by allowing Dr. Halvorsen to discuss the standard of care applicable when a physician uses radiological tools to diagnose a patient. Dr. Halvorsen had the expertise to discuss this subject and was properly admitted as an expert to express such an opinion. The estate had a fair opportunity on cross-examination to clarify the scope of Dr. Halvorsen's expertise and testimony. We conclude that the trial court did not abuse its discretion by permitting Dr. Halvorsen to express this opinion.

E. The Court Did Not Err by Refusing To Impose a Presumption of Negligence Based on the Failure To Prepare a Timely Discharge Summary.

Margaret Zaverl's discharge summary was prepared forty-eight days after her discharge; the estate alleges that this delay violated 7 Alaska Administrative Code (AAC) 12.770(e), which requires that a discharge summary be prepared within fifteen days of discharge and be signed by the attending physician. The estate asserts that the delay hindered its ability to present its case, and that the trial court erred by failing to impose a presumption of negligence and causation. It also argues that a violation of this regulation and an equivalent hospital policy is relevant, and that the trial court erred in preventing the estate from examining Dr. Borden about discharge summary procedures. It does not explain how that ruling prejudiced the trial of its claims.

Under the circumstances of this case, the court did not err by declining to impose a presumption of fault or causation. In *Sweet v. Sisters of Providence in Washington,* we held that a regulatory breach regarding hospital records could give rise to a presumption of negligence. A presumption of negligence is appropriate when the court is convinced that "the absence of the records hinders [the plaintiff's] ability to establish a prima facie case" and that "the essential medical records are missing through the

(continued)

negligence or fault of the adverse party But there the records were entirely absent, not merely late-prepared. Here, by contrast, the discharge summary was ultimately prepared, and no information was missing or withheld. And given that the diagnosis memorialized in the discharge summary was incorrect, it is apparent that Dr. Borden did not use the extra time to improve his position in event of litigation. More importantly, Sweet made out a specific showing of prejudice. In this case, however, the estate advances no plausible theory demonstrating that the delay prejudiced its case. It has not explained what information it expected to find in the discharge summary that is not there, nor has it directed us to evidence that the delay impaired the plaintiff's experts' analyses. *Sweet v. Sisters of Providence in Washington,* 895 P.2d 484, 490-92 (Alaska 1995).

Accordingly, we hold the trial court did not err in failing to assign a presumption of negligence for failure to prepare a timely discharge summary.

The estate's companion argument--that it should have been permitted to inquire about the delay and whether the delay violated state law and hospital procedures--is equally unpersuasive. The estate has not shown what evidence might have been elicited or how it might have altered the verdict.

F. Costs and Fees Awards Are Not Allowable Against Non-Party Statutory Beneficiaries in a Wrongful Death Action.

The trial court awarded Drs. Borden and Hanley attorney's fees and costs totaling $124,973.92. Reasoning that the statutory beneficiaries in wrongful death actions are the actual "parties represented" within the meaning of AS 09.60.040, the court ruled that William Zaverl, individually and as a statutory beneficiary, and the three Zaverl children, individually and as statutory beneficiaries, would be personally liable for these costs and fees. It concluded that the beneficiaries should be liable for costs and fees because the representative of the estate is only a nominal party and the estate is not a party at all. The court entered judgment totaling $124,973.92 in favor of Drs. Borden and Hanley.

Because the children were not named parties to the lawsuit and did not personally appear in the lawsuit and William Zaverl appeared only in his representative capacity, Zaverl argues that it was error to interpret AS 09.60.040 to allow recovery of costs and attorney's fees against him and the three children.

Drs. Borden and Hanley argue that the surviving spouse and children in a wrongful death action are liable for attorney's fees and costs under AS 09.55.and AS 09.60.040. They rely on *In re Soldotna Air Crash Litigation,* in which we reiterated that although estate representatives are nominal parties in wrongful death actions, a wrongful death action is "the [beneficiaries'] cause of action." AS 09.55.580 provides in pertinent part: (a) Except as provided under (f) of this section, when the death of a person is caused by the wrongful act or omission of another, the personal representatives of the former may maintain an action therefor against the latter, if the former might have maintained an action, had the person lived, against latter for an injury done by the same act or omission.... The amount recovered, if any, shall be exclusively for the benefit of the decedent's spouse and children when the decedent is survived by a spouse or children, or other dependents.

Alaska Statute 09.60.040 cannot reasonably be read to permit recovery of attorney's fees and costs against the statutory beneficiaries in this case because they did not appear and did not make claims in their personal capacities. *Soldotna* is distinguishable. We were concerned there with whether a prevailing defendant could recover costs and attorney's fees under AS 09.60.040 against the non-prevailing plaintiff in a wrongful death action. We held that the prevailing defendant could recover its award from the fund created by the plaintiffs' recovery from the other defendants. We left for another day the question whether a

(continued)

prevailing defendant could recover such an award from the statutory beneficiaries in the absence of a fund. We now address that question and answer it in the negative.

The only party plaintiff in this case was William Zaverl, and he appeared only in his representative capacity and not in any personal capacity. We hold that, although the statutory beneficiaries not named in a wrongful death lawsuit are the beneficiaries of any recovery, statutory beneficiaries who are not parties to the wrongful death lawsuit in their personal capacities are not parties for the purpose of responding to awards of costs and attorney's fees. Accordingly, we vacate the trial court's award of costs and attorney's fees against the estate's statutory beneficiaries. The relationship of statutory beneficiaries to the personal representative is analogous to that of the beneficiaries of an estate or trust to an executor or trustee. Estate and trust beneficiaries are ordinarily not considered parties to an action brought by an executor or trustee, nor are they personally responsible for costs and fees if the action proves to be unsuccessful. *See* 97 C.J.S. § 1972 (2001) (devisee liable only as to distributed assets); 90A C.J.S. *Trusts* § 586 (2001); *see also* Restatement (Second) of Trusts § 274 (1959). These rules are subject to an exception if the beneficiary has received property from the estate or trust that should have been available for the payment of costs and fees. *See* Restatement (Second) of Trusts § 274 (1959); AS 13.16.635 (estate distributee not liable for amounts in excess of value of distribution); 97 C.J.S. § 1972 (2001). We applied a similar exception in the case of wrongful death action statutory beneficiaries in *Soldotna,* 835 P.2d at 1221-22.

We REMAND to the trial court to determine whether the error of allowing Dr. Borden to testify at trial about topics he refused to discuss at his deposition prejudiced the estate's claims against either defendant. We also VACATE the joint and several award of costs and attorney's fees against the estate's statutory beneficiaries. We AFFIRM as to all other issues.

In the event the physician is allegedly responsible for the actions of a subordinate, the issue of respondeat superior comes into play. As discussed briefly in Chapter 1, in most cases where an employer is considered to be responsible for the conduct of an employee while acting within the scope of employment, the employer will be held financially responsible for injuries caused by the employee under the theory of respondeat superior. But, in the arena of medical malpractice, the question becomes particularly difficult. As with any civil suit claiming respondeat superior, the essential elements of one acting within the scope of employment or at the direction of a superior must be shown.[2] In the modern-day health care field this question becomes even more complex because more than one superior from various roles of employment may be involved. Also, it is common for a number of medical personnel acting at various levels of independence to come into contact with a patient during treatment. Many health care providers have a significant amount of training and independent judgment which they exercise in the scope of their employment. They may also be subject to the direct and indirect supervision of more than one individual. For example, a lab technician may be directed by a physician with respect to particular tests to be done. That technician may be employed by a different physician, hospital, or laboratory that has a separate contract for services with the physician, hospital, or both. In some instances, an independent physician requesting specific tests for a patient may issue conflicting directions with the physician to whom the technician normally reports. The physicians are typically not present when the technician performs his or her duties and this creates an even greater issue as to the extent of direction versus independent action. These same issues may result with other types of providers such as occupational, physical, and respiratory therapists, nurse anesthetists, physician's assistants, and so on. While, ultimately, the physician may be held accountable for direction, the issue must first be sorted out regarding who was the direct supervisor and employer, and the degree to which the conduct constituted independent judgment.

The increased number of these cases in recent years has resulted in development to better define the relationship among providers. Today, it is a matter of routine that all physicians with privileges to practice in a particular facility such as a hospital, clinic, or treatment center, have clearly written agreements with the facility as to their legal status as an employee or independent contractor. Similarly, subordinate employees such as technicians, nurses, therapists, various types of assistants, and other staff providing medical care, treatment, or services are identified in their employment agreements or job descriptions as independent contractors or employees. If they are employees, there is usually a distinct hierarchy of authority. Regardless of instruction or direction by outsiders, such as physicians who are independent contractors, the ultimate responsibility for direction is placed with the stated individual of authority. Similarly, if an independent contractor physician brings a subordinate staff member into a facility—such as a nurse to assist with treatment of patients—that staff member remains the subordinate of the physician and the facility does not generally accept liability for respondeat superior simply because the individual performs duties within the facility. It should also be noted that a physician is typically not held accountable for an employee's conduct that is considered an intentional tort or an action outside the scope of employment unless there is evidence that the conduct was encouraged or acquiesced to by the superior. Consider the following example in Application 3.5 in which a physician is held accountable for the actions of a subordinate even though the physician is not physically present when the alleged malpractice occurs.

APPLICATION 3.5

Dr. Thompsen makes rounds of hospital patients she has admitted each day. Typically, her employee and physician's assistant, Derek, accompanies her. On a particularly busy morning, Dr. Thompsen delegates Derek to make rounds and examinations of the patients on one floor while Dr. Thompsen sees patients on another. While Derek is making notes in the charts, he fails to acknowledge or examine the leg pain in a post-operative patient that has been noted in the chart by the nurse as ongoing for several hours. The patient was previously scheduled for discharge that day and Dr. Thompsen confirms the discharge order. The patient returns home and subsequently suffers a fatal pulmonary embolism (blood clot to the lung) that initiated in the leg. This is a condition that is readily treatable with timely diagnosis. A medical malpractice suit is commenced. Even though the negligent conduct of the physician's assistant occurred in the hospital, Dr. Thompsen would be responsible under respondeat superior for the actions of the physician's assistant. There may be other causes of action against the hospital, but they would not be likely held accountable for the actions of Derek.

CASES INVOLVING NON-PHYSICIAN MEDICAL PROFESSIONALS

In the previous section, discussion focused on the responsibility of physicians for the acts of subordinate medical personnel. But what of the personal accountability of the non-physician medical professional? Many states now have medical malpractice statutes that govern the procedures for litigation in cases of malpractice. Each state's language varies as to whose conduct is covered by these statutes, but these statutes are largely procedural in their effect. They determine the allowable period of time for bringing suit, methods of commencing and conducting the litigation process in these cases, and in some instances there are limits on the amount that can be recovered. Quite often they do not address the ultimate issue of whether a non-physician can be held liable for professional malfeasance in the delivery of health care, treatment, or services under the statute. Even if a malpractice statute does not include a non-physician, there may still be liability under general principles of civil law. Those acting under the immediate supervision and direction of a physician may aim allegations of malpractice to the physician, but, while there is generally a deeper pocket for recovery with physician malpractice, the subordinate is not always free of liability.

In cases where a non-physician is alleged to have independently committed medical malpractice and no medical malpractice statute is considered applicable, the standard is typically that of ordinary negligence. A nurse, assistant, therapist, or technician or other health care provider is treated essentially the same if a malpractice statute is found to be inapplicable to him or her. The established rule is that if one undertakes to provide care by virtue of specialized skill or training, he or she is held to the standard of one who is competently trained in the same field. For example, a nurse is required to exercise an ordinary degree of care and skill that would be exercised by a nurse of similar training and licensure. The duty is to the patient for whom care has been undertaken and to any others who might be indirectly affected by a failure to adhere to the standard of care. See Application 3.6.

APPLICATION 3.6

Ambrose was a patient in a hospital where he was being treated for pneumonia. During a treatment by the respiratory therapist, Ambrose became quite ill and started choking. He subsequently lost consciousness and stopped breathing. The therapist intubated Ambrose to open his airway and begin artificial ventilation. Unknowingly, the therapist had placed the tube in the esophagus rather than the airway and Ambrose was deprived of oxygen for a significant period of time causing serious brain damage. In this case, the employer of the respiratory therapist would likely be responsible for the actions of its employee. But, what if it were discovered that the therapist had intentionally deprived Ambrose of oxygen so that he could be revived and saved by the therapist? Another possible situation where respondeat superior might not apply would be in a case where the therapist was in a hurry to get off duty and made the decision not to bring the standard and appropriate equipment to the room for treatment so he could finish and leave more quickly. In such a case an intentional tort may apply.

The same essential rules apply to laboratory and other technicians, therapists, assistants, and non-physicians providing health care. As mentioned, it is unusual to find a suit against one of these individuals that does not also make a claim against the employer physician or health care facility under the theory of respondeat superior. However, this theory is not always applicable. As stated with regard to physicians above, an employer is not generally responsible for acts of an employee that constitute intentional torts.[3] A similar rule applies to criminal conduct. The exception is when the employer or facility directed the conduct expressly or by implication. Thus, when framing an action against a provider and evaluating the proper cause of action upon which to base the suit, it is important to consider the possible sources of recovery (i.e., insurance coverage), and whether a cause of action against a particular individual has sufficient evidence to support the case to a successful conclusion. Exactly the opposite is true from a defense perspective. The case must be considered in terms of whether the individual who allegedly committed the malpractice acted in such a way that respondeat superior is rendered inapplicable or subject to exception. There are different exclusionary rules when the non-physician is in a practical setting independent of a physician and/or health care facility.

CASES INVOLVING INDEPENDENT PHARMACISTS, DENTISTS, CHIROPRACTORS, PSYCHOLOGISTS, AND OPTOMETRISTS AND OTHER INDEPENDENT NON-PHYSICIAN HEALTH CARE PROVIDERS

As with subordinate personnel, there is always a question of whether a health care provider is subject to any applicable medical malpractice statute. Once the statute has been defined as to applicability of non-physicians as mentioned above, these statutes are typically procedural in effect both with regard to commencement of the action and, in some instances, limits on damages. Once the procedural requirements are met, whether general civil or pursuant to specialized legislation, the substantive evidence and burden of proof requirements apply in a similar manner. And, as with physicians and subordinate personnel the standards are essentially the same for independent providers of health care services. The general rule is that anyone who accepts responsibility and the inherent trust to provide professional health care services has an obligation to do so with no less than a minimum level of competence. That level is usually one of ordinary care that would be exercised by a competently trained and educated, similarly situated professional. There is, of course, also the requirement that the patient sought out or, at the very least, accepted the professional treatment by the health care provider. It is not necessary that there be a contractual relationship for payment in cases of negligence. Rather, the relationship is based on direct or implied consent of both parties. The consent of the provider generally occurs when he or she undertakes to perform some affirmative act for the benefit of the patient.

There are a number of instances in which a professional relationship does not exist for purposes of a medical malpractice claim.[4] These include situations in which the patient is not a regular patient seeking treatment but rather has limited contact with the professional and no relationship beyond something casual, social, or superficial such as a one-time general verbal recommendation or finite connection. For example, one who receives an employment physical by someone whose contact is contained to that situation with the individual would not usually create a relationship sufficient to support a claim of medical malpractice based on a failed diagnosis or treatment. The occasion for such examinations is generally quite limited in scope and is not conducted for diagnostic or treatment purposes. Also, there is typically no further relationship with the party performing the examination. Finally, there is generally insufficient evidence to support a claim that the plaintiff sought professional medical care and intended to establish a patient relationship. This creates a problem in cases based on both contract and tort with regard to an obligation or duty on the part of the provider. The objective is to obtain some other result such as a satisfactory report to qualify for employment. Thus, there is no intent or duty to the patient to create a professional medical relationship and provide ongoing services. This is one example. But in any situation where the relationship is not based on sought medical care or with the goal of providing medical care, treatment, or services, the question of whether a patient relationship even exists must be clearly established.

> **ASSIGNMENT 3.1**
>
> Examine the following situations and explain why a relationship supporting a case based on medical malpractice would or would not exist.
>
> 1. A chiropractor allegedly negligently provides treatment to an employee and causes injury.
>
> 2. An optometrist receives a phone call from someone who is not a patient of the practice and who describes symptoms of an eye problem and the optometrist advises the individual to call and schedule an appointment with his or her physician.
>
> 3. A female patient of a psychologist enters into a sexual relationship with the psychologist as part of the prescribed therapy and, as a result, the patient's spouse divorces her.
>
> 4. A spouse discovers his wife has entered into a sexual relationship with her psychologist as part of her prescribed therapy and, as a result, the wife decides she wants a divorce in order to pursue her relationship with the psychologist.
>
> 5. A dentist receives a call on a Friday afternoon from a longtime patient who reports significant pain and the dentist tells the patient to come in Monday for an examination. As a result of the delay, an infection sets in and the patient suffers permanent facial nerve damage.
>
> 6. A physician hired to conduct exams for applicants seeking life insurance is discovered to have made rectal exams on hundreds of male patients as a routine part of his examination although it was not required by the insurance company.
>
> 7. An individual involved in a lawsuit based on an automobile accident is required to undergo an examination by a physician hired by the opposition. During the examination the physician notes what appears to be a cancerous lesion, but does not discuss it with the individual.

Once it is established that the relationship exists between a health care provider and patient, the case proceeds as any other case for professional malfeasance. The standard of care is based on the professional capacity in which the individual acted. For example, a chiropractor would be held to a level of skill, training, and education of a chiropractor in a similar setting. The same principle would hold true for any other independent provider such as a dentist, optometrist, psychologist, or other independent therapist. However, as with physicians, one who represents him or herself as having specialized knowledge or training, generates expectations of a higher duty toward the patient. If the skill required exceeds their ability, there is an obligation to refer to a properly trained specialist. Failure to do so may result in a finding of malpractice. Continuing to treat a patient when exceeding one's ability may well result in an imposition of the higher specialist duty on the professional. For example, a dentist who undertakes treatment generally considered within the realm of a more advanced training such as orthodontics, periodontics, or oral surgery, would be held to a standard of skill exercised by one fully trained and educated in that area.

CASE

262 Md. 156, 277 A.2d 67, 51 A.L.R.3d 1268

Court of Appeals of Maryland.

Stanley TEMPCHIN
v.
Enid Deborah Cook SAMPSON et al.

May 13, 1971.

HAMMOND, Chief Judge.

This is a sad case. The appellant, an experienced optometrist, characterized by a leading ophthalmologist as 'the most competent optometrist I have ever dealt with,' was found by the jury, permissibly and justifiably in our view, to have been guilty of professional negligence that was a proximate cause of damage to the eyes of the appellee, a young woman, that may well end in blindness in one eye and possibly in the other.

The sole contention of the appellant is that Judge Moorman erred in ruling that there was sufficient evidence of negligence to go to the jury. We are not persuaded, finding that there was ample evidence.

The appellant Stanley Tempchin is a practicing optometrist, licensed by the Board of Examiners of Optometry for the State of Maryland, and so held himself out. Code (1971 Repl. Vol.), Art. 43, s 372, defines the permitted practice of optometry as:

'the employment of any means, except the use of drugs, medicine or surgery, known to the science of optics for the purpose of determining, correcting and prescribing by means of lenses for any optical condition existing in the human eye, and also the employment of any means, except the use of drugs, medicine or surgery, for the purpose of detecting diseased conditions.'

Section 381 of Art. 43 makes it 'unlawful for any person *158 to knowingly sell to or prescribe glasses for persons with diseased eyes except it be with their knowledge and consent or on an order of or advice from a registered physician.'

Enid Deborah Cook (Mrs. Sampson at the time of trial) was troubled because her eyes tried when she read for a time and because an examiner of the Department of Motor Vehicles advised her to have her eyes examined before she sought a renewal of her driver's license. Her aunt took her to Dr. Tempchin to obtain glasses. Both were aware that he was an optometrist and was not an ophthalmologist. As part of the examination, Dr. Tempchin looked at the internal structures of the eyes with an ophthalmoscope and detected on the lens of each eye what he described as spots or opacities, the abnormality being greater in the right eye. Enid and her aunt both say he told them the spots were evidences of incipient cataracts. Both testified that

(continued)

they inquired as to the need or desirability of consulting a doctor and that they were told that they need not do so as he would check the patient's eyes each year for two or three years and would recommend medical advice when it was needed. Dr. Tempchin prescribed glasses which the patient bought and attempted to use without relief. Enid's eyes deteriorated very rapidly and painfully and some eleven days after her examination and four days after she picked up her glasses, her mother on her own initiative took Enid to an ophthalmologist who immediately diagnosed her condition as a form of uveitis. His diagnosis was confirmed that day by a sub-specialist in the medical specialty of ophthalmology, and that night Enid was taken to the hospital for intense and massive treatments with cortisone and other drugs.

After an extended period of treatment, including a stay at the National Institute of Health, her condition improved but the long range prognosis is probable eventual blindness in the right eye and possible blindness in the left. The ophthalmologist to whom Enid went eleven days after Dr. Tempchin discovered the abnormal or pathological condition of her eyes, testified that he could say with reasonable medical certainty that if he had seen her on September 23, the day Dr. Tempchin saw her, or soon thereafter, instead of October 4, the use of proper drugs, begun at the earlier time would have prevented the acute stage of the disease that had progressed so rapidly and done so much damage by October 4 when he saw and treated her.

The liability of an optometrist to a patient is to be tested by standards analogous to those used to test physicians and surgeons-'whether or not he did fail to exercise the amount of care, skill and diligence as (an optometrist) which is exercised generally in the community * * * in which he was practising by (other practitioners) in the same field.' State, Use of Solomon v. Fishel, 228 Md. 189, 195, 179 A.2d 349, 353. See Lane v. Calvert, 215 Md. 457, 462, 138 A.2d 902; Johns Hopkins Hospital, v. Genda, 255 Md. 616, 258 A.2d 595; 70 C.J.S. Physicians and Surgeons s 41, p. 947; 41 Am.Jur. Physicians & Surgeons s 88, p. 206; Fink v. Steele, 166 Md. 354, 171 A. 49; Hardy v. Dahl, 210 N.C. 530, 187 S.E. 788; Kahn v. Shaw, 65 Ga.App. 563, 16 S.E.2d 99.

There was expert testimony from Dr. Tempchin himself, from the ophthalmologist to whom Enid went for treatment, and from another optometrist called by Dr. Tempchin that optometrists practicing in Montgomery County ordinarily and customarily, if not routinely, refer a patient in whom they discover a pathological condition to a physician for treatment as part of their duty and obligation as optometrists. See Evers v. Buxbaum, 102 U.S.App.D.C. 334, 253 F.2d 356, 361. That this is so flows almost necessarily from the limitations the statutes put on the optometrist. He may and should detect disease but he may not treat it.

The case turned essentially on whether Dr. Tempchin did or did not refer Enid to an ophthalmologist and the parties recognized and accepted this proposition.

Judge Moorman charged the jury:

'it is the duty of optometrists to refer their patients to a physician for a pathological disease or a pathological condition which they realize exists or ought to recognize.

'Now, if you find that the Defendant found a pathological condition and under all the circumstances seasonably and timely informed the patient thereof and he recommended and suggested or directed the patient to obtain competent medical assistance, then the Defendant performed his duty and if you so find, your verdict must be and should be for the Defendant on all the allegations of negligence.

'If, on the other hand, you find that the Defendant found a pathological condition and failed to seasonably and timely inform the patron thereof and (to recommend) the patron obtain competent, medical assistance and such failure was the proximate cause of the injuries complained of, then you should find a verdict for the Plaintiff upon the ground of negligence.'

These instructions were accepted without exception or objection by Enid and Dr. Tempchin, who on the stand had acknowledged the duty to refer but had defended on the ground that he fully performed that duty. He testified that after his examination he told Enid and her aunt that Enid should be seen by an eye specialist and

(continued)

that he suggested a Dr. Dubroff, a qualified ophthalmologist, and that days later he told her mother the same things. This testimony was flatly denied by Enid, her aunt and her mother, and evidently was not believed by the jury since they found specifically, on an issue, that Dr. Tempchin had been negligent. To make this finding the jury had to believe the testimony of the witnesses for the claimant, including that of competent and qualified experts, and that testimony was sufficient prima facie to meet the standards necessary to show professional malpractice and resulting damage.

Judgments affirmed, with costs.

CASES AGAINST HEALTH CARE FACILITIES

A major distinction in cases of malpractice against facilities in contrast to individual health care providers is the standard of care. Generally, allegations of malpractice against individuals go to a very specific set of facts including an identifiable act or omission that produced the injury. The standard to which physicians are held accountable conforms to the education, training, and skill of other members of their profession. With facilities, the facts often may cover a condition that developed over a period of time rather than as an isolated incident. The duty and standard elements of a case are adapted to the particular facts of the case. Facilities may also face liability for specific acts of the employees of the entity under the theory of respondeat superior. A facility is obligated to provide whatever resources are necessary to properly care for patients who are within the facility boundaries, taking into account the individual person's particular ability, or inability, to care for themselves.

The issues facing health care facilities today are becoming increasingly complex. The World War II baby boom has created a large, aging population. Medical technology is extending the average life expectancy of this group, causing an ever increasing population of patients. However, the ability to provide adequate care is challenged by the lack of personnel in many areas. Women are branching out in their own employment choices and no longer feel compelled to choose a nursing career, while men are just beginning to move toward this historically female profession. The result is a continuing shortage of qualified nurses. The competitive forces in the health care industry make it difficult for smaller institutions to financially compete for the services of qualified health care providers. These are just a few of the factors that make providing adequate care within a health care facility a daunting task.

Basic elements of creating a safe and adequate environment within a health care facility is largely governed by statute and the leading accrediting organization, the Joint Commission on Accreditation of Healthcare Organizations (**JCAHO**). This organization provides accreditation to different types of health care facilities. If a facility is statutorily compliant, and has the approval of the JCAHO, there is an initial basis to defend allegations relating to a failure to provide a safe environment with adequate care, monitoring, supervision, and assistance for patients. The difficulty arises when the facts of the particular case allege that the accreditation requirements were not, in fact, met on that occasion.

Generally, a health care facility must possess JCAHO approval to obtain and keep professional liability insurance. This accreditation is a form of assurance to the insurer that the provider meets minimum standards for facility safety. Also, the JCAHO monitors the continuing operation of facilities with standards for operation and periodic reaccreditation. In 2001, the JCAHO issued a controversial standard that requires any unanticipated outcome in the delivery of health care to be disclosed to the patient. Many argued that this would, in fact, drive up the incidence of malpractice by arming patients with information that might support a claim of malpractice. However, the position of the JCAHO is that from an ethical and practical point of view, it creates a more positive and open relationship with patients and in turn reduces the risk of malpractice suits.

Hospitals

The most common defendant in cases against health care facilities in the past has been the hospital. It is only in recent years that there has been a significant growth of other types of health care facilities. Cases alleging hospital malpractice date back nearly as far as cases against physicians in the American legal system. In the early cases, the foundation of suits was most often based on the theory of respondeat superior for the conduct of hospital employees. Specifically, it was common to allege the hospital was responsible for the negligent conduct of physicians or nurses who were employees. While these cases involving physicians are still filed today, they are increasingly less frequent as most hospitals do not employ physicians but rather provide them with practice privileges as independent contractors in a cooperative effort.

In early cases of malpractice against hospitals, many were held immune from liability. Throughout the 1800s and early into the 1900s, if a hospital was a purely charitable organization, it could not be held liable for the negligent acts of employees who had been originally selected and hired with due care. The rationale prevailed that because these hospitals made and kept no profits and turned any income back into the charitable service of the hospital, they were not in a position to pay judgments. This was compounded by the fact that they provided such a valuable service to the public, and especially those in need of charity, that, as a matter of public policy, they should not be subjected to monetary judgments which could jeopardize their very existence.

The rule of charitable immunity continued its popularity throughout the early 1900s. However, it created an avenue of escape from liability for medical facilities regardless of the degree of improper conduct by their employees. The question was no longer one of whether the patient had been injured as the result of the negligence of another. Rather, the patient had to establish that the hospital knew, or should have known, the lack of skill, training, or ability of the employee at the time of hiring. This was next to impossible in most cases and left many injured parties without genuine recourse. They could file an action against the employee as an individual, but most hospital employees were without sufficient assets to satisfy any judgment.

It should be noted that at the time the rule of charitable immunity developed, there was no professional liability insurance for such occurrences. There was also a shortage of facilities to provide adequate health care, especially for those without financial means. The greater public good was served by allowing immunity for those organizations that provided a source of medical care without the objective of personal gain or profit, but over time the circumstances began to change. More and more public funding was used to erect medical facilities such as hospitals. Many were associated with public universities and contributed to medical research and the advancement of medical science. Also, insurance companies began offering liability insurance as a source of funding for potential judgments in cases of alleged malpractice. As a result, the courts began to question the continued need for the charitable immunity rule. In 1957, a court in New York expressly abandoned the rule. For the reasons stated above, the charitable immunity rule was no longer seen as necessary as a matter of public policy. Many courts in other jurisdictions quickly followed suit.

CASE

2 N.Y.2d 656, 143 N.E.2d 3, 163 N.Y.S.2d 3

Court of Appeals of New York.

Isabel BING, Appellant, et al., Plaintiff,
v.
Louis A. THUNIG, Defendant, and St. John's Episcopal Hospital, Respondent.

May 16, 1957.

FULD, Judge.

Following Schloendorff v. Society of New York Hosp., 211 N.Y. 125, 105 N.E. 92, 52 L.R.A.,N.S., 505, a body of law has developed making the liability of a hospital for injuries suffered by a patient, through the negligence of its employees, depend on whether the injury-producing act was 'administrative' or 'medical.' The wisdom and workability of this rule exempting hospitals from the normal operation of the doctrine of respondeat superior have in recent years come under increasing attack. Decision in the present case calls upon us to say whether the rule should longer endure.

The plaintiff, Isabel Bing, was severely burned during the course of an operation, performed at St. John's Episcopal Hospital by her own physician, for correction of a fissure of the anus. She had been made ready for the operation, before the surgeon's appearance, by the hospital anesthetist and by two nurses also in the employ of the hospital. Preparatory to administering spinal anesthesia, the anesthetist painted the lumbar region of the patient's back with an alcoholic antiseptic, tincture of zephiran, an inflammable fluid, reddish in color. Again, after induction of the spinal anesthesia, one of the nurses applied the zephiran solution to the operative area. At that time there were three layers of sheeting under the patient.

The nurses were fully aware that the inflammable antiseptic employed was potentially dangerous. They acknowledged that they had been instructed, not only to exercise care to see that none of the fluid dropped on the linen, but to inspect it and remove any that had become stained or contaiminated. However, they made no inspection, and the sheets originally placed under the patient remained on the table throughout the operation.

The surgeon was not in the operating room when the antiseptic was applied and at least 15 munutes elapsed before he initiated the preoperative draping process. The draping completed, the doctor took a heated electric cautery and touched it to the fissure to mark it before beginning the actual searing of the

(continued)

tissue. There was a 'smell of very hot singed linen' and, 'without waiting to see a flame or smoke', he doused the area with water. Assured that the fire was out, he proceeded with the operation. Subsequent examination of the patient revealed severe burns on her body, later inspection of the linen, several holes burned through the sheet under her.

In the action thereafter brought against the hospital and the surgeon to recover for the injuries suffered, there was a verdict against both. As to the hospital, with whose liability we are alone concerned, the court charged that that defendant could be held liable only if plaintiff's injuries occurred through the negligence of one of its employees while performing an 'administrative,' as contrasted with a 'medical,' act. Upon appeal, the Appellate Division by a closely divided vote reversed and dismissed the complaint. The majority of three, reasoning that the application of the antiseptic was in preparation for the operation and, therefore, part of the operation itself, concluded that the injury resulted from a 'medical' act.

As is apparent, the liability asserted against the hospital is predicated on an independent act or omission of the hospital-employed nurses, and not on any conduct of theirs ordered or directed by a visiting doctor or surgeon or, for that matter, by any physician. The evidence strongly supports the findings, implicit in the jury's verdict, that some of the inflammable zephiran solution had dropped on the sheet beneath the plaintiff's body, that it had left a stain discoverable upon inspection, that the nurses in attendance had had full opportunity, before the beginning of the operation, to remove the stained linen and that the solution (which had dropped on the sheet) had given off a gaseous vapor that ignited upon contact with the heated cautery. In the light of these facts, the jury was thoroughly justified in concluding that the failure of the nurses to remove the contaminated vapor-producing linen constituted the plainest sort of negligence.

But, contends the hospital such negligence occurred during the performance of a 'medical' act and, accordingly, under the so-called Schloendorff rule, the doctrine of respondeat superior may not be applied to subject it to liability. The difficulty of differentiating between the 'medical' and the 'administrative' in this context, highlighted as it is by the disagreement of the judges below, is thus brought into sharp focus.

That difficulty has long plagued the courts and, indeed, as consideration of a few illustrative cases reveals, a consistent and clearly defined distinction between the terms has proved to be highly elusive. Placing an improperly capped hot water bottle on a patient's body is administrative (Iacono v. New York Polyclinic Med. School & Hosp., 296 N.Y. 502, 68 N.E.2d 450), while keeping a hot water bottle too long on a patient's body is medical (Sutherland v. New York Polyclinic Med. School & Hosp., 298 N.Y. 682, 82 N.E.2d 583). Administering blood, by means of a transfusion, to the wrong patient is administrative (Necolayff v. Genesee Hosp., 296 N.Y. 936, 73 N.E.2d 117), while administering the wrong blood to the right patient is medical (Berg v. New York Soc. for Relief of Ruptured & Crippled, 1 N.Y.2d 499, 154 N.Y.S.2d 455, reversing 286 App.Div. 783, 146 N.Y.S.2d 548). Employing an improperly **5 sterilized needle for a hypodermic injection is administrative (Peck v. Charles B. Towns Hosp., 275 App.Div. 302, 89 N.Y.S.2d 190), while improperly administering a hypodermic injection is medical (Bryant v. Presbyterian Hosp. in City of N. Y., 304 N.Y. 538, 110 N.E.2d 391). Failing to place sideboards on a bed after a nurse decided that they were necessary is administrative (Ranelli v. Society of N. Y. Hosp., 295 N.Y. 850, 67 N.E.2d 257), while failing decide that sideboards should be used when the need does exist is medical (Grace v. Manhattan Eye, Ear & Throat Hosp., 301 N.Y. 660, 93 N.E.2d 926).

From distinctions such as these there is to be deduced neither guiding principle nor clear delineation of policy; they cannot help but cause confusion, cannot help but create doubt and uncertainty. And, while the failure of the nurses in the present case to inspect and remove the contaminated linen might, perhaps, be denominated an administrative default, we do not consider it either wise or necessary again to become embroiled in an overnice disputation as to whether it should be labeled administrative or medical. The distinctions, it has been noted, were the result of 'a judicial policy of compromise between the doctrines of respondeat superior and total immunity for charitable institutions.' (Bobbe , Tort Liability of Hospitals in

(continued)

New York, 37 Corn.L.Q. 419, 438.) The better to understand the problem presented, a brief backward glance into historical beginnings proves profitable.

The doctrine declaring charitable institutions immune from liability was first declared in this country in 1876. McDonald v. Massachusetts Gen. Hosp., 120 Mass. 432. Deciding that a charity patient, negligently operated upon by a student doctor, could not hold the hospital responsible, the court reasoned that the public and private donations that supported the charitable hospital constituted a trust fund which could not be diverted. As sole authority for its conclusion, the Massachusetts court relied on an English case (Holliday v. St. Leonard's, 11 C.B.N.S. 192, 142 Eng.Rep. 769), which in turn was based on a dictum in a case decided in 1839 (Duncan v. Findlater, 6 Cl. & Fin. 894, 7 Eng.Rep. 934), failing, apparently, to note that the dictum in the earlier case had been overruled (see Mersey Docks Trustees v. Gibbs, 11 H.L.Cas. 686) and that the decision in the other had been reversed. (See Foreman v. Mayor of Canterbury, 6 Q.B. 214.) At any rate, after the McDonald case was decided (supra, 120 Mass. 432), other courts in this country, through not all on the same theory or for the same reason, followed the lead of Massachusetts in exempting the charitable hospital from liability, and so in time did the courts of New York. (See 4 Scott on Trusts (2d ed., 1956), s 402, p. 2895 et seq.; Bobbe , supra, 37 Corn.L.Q. 419, 420-425.

Although it was not the first case to deal with the general subject in this state, Schloendorff v. New York Hosp. (supra, 211 N.Y. 125, 105 N.E. 92, 52 L.R.A.,N.S., 505) was the most important of the early decisions to be handed down by this court. It was there declared broadly that a charitable hospital was not responsible for the negligence of its physicians and nurses in the treatment of patients. Two reasons were assigned for that conclusion. The first was that one who seeks and accepts charity must be deemed to have waived any right to damages for injuries suffered through the negligence of his benefactor's servants and yet the rule was not limited to charity patients but was expanded to cover both paying patients and a private or profit-making hospital. See Bakal v. University Heights Sanitarium, 302 N.Y. 870, 100 N.E.2d 51, affirming 277 App.Div. 572, 101 N.Y.S.2d 385; Steinert v. Brunswick Home, 172 Misc. 787, 16 N.Y.S.2d 83, affirmed 259 App.Div. 1018, 20 N.Y.S.2d 459, motion for leave to appeal denied 284 N.Y. 822, 31 N.E.2d 517. The second reason which the court advanced was that the principle of respondeat superior was not to be applied to doctors and nurses. It was the court's though that, even though employed by the hospital, they were to be regarded as independent contractors rather than employees because of the skill they exercised and the lack of control exerted over their work and yet, we pause again to interpolate, the special skill of other employees (such as airplane pilots, locomotive engineers, chemists, to mention but a few) has never been the basis for denying the application of respondeat superior and, even more to the point, that very principle has been invoked to render a public hospital accountable for the negligence of its doctors, nurses and other skilled personnel. See Becker v. City of New York, 2 N.Y.2d 226, 159 N.Y.S.2d 174; Liubowsky v. State of New York, 285 N.Y. 701, 34 N.E.2d 385, affirming 260 App.Div. 416, 23 N.Y.S.2d 633.

The Schloendorff rule has pursued an inconstant course, riddled with numerous exceptions and subjected to various qualifications and refinements. While it would serve no useful purpose to trace in detail the doctrinal changes and modifications or the shifting theories advanced to support them, we briefly note two or three of the more striking instances. We have already remarked the qualification which excepts public hospitals, those owned by the state or city, from the operation of the Schloendorff rule and from the application of the medical-administrative distinction. See, e. g., Becker v. City of New York, supra, 2 N.Y.2d 226, 159 N.Y.S.2d 174; Liubowsky v. State of New York, supra, 285 N.Y. 701, 34 N.E.2d 385, affirming 260 App.Div. 416, 23 N.Y.S.2d 633. And in Berg v. New York Soc. for Relief of Ruptured & Crippled, supra, 1 N.Y.2d 499, 154 N.Y.S.2d 455, reversing 286 App.Div. 783, 146 N.Y.S.2d 548, the court carved another large segment out of that rule by holding that those distinctions were to be discarded in every case in which the injury-producing act was performed by a nonprofessional employee.

(continued)

The cases to which we have adverted do not merely illustrate fluctuation of doctrine and the vicissitudes of judgment. They rather demonstrate the inherent incongruity of the immunity rule itself. A distinction unique in the law should rest on stronger foundations than those advanced. Indeed, the first ground stated in Schloendorff, namely, that there is a waiver by the patient of his right to recover for negligent injury, has long been abandoned as 'logically weak' and 'pretty much a fiction.' Phillips v. Buffalo Gen. Hosp., 239 N.Y. 188, 189, 146 N.E. 199; Sheehan v. North Country Community Hosp., 273 N.Y. 163, 166, 7 N.E.2d 28, 29, 109 A.L.R. 1197. The second ground that professional personnel, such as doctors, nurses and internes, **7 should be deemed independent contractors, though salaried employees is inconsistent with what they have been held to be in every other context and, to a large extent, even in this one. For example, the nurse, regarded as an independent contractor when she injures a patient by an act characterized as medical, is considered an employee of the hospital, entitled to compensation, if she should happen to injure herself by that very same act. Bernstein v. Beth Israel Hosp., 236 N.Y. 268, 140 N.E. 694, 30 A.L.R. 598. Further, in holding the city responsible for injuries sustained through the carelessness of members of the staff of a city hospital, not only did we recognize that they were employees, to whom the doctrine of respondeat superior applies, but we noted the anomaly of treating as independent contractors 'persons, who by all other tests are clearly employees'. Becker v. City of New York, supra, 2 N.Y.2d 226, 235, 159 N.Y.S.2d 174, 183; and cf. Mrachek v. Sunshine Biscuit, 308 N.Y. 116, 123 N.E.2d 801.

Nor may the exemption be justified by the fear, the major impetus originally behind the doctrine, that the imposition of liability will do irreparable harm to the charitable hospital. At the time the rule originated, in the middle of the nineteenth century, not only was there the possibility that a substantial award in a single negligence action might destroy the hospital, but concern was felt that a ruling permitting recovery against the funds of charitable institutions might discourage generosity and 'constrain * * * (them), as a measure of self-protection, to limit their activities.' Schloendorff v. New York Hosp., supra, 211 N.Y. 125, 135, 105 N.E. 92, 95, 52 L.R.A.,N.S., 505. Whatever problems today beset the charitable hospital and they are not to be minimized, the dangers just noted have become less acute. Quite apart from the availability of insurance to protect against possible claims and lawsuits, we are not informed that undue hardships or calamities have overtaken them in those jurisdictions where immunity is withheld and liability imposed. See, e. g., President and Directors of Georgetown Coll. v. Hughes, 76 U.S.App.D.C. 123, 130 F.2d 810, 823-824; Cohen v. General Hosp. Soc., 113 Conn. 188, 193, 154 A. 435; Pierce v. Yakima Val. Memorial Hosp. Ass'n, 43 Wash.2d 162, 171- 172, 260 P.2d 765. In any event, today's hospital is quite different from its predecessor of long ago; it receives wide community support, employs a large number of people and necessarily operates its plant in businesslike fashion.

Based on considerations such as those remarked in the preceding pages, and others, the trend of decision throughout the country has more and more been away from nonliability. See, e. g., President and Directors of Georgetown Coll. v. Hughes, supra, 76 U.S.App.D.C. 123, 130 F.2d 810, 818-822; Pierce v. Yakima Val. Memorial Hosp. Ass'n, supra, 43 Wash.2d 162, 175-177, 260 P.2d 765; Note, 25 A.L.R.2d 29. As one court observed, 'American judicial thinking, which formerly gave 'overwhelming' acceptance to the immunity rule, now gives that doctrine a very modest majority.' Pierce v. Yakima Val. Memorial Hosp. Ass'n, supra, 43 Wash.2d 162, 177, 260 P.2d 765, 773. In point of fact, a survey of recent cases those decided since the middle 1940's demonstrates, not only that the immunity rule has been rejected in every jurisdiction where the court was unfettered by precedent but that the doctrine has been overruled and abandoned in a number of state where nonliability had long been the rule.

Although we have hitherto refrained from pronouncing 'the ultimate fate' of the Schloendorff rule (Becker v. City of New York, supra, 2 N.Y.2d 226, 235, 159 N.Y.S.2d 174, 182; Berg v. New York Soc. for Relief of Ruptured & Crippled, supra, 1 N.Y.2d 499, 503, 154 N.Y.S.2d 455, 457), we have long indicated our

(continued)

dissatisfaction with it, and only last year, in further expanding the hospital's liability, the court posed this searching and suggestive question (1 N.Y.2d 499, 502, 154 N.Y.S.2d 455, 456): 'What reason compels us to say that of all employees working in their employers' businesses (including charitable, educational, religious and governmental enterprises) the only ones for whom the employers can escape liability are the employees of hospitals?'

The doctrine of respondeat superior is grounded on firm principles of law and justice. Liability is the rule, immunity the exception. It is not too much to expect that those who serve and minister to members of the public should do so, as do all others, subject to that principle and within the obligation not to injure through carelessness. It is not alone good morals but sound law that individuals and organizations should be just before they are generous, and there is no reason why that should not apply to charitable hospitals. 'Charity suffereth long and is kind, but in the common law it cannot be careless. When it is, it ceases to be kindness and becomes actionable wrongdoing.' President and Directors of Georgetown Coll. v. Hughes, supra, 76 U.S.App.D.C. 123, 130 F.2d 810, 813. Insistence upon respondeat superior and damages for negligent injury serves a two-fold purpose, for it both assures payment of an obligation to the person injured and gives warning that justice and the law demand the exercise of care.

The conception that the hospital does not undertake to treat the patient, does not undertake to act through its doctors and nurses, but undertakes instead simply to procure them to act upon their own responsibility, no longer reflects the fact. Present-day hospitals, as their manner of operation plainly demonstrates, do far more than furnish facilities for treatment. They regularly employ on a salary basis a large staff of physicians, nurses and internes, as well as administrative and manual workers, and they charge patients for medical care and treatment, collecting for such services, if necessary, by legal action. Certainly, the person who avails himself of 'hospital facilities' expects that the hospital will attempt to cure him, not that it nurses or other employees will act on their own responsibility.

Hospitals should, in short, shoulder the responsibilities borne by everyone else. There is no reason to continue their exemption from the universal rule of respondeat superior. The test should be, for these institutions, whether charitable or profit-making, as it is for every other employer, was the person who committed the negligent injury-producing act one of its employees and, if he was, was he acting within the scope of his employment.

The rule of nonliability is out of tune with the life about us, at variance with modern-day needs and with concepts of justice and fair dealing. It should be discarded. To the suggestion that stare decisis compels us to perpetuate it until the legislature acts, a ready answer is at hand. It was intended, not to effect a 'petrifying rigidity,' but to assure the justice that flows from certainty and stability. If, instead, adherence to precedent offers not justice but unfairness, not certainty but doubt and confusion, it loses its right to survive, and no principle constrains us to follow it. On the contrary, as this court, speaking through Judge Desmond in Woods v. Lancet, 303 N.Y. 349, 355, 102 N.E.2d 691, 694, 27 A.L.R.2d 1250, declared, we would be abdicating 'our own function, in a field peculiarly nonstatutory,' were we to insist on legislation and 'refuse to reconsider an old and unsatisfactory court-made rule.'

In sum, then, the doctrine according the hospital an immunity for the negligence of its employees is such a rule, and we abandon it. The hospital's liability must be governed by the same principles of law as apply to all other employers.

The judgment of the Appellate Division should be reversed and a new trial granted, with costs to abide the event.

In recent years, the legislatures have stepped in on many occasions and limited the liability in monetary awards against charitable organizations. The reasoning is much the same as for the original doctrine of charitable immunity. The public service these institutions provide is an important and necessary element of our medical care system. The cost of liability insurance has continued to increase to the point that it threatens the ability of charitable organizations to continue to pay for it. Without such insurance, a single judgment could cause a charitable organization to face bankruptcy. By limiting the awards, the threat of colossal judgments is eliminated, and therefore insurance companies can issue policies at a more reasonable rate. Other statutes limit the liability of hospitals in certain circumstances where they undertake to provide short-term care for patients who are mentally unstable and pose a high risk of danger to themselves or others. The reasoning behind this is that hospitals are providing a public service by accepting such patients as an alternative to being placed in custody and consequently the hospital should not be held accountable if the patient later objects to the method or form of treatment administered while they were considered dangerous and unable to provide consent. This, of course, excludes circumstances when the patient was injured through negligence or deliberate conduct.

111 Cal.App.4th 735, 3 Cal.Rptr.3d 903, (2003)

Court of Appeal, Fourth District, Division 1, California.

Arturo A. GONZALEZ et al., Plaintiffs and Appellants,
v.
PARADISE VALLEY HOSPITAL et al., Defendants and Respondents.
Aug. 26, 2003.

McCONNELL, J.

Arturo had a history of paranoid schizophrenia. On the evening of September 26, 1999, Arturo, after a period of not taking his medication, attempted to choke his mother. National City police officers took him to the Hospital's emergency room and requested that he be detained on a 72-hour hold under section 5150. Arturo was agitated and "clearly psychotic." He ran out the door, but officers returned him to the emergency room where he was placed in restraints and medicated. Dr. Highum, a psychiatrist, ordered that Arturo be transferred to the Hospital's locked psychiatric unit for a 72-hour hold on the ground he posed a threat to others.

The following morning, Dr. Highum examined Arturo and concluded he remained a danger to others. Dr. Highum noted Arturo's "[t]hought content was without current suicidal or homicidal ideation, obsessions or compulsions," but he was suspicious and having auditory hallucinations. Dr. Highum treated Arturo with Haldol Decanoate, which Arturo reported "worked relatively well for him previously."

That afternoon, Arturo broke through a window in the psychiatric unit and escaped. He left the hospital grounds, entered a nearby apartment, which was occupied, and grabbed a kitchen knife and cut his throat and abdomen. Police arrived and Arturo obeyed their order to come outside. However, the police shot him and inflicted mortal wounds.

(continued)

The Gonzalezes sued the Hospital and Dr. Highum for professional malpractice. In a first amended complaint, the Gonzalezes alleged the defendants knew or should have known Arturo was at risk for escape, and they negligently failed to "provide adequate treatment and medication for his mental illness," "failed to provide adequate supervision by observing [him] ... at regular intervals," and "failed to provide adequate restraints, security, and proper facilities," and as a foreseeable consequence of the negligence Arturo was shot and killed by police officers. The Gonzalezes alleged Dr. Highum was acting within the scope of an agency or employment relationship with the Hospital.

The Hospital moved for summary judgment on the grounds it met the applicable standard of care and its conduct was not a legal cause of Arturo's death, and in any event, under section 5278 it is immune from liability for any medical malpractice or other negligence occurring during a proper 72-hour hold. For the latter argument, the Hospital relied on this court's opinion in *Heater, supra,* 42 Cal.App.4th 1068, 49 Cal.Rptr.2d 880.

In opposition to the motion, the Gonzalezes argued *Heater* does not stand for the proposition section 5278 confers absolute immunity on health care providers for negligent treatment of a patient detained on a 72-hour hold. The Gonzalezes also argued there are "triable issues of fact as to whether [the Hospital's] psychiatric lockdown facility was compliant with building codes and the standard of care in the industry," whether Arturo "was properly supervised during his detention, and whether he received the appropriate anti-psychotic medications and care required to treat his condition."

In support, the Gonzalezes submitted the declaration of their expert, psychiatrist Clark E. Smith. In Dr Smith's opinion, Dr. Highum knew or should have known Arturo was "a dangerously unstable, acutely psychotic patient, at extremely high risk for elopement," and he breached the standard of care by not giving Arturo medication "for stabilization for acute psychosis." According to Dr. Smith, Haldol Decanoate is a "short term sedating medication" that "requires six days to reach a peak effect," and the drug is "intended to be used on patients that have been stabilized on short acting antipsychotic medications." Dr. Smith believed it was "extremely unlikely that ... Arturo ... had received any therapeutic effect from the Haldol Decanoate shot given approximately two hours before he died." Further, Dr. Smith believed the Hospital was negligent in placing Arturo "in a room without adequate observation and with breakable windows which allowed the means" for his escape.

Citing *Heater, supra,* 42 Cal.App.4th 1068, 49 Cal.Rptr.2d 880, the court granted the Hospital's motion on the sole ground of immunity under section 5278. Dr. Highum separately moved for summary judgment on the same ground, and the court granted the motion. Judgments for the Hospital and Dr. Highum were entered on February 11, 2002, and April 4, 2002, respectively.

A "party moving for summary judgment bears the burden of persuasion that there is no triable issue of material fact and that he [or she] is entitled to judgment as a matter of law." (*Aguilar v. Atlantic Richfield Co.* (2001) 25 Cal.4th 826, 850, 107 Cal.Rptr.2d 841, 24 P.3d 493.) A defendant satisfies this burden by showing " 'one or more elements of' the 'cause of action' in question 'cannot be established,' or that 'there is a complete defense' " to that cause of action. (*Ibid.*) If the defendant meets his or her initial burden, "the opposing party is then subjected to a burden of production of his [or her] own to make a prima facie showing of the existence of a triable issue of material fact." (*Ibid.*) We review rulings on summary judgment motions independently. (*Rubenstein v. Rubenstein* (2000) 81 Cal.App.4th 1131, 1143, 97 Cal.Rptr.2d 707.)

In California, the Lanterman-Petris-Short Act (LPS Act) (§ 5000 et seq.) governs the involuntary treatment of the mentally disordered. (*Conservatorship of Susan T.* (1994) 8 Cal.4th 1005, 36 Cal.Rptr.2d 40, 884 P.2d 988.) Under the LPS Act, a designated facility may detain a person for up to 72 hours for evaluation and treatment if there is "probable cause to believe that the person is, as a result of mental disorder, a danger to others, or to himself or herself, or gravely disabled." (§ 5150; see also § 5151.) "Each person admitted to a facility for 72-hour treatment and evaluation ... shall receive an evaluation as soon after he or she is

(continued)

admitted as possible and shall receive whatever treatment and care his or her condition requires for the full period that he or she is held." (§ 5152, subd. (a).)

Section 5278 provides in part: "Individuals authorized under this part to detain a person for 72-hour treatment and evaluation pursuant to Article I (commencing with Section 5150) ... shall not be held either criminally or civilly liable for exercising this authority in accordance with the law." The Gonzalezes contend the immunity does not extend to negligent treatment during the confinement. The defendants counter that under *Heater, supra,* 42 Cal.App.4th 1068, 49 Cal.Rptr.2d 880, any negligence committed during a legal 72-hour hold is within section 5278's scope of immunity.

In *Heater,* this court stated "no other conclusion is possible than that section 5278 means precisely what it says it means, and that civil liability, whether for battery, for false imprisonment, or for medical malpractice is precluded insofar as the detention is 'in accordance with the law.' " (*Heater, supra,* 42 Cal.App.4th at p. 1083, 49 Cal.Rptr.2d 880.) In that case, however, the only alleged wrongful act discussed was the administration of a tranquilizer without the plaintiff's consent. The plaintiff's assault and battery cause of action was based on the lack of consent, and there is no suggestion the medical malpractice claim was based on other conduct. In our recent decision in *Jacobs, supra,* 108 Cal.App.4th at page 77, 133 Cal.Rptr.2d 9, we cautioned that *Heater's* discussion of section 5278's applicability to medical malpractice claims is limited to the facts presented there.

The scope of immunity afforded by section 5278 is a legal question governed by rules of statutory construction. "A court's overriding purpose in construing a statute is to ascertain legislative intent and to give the statute a reasonable construction conforming to that intent. [Citation.] In interpreting a statute to determine legislative intent, a court looks first to the words of the statute and gives them their usual and ordinary meaning." (*Home Depot, U.S.A., Inc. v. Contractors' State License Bd.* (1996) 41 Cal.App.4th 1592, 1600, 49 Cal.Rptr.2d 302.) "If the language is clear and unambiguous, the plain meaning of the statute governs." (*Ford v. Norton* (2001) 89 Cal.App.4th 974, 981, 107 Cal.Rptr.2d 776.) "The words of a statute must be construed in context and provisions relating to the same subject matter must be harmonized to the extent possible." (*Ibid.*)

" 'The LPS Act must be construed to promote the intent of the Legislature, among other things, to end the inappropriate, indefinite and involuntary commitment of mentally disordered persons, to provide prompt evaluation and treatment *and to protect mentally disordered persons* (§ 5001).' [Citation.]" (*Jacobs, supra,* 108 Cal.App.4th at p. 75, 133 Cal.Rptr.2d 9, quoting *Michael E.L. v. County of San Diego* (1986) 183 Cal.App.3d 515, 525, 228 Cal.Rptr. 139.)

In *Jacobs,* we concluded that in enacting section 5278, the Legislature did not intend to immunize health care providers from liability for breaches of the applicable standards of care during the period of confinement. (*Jacobs, supra,* 108 Cal.App.4th at p. 79, 133 Cal.Rptr.2d 9.) Here, we affirm our conclusion that section 5278 is inapplicable to actions for negligence stemming from acts or omissions in evaluation or treatment during 72-hour holds.

Section 5278 provides that "[i]ndividuals authorized ... to detain a person for 72-hour treatment and evaluation pursuant to Article 1 (commencing with Section 5150) ... shall not be held either criminally or civilly liable *for exercising this authority in accordance with the law.*" (§ 5278, italics added.) The italicized language shows the Legislature's intent to protect health care providers from any liability for intentional torts arising from the exercise of (1) the statutory authority to involuntarily detain mentally ill persons, upon probable cause, and (2) the statutory mandate to promptly evaluate and treat detained persons. (§ § 5150, 5151; *Jacobs, supra,* 108 Cal.App.4th at p. 78, 133 Cal.Rptr.2d 9.) "Without the immunity provided by

(continued)

section 5278, an involuntary detention and treatment without consent would arguably constitute kidnapping, false imprisonment, or battery." (*Jacobs, supra,* at p. 78, 133 Cal.Rptr.2d 9.)

The protected conduct is confined to the *exercise* of statutory authority to detain, evaluate and treat against the patient's wishes, and does not extend to the *manner* in which evaluation and treatment are carried out. In other words, liability arising from negligent evaluation or treatment is not liability arising from the "exercis[e of] this authority in accordance with the law." (§ 5278.) The interpretation of section 5278 the defendants urge is contrary to its language, and would undermine a purpose of the Legislature in enacting the LPS Act, protection of mentally ill persons. Any intent of the Legislature to confer an immunity that would deny involuntarily detained persons redress for injuries caused by evaluation or treatment falling below the standard of professional care should be expressly stated.

Dr. Highum contends his alleged negligence is immunized because "[k]eeping an involuntarily-detained patient confined in a hospital ... during a 72-hour hold is inherent in a detention pursuant to ... section 5150." Dr. Highum relies on the following language from *Jacobs, supra,* 108 Cal.App.4th at pages 78- 79, 133 Cal.Rptr.2d 9: "[T]he scope of section 5278 immunity extends to claims based on facts that are inherent in an involuntary detention pursuant to section 5150. If there is probable cause for the detention, the statute therefore provides immunity for the decision to detain as well as for the detention and its inherent attributes, including the fact that the patient must necessarily be evaluated and treated without consent.... However, the immunity does not extend to *other* negligent acts, intentional torts, or criminal wrongs committed during the course of the detention, evaluation, or treatment." (Italics added.) We clarify here that the immunity of section 5278 does not extend to any negligent acts, and the inclusion of the word "other" in *Jacobs* was unintended. As we went on to hold in *Jacobs, supra,* at page 79, 133 Cal.Rptr.2d 9, "section 5278 does not provide immunity for injuries proximately caused by negligence."

Additionally, Dr. Highum cites Government Code section 856.2, subdivision (a)(2), which immunizes public entities and their employees from liability for an "injury to, or the wrongful death of, an escaping or escaped person who has been confined for mental illness or addiction." Dr. Highum points out that in *Jacobs,* we found our interpretation of Welfare and Institutions Code section 5278 is consistent with its statutory counterpart, Government Code section 856, which immunizes public entities and their employees from liability for injuries arising from the determination of whether to confine a person for mental illness or addiction, the terms and conditions of the confinement, and whether to release a confined person, if such determinations are "*carr[ied] out with due care.*" (Gov.Code, § 856, subds. (a) & (b), italics added.) "Public employees are specifically *not* exonerated from liability for injuries proximately caused by their negligent or wrongful acts or omissions in carrying out or failing to carry out the specified determinations. (Gov.Code, § 856, subd. (c).)" (*Jacobs, supra,* 108 Cal.App.4th at p. 79, 133 Cal.Rptr.2d 9.) However, the LPS Act includes no provision such as Government Code section 856.2, subdivision (a)(2), and any corresponding immunity for the private sector must come from the Legislature.

The Gonzalezes alleged Arturo's death was proximately caused by defendants' negligence during his detention, specifically, Dr. Highum's failure to appropriately treat his psychosis and the Hospital's failure to adequately supervise and observe him and its provision of inadequate facilities. The Gonzalezes raised triable issues of fact regarding their negligence claims, and thus the summary judgments were improper.

The judgments are reversed. The Gonzalezes are awarded costs on appeal.

More general cases of liability of hospitals frequently allege inadequate care, monitoring, supervision, or medical staff on duty. In all of these cases a common question is considered in the courts. The cases typically turn on the degree to which the patient's medical condition, either naturally occurring or induced by treatment, affects the patient's ability to provide for his or her own safety and care. This means that if a patient, who is in general control of their physical movement and mental ability, happens to be injured while within the confines of a hospital as a result of their own actions and not misconduct or malfeasance of another, there will probably not be a finding of negligence. In Application 3.7, a similar case demonstrates how the outcome of a case can change dramatically with a slight change in facts.

APPLICATION 3.7

Suzanne is admitted to the hospital for the delivery of her first child. Two days after the baby is delivered, Suzanne is scheduled to be discharged. As she waits for the doctor to discharge her, she decides to seize the opportunity for some rest and lowers the rail on her hospital bed and climbs in to lie down. As she naps in her bed and, being used to a king-size bed at home, she rolls out of the bed onto the floor, fracturing her leg. In this case, Suzanne was under no physical or mental disability. She herself had lowered the safety rail on the side of the bed. The viability of her claims would be questionable at best.

However, consider the following change of facts: Suzanne undergoes a complicated Caesarean delivery of her baby and is heavily sedated with pain medication. Shortly after surgery she awakes, locates the call button, and asks for help getting out of bed to go to the bathroom. The nurse responds over the intercom that Suzanne is confined to bedrest for the time being. The nurse states she will be along shortly to help Suzanne. After waiting approximately 20 minutes, Suzanne attempts to use the call button again but finds it has fallen from the bed and she cannot reach it. She tries to get out of bed to go to the bathroom on her own. She falls and is severely injured. In this instance, Suzanne was not able to provide adequately for her own needs and the nursing staff would likely be found to have provided inadequate monitoring, assistance, and supervision. If it can be shown that the hospital unit was inadequately staffed for the number of patients, this may also support a cause of action.

While medical records are an invaluable resource to record incidents involving injuries to patients, they are not always complete. Keep in mind that the very parties documenting the incident are the potential defendants which can lead to records of injuries that may be less than detailed in some cases. The presumption is that the information within them is accurate but it is always advisable to consult all available records for consistency and be particularly suspicious of any alterations or amendments. If records are incomplete, or contrary to what one would expect, it is important to keep in mind the possible use of the theory of res ipsa loquitur. This theory is used by a plaintiff in cases where the plaintiff's own memory of relevant events may not be intact as the result of their medical condition or medication influence at the time of the alleged incident.

Ultimately, hospitals are likely to be defendants when alleged malpractice occurs to a patient who is subject to the care of the hospital. The circumstance may be regarding faulty equipment, employee conduct, or inadequately trained staff; each can result in a lawsuit if the facts support the claimed injury.

Clinics Offering Outpatient Services

Those facilities which offer outpatient services exclusively are under the same obligations with regard to legal principles of medical malpractice as are hospitals. They are required to provide adequate treatment, monitoring, and supervision necessary to the particular ability of the patient who submits to their care. Failure to do so can result in liability. Like hospitals, the clinics may be sued consequent to acts or omissions of employees, faulty equipment, or failure to provide adequately trained staff for the services offered. The only significant difference is that the patient typically does not have the incapacity normally associated with one admitted to a traditional hospital. Now that more and more procedures that were traditionally performed in hospitals are being performed in outpatient facilities, this is an area of increased risk for the clinic. For example, many outpatient facilities now undertake significant surgical procedures such as cosmetic surgery, many orthopedic procedures, and diagnostic procedures that require varying levels of anesthesia. Nevertheless, patients are often discharged on the same day—before they are fully conscious and alert and certainly before they are able to transport themselves home—creating a high risk for claims of malpractice if sufficient steps are not taken to ensure that the patient is discharged from the facility in a safe manner.

Many outpatient facilities offer a variety of less impacting treatments to patients on a continuing basis. These include everything from simple dental care to allergy shots to something more involved, such as kidney dialysis. While the outpatient facility has a high degree of responsibility to care for the needs of these patients and may refer for more involved treatment when appropriate, the facility is not limitless in its responsibility. If the patient suffers from some malady about which the facility is unaware, they cannot be held accountable for failing to discover and treat the illness unless such diagnostic investigation was part of their routine care for the patient. See Application 3.8.

305 A2d 130, 759 NYS2d 65 (2003)
Jacqueline Barker, Respondent,
v.
St. Barnabas Hospital et al., Defendants, and Albert Einstein College of Medicine of Yeshiva University, Appellant.

Supreme Court, Appellate Division, First Department, New York

(May 6, 2003)

Order, Supreme Court, Bronx County (Joseph Giamboi, J.), entered March 7, 2001, which denied defendant Albert Einstein College of Medicine's motion for summary judgment, unanimously reversed, on the law, without costs, and the motion granted. The Clerk is directed to enter judgment in favor of defendant-appellant dismissing the complaint as against it.

Plaintiff's decedent, James Barker, received doses of methadone and provided a urine sample for toxicology screening at a methadone clinic operated by defendant Albert Einstein College of Medicine of Yeshiva University (Yeshiva) from June 1976 until his last visit on July 8, 1993. During his last visit, he also

(continued)

completed a health care proxy as was generally required for all patients. On May 24, 1993, Barker had fallen at his place of employment and fractured his left leg. Initially treated at Our Lady of Mercy Hospital, he was transferred to St. Barnabas Hospital, where he remained until he was discharged on June 2. On his discharge, he was subsequently treated by Dr. Tsamparlis as his primary care physician. On June 14, Barker visited his physician, complaining that his left heel was in pain. On July 14, he returned to that physician with an infection in his left leg and elevated temperature. Admitted to St. Barnabas Hospital, he was diagnosed with sepsis secondary to cellulitis and was treated with antibiotics, and he died on September 2, 1993. This action was then commenced and liability asserted against defendant Yeshiva based on alleged negligent treatment and failure to diagnose and treat. While Barker made weekly visits to Yeshiva's methadone clinic, he never complained about the condition of his leg and never requested medical treatment from Yeshiva. The admission records of St. Barnabas Hospital document that visible symptoms of Barker's leg infection only became evident three days prior to admission, a date subsequent to his last visit to Yeshiva. Yeshiva's summary judgment motion should have been granted since plaintiff's opposition consists of unfounded allegations by counsel regarding either imagined conversations which decedent may have had with Yeshiva's employees or presumed signs and symptoms which decedent might have exhibited during his July 8 visit to Yeshiva. Mere surmise or conclusory allegations are insufficient as a basis to deny summary judgment. There is no evidence of any treatment by Yeshiva with respect to decedent's leg and there is no basis upon which Yeshiva can be held to have had a duty to monitor the treatment being administered by decedent's treating physician (*see Alvarez v Prospect Hosp.*, 68 NY2d 320, 325 [1986]).

APPLICATION 3.8

Heather went to a dental clinic to have what was described to her in advance as a minor procedure to repair a damaged tooth using local anesthesia. The procedure was performed by a general dentist. In fact, the procedure involved oral surgery and typically was done under general anesthesia. Shortly after the procedure, Heather was sent home alone. At home, as the local anesthesia quickly wore off, she began to experience significant pain. She contacted the dental clinic office and was told by the receptionist to take some aspirin or acetaminophen and the pain would be gone by the following day. Heather did as she was directed. Two hours later the pain was becoming increasingly severe. She called again and asked to speak to the dentist. The receptionist repeated the same instruction as before. This time Heather took a much stronger pain medication that she had left over from a previous injury. More than an hour later the pain was becoming unbearable. She took another one of the strong pain pills with no relief. After another hour she called the dental clinic and demanded to be seen. She was now unable to drive due to the pain and influence of medications. It took her almost an hour to locate someone to take her in. When she arrived, the receptionist told Heather to go to the waiting room and she'd be seen when there was an opening. However, Heather's moaning became so loud it was disruptive to other patients and she was taken in for examination. When she was finally examined it was discovered that during the procedure, the dentist had not noticed an exposed nerve root and

(continued)

> had packed dental material on top of it causing serious damage to the nerve root. As a result, the material had to be removed and Heather subsequently had to undergo a root canal. Ultimately, two additional dental surgeries with an oral surgeon were required to correct the damage.
>
> In this case, Heather would likely have an action against the dental clinic based on failure to have adequately trained personnel respond to her concerns when she called in, and potentially an action against the clinic for allowing a general dentist to perform an oral surgery procedure.

Long-Term Care Facilities

The concept of the long-term care facility is something that has developed largely in the twentieth century. In the nineteeth century, prior to the industrial revolution and other changes in society, most families worked in or near their home. At that time, because medical science was at such an early stage of development, serious injuries or illness frequently resulted in either recovery or death in a fairly short period of time. The average life expectancy was also decades shorter than today. Thus, the need for long-term care of the aged, invalid, or infirm was much more limited than today. Most often, the facilities that did exist where patients lived out their lives were few and far between. Often the patients were confined to care for those diseases considered to be highly communicable and terminal such as tuberculosis or leprosy. Throughout the twentieth century, more and more able-bodied adult family members worked outside the home, leaving no one available to provide care for those unable to care for themselves. Medicine advanced dramatically and with it the average life expectancy. As a result, a need arose to provide a place to live for those who were no longer independent and/or who needed medical supervision and treatment. It is estimated that approximately nine million Americans resided in long-term care facilities in 2000 and that number is expected to grow. Today there is a vast array of facilities ranging from those providing care for the comatose to rehabilitation centers as a transitional living environment during recovery. The list also includes Alzheimer and elderly dementia facilities, residential locations for the developmentally disabled or mentally challenged, and traditional nursing homes. Frequently a facility will offer several types of care for patients who require varying levels of care that extend beyond the average hospital stay. The possibility of malpractice is an additional problem these facilities face because the care of such individuals often requires a certain degree of medical skill.

The legislation for long-term care facilities swelled dramatically in the late 1900s. Today, there are extensive regulatory and statutory rules of compliance for facilities providing a place to live and care for those who are not capable of independent living. The legal standards apply to everything from providing a safe physical environment secure from intruders to adequately trained staff—and everything in between. In addition, many states now have statutory "Patient's Bill of Rights" that provide a clear statement of the personal treatment to which every patient is entitled. Similar guarantees are also embodied in federal regulations. Violation of these may support a medical malpractice cause or be a separate basis for a lawsuit depending on the circumstances.

Like other facilities such as hospitals and clinics, claims of medical malpractice are typically predicated on allegations that care was administered improperly, there was a failure of equipment, or there was a lack of adequately trained health care personnel. These cases are litigated in much the same way. However, in the long-term care facility, there is an additional basis for medical malpractice that has generated suits in a large number of jurisdictions. This action arises from the unique characteristics of the long-term care facility. In the traditional hospital or clinic setting, patients present themselves for the primary purpose of medical care, treatment, or services. Their presence in the facility is incident to the primary purpose. However, in the long-term care facility, patients are present for the equal purpose of a safe living environment. Many patients have medical conditions that are permanent and require only basic maintenance. Nevertheless, the patients are incapable of caring for their personal and/or medical needs independently, and the facility is entrusted with the responsibility to monitor the condition of the patient for significant changes.

These changes may occur suddenly or over a period of time. In any event it is the duty and, in some cases, statutory responsibility of the facility staff to make note of changes and to report them either to family members, guardians, or the physician who oversees the patient's care. In some instances, the change may occur as the result of an event. In others, it may be symptomatic of a slow, deteriorating condition. And some patients develop medical conditions secondary to their original status and primary reason for admission to the facility. The origin is not the issue. The liability of the facility is created when there is a failure to duly note changes and properly report them.

In the past, some facilities have defended allegations of failure to report with the fact that the patient was terminal and a deteriorating condition was to be expected. The courts rejected this defense on the basis that the right to choose the proper course of medical treatment belonged to the patient and their guardian and could not be ignored by the facility. The end result of such claims is founded in an allegation of medical malpractice by the personnel of the facility for failure to properly attend to the medical needs of the patient.

In addition to claims of malpractice based on a failure to report, there is also the question of abuse and neglect of patients. Depending on the circumstances, this type of claim may be predicated on general civil law or medical malpractice. Cases supporting claims of malpractice have involved concerns about failure to properly administer medication, physical therapy, occupational therapy, or other medical directives; failure to provide preventive or rehabilitative care for existing conditions (e.g., bedsores), failure to properly monitor fluid and nutritional intake/output when the patient was unable to do so; and any other failure to adequately provide the care for which the facility was entrusted by the patient and guardian.

The issue of pain and suffering is present in virtually any lawsuit for medical malpractice and is discussed in greater detail in subsequent chapters. At this juncture it should be noted that the element of pain and suffering is of particular concern in cases against long-term care facilities. The patients in such facilities are among the most vulnerable in our society. Their medical care and continued existence is dependent upon and confided to the staff of the long-term care facility. Thus, when medical malpractice occurs, there is almost always an accompanying element of pain and suffering for patients who are unable to remove themselves from the situation and are left to the mercy of the very people who inflicted the medical malpractice. When there is a verdict for a plaintiff in a medical malpractice action, the result may be a jury verdict that stretches the limits of the judge and/or jury's authority.

353 Ark. 29, 111 S.W.3d 346
Supreme Court of Arkansas.

ADVOCAT, INC.; Diversicare Leasing Corporation, d/b/a Rich Mountain Nursing and Rehabilitation Center; and Diversicare Management Services Co.
v.
Lon C. SAUER, Individually, and as Administrator of the Estate of Margaretha Sauer, Deceased, and on Behalf of the Wrongful-Death Beneficiaries of Margaretha Sauer.

(continued)

May 1, 2003.

ROBERT L. BROWN, Justice.

On July 19, 1998, Margaretha Sauer died at the Mena Medical Center following a five and one-half year stay at Rich Mountain. She was 93 years old. Mrs. Sauer's discharge summary revealed that the cause of her death was severe electrolyte abnormalities, with contributing factors of "Alzheimer's type, dementia[,]" and protein calorie malnutrition.

The events leading up to Mrs. Sauer's death are these. She had been scheduled for the insertion of a gastro-intestinal feeding tube into her stomach on July 6, 1998, but the surgery was delayed due to the doctor's unavailability. On July 18, 1998, at 8:00 a.m., a nursing note reveals that Mrs. Sauer refused her medication. Her vital signs then began to decline. On July 19, 1998, at 3:30 a.m., her vital signs were still declining, and, according to the nursing staff, she was not "acting right." At 5:00 a.m. that same morning, the nursing staff reported the developments to Dr. David Brown, her treating physician, who ordered that she be taken to the emergency room at the Mena Medical Center. She arrived at the hospital in a semi-comatose condition. She died about sixteen hours later on that same date.

Mrs. Sauer's physical condition at time of death was gleaned from nursing notes. She had lost fifteen pounds in the last month and was in need of a feeding tube. There were signs of bedsores on her body, stemming from lying in urine and excrement. She suffered from contractures from Alzheimer's Disease, which involved contraction of her limbs into her sockets. She also had a urinary infection and had been experiencing a foul vaginal discharge.

On January 12, 2000, the Sauer Estate filed a complaint against the appellants, and included as well Diversicare Corporation of America--Arkansas, and Diversicare Corporation of America as parties defendant. According to the complaint, Advocat was a Pennsylvania corporation and the parent company. Advocat owned eighty-six facilities in the southeast and Canada, sixty-four of which were nursing homes. Diversicare Leasing Corporation was an Arkansas corporation that did business as Rich Mountain Nursing and Rehabilitation Center. Diversicare Management Services Co. was a Tennessee corporation that held the permit for Rich Mountain to operate in the state. The complaint alleged several counts against the named defendants, including negligence, negligence *per se*, tort of outrage, breach of contract, and wrongful death. The complaint prayed for damages for medical expenses and costs, mental anguish, funeral expenses, and for Mrs. Sauer's pain and suffering prior to her death, as well as general and special damages, the costs of litigation, and punitive damages. A first amended complaint filed later dropped the negligence *per se* count and added a new count for medical malpractice.

The appellants generally denied the complaint and asserted affirmative defenses, including failure to allege facts sufficient to state a claim, failure to comply with Ark. R. Civ. P. 9(b) relating to allegations of fraud, negligence of others, pre-existing condition, failure to mitigate, entitlement to set-off from any recovery, no proximate causation, and statute of limitations, among others. On June 13, 2001, the trial began and lasted eight days. Twenty-eight witnesses testified, and there were twenty-four binders of exhibits. At the trial's conclusion, the jury retired to consider four counts: ordinary negligence, medical malpractice, breach of contract, and wrongful death. The jury returned a verdict for the Sauer Estate on all counts submitted. It awarded compensatory damages of $5 million for ordinary negligence, $10 million for medical malpractice, $25,000 for breach of contract, and $100,000 for each of the surviving beneficiaries for wrongful death. The total judgment against the three appellants for compensatory damages was $15,400,000, with joint and several liability. An award of $25,000 was also entered separately against Diversicare Leasing Corporation for breach of contract. Punitive damages in the amount of $21 million were awarded separately against each

(continued)

of the three appellants, without joint and several liability, for a total punitive damage award of $63 million. Combined judgments totaling $78,425,000 were memorialized by order of the court. ...

... The appellants first argue that the damage awards for negligence and medical malpractice are grossly excessive. In support of their position, the appellants assert that the only elements of damage at issue were past medical expenses, conscious pain and suffering, scars and disfigurement, and contract damages. Moreover, they maintain that Mrs. Sauer had no dependents, was unemployed, and had a life expectancy of two years at the time of her death. She had been at Rich Mountain for five and one-half years but was now crippled by Alzheimer's disease and bed-bound.

With respect to pain and suffering, they contend that evidence of such is scarce in the record. They further maintain that the introduction of two Office of Long Term Care surveys, admitted over their objection, inflamed the jury, because the surveys were "replete with statements that there was not enough help in the nursing home to feed, bathe, or clean residents." Additionally, appellants submit that testimony by witnesses that the nursing home had engaged in "false-charting" to show more staff than were actually present was prejudicial, because it suggested the appellants had staffing inadequacies that they tried to conceal from the State.

The appellants also point to the prejudicial testimony of Faye Chamberlain, a former nurse assistant at the home, who wrote to then-President Clinton in 1997 about the nursing home's inadequacies, and the testimony of Mark Hemingway, a former regional vice-president of Diversicare Management, who testified to a change in corporate philosophy in 1996 to stressing profits over care. There was, too, they assert, the prejudicial testimony of a former chief financial officer, Mary Margaret Hamlett, who testified that all three separate appellants were run as one company. The appellants conclude that all of this testimony combined incited the jury to give the largest personal-injury verdict ever awarded in Arkansas and inflamed the jury, not because of Mrs. Sauer's injuries, but because of problems in the nursing home industry as a whole. They add that there was no basis for the jury's award of $5 million for negligence or $10 million for medical malpractice, when Mrs. Sauer's actual medical bills totaled little more than $7,700. Indeed, they contend that in a recent case this court reversed an award of $100,000 for pain and suffering to the estate of an sixty-six-year old woman who died after waiting thirteen hours for a consultation with a surgeon. *Williamson v. Elrod*, 348 Ark. 307,72 S.W.3d 489 (2002).

The appellants further assert that the Sauer Estate is urging the wrong standard of review and that the correct standard is *de novo* review. They contend that the jury awarded the appellee $14,992,291.50 (total compensatory damages less actual medical damages) for pain and suffering associated with pressure sores, contractures, oral hygiene, and lack of food or drink that occurred only during the last 24 to 48 hours of Mrs. Sauer's life. They claim that the Sauer Estate grossly exaggerated the number and severity of Mrs. Sauer's pressure sores and that her contractures and poor oral hygiene do not support such an award for pain and suffering; nor, they urge, was there evidence that Mrs. Sauer's vaginal discharge caused her any pain and suffering. As for her lack of food and water, the appellants contend that had the family permitted a feeding tube earlier, she would have lived.

We, initially, are of the opinion that the Sauer Estate correctly states our standard of review. Where an award of damages is alleged to be excessive, this court reviews the proof and all reasonable inferences most favorably to the appellee and determines whether the verdict is so great as to shock the conscience of the court or demonstrate passion or prejudice on the part of the trier of fact. *See Houston v. Knoedl*,329 Ark. 91, 947 S.W.2d 745 (1997). Remittitur is appropriate when the compensatory damages awarded are excessive and cannot be sustained by the evidence. *See Ellis v. Price*, 337 Ark. 542, 990 S.W.2d 543 (1999). The standard of review in such a case is that appropriate for a new trial motion, *i.e.,* whether there is substantial evidence to support the verdict. *See Johnson v. Gilliland*, 320 Ark. 1, 896 S.W.2d 856 (1995) (citing Ark. R. Civ. P. 59(a)(5) (stating a new trial may be granted on the ground that there was error in the assessment of the amount of recovery, whether too large or too small)). Moreover, Arkansas Rule of Civil Procedure 59(a)(4)

(continued)

provides as one ground for a new trial "excessive damages appearing to have been given under the influence of passion or prejudice."

Here, Mrs. Sauer died in the care of Rich Mountain from severe malnutrition and dehydration. There was evidence presented that she was found at times with dried feces under her fingernails from scratching herself while lying in her own excrement. At other times, she was not "gotten up" out of her bed as she should have been. Often times, Mrs. Sauer's food tray was found in her room, untouched because there was no staff member at the nursing home available to feed her. She was not provided with "range of motion" assistance when the facility was short of staff. On one occasion, her son complained to staff that he had found his mother at 3:00 p.m., still in her gown, wet with urine, disturbed, and upset.

Testimony further revealed that at times, there was not enough hot water with which patients could shower. Mrs. Sauer was often times found wet without being changed in four hours. She had pressure sores on her back, lower buttock, and arms on days she was found sitting in urine and excrement. A former staff member remembered seeing Mrs. Sauer at one time with a pressure sore the size of a softball, which was open. Her sores and blisters became infected. She was frequently double-padded, and even triple-padded, rather than single-padded for her incontinence problems. At times, she had no water pitcher in her room; nor did she receive a bath for a week or longer, due to there not being enough staff at the facility. She was described as "always thirsty" and her nursing notes indicated that she was heard moaning and crying. At the time she was hospitalized prior to her death, she had a severe vaginal infection. When she was in the geriatric chair, she was not "let loose" every two hours, as required by law. Finally, Mrs. Sauer was found to suffer from poor oral hygiene with caked food and debris in her mouth.

We hold that the jury verdicts were not based on passion or prejudice. There was ample testimony and evidence presented to demonstrate that Mrs. Sauer suffered considerably and was not properly cared for, that Rich Mountain was short-staffed, and that the appellants tried to cover this up by "false-charting" and by bringing in additional "employees" on state-inspection days. Mr. Hemingway testified that these deficiencies were due to a shift in corporate philosophy that placed profits over proper patient care. All of this serves to support the Sauer Estate's case that the nursing home, under the auspices of the appellants, knew it had staffing problems and committed negligence as to Mrs. Sauer, because it was short-staffed due to cutbacks.

The second question for this court to resolve is whether the verdict for compensatory damages was so great as to shock the conscience of the court This court has held that there is no definite and satisfactory rule to measure compensation for pain and suffering; the amount of damages must depend on the circumstances of each particular case. See *McElroy v. Benefield*, 299 Ark. 112, 771 S.W.2d 274 (1989). Additionally, we have held that compensation for pain and suffering must be left to the sound discretion of the jury and the conclusion reached by it should not be disturbed unless the award is clearly excessive. See *id.* In this regard, we have observed that where the jury's award is not segmented, it is difficult for this court to surmise what the basis for the jury award was, apart from medical expenses. See *West Union v. Vostatek* 302 Ark. 219, 788 S.W.2d 952 (1990).

The evidence in this case certainly reflects that Mrs. Sauer's estate was entitled to damages for pain and suffering in connection with both negligence and medical malpractice. The question is, in what amount? ...

...One treatise on damages has described the jury's dilemma inherent in any pain-and-suffering evaluation: Pain and suffering have no market price. They are not capable of being exactly and accurately determined, and there is no fixed rule or standard whereby damages for them can be measured. Hence, the amount of damages to be awarded for them must be left to the judgment of the jury, subject only to correction by the courts for abuse and passionate exercise. One of the most difficult decisions facing the jury in a personal injury case is the size of the monetary award for pain and suffering, since there is no objective method of evaluating such damages. The question in any given case is not what sum of money would be

(continued)

sufficient to induce a person to undergo voluntarily the pain and suffering for which recovery is sought or what it would cost to hire someone to undergo such suffering, but what, under all the circumstances, should be allowed the plaintiff in addition to the other items of damage to which he or she is entitled, in reasonable consideration of the pain and suffering necessarily endured or to be endured. The amount allowed must be fair and reasonable, free from sentimental or fanciful standards, and based upon the facts disclosed. 2 *Stein on Personal Injury Damages*, § 8:8, at 8-19 (3d ed.1997) (footnotes omitted). *See also Howard Brill, Arkansas Law of Damages*, § 29-2, pp. 551-52 (4th ed.2002)....

... We hold that while the compensatory damages awarded in this case were not the result of passion or prejudice, they do shock the conscience of this court. Nevertheless, the issue still remains: What is an appropriate measure for reduction? Again, virtually all of the damages awarded were for pain and suffering. The jury awarded $5 million for negligence and $10 million for medical malpractice, with the three appellant corporations to be held jointly and severally liable. No doubt the jury focused on Mrs. Sauer's age and medical condition at the time of her death, the extent of her misery, and the absence of care she received for the period leading up to her death. Testimony by the Sauer Estate's witness, Mary Margaret Hamlett, was clear, though, that the three appellants operated Rich Mountain as one business. This court concludes that the three appellants did operate Rich Mountain as one business, which the circuit court acknowledged in its comments from the bench. We further hold that the circuit court abused its discretion in not granting a new trial based on excessive damages or by ordering a remittitur of damages. Though we are cognizant of the fact that separate verdict forms were returned for each appellant on negligence and medical malpractice, we are persuaded that a reasonable basis for remittitur is to reduce the negligence and medical malpractice awards by two-thirds. We grant the remittitur and reduce the total damage award for negligence and medical malpractice from $15 million to $5 million, with joint and several liability. We affirm the judgment award on condition of remittitur as stated at the conclusion of this opinion.

Appellants next argue that the evidence was insufficient to support an award of punitive damages in that although the testimony presented may have been evidence of negligence, it was not evidence of conscious or reckless disregard of known or probable consequences, from which malice can be inferred, as required for an award of punitive damages under state law. Appellants further contend that the punitive-damage awards are an unlawful taking and violate their due process rights under the United States Constitution under the holding of the United States Supreme Court in *BMW of North America, Inc. v. Gore, supra.*

Appellants' first argument that there was insufficient evidence to support the award of punitive damages in this case is not preserved for this court's review. Arkansas Rule of Civil Procedure 50(e) requires that where "there has been a trial by jury, the failure of a party to move for a directed verdict at the conclusion of all the evidence, because of insufficiency of the evidence will constitute a waiver of any question pertaining to the sufficiency of the evidence to support the jury verdict." We conclude that "at the conclusion of the evidence" means exactly that--when all the evidence is in....

... The appellants contend that the punitive damages are excessive under Arkansas law and, in addition, violate their due process rights under *BMW of North America, Inc. v. Gore, supra*. In 1998, this court set out a compendium of Arkansas law related to remittitur and punitive damages:

When considering the issue of remittitur of punitive damages, we review the issue *de novo*. *See Smith v. Hansen*, 323 Ark. 188, 914 S.W.2d 285 (1996). We consider the extent and enormity of the wrong, the intent of the party committing the wrong, all the circumstances, and the financial and social condition and standing of the erring party. *See United Ins. Co. of America v. Murphy*,331 Ark. 364, 961 S.W.2d 752 (1998. Punitive damages are a penalty for conduct that is malicious or perpetrated with the deliberate intent to injure another. *See United Ins. Co., supra.* When punitive damages are alleged to be excessive, we review the proof

(continued)

and all reasonable inferences in the light most favorable to the appellees, and we determine whether the verdict is so great as to shock the conscience of this court or to demonstrate passion or prejudice on the part of the trier of fact. See *Houston v. Knoedl,* 329 Ark. 91, 947 S.W.2d 745 (1997. It is important that the punitive damages be sufficient to deter others from comparable conduct in the future. See *McLaughlin v. Cox, supra. Routh Wrecker Service v. Washington,* 335 Ark. 232, 240-241, 980 S.W.2d 240, 244 (1998). The conscious indifference of the alleged wrongdoer to the wrong committed is a pertinent factor in assessing punitive damages. See *United Ins. Co. of America v. Murphy,* 331 Ark. 364, 961 S.W.2d 752 (1998).

We begin by observing that the extent and the enormity of the wrong done to Mrs. Sauer are considerable. As already emphasized in this opinion, there was evidence that the appellants knew Rich Mountain was short-staffed, including surveys by the Office of Long Term Care, but took no measures to rectify the situation. Indeed, there were attempts to disguise this fact. Also, the Advocat business enterprise appears to be sizeable. The appellants make much of the fact that they were precluded from offering financial information at a posttrial hearing. But we agree with the circuit court that the appellants could not have it both ways. The appellants first objected to any requirement that they divulge financial information at trial. The circuit court sustained the objection. They cannot now, postverdict, seek a remedy that they themselves shut the door to during the trial. The circuit court correctly disallowed the request. The same holds true of the appellants' passionate argument in favor of a postverdict excessiveness hearing to introduce financial information they objected to at trial. We know of no procedure authorized in this state by rule or statute providing for such an evidentiary hearing under these circumstances. We decline to authorize one in the instant case....

... Viewing all of the pertinent evidence together, we conclude that punitive damages were indeed appropriate in this case. The question, however, as was the case with compensatory damages, is the amount of those damages. We conclude that an award of $63 million in punitive damages shocks the conscience of this court as a civil penalty. We will consider what remittitur is appropriate after an analysis under *BMW of North America, Inc. v. Gore, supra.* Again, what impacts this court is that the three appellants operated Rich Mountain as one business....

... Appellants claim that it ludicrous to conclude that Mrs. Sauer suffered 6,300 violations under the subchapter to substantiate a punitive-damages award of $63 million. However, it appears from the definition of the term "neglect" that it is impossible to know how many violations might have occurred; nor have the appellants suggested a more appropriate number. Moreover, the jury verdicts from other jurisdictions cited in the circuit court's letter opinion do not inform this court about whether those cases were ultimately settled or appealed and affirmed.

The highest punitive-damages award affirmed by this court is $3 million. See *Airco, Inc. v. Simmons First Nat. Bank,* 276 Ark. 486, 638 S.W.2d 660 (1982). The highest punitive-damages award affirmed by our court of appeals on appeal is $4 million. See *Arrow Int'l, Inc. v. Sparks,* 81 Ark.App. 42, 98 S.W.3d 48 (2003). We conclude, as we did with compensatory damages, that the punitive damages awarded, while not the result of passion or prejudice, shock the conscience of this court. They are far and away in excess of any other punitive-damages award in this state, which, while not the determinative factor, is instructive. Under our analysis, the third criterion in *Gore* has not been met.

We hold that the circuit court abused its discretion in not granting a new trial due to excessive punitive-damages awards or, alternatively, in failing to grant a remittitur. We further hold that under Arkansas law and under the three *Gore* factors, $63 million was a grossly excessive award and one that could not have been anticipated by the appellants, particularly since the largest award of punitive damages affirmed in this state on appeal heretofore has been $4 million. We grant the remittitur and reduce the amount of the total punitive damages awarded by two-thirds to $21 million, and provide for joint and several liability. We do so on the basis that this is reasonable under our *de novo* review. We conclude that one business is involved in the

(continued)

management of Rich Mountain and that it shocks the conscience of this court to award the same amount of punitive damages against the parent company and the two subsidiary companies. We will affirm the judgment only on condition of remittitur as stated in the conclusion of this opinion. We hold under Ark. R. Civ. P. 59(a)(4) and (5). If, within eighteen days, the Sauer Estate remits $10 million of the $15 million compensatory damages, leaving a compensatory damage award of $5 million, with joint and several liability, and further remits $42 million of the $63 million punitive damages, leaving a punitive damages award of $21 million, also with joint and several liability, the judgment will be affirmed. Otherwise, the case will be reversed, and the cause will be remanded for a new trial. *See Fisher Trucking, Inc. v. Fleet Lease, Inc.,* 304 Ark. 451, 803 S.W.2d 888 (1991).

Affirmed on condition of remittitur.

CASES INVOLVING NON-TRADITIONAL AND ALTERNATIVE CARE

An increasingly large segment of American society is involved in what are considered non-traditional forms of health care. In some instances, it is pursued in conjunction with traditional methods. But in many instances, individuals seek to cure ailments through more natural methods in a variety of ways. Some of the traditional disciplines have embraced non-traditional methods as supplemental forms of treatment, but a segment of the population places its trust in these alternatives as a primary form of treatment. Non-traditional forms of health care include a variety of methods from acupuncture to homeopathic remedies, nutrition-based care, and care that relies on religious practices and beliefs. It is every individual's right to pursue medical care for their own well-being in the manner they choose. This may be somewhat limited in situations that involve selecting care for children because the court attempts to balance maximum parental freedom against the best interests of the child's physical and emotional welfare. Occasionally, in that instance, courts will step in and disallow certain courses of action. Otherwise, the general rule is to refrain from interfering with individual choices regarding personal health care.

When one undertakes to provide a non-traditional form of health care to others, the legislatures and courts take a much more involved approach. Many non-traditional forms of care are licensed by the state legislatures with regard to minimum qualifications and clinical settings that comply with basic health code requirements. Non-traditional providers are seen as an alternative which citizens are entitled to pursue in furtherance of their own personal well-being. These providers do offer a form of health care, and they are subject to liability for instances when they fail to exercise a reasonable degree of skill associated with their profession, or when their professional conduct exceeds the limits of that profession's standards. In the following case, an alternative care practitioner was held liable for recommending that a cancer patient substitute alternative medicine for conventional medical standards. As the court indicated, it is one thing to suggest an alternative form of treatment. It is another, entirely, to encourage a patient to abandon traditional medical care.

251 A.D.2d 72, 673 N.Y.S.2d 685, (1998).

Supreme Court, Appellate Division, First Department, New York.

Julianne CHARELL, et al., Plaintiffs-Respondents-Appellants,
v.
Nicholas J. GONZALEZ, Defendant-Appellant-Respondent.

June 9, 1998.

MEMORANDUM DECISION.

Judgment, Supreme Court, New York County (Edward Lehner, J.), entered August 7, 1997, upon a jury verdict apportioning liability for plaintiff's injuries 51% against defendant and 49% against plaintiff and awarding plaintiff damages in the amount of $2,500,000 for past pain and suffering, $2,000,000 for future pain and suffering, $125,000 for past loss of earnings, $75,000 for future loss of earnings, and punitive damages of $150,000, such awards being reduced pursuant to CPLR article 14-A and structured pursuant to CPLR article 50-A, and bringing up for review an order of the same court and Justice, entered on or about June 10, 1997, which denied defendant's motion to set aside the verdict and plaintiff's cross motion to set aside that portion of the verdict as found that she assumed a risk of injury to herself, and an order of the same Court (Karla Moskowitz, J.), entered on or about October 17, 1996, which denied defendant's motion for summary judgment, unanimously modified, on the law and the facts, to vacate that portion of the judgment awarding plaintiff punitive damages, and otherwise affirmed, without costs.

In this action for medical malpractice and lack of informed consent in connection with plaintiff's decision to forgo conventional chemotherapy/radiation treatments for her cancer and instead follow defendant's alternative nutritional regimen, the jury found defendant 51% liable for plaintiff's injuries and plaintiff 49% liable for her injuries, based on its conclusion that the treatment provided by defendant was a departure from good and accepted medical practice, which departure was a proximate cause of plaintiff's injuries. The jury also premised its verdict upon the finding that defendant failed to provide plaintiff with appropriate information with respect to the risks *73 of the treatment he offered and the alternatives thereto. It further found that a reasonably prudent person in plaintiff's position would not have agreed to the course of treatment offered by defendant if appropriately advised, but that, even without the benefit of proper advice, plaintiff, at least impliedly, assumed some of the risk of injury entailed by her election to undergo defendant's alternative therapy.

(continued)

According due deference to the jury's determination, which was based upon its opportunity to observe and hear the witnesses, and weighing the conflicting testimony of the parties and their respective experts, it cannot be said that the evidence so preponderated in favor of defendant that the jury could not have reached its conclusion based upon any fair interpretation of the evidence (*Arpino v. Lombardo,* 215 A.D.2d 614, 615, 628 N.Y.S.2d 320). We conclude, then, that the verdict with respect to liability was supported by sufficient evidence and was not against the weight of the evidence (*Cohen v. Hallmark Cards,* 45 N.Y.2d 493, 498-499, 410 N.Y.S.2d 282, 382 N.E.2d 1145; *Nicastro v. Park,* 113 A.D.2d 129, 495 N.Y.S.2d 184). In this connection, we are of the view that, based upon the evidence that plaintiff refused the treatment plan recommended to her by conventional oncological specialists and elected instead to follow defendant's alternative protocol, the jury's finding that plaintiff impliedly accepted a substantial part of the risk entailed by the alternative protocol is sustainable, notwithstanding the jury's concurrent finding that defendant did not discharge his duty to advise plaintiff respecting the risks of pursuing the alternative protocol.

We modify only to the extent of vacating the award of punitive damages. Defendant's conduct was not so wantonly dishonest (*Moskowitz v. Spitz,* 243 A.D.2d 357, 664 N.Y.S.2d 545), grossly indifferent to patient care (*Pascazi v. Pelton,* 210 A.D.2d 910, 621 N.Y.S.2d 979), or so malicious and/or reckless (*see, Camillo v. Geer,* 185 A.D.2d 192, 587 N.Y.S.2d 306) as to warrant such an award. We have considered the parties' remaining contentions for affirmative relief and find them to be without merit.

In many ways, alternative medicine practitioners are under the same duties as their traditional medicine counterparts. There is always the obligation to comply with all aspects of licensure and/or certification. Like other health care providers, there is the responsibility to act in a manner reasonable and consistent with other similarly situated professionals. However, in addition to these, the practitioner of alternative medicine has a particular duty to refrain from discouraging clients from seeking traditional medical care as demonstrated in the case above.

CASES RESULTING FROM DEFECTIVE PRODUCTS/EQUIPMENT

Historically, products liability actions impose strict liability, or no-fault, principles against those who are engaged in the commerce of defective and/or dangerous products. The rationale is that an unsuspecting public does not generally have the knowledge or skill necessary to determine the safety of finished products. Their trust is placed in those engaged in the manufacture and sale of the products. The public cannot protect themselves from unknown dangers, but those engaged in the commerce of such products who benefit from their sale, must also bear the cost of injuries.

In recent years though, the courts have largely rejected the concept of holding health care providers as part of the group responsible for defective medical products. This is true even in cases when the practitioner directly provided the product or used the equipment on the patient that caused the injury. The court's reasoning is that the health care provider is not usually in the business of selling the product, but rather of providing medical care, treatment, or services. The product or equipment use was only incidental to the professional duties of the provider. Repeatedly, the courts have held that the hospitals and physicians are mere consumers that use the product in the delivery of health care. As such, they are not within the chain of commerce.

A significant component of the reluctance by courts to include health care providers in the possible defendants associated with a products liability claim is the trend to limit, as much as reasonably possible, claims against such providers in matters not directly involved with the breach of contract or negligent delivery of health care. When this is combined with the approach that health care providers are not "dealers" in the sale of products, many courts have resisted allowing products liability actions against such providers. However, there are exceptions to this trend.

312 N.J.Super. 81, 711 A.2d 352

Superior Court of New Jersey,
Appellate Division.

The ESTATE OF Angelina A. CHIN by Robert CHIN as Administrator and Administrator Ad Prosequendum of the Estate of Angelina A. Chin, and Robert Chin, individually, Plaintiffs-Respondents,
v.
ST. BARNABAS MEDICAL CENTER, Immacula Louis-Charles, Teresa Leib, and Nancy Hofgesang, Defendants-Respondents,
and
Dr. Herbert Goldfarb, Defendant-Appellant,
and
C.R. Bard, Inc., Defendant.

Decided May 27, 1998.

D'ANNUNZIO, J.A.D.

This claim arises out of the tragic and avoidable death of Angelina Chin during a hysteroscopy, a diagnostic procedure in which death is not an anticipated risk. The trial court submitted the case to the jury under the principles announced in *Anderson v. Somberg*, 67 *N.J.* 291, 338 *A.2d* 1, *cert. denied*, 423 *U.S.* 929, 96 *S.Ct.* 279, 46 *L. Ed.*2d 258 (1975). The jury awarded two million dollars in damages and apportioned liability as follows: twenty percent to Dr. Goldfarb; twenty percent to nurse Leib; twenty-five percent to nurse Hofgesang; thirty-five percent to St. Barnabas Medical Center; and zero percent to nurse Charles. The trial court had granted defendant C.R. Bard, Inc.'s motion for judgment at the close of the evidence.

After the jury announced its verdict, the court granted the motion of the hospital and the nurses for judgment notwithstanding the verdict. *R.* 4:40- 2(b). The court entered judgment against Dr. Goldfarb alone for the entire amount of two million dollars plus interest. Dr. Goldfarb appeals. There are no cross-appeals. No one challenges plaintiff's right to judgment or to the two million dollar damages award. The only dispute is between the hospital and the nurses on the one hand, hereinafter sometimes referred to as the hospital defendants, and defendant Goldfarb.

(continued)

A hysteroscopy is a diagnostic procedure whereby the uterus is observed utilizing a scope, a wand-like instrument with a television lens at its functioning end. The uterus can then be visualized on a television monitor. The physician's view is enhanced by stretching the uterus. This is achieved with the flow of fluid into the uterus. The flow can be by gravity or by the use of a pump which introduces the fluid into the uterus under pressure.

In the present case, the procedure was performed using a Bard Hystero-Flo Pump, a device manufactured by defendant C.R. Bard, Inc. The device consists of several tubes and a pump. Two of the tubes, located at one end of the device, are inserted into bags of fluid suspended from an IV pole. Fluid flows from the *85 bags through the tubes to a point where they connect at what is called a Y-adaptor. Below the Y-adaptor is a diaphragm pump. A single tube leads from the pump, bringing fluid to the scope and then into the uterus.

The pump is energized by gas. In this case, defendants used a supply of nitrogen gas located in the ceiling of the operating room. The gas flows from its source to a regulator and from the regulator the gas moves through a tube, the gas line, to the diaphragm pump. Gas that has powered the pump then flows out of the system through an open exhaust line into the atmosphere.

As previously indicated, the scope has a lens on its functioning end. There are two ports in the wall of the scope upstream from the functioning end. One port is the inflow port, *i.e.*, it is connected to the line carrying fluid from the diaphragm pump. The fluid, under pressure, enters the uterus through a fitting on the end of the scope. The second port is the outflow port. Excess fluid is evacuated from the uterus through suction tubing attached to the outflow port. Sometimes gravity is used to evacuate the fluid, and the excess fluid flows through the suction tubing into a pail. On other occasions, a suction canister is used to facilitate evacuation.

In the present case, gas entered through Angelina Chin's body cavity and into her circulatory system. Air bubbles formed in her blood vessels and killed her almost immediately. All parties accept the theory that the exhaust line was the source of the gas which killed Mrs. Chin.

The evidence established that the exhaust line, when it comes from the manufacturer, is clipped to the gas line, *i.e.*, the line that carries gas from the regulator to the diaphragm pump. The exhaust line begins at the diaphragm pump, and it is forty-five inches long. Three clips hold the exhaust line to the gas line and the last clip is within an inch of the outflow end of the exhaust line. The evidence established that the exhaust line was properly clipped when it left the manufacturer, but the last clip was not on the apparatus when it was used in the Chin procedure. The absence of the last clip caused twenty-seven inches of the exhaust line to hang loose. The theory is that in its loose state the exhaust line could have been mistaken for a suction line. A jury could conclude that one of the nurses removed the clip or caused it to come off the line. There is evidence from which a jury could conclude that Dr. Goldfarb attached the loose exhaust line to the outflow port, although Dr. Goldfarb denied that he did so. There is evidence from which a jury could conclude that one or more of the nurses assisting in the procedure unclipped the exhaust line and made it possible for that line to be within the operative field, thereby facilitating its erroneous connection to the outflow port. There is also evidence to support a finding that one of the nurses connected the loose exhaust line to a suction canister which may have been connected to the scope through suction tubing.

The evidence established that the two nurses the hospital assigned to assist in the procedure, nurse Charles and nurse Leib, had no experience regarding the use of the Bard apparatus and had not attended hospital

(continued)

training sessions regarding its use. The evidence established that the supervising nurse who made the assignments was unaware of the experience or lack thereof of nurses Charles and Leib regarding this equipment. The evidence also established that, because of their inexperience, Charles or Leib asked nurse Hofgesang to assist them. During the procedure, Hofgesang, located to the patient's left, received the apparatus from Charles, the scrub or sterile nurse, who was located on the patient's right. Charles had removed the equipment from the Bard package, which Leib had opened, and handed the apparatus to Hofgesang who connected the tubes to the fluid bags and also connected the hospital's gas line to the regulator.

As previously indicated, the trial court ruled that this case is governed by the principles of *Anderson v. Somberg, supra,* and we begin our analysis with a discussion of it. *Anderson* arose out of back surgery performed by defendant, Dr. Somberg. During the procedure the tip of an instrument, an angulated pituitary rongeur, broke off in Anderson's spinal canal and lodged in his spine. 67 *N.J.* at 294, 338 *A.2d* 1. He sued Dr. Somberg, the hospital, the manufacturer of the rongeur and the rongeur's distributer. *Id.* at 295, 338 *A.2d* 1.

A jury returned a verdict of no cause as to each defendant. The Appellate Division reversed, on the ground that the trial court's instruction to the jury was inadequate. *Anderson v. Somberg,* 134 *N.J.Super.* 1, 5, 338 *A.2d* 35 (App.Div.1973). The majority opinion stated:
> Reason and common sense dictate that the jury additionally should be charged that under the peculiar circumstances of this case the occurrence itself indicates liability on the part of one or more of the defendants, and that the burden should be shifted to defendants as they are most likely to possess knowledge of the cause of the accident. Each defendant has the duty to come forward with explanatory evidence. *Nopco Chemical Div. v. Blaw-Knox Co.,* 59 *N.J.* 274, 282-283, 281 *A.2d* 793 (1971). *Cf. Magner v. Beth Israel Hospital,* 120 *N.J.Super.* 529, 534, 295 *A.2d* 363 (App.Div.1972).
>
> For the reasons expressed the matter is reversed and remanded for a new trial as to all defendants. [*Id.* at 5-6, 338 *A.2d* 35.]

Judge Seidman concurred in the reversal and remand for a new trial on the ground that the jury instruction "was so structured that they may well have been misled or confused thereby." *Id.* at 6, 338 *A.2d* 35 (Seidman, J., concurring). Judge Seidman disagreed with the majority's ruling that the jury should be instructed that the circumstances established liability on one or more defendants. *Ibid.* In his view, the circumstances supported an inference of negligence which protected plaintiff from dismissal at the conclusion of plaintiff's proofs. *Id.* at 7, 338 *A.2d* 35. He would have shifted "the burden ... to each defendant to come forward with proof," *id.* at 8, 338 *A.2d* 35, leaving it to the jury "to determine whether in the final analysis the inference of fault outweighs the explanation." *Ibid.*

The Supreme Court affirmed in a four to three vote. Of the four voting to affirm, Justice Jacobs wrote no separate opinion "but vote[d] to affirm on the majority opinion rendered in the Appellate Division." *Anderson, supra,* 67 *N.J.* at 305, 338 *A.2d* 1.

In affirming the Appellate Division, Justice Pashman, writing for the plurality, stated:
> The position adopted by the Appellate Division majority seems to us substantially correct; that is, at the close of all the evidence, it was apparent that at least one of the defendants was liable for plaintiff's injury, because no alternative theory of liability was within reasonable contemplation. Since defendants had engaged in conduct which activated legal obligations by each of them to plaintiff, the jury should have been instructed that *the failure of any defendant to prove his nonculpability would trigger liability;*

(continued)

> *and further, that since at least one of the defendants could not sustain his burden of proof, at least one would be liable.* A no cause of action verdict against all primary and third-party defendants will be unacceptable and would work a miscarriage of justice sufficient to require a new trial. R. 2:10-1.

In the ordinary case, the law will not assist an innocent plaintiff at the expense of an innocent defendant. However, in the type of case we consider here, where an unconscious or helpless patient suffers an admitted mishap not reasonably foreseeable and unrelated to the scope of the surgery (such as cases where foreign objects are left in the body of a patient), those who had custody of the patient, and who owed him a duty of care as to medical treatment, or not to furnish a defective instrument for use in such treatment can be called to account for their default. *They must prove their nonculpability, or else risk liability for the injuries suffered.* [*Id.* at 298, 338 A.2d 1 (emphasis added).] The plurality explained that the actual burden of proof shifted to defendant, not merely the burden of going forward. *Id.* at 300, 338 A.2d 1.

We have engaged in this lengthy examination of *Anderson* because a recent Appellate Division opinion has suggested that *Anderson* does not result in a shifting of the burden of persuasion to defendants, but merely the burden of going forward. *Maciag v. Strato Medical Corp.,* 274 *N.J.Super.* 447, 459, 644 A.2d 647 (App.Div.1994). We disagree with the *Maciag* court's analysis of *Anderson*.

Maciag states, erroneously, that the "plurality opinion of the Supreme Court built upon Judge Seidman's concurring opinion in the Appellate Division." *Maciag, supra,* 274 *N.J.Super.* at 456 n. 3, 644 A.2d 647. Not so. As previously indicated, under Judge Seidman's analysis, a plaintiff could lose. Under the majority opinion in the Appellate Division, and the Supreme Court's plurality opinion, plaintiff could not lose. Judge Seidman expressly recognized this difference when he observed that the jury instruction crafted by the majority "in effect, instructs the jury that someone is liable and mandates that they return a verdict in favor of the plaintiff and against one or more of the defendants." *Anderson, supra,* 134 *N.J.Super.* at 6, 338 A.2d 35.

Maciag states that because the Supreme Court's opinion was only a plurality, "[t]he decision actually did nothing more than affirm the Appellate Division decision that the burden of coming forward with evidence should shift to the defendants based on the principles described by the Supreme Court in *Nopco Chem. Div. v. Blaw-Knox Co.*" 274 *N.J.Super.* at 456, 644 A.2d 647 (citations omitted). Accepting the premise that the plurality opinion in effect "did nothing more than affirm the Appellate Division," *ibid.*, the Appellate Division majority, as we have demonstrated, held that plaintiff could not lose, *i.e.,* plaintiff was entitled to a liability verdict and the jury was to be so instructed. *Anderson, supra,* 134 *N.J.Super.* at 5- 6, 338 A.2d 35. Under *Maciag*'s analysis, a plaintiff in an *Anderson*-type case could lose. *Maciag, supra,* 274 *N.J.Super.* at 462, 644 A.2d 647. That is not what the Appellate Division majority held in *Anderson*. The point is, if the plaintiff cannot lose, then the burden of persuasion must shift to each defendant, *vis-a-vis the other defendants,* to exculpate himself or herself.

The Supreme Court has not repudiated the *Anderson* principle that, in cases to which it applies, plaintiff is entitled to a judgment and the burden of persuasion shifts to the defendants. The Court had an opportunity to repudiate our reading of *Anderson* in *Shackil v. Lederle Labs.,* 116 *N.J.* 155, 561 A.2d 511 (1989), in which it rejected a theory of market-share liability in pharmaceutical product liability cases. The Court, noting that *Anderson* shifted the burden of persuasion, limited *Anderson* "to one factual context." *Id.* at 173, 561 A.2d 511. In a dissenting opinion, Justice O'Hern, in support of a market-share theory of liability, observed that the "*Anderson* judgment has stood the test of time. When one of multiple tortfeasors has most probably caused plaintiff's injury, the law does not permit those tortfeasors to exonerate themselves by

(continued)

insisting that the plaintiff's inability to prove which of them caused the injury is a total bar in law to recovery." *Id.* at 199-200, 561 *A.*2d 511 (O'Hern, J., dissenting).

Additionally, many appellate opinions have discussed *Anderson,* understood it to shift the burden of persuasion in cases to which it applied, and have not suggested the revisionist evaluation of *Anderson* contained in *Maciag. See Blitz v. Hutchinson,* 252 *N.J.Super.* 580, 588-89, 600 *A.*2d 485 (App.Div.1991); *Wagner v. Deborah Heart & Lung Ctr.,* 247 *N.J.Super.* 72, 78- 79, 588 *A.*2d 860 (App.Div.1991); *Sholtis v. American Cyanamid Co.,* 238 *N.J.Super.* 8, 21, 568 *A.*2d 1196 (App.Div.1989); *Namm v. Charles E. Frosst & Co.,* 178 *N.J.Super.* 19, 30-31, 427 *A.*2d 1121 (App.Div.1981); *Maslonka v. Hermann,* 173 *N.J.Super.* 566, 573, 575-76, 414 *A.*2d 1350 (App.Div.1980), *rev'd on dissent,* 85 *N.J.* 533, 428 *A.*2d 504 (1981); *see also Huddell v. Levin,* 537 *F.*2d 726, 746 (3d Cir.1976)(Rosenn, J., concurring).

We conclude that *Anderson* applies to the present case; plaintiff's decedent was a blameless, helpless, anesthetized victim of an event that was not reasonably foreseeable or anticipated and that would not have occurred in the absence of wrongdoing by one or more of these defendants. Each defendant, therefore, had the burden of persuading the jury that, as compared with the other defendants, he or she was blameless. With one exception, the parties acquiesced in trying this case as an *Anderson* case and in the shifting of the burden of persuasion.

The hospital defendants contended below, and contend on appeal, that once the trial court granted judgment to Bard, *Anderson* no longer applied. We disagree. Initially, the court denied Bard's motion for judgment made at the close of its codefendants' evidence. Bard then presented the testimony of its quality assurance manager and a consulting engineer. Thereafter, Bard renewed its motion, which the court granted. No party has appealed from the judgment in favor of Bard, and we conclude that the trial court correctly granted the motion. The apparatus did not malfunction or break, and there was no expert evidence to establish a design defect. The parties conceded that all three clips attaching the exhaust line to the gas line were in place when the apparatus left the manufacturer. The trial court, in essence, determined correctly that Bard had carried its burden of persuasion regarding its non-culpability. *Anderson* contemplated such an eventuality. *Anderson, supra,* 67 *N.J.* at 303, 338 *A.*2d 1.

As previously indicated, the trial court granted judgment to the hospital defendants notwithstanding the jury's verdict. In so ruling, the court stated:
> I'm granting that motion. I find there was no basis for the jury to return a, to even go to the jury as to the nurses. I believe I was in error in giving them the standard to use their common knowledge. There was no basis for that, for them to have common knowledge as to what goes on in the, in the hospital setting under the circumstances of this case.

In deciding a motion for judgment notwithstanding the verdict under *R.* 4:40-2(b) in a typical case, the trial court " 'must accept as true all the evidence which supports the position of the party defending against the motion and must accord him the benefit of all legitimate inferences which can be deduced therefrom, and if reasonable minds could differ, the motion must be denied.' " *Lanzet v. Greenberg,* 126 *N.J.* 168, 174, 594 *A.*2d 1309 (1991) (citation omitted); *Dolson v. Anastasia,* 55 *N.J.* 2, 5, 258 *A.*2d 706 (1969). The judicial function is "quite a mechanical one" as the trial court is "not concerned with the worth, nature or extent (beyond a scintilla) of the evidence, but only with its existence, viewed most favorably to the party opposing the motion." *Dolson, supra,* 55 *N.J.* at 5, 258 *A.*2d 706.

(continued)

Thus, a reviewing court should not disturb a trial court's denial of the motion if the evidence, along with all legitimate inferences therefrom, could uphold a judgment in favor of the non-moving party. *Lanzet, supra,* 126 *N.J.* at 174, 594 *A.*2d 1309; *Dolson, supra,* 55 *N.J.* at 5, 258 *A.*2d 706.

We are persuaded that the judgment cannot withstand the application of *Anderson.* Before we apply *Anderson,* however, we will review briefly the law regarding professional standards in malpractice cases.

Ordinarily, a medical malpractice claim requires that " 'the standard of practice to which [the defendant] failed to adhere must be established by expert testimony,' " *Kelly v. Berlin,* 300 *N.J.Super.* 256, 264-65, 692 *A.*2d 552 (App.Div.1997) (quoting *Rosenberg ex rel. Rosenberg v. Cahill,* 99 *N.J.* 318, 325, 492 *A.*2d 371 (1985)). However, experts are not needed to establish professional standards of care where either the doctrine of *res ipsa loquitur* or the doctrine of common knowledge applies. *Id.* at 265, 692 *A.*2d 552. *Res ipsa loquitur* allows an inference of negligence where: (1) the accident which produced a person's injury was one which ordinarily does not happen unless someone was negligent; (2) the instrumentality or agent which caused the accident was within the defendant's exclusive control; and (3) there is no indication in the circumstances that the injury was the result of plaintiff's own voluntary act or neglect. *Buckelew v. Grossbard,* 87 *N.J.* 512, 525, 435 *A.*2d 1150 (1981); *Maciag, supra,* 274 *N.J.Super.* at 460, 644 *A.*2d 647.

The common knowledge doctrine applies when "[t]he facts of a given case [are] such that the common knowledge and experience possessed by lay [persons] ... enable a jury to conclude, without expert testimony, in a malpractice action as in any other negligence action that a duty of care has been breached." *Kelly, supra,* 300 *N.J.Super.* at 265, 692 *A.*2d 552 (citing *Klimko v. Rose,* 84 *N.J.* 496, 503-04, 422 *A.*2d 418 (1980)). The trial of a common knowledge case is essentially the same as an ordinary negligence case, and the jury is permitted to supply the applicable standard of care. *Rosenberg, supra,* 99 *N.J.* at 325, 492 *A.*2d 371 (citations omitted).

Although related, *res ipsa* and common knowledge doctrine cases are different, as explained by our Supreme Court in *Sanzari v. Rosenfeld,* 34 *N.J.* 128, 167 *A.*2d 625 (1961):

> In *res ipsa* cases, plaintiff need only prove his injury, and need not prove a standard of care or a specific act or omission. Ordinarily, the common knowledge doctrine is applied in a malpractice case after the plaintiff proves his injury *and* a causally related act or omission by the defendant.
> [*Id.* at 141, 167 *A.*2d 625 (emphasis added).]

Thus, *res ipsa* cases only require plaintiff's showing of an injury; the establishment of a standard of care is not part of the plaintiff's case. By contrast, a common knowledge case requires plaintiff's proof of an injury and some act or failure to act by defendant that led to the injury.

All defendants in the present case accepted the premise that gas was pumped into Mrs. Chin through the exhaust line. We observe, therefore, that the case hinged primarily on the jury's determinations regarding who did what with the exhaust line, rather than with regard to professional standards of care. Indeed, during colloquy preceding the testimony of plaintiff's expert, Dr. Piver, counsel for the hospital defendants conceded that this case is a common knowledge case "to the extent that if there is an incorrect hook-up, the jury can figure that out." We are persuaded, therefore, that the court did not err in submitting the case against the hospital defendants to the jury based on a common knowledge standard.

The hospital defendants contend that the trial court erred in not submitting the case against Dr. Goldfarb to the jury based on common knowledge, rather than on a standard of care to be supplied by expert testimony.

(continued)

To the extent that the court may have erred in this regard we conclude that the error was not "clearly capable of producing an unjust result." R. 2:10-2. Dr. Piver testified as an expert against Dr. Goldfarb. According to Dr. Piver, Mrs. Chin's death was the result of an improper connection of the Bard device to the hysteroscope, causing the introduction of gas into the uterus and the bloodstream. Dr. Piver opined that Dr. Goldfarb made the fatally incorrect connection. He also testified that Dr. Goldfarb had "a duty to observe, and should have observed, that the hook-up was not correct." Thus, the expert testimony against Dr. Goldfarb coincided with the theory accepted by all parties, that the incorrect connection of the exhaust line caused Mrs. Chin's death. In addition, Dr. Piver's testimony directly pointed the finger of blame at Dr. Goldfarb. In these circumstances, we perceive no harmful error.

We deem it unnecessary to describe in detail the testimony and evidence in this case. We are satisfied that the direct and circumstantial evidence and the inferences which reasonably could have been drawn from the evidence would have supported several theories of liability.

The jury could have determined that Dr. Goldfarb connected the exhaust line to the scope's outflow port. Alternatively, the jury could have found that Dr. Goldfarb did not connect the exhaust line to the outflow port, but bore some responsibility for Mrs. Chin's death because he did not recognize that gas was being pumped into his patient.

Regarding the nurses, the jury could have determined that one of them was responsible for the missing third clip on the exhaust line and that the disconnection of the exhaust line from the gas line facilitated the mistaken use of the exhaust line by Dr. Goldfarb or by a nurse. The jury could have found that the nurses were not qualified to work with the equipment; that one of them connected the exhaust line to a suction canister to which the suction tubing was attached; or that one of them left the loose exhaust line in a position where Dr. Goldfarb could have mistaken it for a suction tube. The jury could have determined that the hospital, through one of its employees, had assigned unqualified people to this procedure and had not required nurse Leib to attend a training session regarding the Bard apparatus.

The evidence was conflicting and inconsistent. Leib's testimony and reasonable inferences drawn from it would have supported a finding that the exhaust line had been connected to the outflow port on the scope, and that Dr. Goldfarb had made the connection. Dr. Goldfarb denied that he had connected the exhaust line. His expert witness, Dr. Lefler, placed the blame on one of the nurses for allegedly connecting the exhaust line to the suction canister. Dr. Lefler's testimony was admissible because it was based, at least implicitly, on Dr. Goldfarb's testimony that he had not connected the exhaust line to the outflow port. Thus, if the jury found Dr. Goldfarb's testimony in this regard to be credible, it could have relied on Lefler's theory.

The jury, of course, had to make credibility decisions. They could have accepted some of a witnesses's testimony as credible and rejected the rest of it. They could have found the testimony of a witness to be entirely credible or incredible. The point is, there was no "smoking gun" in this case. There was no obvious resolution of what happened in the operating room. There are only theories, the acceptance of which depended on the jury's evaluation of credibility and the inferences to be drawn from facts as found by them.

In these circumstances, the applicability of *Anderson* renders the jury's verdict virtually unassailable because each defendant had the burden of persuading the jury that it was not culpable. Thus, the verdict represents

(continued)

the jury's determination that Goldfarb, Leib, Hofgesang, and the hospital did not completely carry their burdens of exculpation. It is a determination which is rationally related to the evidence.

The judgment solely against Dr. Goldfarb is reversed. The case is remanded for entry of a judgment against the hospital defendants and Dr. Goldfarb in accordance with the jury's verdict.

ASSIGNMENT 3.2

Based on the reasoning in the case above, create a factual situation in which an unsafe product used in a health care setting would support a claim for malpractice under a products liability theory. Assume there is no medical malpractice legislation in your jurisdiction.

As medical providers become more and more comprehensive in their delivery of products and services, the patient as a consumer is placed at an increasingly distant point from the manufacturer of medically based products. Additionally, if the provider regularly obtains such products and supplies them to patients at a profit, the provider becomes more and more similar to a member of the stream of commerce. Combined with the increasing complexity and advanced nature of such products and the patient's total inability to determine safety versus the provider's increased knowledge and opportunity to inspect the product, it is likely that more courts will join in a trend to permit such actions against providers. In the context of medical malpractice litigation, a crucial consideration for the legal professional is to determine whether the case sounds in products liability or negligence as the result of medical malpractice. This distinction at the outset will often determine the path of litigation as the two areas are often governed by different statutory requirements (e.g., statutes of limitation, damages, pretrial procedures, etc.).

Problem 3.1

Complete 3.1 of the Comprehensive Problem in Appendix A.

CHAPTER SUMMARY

This chapter explored many of the ways in which medical malpractice cases develop and how the parties are involved. Dispelling the common misconception that these cases are confined to physicians and their patients, the text shows that medical malpractice can involve various types of independent providers such as optometrists, dentists, therapists, and other professionals who provide medical care, treatment or services. Actions against organizations are not uncommon and may include hospitals, clinics, and even long-term care facilities such as rehabilitation centers and nursing homes. Cases involve not only negligence in the physical delivery of services, but also ethical violations and failure to provide a safe environment. Products cases based on strict liability, traditionally confined to the manufacturers and dealers, have seen some extension to providers who routinely use products and sell them to patients at a profit. Changes in society over the past century have seen malpractice principles create and abandon such doctrines as charitable immunity. Additionally, working for change continues in the courts and through legislation in an attempt to reduce tremendous monetary judgments and create some form of control over the medical malpractice epidemic.

Key Terms

alternative health care	JCAHO
criminal conduct	respondeat superior
ethics	specialist
HIPAA	

End Notes

[1] Coverage of Professional Liability or Indemnity Policy For Sexual Contact With Patients By Physicians, Surgeons, and Other Healers, 60 A.L.R. 5th 239.

[2] Hull v. Foley, 17 Mass.L.Rptr. 187, 2004 WL 65287 (Mass. Supp.)

[3] Groner v. DeLevie, 2001 WL 438701 (Ohio App.)

[4] What Constitutes Physician-Patient Relationship For Malpractice Purposes, 17 A.L.R. 4th 132.

 For additional resources, go to http://www.westlegalstudies.com.

CHAPTER 4

Risk Management Issues In the Health Care Industry

CHAPTER OBJECTIVES

When you complete this chapter, you should be able to:

- Explain the doctrine of informed consent

- Describe the need for legal protection of confidentiality and patient privilege

- Discuss the important benefits of proper documentation of health care and the dangers associated with improper documentation

- Describe how provider qualifications and compliance with legal standards are established

- Discuss the importance of the safe environment in the health care facility

RISK MANAGEMENT AS PART OF THE DELIVERY OF HEALTH CARE

Although medical malpractice has existed almost as long as the American legal system, the concept of taking proactive measures to reduce the chances of injuries, and consequently successful malpractice claims, is a fairly recent development. The concept has quickly become a major component in the delivery of health care in the United States. Even though formalized **risk management** measures did not even exist on a wide scale until the latter half of the twentieth century, the growth was swift. Today, risk management is a lucrative career in and of itself with colleges and universities across the country offering undergraduate and graduate degree programs.

Most health care facilities of even moderate size employ individuals whose sole purpose is to deal with risk management issues. Larger facilities may have an entire department staffed to handle these matters. Others contract with independent consulting firms that evaluate, make recommendations, and in some cases implement measures with respect to matters involving risk management. Effective risk management is a three step process. First, it is necessary to identify potential dangers of all kinds and implement whatever measures are necessary to eliminate or, at the very least, minimize the chance of injury of any kind. Second, steps must be taken to maintain a safe environment from not only a physical but a legal viewpoint. This may include periodic inspections, training, and updating of staff, procedures, systems, and equipment. Finally, risk management is used to respond to incidents which may give rise to litigation. These issues range from written reports to record the circumstances of physical injuries, to the correction of problems discovered in recordkeeping, equipment, the facility itself, and staffing. While risk management issues apply to patients, staff, and others who may be in contact with a provider or facility in a professional capacity, this chapter will focus on issues dealing with the patients of health care providers.

Today, state and federal law impacts risk management issues directly. Jurisdictions employ statutes and regulations that establish and require compliance with minimum standards for issues such as record creation and maintenance, communication between patients and providers, **confidentiality**, continued medical education by providers, and periodic review of services provided by the health care professionals. State and federal regulatory agencies such as the CDC, OSHA, and others require various measures of compliance to maximize safety. Failure to abide by these legal standards can have a direct impact on the ability of a facility and/or provider to continue in a professional capacity. Additionally, there are many instances where the failure to comply may well be used as evidence against a provider in a malpractice action. Also, various agencies and organizations that offer accreditation independent of government, such as JCAHO, employ a variety of measures that are required to ensure appropriate risk management procedure within the health care facility.

INFORMED CONSENT

While perhaps not the oldest basis for medical malpractice actions, there is little question that the issue of **informed consent** has seen the highest volume and most rapid growth of all the causes of action in medical malpractice cases. Throughout the mid 1900s, the question of what constituted informed consent arose in virtually every jurisdiction in America. The doctrine of informed consent essentially maintains that, short of an emergency situation, a patient (or one who is legally authorized if the patient is incapacitated) has the right to receive and understand the following information before making a determination of whether to proceed:

1. diagnosis (and any other possible diagnosis);
2. course of recommended treatment;
3. alternative options for treatment;
4. significant risks and benefits of recommended treatment plan;
5. expected result of recommended treatment.[1]

Initially, the standard was measured against what information a reasonable physician would provide under the circumstances.[2] In each case, the court considered what a reasonably skilled provider would disclose to a patient prior to a particular service or treatment. The focus was on what and how much the professional community thought the patient ought to be told. This was supported by the traditional view of health care providers as having specialized knowledge far beyond that of the patient. As such, the provider was deemed to be the party most appropriate to decide what was in the patient's best interest. In the latter part of the twentieth century and now, in the early twenty-first century, this standard has been abandoned by most jurisdictions in favor of one focused on the patient. Many jurisdictions have enacted legislation that requires informed consent; the majority of jurisdictions interpret the doctrine as one which requires a health care provider to consider the patient's right to know all significant benefits and risks before proceeding with treatment.[3] Most health-care-based professions have also amended their own codes of ethics to impose a duty to communicate the risks and benefits of proposed treatments, care or services to the patient and obtain consent to proceed. The end result is a much broader disclosure to the patient and ample opportunity for the patient to have the controlling role in his or her health care decisions. In fact, in 1990, Congress responded to legal issues regarding informed consent by passing the *Patient Self Determination Act, 42 U.S.C.A. Section 1395, et.seq.* With this legislation, Congress supported all state law that required disclosure of information to patients. From a practical standpoint, the legislation responded to the growing concern about a patient and/or legally authorized representative's right to determine whether life-prolonging procedures should be administered. It also had an impact on the everyday delivery of health care by mandating compliance with legal principles of informed consent. With federal legislation in place, providers who failed to comply could jeopardize federal funding through various programs, both state and federal, including Medicare and Medicaid. From a risk management point of view, this legislation, along with the many state statutes, has sent a clear message to providers that an informed consent should always be obtained prior to delivery of any type of health care, treatment or services.

Despite the technological revolution and increased computer use in our society, when it comes to legal issues America is still largely a paper society. In most transactions involving interaction with others there is a paper record. In the case of anything that is, or could potentially result in, a legal issue requires a signature. Even computerized systems such as retail store credit card processors often require a photo image of one's signature, which is accomplished by signing a screen. With regard to health care records, signatures are often necessary for documents that are lengthy or full of technical and legal terminology. Anyone who has ever been hospitalized can attest to the numerous papers that must be signed to get in—and even get out of—the facility. As a result, it is not uncommon for consent to care, treatment, and services to be buried amidst the various other documents relating to insurance, billing, etc. Nevertheless, it is an essential risk management procedure that any consent to treatment be identified as such and be as specific as possible. Additionally, someone with the ability to explain the various terms of the document should be readily available to the patient.

One response to the increase in cases regarding informed consent was to develop patient education materials. It is rare these days to enter any type of health care facility—a large hospital or, a physicians clinic—and not find such materials. These educational materials may be general information or pamphlets focused on specific procedures and treatments. The educational materials are presented in a variety of formats including papers, pamphlets, audio tapes, and video materials. Some are interactive and require the patient to answer questions or make comments. Such features are not for entertainment but rather, to assist the patient's education and, ultimately, risk management. The more evidence presented that a patient participated in educational sessions decreases the likelihood of a claim of lack of informed consent. However, regardless of the amount or level of sophistication of patient education materials provided, this alone is insufficient to prove there is informed consent. The doctrine requires that the provider, or knowledgeable person, meet with the patient and discuss the procedure as well as answer any questions.[4] If the patient refuses, there is a corresponding obligation to discuss the possible outcomes of the refusal. Also, a general consent to receive medical care, treatment, and services at a facility is not the same as an informed consent. The latter requires disclosure and discussion of information about the specific treatment plan.

There are circumstances where informed consent is not required. It is generally accepted that informed consent is present when the patient submits to procedures and treatment that are considered simple and common. Typically these are routinely performed procedures that are not considered to be invasive in terms of entering body cavities and/or accompanied by a significant risk of serious injury. Examples might include taking of vital signs such as blood pressure, temperature, height, and weight; blood draws; and injections of regularly used low-risk medications. Conversely, the administration of high-risk drugs such as chemotherapy and blood products, or performing procedures so significant as to require sedation or invasion that requires opening of the skin beyond something such as a superficial needle puncture, are those which ordinarily warrant an informed consent.

In addition to the question of whether the procedure itself warrants consent, there are certain circumstances in which the patient's condition eliminates the requirement for informed consent. The obvious situation—an emergency—is described as one of the key elements of the doctrine of informed consent.

If the patient's condition is such that they are unable to give consent and no legally authorized representative is available, the treatment may be administered if it is necessary to save the patient's life or prevent an irreversible deterioration of their condition. There are other circumstances in which consent may not be required. Most often this occurs with patients whose mental condition is such that a disclosure of necessary medical care may cause greater risk of harm than any benefit achieved by the procedure of informed consent.[5] However, most jurisdictions with informed consent statutes require documentation that more than one provider considered the circumstance and agreed that, for therapeutic reasons, it is best that the patient not be provided with full disclosure of the treatment plan risks and benefits. As always in the case of a patient's incapacity, consent of a legally authorized representative should be sought whenever possible. In some circumstances, this may even require that steps be taken to legally obtain such authorization. For example, if an adult child is mentally challenged but no legal guardianship has been established, it may be necessary to obtain court approved authority in order to properly give an informed consent. Also, in the case of a minor who has not been legally emancipated, parental consent is typically required except in very specific circumstances. These are usually identified by statute and vary from state to state. However, it is now more common that minors do not need parental consent for contraceptive or pregnancy-related treatment (other than sterilization), substance abuse treatment, and sexually transmitted disease diagnosis/treatment.

APPLICATION 4.1

Miranda, 29 years old, is admitted to a busy urban hospital after receiving serious injuries in an automobile accident. She is in a great deal of pain but is conscious. A nurse enters the emergency room and hands Miranda a clipboard with a number of documents to sign. The nurse asks Miranda to sign on the line marked with an "X" on each of the documents and without further explanation leaves the room. Among the many documents is a two-page consent to surgery for her injuries with a specific statement permitting all necessary procedures including a hysterectomy if the internal injuries cannot be adequately repaired in surgery. Unaware of the content of the documents, Miranda does as she is asked and signs each line marked with an "X." The hysterectomy is in fact performed during surgery and eliminates the possibility Miranda will ever have children. When she awakens she claims to have never given consent for such drastic measures.

Proper risk management policies would never encourage a situation such as that described above. Someone should have assessed whether the patient's physical condition left her with the ability to give consent for the full scope of her treatment. If not, and if her life was not in immediate danger, her legally authorized representative should have been contacted to advise her about consent. With respect to the consent, the party signing should have been given specific information as to the nature of the document, adequate opportunity to examine it, and to discuss the contents with someone who could properly explain the treatment plan, possible outcomes, and various associated risks and benefits.

The situation such as that described in Application 4.1 was once the standard procedure in many health care facilities. As a result, many lawsuits were filed by patients who alleged they did not have adequate information and opportunity to make in informed decision regarding their health care. In fact, many patients claimed to have not even been aware that their signature on the stack of forms included a consent to treatment. As a body of law developed from the many malpractice cases filed, some basic standards for evaluating allegations regarding informed consent evolved. Today, when a patient alleges that the provider failed to obtain informed consent prior to a procedure, there are basic questions that must be considered:

- Was there an emergency situation or unanticipated circumstance that required immediate treatment regardless of consent?
- Was a competent patient or legally authorized representative given adequate information as well as other reasonable alternatives of all significant risks and benefits of the proposed treatment?
- If the consent was provided by the patient, was it given at a time and under circumstances wherein the patient could think clearly and properly process the information provided (e.g., not under the influence of medication)?
- Was the patient or legally authorized representative given adequate opportunity to ask questions and receive responses regarding the proposed treatment, risks, and benefits.
- Is there evidence to support a reasonable finding that if the patient or legally authorized representative had been given appropriate information and the opportunity to inquire about the proposed treatment, the treatment would have been refused?

All of these are important questions in making the determination of whether an informed consent was actually obtained. The first line of defense would be a signed authorization, but that can be negated if there is evidence that the patient did not fully understand the consent being provided, did not have opportunity to properly discuss the proposed treatment, did not have a clear mind at the time of the consent, or evidence indicated that the patient would have been opposed to the proposed treatment. As a result, the continuing trend in risk management has been to encourage thorough handling of any documents dealing with consent to medical care, treatment or services.

The illustration that follows is a sample document similar to those commonly used in medical facilities. See Exhibit 4.1

Exhibit 4.1   Sample Informed Consent Document

INFORMED CONSENT FOR MEDICAL PROCEDURE

1. I,_____, hereby authorize and direct_____, and/or associates of his/her choosing and at his/her direction to perform the following operation(s) or procedure(s):

_____

_____

2. I state that I have been informed of the significant risks and benefits associated with the above operation(s) or procedure(s) and, that I have had full opportunity to question and discuss the operation(s) or procedure(s), risks

(continued)

Exhibit 4.1, continued

and benefits, alternative treatments, and anticipated outcomes. I understand that the significant risks associated with the above operation(s) or procedure(s) may include but are not limited to the following:

_____

_____

_____

3. I further understand that all operations and procedures involved risks from unforeseen circumstances and from known possibilities including, but not limited to, unsuccessful results, complications, injury and death in addition to those normally associated with the particular operation or procedure.

4. I have been informed of whether my physician stands to benefit in any way either directly or indirectly economically or professionally, beyond ordinary interests from the performance of the operation(s) or procedure(s) named above.

5. I am aware that there may be other health care providers or authorized persons in the operating room during the above operation(s) or procedure(s) for the purpose education or of providing technical support. I consent to their presence at the discretion of this facility and the health care provider whom I have designated to perform this operation(s) or procedure(s).

    I specifically do not consent to the presence of persons in the operating room other than the health care providers necessary to properly complete the above operation(s) or procedure(s)

_____

6. I understand and authorize the above health care provider to provide or arrange for the provision of such additional services and/or related procedures which he/she deems appropriate and necessarily incident to the above operation(s) or procedure(s) including, but not limited to pathology and radiological services.

ASSIGNMENT 4.1

Consider the following situations and determine whether it would be necessary and recommended to obtain a written informed consent. Explain your answer as to why the situation may or may not warrant documentation of consent.

1. An unidentified minor is brought in after being struck by a car. The child is approximately 10 years of age. He suffers from a badly broken jaw and two broken arms with a crushed right hand and possible head injury. All of the injuries require surgical intervention. He is unable to talk or write because of his injuries.

(continued)

2. A 17-year-old boy (a minor by state law) presents himself to his family physician and requests that he be sterilized.

3. A patient previously diagnosed as paranoid schizophrenic is in need of surgery to remove a tumor from her intestine. She has told her doctor many times that she is convinced that general anesthesia is used by aliens who want to remove the brain of victims for their research. Therefore, she would like a local anesthetic to be used for her abdominal surgery.

4. A patient is scheduled to receive an experimental vaccine to prevent the common cold.

5. A doctor treating an elderly patient in a nursing home for a contagious disease has blood samples removed daily even though the patient stated clearly that he does not want to have this procedure performed.

It should be apparent at this point that the doctrine of informed consent alone poses a continuing challenge for risk managers. When properly administered, informed consent is a relatively simple task to accomplish in most situations. But, despite its simplicity, it is something that must be an integral part of the delivery of health care. It is something that requires active participation by the provider and patient. The failure to do so can result in significant liability for the provider and facility.

CONFIDENTIALITY AND PATIENT PRIVILEGE

It has long been held that the relationship between a patient and his or her health care provider is a fiduciary one. This type of relationship is one in which there is an inherent element of trust. It may exist between anyone who has what is considered to be a legal and/or ethical duty to respect the trust placed in them by another. In the case of health care, that trust presumes an element of privacy. The reasoning is that an important part of proper health care is full disclosure by a patient to the provider of all relevant information. However, patients may find some of the information they should disclose embarrassing or uncomfortably personal. To encourage disclosure of embarrassing or very personal information, the provider has an ethical and legal obligation to maintain such information as confidential as it pertains to a specific patient. Over time, this obligation has been relaxed and then restricted again but has always been present in some form as a cornerstone of the relationship between provider and patient.

As with other types of malpractice actions, cases alleging an improper dissemination of personal information by a provider have also increased in number in recent years. As a result, a body of common law, and in many states legislation, has developed to guide health care providers as to what constitutes appropriate and inappropriate disclosure of personal patient information. This became a particularly volatile issue with the advent of the AIDS (Acquired Immune Deficiency Syndrome) epidemic in this country. The problems associated with the AIDS crisis and treatment of individuals who tested positive for HIV (the disease that causes AIDS) became so serious that legal standards were created specifically to protect the confidentiality of this information.

A split objective came to the forefront with the advent of the AIDS crisis. On the one hand, AIDS testing for early diagnosis and effective treatment is paramount. A percentage of infections are the result of unprotected sexual contact or hypodermic needle use. As a result, many individuals are less than anxious to come forward for testing with respect to a disease that has such socially negative connotations affiliated with it. The government and health care industry want to encourage any individual who has been placed at risk to be tested. Thus, the promise of confidentiality is especially important. Conversely, there is the real need to identify and communicate with all who are known to be at risk given the highly communicable aspects of the disease under certain circumstances. This would require informing such individuals that they have had sufficient contact with individuals testing positive for HIV, but that compromises the confidentiality issue. The majority of jurisdictions continue to address these issues in the various circumstances in which they occur. As a result, this area of law is still in its infancy stage as the courts and legislatures attempt to strike a balance between the need for public welfare and the very personal right to privacy.

The increase in cases alleging medical malpractice and the specific focus on confidentiality generated by the AIDS crisis caused the entire approach toward patient rights to confidentiality to be addressed nationwide. In 2003, federal regulations impacted the entire issue of privacy through the new HIPAA regulations discussed earlier in Chapter 2. Prior to this, a number of jurisdictions adopted very general statutes and/or a case-by-case approach because the circumstances were so varied. While it was universally agreed that public disclosures of personal medical information that were specific to a particular identified patient would be improper, there were other situations that fell into a gray area. Some of the questions regarding patient confidentiality that arose and received different answers in different jurisdictions include, but are not limited to, the following:

- If an employer sent a patient to a physician and paid for diagnosis and treatment of a condition that impacted the patient's employability, should the employer be entitled to that information?
- Are family members such as spouses or legally authorized representatives entitled to private information?
- If the patient's name is not given, can film footage or photographs of conditions or treatment be published?
- Is the privacy requirement presumed or should there be consent or restriction by the patient and, if not, should the patient's request be in writing?
- Can medical test results be disseminated to a government official if they are relevant to a criminal prosecution?

While many of the courts reached different conclusions in various jurisdictions, it is not an entirely volatile area of law without established standards. Rather, when an issue regarding an alleged breach of patient confidentiality occurs, the case often turns on the specific circumstances of the case. In these types of suits some of the questions frequently considered and discussed by the courts in their opinions include the following:

- Was there any specific regulatory or statutory protection of the information that was communicated?
- Was the disclosure of specific information regarding to the patient's particular medical condition or was it information of a more general nature?
- Was the patient's identity communicated along with specific facts about their medical condition or were general statements made that precluded the recipient of the information from deducing the patient's actual identity?
- Did the party receiving the information have a legitimate interest in the patient's medical condition and circumstances which would warrant the disclosure?

Most often, if a provider disclosed the identity and medical information that the patient would have reasonably expected to be private and which had not been disclosed by the patient previously, then there is an obligation to keep such information private. There are, of course, exceptions which have been previously mentioned. These include consent, or disclosure by request, disclosure necessary to facilitate the patient's treatment, protected public health interests, and cases in which the patient has placed their medical condition in issue as part of litigation. There may be other circumstances as well but these are the most common.

Under the new HIPAA regulations, risk managers were given a great deal of direction and support from federal regulations that specifically set forth privacy standards for health care providers. As a result, formal written statements were prepared and are now routinely provided to patients as a clear and unequivocal statement of the rights and duties of the provider and patient with respect to personal information. The objective is to protect personal privacy, reduce the number of instances in which information is improperly disseminated and in turn reduce the number of lawsuits that result from the disclosure. Additionally, patients who receive these statements have much clearer expectations of what can and cannot be passed on to third parties. From a risk management perspective, the statements are a tremendous advantage. And, unlike the informed consent issue, the effectiveness of the privacy statements are not conditioned on an interaction between the provider and patient. If the patient signs a document that they've received the statement, and the provider abides by its terms, the privacy policies of providers should be a valuable risk management tool. Exhibit 4.2 is an example of a comprehensive privacy policy document similar to that used by providers following the issuance of the new HIPAA regulations.

Exhibit 4.2 Sample Privacy Policy

PRIVACY POLICY

HOW MEDICAL INFORMATION ABOUT YOU MAY BE USED AND DISCLOSED AND YOUR RIGHTS TO ACCESSES THIS INFORMATION. PLEASE READ CAREFULLY.

EFFECTIVE APRIL 1, 2003.

The following is the privacy policy("Privacy Policy") for this facility and its employees ("Covered Entity") as described in the Health Insurance Portability and Accountability Act of 1996 ("HIPAA") and all regulations promulgated thereunder. HIPAA requires by law that the Covered Entity maintain the privacy of your personal health information. It further requires that you be provided with notice of the legal duties of the Covered Entity and all privacy policies with respect to your personal health information.

The Covered Entity collects personal health information through treatment, payment and related healthcare operations, the application and enrollment process, and/or health care plans, health care providers, and other means. Your personal health information that is protected by law includes all information, oral, written, or recorded, that is created or received by certain health care entities, including, but not limited to, health care providers, such as physicians and hospitals, as well as health insurance companies or plans. HIPAA specifically protects person health information that contains identifying data that could be used to identify you as the individual associated with that information.

(continued)

Exhibit 4.2, continued

Unless otherwise subject to legal exception, your personal health information may not be disclosed without your permission. If permitted, disclosures of personal health information is limited to the scope and specific terms of the permission. In addition to permitted disclosure, the following lists some of those circumstances in which disclosure may be made:

a) Incidental disclosure relevant to the delivery of care within the office setting by conversations among health care staff and physicians.

b) As necessary to provide adequate services and or treatment that is required or requested.

c) To collect payment for services through any government or private insurance or reimbursement plan.

d) For the development of clinical guidelines, review of the qualifications of and training for health care professionals, general administrative activities including, but not limited to, customer service and data analysis.

Your personal health information may be disclosed to the extent it is required by law including, but not limited to:

a) public health requirements to prevent or control disease or other injury; public health surveillance and/or investigations with regard to the workplace, reporting adverse conditions with regard to food or dietary supplements or product defects to the Food and Drug Administration,

b) disclosures regarding victims of abuse, neglect, or domestic violence,

c) judicial and administrative proceedings in response to legal requirements such as warrant, subpoena, court order, discovery requests or other lawful purpose,

d) disclosures with respect to decedents for the purpose of organ, eye, tissue donation,

e) governmentally authorized research, military, national security, intelligence, and protection of government officers purposes,

f) government authorized programs providing benefits for the public and worker's compensation funds.

With the exception of those matters above, your personal health information may not be disclosed absent your express written authorization. Any such disclosure shall be in accordance with the terms of such authorization. Your authorization may be revoked unless it was conditional for obtainment of health insurance coverage.

(continued)

Exhibit 4.2, continued

You may be contacted and personal health information discussed with you for the purpose of scheduling, appointment reminder, treatment alternatives, and other health benefits and services that may be relevant to you. You may also be contacted for the purposes of fundraising for purposes related to the Covered Entity.

You may request restrictions on the use and disclosure of your personal health information with regard to who is provided such information. It is not mandatory that such restrictions be followed unless you receive a written consent to such restrictions.

You have the right to confidential communication of your personal health information. Such confidentiality may be conditional upon compliance with established rules for establishing method of contact, payment for services, and acknowledgment that the restriction of such confidentiality could endanger you.

You have the right to inspect and obtain copies of your personal health information including medical and billing records, insurance enrollment, claims adjudication, and case or medical management records systems except for: a) information prepared in reasonable anticipation of, or for use in judicial or administrative proceedings, b) information that may be withheld by law, c) psychotherapy notes. You may be required to complete a written request for access and/or copies of your personal health information. Such request must be complied with by us in a reasonable and timely manner. You may be charged a reasonable cost-based fee for preparation of the records.

This privacy policy may be revised or amended at any time. Such revisions or amendments may be effective for all existing and future personal health information and records. Such revisions and amendments will be available for 60 days following said change at the primary care delivery sites and administrative offices. At any time, a current copy of the effective privacy policy may be obtained at the primary care delivery sites and administrative offices.

Documents like the one above are appearing in health care provider offices and facilities—including not only doctors and hospitals, but also dentists, clinics, chiropractors, long-term-care facilities, and other types of organizations—that are in the business of dealing with individual health care needs. While they contribute to what may already seem like the mountain of paper patients must deal with, they are an important aspect of risk management. When evaluating a potential case of malpractice, it is important to note the policies, procedures, and actual level of compliance with regard to patient confidentiality. Even though this may not be an issue in some specific cases, the practices of a provider give some insight as to the carefulness with which services are delivered as a whole.

CASE

335 Ill.App.3d 809, 781 N.E.2d 340, 269 Ill.Dec. 543

Appellate Court of Illinois,
Fifth District.

Jane DOE, Plaintiff-Appellee,
v.
Santosh P. CHAND, M.D., and Santosh P. Chand, M.D., Ltd., Defendants-Appellants.

Sept. 4, 2002.

Justice RARICK delivered the opinion of the court:

The plaintiff, Jane Doe, filed a multicount complaint in the circuit court of St. Clair County against Dr. Santosh P. Chand and Dr. Santosh P. Chand, M.D., Ltd. (defendants), alleging, *inter alia*, a violation of the AIDS Confidentiality Act (Act) (410 ILCS 305/1 *et seq.* (West 1998)).

Doe testified that in February 1999 she learned that her husband had tested positive for the human immunodeficiency virus (HIV). She stated that she did not immediately seek to be tested because she was certain what the results would be and she was not ready to find out. On April 17, 1999, Doe went to Dr. Chand's office to pick up her mother, who was also a patient of Dr. Chand's. When Doe told Dr. Chand about her husband, Dr. Chand suggested that she be tested, and she agreed. Doe testified that Dr. Chand did not provide a written consent form or give her any written information concerning the testing or the availability of counseling. Doe stated that she called Dr. Chand's office on several occasions to inquire about the results of her HIV test. Each time she was told that the test results were not in. Doe stated that she learned of the results from her sister, Pamela Randolph. Doe and her mother had gone to Randolph's house. When they arrived, Randolph told her that she had been informed by Dr. Chand that Doe had tested positive for HIV. Doe also testified that she had spoken with several other persons who stated that they knew Doe had HIV or AIDS and that they had learned of such from Dr. Chand.

Doe further testified that in May 2000 she took a leave of absence from her job as a loan processor at the local credit union. Doe stated that many of Dr. Chand's patients were customers of the credit union and that she was constantly worried about whether they knew of her condition. Doe moved to Chicago and lived with a friend. While there, she worked as a bank teller. Prior to trial, Doe relocated to Champaign, Illinois.

Barbara Fergeson testified that she was a patient of Dr. Chand's and knew Doe. In July 1999 she encountered Doe in a local shopping mall. During their conversation, Doe disclosed that her husband had AIDS

(continued)

and that he had given her AIDS. Fergeson stated that about a month later she was in Dr. Chand's office and mentioned that she had seen Doe. At that time Dr. Chand stated that Doe had AIDS. Lisa Mohammed, Dr. Chand's phlebotomist, and Angela Hubbard, the receptionist, were present at the time.

Pamela Randolph, Doe's sister, testified that Dr. Chand called her at home and told her that Doe had tested positive for HIV. According to Randolph, Dr. Chand felt that Doe should get the news from a family member. Randolph further testified that several months later she noticed that Doe was very upset. When Randolph asked why, Doe stated that she had been hearing rumors that others knew of her condition and that Dr. Chand had obviously told other people.

Nancy White testified that she was a patient of Dr. Chand's and knew Doe from Dr. Chand's office. White testified that she was in Dr. Chand's office when Dr. Chand called her back into an examining room and told her to stay away from Doe because she had AIDS.

Lisa Mohammed testified that she was a phlebotomist and worked in Dr. Chand's office. Mohammed stated that after being informed that Doe's test results were positive, Dr. Chand asked her if she should call Doe's sister because she did not know how Doe would handle the information. Mohammed responded that Dr. Chand knew best how to handle her patients. Mohammed did not remember Dr. Chand telling Barbara Fergeson that Doe had AIDS.

Natasha Thornton testified that she was a patient of Dr. Chand's. She was seeing Dr. Chand in an effort to get pregnant. She testified that Dr. Chand had called her and asked her to come to the office. Once she was there, Dr. Chand informed her that she had tested positive for a sexually transmitted disease. When Thornton disputed the test results, Dr. Chand said that she was just like Doe, who did not want to believe that she had AIDS.

Over defendant's objections, Doe introduced the testimony of Judith Murashige, an art therapist. Murashige testified that she had treated Doe for emotional issues related to having been diagnosed HIV positive and to Dr. Chand's disclosure of her HIV status.

Introduced into evidence was the deposition of Dr. Paul L'Ecuyer, an infectious-disease specialist. Dr. L'Ecuyer testified that Doe was his patient and had been referred to him by her insurance company for treatment of her HIV infection. He first saw Doe on May 28, 1999. Doe continued to see Dr. L'Ecuyer on a regular basis. At one of their follow-up appointments, Doe stated that she was upset with Dr. Chand for having disclosed to several people that she was HIV positive. Dr. L'Ecuyer opined that Doe suffered from anxiety and depression and that Dr. Chand's disclosure of Doe's HIV status was a contributing cause.

Dr. Chand testified that she called Doe at home. Doe's mother answered the phone and asked about the test results. Dr. Chand told her mother that she did not know what to say, that they should talk to Doe, and that she was not happy. Dr. Chand testified that Pamela Randolph called. Dr. Chand told Randolph that she was not happy and to have Doe call her because she needed to get some more work-up done on her.

On May 13, 1999, Doe came to Dr. Chand's office for further testing. Dr. Chand discussed the results of the test with Doe and the need for follow-up testing. Dr. Chand denied disclosing the results of the test to Doe's mother, her sister, or anyone else.

(continued)

Prior to trial, Doe voluntarily dismissed all but the count under the Act. Dr. Chand's request for a jury trial was subsequently denied by the trial court. After a bench trial, the trial court found that Doe had proved "numerous" violations of the Act, some of which were negligent and some of which were intentional or reckless, and that she had suffered emotional and nonemotional damages as a result. Based upon these findings, the trial court awarded Doe $600,000 in actual damages and $300,000 in punitive damages.

On appeal, defendants argue first that Doe's counsel, JoeDee Favre, should have been disqualified. Defendants contend that from June 1996 through January 1998, attorney Favre represented defendants on numerous matters relating to Dr. Chand's suspension of privileges at numerous hospitals for inadequate record-keeping, complaints brought by the Illinois Department of Professional Regulation regarding Dr. Chand's license and record-keeping, a social security matter involving an order of protection with a former patient, and a medical malpractice matter. Defendants maintain that during this time, attorney Favre was provided with unrestricted access to defendant's private office and that defendants' employees provided attorney Favre with patient records. Because of the prior representation, defendants argue, attorney Favre had valuable insight into the policies and procedures of defendants' office, including the manner in which records were maintained, which is the subject matter of several of the allegations made by Doe.

The determination of whether counsel should be disqualified is directed to the sound discretion of the trial court and will not be disturbed on appeal absent an abuse of that discretion. *Franzoni v. Hart Schaffner & Marx,* 312 Ill.App.3d 394, 244 Ill.Dec. 744, 726 N.E.2d 719 (2000). An abuse of discretion occurs when no reasonable person would agree with the position adopted by the trial court. *Gerber v. Hamilton,* 276 Ill.App.3d 1091, 213 Ill.Dec. 527, 659 N.E.2d 443 (1995). Where the question on appeal involves the resolution of factual issues, the trial court's determinations will not be disturbed unless they are unsupported by the evidence in the record. *International Insurance Co. v. City of Chicago Heights,* 268 Ill.App.3d 289, 205 Ill.Dec. 698, 643 N.E.2d 1305 (1994).

Rule 1.9 of the Illinois Rules of Professional Conduct, which defines the scope of an attorney's obligation to refrain from representing a person with interests that are materially adverse to the interest of a former client, provides:
   "(a) A lawyer who has formerly represented a client in a matter shall not thereafter:
   (1) represent another person in the same or a substantially related matter in which that person's interests are materially adverse to the interests of the former client, unless the former client consents after disclosure; or
   (2) use information relating to the representation to the disadvantage of the former client, unless:
   (A) such use is permitted by Rule 1.6; or
   (B) the information has become generally known." 134 Ill.2d R. 1.9.

In *Schwartz v. Cortelloni,* 177 Ill.2d 166, 226 Ill.Dec. 416, 685 N.E.2d 871 (1997), our supreme court held:
   "Under Rule 1.9 * * * an attorney's subsequent representation of a person with interests adverse to a former client is prohibited only if the matters involved in the two representations are the same or substantially related. The party seeking disqualification bears the burden of establishing that the present and former representations are substantially related. If a substantial relationship between the two matters is not shown, then no breach of the duty of confidentiality will be found. Attorney disqualification is a drastic measure because it destroys the attorney-client relationship by prohibiting a party from

(continued)

representation by counsel of his or her choosing. Thus, caution must be exercised to guard against motions to disqualify being used as tools for harassment." *Schwartz,* 177 Ill.2d at 177-78, 226 Ill.Dec. 416, 685 N.E.2d at 877.

In determining whether a substantial relationship exists between two representations, a careful examination of the factual context of the judgment matters of both representations is necessary in order to determine whether disqualification is required. See *Hannan v. Watt,* 147 Ill.App.3d 456, 100 Ill.Dec. 945, 497 N.E.2d 1307 (1986). In *Schwartz,* our supreme court adopted the three-step analysis set forth in *LaSalle National Bank v. County of Lake,* 703 F.2d 252 (7th Cir.1983), for making such determination. Under the *LaSalle* inquiry, the court must first make a factual reconstruction of the scope of the former representation. It must then determine whether it is reasonable to infer that the confidential information allegedly given would have been given to a lawyer representing a client on those matters. Finally, the court must consider whether the information is relevant to the issues raised in the litigation pending against the former client. *Schwartz,* 177 Ill.2d at 178, 226 Ill.Dec. 416, 685 N.E.2d at 877 (citing *LaSalle,* 703 F.2d at 256).

In the present case, defendants filed a motion to disqualify attorney Favre, arguing that through her prior representation of Dr. Chand, she learned confidential information, including: (1) Dr. Chand's dealing with the National Practitioner Databank, (2) information from current and former employees concerning Doe and Doe's witnesses, (3) the manner in which Dr. Chand tested patients for HIV or AIDS and informed them of the results, and (4) Dr. Chand's dealings with various hospitals concerning staff privileges and her record-keeping. Both parties submitted affidavits. In her affidavit in support of the motion to disqualify, Dr. Chand averred that Favre visited her office frequently, visiting both her and her staff. Dr. Chand further averred that as a result, Favre had the opportunity to observe how laboratory results were delivered and placed in patient records. Dr. Chand also made that statement because through her representation Favre became familiar with how Dr. Chand's office maintained records and confidential patient information. In her affidavit, attorney Favre disputed the frequency with which she visited Dr. Chand's office and denied seeing or having any knowledge of how test results were handled or how patients were tested for HIV or AIDS or how they were informed of the results.

Reviewing the record, we cannot say that the trial court abused its discretion in denying the motion to disqualify. Defendants offer only the vaguest allegations that attorney Favre obtained confidential information relevant to the current litigation, and they offer no specifics as to the nature of this confidential information or how it is relevant to the current litigation. Defendants contend that attorney Favre was in a position to see how Dr. Chand maintained her records and received and reported test results. Favre denied these allegations, however, and the trial court apparently found her more credible on this issue. In any event, such generalized allegations are wholly insufficient to meet the defendants' burden of demonstrating a substantial relationship between the current and former representations or to justify the drastic step of disqualifying Doe's chosen counsel.

Defendants argue next that they were entitled to a trial by jury. Defendants maintain that the essence of Doe's complaint is that the defendants improperly disclosed that Doe had tested positive for HIV and that she suffered from AIDS, that such disclosures were false, and that defendants tested Doe for HIV without obtaining her informed consent. Defendants contend that Doe could have sought relief for each of these claims through the common law causes of action for breach of contract, invasion of privacy, false light, or

(continued)

the tort of outrage, each of which Doe included her original complaint. Defendants maintain that the ACA did not create any new causes of action but that it merely codified existing causes of action and set forth requirements for a written informed consent. We do not agree.

In Illinois, the right to a trial by jury "only attaches in those actions where such right existed under the English common law at the time the constitution was adopted." *Martin v. Heinold Commodities, Inc.*, 163 Ill.2d 33, 73-74, 205 Ill.Dec. 443, 643 N.E.2d 734, 753 (1994). The test of whether or not the right to a jury trial exists in a given case depends on the nature of the controversy rather than the form of the action. *Flaherty v. Murphy,* 291 Ill. 595, 126 N.E. 553 (1920).

Section 13 of the Act (410 ILCS 305/13 (West 1998)) provides for a right of action for any violation of the Act itself or for a violation of any regulation promulgated by the Department of Public Health pursuant to section 16 thereof (410 ILCS 305/16 (West 1998)). There are numerous provisions of the Act the violation of which gives rise to no cause of action at common law. For example, section 5 of the Act provides that no physician may order an HIV test without making available to the person being tested information about the meaning of the test results, the availability of additional testing, and the availability of referrals for future information or counseling. 410 ILCS 305/5 (West 1998). No action for failure to provide such information exists at common law. Section 9 of the Act bars, with few exceptions, any person from disclosing the identity of anyone who has submitted to an HIV test, or the results thereof. 410 ILCS 305/9 (West 1998). No such broad right exists at common law for a person submitting to an HIV test. Section 10 provides that no person to whom test results have been disclosed may disclose the test results to another person, except as authorized by section 9. 410 ILCS 305/10 (West 1998). Section 6 requires that written informed consent be provided by using a coded system which does not link the identity of the individual with the test result. 410 ILCS 305/6 (West 1998). There is no requirement at common law that such a system be used to give informed consent. Moreover, section 3(d) of the Act provides:

> " 'Written informed consent' means an agreement in writing executed by the subject of a test or the subject's legally authorized representative without undue inducement or any element of force, fraud, deceit, duress or other form of constraint or coercion, which entails at least the following:
> (1) a fair explanation of the test, including its purpose, potential uses, limitations and the meaning of its results; and
> (2) a fair explanation of the procedures to be followed, including the voluntary nature of the test, the right to withdraw consent to the testing process at any time, the right to anonymity to the extent provided by law with respect to participation in the test and disclosure of test results, and the right to confidential treatment of information identifying the subject of the test and the results of the test, to the extent provided by law." 410 ILCS 305/3(d) (West 1998).

In a common law action based upon failure to obtain informed consent, "informed consent" means consent obtained from a patient by a health care provider after the disclosure by such provider of those factors which a reasonably well-qualified provider would disclose under the same or similar circumstances. See Illinois Pattern Jury Instructions, Civil, No. 105. 07.01 (3d ed.1990). The requirement for obtaining informed consent under the Act is both more comprehensive and more specific. Finally, in section 2(2) our legislature found, as one of its reasons for enacting the Act, that "[d]espite existing laws, regulations[,] and professional standards which require or promote the informed, voluntary[,] and confidential use of tests designed to reveal HIV infection, many members of the public are deterred from seeking such testing because they misunderstand the nature of the test or fear that test results will be disclosed without their consent." 410 ILCS 305/2(2)

(continued)

(West 1998). Clearly, our legislature felt that additional protection was needed to ensure the confidentiality of HIV testing. We conclude that in enacting the Act, our legislature created new rights for persons wishing to obtain confidential HIV testing and a new cause of action unknown at common law to protect those rights.

Defendants next argue that the trial court erred in awarding Doe punitive damages. Defendants contend that Doe was not entitled to punitive damages because the plain language of the Act does not provide for an award of punitive damages.

Section 13 of the Act provides:
"Any person aggrieved by a violation of this Act or of a regulation promulgated hereunder shall have a right of action in the circuit court and may recover for each violation:
(1) Against any person who negligently violates a provision of this Act or the regulations promulgated hereunder, liquidated damages of $1000 or actual damages, whichever is greater.
(2) Against any person who intentionally or recklessly violates a provision of this Act or the regulations promulgated hereunder, liquidated damages of $5000 or actual damages, whichever is greater.
(3) Reasonable attorney fees.
(4) Such other relief, including an injunction, as the court may deem appropriate." 410 ILCS 305/13 (West 1998).

It is well-settled that the cardinal rule of statutory construction is to ascertain and give effect to the intent of the legislature. *American Standard Insurance Co. of Wisconsin v. Gnojewski*, 319 Ill.App.3d 970, 254 Ill.Dec. 327, 747 N.E.2d 367 (2001). The most reliable indicator of legislative intent is the language of the statute, which is given its plain and ordinary meaning. *First Bank & Trust Co. of O'Fallon v. King*, 311 Ill.App.3d 1053, 244 Ill.Dec. 646, 726 N.E.2d 621 (2000). Where the language of the statute is clear and unambiguous, the statute will be enforced as written *819 and courts will not resort to other aids for construction. *Goff v. Teachers' Retirement System*, 305 Ill.App.3d 190, 239 Ill.Dec. 47, 713 N.E.2d 578 (1999). When ascertaining legislative intent from the language of the statute, a court will examine the language of the statute as a whole, considering each part of section in connection with every other part or section. **349***552*Monat v. County of Cook*, 322 Ill.App.3d 499, 255 Ill.Dec. 679, 750 N.E.2d 260 (2001).

Section 13 provides for liquidated or actual damages but does not specifically provide for punitive damages. It does, however, provide for "[s]uch other relief * * * as the court may deem appropriate." 410 ILCS 305/13 (West 1998). The question then becomes: Does "such other relief" include punitive damages? We conclude that it does not. Punitive damages are warranted where an otherwise negligent act is accompanied by outrageous conduct or acts committed with malice or reckless indifference to the rights of others. *McCann v. Presswood*, 308 Ill.App.3d 1068, 242 Ill.Dec. 532, 721 N.E.2d 811 (1999). Section 13 provides for liquidated damages of $1,000 for negligent violations and $5,000 where the violation is intentional or reckless. In other words, the statute specifically provides for increased damages where the disclosure is the result of conduct which typically warrants the imposition of punitive damages, but it does not provide for the imposition of punitive damages for such disclosures. Moreover, it is well-settled that punitive damages, because of their penal nature, are not favored is the law. *Ainsworth v. Century Supply Co.*, 295 Ill.App.3d 644, 230 Ill.Dec. 381, 693 N.E.2d 510 (1998). We conclude that our legislature chose not to provide for the recovery of punitive damages for violation of the Act.

(continued)

Finally, defendants argue that the amount of actual damages awarded was improper because it was based upon evidence obtained as the result of a serious discovery violation and opinion testimony from a witness unqualified to provide such testimony. Defendants also argue that the amount of actual damages was excessive and contrary to the manifest weight of the evidence.

With respect to the discovery violation, defendants contend that at no time during the discovery process did Doe reveal that she was being treated by Dr. Clay. Defendants maintain that because Doe was seeking to recover expenses related to her treatment for mental anguish, any information Dr. Clay had regarding Doe's emotional condition was relevant to the issue of damages.

In written interrogatories propounded to Doe, defendants asked her to state whether she had received any medical treatment from any physician or other health care provider for any medical, physical, or mental condition "referred to in any way in Plaintiff's First Amended Complaint," during the period "beginning ten years prior to the alleged improper disclosures, and continuing up to the present," and to state the name and address of each provider, the date and nature of each treatment or service, and the cost thereof. In response, Doe identified Dr. Paul L'Ecuyer, Judy Murashige, and Wal-Mart Pharmacy. At trial, Doe's attorney asked her whether she was " currently" being treated for depression and who her current treating doctors were. Doe responded that her physicians were Drs. L'Ecuyer and Clay.

Pursuant to Supreme Court Rule 213(i), a party has an ongoing duty to supplement or amend any prior answer or response to written interrogatories whenever new or additional information subsequently becomes known to that party. 177 Ill.2d R. 213(i). Thus, Doe had an obligation to disclose the fact that she had begun treating with Dr. Clay and her failure to do so was technically a violation of Rule 213. We note, however, that Doe did not call Dr. Clay to testify at trial, nor did she seek to admit any evidence deposition or medical records of Dr. Clay. Furthermore, Doe did not seek reimbursement for any expenses related to Dr. Clay's treatment.. Indeed, the *only* reference to Dr. Clay is Doe's testimony that she was currently treating with him. The standard for determining whether a trial court should grant a mistrial as a sanction for a discovery violation is whether the violation is of such character and magnitude as to deprive a party of a fair trial and the party seeking the mistrial demonstrates actual prejudice as a result. *Copeland v. Stebco Products Corp.,* 316 Ill.App.3d 932, 250 Ill.Dec. 235, 738 N.E.2d 199 (2000). No evidence regarding Dr. Clay's diagnosis, treatment, or opinion was introduced at trial; defendants therefore could not have and did not suffer any prejudice as a result of Doe's failure to disclose the fact that she was being treated by Dr. Clay, and a new trial is not warranted.

Defendants also argue that the trial court erred in admitting the testimony of Judy Murashige, as an expert, into evidence. Defendants contend that Murashige was permitted to render opinion testimony that she was not qualified to provide. Specifically, defendants contend that art therapists are not qualified to diagnose or treat medical or mental conditions or to render an opinion to a reasonable degree of medical certainty, that Murashige was not a licensed art therapist, and that Murashige should not have been qualified as an expert because she did not utilize any objective standards but merely recited Doe's unsubstantiated statements.

Expert testimony is admissible if the proffered expert is qualified as an expert by knowledge, skill, expertise, training, or education and the testimony will assist the trier of fact in understanding the evidence. *Dotto v. Okan,* 269 Ill.App.3d 808, 207 Ill.Dec. 190, 646 N.E.2d 1277 (1995). It is incumbent upon the party offering

(continued)

the witness to demonstrate *821 that the witness possesses the necessary learning, knowledge, skill, or practical experience to enable such witness to testify as an expert. *Lombardo v. Reliance Elevator Co.,* 315 Ill.App.3d 111, 248 Ill.Dec. 199, 733 N.E.2d 874 (2000). The determination of whether a witness is qualified to render an expert opinion and the decision to admit expert opinion testimony are matters that rest with the sound discretion of the trial court, and its ruling thereon will not be disturbed on appeal absent an abuse of discretion. *Seef v. Ingalls Memorial Hospital,* 311 Ill.App.3d 7, 243 Ill.Dec. 806, 724 N.E.2d 115 (1999). An abuse of discretion occurs where the trial court acted arbitrarily and without the employment of conscientious judgment or, in view of all the surrounding circumstances, exceeded the bounds of reason and ignored recognized principles of law, such that substantial prejudice resulted. *May v. SmithKline Beecham Clinical Laboratories, Inc.,* 304 Ill.App.3d 242, 237 Ill.Dec. 830, 710 N.E.2d 460 (1999).

Murashige testified that she was a registered art therapist. Murashige explained that to become a registered art therapist, a person was required to have a master's degree and complete a period of clinical experience under the supervision of a registered art therapist. Murashige testified that she had a bachelor's degree in secondary education and a master's degree in adult education. After working as an academic adviser and counselor, she subsequently enrolled in the art therapy program at Southern Illinois University at Edwardsville. Murashige stated that an art therapist was trained in all the psychological course work that a regular family therapist would have but also had an art background and was taught to use art as a diagnostic tool. Although she did not have a master's degree in art therapy, Murashige explained that she had completed all of the course work for a master's degree in art therapy and that, because she already **351 ***554 had a master's degree, was not required to get a second master's degree in order to become an art therapist. She subsequently worked for two years under the supervision of a registered art therapist. Murashige explained that there was no exam or licensing requirement in order to become a registered art therapist. Prior to treating Doe, Murashige had spent the previous eight years working at an HIV resource center, counseling people with HIV.

Given Murashige's educational background and experience in counseling HIV patients, we cannot say that the trial court abused its discretion in admitting her testimony. Murashige had the required education and training to become a registered art therapist, and she had eight years' experience in counseling HIV patients. Murashige did not diagnose depression or any other psychological condition. She merely testified that she treated Doe for emotional problems related to Dr. Chand's disclosure of her HIV status and that Dr. Chand's disclosures caused or contributed to the condition for which Murashige provided treatment.

Finally, defendants argue that the amount of actual damages was speculative and excessive because there was no objective evidence to support it. They request a new trial on actual damages. A trial court's determination on damages will not be disturbed on review unless that determination is contrary to the manifest weight of the evidence. *Lanterman v. Edwards,* 294 Ill.App.3d 351, 228 Ill.Dec. 800, 689 N.E.2d 1221 (1998). Reviewing the record as a whole, we conclude that the trial court's award of actual damages was contrary to the manifest weight of the evidence.

As noted above, section 13 of the Act provides that a person may recover liquidated damages in the amount of $1,000 for negligent violations of the Act and $5,000 for intentional or reckless violations. Such amounts can be recovered without proof of damages. Our legislature further provided that a plaintiff could recover actual damages if such damages exceeded the amounts provided for in section 13. 410 ILCS 305/13 (West 1998). In

(continued)

the present case, the trial court found that Doe had proved numerous violations of the Act, but the court did not specify what these violations were, how many there were, or which violations were negligent and which were intentional or reckless. Moreover, Doe did not submit any evidence of or seek compensation for any medical bills, lost wages, or other out-of-pocket expenses. We conclude that the record simply does not support the finding that Doe's actual damages were $600,000.

For the foregoing reasons, the judgment of the circuit court of St. Clair County is affirmed with respect to its determination that Dr. Chand violated various provisions of the Act and with respect to the denial of defendant's motion for a jury trial. The award of punitive damages is reversed. The award of actual damages is vacated, and the cause remanded for a new trial on actual damages.

Affirmed in part, vacated in part, and reversed in part and cause remanded.

DOCUMENTATION

One of the most significant elements in any medical malpractice action is the patient record showing evidence that supports or defends the action. This is often an area that gets woefully inadequate attention during the training of health care providers and in actual practice. Providers have finally begun to acknowledge the importance of the proper documentation methods with respect to patient interaction and treatment owing to media attention given to the growing number of malpractice suits in recent years. As a result many records are becoming clearer and more detailed than in the past.

The documentation associated with providing patient care benefits the patient during care because it can improve the comprehensive level of care. The demands on health care providers are great as the amount of necessary knowledge constantly changes and increases. The number of patients needing care seems to be growing as well. These demands often interfere with the amount of time a provider spends creating a documented record. Yet, without the record, there is little a provider can do to support his or her actions as appropriate and warranted in the care, treatment or services delivered. From a health care perspective, thorough documentation is important to establish an ongoing course of care and a logical progression of diagnosis and treatment. From a risk management perspective, proper documentation is essential to establish that the provider acted in a manner similar to that of other similarly situated providers and thus fell clearly within the standard of care. No doubt, proper documentation can make or break an allegation of medical malpractice early in the process and greatly diminish the time and expense of litigating a case to trial.

From a risk management perspective, what is important in the creation of patient records? The following list, while certainly not exhaustive, gives some insight into the elements necessary to create an appropriate and complete patient record:

- Timely and legible entries
- Accurate and complete entries
- A logical progression of entries with reference to concurrent records and former entries

- Proper correction technique
- Omission of inappropriate entries

In order to produce a proper patient record, it is important that the provider create the documentation within a reasonable period after the information is generated. On a daily basis, the provider is faced with the daunting tasks of interacting with numerous patients (sometimes at more than one location); dealing with issues relating to the business of health care; interacting professionally with other providers regarding patients; reviewing results of tests, procedures, and previous documentation; and dedicating time to keeping abreast of developments and changes in the profession. The provider is also expected to find time to document the observations and results of the patients seen that day. From a risk management view, documentation of records should be done as close to the actual visit as possible, but many providers make brief notes and come back at a later time to create the actual record. In a case of alleged malpractice, this practice can be devastating. It is not unreasonable for a jury to find that a significant lapse of time between the patient interaction and the creation of the record lends itself to unreliable and possible inaccurate or incomplete documentation. Consider the following example in Application 4.2 of the standard practice of an actual physician (unknown to patients and insurers).

APPLICATION 4.2

Dr. J had a busy medical practice and small children at home. Her days were very full. On an average day she would spend one to two hours making rounds at the hospital. She would also see 40 to 50 patients in the office. As a standard practice she would place a sticky note in the chart with the date, and two to four words as reminders of what occurred during the visit. Then, about every three months she would spend an entire weekend in the office going through all the charts and dictating her notes based on the various sticky notes that accumulated in them, any test results that might have been generated elsewhere, and the documentation regarding vital statistics and reported symptoms that the nurses recorded in the charts.

The practice outlined above would be a dream situation for a malpractice attorney representing a plaintiff. The documentation practice in and of itself is probably as bad as, or worse than, no documentation at all. The odds that a jury would believe that a physician could accurately recall the details of every patient exam averaging 200 per week over a three-month period are nonexistent. Additionally, this regular course of conduct could be used to imply an ongoing pattern of professional practice that is clearly below the standard of practice for the average practitioner.

The issue of proper documentation is one that frequently arises in cases of alleged malpractice. As can be seen in the example and discussion above, the demands on most providers is significant. Time management and organizational skills are absolutely essential in today's health care system. It is far too easy to push aside those matters that do not require immediate personal contact. The result is that errors occur which would have been avoided had documentary matters been attended to as readily as the other requirements of the day. From the perspective of risk management, providers should be kept aware, on a continuing basis, of the importance of timely and thorough documentation. Just as important is correction documentation.

The manner in which medical records are created varies widely. Some providers make handwritten notes. Others dictate onto audio tape and the material is then transcribed into a written record. There are some providers who use specially designed software that allows them to either type or speak their notes directly into the computer. While it is extremely important that the medical record be created as completely and timely as possible, it is just as important that the information be accurate. All medical records should be reviewed by the provider once they are created. If errors are discovered, it is a fundamental rule that the corrections be properly made. At this point in time, the majority of medical records are still maintained in hard copy contained within paper files. This will most likely change to a paperless system in the future as technology makes the process more efficient. In most cases, the patient record is reviewed once the hard copy is created.

If an error is discovered in the record, it is of the utmost importance that it not be covered up or obliterated. In the event the medical record of the patient is ever considered as evidence in any kind of litigation, covering or destroying information is perceived as an attempt to hide information when in fact it may be something as simple as a clerical error. Rather, any corrections in any form of legal document, including medical records, should be clearly marked in such a way that they are legible, but noted as a correction. The date and identity of the party making the correction should also be indicated. By using this system, the correction of clerical errors appear as just that and not a blatant attempt to alter a medical record to strengthen a defense.

Finally, what information should be included within a medical record? The answer obviously varies with the situation, however, it is always important to keep personal opinions regarding the patient as an individual personality to a minimum. Even mental evaluations should be phrased in an objective tone rather than what might be interpreted as derogatory remarks. Such records often translate to a negative and judgmental approach. Members of the jury may well put themselves in the shoes of the patient when considering a case. If such negative remarks are made, they might well be interpreted on a personal basis and create an emotional response. It is important that providers base all assessments on actual facts and whenever possible diagnoses should be supported with scientific evidence. From the perspective of the plaintiff involved in litigation, records should be examined for any remarks that indicate an emotional or personal judgment rather than one based in sound logic and scientific fact. As for the risk manager, the importance of objectivity in the creation of medical records should be continually stressed to the provider.

Matters as simple as the manner in which corrections are made, the tone of the language used, or the procedure for creating records come within the realm of risk management. As stated at the outset, risk management consists of procedures to prevent the basis for litigation and to present the best possible approach for the defense in the event such issues do arise.

PROVIDER QUALIFICATIONS AND COMPLIANCE WITH STANDARDS

For hundreds of years the appropriateness of the professional conduct of a health care provider was only considered after the fact. That is to say, consideration was made after a question of malpractice arose and litigation ensued. Another byproduct of the dramatic increase in medical malpractice lawsuits throughout the twentieth century is a more proactive risk management approach. Today, at virtually every stage of a health care provider's training and career, qualifications as well as personal and professional conduct are considered. For example, virtually anyone seeking any level of government licensure or certification in the health care field must pass a variety of screenings. These may include past criminal history, a variety of medical tests for highly communicable diseases, and even immigration status. Education and training is verified through official transcripts, records, and letters from the education and training organizations. As discussed earlier in the text, completion of testing to demonstrate an appropriate level of knowledge and skill is also expected. As health care providers move through their professional careers, these matters are typically verified at each stage, such as when employment changes. Most liability insurers of facilities and providers require proof of licensure or certification in good standing of all providers employed, and, traditionally, once providers achieved proper licensure or certification they were free to go about their careers. However, that situation continues to change dramatically for today's health care professionals. One example is the ever increasing requirements of **continuing medical education** to remain abreast of the most current developments.

Some discussion was given earlier to databanks and information exchanges that allow states and health care facilities to share information about disciplinary actions against health care providers. These are important tools in risk management and greatly impede the attempts by providers with a history of professional malfeasance or disciplinary investigations/actions to move freely about the country as they avoid the responsibility and effects of past actions.

A number of other measures also help to minimize the possibility of malpractice and protect a largely unsuspecting public from incompetence by health care providers. A feature common to most health care facilities are peer review and medical review boards. These are groups made up of health care professionals that regularly consider cases of the providers serving the facility. In some instances, they consider questionable cases or practices. In others, they consider random cases or cases involving unexpected or undesirable outcomes as well as incidents that may occur within the facility. The peer review committee considers the cases and determines if the end result was appropriate or the product of a failure to abide by a reasonable standard of care and established risk management policies and procedures. The committee can then approve the handling of the case or make recommendations. In many situations, the peer review committee is the first line of defense in discovering providers who are less than capable on the job or who have engaged in inappropriate practices, such as subjecting patients to unnecessary treatments or procedures in order to generate revenue. This circumstance is demonstrated in the following Application 4.3.

APPLICATION 4.3

A hospital peer review committee considers the conduct of a radiologist. It appears that in a strikingly high percentage of cases, approximately one of every two, when an X ray is ordered, the radiologist determines the result inconclusive and orders follow up diagnostic tests in the form of a CT Scan or MRI. This percentage is high above the national and even community standard. The committee selects a number of such cases and asks an independent radiologist to review the initial X rays. The result of the review is that nearly 50 percent of the cases in which additional tests were ordered are deemed unnecessary.

In a case such as that described, the peer review committee must make a determination as to whether the radiologist's qualifications to read X rays are substandard and/or whether the ordering of additional tests is purely to generate additional revenues. Either is inappropriate, but the recommendation of the committee may be different dependent on the findings. In any event, the facility then has a number of options are available. The committee/facility can recommend additional training, it can suspend or terminate privileges, petition the state for disciplinary action, or pursue any other legal option which eliminates the problem. The point is that the facility has a risk management tool in place to deal with such situations as they are discovered.

Peer or medical review committees are intended as a means by which providers can effectively police themselves and implement an effective risk management measure. These committees were not created, and are not in place, to assist plaintiffs in medical malpractice litigation. If that were so, most providers would be hesitant to participate and cooperate fully with the committee. For this reason, jurisdictions typically have legislation or regulatory provisions in place that make the records of peer review committees privileged and confidential and not available to outsiders—short of an express waiver by the committee.[6] This may seem unfair to an injured party as what might be valuable evidence of malfeasance is unavailable to the plaintiff. However, the courts have determined, as have the legislatures in many jurisdictions, that the greater good is served by an unhindered committee that can help to protect the entire population of patients without fear of being turned into unwilling witnesses in individual cases.

GOOD SAMARITAN DOCTRINE

A common question among health care providers is about their duty to use their professional skills in situations outside of their normal professional practice. Most providers would agree that there is an ethical obligation to render assistance when it is needed and one can help another who is in trouble. In light of the risk of litigation, if the assistance does not generate a completely successful result, many providers are hesitant to step forward. This obviously is not consistent with the strong objective of society to help those in need. With advanced technology and medical treatment alternatives available in nontraditional healthcare settings or circumstances, it is no longer sufficient to assume a general ethical duty as a comprehensive method to deal with the situations that arise.

There is no universally accepted legal obligation for all health care providers or the general population to provide assistance to strangers who are experiencing an emergency situation. As a means to encourage individuals to help one another, many jurisdictions long ago adopted a common-law principle which stated that strangers who offer genuine and well-intended assistance to those in need cannot be held accountable for any negative results that might result from their assistance. These have become known as **Good Samaritan** rules. This principle was questioned when the person offering assistance was a medical professional. There was some thought that such individuals should be held to a higher standard in terms of the aid rendered. Response to this concern began in 1959 and has since been dealt with in all 50 states. The state legislatures enacted statutory law that provided exemption from liability to all, but especially those health care professionals who provided aid to strangers in medical need. Because there is no nationally accepted standard, it is essential to consider the laws and legal principles established in the particular jurisdiction where a question arises.

172 N.J. 240, 798 A.2d 51

Supreme Court of New Jersey.

Conor VELAZQUEZ, an infant by his mother and natural guardian, Charmaine VELAZQUEZ, Charmaine Velazquez, individually and as Administratrix of the

(continued)

Estate of Conor Velazquez, and Jose Velazquez, individually and as
Administrator of the Estate of Conor Velazquez, Plaintiffs-Respondents,
v.
Teresa JIMINEZ, M.D., St. Peter's Medical Center, Ellen Maak, R.N., Jeanine
Healy, R.N., and John Does, M.D., Defendants,
and
Angela C. Ranzini, M.D., Defendant-Appellant.
Decided May 29, 2002.

LONG, J.

New Jersey's Good Samaritan Act, *N.J.S.A.* 2A:62A-1, provides:
> Any individual, including a person licensed to practice any method of treatment of human ailments, disease, pain, injury, deformity, mental or physical condition, or licensed to render services ancillary thereto, or any person who is a volunteer member of a duly incorporated first aid and emergency or volunteer ambulance or rescue squad association, who in good faith renders emergency care at the scene of an accident or emergency to the victim or victims thereof, or while transporting the victim or victims thereof to a hospital or other facility where treatment or care is to be rendered, shall not be liable for any civil damages as a result of any acts or omissions by such person in rendering the emergency care.

In July 1994, Charmaine and Jose Velazquez (collectively, plaintiffs), individually and as representatives of the estate of their deceased son, Conor, sued St. Peter's Medical Center (Medical Center) and its staff members, Teresa Jiminez, M.D., Angela C. Ranzini, M.D., Ellen Maak, R.N., Jeanine Healy, R.N., and unnamed residents, for damages resulting from their negligence during Conor's delivery.

Before trial, Dr. Jiminez, the Medical Center and the nurses settled with plaintiffs who, in turn, voluntarily dismissed the residents. Dr. Ranzini moved for summary judgment under the Good Samaritan Act, *N.J.S.A.* 2A:62A-1 to -2. The trial court denied the motion as a matter of law, holding that the Act does not immunize physicians responding to emergencies within a hospital. Dr. Ranzini went to trial alone.

The facts established at trial are detailed in the Appellate Division opinion, *Velazquez v. Jiminez*, 336 *N.J.Super.* 10, 18-28, 763 *A.*2d 753 (2000), and are incorporated as if more fully set forth. Mrs. Velazquez was a patient at the Medical Center for the purpose of delivering a baby. Dr. Jiminez was her attending physician. Complications occurred during the delivery because Mrs. Velazquez's baby was suffering from bilateral shoulder dystocia (both of his shoulders were lodged against his mother's pubic bone). After delivering the baby's head, Dr. Jiminez was unable to deliver the rest of the baby's body. She rang for assistance and Dr. Ranzini responded.

Dr. Ranzini had no prior relationship with or connection to Mrs. Velazquez. Dr. Ranzini was an Assistant Professor of Clinical Obstetrics and Gynecology at the University of Medicine and Dentistry of New Jersey (UMDNJ), assigned to the Maternal Fetal Care Unit (MFCU) at the Medical Center. She specializes in maternal fetal medicine and was responsible both for attending to high-risk patients in the MFCU and for supervising resident physicians who cared for their own UMDNJ clinical patients at the Medical Center. Mrs. Velazquez was neither an MFCU nor a clinical patient. Rather, she was the patient of Dr. Jiminez, an attending physician with staff privileges at the Medical Center.

(continued)

Dr. Ranzini first attempted to complete the delivery vaginally. When those efforts proved unsuccessful, Dr. Ranzini assisted in preparing Mrs. Velazquez and the baby--who was, by virtue of his position, at risk of suffering from hypoxia (a loss of oxygen)--for an emergency Caesarean section. The baby, Conor, ultimately was born severely brain damaged, spent his life in a dependent state and died of pneumonia before reaching his third birthday.

As might be expected in a medical malpractice case, the trial essentially was a battle of experts. Plaintiffs' experts testified that Dr. Ranzini deviated from the standard of care. Dr. Ranzini's experts testified, in essence, that her conduct conformed to all applicable medical standards and that Conor's condition resulted from the negligence of Dr. Jiminez. The details of that testimony need not be recounted here because the issue before us is Dr. Ranzini's amenability to suit and not the substance of the care that she rendered.

The jury returned a verdict in favor of plaintiffs and assigned three percent of the liability to Dr. Ranzini. The trial court, *sua sponte,* entered judgment notwithstanding the verdict (j.n.o.v.) in favor of Dr. Ranzini. The court ruled that under *Scafidi v. Seiler,* 119 *N.J.* 93, 574 A.2d 398 (1990), Dr. Ranzini's liability could not be regarded as a substantial factor in the harm that resulted to Conor. In so ruling, the court reiterated that the Good Samaritan Act did not operate to insulate Dr. Ranzini from suit.

Plaintiffs appealed, challenging the j.n.o.v., among other trial errors. Dr. Ranzini cross-appealed from the trial court's ruling that the Good Samaritan Act did not immunize her from suit. The Appellate Division reversed the j.n.o.v. (an issue not before us) and rejected Dr. Ranzini's cross-appeal on the ground that, as a matter of law, the Good Samaritan Act does not apply to physicians working within a hospital. *Velazquez, supra,* 336 *N.J.Super.* at 16, 52, 763 A.2d 753.

We granted Dr. Ranzini's petition for certification regarding the applicability of the Good Samaritan Act to emergencies involving a patient occurring within a hospital. 169 *N.J.* 604, 782 A.2d 422 (2001).

Dr. Ranzini argues that the Appellate Division erred in concluding that the protections of the Good Samaritan statute stop at the door of the hospital. According to her, the location of an emergency is of no consequence; a physician is immunized so long as he or she acts in the absence of a prior duty to do so. She further contends that the weight of out-of-state authority supports her interpretation, which she claims will encourage physicians to assist in a hospital emergency. Finally, she argues that she had no prior duty to Mrs. Velazquez and thus was entitled to the shield of *N.J.S.A.* 2A:62A-1 as a volunteer.

Plaintiffs counter that Dr. Ranzini's construction of the Act is inconsistent with its plain meaning and legislative purpose. They contend that it would be illogical for the Legislature to have intended the original "scene of an accident or emergency" language to include care rendered in a hospital if, in 1987, it conferred an additional grant of immunity to Good Samaritans while they transport victims *from* the scene *to* the hospital. Plaintiffs additionally dispute that most other jurisdictions have immunized physicians in hospitals. Finally, plaintiffs assert that Dr. Ranzini had a pre-existing duty to assist Mrs. Velazquez....

...in 1959, California became the first state to adopt a Good Samaritan statute immunizing from tort liability a physician who "in good faith renders emergency care at the scene of the emergency." Mapel & Weigel, *supra,* 21 *S. Tex. L.Rev.* at 329 (quoting A.B. 2873, *Cal. Stats.* 1959, ch. 1507 (current version at *Cal. Bus. & Prof.Code* § 2395)). An early California decision explained the rationale underpinning Good Samaritan legislation:

[The statutes] were enacted to aid the class of individuals though requiring immediate medical care were not receiving it. Typically, it was the roadside accident victim who, as a result of the strictures of the common law malpractice doctrines, was left uncared for. However, hospital patients, such as the decedent[,] have historically enjoyed the benefits of full medical attention. There is no need for special legislation to encourage physicians to treat this class of individuals. ....

(continued)

[The Good Samaritan] sections were directed towards physicians who, by chance and on an irregular basis, come upon or are called to render emergency medical care. Often, under these circumstances, the medical needs of the individual would not be matched by the expertise of the physician and facilities could be severely limited.... [*Colby v. Schwartz*, 78 *Cal.App.*3d 885, 892, 144 *Cal.Rptr.* 624, 628 (Cal.Ct.App.1978).]

... In sum, Good Samaritan legislation has, at its core, the goal of encouraging the rendering of medical care to those who need it but otherwise might not receive it (ordinarily roadside accident victims), by persons who come upon such victims by chance, without the accoutrements provided in a medical facility, including expertise, assistance, sanitation or equipment.

All fifty states and the District of Columbia have now enacted some form of Good Samaritan legislation. As of 1987, "117 statutes provide[d] varying degrees of immunity to different classes of rescuers under a multitude of settings." Reuter, *supra*, 20 *J. Legal Med.* at 157 (quoting Robert A. Mason, *Good Samaritan Laws--Legal Disarray: An Update*, 38 Mercer L.Rev. 1439, 1442 (1987)). Moreover, "no two states are alike. This is in part due to disparate policies behind their enactment and in part because of the ambiguous terminology used in their manufacture." Mapel & Weigel, *supra*, 21 *S. Tex. L.Rev.* at 331 (footnote omitted). *See also* Eric A. Brandt, Comment, *Good Samaritan Laws--The Legal Placebo: A Current Analysis*, 17 *Akron L. Rev.* 303, 304 (1983) ("[M]any of the 109 Good Samaritan statutes effective today are so confusing and ambiguous that the people whom they are meant to protect either do not know that they are covered under a particular statute or cannot understand the extent of their protection.") (footnotes omitted). The country's Good Samaritan statutes broadly can be classified as falling into one of three categories: those that expressly exclude hospital care; those that expressly include hospital care; and those, like New Jersey's, that contain no explicit provision one way or the other....

New Jersey is among twenty-nine states ... that does not explicitly address whether in-hospital care can be shielded from liability under a Good Samaritan statute. By way of example, some statutes in that class immunize care provided "at the scene of an accident or emergency to the victim or victims thereof," *Ga.Code Ann.* § 51-1-29 (2000); *N.J.S.A.* 2A:62A-1.1; "at the scene of the emergency," *Del.Code Ann.* tit. 24, § 1767 (1997); "at the scene of an accident, fire, or any life-threatening emergency," *Va.Code Ann.* § 8.01-225(A)(1) (Michie 2000); or "at the scene of an accident, casualty, or disaster." *Ala.Code* § 6-5-332(a) (Michie Supp.2001). ...

Finally, some general-language jurisdictions (including New Jersey) provide express immunity for medical care rendered while transporting an injured person from "the scene" to a hospital. *See, e.g., Iowa Code* § 613.17 (West 1999) ("at the place of an emergency or accident or while the person is in transit to or from the emergency or accident"); *N.D. Cent.Code* § 39-08-04.1 (1997) ("en route [from the scene of an accident, disaster, or other emergency] to a treatment facility"); *Va.Code Ann.* § 8.01- 225(A)(1) ("en route therefrom [from the scene of an accident, fire or any life-threatening emergency] to any hospital, medical clinic or doctor's office"); *Wash. Rev.Code Ann.* § 4.24.300 (West 1988) ("in transporting, not for compensation, therefrom [from the scene of an emergency] an injured person or persons for emergency medical treatment").

In 1996 and 1998, our Legislature added two new Good Samaritan provisions specifically protecting law enforcement officers and firefighters, respectively. *N.J.S.A.* 2A:62A-1.1 and -1.2. Each of those sections immunizes good faith emergency care given "at the scene of an accident or emergency to any victim thereof, or in transporting any such victim *to a hospital* or other facility where treatment is to be rendered[.]" *Ibid.* (emphasis added).

... The few judicial decisions interpreting the category of statutes that neither expressly excludes nor expressly includes in-hospital emergency medical care are in equipoise. On the one hand, cases from

(continued)

Arizona, Indiana and Oklahoma support the proposition that Good Samaritan statutes do not immunize emergency care provided in a hospital to a patient. *Guerrero v. Copper Queen Hosp.,* 112 *Ariz.* 104, 537 *P.*2d 1329, 1331 (1975); *Steffey v. King,* 614 *N.E.*2d 615, 617 (Ind.Ct.App.1993); *Jackson v. Mercy Health Ctr., Inc.,* 864 *P.*2d 839, 844 (Okla.1993). On the other, courts in Georgia, Illinois, and Utah have interpreted their state's Good Samaritan statutes as protecting physicians who render emergency medical care in a hospital setting. *Clayton v. Kelly,* 183 *Ga.App.* 45, 357 *S.E.*2d 865, 868 (1987); *Johnson v. Matviuw,* 176 *Ill.App.*3d 907, 126 *Ill.Dec.* 343, 531 *N.E.*2d 970, 972, 975-76 (1988), *appeal denied,* 125 *Ill.*2d 566, 130 *Ill.Dec.* 481, 537 *N.E.*2d 810 (1989); *Hirpa v. IHC Hosps., Inc.,* 948 *P.*2d 785, 788 (Utah 1997). The difference in outcome between the cases is based, in great measure, on whether the statutes were broadly or narrowly interpreted.

In any event, it would be fair to say that there is no universal interpretation of general statutory language among our sister jurisdictions, no roadmap to follow. Thus, to the extent that the parties in this case rely on the weight of out-of-state authority in support of their positions, they have vastly overstated the case.

In interpreting a legislative enactment, the starting point is the language of the statute itself. If the language is clear, " ' 'the sole function of the courts is to enforce it according to its terms.' ' " *Hubbard ex rel. Hubbard v. Reed,* 168 *N.J.* 387, 392, 774 *A.*2d 495 (2001) (quoting *Sheeran v. Nationwide Mut. Ins. Co.,* 80 *N.J.* 548, 556, 404 *A.*2d 625 (1979) (quoting *Caminetti v. United States,* 242 *U.S.* 470, 485, 37 *S.Ct.* 192, 194, 61 *L.Ed.* 442, 452 (1917))). All terms in a statute should be accorded their normal sense and significance. *Stryker Corp. v. Director, Div. of Taxation,* 168 *N.J.* 138, 156, 773 *A.*2d 674 (2001). When a statute is subject to more than one plausible reading, our role is "to effectuate the legislative intent in light of the language used and the objects sought to be achieved." *State v. Hoffman,* 149 *N.J.* 564, 578, 695 *A.*2d 236 (1997) (internal citations omitted).

Further, a statute enacted in derogation of the common law must be construed narrowly. *Oswin v. Shaw,* 129 *N.J.* 290, 310, 609 *A.*2d 415 (1992). Where a statute alters the common law, the most circumscribed reading of it that achieves its purpose is the one that should be adopted. Doubt about its meaning should be resolved in favor of the effect which makes the least rather than the most change in the common law. The rule has been declared by the United States Supreme Court, as follows: "No statute is to be construed as altering the common law, farther than its words import. It is not to be construed as making any innovation upon the common law which it does not fairly express." [*Ibid.* (quoting 3 Norman J. Singer, *Sutherland Statutory Construction* § 61.01, at 77 (4th ed.1986) ...

With those general principles in mind, we look now to our Good Samaritan statute, enacted in 1963, following California's lead. Originally, the statute included only health care practitioners; it was amended in 1968 to extend immunity to "any individual,"
including a person licensed to practice any method of treatment of human ailments, disease, pain, injury, deformity, mental or physical condition, or licensed to render services ancillary thereto, who in good faith renders emergency care at the scene of an accident or emergency to the victim or victims thereof.... *N.J.S.A.* 2A:62A-1.]

... Thus, in derogation of the basic common law principle that one who volunteers to render assistance must do so reasonably, anyone who rendered care at the scene of an accident or emergency was immunized from civil liability.

... Although the statute in its original form was silent regarding whether "the scene of an accident or emergency" is limited in any way, it was most recently amended to "clarify" that volunteer members of a first aid or ambulance squad are granted "*the same immunity* " as all other individuals. Assembly Law, Public Safety, Defense & Corrections Committee Statement accompanying Bill No. 2467--L. 1987, c. 296 (emphasis added). In its present form, the statute immunizes any Good Samaritan who "renders emergency care at

(continued)

the scene of an accident or emergency to the victim or victims thereof, or while transporting the victim or victims thereof to a hospital or other facility where treatment or care is to be rendered." *N.J.S.A.* 2A:62A-1.

The Appellate Division read that new language as revelatory of a legislative understanding that "the scene of an accident or emergency" is somewhere other than a hospital or treatment facility, which is staffed and equipped to render medical care. *Velazquez, supra,* 336 *N.J.Super.* at 48, 763 *A.*2d 753. That is certainly one fair interpretation of the statute, which scholars have approved. "By distinguishing between these two types of places, the legislature operationally defined 'scene of an emergency' as a place other than a hospital...." Roger L. Tuttle, *Hospital Emergency Rooms--Application of Good Samaritan Laws,* 31 *Med. Trial Tech. Q.* 145, 157 (Fred Lane ed., 1985) (discussing *Miss.Code Ann.* § 73-25-37). More fundamental to us is the notion that if the Legislature had intended the locationally unlimited immunity urged by Dr. Ranzini, it simply could have said so. *See, e.g., Okla. Stat. Ann.* tit. 76, § 5(a)(1) (immunizing medical practitioner who "voluntarily and without compensation, renders or attempts to render emergency care to an injured person or any person who is in need of immediate medical aid, *wherever required* ") (emphasis added). There would have been no reason for it to include, at the Act's inception, the limiting language "at the scene of an accident or emergency." There likewise would have been no subsequent need to extend immunity explicitly to persons rendering emergency care while transporting a victim to a medical facility. All of those circumstances would have been encompassed by a statute that immunized anyone rendering emergency medical care. The Legislature apparently intended a circumscription of Good Samaritan immunity as evidenced by the limiting language it chose.

That narrowly tailored interpretation does the least violence to our citizens' common-law right to institute tort actions against those whose negligence injures them. It thus conforms to our rules regarding the interpretation of statutes in derogation of the common law and statutes granting immunity. Moreover, it gives full throat to the goals underlying the legislation: to encourage the rendering of medical care to those who would not otherwise receive it, by physicians who come upon such patients by chance, without the benefit of the expertise, assistance, equipment or sanitation that is available in a hospital or medical setting. *Colby v. Schwartz, supra,* 78 *Cal.App.*3d at 892, 144 *Cal.Rptr.* at 628; Reuter, *supra,* 20 *J. Legal Med.* at 189; Groninger, *supra,* 26 *Pepp. L.Rev.* at 364; Burke, *supra,* 1 *Annals Health L.* at 140; Dyke, *supra,* 15 *How. L.J.* at 676; Note, *supra,* 64 *Colum. L.Rev.* at 1307.

Obviously, in enacting our Good Samaritan law, the Legislature was aware that a hospital patient is present in that venue for the very purpose of receiving medical care and is not a person who ordinarily would lack care in the absence of Good Samaritan immunity. Further, physicians in a hospital ordinarily do not come upon a hospital patient "by chance" as would be the case if an accident or emergency occurred on a roadway. Most importantly, our Legislature knew that the fundamental problem facing a Good Samaritan on the street (the ability to do little more than render first aid under less than optimal circumstances) is not present in a fully staffed and equipped facility like a hospital, whose very purpose is "to make available[ ] the human skill and physical materiel of medical science to the end that the patient's health be restored." *Perlmutter v. Beth David Hospital,* 308 *N.Y.* 100, 123 *N.E.*2d 792, 794 (1954). As Stewart R. Reuter has observed in "Physicians as Good Samaritans," 20 *J. Legal Med.* 157, 189 (1999):

> [P]hysicians who care for patients in hospitals are not volunteers in the sense of the person who by chance comes upon the scene of an accident. Moreover, physicians who provide emergency care in hospitals have at their disposal all the modern diagnostic and therapeutic equipment. Granted, they may not be familiar with the patient's medical history or disease and are at somewhat of a disadvantage when compared with the patient's personal physician. However, this disadvantage does not rise to the level

(continued)

of the difficulty that confronts the physician who stops at the site of a roadside accident, who can provide little more than first-aid until the EMS team arrives. In many cases, the physician or surgeon whose expertise is being requested in a hospital emergency will work with a physician or with hospital personnel who have excellent knowledge of the patient's condition and problems. Even if no other physician is already involved in the emergency, the duration of care provided generally is short--until the hospital's trained Code Blue team arrives. ...

Dr. Ranzini's suggestion that she qualifies as a Good Samaritan because she had no prior duty to Mrs. Velazquez misconceives the Good Samaritan Act entirely. Although the absence of a pre-existing duty is one element that volunteers must establish to qualify for Good Samaritan immunity, *Praet v. Borough of Sayreville*, 218 *N.J.Super.* 218, 223, 527 *A.*2d 486 (App.Div.), *certif. denied*, 108 *N.J.* 681, 532 *A.*2d 253 (1987), standing alone it does not satisfy the statute. It is the reduced circumstances in which the volunteer finds himself or herself that the Legislature recognized, and it is the rendering of care in the face of those restrictions that it desired to immunize from suit. Had the Legislature intended to insulate *anyone* rendering emergency care under *any circumstances* where no pre-existing duty to render aid exists, it could have done so simply and directly. *See, e.g., Conn. Gen.Stat.* § 52-557b(a) (West Supp.2002) (immunizing medical practitioner "who, voluntarily and gratuitously and other than in the ordinary course of such person's employment or practice, renders emergency medical or professional assistance to a person in need thereof"); *Nev.Rev.Stat.* § 41.500(1) (2001) (immunizing "any person in this state who renders emergency care or assistance in an emergency, gratuitously and in good faith").

We think it is important as well that five out of the seven state statutes that now expressly immunize emergency care in a hospital setting contained, at their inception, general language like ours. *Supra* at 251 n. 3, 798 *A.*2d at 58 n. 3. Likewise, the legislatures in states that have immunized obstetrical care rendered in a hospital have done so with a specific enactment, altering or supplementing a general statute like our own. *Supra* op. at 254-255, 798 *A.*2d at 60. Presumably, the legislatures of those states recognized that in-hospital emergency care is not within the contemplation of a general language Good Samaritan act. Karen H. Rothenberg, *Who Cares?: The Evolution of the Legal Duty to Provide Emergency Care*, 26 *Hous. L.Rev.* 21, 72 (1989) (noting that Virginia emergency obstetrical care provision, adopted after general statute, was enacted in response to obstetricians' threats to boycott on-call emergency room services).

Dr. Ranzini's contention that by not extending Good Samaritan immunity to a hospital we will encourage physicians to simply stand by and allow patients to suffer or die is equally unpersuasive. First, we will not impute such conduct to the highly respected medical profession. Moreover, we note that scholars suggest that physicians' contracts, hospital protocols, ethical rules, regulatory standards and physicians' personal relationships operate to make that potential extremely unrealistic relative to a hospital patient. Reuter, *supra*, 20 *J. Leg. Med.* at 187, 189. To be sure, the Legislature is free to immunize all persons who render emergency medical treatment without a prior duty to do so, including those who volunteer to act within the walls of a hospital. We tilt neither against nor in favor of such an extension of immunity. We simply are persuaded that the choice is one for the Legislature, and we are unconvinced that the current statute reflects a legislative choice in favor of such immunity.

In sum, Good Samaritan immunity under *N.J.S.A.* 2A:62A-1 encompasses only those situations in which a physician (or other volunteer) comes, by chance, upon a victim who requires immediate emergency medical care, at a location compromised by lack of adequate facilities, equipment, expertise, sanitation and staff. A hospital or medical center does not qualify under the terms of the Good Samaritan Act in its present form.

(continued)

One final note. It is important to recognize that it simply does not follow that because a party is amenable to suit, he or she will be liable. The Good Samaritan Act renders a very circumscribed population of emergency volunteers immune from suit. The remainder of our citizens are subject to the ordinary common law rules governing conduct. Thus, for example, if a party has a pre-existing duty to act and breaches it, either by failing to act or performing in a negligent manner, the breach will be actionable. *Restatement (Second) of Torts*, Division Two, Ch. 12, Topic 4, Scope Note, at 65-66 (1965). In the absence of a pre- existing legal duty, if a party undertakes to act and does so in an unreasonable manner, that conduct will be actionable. *Dawson v. Bunker Hill Plaza Assocs.*, 289 N.J.Super. 309, 327, 673 A.2d 847 (App.Div.), *certif. denied*, 146 N.J. 569, 683 A.2d 1164 (1996); *O'Neill v. Suburban Terrace Apartments, Inc.*, 110 N.J.Super. 541, 545, 266 A.2d 304 (App.Div.), *certif. denied*, 57 N.J. 138, 270 A.2d 40 (1970). Whether a volunteer's conduct is reasonable depends upon the circumstances, including his or her experience and training. The standard of care to be imposed "will vary with ... the level of skill of the individual," Mapel & Weigel, *supra*, 21 S. Tex. L.Rev. at 328, and requires "careful consideration of all the attending circumstances, including any disability under which the rescuer might be operating--e.g., physical incapacity as well as the urgency of the situation and the concomitant need to act quickly." Brandt, *supra*, 17 *Akron L.Rev.* at 305 (citing *Restatement (Second) of Torts* § § 283C, 296(1) (1977)). No party is *required* to volunteer in the absence of a pre-existing duty to do so. *O'Neill, supra*, 110 *N.J.Super.* at 545, 266 A.2d 304. The question of duty is one of law to be decided on a case-by-case basis. *Pfenninger v. Hunterdon Cent. Reg'l High School*, 167 N.J. 230, 240-41, 770 A.2d 1126 (2001); *Wlasiuk v. McElwee*, 334 N.J.Super. 661, 666, 760 A.2d 829 (App.Div.2000).

Because Dr. Ranzini rendered aid to Mrs. Velazquez in a fully equipped and staffed hospital to which Mrs. Velazquez had been admitted for the purpose of receiving medical care, the Good Samaritan Act did not immunize her from suit. When she assisted in Mrs. Velazquez's delivery, our law imposed on her the obligation to do so in accordance with the applicable standard of care. A jury found her to be negligent to a minimal degree. The Appellate Division upheld that judgment and we see no warrant to interfere with it. Thus, we affirm.

With the advent of legislation in all 50 states, there are numerous significant differences in which people and what circumstances are afforded immunity from liability for rendering aid. But there are also a number of common themes found in a majority of jurisdictions. Some of the standards found across the states on a more consistent basis include the following:

- There can be no expectation of remuneration for the assistance provided;
- The assistance cannot be reasonably objected to by the patient;
- Assistance must be offered in good faith;
- Assistance must be warranted by an emergency circumstance (jurisdictions vary on definition of "emergency");
- Emergency situation must not have been created by the individual rendering assistance;
- Assistance rendered must not be willfully or wantonly in violation of professional standards of care;
- Assistance rendered must not be part of a preexisting duty.

The states have been somewhat divided on whether this immunity extended to aid rendered within health care facilities. The argument is that those within a health care facility who provide their professional expertise to strangers must do so at the same standard of practice as with established patients. Many courts have held that the professional presence of the provider in a health care facility gives them a preexisting duty to render aid and, since immunity is to encourage aid, it is not necessary in that setting. However, the viewpoint of the providers is that when called into an emergency situation whether on the street or at a hospital, they are not always presented with the same situation as they encounter with an established patient such as the type of professional care they are primarily trained for and ordinarily render, which includes proper technical support, patient history, details pertinent to the emergency, etc. For this reason, some states have granted immunity from litigation to providers who render emergency assistance, regardless of location. Other states require the providers to render an appropriate level of care. Consider the following Application 4.4 which recalls an actual occurrence.

APPLICATION 4.4

Dr. K undertook to perform a routine surgical procedure on his patient. The procedure involved cleaning the interior wall of the uterus through a scraping procedure. The patient was placed under anesthesia and Dr. K began. Approximately halfway through the procedure, he perforated the wall of the uterus and, due to the compacted nature of the abdominal cavity, the opening caused a release of pressure and the patient's intestine came pouring through the uterus and the surgical opening onto the operating table. The doctor immediately declared a medical emergency and requested assistance from any physician in the hospital willing to help.

At the time of the occurrence there was no statutory immunity for health care providers when working within a health care facility. Thus, when faced with a situation that had the clear potential for a medical malpractice action, no provider was willing to come to the aid of the operating physician. The patient suffered the loss of most of her intestine and eventually died some years later from her injuries received during the surgery.

In the above situation, the risk of liability was so severe it prevented trained health care professionals from rendering aid in a life-threatening situation. In this circumstance a Good Samaritan rule of immunity within hospitals might well have produced a different outcome and have possibly saved a life. On the other hand, it could have provided immunity to those who did not meet the standard of care within the confines of their professional setting and could have jeopardized competent medical care.

From a risk management perspective, Good Samaritan laws can be both a help and a hindrance. First and foremost it is important for the providers and risk managers to be well versed in the statutory language and judicial interpretation of Good Samaritan laws in the jurisdiction in which services are provided. Just as with informed consent, confidentiality, and other laws that affect the delivery of health care, Good Samaritan laws must be integrated with the ethical obligations and moral standards of the providers as they proceed in their professional practice.

FACILITY SAFETY

A key question that arises in cases that involve injuries resulting from an occurrence within a facility, rather than directly from medical treatment, is whether applicable medical malpractice statutes apply. Clearly, this can have an enormous impact on the outcome of a lawsuit and thus is a hotly contested issue in most cases of this nature. The following example, based on a real-life malpractice suit, demonstrates how the conditions in a facility can directly contribute to the delivery of health care. See Application 4.5.

APPLICATION 4.5

Gregorio is a patient in the hospital who has undergone a recent amputation of his lower left leg. He has been encouraged by the nursing staff to ambulate on his own whenever possible. On a day when his roommate has several visitors (in excess of the stated policy of two visitors per patient), Gregorio attempts to use his crutches to walk to the bathroom. He trips over a chair occupied by one of the visitors and falls causing serious injuries to the surgical site. Gregorio requires additional surgery and the removal of another portion of his leg. He files suit against the hospital.

In this particular jurisdiction there is a medical malpractice statute that limits damages. If it is determined that the state medical malpractice statute applies, and that Gregorio's fall was the proximate result of malpractice by the hospital, his damages under the statute would be limited to the statutory cap on damages in malpractice actions. If the statute is found not to apply to these circumstances and that ordinary negligence is the proper cause of action for the suit, the damage award by a jury would be unlimited.

Questions of whether or not malpractice statutes apply in cases against medical facilities are raised and debated nationally and even within jurisdictions. For this reason, it is essential to closely examine the legislation and case law of a particular jurisdiction when evaluating a claim against a health care facility. There are no firmly established principles of law in this area, but it is becoming clear, as the body of law develops, that the more closely related the cause of injury is to the administration of medical care, treatment, or services, the more likely it is to be considered within the definition of any applicable medical malpractice statute. If the injuries are not directly related to the receipt of medical care then it isn't likely to apply. For example, if someone is walking through a hospital on their way to visit a patient and falls, the claim for injury would likely not be subject to medical malpractice statutes; this case would ordinarily proceed under a claim of negligence based on premises liability. However, if a hospital patient is injured when a wheelchair collapses during transport from one hospital department to another to receive medical tests, the question of applicability is much greater. Finally, if a hospital patient is in the process of delivering a baby with a physician's assistance and a specially constructed bed for deliveries breaks causing the patient to fall from the bed and thereby injure herself and the baby, it is much more likely that a medical malpractice statute would apply.

RISK MANAGEMENT ISSUES IN THE HEALTH CARE INDUSTRY 165

ASSIGNMENT 4.2

Consider the following situations and explain why or why not a medical malpractice statute would be likely to apply.

1. A patient is walking in a hospital hallway when he slips and falls on a recently mopped floor. The patient has no impediments to walking.

2. A patient in a nursing home is being assisted to the shower with the use of a special belt that allows the hospital personnel to support the patient's weight. The belt breaks and the patient falls.

3. A doctor issues orders to restrain a particular patient admitted for medical evaluation. The patient convinces the nurse she is quite lucid and competent. The nurse does not follow the order for restraint. The patient proceeds to jump out a window and falls to her death.

4. A heavily medicated patient is alone in his room which is some distance from the nurse's station and near an exit. There is a video surveillance system at the nurse's station. It scans several areas of the facility and shows any given area approximately every two minutes. The patient awakens disoriented and leaves his room during the night. He enters a stairway and falls, suffering serious injuries.

5. A patient comes to a medical laboratory for a blood test. It is the first time he has ever given blood and upon seeing the blood flow from his arm he passes out and falls from the chair onto the floor and suffers a serious head trauma.

Included below are two judicial opinions. Both involve falls within a medical facility. Both are subject to the same medical malpractice statute in the same jurisdiction. In the first case, the medical malpractice statute is found to be applicable. In the second it is found not to apply. Consider the rationale of both courts as they reach their decisions and consider how they came to such opposite results.

CASE

438 N.E.2d 315

Court of Appeals of Indiana,
Fourth District.

(continued)

METHODIST HOSPITAL OF INDIANA, INC., Appellant (Defendant Below),
v.
Mabel D. RIOUX and Charles E. Rioux, Appellees (Plaintiffs Below).

Aug. 9, 1982.

YOUNG, Presiding Judge.

Appellant-defendant Methodist Hospital of Indiana, Inc. brings this interlocutory appeal contending the trial court erroneously denied its Motion for Summary Judgment. Ind.Rules of Procedure, Trial Rule 56. We reverse.

Because of the early point in the proceedings at which this appeal was taken, the details before us are limited. Plaintiff-appellee Mabel D. Rioux was a patient at the hospital when she fell and broke her hip. She alleges the defendant "negligently and carelessly failed to properly provide appropriate care ... to prevent said fall and injury." Complaint R. 6. The hospital filed a Motion for Summary Judgment accompanied by an affidavit demonstrating that no opinion of the medical review panel had been rendered as required by Ind.Code 16-9.5-9-2. The trial court denied the motion. The hospital brought this interlocutory appeal.

In essence, Riouxes claim the hospital negligently and carelessly failed to provide appropriate care to prevent a fall. No facts are before the court other than the affidavit of the insurance commissioner filed by the hospital that no medical review panel opinion had been rendered. The issue before us is whether the Medical Malpractice Act, Ind.Code 16-9.5-1-1 *et seq.*, requires the plaintiffs in this case to file a proposed complaint with the medical review panel and to have an opinion rendered by the panel before a complaint can be filed in any court. The hospital argues the Act does apply and such a filing is required. Riouxes argue the complaint is not one for medical malpractice against a health care provider, but is a suit for ordinary negligence and therefore not subject to the Act. It is not disputed that the hospital is a hospital within the Act. Nor is there a dispute that Mabel was a patient injured during confinement in the hospital.

As a prerequisite to an action in any court of this state against a health care provider, the Act requires that a proposed complaint be presented to a medical review panel and an opinion rendered by the panel. Ind.Code 16-9.5-9-2. The medical review panel reviews all proposed malpractice complaints against health care providers covered by the Act. Ind.Code 16-9.5-9-1. A health care provider is "[A] person, partnership, corporation, professional corporation, facility or institution licensed or legally authorized by this state to provide health care or professional services as a physician, psychiatric hospital, hospital, ... or an officer, employee or agent thereof acting in the course and scope of his employment ...." Ind.Code 16-9.5-1-1(a)(1). Health care is "any act, or treatment performed or furnished, or which should have been performed or furnished, by any health care provider for, to, or on behalf of a patient during the patient's medical care, treatment or confinement." Ind.Code 16-9.5-1-1(i). Malpractice means "any tort or breach of contract based on health care or professional services rendered, or which should have been rendered, by a health care provider, to a patient." Ind.Code 16-9.5-1-1(h). Tort is defined as "any legal wrong, breach of duty, or negligent or unlawful act or omission proximately causing injury or damage to another." Ind.Code 16-9.5-1-1(g). Thus the Act applies to any legal wrong, breach of duty, or negligent or unlawful act or omission proximately causing injury to another based on any act or treatment performed or furnished, or which

(continued)

should have been performed or furnished by the hospital for, to, or on behalf of a patient during the patient's medical care, treatment or confinement.

The complaint alleges that the hospital negligently and carelessly failed to provide appropriate care for the patient during her confinement to prevent her fall and injury. This falls within the broad language of the statute. When the hospital filed its Motion for Summary Judgment with accompanying affidavit demonstrating no medical review panel opinion had been rendered, Riouxes did nothing to place in issue facts to take the complaint out of the Act. When a motion for summary judgment is made and supported as provided in T.R. 56, an adverse party may not rest upon his pleadings but must, as provided by the rule, set forth facts showing there is a genuine issue for trial. T.R. 56(E). In their memorandum in opposition, Riouxes claim the negligence was of a non-medical nature removing them from the Act. However, the complaint places in issue appropriate care by the hospital during confinement which is subject to the Act. Statements of fact in the memorandum in opposition cannot be relied upon to demonstrate genuine issues of fact. *Bell v. Horton*, (1980) Ind.App., 411 N.E.2d 648.

There is no genuine issue of material fact presented. The Act is drafted in very broad terms, as shown by the definitions set out above. Applying the definitions of the Act, filing a proposed complaint and an opinion of the medical review panel were necessary prerequisites to filing suit in the trial court. Hence, summary judgment was appropriate and should have been granted. The trial court erred in its application of the law to the facts and the legal issue before it. We must reverse and remand for proceedings consistent with this opinion.

Reversed.

CASE

465 N.E.2d 731
Court of Appeals of Indiana,
Fourth District.

WINONA MEMORIAL FOUNDATION OF INDIANAPOLIS and Winona Memorial Hospital,
Appellants (Defendants Below),
v.
Rochelle A. LOMAX, Appellee (Plaintiff Below).
June 25, 1984.

(continued)

MILLER, Judge.

On February 7, 1979, Lomax was in Winona Memorial Hospital to receive physical therapy treatment prescribed by her doctor. On that date, Winona was qualified as a health care provider within the meaning of the Medical Malpractice Act, IND.CODE 16-9.5-2-1. For the purposes of this appeal, it may be presumed Lomax was a patient, as defined in the Act. *See,* IND.CODE 16-9.5-1-1(c).

Before receiving her therapy, which was to be conducted in a large pool, Lomax was instructed to change her clothes in a dressing room with a board floor adjacent to the pool area. She did so, unattended by any of Winona's employees. On her way from the dressing room to the pool area, Lomax tripped and fell when she caught her foot on a floorboard that protruded above floor level. No employee of Winona was assisting Lomax at the time of her fall, and no medical or physical therapy treatment was rendered to her before or at the time of her fall.

On August 8, 1979, Lomax filed her complaint in court, alleging Winona's negligent maintenance of the floor adjacent to the pool area was the cause of her fall and of her injuries, including a herniated disc in her lower back and a numbing of the right side of her body. Winona moved to dismiss the complaint on the grounds that Lomax had failed to comply with the Medical Malpractice Act by failing to present a proposed complaint to the Insurance Commission for review by a medical review panel before commencing her action in court. *See* IND.CODE 16-9.5-9-2. Winona's motion to dismiss was denied on April 23, 1981.

On October 21, 1982, Winona filed a motion for summary judgment on the same grounds as its motion to dismiss. The summary judgment motion was supported by the Affidavit of the Chief Deputy Insurance Commissioner stating that Winona was a qualified health care provider and that the Insurance Commission had not received an opinion from any medical review panel concerning Lomax's allegations of negligence. Lomax responded with an affidavit of her own, swearing to the circumstances surrounding her fall and disclaiming that her injuries resulted from malpractice or from professional services rendered or not rendered. The trial court held Lomax's claim was not within the Medical Malpractice Act and, therefore, was not subject to the precondition of review by a medical review panel. Winona's motion for summary judgment was thus denied, and, pursuant to T.R. 56(B), the trial court entered summary judgment for Lomax on the issue of whether her claim was within the scope of the Act.

... Because it is undisputed that Lomax was a patient (R. 2, 31) and Winona was a qualified health care provider (R. 20, 87) within the meaning of the Medical Malpractice Act, the only issue for decision on this appeal is whether the trial court properly determined, as a matter of law, that Lomax's claim of Winona's negligent failure to maintain its premises in a reasonably safe condition was not within the scope of the Act. Winona essentially argues: (1) the language of the Act is clear on its face, without need of construction, and broad enough to encompass Lomax's claim; (2) the purpose of the Act requires that all claims by a patient against a health care provider be included within the Act; and (3) this court's decision in *Methodist Hospital of Indiana, Inc. v. Rioux,* (1982) Ind.App., 438 N.E.2d 315, is direct and controlling authority for the inclusion of Lomax's claim within the Act. Lomax, on the other hand, contends: (1) literal application of the supposedly clear language of the Medical Malpractice Act would lead to absurd and contradictory results, which can be avoided only by proper statutory construction; (2) the purpose and structure of the Act require exclusion of Lomax's claim from its coverage; and (3) the language of the *Rioux* decision on which Winona relies is dicta and, therefore, not controlling in the present case. We agree with the arguments made by Lomax and affirm the trial court.

Winona's argument begins with the proposition that a statute that is "clear and unambiguous on its face need not and cannot be interpreted by a court." *Indiana Board of Tax Commissioners v. Holthouse Realty*

(continued)

Corp. (1976) 170 Ind.App. 232, 239, 352 N.E.2d 535, 539. Winona contends the language of the definitional section of the Medical Malpractice Act, IC 16-9.5-1-1, clearly and unambiguously defines Lomax's claim as being within the Act. Specifically, Winona points to the following definitions:

" 'Malpractice' means any tort or breach of contract based on health care or professional services rendered, or which should have been rendered, by a health care provider, to a patient."
IC 16-9.5-1-1(h).
" 'Tort' means any legal wrong, breach of duty, or negligent or unlawful act or omission proximately causing injury or damage to another."

Id. § 1(g).
" 'Health care' means any act, or treatment performed or furnished, or which should have been performed or furnished, by any health care provider for, to, or on behalf of a patient during the patient's medical care, treatment or confinement."

Id. § 1(i). Winona places special emphasis on the words "any act" in this definition. Also relevant is the following:

" 'Health care provider' means:
(1) a person, partnership, corporation, professional corporation, facility or institution licensed or legally authorized by this state to provide health care or professional services as a physician, psychiatric hospital, hospital, dentist, registered or licensed practical nurse, optometrist, podiatrist, chiropractor, physical therapist or psychologist, or an officer, employee or agent thereof acting in the course and scope of his employment."

Id. § 1(a)(1).

Putting these definitions together, Winona concludes: "Malpractice, then, by definition is any breach of duty or negligent act or omission by a health care provider to a patient." Appellants' Brief at 14. Winona argues the clear, unambiguous effect of these definitions is to place Lomax's claim squarely within the Medical Malpractice Act without the need, or even permissibility, of statutory construction, and to reject the distinction Lomax attempts to draw between "classical" medical malpractice, which she admits is within the Medical Malpractice Act, and ordinary negligence, which she contends is not.

The basis for Lomax's contention is the absurd and contradictory results she claims would arise from application of the Act to "premises liability" or "ordinary negligence" claims such as hers. She points out that, presumably, "the Legislature does not intend an absurdity, and such a result will be avoided if the terms of the act admit of it by a reasonable construction." *In re Estate of Pickens,* (1970) 255 Ind. 119, 128, 263 N.E.2d 151, 156.

Lomax contends that Winona's position that every claim by a patient against a qualified health care provider comes within the Medical Malpractice Act leads to absurd results. For example, under that construction of the Act, all of the following claims would be subject to the requirements and procedures of the Act: (1) the claim of a patient who was injured when a light fixture fell on him in his hospital bed; (2) the claim of an ambulatory patient who, while walking down a hospital hallway with *735 a visiting friend, was injured when he slipped and fell on soapy water left on the floor by a hospital janitor, even though the visitor's claim would not be subject to the Act if he also fell and was injured; (3) the claim of a patient who was slandered by a hospital employee; and (4) the claim of a patient who was assaulted by a hospital employee.

Lomax also argues that application of the Act to her complaint would achieve a contradictory result with regard to the admissibility of expert witness testimony under Indiana law. As previously noted, the Medical Malpractice Act requires a claimant to submit a proposed complaint to the Insurance Commission for review by and an opinion of a medical review panel as a condition precedent to filing an action in court. IC 16-9.5-9-2. The Act charges the review panel with "the sole duty to express its expert opinion as to

(continued)

whether or not the evidence supports the conclusion that the defendant or defendants acted or failed to act within the appropriate standards of care as charged in the complaint." IND.CODE 16-9.5-9-7. Further, the Act provides: "Any report of the expert opinion reached by the medical review panel shall be admissible as evidence in any action subsequently brought by the claimant in a court of law ...." IND.CODE 16-9.5-9-9. Lomax first argues that health care providers, who must be included on the medical review panel, are not expert in such matters as the maintenance of reasonably safe premises. Secondly, Lomax argues that such matters are within the common knowledge and experience of juries, and thus, expert testimony regarding the exercise of reasonable care is improper and should be excluded. *Emig v. Physicians' Physical Therapy Service,* (1982) Ind.App., 432 N.E.2d 52 (case not decided under Medical Malpractice Act); *see also Rosenbalm v. Winski,* (1975) 165 Ind.App. 378, 332 N.E.2d 249; *Brunker v. Cummins,* (1892) 133 Ind. 443, 32 N.E. 732. Thus, Lomax contends, inclusion within the Act of a claim such as hers would cause a contradiction between a longstanding rule of evidence under Indiana law and Code section 16-9.5-9-9. She contends the legislature could not have intended such a result.

The rules that determine when judicial construction of a statute is appropriate were reviewed in *Sue Yee Lee v. Lafayette Home Hospital, Inc.,* (1980) Ind.App., 410 N.E.2d 1319:

"In determining the meaning of statutes there are certain rules which we are bound to follow. It has been consistently held in Indiana that judicial construction of a statute is permissible only where the statute is ambiguous and of doubtful meaning. *Bowen v. Review Board of Indiana Employment Security Division,* (1977) [173] Ind.App. [166] 362 N.E.2d 1178; *Ott v. Johnson,* (1974) 262 Ind. 548, 319 N.E.2d 622; 26 I.L.E., *Statutes,* § 101. If the language of the statute is plain and unambiguous, judicial interpretation is inappropriate and the courts will adopt the meaning clearly expressed. *Bowen, supra; Town of Merrillville v. Lincoln Utilities, Inc.,* (1976) [171] Ind.App. [224] 355 N.E.2d 851. If however, a statute is ambiguous and its meaning is not clear from the words used, judicial construction is proper. In such cases, the purpose and goal of judicial construction is to give effect to the intention of the legislature. *Gonser v. Board of Commissioners for Owen County,* (1978) [177] Ind.App. [74] 378 N.E.2d 425. A statute should be construed to accomplish the end for which it was enacted. *Wilfong v. Indiana Gas Co.,* (1980) Ind.App., 399 N.E.2d 788."

Id. at 1322-23; *see also Field v. Area Plan Commission,* (1981) Ind.App., 421 N.E.2d 1132, 1137.

Sue Yee Lee was decided under the Medical Malpractice Act and contains a number of factual similarities to the present case. There, the parents of a young girl sought to recover damages for loss of services and medical expenses of their daughter, allegedly caused by the medical malpractice of the defendants. The defendants were awarded summary judgment on the grounds that the parents had failed to obtain the opinion of a medical review panel prior to commencing their action in court, as required by the Act, IC 16-9.5-9-2. The parents argued that because the Act referred only to actions by "a patient or his representative," IND.CODE 16-9.5-1-6, their independent action as parents was excluded from the coverage of the Act because not specifically mentioned--*expressio unius est exclusio alterius.* The defendants contended that because the statutory definition of the term "representative" included the "parent ... of the patient," IC 16-9.5-1-1(f), the action by the parents was clearly within the Act. Despite the court's eventual conclusion that the parents' claim was within the Act and despite the facially unambiguous effect of the interaction of the definition of the term "representative" with the authorization of an action by "a patient or his representative," the court in *Sue Yee Lee* held the Medical Malpractice Act "to be ambiguous and unclear *in meaning* with regard to whether or not the action of parents for loss of services of, and medical expenses for, a minor child is subject to the Act." 410 N.E.2d at 1319 (emphasis added).

(continued)

..."In construing an Indiana statute, our duty is to ascertain and give effect to the intent of the legislature. In doing so, we must give meaning to the language used, where that meaning is clear and unambiguous. Where the *meaning of the statute* is ambiguous, however, or where one or more constructions are apparently possible, we must construe the statute so as to arrive at the apparent intention of the legislature which is consistently revealed in all sections of the act, and consistent with all other statutes passed by the legislature." 418 N.E.2d at 210 (emphasis added.)

...The meaning and intention of the legislature are to be ascertained not only from the phraseology of the statute but also by considering its design, its nature and the consequences that flow from the various interpretations. ....

Our role in construing this statute is well stated in Crawford, Statutory Construction § 261, p. 516: 'In other words, the court will determine whether a particular provision must be followed. It will do this, even though the statute on its face is clear, just as it will determine whether an unambiguous statute will include or exclude a given case from its operation if construed strictly or liberally. * * * Both are used to avoid a strict and literal adherence to the letter and form of a statute in order that the statute may produce no absurd or mischievous results. * * * And, of course, the justification for this attitude is found in the maxim that it is presumed that the legislature does not intend to enact a law which will operate absurdly or mischievously. Consequently, in avoiding such results, the court is actually giving effect to the legislative intent.' " 253 Ind. at 184-85, 252 N.E.2d at 427.

As the cases above instruct, it is not the clarity or ambiguity of the words used in a statute that determine whether judicial construction of the statute is appropriate; rather it is the clarity or ambiguity of *the meaning* those words give to the statute as a whole. We hold the Medical Malpractice Act is ambiguous and unclear in meaning as to whether a claim for premises liability by a patient against a qualified health care provider is within the scope of the Act. As such we must seek the intention of the legislature in passing the Act in order to give it proper construction to accomplish the end it was enacted to attain. *Wilfong v. Indiana Gas Co.*, (1980) Ind.App., 399 N.E.2d 788, 791.

Winona contends that the legislative purpose in enacting the Medical Malpractice Act was to control "the overwhelming potential financial liability arising out of the patient/health care provider relationship." Appellant's Brief at 10. In Winona's view, all that is necessary for the application of the Act is that the parties stand in the relationship of patient and qualified health care provider. Lomax, however, views the purpose of the Act more narrowly, arguing that the legislature intended to control the potential liability of health care providers only for what Lomax terms "classic" medical malpractice, i.e., "the negligent rendition or failure to render professional medical and hospital care." Appellee's Brief 7-8.

The historical background leading to the enactment of the Medical Malpractice Act in 1975 is an appropriate place to begin in ascertaining the legislative purpose behind the Act. In the early 1970's, the problem of expensive medical malpractice insurance, which had been simmering for over a decade, came to a boil and threatened to make such insurance completely unavailable. *See* Note, *A Study of Medical Malpractice Insurance: Maintaining Rates and Availability*, 9 IND.L.REV. 594 (1976); Note, *The Indiana Medical Malpractice Act: Legislative Surgery on Patients' Rights*, 10 VAL U.L.REV. 303 (1976). In *Johnson v. St. Vincent Hospital*, (1980) 273 Ind. 374, 404 N.E.2d 585, upon which both Winona and Lomax rely, our supreme court affirmed the constitutionality of the Indiana General Assembly's response to this nationwide problem, the Medical Malpractice Act. In upholding the Act, the court surveyed the conditions that spurred its enactment:

"In the Mansur case [one of the four cases consolidated before the court for argument and opinion] a great deal of proof descriptive of the conditions in the health care and insurance industries which gave rise to the Act was brought forth and developed at a trial for constitutional purposes. Immediately

(continued)

prior to its enactment seven of the ten insurance companies writing the majority of medical malpractice insurance policies in the State ceased or limited writing such insurance because of unprofitability or an inability to calculate an adequate premium. Premiums had already increased as much as 1200 percent over a period of fifteen years because of the increase in the number and size of claims. Physicians practicing high risk specialties such as anesthesiology were hard pressed or totally unable to purchase insurance coverage. In some rural areas surgery was reported cancelled. Emergency services were discontinued at some hospitals. Health care providers had become fearful of the exposure to malpractice claims and at the same time were unable to obtain adequate malpractice insurance coverage at reasonable prices.

According to the Legislature's appraisal, these conditions implicated the vital interests of the community in the availability of the professional services of physicians and other health care providers. The Legislature responded with this Act in an effort to preserve those services and thereby to protect the public health and wellbeing of the community. It reflects a specific legislative judgment that a causal relationship existed at the time between the settlement and prosecution of malpractice claims against health care providers and the actual and threatened diminuation [sic] of health care services. The exceptionally high cost and even unavailability of malpractice insurance were major links in the relational chain. They in turn were connected through the large settlements and judgments being paid to patients. To the extent that these sums were excessive or unjustifiable, they had become so large because the processes by which evidence of negligent conduct was being gathered, evaluated, and used were faulty. Subsidiarily, these sums were being unnecessarily increased because the habitually negligent health care providers were not being identified and dealt with, very large attorney fees were being charged, and the time limitations upon bringing malpractice actions were too long.

With these judgments as its basis the Act created voluntary state-sponsored liability insurance for doctors and other health care providers, created a patient compensation fund, took measures to prevent injuries to patients through the negligence of health care providers, and subjected negligence claims against health care providers to special controls limiting patient remedies." 404 N.E.2d at 589-90.

Despite the language at the end of this passage referring generally to "negligence claims against health care providers," it is clear from reading this passage *as a whole* that the Medical Malpractice Act was the legislative response to the crisis in the availability of medical malpractice insurance, which, in turn, was threatening the availability of health care services to the public. The supreme court's review of the historical background of the Act does not indicate the legislature was aware of any difficulties of health care providers in obtaining general liability insurance coverage for ordinary non-medical accidents on their premises. No threatened unavailability of such insurance existed as a link in the relational chain to the threatened diminution of health care services. The legislature was responding only to a crisis in the ability of health care providers to obtain medical malpractice insurance coverage (which did not cover non-medical accidents) and thus to continue providing health care services to the public. *See Sue Yee Lee,* 410 N.E.2d at 1324.

Thus, the conditions that were the impetus for the legislature's enactment of the Medical Malpractice Act had nothing to do with the sort of liability any health care provider--whether a hospital or a private practitioner--risks when a patient, or anyone else, is injured by the negligent maintenance of the provider's business premises. That not being the sort of liability that brought about passage of the Act, it is absurd to believe the legislature would have reached out to restrict such liability by including it within the Act.

That the legislature did not intend to include such claims as Lomax's within the Act is further supported by the design and procedures of the Act. As Lomax points out above, the provisions of IC 16-9.5-9-7, charging the medical review panel with the sole duty of expressing its expert opinion on whether the

(continued)

defendant acted within the appropriate standard of care, and IC 16-9.5-9-9, mandating the admissibility of that opinion in the claimant's subsequent court action, would conflict with well-established principles of Indiana evidence law if applied to a claim such as Lomax's. Such matters as the maintenance of reasonably safe premises are within the common knowledge and experience of the average person. Health care providers, who must make up the medical review panel under IC 16-9.5-9-3, are no more qualified as experts on such matters than the average juror. And as we have stated: "When ... the matters at issue are within the common knowledge and experience of the jury, expert testimony regarding the exercise of reasonable care is improper and should be excluded." *Emig v. Physicians' Physical Therapy Service, Inc.,* 432 N.E.2d at 53 (citing *Rosenbalm v. Winski,* (1975) 165 Ind.App. 378, 332 N.E.2d 249). Thus, the consequences that flow from the interpretation of the Act argued for by Winona lead to a conflict with established law of evidence. It is presumed the legislature did not intend such a problematic result. *See Allen County Department of Public Welfare, supra.*

Thus, in examining the historical background leading to the enactment of the Medical Malpractice Act and the legislature's design of the Act, two important factors relevant to the legislative intent behind the Act become clear. First, the underlying problem that confronted the legislature at the time it passed the Act was the extremely high cost of medical malpractice insurance, which threatened the continued availability of health care services because the providers of such services were forced either to pay exorbitant malpractice insurance premiums or to provide care and treatment without insurance or to refuse to provide treatment at all. There is no indication in the background of the Act that health care providers had any problem obtaining the sort of general liability insurance that would cover a premises liability claim such as Lomax's or that the legislature was concerned with any such problem. Secondly, the system designed by the legislature to solve the medical malpractice insurance problem, if applied to a claim such as Lomax's, creates conflicts with established Indiana law of evidence, and there is no indication the legislature intended to overrule the established law.   Given these considerations, it seems clear the legislature did not intend a premises liability claim such as Lomax's to come within the coverage of the Act. Nevertheless, this court expressed an apparently contrary view in *Methodist Hospital of Indiana, Inc. v. Rioux,* (1982) Ind.App., 438 N.E.2d 315. It is to that opinion we now must turn..

The crux of the issue raised by the *Rioux* decision can best be introduced by quoting the critical segment of our opinion in that case:
"The complaint alleges that the hospital negligently and carelessly failed to provide appropriate care for the patient during her confinement to prevent her fall and injury. This falls within the broad language of the statute.2
When the hospital filed its Motion for Summary Judgment [footnote omitted] with accompanying affidavit demonstrating no medical review panel opinion had been rendered, Riouxes did nothing to place in issue facts to take the complaint out of the Act. When a motion for summary judgment is made and supported as provided in T.R. 56, an adverse party may not rest upon his pleadings but must, as provided by the rule, set forth facts showing there is a genuine issue for trial. T.R. 56(E). In their memorandum in opposition, Riouxes claim the negligence was of a non-medical nature removing them from the Act. However, the complaint places in issue appropriate care by the hospital during confinement which is subject to the Act. Statements of fact in the memorandum in opposition cannot be relied upon to demonstrate genuine issues of fact. *Bell v. Horton,* (1980) Ind.App., 411 N.E.2d 648.
There is no genuine issue of material fact presented. The Act is drafted in very broad terms as shown

(continued)

by the definitions set out above. Applying the definitions of the Act, filing a proposed complaint and an opinion of the medical review panel were necessary prerequisites to filing suit in the trial court. Hence, summary judgment was appropriate and should have been granted. The trial court erred in its application of the law to the facts and the legal issue before it. We must reverse and remand for proceedings consistent with this opinion."

Methodist Hospital is a hospital facility authorized to provide professional services and health care. It is the professional duty of a hospital to provide a safe environment within which to diagnose and treat patients. Failure to keep the hospital premises in a safe condition is a breach of the duty of a hospital. *Murillo v. Good Samaritan Hospital,* (1979) 99 Cal.App.3d 50, 160 Cal.Rptr. 33. Thus by definition, the injury or damage complained of falls within the Act. Ind.Code 16-9.5-1-1.] 438 N.E.2d at 316-17. On these grounds, the trial court's denial of the hospital's motion for summary judgment was reversed.

Winona contends *Rioux* is "four square" on the facts and determinative of the present case. To support this argument, Winona quotes from the appellate brief filed by the plaintiffs in *Rioux,* wherein the plaintiffs charged the hospital with "negligence in failing to properly maintain the floor of the bathroom where Mrs. Rioux fell," and disclaimed that their action was one for medical malpractice. Appellant's Brief at 16. Lomax argues *Rioux* was decided solely on the allegation in the complaint that the hospital "negligently and carelessly failed to provide appropriate care ... to prevent said fall and injury." Appellee's Brief at 16-17, quoting 438 N.E.2d at 316. Thus, Lomax contends that, whatever the plaintiffs in *Rioux* may have claimed in their brief regarding the condition of the hospital floor, it was not properly before this court, and that *Rioux* is thus distinguished from the present case.

Lomax is correct, as should have been clear from our holding that statements of fact in a memorandum in opposition to a motion for summary judgment (or in an Appellee's Brief, for that matter) cannot be relied upon to create a genuine issue of fact sufficient to withstand the motion. *Rioux* was decided only on the allegation of failure of appropriate care as charged in the complaint. This court had no evidence *properly before it* to remove that allegation from the coverage of the Act.

Here, however, Lomax did two things that the plaintiffs in *Rioux* failed to do that removed this complaint from the coverage of the Medical Malpractice Act and saved her from an adverse summary judgment. First, she alleged in her complaint more than a mere failure of "appropriate care" on the part of Winona; rather, she alleged, in what is clearly and unambiguously a premises liability claim, that "she fell as a proximate result of defendant's negligent maintenance of the floor ... in allowing a broken board to stick up in said floor ...." R. 2. Unlike the complaint in *Rioux,* this cannot possibly be construed as alleging the sort of negligence that the Medical Malpractice Act was intended to cover.

Secondly, unlike the plaintiffs in *Rioux,* Lomax did not simply rest on her pleadings in the face of Winona's motion for summary judgment supported by affidavit. Rather, Lomax filed an affidavit of her own that showed she was unattended by any of Winona's employees at the time of her fall, i.e., she clearly was not receiving care or treatment at that time. This served to further clarify that her claim was not within the coverage of the Act. The *Rioux* plaintiffs' failure to present such evidence on the record in a form allowed for by the Trial Rules left this court with no option but to hold that the trial court should have granted the hospital's motion for summary judgment pursuant to Trial Rule 56(E).

A premises liability claim by a patient against a health care provider, such as Lomax's claim against Winona, is not within the coverage of the Medical Malpractice Act. Anything in *Rioux* to the contrary is

(continued)

dicta and does not control this case. Thus, we hold that the trial court properly determined that Lomax was entitled to partial summary judgment.

Affirmed.

Ultimately, the question of medical malpractice actions against a facility is one that must be considered case by case and jurisdiction by jurisdiction. There is little question that a facility can be held responsible for negligence in property maintenance, defective equipment, unsafe conditions, and failure to competently provide the services which are the purpose of the facility. However, when determining how to proceed with such an action, any legislation that might affect the suit must be closely examined as well as any applicable case law. These must be compared closely to the facts of the particular case to evaluate how the action should proceed. While the jurisdictions are heavily divided on the issues of applicability of medical malpractice statutes, the trend is clear to apply the statutes whenever the cause of injury is closely connected to the professional delivery of medical care, treatment, or services. From the perspective of risk management, facilities must focus an equal amount of attention, if not more, to the policies and procedures for the physical maintenance and movement within the facility as they give to delivery of professional services. This is especially true for those facilities within jurisdictions in which issues of facility liability tend to be excluded from medical malpractice statutes as they do not receive the protection of the statutes intended to limit the number of suits and amount of damages awarded.

In the event an incident does occur in spite of proactive measures to create and maintain a safe facility, effective risk management is crucial to contain potential damages. For example, it is important to thoroughly document all aspects of any incident including complete statements from all those involved, steps taken to assist the injured, and any information that might demonstrate contributory negligence on the part of the injured party.

Problem 4.1

Complete 4.1 of the Comprehensive Problem in Appendix A.

CHAPTER SUMMARY

Risk management is a core element of the delivery of health care in today's society. It is a totally separate issue but is an integral part of the delivery of health care, treatment, and services. When accomplished in an effective manner it can reduce the number of incidents and properly contain the potential damage when an incident occurs. The concept of risk management developed largely within the twentieth century and continues to evolve. Risk management is the concern of providers, employees, and facilities. The scope is broad and far-reaching. It involves proactive measures such as stated policies and procedures for everything ranging from continuing medical education of professionals to a preventive maintenance schedule for the facility and all equipment. Good risk managers also follow up to see that policies and procedures are followed on a regular and consistent basis. In the event an incident does occur, the tone of risk management turns to one of reactive procedures to implement damage control and limitation of liability.

Key Terms

risk management	privilege
confidentiality	continuing medical education (CME)
informed consent	Good Samaritan

End Notes

[1] Soileau v. Med-Express Ambulance Service Inc., 856 So.2d 92 (La.App. 3, 2003).

[2] Doty v. Lutheran Hosp. Assoc. 110 Neb. 467, 194 NW 444 (1923).

[3] Phelps v. Dempsey, 656 So.2d 377 (Ala. 1995).

[4] Clark v. McEnany, 674 N.W.2d 780 (Wis.App. 2003).

[5] Miller v. Rhode Island Hosp. 625 A.2d 778 (R.I. 1993).

[6] Germanoff v. Aultman Hosp., 2002 WL 311116696 (Ohio App. 5).

 For additional resources, go to http://www.westlegalstudies.com.

5 CHAPTER

The Role of Insurance in Medical Malpractice Claims

As your insurer, we will pay any and all amounts up to the limit of liability you are legally obligated to pay as a result of patient injury or damage during the coverage term of the policy. The injury or damage must be caused by a medical incident arising out of the supplying of or failure to supply professional services by you ...

CHAPTER OBJECTIVES
When you complete this chapter, you should be able to:

- Explain the function of medical malpractice insurance

- Distinguish policies based on "claims made," "occurrence," and "tail" coverage

- Discuss the role of patient insurance in medical malpractice risk management and litigation

A highly controversial subject in American society, and a frequent topic of political discussion, is insurance. For the medical professional, insurance against claims of medical malpractice is an absolute element of the business of medicine. For the individual, the availability of insurance is an important concern given the potential for a personal medical crisis that can quickly result in astronomical medical expenses. Unfortunately, estimates of Americans for whom health insurance is either unavailable or unaffordable reach into the tens of millions. In this chapter, both issues are discussed as they affect and are affected by the question of medical malpractice.

PROFESSIONAL LIABILITY INSURANCE

Most individuals are familiar with the concept of insurance. A company identifies a potential risk. It evaluates the possible monetary damages associated with the risk if it should, in fact, occur. The next step is an evaluation of the likelihood of the risk occurring. This is then spread across the total number of parties who would be likely to purchase the insurance against the risk occurrence. That figure, plus a percentage of profit, determines the cost of the insurance. Medical malpractice liability insurance is essentially the same in its premise. However, there are additional factors to be considered. The purpose of this chapter is to consider these factors and how they affect the parties involved in medical malpractice litigation.

As with other types of insurance, companies that issue medical malpractice coverage offer financial protection to their consumers (health care professionals and facilities) in the event of a malpractice claim. The health care provider should always keep in mind that the primary goal of the insurance companies is always profit. They must take in more money in premiums than is paid out in judgments, settlements, and costs associated with administration of policies and litigation. Conversely, health care professionals turn to malpractice insurance as a means to protect their own personal and professional assets in the event of litigation brought against them. While both objectives are not mutually exclusive, it is important for all parties concerned to be fully aware that they are also not always mutually supportive.

The typical medical malpractice insurance policy furnishes monetary protection against litigation and ultimately damages for errors committed within the scope of the delivery of medical care, treatment, and services. As part of this protection, the insurer typically provides legal representation with respect to the policy. An extremely important concept that many health care providers fail to distinguish is the role of the legal professional. The legal representation is that of the insurance company's interests with respect to the policy and any potential payout. Because the health care provider or facility holds the policy of insurance, the representation is of their rights to the insurance and not of the provider or facility personally. While both the provider and the insurance carrier have the objective of avoiding or minimizing the insurance payout, the joint interest ends there. The example in Application 5.1 demonstrates how an insured and insurer can quickly be at odds in a situation in which both should be on the same side of the issue.

APPLICATION 5.1

A physical therapist is sued for malpractice as the result of injuries received by a client receiving physical therapy. The client was a middle-aged woman who was recovering from a recent stroke which had left her paralyzed on one side of her body and sometimes confused. On a particularly busy day she was first seen by one physical therapist. The client was then asked to go to another part of the room to work with another therapist. As she attempted to cross the room unassisted she fell and struck her head, suffering fatal injuries.

The family sued the provider. There were no applicable medical malpractice statutory limits on damages within the jurisdiction. The insurance company evaluated the case and determined that the possibility of a judgment at trial for the full amount of the policy was remote because the woman did not elect to use her walker when she attempted to cross the room. Thus, they were unwilling to offer a sum for the entire amount of the policy since that is the most they could be ordered to pay anyway after a trial. At trial, a verdict was, in fact, rendered for the plaintiffs based on a lack of supervision given the patient's mental and physical condition at the time she arrived for therapy. Further, the jury awarded damages in an amount that was approximately triple the amount of the physical therapist's insurance of one million dollars. The provider would be accountable for amounts of an award beyond the amount of insurance. In a case such as this, the award could well be enough to destroy the provider's financial status personally and professionally.

Typically, there are three types of **professional liability insurance** for health care providers.

First is the **"occurrence" policy**. This type of insurance is frequently the most expensive. It provides insurance coverage for claims that occur against a provider for acts during the period of coverage regardless of when the claims are asserted. This type of insurance applies even if the provider no longer has the particular policy in effect at the time the claim is made, which means that insurance companies are providing coverage for a period beyond that in which the policy was actually in effect.

Another type of policy is known as "**claims made**." This type of insurance covers only claims made while the policy is in effect. It should be noted that it is not unusual for claims to develop well after the injury either because the plaintiff was unaware or for various reasons that could cause a delay of as much as several years. If a provider moved to a different area and obtained a policy from a different company, any claims made on conduct that occurred at the prior location would not be covered once the policy at that first location had ceased to be effective. Exhibit 5.1 provides sample policy language that demonstrates the difference between a "claims made" and "occurrence" policy.

Exhibit 5.1 Sample policy language demonstrating the difference between a "claims made" and an "occurrence" policy

Occurrence:

This policy is applicable to those claims resulting directly from medical incidents occurring on or after the effective coverage date and prior to the final coverage date as stated on the certificate of insurance.

Claims Made:

This policy is applicable to those claims resulting directly from medical incidents that occur, and for which said claims are first made, on or after the effective coverage date and prior to the final coverage date as stated on the certificate of insurance. There shall be no coverage for claims first issued after the final coverage date regardless of the date of the medical incident which is the subject of such claim.

A third type of policy is commonly referred to as **"tail" coverage**. These are supplemental policies for the "claims made" type of insurance. If a health care provider terminates a policy of insurance, for whatever reason, he or she may elect to purchase a "tail" policy. This additional policy provides coverage for a stated period of time to deal with potential allegations of malpractice arising from conduct that occurred during the term of the now-ended "claims made" policy. Regardless of the type of professional liability insurance in effect, the ultimate questions for the insurance carrier in the event of a claim of professional malfeasance remain the same. These questions are whether or not medical malpractice law applies and whether or not the allegedly wrongful conduct is subject to the terms of the policy.

The statutory limits in connection with medical malpractice actions have been discussed throughout this text. In many jurisdictions, these limits restrict the amount of a judgment in a medical malpractice case, however, not all jurisdictions employ statutory limits. At the time of this publication, the efforts for federal legislation to limit noneconomic damages (e.g., pain and suffering), have been unsuccessful. In the event such legislation does go into effect, the amount of the judgments permitted is still likely to be significant in order to accommodate cases of extreme and/or long-term injury. That said, the cost of malpractice insurance is not likely to decrease. As reported in earlier chapters, not all cases brought against health care providers and facilities are found to be subject to medical malpractice statutes, and judgments are not subject to the statutory limits of medical malpractice laws. In such cases, the question is raised regarding coverage under the professional liability insurance policy. Availability of adequate and, especially, applicable insurance is a critical issue to those engaged in the health care professions and businesses.

In the event a health care professional becomes aware of a potential claim for malpractice, most policies require that he or she informs the professional liability insurer immediately. This allows the insurer to evaluate the potential claim and consider all existing evidence, interview witnesses, etc. In the event a claim of malpractice is actually made against the provider, it is wise to also immediately engage personal legal counsel to work in conjunction with the counsel representing the insurance company. The importance of personal legal counsel is apparent in the scores of cases in which insured health care providers have sued their own insurers following claims of malpractice. In some instances, the insured alleges that the insurance company failed to make reasonable attempts to settle, thereby exposing the provider to financial liability for judgment amounts exceeding the insurance. In other situations, the insured alleges the insurance company settled a case prematurely when the provider believed he or she would have prevailed in the suit. The typical complaints in this type of action are that the settlement exposed the provider to damage to reputation, higher premiums for malpractice insurance, and even loss of income or employment as the result of having a case against them settled rather than dismissed as unfounded. In matters of medical malpractice, the insurance carrier is only obligated to act in "good faith" with respect to the interests of the insured. This term is ambiguous at best and subject to a wide variety of interpretations. Consequently, this is an important reason for providers faced with allegations of medical malpractice to employ their own personal legal counsel to protect and defend what is, in fact, in their best interest.

22 Kan.App.2d 259, 915 P.2d 129
Court of Appeals of Kansas.

Lydia SAUCEDO, Appellee,
v.
Ray WINGER, M.D., Appellant.

April 19, 1996.

[by the Court

RULON, Presiding Judge:

The facts of this case are not in dispute. This is the second time this case has been presented to the Kansas appellate courts. The background facts leading up to this dispute are detailed in *Saucedo v. Winger*, 252 Kan. 718, 850 P.2d 908 (1993).

Plaintiff Lydia Saucedo originally sued defendant for alleged medical malpractice surrounding the death of her husband, Pablo. The case was tried to a jury which found that, although defendant's actions fell below

(continued)

the required professional standard of care, his actions or lack thereof, did not cause or substantially contribute to Pablo's death. Consequently, the trial court entered a verdict in favor of defendant.

Plaintiff sought to set the judgment aside, claiming juror misconduct. The district court denied her request for a new trial and this court affirmed that decision in an unpublished opinion. Our Supreme Court granted review and reversed and remanded for a new trial. 252 Kan. at 733, 850 P.2d 908.

On remand, before a new trial could be held, defendant's malpractice insurance carrier, Medical Protective Company (Medpro), entered into a settlement agreement with plaintiff. Defendant filed a motion asking that the settlement not be approved on the basis that Medpro was not a party to the suit and did not have authority to settle. The district court rejected defendant's argument and approved the settlement. The insurance company agreed to settle for $145,000. The policy limit was $200,000.

THE SETTLEMENT AGREEMENT

"Interpretation of an insurance policy, like the construction of any written instrument, is a question of law.... The appellate court's review of questions of law is unlimited." *Levier v. Koppenheffer,* 19 Kan.App.2d 971, 976, 879 P.2d 40 *rev. denied* 255 Kan. 1002 (1994). When an insurance policy is not ambiguous, the court may not make another contract for the parties. *Catholic Diocese of Dodge City v. Raymer,* 251 Kan. 689, 693, 840 P.2d 456 (1992). Whether ambiguity exists in a written instrument is a question of law to be decided by the court. 251 Kan. at 691, 840 P.2d 456.

The language of a policy of insurance, like any other contract, must, if possible, be construed in such manner as to give effect to the intention of the parties. Where the terms of a policy of insurance are ambiguous or uncertain, conflicting, or susceptible of more than one construction, the construction most favorable to the insured must prevail. Since the insurer prepares its own contracts, it has a duty to make the meaning clear." 251 Kan. at 693, 840 P.2d 456.

"The test to determine whether an insurance contract is ambiguous is not what the insurer intends the language to mean, but what a reasonably prudent insured would understand the language to mean." *Farm Bur. Mut. Ins. Co. v. Winters,* 248 Kan. 295, Syl. ¶ 1, 806 P.2d 993 (1991). "A contract of insurance should not be construed through the magnifying eye of the technical lawyer but rather from the standpoint of what an ordinary [person] would believe it to mean." *Wheeler v. Employer's Mutual Casualty Co.,* 211 Kan. 100, 104-05, 505 P.2d 768 (1973).

The outcome of this case turns on what authority the insurance carrier, MedPro, did or did not have under the terms of the policy with defendant. The policy reads in material part:

"In Consideration of the payment of the premium, receipt of which is hereby acknowledged, and subject to the limits of liability and other terms of this policy, the Company hereby agrees to DEFEND and PAY DAMAGES, in the name and on behalf of the Insured or his estate. ....

"B. Upon receipt of notice the Company shall immediately assume its responsibility for the defense of any such claim. Such defense shall be maintained until final judgment in favor of the Insured shall have been obtained or until all remedies by appeal, writ of error or other legal proceedings deemed reasonable and appropriate by the Company shall have been exhausted at the Company's cost and without limit as to the amount expended. However, the Company shall not be obligated to defend any claim after the applicable limit of the Company's liability has been exhausted by payment of judgments or settlements. ....

(continued)

"2. The Insured shall not (a) make any hold harmless agreements or contract any expense nor voluntarily assume any liability in any situation nor (b) make or contract any settlement of a claim hereunder, except at his own cost and responsibility, without the written authorization of the Company. The Insured shall at all times fully cooperate with the Company in any claim hereunder and shall attend and assist in the preparation and trial of any such claim."

In district court, defendant argued that most insurance policies explicitly provide that the insurer has the right to settle without the insured's consent. This policy, however, does not have such a provision. According to defendant, Medpro was without authority to settle this action without defendant's consent and, consequently, the district court should not have approved the settlement. Importantly, Medpro did not intervene and offered no argument either in district court or on appeal. The only opposing argument in the district court came from plaintiff, whose position was that any dispute over the terms of the insurance policy were between defendant and Medpro and that she had no interest in such dispute because she had a valid settlement agreement with the insurer. Plaintiff further argued that the policy provides both express and apparent authority for Medpro to settle this suit and all that was left for the district court to do was to approve the attorney fees.

Under the terms of the policy before us, defendant could not make any hold harmless agreements or voluntarily assume liability. Defendant could not, except at his own expense, settle without the written consent of Medpro. Finally, defendant was required to fully cooperate with Medpro in any claim and attend and assist in the preparation of any trial.

Medpro, in consideration of payment of the premium paid by defendant, was required to assume the responsibility to defend any claim which was covered by the policy. Such defense was required to be maintained until a judgment favorable to defendant was obtained or until all appeals had been exhausted. However, Medpro was not obligated to defend any suit after the extent of the company's liability had been exhausted by payment of judgment or settlement.

Clearly, the policy before us does not give Medpro the express right to settle without defendant's consent. The policy does not specifically require that defendant give his consent to any settlement. This policy, however, specifically prohibits defendant from settling without Medpro's consent unless he **133 assumes all responsibility for such a settlement.

There are several treatises that discuss the issue before us in general terms.

One treatise states:

"An insurance company is free to exercise its own judgment as to whether to enter into a settlement. It can, therefore, absent an express policy provision to the contrary, settle a case despite the insured's request that it not do so. The only limitation is that the insurer act in good faith." 1 Windt, Insurance Claims & Disputes: Representation of Insurance Companies and Insureds § 5.03, pp. 306-07 (3d ed.1995).

Interestingly, none of the cases this source relies upon states such a legal proposition. All the cited cases involved situations where the insurance policies *expressly* gave the insurer the right to settle within policy limits at the insurer's discretion. See *Ins. Co. of North America v. Medical Protective Co.*, 768 F.2d 315 (10th Cir.1985); *Puritan Ins. Co. v. Canadian Universal Ins. Co* 586 F.Supp. 84 (E.D.Pa.1984), *rev'd on other grounds* 775 F.2d 76 (3d Cir.1985); ...

Similarly, 7C Appleman, Insurance Law and Practice § 4711, pp. 367-69 (1979) states:

"It was early stated that an insurer has the right to make a compromise or settlement of any claims against the insured, and that it is not bound to consult the interests of the insured to its own prejudice. The law favors settlement without recourse to litigation.

(continued)

"Liability insurance contracts have been held to give the insurer absolute authority to settle claims within the policy limits, and the insured has no power either to compel the insurer to make such settlements, or to prevent it from doing so."...

Again, the cases cited for the principle that the insured cannot complain if the insurer settles for equal to or less than policy limits do not support that position. In these cases the insurance policy in question had *express* language giving the insurer the right to settle at its discretion. See *Martin v. Levinson,* 409 N.E.2d 1239 (Ind.App.1980); *Marginian* 18 Ohio St.3d 345, 481 N.E.2d 600. Long also notes that most medical malpractice policies contain provisions requiring the insurer to obtain the insured's consent prior to settling with a plaintiff. 2 Long, The Law of Liability Insurance § 12.05[2], p. 12-99 (1993).

There is, however, one reported case that supports the position that an insurer can settle a claim with a plaintiff even though the policy does not give the insurer the express power to do so. In *Kaudern v. Allstate Insurance Company,* 277 F.Supp. 83 (D.N.J.1967), the plaintiff sued his insurer Allstate, alleging it had improperly investigated a case arising out of an automobile accident in which the plaintiff was involved.

After the initial investigation, Allstate determined that this was a "no liability" case. Allstate, however, was obligated under the terms of its policy to provide legal assistance to its insured in the matter.

During two settlement conferences, after receiving statements of damages, medical reports, and depositions, Allstate refused to make any contribution towards any settlement. Allstate's insured was not informed of the existence of these conferences. Subsequently, the injured parties sent a letter to the attorney hired by Allstate and offered to settle for $10,000, Allstate's policy limits. Allstate did not answer the offer or inform its insured of the offer. Just prior to trial, Allstate offered to settle for $5,500. The offer was rejected. The case subsequently went to trial and a verdict was entered against Allstate's insured for damages totaling $175,000. Allstate appealed the decision, lost, and then made payment of $24,575 on behalf of its insured. The payment consisted of its $10,000 policy liability limit plus interest.

The insured then sued Allstate, alleging that Allstate exercised bad faith in the preparation, investigation, and settlement negotiations which resulted in a judgment greatly in excess of the policy limits. The court discussed the two competing standards of conduct in judging an insurer's action in deciding whether to settle a case--the negligence theory and the bad faith theory. At the start of its analysis of the insurer's duty, the court stated:

"The problems in this area arise from the standard clause in a liability insurance policy, present here, which provides that the insurer will defend in the name of and on behalf of the insured any claims for injuries to persons by reason of the operation of the motor vehicle owned by the insured. *This clause naturally encompasses the negotiation of any settlement claim prior to trial.*" (Emphasis added.) 277 F.Supp. at 87.

Kaudern is distinguishable for several reasons. First, the issue of whether Allstate had the right to settle was not at issue; thus, the above highlighted sentence is dicta. Second, the trial court made this statement without citation to any authority. Third, nowhere in the case were the actual terms of the policy enumerated. Last, this involved an automobile liability policy, and if Allstate had settled there would be virtually no financial impact on its insured.

We believe the rule is more appropriately stated as, where an insurance policy explicitly reserves the right to settle to the insurer, an insured cannot complain that the insurer settles or refuses to settle within policy limits absent a showing of bad faith or negligence on the part of the insurer. However, where the policy requires the consent of the insured prior to entering into a settlement with the plaintiff, the insured should not be allowed to withhold consent except at his or her own risk. See 1 Windt, Insurance Claims & Disputes: Representation of Insurance Companies and Insureds § 5.03, p. 307 (3d ed.1995).

(continued)

The question remains, what rule applies where there is no policy language expressly giving either the insurer or the insured the express right to settle?

A somewhat analogous situation was presented in *Lieberman v. Employers Ins. of Wausau*, 84 N.J. 325, 419 A.2d 417 (1980). In *Lieberman*, a physician brought an action against his medical malpractice liability insurer, alleging the insurer settled a claim against him without his consent in violation of the terms of the policy. The facts of that case show that the policy expressly provided that the insurer was empowered to investigate and negotiate settlement of any claim with written consent of the insured.

Initially, Lieberman gave his consent for the insurer to discuss settlement with the plaintiff. However, Lieberman subsequently obtained information that indicated that the plaintiff was not injured to the extent claimed. Lieberman then sent a certified letter to the insurer withdrawing his consent to settle and expressing his wish that the case proceed to trial. The insurer replied that because negotiations had already been commenced, it was unable to comply with Lieberman's request. Employers subsequently settled the case with the plaintiff.

At trial, Employers argued that it had relied on Lieberman's initial consent and was not required to accede to any attempt to revoke said consent. Therefore, its settlement with the plaintiff was proper.

On appeal, in reviewing an insured's right to withdraw his or her consent to settle, the court concluded: "When the insurance contract calls for the consent of the insured as a condition for settlement but is silent as to the irrevocability of that consent, we must be guided in the interpretation of the insurance contract by the overriding fiduciary responsibilities of the insurer. In terms of whether the insured has the contractual right to revoke a consent once given, our interpretation of the insurance policy should be harmonized with the fundamental notion that the insurer acts as a fiduciary for the insured and must in good faith be responsive to the insured's interests. [Citations omitted.] ...

"In this case, it should be emphasized that the insurance contract contained no express provision that would either render the insured's consent to settlement irrevocable or prevent such a consent from being withdrawn once it has been given. The omission of such an express provision in a policy which explicitly requires the insured's consent to settle creates at the very least an ambiguity as to the revocability of an insured's consent. That ambiguity is to be resolved in favor of the insured. [Citations omitted.] "We therefore hold that consent of the insured to authorize the insurer to effect a settlement is revocable in the absence of a contrary provision." 84 N.J. at 336-37, 419 A.2d 417.

As we understand, the New Jersey court said that if the insurance policy is silent on an issue of consent to settle or consent to withdraw a consent to settle, the interpretation must be resolved in favor of the insured.

We note that in *Harrison v. Long*, 241 Kan. 174, 734 P.2d 1155 (1987), a physician, Dr. Long, argued that certain provisions of the Health Care Provider Insurance Act, K.S.A. 40-4301 *et seq.*, were unconstitutional. Specifically, Dr. Long argued that the provision of the statute authorizing the Fund to settle with a plaintiff, without the health care provider's approval, after the primary insurer had tendered the policy limits of its liability, deprived him of a property right and was a denial of his right to due process of law. The *Harrison* court concluded that the Kansas Constitution did not require that a plaintiff's action be allowed to continue to trial to allow the defendant to vindicate himself or herself. Thus, there was no property right. 241 Kan. at 179, 734 P.2d 1155. The court further concluded that the Act provides a procedural framework that allows the physician an opportunity to represent his interest to the court at a settlement hearing, thus maintaining due process of law. 241 Kan. at 181, 734 P.2d 1155. Finally, the court found that where the primary insurer had settled for its policy limits, the physician could not complain that the Fund settled with the plaintiff because

(continued)

the State had a significant overriding countervailing interest in making sure that there was adequate liability insurance available to health care providers in the state. The *Harrison* court said:

> "It is the public policy of the State to assure an adequate supply of health care providers and provide protection to patients who may be injured as a result of medical malpractice. Under the Act, it is the Fund, not the provider, which is responsible for paying any difference above the coverage of liability insurance. It is, therefore, implicit in the Act that the provider relinquish his right to prevent a settlement. To allow physicians to control the defense of malpractice claims against them and reach their own decisions to continue or to settle the action would undermine the whole purpose and the financial structure of the Act." 241 Kan. at 181, 734 P.2d 1155.

Harrison is also distinguishable from the facts presented here. In *Harrison* the question involved the Fund's ability to settle with a plaintiff when the primary insurer had already tendered the policy limits. Language in the opinion suggests that Dr. Long's policy with his insurer gave the insurer the exclusive right to settle at its discretion. See 241 Kan. at 180, 734 P.2d 1155. Here, Medpro has not tendered its policy limits. Also, in *Harrison* there was a distinct public policy in protecting the Fund against actions that could lead to its financial downfall. Here, Medpro is not a state-created fund, and there is no significant, countervailing, or overriding interest in protecting it.

In the final analysis, this case boils down to a simple matter of contract interpretation. As stated above, if the language is ambiguous, the policy must be interpreted in favor of the insured--in this case, defendant. The policy at issue simply does not say if Medpro has the exclusive right to settle and consequently must be interpreted to mean that Medpro cannot settle for less than the policy limits without the consent of defendant. This court is not free to insert terms and conditions that the parties did not provide for themselves. *Koehn v. Central National Ins. Co.*, 187 Kan. 192, 196-200, 354 P.2d 352 (1960).

At the settlement hearing, plaintiff argued that Medpro had apparent authority to settle this case and therefore the district court should approve the settlement. However, faced with defendant's expressed opposition to settlement of the case prior to and at the settlement hearing, plaintiff could not reasonably rely on Medpro's apparent authority. As such, defendant cannot be estopped from challenging the settlement. See *Tucker v. Hugoton Energy Corp* 253 Kan. 373, 382-83, 855 P.2d 929 (1993).

Reversed and remanded with directions that the district court vacate the order which approved the settlement between plaintiff and Medpro.

The various medical malpractice statutory provisions have been enacted largely in response to the dramatic increases in the cost and availability of medical malpractice coverage. Throughout the country there are geographical areas with a strikingly higher incidence of claims of medical malpractice than in other jurisdictions. There are also jurisdictions that have earned a reputation for jury verdicts that are substantially higher than the national average in similar types of cases. Both of these factors lead to increased costs for insurance companies as they litigate, settle claims, and pay judgments. Those expenses are then passed on to the physicians and health care professionals in the form of increased premiums. In some instances, the increases are so regular and significant that providers have been inclined to relocate to an area where the insurance is more affordable. Other providers limit their practice to situations where the risk of allegations of malpractice is lower and even refuse to offer certain procedures and treatments, which, in turn, limits the availability of certain types of health care in some areas. Some physicians admit they now order many more extensive diagnostic tests than in the past as a means of practicing defensive medicine against claims of negligent care or treatment. In extreme cases, some providers have left their professional practice entirely and pursued other career alternatives. While there has been no documented mass exodus from the health care professions, there is an increasing difficulty in recruitment to certain locales and for some subspecialties of health care. All of these occurrences are negative outcomes of the increasing cost and unavailability of medical malpractice coverage.

There are many who allege that the malpractice "crisis" is an inflated concept and has been largely created by insurance companies as a basis to increase premiums and profits. The argument continues with strong advocates on both sides. Regardless of the cause or contributing factors, the ultimate result currently is that premiums are going up at a dramatic rate and having a direct effect on the health care industry.

When there is more than one type of insurance in place, concern arises regarding the applicability of insurance policies. Most health care facilities, whether it be hospital, dentist office, chiropractic clinic, laboratory, or any other type of health care facility, contract for more than just professional liability insurance. Any business owner may be subject to liability for injuries received on their property. This is in addition to the risk of injury in the delivery of medical care, treatment, or services. There are many situations in which an injury might occur that is clearly not the result of medical malpractice, such as injury to a nonpatient who happens to be on the property of the provider and suffers injury from some event like a slip or fall. Other circumstances are less clearly defined. Those cases include situations in which the patient is injured as the result of an ancillary occurrence within the facility of the provider that is not the direct result of treatment. In this case, it must be determined whether the patient's injuries are covered under a professional liability policy for medical malpractice or a policy of liability for injuries received on the provider's premises. This is often referred to as a "businessowner's" or "premises" liability insurance policy. When evaluating whether a case is subject to the requirements and limitations of a medical malpractice statute and which insurance policy should the claim be made under, it is important to establish whether the injury was, in fact, the result of the delivery of medical treatment, as demonstrated in Application 5.2.

APPLICATION 5.2

Dr. T practiced as an OB/GYN. He had been in practice for approximately 10 years when he was sued for four million by a patient alleging malpractice as the result of inappropriate sexual contact during a routine pelvic medical exam. The doctor vehemently denied the accusations. However, on the day of the occurrence the office staff was shorthanded and the doctor conducted his usual and routine exams without the presence of a nurse. The only persons in the room at the time of alleged impropriety were the doctor and the patient. The insurance company provided a legal defense for the doctor but also claimed that, if proven, the allegedly wrongful conduct fell outside the policy coverage. The case went to trial. During the trial the jury found that the conduct was indeed of an inappropriate sexual nature. The plaintiff was awarded two million dollars in damages. The insurance company then filed an action to have the applicability of the policy determined. The court found the plaintiff a more credible witness and determined that the conduct of the doctor was not part of the delivery of medical care and as such was not medical malpractice by definition. Therefore, no medical malpractice statutory limits applied. Further, the insurance company was relieved of any responsibility to pay the damage award under the policy of coverage for medical malpractice by the physician. The doctor was ordered to pay the plaintiff two million dollars. As a result, the doctor closed his practice and accepted a position teaching at a university.

(continued)

In this situation, the malpractice coverage was determined inapplicable even though the occurrence took place while the doctor alleged he was practicing in his regular office routine. Additionally, because the conduct was not considered malpractice by statutory definition, the doctor was also not able to stand behind the protection of statutory limits.

ASSIGNMENT 5.1

Consider the following situations and explain why they are likely or not likely to be included in a) the definition of malpractice; and b) subject to coverage by a professional liability insurance policy.

a) Dr. Eve, a surgeon, is sued by a nurse anesthetist because he routinely speaks of sexually graphic situations to the nurse while patients are under anesthesia and the nurse anesthetist is unable to leave the patient without endangering them.

b) Sue is injured when she falls asleep in an exam room at the doctor's office and falls off the table while waiting for the doctor.

c) Dr. Wavier, a chiropractor, is sued when he does not refer a patient with a palpable mass in the middle of his spinal column to a physician, and instead continues to treat through chiropractic methods.

d) Corinna is a patient sent by her doctor to a hospital for tests. A gel-like fluid is used on her abdomen by the technician to assist in performing an ultrasound. The warmer for the gel has malfunctioned and Corinna suffers third-degree burns.

e) Max, a 9-year-old boy, is left alone in an exam room at the doctor's office while some X rays are developed. The little boy opens a container of used syringes and accidentally sticks himself with a contaminated needle that results in his contracting hepatitis.

PATIENT INSURANCE

Much of the media coverage that involves individual health insurance focuses on the unavailability and/or unaffordability for the average American citizen to obtain adequate health insurance coverage. Attention is not paid to the significant role of individual health insurance policies in the law of medical malpractice. Proponents of medical malpractice legislation frequently argue that the high cost of individual health coverage is a direct result of increased health care costs, which relate to increased professional liability premiums caused by malpractice lawsuits. There are also those who raise the alternative explanation of increased profits of insurers. As with the arguments regarding professional liability insurance, there are two sides to this issue and both are well represented with statistical data and logic. However, for the purposes of this discussion, the topic will be confined to the direct role of patient insurance as it relates to medical malpractice.

The chapter on risk management began the discussion of the role of insurance companies as they interact with specific providers. That discussion will be expanded here. Most individuals are familiar with the process of presenting proof of insurance to a health care provider in exchange for services. What most are not aware of is the intricate relationship that must be established and maintained between a provider and insurance company in order for patients to receive health care from a provider with at least part of the payment for these services coming from an insurer.

There are many types of insurance, ranging widely from open care where the individual selects his or her provider and treatments with few or no limitations, to totally managed care policies where the insured must select from a pool of approved providers and virtually all treatment must be approved (often in advance) before payment is issued. Based on the types of policies an insurance company sells to its consumers, a provider may have more than one type of agreement with the same insurance company for reimbursements. The terms of each must be followed with respect to the specific policy terms of each insured patient. Prior to any payment for services provided to insured patients, most providers must establish a relationship with the insurance company. Typically, this includes completing applications, providing proof of current licensure in good standing of the primary health care professionals, evidence of proper certifications and credentials for equipment and staff, and effective malpractice insurance. The provider also typically agrees to accept a stated amount for each of the various services offered regardless of the provider's usual and customary charge for the service. Providers are encouraged to accept the often lower amount in exchange for the regular and consistent payment by the insurance company on behalf of the insured. Insurance companies offer payments at the stated amounts in exchange for providing their insured clients with availability of quality health care at a controlled cost. A provider that is not established with a particular insurance company or type of policy within the company may charge what they wish to patients, but they have no guarantee of payment for services rendered. As a result, the provider faces the possibility of having to collect fees from the patient directly in the event insurance does not cover the charges. Because of the high cost of health care, patients can rapidly accumulate extensive debt for medical care, treatment, and services. For the provider, individual collection is often a difficult and long-term process. As a consequence, providers are usually more than willing to accept a lower fee schedule as part of their agreement with the insurance company. In some situations, the insurance company requires the provider to accept all of their insured clients regardless of the number of existing patients being served by the provider. Thus, in some instances a provider may be required to refuse new patients from other sources in order to accommodate the insured patients of a particular insurance company. The business of individual insurance is a complex web of contractual terms and policy procedures that must be followed for each and every patient and type of policy.

From another perspective, the contractual relationship between provider and patient insurer has a certain amount of evidentiary value in claims of malpractice. If a provider has such an agreement, they may well have been the subject of audits. The results of these audits are often a valuable tool in considering whether a claim of malpractice is based on an ongoing policy or practice that is a pattern of conduct demonstrating a negligent professional. Thus, in the evaluation of an allegation of malpractice, it is important for both the plaintiff and defendant to review the results of any past audits by patient insurers, and the history of all relevant inspections and certifications of the facility and staff.

In addition to the obvious economic benefits of providing medical care, treatment, and services to insured patients, there are other considerations as well. Patients who are uninsured often find themselves personally responsible for all of the costs associated with health care. As a practical matter, these increased personal costs result in patients who demonstrate a higher incidence of not following through with recommended treatments and in turn have an increased risk of poor outcomes. Statistically, patients with poor outcomes—regardless of cause—have a greater incentive to sue the provider, even though a percentage of the negative outcome may be attributed to the patient's own noncompliance. Proof of such contributory or comparative negligence typically reduces damages but often does not eliminate them entirely in a case of alleged malpractice. This is especially true when the plaintiff responds to the defense with the claim that the provider knew, or should have known, that uninsured patients are at greater risk for noncompliance and poor outcome when complicated or extensive treatments are prescribed. Even in the event that the case is won by the provider, there are still litigation costs associated with the matter in presenting a successful defense. To combat this type of situation, many states have established panels and review boards or other measures that require the matter to be considered with respect to allegations of malpractice first, before the case is permitted to proceed into the courts. While this does not eliminate costs of defense, it greatly decreases them. An additional defensive measure of providers is to not accept patients without medical insurance who are not in life-threatening situations. This, however, creates an entirely new set of issues for American citizens who need health care and nonacceptance contributes to a negative relationship between providers and patients, setting the scene for even more allegations of malpractice.

In 1985, federal legislation was passed as an attempt to protect the general public from an alarming practice that had developed. Many providers had begun to refuse or "dump" patients who did not have medical insurance. With the advent of this legislation, it became illegal for any provider, who received government Medicare benefits for services rendered, to refuse emergency medical care to patients regardless of the ability to pay. In the case below, the patient had insurance, but emergency care was not provided. The opinion provides a discussion of the federal legislation that is a thorough examination of how this law has been applied since its inception. It is clear from the decision of the court that the providers have an obligation to provide immediate and basic emergency care without regard to the ability of a patient to pay or the likelihood of survival.

596 NW2d 391, 227 Wis.3d 811 (1999).

Supreme Court of Wisconsin.

Shemika A. BURKS, and PrimeCare Health Plan, Inc., Plaintiffs,
v.
ST. JOSEPH'S HOSPITAL, Defendant-Appellant,
Wisconsin Patients Compensation Fund, Defendant-Respondent-Petitioner.

Argued May 27, 1999.
Decided July 8, 1999.

DAVID T. PROSSER, J.

The Wisconsin Patients Compensation Fund (Fund) seeks review of an unpublished court of appeals decision reversing the circuit court's conclusion that the Fund does not provide coverage for violations of the federal Emergency Medical Treatment and Active Labor Act (EMTALA). The issue presented is whether the Fund is required to provide excess coverage for damages resulting from a hospital's refusal or failure to provide medical treatment to a severely premature infant, an alleged violation of EMTALA.

On April 1, 1993, Shemika A. Burks (Burks) arrived at the emergency room of St. Joseph's Hospital in Milwaukee, complaining of cramps and contractions. The time was approximately 6:40 a.m. Burks was 22 weeks pregnant and not expecting to deliver until August 10, 1993, almost 19 weeks later.

(continued)

3 One hour after she arrived, Burks gave birth to a baby daughter, Comelethaa, who weighed only 200 grams (approximately 7 oz.) and measured 11 inches long. The baby died at 10:15 a.m., two and a half hours after delivery.

In a subsequent lawsuit against the hospital, Burks alleged that her daughter was breathing and had a heartbeat at birth. She claimed the hospital staff denied her requests for medical assistance to the infant after birth and that the baby died in her arms.

St. Joseph's Hospital contended that it would not have been appropriate to resuscitate such a severely premature baby. In an affidavit filed later in the circuit court, Dr. Karlo Raab, a neonatologist at St. Joseph's Hospital, stated that "no attempt was made to resuscitate Shemika Burks' fetus" and that "resuscitation was not medically indicated for Shemika Burks' fetus and in fact is medically inappropriate for any fetus weighing 200 grams."

6 On March 30, 1995, Burks and her health insurer, PrimeCare Health Plan, Inc., filed a complaint against St. Joseph's Hospital and the Wisconsin Patient Compensation Fund (Fund) in Milwaukee County Circuit Court. The complaint alleged three causes of action. First, Burks alleged that St. Joseph's Hospital, acting through its agents and employees, and vicariously**393** through its staff physicians, was negligent in caring for her daughter. Second, Burks accused the hospital of negligent infliction of emotional distress. Third, Burks asserted a violation by the hospital of EMTALA by "refusing to provide treatment" for the baby, especially for refusing to resuscitate her.

7 On September 17, 1996, the Fund filed a motion for partial summary judgment, asking the circuit court to excuse the Fund from any liability for excess coverage on the third cause of action regarding EMTALA because the EMTALA claim was not a medical malpractice claim. The court heard the Fund's motion on October 21, 1996, and on November 19, 1996, it issued a written decision which granted the motion.

Following the court's written decision, the parties entered into a stipulation and order for partial dismissal, which dismissed the first two causes of action in the complaint. Thereafter, the only claim that remained was the EMTALA claim against the hospital.

Because the circuit court had previously granted the Fund's motion for partial summary judgment determining that the Fund did not provide coverage for EMTALA violations, the Fund submitted *815 an order for judgment and judgment to the court, asking that the Fund be dismissed entirely from the case. The order for judgment and judgment were both entered on January 21, 1997. St. Joseph's Hospital filed a Notice of Appeal from a final judgment on February 10, 1997.

The court of appeals reversed the decision of the circuit court and concluded that the Fund must provide coverage for EMTALA violations. The majority opinion, authored by Judge Charles Schudson, relied primarily on Wis. Admin. Code § Ins 17.35(2)(a) which requires that a health care liability insurance policy include "[c]overage for providing or failing to provide health care services to a patient." Because the cause of action regarding a violation of EMTALA alleged that St. Joseph's Hospital failed to provide certain health care services to a patient, the court of appeals determined that such a violation should be covered by the Fund.

Judge Schudson also wrote a concurring and dissenting opinion, signaling that the issue was close and difficult. He stated that *McEvoy v. Group Health Cooperative,*HYPERLINK *"http://www.westlaw.com/Find/Default.wl?rs=++++1.0&vr=2.0&DB=595&FindType=Y&SerialNum=1997226486"* 213 Wis.2d 507, 570 N.W.2d 397 (1997), was the controlling authority. Judge Schudson argued that in *McEvoy* this court stated that chapter 655, the chapter under which the Fund operates, covers only medical malpractice claims. Because the remaining claim was for a violation of EMTALA, not a medical malpractice claim, the concurring/dissenting opinion would have affirmed the circuit court's entry of judgment in favor of the Fund.

(continued)

We granted the Fund's petition for review to consider whether the Fund is required to provide excess coverage for damages resulting from a hospital's refusal or failure to provide care to a severely premature infant, an alleged violation of the EMTALA statute.

We begin with a review of the state and federal statutory provisions at issue in this case.

The Wisconsin legislature created the Wisconsin Patients Compensation Fund in 1975. § 9, chapter 37, Laws of 1975 The Fund was created "for the purpose of paying that portion of a medical malpractice claim which is in excess of the limits expressed in s. 655.23(4) or the maximum liability limit for which the health care provider is insured, whichever limit is greater ..." Wis. Stat. § 655.27(1). In other words, "Chapter 655 created the Fund to curb the rising costs of health care by financing part of the liability incurred by health care providers as a result of medical malpractice claims." *Patients Compensation Fund v. Lutheran Hospital-LaCrosse, Inc* 223 Wis.2d 439, 452, 588 N.W.2d 35 (1999). It is the responsibility of the health care provider to provide coverage for medical malpractice claims up to the amounts set out in § 655.23(4) through its own health care liability insurance, self-insurance, or a cash or surety bond.

Congress enacted EMTALA as part of the Comprehensive Omnibus Budget Reconciliation Act of 1985 (COBRA) to prevent "patient dumping" i.e., refusing medical treatment or transferring indigent and uninsured patients from private to public hospitals to avoid the costs of treatment. *Marshall on Behalf of Marshall v. East Carroll Parish Hosp. Service Dist.,*134 F.3d 319, 322 (5th Cir.1998). EMTALA provides that hospitals that have entered into Medicare provider agreements are prohibited from inappropriately transferring or refusing to provide medical care to "any individual" with an emergency medical condition. 42 U.S.C. § 1395dd(a). It "places obligations of screening and stabilization upon hospitals and emergency rooms who receive patients suffering from an 'emergency medical condition.' " *Roberts v. Galen of Virginia, Inc* 525 U.S. 249, 119 S.Ct. 685, 142 L.Ed.2d 648 (1999) (per curiam).

16 Under EMTALA, hospitals with emergency departments that have entered into Medicare provider agreements have two obligations. First, if any individual comes to the emergency department requesting examination or treatment, a hospital must provide for "an appropriate medical screening examination within the capability of the hospital's emergency department." 42 U.S.C. § 1395dd(a). Second, if the hospital "determines that the individual has an emergency medical condition," it must provide "within the staff and facilities available at the hospital" for "such treatment as may be required to stabilize the medical condition" and may not transfer such a patient until the condition is stabilized or other statutory criteria are fulfilled. 42 U.S.C. § § 1395dd(b), (c).

A person who "suffers personal harm as a direct result" of a hospital's failure to meet the requirements under EMTALA may bring a civil action seeking damages and appropriate equitable relief against the participating hospital. 42 U.S.C. § 1395dd(d)(2)(A).

The relationship between chapter 655 and EMTALA presents an important issue for this court. To what extent do these two statutes intersect? To what extent, if any, does a federal EMTALA claim come under Wisconsin's Patient Compensation Fund, so that the Fund is required to pay excess liability for an EMTALA violation?

The Fund asserts that its coverage is limited to medical malpractice claims and that a tort claim for medical malpractice under state law is separate and distinct from an EMTALA claim grounded in federal statute. Consequently, the Fund argues that it has absolutely no responsibility to cover any EMTALA violation.

The Fund cites *McEvoy v. Group Health Coop. of Eau Claire* 213 Wis.2d 507, 570 N.W.2d 397 (1997), to support its position. In *McEvoy,* this court examined the scope and application of chapter 655 to determine whether the chapter precluded Fund coverage for a "bad faith" tort claim against an HMO. In holding that such a claim was precluded, this court said that "an examination of the language of chapter 655 reveals that

(continued)

the legislature did not intend to go beyond regulating claims for medical malpractice." *Id.* at 529, 570 N.W.2d 397. "We conclude that ch. 655 applies only to negligent medical acts or decisions made in the course of rendering professional medical care." *Id.* at 530, 570 N.W.2d 397.

The Fund relies on several cases for the proposition that EMTALA is not a federal malpractice act. *Brooks v. Maryland General Hosp., Inc* 996 F.2d 708, 710 (4th Cir.1993). A hospital's liability is not grounded upon tort concepts. *Griffith v. Mt. Carmel Medical Center* 842 F.Supp. 1359, 1365 (D.Kan.1994).EMTALA, the Fund argues, is a strict liability law created to prevent patient dumping, without any regard to whether malpractice occurred. The Fund also claims that providing coverage under the Fund for EMTALA violations conflicts with *Rineck v. Johnson,* 155 Wis.2d 659, 456 N.W.2d 336 (1990), which it says makes clear that for other statutes to apply to the Fund they must be specifically incorporated into chapter 655.

Finally, the Fund argues that it is error to conclude that Wis. Admin. Code § Ins. 17.35(2)(a), and therefore chapter 655, applies any time there is liability for providing or failing to provide health care services to a patient, regardless of whether there is medical malpractice. The Fund asserts that § Ins 17.35(2)(a) applies to medical malpractice cases only, since the rule implements Wis. Stat. § 655.23. The rule is limited to what § 655.23 covers insurance for medical malpractice claims.

In sum, the Fund asserts EMTALA is a federal statute that "imposes two requirements on any hospital which participates in the Medicare program: (1) the hospital must conduct appropriate medical screening to persons visiting the hospital's emergency room; and (2) the hospital may not ... transfer out of the hospital a patient whose medical condition has not been stabilized." *Brewer v. Miami County Hosp.,*862 F.Supp. 305, 307 (D.Kan.1994). A malpractice claim requires a violation of a standard of care. This requires negligence. An action under EMTALA requires proof of a violation of the federal statute, nothing more. Consequently, the Fund argues that *no* EMTALA violations come under the Fund.

St. Joseph's Hospital takes exactly the opposite position. It asserts that all violations of EMTALA must be covered by the Fund. "EMTALA claims are failure to treat claims," St. Joseph's argues. "They all involve allegations of inadequate or inappropriate medical care against hospitals that pay assessments to the Fund with the reasonable expectation of coverage for such claims." Respondent's Br. at 4. Because EMTALA claims are not unlike medical malpractice claims, St. Joseph's declares, the legislature intended to provide coverage for an allegation that a health care provider failed to examine or stabilize a patient.

St. Joseph's Hospital maintains that chapter 655 does not define "medical malpractice" and does not consistently refer to coverage only for "medical malpractice." It cites several examples of other language in chapter 655 such as Wis. Stat. § 655.017 (limitation on noneconomic damages applies to "damages recoverable by a claimant or plaintiff under this chapter for acts or omissions of a health care provider ...") and § 655.27(1) "The fund shall provide occurrence coverage for claims against health care providers that have complied with this chapter ..."). It also asserts that because EMTALA is interpreted to incorporate state medical malpractice damage caps, the federal statute should also be interpreted to incorporate Wisconsin's requirement that the Fund cover claims against health care providers who comply with chapter 655. St. Joseph's Hospital also cites Wis. Admin. § Ins 17.35(2)(a) in support of its position. According to St. Joseph's, because § Ins 17.35(2)(a) defines the minimum coverage a primary health care liability policy must contain, the Fund, which provides excess coverage, should not provide less coverage than the provider's primary insurer.

St. Joseph's Hospital distinguishes *Rineck* and *McEvoy:* *Rineck* did not say anything about the extent of the Fund's coverage obligations but instead held that the Fund supersedes any contrary rule in other statutes or the common law. *McEvoy* never addressed the extent of the Fund's coverage obligations or whether the Fund covers EMTALA claims but instead addressed the issue whether the denial of HMO benefits is a chapter 655 medical malpractice claim.

(continued)

St. Joseph's Hospital points out that *McEvoy* dealt with an administrative decision to deny coverage for health care services, while this case involves an allegedly "improper medical action or decision" made in the course of rendering professional care. St. Joseph's stresses that this case is not an administrator's breach of contract, as in *McEvoy*, but a health care provider's medical decision that medical treatment was not appropriate and should not be rendered.

In sum, St. Joseph's asserts that the Fund was created to address the increase in claims arising out of the delivery of health care services. EMTALA claims arise out of the delivery or failure to deliver health care services. Hence, St. Joseph's argues that *all* EMTALA claims come under the Fund.

Both parties make compelling arguments, and both parties can point to cases from other jurisdictions to support their respective positions.

Our ultimate objective in this case is to interpret the scope of chapter 655, a Wisconsin statute. The interpretation and application of a statute presents a question of law that this court reviews *de novo*. *Patients Compensation Fund v. Lutheran Hospital*, 223 Wis.2d at 454, 588 N.W.2d 35; *Wisconsin Patients Compensation Fund v. Wisconsin Health Care Liab. Ins. Plan*, 200 Wis.2d 599, 606, 547 N.W.2d 578 (1996).

The Patients Compensation Fund provides excess coverage for medical malpractice claims. Wisconsin Stat. § 655.27(1) provides:

There is created a patients compensation fund for the purpose of paying that portion of a *medical malpractice claim* which is in excess of the limits expressed in s. 655.23(4) or the maximum liability limit for which the health care provider is insured, whichever limit is greater, paying future medical expense payments under s. 655.015 and paying claims under sub. (1m). The fund shall provide occurrence coverage for claims against health care providers that have complied with this chapter, and against employes of those health care providers, and for reasonable and necessary expenses incurred in payment of claims and fund administrative expenses.... (Emphasis supplied).

In *McEvoy*, after citing five references to *malpractice* in the chapter, this court said: "We conclude that ch. 655 applies only to negligent medical acts or decisions made in the course of rendering professional medical care. To hold otherwise would exceed the bounds of the chapter and would grant seeming immunity from non-ch. 655 suits to those with a medical degree." *McEvoy*, 213 Wis.2d at 530,

We know that chapter 655 applies only to medical malpractice claims, but this begs the question. What is a medical malpractice claim? Chapter 655 does not define medical malpractice. The Wisconsin Jury Instruction-- Civil 1023 states that the standard to determine medical malpractice is "whether (doctor) failed to use the degree of care, skill, and judgment which reasonable (general practitioners) (specialists) would exercise given the state of medical knowledge at the time of the (treatment) (diagnosis) in issue."

The phrase "state of medical knowledge at the time of" in the instruction implies that the standard of care for general practitioners or specialists is constantly evolving as the state of medical knowledge advances. *Cf. Nowatske v. Osterloh*, 198 Wis.2d 419, 438-39, 543 N.W.2d 265 (1996). The state of medical knowledge is not static. It may in certain circumstances require an understanding of statutory requirements. The Informed Consent Statute is one example. *See* Wis. Stat. § 448.30.

The failure to provide health care services can be a component of medical malpractice. Wisconsin Stat. § 655.005(1) refers to "damages for bodily injury or death due to acts or *omissions* ..." and subsection (2) refers to "claims against the health care provider or the employe of the health care provider due to the acts or *omissions* of the employe acting within the scope of his or her employment and providing health care services." (Emphasis supplied). Wisconsin Stat. § 655.44(1) refers to persons having "a claim or a derivative claim under this chapter for bodily injury or death because of a tort ... based on professional services rendered *or that should have been rendered* by a health care provider ..."

(continued)

Given this statutory language it makes perfect sense for Wis. Admin. § Ins 17.35(2)(a) to require that a health care liability insurance policy, providing the primary coverage for a health care provider, include "[c]overage for providing or failing to provide health care services to a patient."

In *Steinberg v. Arcilla*," _194 Wis.2d 759, 773, 535 N.W.2d 444 (Ct.App.1995), the court of appeals accepted a jury instruction which read in part: A physician fails to exercise reasonable and ordinary care when, without intending to do any wrong, he does an act *or omits to act* under circumstances in which a physician ought reasonably to foresee that such action or *omission* will subject his patient to an unreasonable risk [of] injury or damage. This instruction is cited by this court in *Nowatske,* 198 Wis.2d at 434-35 n. 8, 543 N.W.2d 265. Medical malpractice includes omissions, failures to provide health care services, and professional services that should have been rendered when these deficiencies violate the standard of care required from a health care provider. The failure to provide health care services to a patient can, in appropriate circumstances, be negligence.

The announced objective of EMTALA was to prohibit hospitals that receive Medicare funds from engaging in "patient dumping." Elizabeth Larson, Note, *Did Congress Intend to Give Patients The Right to Demand and Receive Inappropriate Medical Treatments?: EMTALA Reexamined in Light of Baby K,* 1995 Wis. L.Rev. 1425. "Patient dumping is the refusal by a hospital to provide necessary emergency medical treatment to someone based upon that person's inability to pay." *Id.*

While Congress may have intended to focus on the indigent and uninsured when it passed EMTALA, the language it used was conducive to a much broader interpretation. In recent years EMTALA has been construed to apply to all patients, irrespective of their ability to pay. Most courts that have considered the question have ruled that EMTALA does not contain an express or implied "improper motive" requirement. A person need not show any medical malpractice to prove an EMTALA violation. In fact, two courts have required medical treatment outside the prevailing standard of care, treatment that is at least arguably medically inappropriate

In a persuasive article, Elizabeth A. Larson writes that even the fully insured may bring suit under EMTALA.

However, with the element of economic discrimination absent from such a case, it is difficult to determine exactly what role EMTALA should play. The courts ... have established a variety of tests for finding a violation in such cases. While these tests differ from one another, they share a common goal: to determine whether a particular hospital failed to adequately screen the patient for an emergency medical condition and, if such a condition was found, whether the hospital stabilized it before releasing or transferring the patient.

The goal of these tests is effectively indistinguishable from that of state malpractice laws: to determine whether the established standard of care was breached. But while the common law of malpractice takes individual factors into account, EMTALA is brief, vaguely written, and provides no guidance for determining a standard of care. Larson, 1995 Wis. L.Rev. at 1426-27 (emphasis supplied).

Larson writes that "The majority rule ... holds that EMTALA does not guarantee a correct diagnosis and does not create a federal malpractice law. Despite the courts' claims, plaintiffs seem to have noticed that the majority rule does in effect create a federal malpractice law." *Id.* at 1457.

Larson is not the only commentator to suggest that EMTALA has made incursions into traditional areas of state malpractice law. Congress has created "a federal standard for emergency care." Scott B. Smith, *The Critical Condition of the Emergency Medical Treatment and Active Labor Act: A Proposed Amendment to the Act After In the Matter of Baby K* 48 Vand. L.Rev. 1491, 1507 (1995). "COBRA's imposition of federal standards on the states represents a radical change from the status quo. Previously state and local governments

(continued)

generally determined the regulation of emergency care." Karen I. Treiger, *Preventing Patient Dumping: Sharpening the COBRA's Fangs*, 61 N.Y.U. L.Rev. 1186, 1209 (1986).

"In the broadest terms, EMTALA imposes a legal duty on hospitals pertaining to the care and subsequent transfer of individuals with emergency medical conditions." Alicia Dowdy, et al., *The Anatomy of EMTALA: A Litigator's Guide* 27 St. Mary's L.J. 463, 470 (1996). "Courts determining the standard of liability under EMTALA have looked to and applied the duties outlined by the statute itself. When a statute like EMTALA creates a duty of care, a violation of the statutory duty is categorized as 'negligence per se' or 'statutory liability.' " *Id.* at 489. EMTALA imposes a duty on hospitals regarding emergency department screening, actual knowledge of medical conditions, stabilization, and transfer, and courts have noted that the statute itself describes the type of conduct required with respect to each of these provisions. Thus, in determining whether a hospital has departed from the statutorily imposed duties, courts reduce the statute to its elements and examine the duty of care for each element.
Id. at 489-90.

There is ample evidence that medical malpractice claims and EMTALA claims are being filed in the same lawsuit. Multiple claims have been encouragedState and federal courts have concurrent jurisdiction over EMTALA claims"It is hornbook law that district courts have discretion to exercise supplemental jurisdiction over the state law claims where the state and federal claims derive from a common nucleus of operative facts." *Lopez-Soto v. Hawayek* 988 F.Supp. 41, 46 (D.P.R.1997) (citing 28 U.S.C. § 1367 and *United Mine Workers v. Gibbs*, 383 U.S. 715, 725, 86 S.Ct. 1130, 16 L.Ed.2d 218 (1966)), *reversed on other grounds*, 175 F.3d 170 (1st Cir.1999).

EMTALA violations frequently have a malpractice element. *See, e.g., Power v. Arlington Hospital Assoc.*, 42 F.3d 851 (4th Cir.1994);*Reid v. Indianapolis Osteopathic Med. Hosp., Inc.*,709 F.Supp. 853, 855 (S.D.Ind.1989); *Barris v. County of Los Angeles* 20 Cal.4th 101, 83 Cal.Rptr.2d 145, 972 P.2d 966, 972 (1999).

To illustrate, in *Power v. Arlington Hospital Assoc.*, 42 F.3d 851 (4th Cir.1994), Susan Power came to the Arlington Hospital emergency room complaining of pain in her left hip, her lower left abdomen, and in her back running down her leg, and reported she was unable to walk, was shaking, and had severe chills. *Id.* at 853. She was eventually given some pain medication and dismissed after seeing two nurses and two physicians. *Id.* She returned to the hospital the next day in an unstable condition with virtually no blood pressure. *Id.* She was diagnosed as suffering from septic shock and immediately admitted into intensive care where she remained for over four months. *Id.* She eventually had both of her legs amputated below the knee, lost sight in one eye, and experienced severe permanent lung damage. *Id.* She was eventually transferred to a hospital in her hometown in England. *Id.*

Power sued Arlington Hospital alleging that the hospital violated EMTALA by failing to provide her an "appropriate medical screening" when she initially arrived at the emergency room. *Id.* at 853-54. She also claimed that the hospital violated EMTALA by transferring her to the hospital in England while she was still in an unstable condition. *Id.* at 854. A jury returned a verdict in favor of Power on the appropriate medical screening claim and awarded actual damages of $5 million. *Id.* The jury found in favor of the hospital on the inappropriate transfer claim. *Id.*

The hospital appealed, raising questions about the appropriate legal standard for recovery in an EMTALA claim and EMTALA's interrelationship with a Virginia statute that caps damages from medical malpractice suits. *Id.* The hospital argued that the court of appeals should adopt a standard that requires proof of non-medical reason or an improper motive for a hospital's treatment or discharge decision before a plaintiff can recover for a breach of EMTALA. *Id.* at 856. The hospital also asserted that damages in the action should be limited by Virginia's malpractice damages cap. *Id.*

(continued)

With respect to the claim that proof of non-medical reason or improper motive is required for an EMTALA claim, the Fourth Circuit stated:

[T]his is not a case in which the EMTALA claim is based solely on allegations that emergency room personnel failed to make a proper diagnosis.... Power has clearly presented evidence from which a jury could conclude that she was treated differently from other patients presenting to the Arlington Hospital emergency room, and that the Hospital did not apply its standard screening procedure, such that it was, uniformly. Although the facts might also give rise to a claim under state law for misdiagnosis or malpractice, that is not what Power has alleged or argued here. Her evidence is sufficient to meet the threshold requirement of an EMTALA claim, namely that the screening she was provided by Arlington Hospital deviated from that given to other patients. *Id.*at 856-57 (citation omitted).

he Fourth Circuit determined that "Power's EMTALA claim would be deemed a malpractice claim under the Virginia Medical Malpractice Act, despite the fact that it does not allege a breach of the prevailing professional standard of care generally associated with a malpractice claim." *Id.* at 861.

Power demonstrates that the scope of EMTALA extends beyond a refusal to treat based on economic reasons. The argument that the hospital failed to screen Power for economic reasons was tenuous, yet the Fourth Circuit still recognized that a valid EMTALA claim existed. The potential scope of EMTALA is extremely broad, and is not limited to the refusal to provide care to persons without insurance. *See, e.g., Lopez-Soto v. Hawayek,* 175 F.3d 170 (1st Cir.1999); *Summers v. Baptist Medical Center Arkadelphia,* 91 F.3d 1132 (8th Cir.1996); *Carodenuto v. New York City Health & Hospitals Corp.,*156 Misc.2d 361, 593 N.Y.S.2d 442 (N.Y.Sup.Ct.1992).

EMTALA claims are not limited to persons who are indigent and uninsured. Hospitals can violate EMTALA without improper motives by "negligently" failing to satisfy the standards of emergency care established in federal law. Commentators have stated that EMTALA overlaps state malpractice law State malpractice law can include failure to provide health care services. Consequently, the conclusion is inescapable that at least some EMTALA violations are medical malpractice claims.

Permitting the label on a cause of action to dictate whether a health care provider receives excess coverage from the Patients Compensation Fund would be elevating form over substance and negating the purpose of the Fund. Hence, we look to the test in *McEvoy* and hold that when a hospital's violation of EMTALA results from a negligent medical act or from a decision made in the course of rendering professional medical care, the Fund has an obligation to provide excess coverage. Conversely, when a hospital's violation of EMTALA results from an economic decision, the Fund has no duty to provide coverage.

In determining whether a violation of EMTALA was medically-based or economically-based, the first factor to consider is whether the patient had health care insurance coverage. The presence of insurance coverage permits the inference that the violation was not economically-based. The absence of coverage creates an implication that the violation may have been economically-based. Other factors to consider are whether the patient was given screening and other medical treatment, whether the screening was consistent with the usual practice at the hospital, whether a decision to transfer was made in consultation with another hospital, whether the action complained of resulted from the decision of a doctor or an administrator, and whether the patient has also made a malpractice claim.

Under the facts in this case, coverage under the Fund exists for Burks' claimed EMTALA violation. There was testimony that a medical decision was made not to treat Burks' newborn because medically the baby could not survive. In addition, several of the indicia described above existed in this case. Burks had medical insurance with PrimeCare Health Plan, Inc. Doctors made the decision not to treat Burks' newborn. This was not a case in which a non-medical administrator of the hospital made a decision not to treat based

(continued)

on economics. Burks began her suit claiming both an EMTALA violation and medical malpractice. Without reaching the merits of Burks' EMTALA violation claim, we conclude that coverage under the Fund exists. Therefore, we affirm the decision of the court of appeals.

The decision of the court of appeals is affirmed.

A fairly recent development in the area of medical malpractice cases that involves patient insurance deals with **managed care** policies. In managed care, costs are contained by strict supervision of the insurance companies over the delivery of medical care, treatment, and services. Many policies require a referral of need from a primary physician before a specialist can be consulted. Other common elements have established time limits for hospitalization based on the reason for the admission. These standardized rules are designed to eliminate unnecessary consultations, hospitalizations, or hospital stays that exceed the established norm. Advocates of managed care assert that it is the best method to keep rising health care costs down. However, opponents of the managed care system claim that it does not consider unique or unanticipated circumstances patients may encounter. As a result, it is alleged that patients may suffer further injury because of delayed access to specialist care, no access to certain types of providers, or premature dismissal from hospitals. Consider Application 5.3 based on a real occurrence.

APPLICATION 5.3

Kimber was a 10-year-old, apparently healthy girl. A teacher noticed mid-year that Kimber appeared to have developed difficulty seeing the blackboard and sometimes appeared to lose her balance on the playground. The teacher suggested having an eye exam. Kimber's mother took her to their family physician to obtain a referral to a specialist as required by their managed care policy of insurance. Specifically, her mother was concerned about the balance issue and wanted her daughter seen by a pediatric ophthalmologist who specialized in medical care of children with eye problems. Kimber was seen by the family practitioner who recommend she see a local optometrist (generally much less expensive). The family doctor did not perform a medical evaluation of Kimber. She was fitted for glasses by the optometrist who was not medically trained. However, after about a month, the problems seemed to be worsening and Kimber began to complain of headaches and dizziness. Her mother again took her to the family doctor. This time she was seen by the physician's assistant in the office who concluded a poor fit on the eyeglass prescription and recommended they go back to the optometrist. Again, no medical evaluation was done. Kimber rapidly deteriorated and within days was suffering extreme headaches and was so dizzy it was difficult to walk. Her mother took her to the emergency room where she was seen by the pediatrician on call. He did a medical exam and ordered radiological tests. Within a matter of a few hours it was discovered Kimber had a brain tumor in

(continued)

advanced stages. The tumor would have been highly treatable had it been discovered in its early stages. However, at the time it was discovered, the condition had advanced to the point where Kimber only lived a few months longer.

The mother sued the family practitioner and the managed care policy administrator for medical malpractice by restricting her access to specialist care that might have saved her daughter's life. The managed care company's position was that it was not responsible for the acts the family practitioner. And, that if every patient were allowed to bypass an initial evaluation and proceed to specialists, who were unnecessary in a large percentage of cases, the costs of health care would rise so quickly that most individuals would be unable to afford any type of insurance at all.

During the 1990s, a number of states passed legislation permitting insurance companies of managed care policies to be sued for malpractice. The insurance companies on the other hand claimed that such laws violated federal law. Prior to the emergence of managed care, federal legislation permitted patients to obtain only an insurance benefit previously denied by an insurance carrier. It did not permit recovery of monetary damages. Additionally, cases under federal law can be compelled into the federal judicial system. Plaintiff's lawyers typically prefer the state courts where there is often a greater possibility for higher jury verdicts and, in many states, punitive damages. The courts have been split over the issue of whether this law applies to cases involving denial of health care by a managed care policy administrator since they were not in effect at the time the legislation was passed. In 2004, the United States Supreme Court considered this issue and rendered its decision.

CASE

124 S.Ct. 2488 (2004).
Supreme Court of the United States

AETNA HEALTH INC., fka Aetna U.S. Healthcare Inc. and Aetna U.S. Healthcare of North Texas, Inc., Petitioner,
v.
Juan DAVILA.
Cigna HealthCare of Texas, Inc., dba Cigna Corporation, Petitioner,
v.
Ruby R. CALAD, et al.

Decided June 21, 2004.

THOMAS, J., delivered the opinion for a unanimous Court. GINSBURG, J., filed a concurring opinion, in which BREYER, J., joined.

(continued)

...Respondent Juan Davila is a participant, and respondent Ruby Calad is a beneficiary, in ERISA-regulated employee benefit plans. Their respective plan sponsors had entered into agreements with petitioners, Aetna Health Inc. and CIGNA Healthcare of Texas, Inc., to administer the plans. Under Davila's plan, for instance, Aetna reviews requests for coverage and pays providers, such as doctors, hospitals, and nursing homes, which perform covered services for members; under Calad's plan sponsor's agreement, CIGNA is responsible for plan benefits and coverage decisions.

Respondents both suffered injuries allegedly arising from Aetna's and CIGNA's decisions not to provide coverage for certain treatment and services recommended by respondents' treating physicians. Davila's treating physician prescribed Vioxx to remedy Davila's arthritis pain, but Aetna refused to pay for it. Davila did not appeal or contest this decision, nor did he purchase Vioxx with his own resources and seek reimbursement. Instead, Davila began taking Naprosyn, from which he allegedly suffered a severe reaction that required extensive treatment and hospitalization. Calad underwent surgery, and although her treating physician recommended an extended hospital stay, a CIGNA discharge nurse determined that Calad did not meet the plan's criteria for a continued hospital stay. CIGNA consequently denied coverage for the extended hospital stay. Calad experienced postsurgery complications forcing her to return to the hospital. She alleges that these complications would not have occurred had CIGNA approved coverage for a longer hospital stay.

Respondents brought separate suits in Texas state court against petitioners. Invoking THCLA § 88.002(a), respondents argued that petitioners' refusal to cover the requested services violated their "duty to exercise ordinary care when making health care treatment decisions," and that these refusals "proximately caused" their injuries. *Ibid*. Petitioners removed the cases to Federal District Courts, arguing that respondents' causes of action fit within the scope of, and were therefore completely pre-empted by, ERISA § 502(a). The respective District Courts agreed, and declined to remand the cases to state court. Because respondents refused to amend their complaints to bring explicit ERISA claims, the District Courts dismissed the complaints with prejudice.

Both Davila and Calad appealed the refusals to remand to state court. The United States Court of Appeals for the Fifth Circuit consolidated their cases with several others raising similar issues. The Court of Appeals recognized that state causes of action that "duplicat[e] or fal[l] within the scope of an ERISA § 502(a) remedy" are completely pre-empted and hence removable to federal court. *Roark v. Humana, Inc.*, 307 F.3d 298, 305 (2002) (internal quotation marks and citations omitted). After examining the causes of action available under § 502(a), the Court of Appeals determined that respondents' claims could possibly fall under only two: § 502(a)(1)(B), which provides a cause of action for the recovery of wrongfully denied benefits, and § 502(a)(2), which allows suit against a plan fiduciary for breaches of fiduciary duty to the plan.

Analyzing § 502(a)(2) first, the Court of Appeals concluded that, under *Pegram v. Herdrich*, 530 U.S. 211, 120 S.Ct. 2143, 147 L.Ed.2d 164 (2000), the decisions for which petitioners were being sued were "mixed eligibility and treatment decisions" and hence were not fiduciary in nature. 307 F.3d, at 307-308. The Court of Appeals next determined that respondents' claims did not fall within § 502(a)(1)(B)'s scope. It found significant that respondents "assert tort claims," while § 502(a)(1)(B) "creates a cause of action for breach of contract," *id.*, at 309, and also that respondents "are not seeking reimbursement for benefits denied them," but rather request "tort damages" arising from "an external, statutorily imposed duty of 'ordinary care.'" *Ibid*. From *Rush Prudential HMO, Inc. v. Moran*, 536 U.S. 355, 122 S.Ct. 2151, 153 L.Ed.2d 375 (2002), the Court of Appeals derived the principle that complete pre-emption is limited to situations in which "States ... duplicate the causes of action listed in ERISA § 502(a)," and concluded that "[b]ecause the THCLA does not provide an action for collecting benefits," it fell outside the scope of § 502(a)(1)(B). 307 F.3d, at 310-311.

(continued)

Under the removal statute, "any civil action brought in a State court of which the district courts of the United States have original jurisdiction, may be removed by the defendant" to federal court. 28 U.S.C. § 1441(a). One category of cases of which district courts have original jurisdiction are "federal question" cases: cases "arising under the Constitution, laws, or treaties of the United States." § 1331. We face in these cases the issue whether respondents' causes of action arise under federal law.

Ordinarily, determining whether a particular case arises under federal law turns on the " 'well-pleaded complaint' " rule. *Franchise Tax Bd. of Cal. v. Construction Laborers Vacation Trust for Southern Cal.*, 463 U.S. 1, 9-10, 103 S.Ct. 2841, 77 L.Ed.2d 420 (1983). The Court has explained that

"whether a case is one arising under the Constitution or a law or treaty of the United States, in the sense of the jurisdictional statute[,] ... must be determined from what necessarily appears in the plaintiff's statement of his own claim in the bill or declaration, unaided by anything alleged in anticipation of avoidance of defenses which it is thought the defendant may interpose." *Taylor v. Anderson*, 234 U.S. 74, 75-76, 34 S.Ct. 724, 58 L.Ed. 1218 (1914).

In particular, the existence of a federal defense normally does not create statutory "arising under" jurisdiction, *Louisville & Nashville R. Co. v. Mottley*, 211 U.S. 149, 29 S.Ct. 42, 53 L.Ed. 126 (1908), and "a defendant may not [generally] remove a case to federal court unless the *plaintiff's* complaint establishes that the case 'arises under' federal law." *Franchise Tax Bd., supra*, at 10, 103 S.Ct. 2841. There is an exception, however, to the well-pleaded complaint rule. "[W]hen a federal statute wholly displaces the state-law cause of action through complete pre-emption," the state claim can be removed. *Beneficial Nat. Bank v. Anderson*, 539 U.S. 1, 8, 123 S.Ct. 2058, 156 L.Ed.2d 1 (2003). This is so because "[w]hen the federal statute completely pre-empts the state-law cause of action, a claim which comes within the scope of that cause of action, even if pleaded in terms of state law, is in reality based on federal law." *Ibid.* ERISA is one of these statutes.

Congress enacted ERISA to "protect ... the interests of participants in employee benefit plans and their beneficiaries" by setting out substantive regulatory requirements for employee benefit plans and to "provid[e] for appropriate remedies, sanctions, and ready access to the Federal courts." 29 U.S.C. § 1001(b). The purpose of ERISA is to provide a uniform regulatory regime over employee benefit plans. To this end, ERISA includes expansive pre-emption provisions, see ERISA § 514, 29 U.S.C. § 1144, which are intended to ensure that employee benefit plan regulation would be "exclusively a federal concern." *Alessi v. Raybestos-Manhattan, Inc.*, 451 U.S. 504, 523, 101 S.Ct. 1895, 68 L.Ed.2d 402 (1981).

ERISA's "comprehensive legislative scheme" includes "an integrated system of procedures for enforcement." *Russell*, 473 U.S., at 147, 105 S.Ct. 3085 (internal quotation marks and citation omitted). This integrated enforcement mechanism, ERISA § 502(a), 29 U.S.C. § 1132(a), is a distinctive feature of ERISA, and essential to accomplish Congress' purpose of creating a comprehensive statute for the regulation of employee benefit plans. As the Court said in *Pilot Life Ins. Co. v. Dedeaux*, 481 U.S. 41, 107 S.Ct. 1549, 95 L.Ed.2d 39 (1987):

"[T]he detailed provisions of § 502(a) set forth a comprehensive civil enforcement scheme that represents a careful balancing of the need for prompt and fair claims settlement procedures against the public interest in encouraging the formation of employee benefit plans. The policy choices reflected in the inclusion of certain remedies and the exclusion of others under the federal scheme would be completely undermined if ERISA-plan participants and beneficiaries were free to obtain remedies under state law that Congress rejected in ERISA. 'The six carefully integrated civil enforcement provisions found in § 502(a) of the statute as finally enacted ... provide strong evidence that Congress did *not* intend to authorize other remedies that it simply forgot to incorporate expressly.' " *Id.*, at 54, 107 S.Ct. 1549 (quoting *Russell, supra*, at 146, 105 S.Ct. 3085).

(continued)

Therefore, any state-law cause of action that duplicates, supplements, or supplants the ERISA civil enforcement remedy conflicts with the clear congressional intent to make the ERISA remedy exclusive and is therefore pre-empted. See 481 U.S., at 54-56, 107 S.Ct. 1549; see also *Ingersoll-Rand Co. v. McClendon*, 498 U.S. 133, 143-145, 111 S.Ct. 478, 112 L.Ed.2d 474 (1990).

The pre-emptive force of ERISA § 502(a) is still stronger. In *Metropolitan Life Ins. Co. v. Taylor*, 481 U.S. 58, 65-66, 107 S.Ct. 1542, 95 L.Ed.2d 55 (1987), the Court determined that the similarity of the language used in the Labor Management Relations Act, 1947 (LMRA), and ERISA, combined with the "clear intention" of Congress "to make § 502(a)(1)(B) suits brought by participants or beneficiaries federal questions for the purposes of federal court jurisdiction in like manner as § 301 of the LMRA," established that ERISA § 502(a)(1)(B)'s pre-emptive force mirrored the pre-emptive force of LMRA § 301. Since LMRA § 301 converts state causes of action into federal ones for purposes of determining the propriety of removal, see *Avco Corp. v. Machinists*, 390 U.S. 557, 88 S.Ct. 1235, 20 L.Ed.2d 126 (1968), so too does ERISA § 502(a)(1)(B). Thus, the ERISA civil enforcement mechanism is one of those provisions with such "extraordinary pre-emptive power" that it "converts an ordinary state common law complaint into one stating a federal claim for purposes of the well-pleaded complaint rule." *Metropolitan Life*, 481 U.S., at 65-66, 107 S.Ct. 1542. Hence, "causes of action within the scope of the civil enforcement provisions of § 502(a) [are] removable to federal court." *Id.*, at 66, 107 S.Ct. 1542.

ERISA § 502(a)(1)(B) provides:

"A civil action may be brought--(1) by a participant or beneficiary--... (B) to recover benefits due to him under the terms of his plan, to enforce his rights under the terms of the plan, or to clarify his rights to future benefits under the terms of the plan." 29 U.S.C. § 1132(a)(1)(B).

This provision is relatively straightforward. If a participant or beneficiary believes that benefits promised to him under the terms of the plan are not provided, he can bring suit seeking provision of those benefits. A participant or beneficiary can also bring suit generically to "enforce his rights" under the plan, or to clarify any of his rights to future benefits. Any dispute over the precise terms of the plan is resolved by a court under a *de novo* review standard, unless the terms of the plan "giv[e] the administrator or fiduciary discretionary authority to determine eligibility for benefits or to construe the terms of the plan." *Firestone Tire & Rubber Co. v. Bruch*, 489 U.S. 101, 115, 109 S.Ct. 948, 103 L.Ed.2d 80 (1989).

It follows that if an individual brings suit complaining of a denial of coverage for medical care, where the individual is entitled to such coverage only because of the terms of an ERISA-regulated employee benefit plan, and where no legal duty (state or federal) independent of ERISA or the plan terms is violated, then the suit falls "within the scope of" ERISA § 502(a)(1)(B). *Metropolitan Life, supra*, at 66, 107 S.Ct. 1542. In other words, if an individual, at some point in time, could have brought his claim under ERISA § 502(a)(1)(B), and where there is no other independent legal duty that is implicated by a defendant's actions, then the individual's cause of action is completely pre-empted by ERISA § 502(a)(1)(B).

To determine whether respondents' causes of action fall "within the scope" of ERISA § 502(a)(1)(B), we must examine respondents' complaints, the statute on which their claims are based (the THCLA), and the various plan documents. Davila alleges that Aetna provides health coverage under his employer's health benefits plan. App. H to Pet. for Cert. in No. 02-1845, p. 67a. Davila also alleges that after his primary care physician prescribed Vioxx, Aetna refused to pay for it. *Id.*, at 67a. The only action complained of was Aetna's refusal to approve payment for Davila's Vioxx prescription. Further, the only relationship Aetna had with Davila was its partial administration of Davila's employer's benefit plan. See App. 25, 31, 39-40, 45-48, 108.

Similarly, Calad alleges that she receives, as her husband's beneficiary under an ERISA-regulated benefit plan, health coverage from CIGNA. *Id.*, at 184. She alleges that she was informed by CIGNA, upon admittance

(continued)

into a hospital for major surgery, that she would be authorized to stay for only one day. *Id.,* at 184. She also alleges that CIGNA, acting through a discharge nurse, refused to authorize more than a single day despite the advice and recommendation of her treating physician. *Id.,* at 185. Calad contests only CIGNA's decision to refuse coverage for her hospital stay. *Id.,* at 185. And, as in Davila's case, the only connection between Calad and CIGNA is CIGNA's administration of portions of Calad's ERISA-regulated benefit plan. *Id.,* at 219-221.

It is clear, then, that respondents complain only about denials of coverage promised under the terms of ERISA-regulated employee benefit plans. Upon the denial of benefits, respondents could have paid for the treatment themselves and then sought reimbursement through a § 502(a)(1)(B) action, or sought a preliminary injunction, see *Pryzbowski v. U.S. Healthcare, Inc.,* 245 F.3d 266, 274 (C.A.3 2001) (giving examples where federal courts have issued such preliminary injunctions).

Respondents contend, however, that the complained-of actions violate legal duties that arise independently of ERISA or the terms of the employee benefit plans at issue in these cases. Both respondents brought suit specifically under the THCLA, alleging that petitioners "controlled, influenced, participated in and made decisions which affected the quality of the diagnosis, care, and treatment provided" in a manner that violated "the duty of ordinary care set forth in §§ 88.001 and 88.002." App. H to Pet. for Cert. in No. 02-1845, at 69a, & ¶ 18; see also App. 187, & ¶ 28. Respondents contend that this duty of ordinary care is an independent legal duty. They analogize to this Court's decisions interpreting LMRA § 301, 29 U.S.C. § 1081, with particular focus on *Caterpillar Inc. v. Williams,* 482 U.S. 386, 107 S.Ct. 2425, 96 L.Ed.2d 318 (1987) (suit for breach of individual employment contract, even if defendant's action also constituted a breach of an entirely separate collective bargaining agreement, not pre-empted by LMRA § 301). Because this duty of ordinary care arises independently of any duty imposed by ERISA or the plan terms, the argument goes, any civil action to enforce this duty is not within the scope of the ERISA civil enforcement mechanism.

The duties imposed by the THCLA in the context of these cases, however, do not arise independently of ERISA or the plan terms. The THCLA does impose a duty on managed care entities to "exercise ordinary care when making health care treatment decisions," and makes them liable for damages proximately caused by failures to abide by that duty. § 88.002(a). However, if a managed care entity correctly concluded that, under the terms of the relevant plan, a particular treatment was not covered, the managed care entity's denial of coverage would not be a proximate cause of any injuries arising from the denial. Rather, the failure of the plan itself to cover the requested treatment would be the proximate cause. More significantly, the THCLA clearly states that "[t]he standards in Subsections (a) and (b) create no obligation on the part of the health insurance carrier, health maintenance organization, or other managed care entity to provide to an insured or enrollee treatment which is not covered by the health care plan of the entity." § 88.002(d). Hence, a managed care entity could not be subject to liability under the THCLA if it denied coverage for any treatment not covered by the health care plan that it was administering.

Thus, interpretation of the terms of respondents' benefit plans forms an essential part of their THCLA claim, and THCLA liability would exist here only because of petitioners' administration of ERISA-regulated benefit plans. Petitioners' potential liability under the THCLA in these cases, then, derives entirely from the particular rights and obligations established by the benefit plans. So, unlike the state-law claims in *Caterpillar, supra,* respondents' THCLA causes of action are not entirely independent of the federally regulated contract itself. Cf. *Allis-Chalmers Corp. v. Lueck,* 471 U.S. 202, 217, 105 S.Ct. 1904, 85 L.Ed.2d 206 (1985) (state-law tort of bad faith handling of insurance claim pre-empted by LMRA § 301, since the "duties imposed and rights established through the state tort ... derive[d] from the rights and obligations established by the contract"); *Steelworkers v. Rawson,* 495 U.S. 362, 371, 110 S.Ct. 1904, 109 L.Ed.2d 362 (1990) (state-law tort action

(continued)

brought due to alleged negligence in the inspection of a mine was pre-empted, as the duty to inspect the mine arose solely out of the collective-bargaining agreement).

Hence, respondents bring suit only to rectify a wrongful denial of benefits promised under ERISA-regulated plans, and do not attempt to remedy any violation of a legal duty independent of ERISA. We hold that respondents' state causes of action fall "within the scope of" ERISA § 502(a)(1)(B), *Metropolitan Life*, 481 U.S., at 66, 107 S.Ct. 1542, and are therefore completely pre-empted by ERISA § 502 and removable to federal district court.

The Court of Appeals came to a contrary conclusion for several reasons, all of them erroneous. First, the Court of Appeals found significant that respondents "assert a tort claim for tort damages" rather than "a contract claim for contract damages," and that respondents "are not seeking reimbursement for benefits denied them." 307 F.3d, at 309. But, distinguishing between pre-empted and non-pre-empted claims based on the particular label affixed to them would "elevate form over substance and allow parties to evade" the pre-emptive scope of ERISA simply "by relabeling their contract claims as claims for tortious breach of contract." *Allis-Chalmers, supra*, at 211, 105 S.Ct. 1904. Nor can the mere fact that the state cause of action attempts to authorize remedies beyond those authorized by ERISA § 502(a) put the cause of action outside the scope of the ERISA civil enforcement mechanism. In *Pilot Life, Metropolitan Life*, and *Ingersoll-Rand*, the plaintiffs all brought state claims that were labeled either tort or tort-like. See *Pilot Life*, 481 U.S., at 43, 107 S.Ct. 1549 (suit for, *inter alia*, "Tortious Breach of Contract"); *Metropolitan Life, supra*, at 61-62, 107 S.Ct. 1542 (suit requesting damages for "mental anguish caused by breach of [the] contract"); *Ingersoll-Rand*, 498 U.S., at 136, 111 S.Ct. 478 (suit brought under various tort and contract theories). And, the plaintiffs in these three cases all sought remedies beyond those authorized under ERISA. See *Pilot Life, supra*, at 43, 107 S.Ct. 1549 (compensatory and punitive damages); *Metropolitan Life, supra*, at 61, 107 S.Ct. 1542 (mental anguish); *Ingersoll-Rand, supra*, at 136, 111 S.Ct. 478 (punitive damages, mental anguish). And, in all these cases, the plaintiffs' claims were pre-empted. The limited remedies available under ERISA are an inherent part of the "careful balancing" between ensuring fair and prompt enforcement of rights under a plan and the encouragement of the creation of such plans. *Pilot Life, supra*, at 55, 107 S.Ct. 1549.

Second, the Court of Appeals believed that "the wording of [respondents'] plans is immaterial" to their claims, as "they invoke an external, statutorily imposed duty of 'ordinary care.'" 307 F.3d, at 309. But as we have already discussed, the wording of the plans is certainly material to their state causes of action, and the duty of "ordinary care" that the THCLA creates is not external to their rights under their respective plans.

Ultimately, the Court of Appeals rested its decision on one line from *Rush Prudential*. There, we described our holding in *Ingersoll-Rand* as follows: "[W]hile state law duplicated the elements of a claim available under ERISA, it converted the remedy from an equitable one under § 1132(a)(3) (available exclusively in federal district courts) into a legal one for money damages (available in a state tribunal)." 536 U.S., at 379, 122 S.Ct. 2151. The point of this sentence was to describe why the state cause of action in *Ingersoll-Rand* was pre-empted by ERISA § 502(a): It was pre-empted because it attempted to convert an equitable remedy into a legal remedy. Nowhere in *Rush Prudential* did we suggest that the pre-emptive force of ERISA § 502(a) is limited to the situation in which a state cause of action precisely duplicates a cause of action under ERISA § 502(a).

Nor would it be consistent with our precedent to conclude that only strictly duplicative state causes of action are pre-empted. Frequently, in order to receive exemplary damages on a state claim, a plaintiff must prove facts beyond the bare minimum necessary to establish entitlement to an award. Cf. *Allis-Chalmers*, 471 U.S., at 217, 105 S.Ct. 1904 (bad-faith refusal to honor a claim needed to be proved in order to recover exemplary damages). In order to recover for mental anguish, for instance, the plaintiffs in *Ingersoll-Rand*

(continued)

and *Metropolitan Life* would presumably have had to prove the existence of mental anguish; there is no such element in an ordinary suit brought under ERISA § 502(a)(1)(B). See *Ingersoll-Rand, supra*, at 136, 111 S.Ct. 478; *Metropolitan Life, supra*, at 61, 107 S.Ct. 1542. This did not save these state causes of action from pre-emption. Congress' intent to make the ERISA civil enforcement mechanism exclusive would be undermined if state causes of action that supplement the ERISA § 502(a) remedies were permitted, even if the elements of the state cause of action did not precisely duplicate the elements of an ERISA claim.

Respondents also argue--for the first time in their brief to this Court--that the THCLA is a law that regulates insurance, and hence that ERISA § 514(b)(2)(A) saves their causes of action from pre-emption (and thereby from complete pre-emption) This argument is unavailing. The existence of a comprehensive remedial scheme can demonstrate an "overpowering federal policy" that determines the interpretation of a statutory provision designed to save state law from being pre-empted. *Rush Prudential*, 536 U.S., at 375, 122 S.Ct. 2151. ERISA's civil enforcement provision is one such example. See *ibid*.

As this Court stated in *Pilot Life*, "our understanding of [§ 514(b)(2)(A)] must be informed by the legislative intent concerning the civil enforcement provisions provided by ERISA § 502(a), 29 U.S.C. § 1132(a)." 481 U.S., at 52, 107 S.Ct. 1549. The Court concluded that "[t]he policy choices reflected in the inclusion of certain remedies and the exclusion of others under the federal scheme would be completely undermined if ERISA-plan participants and beneficiaries were free to obtain remedies under state law that Congress rejected in ERISA." *Id.*, at 54, 107 S.Ct. 1549. The Court then held, based on

"the common-sense understanding of the saving clause, the McCarran-Ferguson Act factors defining the business of insurance, and, *most importantly*, the clear expression of congressional intent that ERISA's civil enforcement scheme be exclusive, ... that [the plaintiff's] state law suit asserting improper processing of a claim for benefits under an ERISA-regulated plan is not saved by § 514(b)(2)(A)." *Id.*, at 57, 107 S.Ct. 1549 (emphasis added).

Pilot Life's reasoning applies here with full force. Allowing respondents to proceed with their state-law suits would "pose an obstacle to the purposes and objectives of Congress." *Id.*, at 52, 107 S.Ct. 1549. As this Court has recognized in both *Rush Prudential* and *Pilot Life*, ERISA § 514(b)(2)(A) must be interpreted in light of the congressional intent to create an exclusive federal remedy in ERISA § 502(a). Under ordinary principles of conflict pre-emption, then, even a state law that can arguably be characterized as "regulating insurance" will be pre-empted if it provides a separate vehicle to assert a claim for benefits outside of, or in addition to, ERISA's remedial scheme.

Respondents, their *amici*, and some Courts of Appeals have relied heavily upon *Pegram v. Herdrich*, 530 U.S. 211, 120 S.Ct. 2143, 147 L.Ed.2d 164 (2000), in arguing that ERISA does not pre-empt or completely pre-empt state suits such as respondents'. They contend that *Pegram* makes it clear that causes of action such as respondents' do not "relate to [an] employee benefit plan," ERISA § 514(a), 29 U.S.C. § 1144(a), and hence are not pre-empted. See Brief for Respondents 35-38; *Cicio v. Does*, 321 F.3d 83, 100-104 (C.A.2 2003); see also *Land v. CIGNA Healthcare*, 339 F.3d 1286, 1292-1294 (C.A.11 2003).

Pegram cannot be read so broadly. In *Pegram*, the plaintiff sued her physician-owned-and-operated HMO (which provided medical coverage through plaintiff's employer pursuant to an ERISA-regulated benefit plan) and her treating physician, both for medical malpractice and for a breach of an ERISA fiduciary duty. See 530 U.S., at 215-216, 120 S.Ct. 2143. The plaintiff's treating physician was also the person charged with administering plaintiff's benefits; it was she who decided whether certain treatments were covered. See *id.*, at 228, 120 S.Ct. 2143. We reasoned that the physician's "eligibility decision and the treatment decision were inextricably mixed." *Id.*, at 229, 120 S.Ct. 2143. We concluded that "Congress did not intend [the

(continued)

defendant HMO] or any other HMO to be treated as a fiduciary to the extent that it makes mixed eligibility decisions acting through its physicians." *Id.,* at 231, 120 S.Ct. 2143.

A benefit determination under ERISA, though, is generally a fiduciary act. See *Bruch,* 489 U.S., at 111-113, 109 S.Ct. 948. "At common law, fiduciary duties characteristically attach to decisions about managing assets and distributing property to beneficiaries." *Pegram, supra,* at 231, 120 S.Ct. 2143; cf. 2A A. Scott & W. Fratcher, Law of Trusts §§ 182, 183 (4th ed.1987); G. Bogert & G. Bogert, Law of Trusts & Trustees § 541 (rev.2d ed.1993). Hence, a benefit determination is part and parcel of the ordinary fiduciary responsibilities connected to the administration of a plan. See *Varity Corp. v. Howe,* 516 U.S. 489, 512, 116 S.Ct. 1065, 134 L.Ed.2d 130 (1996) (relevant plan fiduciaries owe a "fiduciary duty with respect to the interpretation of plan documents and the payment of claims"). The fact that a benefits determination is infused with medical judgments does not alter this result.

Pegram itself recognized this principle. *Pegram,* in highlighting its conclusion that "mixed eligibility decisions" were not fiduciary in nature, contrasted the operation of "[t]raditional trustees administer[ing] a medical trust" and "physicians through whom HMOs act." 530 U.S., at 231-232, 120 S.Ct. 2143. A traditional medical trust is administered by "paying out money to buy medical care, whereas physicians making mixed eligibility decisions consume the money as well." *Ibid.* And, significantly, the Court stated that "[p]rivate trustees do not make treatment judgments." *Id.,* at 232, 120 S.Ct. 2143. But a trustee managing a medical trust undoubtedly must make administrative decisions that require the exercise of medical judgment. Petitioners are not the employers of respondents' treating physicians and are therefore in an analogous position to that of a trustee for a traditional medical trust.

"ERISA itself and its implementing regulations confirm this interpretation. ERISA defines a fiduciary as any person "to the extent ... he has any discretionary authority or discretionary responsibility in the administration of [an employee benefit] plan." § 3(21)(A)(iii), 29 U.S.C. § 1002(21)(A)(iii). When administering employee benefit plans, HMOs must make discretionary decisions regarding eligibility for plan benefits, and, in this regard, must be treated as plan fiduciaries. See *Varity Corp., supra,* at 511, 116 S.Ct. 1065 (plan administrator "engages in a fiduciary act when making a discretionary determination about whether a claimant is entitled to benefits under the terms of the plan documents"). Also, ERISA § 503, which specifies minimum requirements for a plan's claim procedure, requires plans to "afford a reasonable opportunity to any participant whose claim for benefits has been denied for a full and fair review by the appropriate named fiduciary of the decision denying the claim." 29 U.S.C. § 1133(2). This strongly suggests that the ultimate decisionmaker in a plan regarding an award of benefits must be a fiduciary and must be acting as a fiduciary when determining a participant's or beneficiary's claim. The relevant regulations also establish extensive requirements to ensure full and fair review of benefit denials. See 29 CFR § 2560.503-1 (2004). These regulations, on their face, apply equally to health benefit plans and other plans, and do not draw distinctions between medical and nonmedical benefits determinations. Indeed, the regulations strongly imply that benefits determinations involving medical judgments are, just as much as any other benefits determinations, actions by plan fiduciaries. See, *e.g.,* § 2560.503-1(h)(3)(iii). Classifying any entity with discretionary authority over benefits determinations as anything but a plan fiduciary would thus conflict with ERISA's statutory and regulatory scheme.

Since administrators making benefits determinations, even determinations based extensively on medical judgments, are ordinarily acting as plan fiduciaries, it was essential to *Pegram*'s conclusion that the decisions challenged there were truly "mixed eligibility and treatment decisions," 530 U.S., at 229, 120 S.Ct. 2143, *i.e.,* medical necessity decisions made by the plaintiff's treating physician *qua* treating physician and *qua* benefits administrator. Put another way, the reasoning of *Pegram* "only make[s] sense where the underlying

(continued)

negligence also plausibly constitutes medical maltreatment by a party who can be deemed to be a treating physician or such a physician's employer." *Cicio*, 321 F.3d, at 109 (Calabresi, J., dissenting in part). Here, however, petitioners are neither respondents' treating physicians nor the employers of respondents' treating physicians. Petitioners' coverage decisions, then, are pure eligibility decisions, and *Pegram* is not implicated.

We hold that respondents' causes of action, brought to remedy only the denial of benefits under ERISA-regulated benefit plans, fall within the scope of, and are completely pre-empted by, ERISA § 502(a)(1)(B), and thus removable to federal district court. The judgment of the Court of Appeals is reversed, and the cases are remanded for further proceedings consistent with this opinion.

It is so ordered.

Problem 5.1

Complete 5.1 of the Comprehensive Problem in Appendix A.

CHAPTER SUMMARY

The discussion and examples demonstrate the enormous impact that medical malpractice insurance, statutes, and cases have had on the delivery of health care in the United States. The most visible changes have been in the costs of professional liability insurance and health care. Additional changes include an increasing number of risk managers employed to cope with the risks of practice, a redirection of health care provider's professional practices from a practical and geographical perspective, a continuing increase in legislation and regulation of the health care industry, and remodeled ethical standards.

Insurance is one of the major industries in America and its impact on the health care system cannot be placed in a quantitative measurement. Professional liability insurance is absolutely necessary for providers of health care. Without it, a single suit could render their professional career at an end. However, the provider needs to maintain a constant awareness of the common and separate objectives they share with the insurer in regard to claims of malpractice. For this reason, it is highly advisable that all providers retain their own legal counsel in the event of a claim of malpractice.

With respect to patient insurance, the companies who provide these policies have a significant role in the development of the law of malpractice. They are often in much greater control of information regarding the professional practices of the provider than is the professional liability insurer. The existence of patient insurance has a proven and dramatic effect on both the conduct of the provider and the compliance of patients. The degree of authority patient insurers have in the decisions regarding health care, treatment, and services received by their insureds is the ongoing question.

Key Terms

professional liability insurance
occurrence policy
claims made policy

tail coverage
managed care insurance

 For additional resources, go to http://www.westlegalstudies.com.

PART 2
ANATOMY OF A LAWSUIT: THE MEDICAL MALPRACTICE CASE

Part 2

Part 2 of the text examines the progression of the medical malpractice action from the origins of injury throughout the legal process. In the early days, lawsuits based in tort law were usually quite straightforward in their approach. The plaintiff would suffer an alleged injury as a proximate result of a known act by the defendant. The plaintiff's awareness of injury was almost always immediate. Knowledge of the defendant's conduct was also generally understood. Once duty and foreseeability on the part of the defendant were established, often the only real questions lay in connecting the causal links and proving the amount of damage. However, as in so many areas of technology, the scientific advancements in medicine throughout the nineteenth and twentieth centuries made the relationship between patient and health care provider more complex and, in many instances, more remote. In some circumstances, the plaintiff had no reason to be immediately aware of malfeasance or injury. This created an entirely new procedural issue.

In all jurisdictions, both state and federal, there are statutes of limitations for all types of cases filed. A statute of limitation is a legislative statement that clearly establishes a time limit for bringing a lawsuit arising out of damage caused by the actions of another. The rationale is that individuals should not be subject indefinitely to the risk of lawsuits. Over time, evidence can be lost or destroyed, witnesses could disappear or lose much of the detail of their recollection. This would make it almost impossible for a defendant to adequately present his or her side of the case and would give plaintiffs who lay in wait an unfair advantage. Medical malpractice cases are no different. All actions sounding in tort are subject to statutory limitation of actions. In many jurisdictions there are special statutes of limitation for actions based in medical malpractice, further limiting the time frame for lawsuits. This narrow window of opportunity for plaintiffs is meant to reduce the potential liability for providers and their insurance companies to contain costs. An action can be brought only when there is a specified time frame and an end date, but in cases of medical malpractice the question is when does the cause of action arise and the time begin to run? And, once suit is filed, does it progress any differently than an ordinary civil suit?

CHAPTER 6
Discovery/Disclosure of the Injury

CHAPTER OBJECTIVES
When you complete this chapter, you should be able to:

- Discuss the discovery rule and its potential impact on a valid claim of malpractice

- Explain the rationale for giving special treatment to those found legally incompetent, as minors

- Discuss the reason for tolling a statute of limitations in some jurisdictions based on a lack of mental competency.

THE DISCOVERY RULE

In most cases of ordinary negligence and other torts, the moment and impact of injury are simultaneous and obvious to the injured party. For example, when someone is involved in a car accident, their injuries are generally immediate. Even those injuries that develop in the time shortly following the event, such as sore muscles and soft tissue injuries, can generally be traced easily to the collision. In cases of medical malpractice, however, it is not always so obvious that there has been an unanticipated result of the medical care, treatment, or services. Consider Application 6.1 below.

APPLICATION 6.1

Cyrus underwent emergency surgery at age 19 for a ruptured appendix. At age 22 he took up horseback riding. A few months later he developed random sharp pains in his abdomen. He saw his family doctor, who ordered tests. It appeared that during Cyrus' appendectomy more than three years earlier (the only surgical procedure in his life), a surgical instrument had been left in his abdomen. It remained there unnoticed until his hobby of horseback riding caused it to dislodge and travel through his abdomen. Cyrus was required to undergo a second surgery to remove the instrument and repair the damage it had caused.

(continued)

> In this case, the injury occurred on the date of the initial surgery. However, Cyrus was unaware of the malfeasance and the damage, both real and potential, until more than three years later. In many jurisdictions this would exceed the time period for an ordinary tort action, not to mention the often shortened medical malpractice statutory limitation. But, under the traditional discovery rule it would be considered unfair to the patient if their cause of action were denied because the provider failed to realize the error through proper instrument counts or by deliberately withholding the information from the patient. Many jurisdictions that have shortened limitations periods extend them to some extent for a reasonable discovery period.

As discussed above, the rationale for the statutes of limitation is that a defendant should be advised of potential liability within an amount of time that allows a reasonable opportunity to develop and present a defense of relevant evidence while it still exists. Plaintiffs cannot preserve their own evidence and then wait until the body of evidence for the defense has deteriorated to the point that an unsuspecting defendant is unfairly disadvantaged. The **discovery rule** is similar in its purpose, but works in favor of the plaintiff.

The discovery rule is generally accepted in tort causes of action and is often specifically addressed in medical malpractice statutes. Essentially, the discovery rule states that the statute of limitations in such actions may be extended and does not begin to run until such time as the plaintiff has a reasonable opportunity to obtain constructive knowledge of a potential injury and/or cause of action. Regardless of whether a defendant is affirmatively concealing malfeasance or knows it occurred, a plaintiff is not penalized for failing to bring a cause of action before he or she knows or should know it has accrued. However, in many jurisdictions the discovery rule is not without its own limitations.

In many, but not all, statutes of limitation that apply a discovery rule, the plaintiff is given a finite time to actually discover injuries and/or causes of action. For example, a statute of limitation creating a discovery rule may state that a cause of action must be brought within two years of the time the plaintiff should have reasonably ascertained or suspected tortious conduct, but in no case more than five years from the actual conduct of the defendant that was allegedly tortious. This is intended to provide a balance between the plaintiff's right to sue for injuries caused by a defendant and allow potential defendants some finality to the window of opportunity for claims against them. Statutes with absolute time frames not subject to tolling (stopping) by application of a discovery rule are known as Statutes of Repose. Consider the preceding example. If the jurisdiction where the case is brought has a medical malpractice statute that limits discovery to three years, Cyrus would still be precluded from bringing suit. However, if the applicable statute of limitations was three years or five years from reasonable discovery, his cause of action would likely be preserved.

6 Cal.Rptr.3d 300 (Cap.App.5Dist. 2003).

Court of Appeal, Fifth District, California.

(continued)

Brandi R. FOX, Plaintiff and Appellant,
v.
ETHICON ENDO-SURGICAL, INC., Defendant and Respondent.

As Modified on Denial of Rehearing
Nov. 20, 2003.

VARTABEDIAN, J.

On April 10, 1999, Fox underwent gastric bypass surgery performed by Dr. Herbert Gladen. During this surgery, Fox was unconscious as the result of general anesthesia and, thus, did not observe the procedures or equipment used. After the surgery--the record is not clear as to the exact length of time--Fox went home. However, she returned to the hospital a few days after the surgery because she did not feel well. Her condition deteriorated, and she was taken to the operating room for exploratory surgery. Dr. Gladen found a perforation or leak at the staple closure of the proximal jejunum and attempted to close it. Dr. Gladen's operative report for the exploration and remedial action states, "no reason could be identified for the perforation." Subsequently, Fox remained hospitalized until March 4, 2000, and apparently required additional surgeries.

On April 6, 2000, in accordance with Code of Civil Procedure section 364 Fox served a "Notice of Intent to Commence Action" on Dr. Gladen and the two hospitals where the surgery and subsequent care took place. Prelitigation discussions with these health care providers did not resolve Fox's claim of professional negligence.

On June 28, 2000, Fox filed a complaint in Fresno County Superior Court for medical malpractice against Dr. Gladen and the two hospitals alleging that "Defendants lacked the necessary knowledge and skill to properly care for [Fox's] condition and were negligent and unskillful in the diagnosis, treatment and prescription procedures utilized in treating [her] condition. The negligence claimed is for negligently performing pre-surgical, surgical, and post-surgical care so as to cause injuries and damages to ... Fox."

The complaint was filed on the Judicial Council form for personal injury complaints and named as defendants Dr. Gladen, the two hospitals, and Does 1 to 100, inclusive. The complaint alleged, "[a]t all times herein mentioned, the defendants named herein as DOES 1 through 100, inclusive, were the agents, servants, and employees of each of the remaining defendants, and in doing the things hereinafter alleged, were acting within the course and scope of their authority as such agents, servants and employees, and with the permission and consent of their co-defendants."

During his August 13, 2001, deposition, Dr. Gladen testified that when he performed a postsurgery exploration of Fox's abdomen he found a leak at the staple closure of the small intestine. Dr. Gladen further testified that the bowel had been stapled using an Ethicon GIA-type stapler, the stapler had been furnished by the hospital, and he had experienced occasions where the this type of Ethicon stapler was used and subsequent leaks occurred.

On November 28, 2001, Fox filed a first amended complaint that restated her negligence cause of action against Dr. Gladen and the hospitals, added Ethicon as a named defendant, and added a products liability cause of action against Ethicon that alleged she was injured by an Ethicon GIA-type stapler on or about April 10, 1999. The claims against Ethicon were set forth on the Judicial Council form for a products liability cause of action; Fox checked the boxes relating to "counts" for (1) strict liability concerning the design, manufacture and assembly of the product, (2) negligence, and (3) breach of implied warranty.

The first amended complaint also added the allegation that Fox "did not discover, nor suspect, nor was there any means through which her reasonable diligence would have revealed, or through which she would

(continued)

have suspected the Ethicon GIA-type Stapler as a cause of her injury until the deposition of [Dr. Gladen] was taken on August 13, 2001." The first amended complaint continued to name as defendants Does 1 through 100.

Ethicon filed a demurrer to the first amended complaint on the ground that the products liability cause of action against Ethicon showed on its face that it was time-barred by the one-year statute of limitations contained in former section 340, subdivision (3).

In her declaration opposing the demurrer, Fox stated that she (1) was never told during the course of her care and treatment subsequent to the gastric bypass surgery that the stapler had malfunctioned in any way or was responsible for the postsurgery problems she suffered; (2) did not believe she was told that a stapler type instrument was to be used on her during the gastric bypass surgery; and (3) first became aware of a possible stapler malfunction when her attorneys told her about the doctor's testimony after his deposition. Fox's declaration also states her willingness to file a second amended complaint to clarify the facts that support her position that until the deposition of her doctor she had no suspicions, and no basis on which a reasonable person would have had suspicions, that Ethicon's stapler had malfunctioned.

Fox's attorney filed a declaration stating that neither the operative report nor the reparative operative report indicated that the stapler had malfunctioned or misfired. The declaration also asserts that (1) Dr. Gladen's deposition was taken during the normal course of discovery in a medical malpractice lawsuit, (2) Fox pursued the lawsuit and discovery with reasonable diligence, and (3) Fox could allege that during the entire time of Dr. Gladen's care of Fox after the surgery he never mentioned to Fox a malfunction or defect in the stapler he used in her surgery.

On May 15, 2002, the trial court issued a tentative ruling indicating its intention to sustain the demurrer without leave to amend. In concluding the products liability cause of action was time barred, the trial court relied upon *Norgart v. Upjohn Co., supra,* 21 Cal.4th 383, 87 Cal.Rptr.2d 453, 981 P.2d 79 (*Norgart*); and *Bristol-Myers Squibb Co. v. Superior Court, supra,* 32 Cal.App.4th 959, 38 Cal.Rptr.2d 298 (*Bristol-Myers Squibb*). In applying those cases, the trial court determined that when a plaintiff has cause to sue based on knowledge or suspicion of negligence (in this case suspicion of medical malpractice by the doctor and hospitals), the statute of limitations begins to run as to all defendants, including a manufacturer subject to a products liability claim. The tentative ruling also stated Fox failed to show that an amendment could overcome the statute of limitations defense.

After hearing argument from counsel, the trial court adopted the tentative ruling as its order; the demurrer was sustained without leave to amend. Subsequently, a judgment was entered in favor of Ethicon. Fox appeals from that judgment.

On appeal from a judgment sustaining a demurrer without leave to amend, the reviewing court gives the complaint a reasonable interpretation and treats the demurrer as admitting all material facts properly pleaded. (*Aubry v. Tri-City Hospital Dist.* (1992) 2 Cal.4th 962, 966-967, 9 Cal.Rptr.2d 92, 831 P.2d 317.) The reviewing court must reverse the judgment if (1) the plaintiff has stated a cause of action under any possible legal theory, or (2) the plaintiff shows there is a reasonable possibility any defect identified by the defendant can be cured by amendment. (*Blank v. Kirwan* (1985) 39 Cal.3d 311, 318, 216 Cal.Rptr. 718, 703 P.2d 58.) The burden of proving a reasonable possibility of cure is squarely on the plaintiff. (*Ibid.*)

Under the statute of limitations for personal injury actions in effect at the time Fox filed her complaint (see former § 340, subd. (3), as amended by Stats.1982, ch. 517, § 97, pp. 2334-2335, Fox was required to bring her products liability cause of action within one year after its accrual. (*Norgart, supra,* 21 Cal.4th at pp. 397, 404, 87 Cal.Rptr.2d 453, 981 P.2d 79 [wrongful death]; *G.D. Searle & Co. v. Superior Court* (1975) 49 Cal.App.3d 22, 122 Cal.Rptr. 218 [personal injury]). The general rule for the accrual of a cause of action "sets the date as the time when the cause of action is complete with all of it elements." (*Norgart* at p. 397, 87 Cal.Rptr.2d 453, 981 P.2d 79.) The essential elements of a cause of action are described generically by the Supreme Court as (1) wrongdoing or wrongful conduct, (2) cause or causation, and (3) harm or injury. (*Ibid.*)

(continued)

The general rule regarding accrual of a cause of action for purposes of former section 340, subdivision (3) is subject to an exception referred to as the "discovery rule." (*Jolly v. Eli Lilly & Co.* (1988) 44 Cal.3d 1103, 1109, 245 Cal.Rptr. 658, 751 P.2d 923 [personal injury allegedly caused by defective drug] (*Jolly*).) Under the discovery rule, the accrual of the cause of action is postponed "until the plaintiff discovers, or has reason to discover, the cause of action." (*Norgart, supra*, 21 Cal.4th at p. 397, 87 Cal.Rptr.2d 453, 981 P.2d 79.) A reason to discover the cause of action exists when the plaintiff "has reason at least to suspect a factual basis for its elements." (*Id.* at p. 398).

A reason to suspect a factual basis for the elements of a cause of action exists when the plaintiff has notice or information of circumstances to put a reasonable person on inquiry. (*Norgart, supra*, 21 Cal.4th at p. 398, 87 Cal.Rptr.2d 453, 981 P.2d 79; *Jolly, supra*, 44 Cal.3d at pp. 1110-1111, 245 Cal.Rptr. 658, 751 P.2d 923.) Ignorance of legal theories or the legal significance of facts does not delay the running of the statute. (*Norgart* at p. 397, 87 Cal.Rptr.2d 453, 981 P.2d 79; *Jolly* at p. 1110, 245 Cal.Rptr. 658, 751 P.2d 923.) Furthermore, a "plaintiff need not be aware of the specific 'facts' necessary to establish the claim; that is a process contemplated by pretrial discovery. Once the plaintiff has a suspicion of wrongdoing, and therefore an incentive to sue, she must decide whether to file suit or sit on her rights. So long as a suspicion exists, it is clear that the plaintiff must go find the facts; she cannot wait for the facts to find her." (*Jolly* at p. 1111, 245 Cal.Rptr. 658, 751 P.2d 923.)

The language used by the Supreme Court in articulating the discovery rule--"plaintiff discovers, or has reason to discover" (*Norgart, supra*, 21 Cal.4th at p. 397, 87 Cal.Rptr.2d 453, 981 P.2d 79) and "plaintiff suspects or should suspect" (*Jolly, supra*, 44 Cal.3d at p. 1110, 245 Cal.Rptr. 658, 751 P.2d 923)--clearly indicates that the discovery rule contains a subjective alternative and an objective alternative. The words "plaintiff suspects" refer to "a subjective test requiring actual suspicion by the plaintiff that the injury was caused by wrongdoing." (*Kitzig v. Nordquist* (2000) 81 Cal.App.4th 1384, 1391, 97 Cal.Rptr.2d 762, citing *Jolly* at p. 1110, 245 Cal.Rptr. 658, 751 P.2d 923.) The words "plaintiff should suspect" refer to "an objective test requiring a showing that a reasonable person would have suspected the injury was caused by wrongdoing." (*Kitzig* at p. 1391, 97 Cal.Rptr.2d 762.)

Applying the subjective and objective alternatives to a particular case is recognized as "presumptively in the domain of the jury" (*Bristol-Myers Squibb, supra*, 32 Cal.App.4th at p. 964, 38 Cal.Rptr.2d 298) or "usually ... for the trier of fact" (*Rose v. Fife* (1989) 207 Cal.App.3d 760, 771, 255 Cal.Rptr. 440). Nevertheless, these issues may be resolved by the court as a matter of law in certain circumstances. "While resolution of the statute of limitations issue is normally a question of fact, where the uncontradicted facts established through discovery are susceptible of only one legitimate inference, summary judgment is proper." (*Jolly, supra*, 44 Cal.3d at p. 1112, 245 Cal.Rptr. 658, 751 P.2d 923.) For example, *Norgart, Jolly, Bristol-Myers Squibb*, and *Rose v. Fife* are all cases in which the application of the discovery rule was decided in favor of the defendants as a matter of law on motions for summary judgment.

Based on the foregoing principles concerning the discovery rule and the elements of a cause of action, a fundamental or basic approach to the delayed accrual of a cause of action for purposes of former section 340, subdivision (3) involves the following steps. First, the identification of each element of the cause of action--a question of law. Second, as to each element, a determination of whether or not the plaintiff had actual knowledge of the factual basis for that element--a question of fact. Third, as to the remaining elements, a determination of whether or not the plaintiff had an actual suspicion of the factual basis for those elements--a question of fact. Fourth, as to the remaining elements of the cause of action not actually known or suspected by the plaintiff, a determination of whether a reasonable person would have suspected the factual basis for each such element--generally a question of fact. (See *Rose v. Fife, supra*, 207 Cal.App.3d at p. 770, 255 Cal.Rptr. 440 [reasonability is generally a question of fact].) This four-step method of analysis subsequently will be referred to as the "Basic Approach" to the discovery rule.

(continued)

In *Rose v. Fife, supra,* the Second District applied the discovery rule to a medical malpractice cause of action and a products liability cause of action using the Basic Approach, although it did not label its method or number its steps. The Second District found as a matter of law that the plaintiff suspected or should have suspected that (1) the manufacturer of her intrauterine device (IUD) wronged her by supplying a defective product, and (2) her doctor wronged her by prescribing it. (*Rose v. Fife, supra,* 207 Cal.App.3d at p. 771, 255 Cal.Rptr. 440.) As to the elements of injury and causation, when plaintiff was hospitalized with a pelvic infection she was told by two doctors that the IUD caused the infection and one of those doctors told her that she was "no doubt sterile" because of her infection and high fever. (*Id.* at p. 766, 255 Cal.Rptr. 440.) As to the element of wrongdoing by the manufacturer--the remaining element of her products liability cause of action--more than one year before filing her lawsuit, plaintiff was suspicious of IUD's per se, worried about using one without having had children, and alerted to the dangers of IUDs by the media. (*Id.* at p. 771, 255 Cal.Rptr. 440.) The Second District inferred from this uncontradicted evidence plaintiff suspected or should have suspected the manufacturer of her IUD of wrongdoing and issued a writ of mandate directing the trial court to grant the manufacturer's motion for summary judgment. (*Id.* at pp. 771-773, 255 Cal.Rptr. 440.)

In the *Bristol-Myers Squibb* case, the Fourth District did not use the Basic Approach to determine if there was a delay in the plaintiff's discovery of a products liability cause of action against the manufacturer of her silicone breast implants. Instead, the Fourth District "reinterpreted the *Jolly* test" to create the following version of the discovery rule: "When a plaintiff has cause to sue based on knowledge or suspicion of negligence the statute starts to run as to *all* potential defendants" (BMS rule). (*Bristol-Myers Squibb, supra,* 32 Cal.App.4th at p. 966, 38 Cal.Rptr.2d 298, italics in original.) It appears the *Jolly* test referred to by the Fourth District is the often quoted statement that " 'the statute of limitations begins to run when the plaintiff suspects or should suspect that her injury was caused by wrongdoing, *that someone had done something wrong to her.*' " (*Bernson v. Browning-Ferris Industries* (1994) 7 Cal.4th at 926, 932, 30 Cal.Rptr.2d 440, 873 P.2d 613, italics added (*Bernson*), quoting *Jolly, supra,* 44 Cal.3d at p. 1110, 245 Cal.Rptr. 658, 751 P.2d 923.)

Because the *BMS* rule is based on the discussion and holding in *Jolly,* we first consider whether the *BMS* rule was mandated by the holding in *Jolly* and subsequent decisions by the Supreme Court.

In *Norgart,* the Supreme Court's most recent decision applying the delayed discovery rule to a products liability cause of action, the Supreme Court had the opportunity to approve and apply the *BMS* rule, but left its status undecided. (See *Norgart, supra,* 21 Cal.4th 383, 87 Cal.Rptr.2d 453, 981 P.2d 79.)

In *Norgart,* parents sued the manufacturer of the prescription drug Halcion for the wrongful death of their daughter six years after the daughter's suicide was allegedly caused by the drug's side effects. At the time of the daughter's death in 1985, the father suspected some outside agent had caused her to commit suicide. Prior to the death, the parents were aware of their daughter's depression and prior suicide attempts. Soon after her death, the father had reason to learn of a connection between her suicide and Halcion because the connection was disclosed by the package insert Upjohn Co. prepared. The insert cautioned about the possibility the drug could intensify depression and mentioned suicide and intentional overdoses. Under these circumstances, the Supreme Court found as a matter of law that the parents had reason to suspect wrongdoing by Upjohn Co. in manufacturing and distributing Halcion soon after their daughter's suicide. (*Norgart, supra,* 21 Cal.4th at pp. 406-407, 87 Cal.Rptr.2d 453, 981 P.2d 79.)

The Supreme Court mentioned the *BMS* rule in *Norgart* but did not explicitly approve or disapprove it: "[W]e need not resolve any conflict between the holding of the Court of Appeal in *Bristol-Myers Squibb* and the holding of the Court of Appeal below." (*Norgart, supra,* 21 Cal.4th at p. 406, 87 Cal.Rptr.2d 453, 981 P.2d 79.) However, the Supreme Court did disapprove of another aspect of the *Bristol-Myers Squibb* court's reading of *Jolly.* (See *Norgart, supra,* 21 Cal.4th at p. 410, fn. 8, 87 Cal.Rptr.2d 453, 981 P.2d 79 [a plaintiff is not required to do more than suspect a factual basis for the elements of a cause of action to discover it].) In

(continued)

Norgart, the Supreme Court did not need to address the status of the *BMS* rule or rely on imputed simultaneous discovery of causes of action because it determined that, even under the version of the discovery rule the First District had adopted below in *Norgart*, the start of the limitation period was not sufficiently delayed to save plaintiffs' causes of action. (*Norgart, supra*, 21 Cal.4th at pp. 406-407, 87 Cal.Rptr. 2d 453, 981 P.2d 79.) Furthermore, the Supreme Court found the undisputed facts showed the parents should have suspected the alleged wrongdoing by Upjohn Co. soon after their daughter's suicide. (*Id.* at p. 407, 87 Cal.Rptr.2d 453, 981 P.2d 79.) If the BMS rule had been mandated by *Jolly* or other Supreme Court decisions, it is unlikely that the Supreme Court would have expressly left its status undecided in *Norgart*. A closer look at *Jolly* will be helpful.

A direct analysis of *Jolly* shows that the *BMS* rule is an extension of its holding. The *Jolly* case concerned a drug, diethylstilbestrol (DES), that the plaintiff's mother had taken during her pregnancy to prevent miscarriage. Plaintiff, who was born in 1951, learned in 1972 that her mother had taken DES and that DES daughters could suffer injuries. Plaintiff had a checkup in 1972 and was diagnosed as having adenosis, a precancerous condition that required monitoring. In 1976, plaintiff underwent surgery to remove abnormal tissue and in 1978 underwent a complete hysterectomy and partial vaginectomy to remove malignancy. (*Jolly, supra*, 44 Cal.3d at p. 1107, 245 Cal.Rptr. 658, 751 P.2d 923.) During her deposition, plaintiff testified that in 1978 she believed (1) DES was a defective drug, (2) someone had done something wrong to her, and (3) she should be compensated. (*Jolly, supra*, 44 Cal.3d at p. 1112, fn. 9, 245 Cal.Rptr. 658, 751 P.2d 923.) Also during 1978, plaintiff was aware of lawsuits against DES manufacturers, but she believed she had no cause of action because she could not identify the particular manufacturer of the drug her mother took during pregnancy. (*Id.* at p. 1108, 245 Cal.Rptr. 658, 751 P.2d 923.) Plaintiff did not file her lawsuit until nearly a year after the Supreme Court decided *Sindell v. Abbott Laboratories* (1980) 26 Cal.3d 588, 163 Cal.Rptr. 132, 607 P.2d 924, and held that a plaintiff who is unable to identify the particular manufacturer of the DES that injured her may jointly sue all the manufacturers of that drug on the theory of enterprise liability.

In *Jolly*, the Supreme Court held that plaintiff's cause of action did not accrue when she learned of the *Sindell* decision. (*Jolly, supra*, 44 Cal.3d at pp. 1113-1114, 245 Cal.Rptr. 658, 751 P.2d 923.) Furthermore, plaintiff's ignorance of the identity of the particular manufacturer of the DES used by plaintiff's mother did not delay the accrual of her cause of action. Subsequently, in *Bernson*, the Supreme Court stated that "the rationale for distinguishing between ignorance of the wrongdoer and ignorance of the injury itself appears to be premised on the commonsense assumption that once the plaintiff is aware of the injury, the applicable limitations period (often effectively extended by the filing of a Doe complaint) normally affords sufficient opportunity to discover the identity of all the wrongdoers." (*Bernson, supra*, 7 Cal.4th at p. 932, 30 Cal.Rptr.2d 440, 873 P.2d 613 [cause of action for libel against persons who allegedly concealed their identities].)

On one hand, the *BMS* rule can be derived from a literal reading of the statement in *Jolly* that a statute of limitations starts to runs when the plaintiff suspects or should suspect "that someone had done something wrong to [plaintiff]." Also, the *BMS* rule appears consistent with the rationale stated in *Bernson* that "once the plaintiff is aware of the injury, the applicable limitations period (often effectively extended by the filing of a Doe complaint) normally affords sufficient opportunity to discover the identity of all the wrongdoers." (*Bernson, supra*, 7 Cal.4th at p. 932, 30 Cal.Rptr.2d 440, 873 P.2d 613.) The *BMS* rule is supported by broadly interpreting this statement of rationale, particularly the phrase "identity of all the wrongdoers," to mean that the applicable discovery period is normally sufficient not only to discover the identity of the person who committed the *suspected* wrong but also to discover *unsuspected* wrongs.

On the other hand, the Fourth District in *Bristol-Myers Squibb* went beyond the facts of *Jolly* when it created a rule of imputed simultaneous discovery of causes of action for medical malpractice and products liability. In both *Bernson* and *Jolly*, the plaintiffs actually suspected the wrongdoing but could not identify the person

(continued)

who did the wrong. (*Bernson, supra,* 7 Cal.4th at p. 929, 30 Cal.Rptr.2d 440, 873 P.2d 613 [plaintiff had a copy of the libelous document, but not know its author or distributor]; *Jolly, supra,* 44 Cal.3d at p. 1112, 245 Cal.Rptr. 658, 751 P.2d 923 [plaintiff actually suspected DES was a defective drug but could not identity which manufacturer made it].) In *Bristol-Myers Squibb,* the plaintiff claimed she did not suspect the manufacturer of her silicone breast implant did anything wrong because she did not actually suspect a defect in the product.

This factual difference between ignorance of the identity of who did a suspected wrong and ignorance of the wrong itself is legally significant. The identity of the manufacturer-wrongdoer that made a defective product is not an essential element of a products liability cause of action and therefore ignorance of wrongdoer's identity will not delay the running of the statute of limitations. (*Bernson, supra,* 7 Cal.4th at p. 932, 30 Cal.Rptr.2d 440, 873 P.2d 613.) In contrast, the existence of the potential defect in the product, i.e., the manufacturer's wrongdoing, is one of the three generic elements essential to a cause of action. (E.g. *Clark v. Baxter Healthcare Corp., supra,* 83 Cal.App.4th at p. 1060, 100 Cal.Rptr.2d 223 [triable issue of fact as to when plaintiff knew or suspected wrongfulness component of cause of action regarding defective manufacture of latex gloves]; see *Norgart, supra,* 21 Cal.4th at p. 397, 87 Cal.Rptr.2d 453, 981 P.2d 79 [regarding generic elements].) Moreover, the significance of this distinction was recognized by the Supreme Court when it stated the "failure to discover, or have reason to discover, the identity of the defendant does not postpone the accrual of a cause of action, whereas a like failure concerning the cause of action itself does." (*Id.* at p. 399, 87 Cal.Rptr.2d 453, 981 P.2d 79.)

In addition, the complaint in *Jolly* asserted a single type of wrongdoing-- the manufacture and distribution of defective DES--for which all of the defendants potentially shared liability under the market share or enterprise liability theory recognized by the Supreme Court in *Sindell v. Abbott Laboratories, supra,* 26 Cal.3d 588, 163 Cal.Rptr. 132, 607 P.2d 924. In contrast, *Bristol-Myers Squibb* involved two types of potential wrongdoing-- negligence by plaintiff's treating physician and production of a defective silicone breast implant by the manufacturer.

Thus, we conclude the factual differences between *Bristol-Myers Squibb* and *Jolly* lead to the conclusion that the *BMS* rule is not a principle inherent in the *Jolly* holding, but is an extension of that holding. Having determined that the *BMS* rule is not mandated by prior Supreme Court holdings, we next discuss why we find it inappropriate to adopt and apply the bright line *BMS* rule in this case. Instead, we follow the method of analysis used by the Second District in *Rose v. Fife, supra,* which is essentially the Basic Approach we have outlined.

The trial court here decided to apply the *BMS* rule to the facts of this case, causing it to sustain Ethicon's demurrer. Ethicon argues we should follow the *BMS* rule because it is a viable and unblemished rule of law since the Supreme Court did not criticize or disapprove it in *Norgart.* In response, Fox argues the facts of this case are distinguishable from the facts of *Bristol-Myers Squibb* and the holding in *Bristol-Myers Squibb* should not be extended to apply to a case where the plaintiff did not know a particular product was to be used on her, could not observe the injury the product may have caused, and did not learn of the possibility of wrongdoing connected to the product, i.e., a product defect, until the doctor who performed the operation and used the product testified about that possible defect in his deposition. One method of analyzing the *BMS* rule of imputed simultaneous discovery is to restate the actual holding as well as the rule itself in terms of the Basic Approach.

Bristol-Myers Squibb held the limitation period on the plaintiff's products liability cause of action against the manufacturer of her silicone breast implant began to run at the same time plaintiff suspected negligence by her treating physician. (*Bristol-Myers Squibb, supra,* 32 Cal.App.4th at p. 967, 38 Cal.Rptr.2d 298.) Because it would be highly fictionalized to restate this holding in terms of the subjective alternative of the discovery rule (actual suspicion), we will use the objective alternative. Stated in terms of what a reasonable person should have suspected, the Fourth District in effect held that based on the information available

(continued)

to plaintiff when she suspected professional negligence by her treating physician, she also should have suspected that her implant was defective.

It appears the result in *Bristol-Myers Squibb* would have been the same if the Fourth District had applied the Basic Approach because the facts of that case showed that plaintiff should have suspected her implant was defective. In *Bristol-Myers Squibb,* the plaintiff's implant was ruptured in an altercation in 1982. By 1984, plaintiff knew that the implant had ruptured, that silicone was migrating down her arm and that the silicone was a cause of physical injury in the form of ulcerations. (*Bristol-Myers Squibb, supra,* 32 Cal.App.4th at p. 962, 38 Cal.Rptr.2d 298.) Plaintiff argued she did not actually suspect the manufacturer of the implant of wrongdoing because she had been told that silicone was an inert substance that could do no harm by itself. (*Id.* at p. 966, 38 Cal.Rptr.2d 298.) Instead of applying a rule of simultaneous discovery of causes of action, the Fourth District could have held that a reasonable person should have suspected the implant was defective at some point prior to April 1990, one year before she filed her complaint, because plaintiff should have suspected that what she had been told about silicone doing no harm was not true since she knew the silicone was a cause of her ulcerations.

With respect to the *BMS* rule itself, it can be restated using the objective alternative in the Basic Approach as follows: When a plaintiff knows, suspects or has reason to suspect a factual basis for negligence by one potential defendant, then a plaintiff also has, as a matter of law, reason to suspect a factual basis for all potential wrongdoing by all potential defendants.

When the consequences that flow from this restatement of the *BMS* rule are examined, we find the rule is too broad to be accepted without limitation. For example, if a reasonable plaintiff suspects malpractice by the surgeon in connection with an operation, then that plaintiff, to be objectively reasonable in the eyes of the *BMS* rule, must also suspect every manufacturer of every piece of equipment and each material used in connection with the operation. This suspicion would include manufacturers of scalpels, clamps, sponges, latex gloves, staplers, sutures and other items. For example, applying the *BMS* rule to this case would imply that Fox also should have suspected her slow healing after the operation was caused by a material that was toxic or to which she was allergic and that this material was one of the items used in her surgery. (Cf. *Clark v. Baxter Healthcare Corp., supra,* 83 Cal.App.4th at p. 1060, 100 Cal.Rptr.2d 223 [plaintiff not aware that chemical substances may have been added to latex gloves that cause her severe allergic reaction; a triable issue of fact existed with respect to when she should have suspected the latex gloves might have been defectively manufactured].) Similarly, in the context of accidents involving negligence, the *BMS* rule also would require the injured plaintiff to suspect a defect in every manufactured item involved in the accident or the causal chain of events leading to the accident.

Requiring as a rule of law that a plaintiff exercise such a high degree of suspicion, without regard to the actual facts known or available to the plaintiff (and perhaps in contradiction to those facts), disconnects the discovery rule from the facts of the case. Because the imputed suspicions of the *BMS* rule are disconnected from the facts, that rule will produce a different result than the Basic Approach in cases where the trier of fact would have found the cause of action was (1) timely, i.e., the plaintiff had no reason to suspect its factual basis before the applicable limitations period, and (2) meritorious. Furthermore, to deal with such imputed suspicions, drafters of complaints seeking to comply with the view of objective reasonableness embodied in the *BMS* rule would be required to include allegations that would reach all potential wrongdoing by all potential wrongdoers. These pleading requirements necessitated by the *BMS* rule would be a regression to the more formalistic pleading requirements of bygone years.

In addition, requiring the pleading of all potential wrongs committed by all potential defendants in order to take advantage of relation back would result in an expansion of section 474 beyond its literal terms. Section 474 addresses Doe pleading when a plaintiff is "ignorant of the name of a defendant" (§ 474), but does not mention situations where the plaintiff does not know or actually suspect (1) wrongdoing of a known person or (2) wrongdoing of an unknown person.

(continued)

In addition to the foregoing implications of the *BMS* rule, that rule also creates a pitfall in cases where the plaintiff has relied upon the 90-day extension in section 364 to extend the time for filing a professional negligence action against a health care provider beyond the one-year period set forth in section 340.5. Subdivision (d) of section 364 does not appear to extend the statute of limitations for causes of action other than professional negligence. (See *Noble v. Superior Court* (1987) 191 Cal.App.3d 1189, 1192-1193, 237 Cal.Rptr. 38 [§ 364, subd. (d) does not extend limitation period for intentional tort of battery].) Thus, a plaintiff who did not file his or her lawsuit within one year of discovering or suspecting professional negligence would be barred from asserting any other causes of action subject to a one-year limitation period, such as a personal injury claim based on products liability. For example, in the present case, plaintiff did not file her complaint until June 28, 2000, which was more than one year after her April 10, 1999, operation. The claim of professional negligence is timely because of the extension granted by section 364, subdivision (d). However, even if Fox has the benefit of the relation-back doctrine, if she is held to have simultaneously discovered the products liability cause of action against Ethicon when she suspected professional negligence, i.e., shortly after the initial operation, her products liability cause of action would be time barred.

To avoid this pitfall, an objectively reasonable plaintiff, who is required by the *BMS* rule to suspect other types of wrongdoing simultaneously with suspicions of professional negligence, would never rely on the provisions of subdivision (d) of section 364 to extend the time for filing the lawsuit. Thus, one consequence of the *BMS* rule would be to eliminate the use of the extension and undermine the purpose served by the extension. The legislative purpose of the 90-day waiting period is to encourage negotiated resolution of medical malpractice disputes outside the formal litigation process. (*Russell v. Stanford University Hospital* (1997) 15 Cal.4th 783, 788, 64 Cal.Rptr.2d 97, 937 P.2d 640.) Accordingly, to avoid disharmony between section 364 and former section 340, subdivision (3), as interpreted and applied through the *BMS* rule, we conclude that application of the *BMS* rule should not be extended beyond those situations where the plaintiff actually suspects or has reason to suspect a factual basis for the wrongdoing on the part of the product manufacturer. The practical effect of this limitation is that the BMS rule has no independent application beyond situations covered by the Basic Approach.

In summary, we conclude a bright line rule that imputes the simultaneous discovery of a products liability cause of action with the discovery of a professional negligence cause of action should not be applied in this case. Instead, we adopt the more reliable Basic Approach, which is dependent upon the facts and circumstances surrounding the products liability claim and its delayed discovery.

The next question is whether Ethicon's demurrer should be sustained under the Basic Approach to the discovery rule. Specifically, did Fox know, actually suspect, or have reason to suspect a factual basis for the three elements of her products liability cause of action against Ethicon more than one year prior to the November 28, 2001, filing of her first amended complaint?

Fox's opening appellate brief states that she "proceeded to file a timely claim for medical malpractice against her health care providers since she knew or suspected when she awoke from the anesthesia utilized in the initial surgery on April 10, 1999 that professional negligence occurred." Thus, Fox concedes an actual suspicion of wrongdoing in the form of professional negligence shortly after her initial operation. Notwithstanding her suspicion of professional negligence, Fox's declaration indicates that until the deposition of Dr. Gladen she had no actual suspicion that Ethicon's stapler had malfunctioned. Similarly, Fox's first amended complaint states that she did not discover or suspect "the Ethicon GIA-type Stapler was a cause of her injuries until the deposition of [Dr. Gladen] was taken on August 13, 2001."

Fox's pleading of her products liability cause of action does not contain separate allegations with respect to the injury for which recovery is sought. For purposes of Ethicon's demurrer, the reasonable inference is that the injury is the same as set forth in her professional negligence cause of action and that she suspected

(continued)

the injury shortly after her initial surgery. Therefore, the following application of the Basic Approach will focus on when Fox actually suspected or should have suspected (1) a defective product and (2) causation.

As to the causation and wrongdoing elements of Fox's products liability cause of action against Ethicon, we cannot reasonably infer from the record before us that Fox actually suspected a factual basis for either of these elements prior to November 28, 2000, i.e., one year before the date her first amended complaint was filed. Rather, accepting Fox's allegation of actual suspicion as true, it appears for purposes of the demurrer that Fox did not actually suspect a stapler defect until August 13, 2001. In parallel to her allegations regarding actual suspicion, Fox's first amended complaint alleges that there were not any means through which her reasonable diligence would have revealed or through which she would have suspected the Ethicon GIA-type stapler was a cause of her injuries until the deposition of Dr. Gladen.

The adequacy of these allegations of delayed discovery is tested under the following rule. "A plaintiff whose complaint shows on its face that [the] claim would be barred without the benefit of the discovery rule must specifically plead facts to show (1) the time and manner of discovery *and* (2) the inability to have made earlier discovery despite reasonable diligence. The burden is on the plaintiff to show diligence, and conclusory allegations will not withstand demurrer. [Citations.]" (*McKelvey v. Boeing North American, Inc.* (1999) 74 Cal.App.4th 151, 160, 86 Cal.Rptr.2d 645; *G.D. Searle & Co. v. Superior Court, supra,* 49 Cal.App.3d at p. 26, 122 Cal.Rptr. 218 [mandamus issued to compel trial court to sustain, with leave to amend, demurrer to products liability complaint against drug manufacturer].) Fox's allegations about Dr. Gladen's deposition comply with the first requirement regarding the time and manner of actual discovery. However, Fox's allegations regarding the circumstance justifying delayed discovery are conclusory. (Cf. *Frederick v. Calbio Pharmaceuticals* (1979) 89 Cal.App.3d 49, 59, 152 Cal.Rptr. 292 [conclusory allegations of discovery].) Therefore, the question becomes whether Fox showed a reasonable possibility of curing the defect.

Fox and her attorney both filed declarations opposing the demurrer that set forth some facts explaining why the discovery of the potentially defective stapler was not made earlier. In addition to the facts set forth in the declarations, Fox may be able to include allegations about whether or not a timely investigation would have disclosed (1) articles in the media concerning defective staplers (see *Jolly, supra,* 44 Cal.3d at pp. 1112-1113, 245 Cal.Rptr. 658, 751 P.2d 923 [numerous articles concerning DES]; see also *Norgart, supra,* 21 Cal.4th at p. 408, 87 Cal.Rptr.2d 453, 981 P.2d 79 [controversy about drug Halcion had arisen in popular press]); (2) lawsuits alleging wrongdoing in connection with the stapler (see *Jolly, supra,* 44 Cal.3d at p. 1113, 245 Cal.Rptr. 658, 751 P.2d 923 [many DES suits filed throughout the country alleged wrongdoing]); (3) a support group with information about the alleged defect (see *Clark v. Baxter Healthcare Corp., supra,* 83 Cal.App.4th at p. 1054, 100 Cal.Rptr.2d 223); or (4) a manufacturer warning regarding the use of the product (see *Norgart* at p. 407, 87 Cal.Rptr.2d 453, 981 P.2d 79 [written precaution inserted in drug packaging]; see generally *Frederick v. Calbio Pharmaceuticals, supra,* 89 Cal.App.3d at p. 59, 152 Cal.Rptr. 292).

Fox's awareness of her injury is not enough by itself to find, as a matter of law, that she reasonably should have suspected a factual basis for wrongdoing related to the stapler and causation. (See *Bristol-Myers Squibb, supra,* 32 Cal.App.4th at pp. 964-965, 38 Cal.Rptr.2d 298; *Kilburn v. Pineda* (1982) 137 Cal.App.3d 1046, 187 Cal.Rptr. 548 [negligence not inferred where operation leads to rare and unforeseen injuries]; cf. *Barrett v. Atlas Powder Company* (1978) 86 Cal.App.3d 560, 150 Cal.Rptr. 339 [doctrine of res ipsa loquitur does not apply in strict liability actions].)

In light of the foregoing, Fox has shown a reasonable probability of alleging facts explaining why a reasonable person would not have suspected the causation and wrongdoing elements of her cause of action before November 28, 2000. Therefore, those factual issues cannot be decided as a matter law at this stage of

(continued)

the proceeding. Because Fox may be able to cure the defects in her first amended complaint, the trial court should have granted her leave to amend.

The judgment is reversed and the case remanded to the trial court with directions to vacate its order sustaining the demurrer without leave to amend and to enter an order sustaining the demurrer with leave to amend the cause of action for products liability. Fox is awarded her costs on appeal.

Whether or not a discovery rule is applied to toll the running of the statute of limitations for an additional period of time is based on the circumstances of the specific case. Typically, before a discovery rule can be applied to extend the time for filing suit by a plaintiff, evidence of one of two situations must be demonstrated. These circumstances occur when:

- the discovery rule is mandated by statute and the facts of the case fall within the statutory definition;
- there is evidence the defendant deliberately concealed or misled the plaintiff regarding information supporting the cause of action to prevent awareness.

In the first instance, where the discovery rule is a statutory privilege, it is not without limitation. The plaintiff must establish compliance with the rule of the jurisdiction regarding the actual discovery of the injury. It is possible for the statute to begin to run from the last date of treatment, which might be a significant period of time after the alleged malfeasance. For example, if a provider continues to provide treatment, a patient may be unaware that malfeasance has occurred and merely believe that the new symptoms are part of the routine risks and procedures of treating the original condition. Consider the example in a previous chapter when a pharmacist filled a doctor's prescription incorrectly and provided the patient with the wrong prescription drug for cancer treatment. The patient, unfamiliar with the drug and chemotherapy, had no preconceived ideas regarding the effects that should have been produced by the correct drug. Thus, it was some time before the patient was aware of the date he ascertained constructive knowledge that he had been taking the wrong drug (and then only as the result of a hospital admission). In that case, it would be unfair to relate the statute of limitations back to the first date the prescription was filled incorrectly. Instead, the more appropriate date for an awareness of the potential malfeasance was at the time the patient first had the opportunity to be aware that the wrong drug had been received, specifically upon discovery of the fact at the hospital months later.

In the second situation, the discovery rule is much more easily understood. Anyone with a basic sense of fairness would conclude that a defendant should not benefit from a statute of limitations when information about the basis for a suit has been deliberately concealed and kept from the potential plaintiff. This is sometimes referred to as **fraudulent concealment**. As mentioned in Chapter 2, the JCAHO recently issued a ruling that all unanticipated results must be disclosed to patients. However, this rule only applies to medical facilities certified by the JCAHO. All other health care providers are faced with their own ethical dilemma of whether to disclose unexpected outcomes to their patients. Application 6.2 describes a situation very similar to an actual occurrence in 2002 that received a great deal of media attention.

APPLICATION 6.2

Dr. L was an oncologist and operated an outpatient clinic in the Midwest where cancer patients came to receive chemotherapy. Many patients had an indwelling port placed just under the skin's surface and leading into the bloodstream. These ports have a small cap extending just below or above the skin where an intravenous line can be easily attached without inserting a needle into the patient's vein through a new injection site each time chemotherapy is administered. The common procedure is to flush the port with a small amount of sterile saline (salt water) solution by inserting it deep into the port under the skin through a syringe. This clears the line before administering the chemotherapy. On one occasion the nurse was hurriedly preparing several patients for chemotherapy. In her rush, instead of using a different syringe for each patient, she reused a syringe for at least one patient as she obtained the saline solution from a large container. Unfortunately, the first patient suffered from hepatitis C in addition to cancer. The syringe was infected with the hepatitis C when the syringe was inserted through the port to the bloodstream. This needle was then injected into the container of saline solution when the syringe was reused. The entire bag was contaminated and as a result more than 70 cancer patients contracted hepatitis C.

In this case, the patients were not initially informed of how they contracted the disease. However, because the disease is highly infectious, it is one that by law must be reported to the authorities when diagnosed. In this instance the alarming number of patients contracting it in a short time from the same small community resulted in an investigation and public disclosure of what had occurred. The results included many lawsuits and disciplinary action for both the supervising physician and nurse. Ultimately, the physician left the United States entirely.

In the situation described above, once the error was discovered, the health care providers were faced with the dilemma of informing all of the patients who had received treatment that included the use of saline from the container which held approximately 400 doses. The circumstances were so grave that there is little doubt the providers were aware of the risk of a professionally devastating result. Instead, they chose initially to keep quiet. The risk chosen was that those infected did not contract the disease, or at the very least, the number of infected individuals would be minimal and the cause would not be discovered. However, the infectious nature of the disease and the decreased immune system of the patients who were exposed combined to create a tragic result. Had the state investigating body not become involved and the matter made public knowledge, it is highly possible many of the patients would not have discovered the error within the statute of limitations or even within an extended period allowed by the discovery rule.

When a provider is aware that an occurrence may lead to claims of malpractice, and the patient is not readily aware of the fact, the provider is faced with a very difficult decision. He or she must consider whether there is a moral obligation to inform the patient and risk an allegation of malpractice versus keeping silent about injuries he or she had a role in producing and thus minimizing their chances of being sued. To date, the majority of jurisdictions have not gone so far as to require individual health care providers to disclose their own mistakes to patients. However, they are encouraged to do so by a majority rule that extends the statute of limitations even further for plaintiffs who are not only the victims of alleged malpractice, but are also victims of the concealment of evidence by the defendants as well.

CASE

56 SW3d 683 (ARK 2001).
Court of Appeals of Tennessee.

Almeda Zolia GREEN
v.
Eugene I. SACKS.

March 15, 2001.

KOCH, J.

Almeda Green is in her seventies and lives in Rutherford County. She had experienced stomach problems for a number of years, including reflux esophagitis, a painful condition that allows gastric fluid from her stomach to enter her esophagus. As a result of these problems, she has undergone multiple surgeries on and around her stomach. One of these surgeries, performed in 1980, involved wrapping part of her stomach tissue around the bottom of her esophagus. This procedure left her stomach tubular shaped.

In early 1987, Ms. Green consulted Eugene I. Sacks, a general surgeon practicing in Nashville, because she was continuing to experience discomfort from reflux esophagitis. Dr. Sacks treated Ms. Green conservatively with medication for approximately eighteen months. In June 1988, when it became evident that the medication was not alleviating Ms. Green's discomfort, Dr. Sacks broached the possibility of surgery. Ms. Green was reluctant to have further surgery in light of the previous surgeries that had not alleviated her problem.

Ensuing events eroded Ms. Green's reluctance about further surgery. In August 1997, she was taken to the emergency room of the Smyrna Medical Center with upper gastrointestinal bleeding. Based on Ms. Green's persisting symptoms, the long and complicated history of her gastrointestinal problems, and the failure of more conservative treatment, Dr. Sacks recommended the surgical insertion of an Angelchik prosthesis. An Angelchik prosthesis is a doughnut-shaped device containing silicone gel that is wrapped around the esophagus at the gastroesophageal junction (where the stomach and esophagus meet) for the purpose of limiting gastric reflux into the esophagus. After insertion, the device rests on the upper part of the stomach where the stomach becomes wider than the device's inner circumference. Ms. Green consented to the surgery because she was concerned that her condition seemed to be getting worse.

Dr. Sacks operated on Ms. Green on September 8, 1988, at Southern Hills Medical Center in Nashville. During the procedure, Dr. Sacks determined that the configuration of Ms. Green's alimentary canal required him to vary the procedure he had planned to perform. As Dr. Sacks describes it: "Because earlier operations had made the top part of Ms. Green's stomach somewhat tubular in shape and indistinguishable from the lower part of the esophagus, I placed the Angelchik below her gastroesophageal junction, allowing it to rest on the part of her stomach that is wider than the inner circumference of the device. The device could not be placed at a higher position." Dr. Sacks never informed Ms. Green that he had placed the Angelchik around her stomach rather than at the gastroesophageal junction.

On September 19, 1988, while Ms. Green was recuperating from surgery, Dr. Sacks conducted an x-ray study revealing that Ms. Green had some continuing reflux above the Angelchik prosthesis. The study also confirmed that the Angelchik was around Ms. Green's stomach below the gastroesophageal junction. At

(continued)

this point, Dr. Sacks decided that it was best, in his words, to "leave the prosthesis in place ... and see how she did." He discharged Ms. Green from the hospital without informing her about the location of the Angelchik.

Dr. Sacks continued to follow Ms. Green postoperatively until November 1991. He continued to monitor the Angelchik's location with x-rays in May 1989 and September 1990. During this time, Ms. Green's reflux problems remained essentially unchanged. In November 1991, Dr. Sacks referred Ms. Green to another physician for continuing treatment.

Ms. Green was taken to Vanderbilt University Medical Center in June 1992 after she passed out. An upper GI endoscopy and an upper GI series revealed that the Angelchik prosthesis had partially eroded into Ms. Green's stomach. Document1zzFN_B0022 The Vanderbilt physician treating Ms. Green referred her back to Dr. Sacks. Dr. Sacks determined that the prosthesis should be removed but referred Ms. Green to another surgeon because he was in the process of closing his medical practice. In mid-July 1992 Ms. Green underwent surgery to remove the Angelchik.

On May 28, 1993, Ms. Green filed a medical malpractice action against Dr. Sacks in the Circuit Court for Davidson County. She also asserted a products liability claim against Mentor Corporation, the Angelchik's manufacturer. Dr. Sacks and Mentor jointly removed the suit to the United States District Court for the Middle District of Tennessee on the ground that Ms. Green's claims against Mentor were pre-empted by the federal Food, Drug, and Cosmetic Act. Shortly after removal, Ms. Green voluntarily dismissed her claim against Mentor, leaving only the medical malpractice action against Dr. Sacks. Dr. Sacks obtained summary judgment on that claim in the United States District Court, but in August 1996, the United States Court of Appeals for the Sixth Circuit vacated the district court's judgment and dismissed the entire case for lack of subject matter jurisdiction. Thereafter, the case was returned to the trial court for further proceedings.

After the case returned to the trial court, Dr. Sacks renewed his motion for summary judgment on the ground that Ms. Green's medical malpractice claim was barred by the statute of limitations in Tenn.Code Ann. § 29-26- 116(a)(1), (2) and by the statute of repose in Tenn.Code Ann. § 29-26- 116(a)(3). Ms. Green responded to the motion by asserting that the statute of repose should be tolled because Dr. Sacks had fraudulently concealed the details of the Angelchik procedure from her, and that she had filed her suit within one year after discovering her injury. The trial court disagreed and granted Dr. Sacks's summary judgment motion, expressly adopting the reasoning in the United States District Court's earlier order granting Dr. Sacks a summary judgment. On this appeal, Ms. Green asserts that Dr. Sacks was not entitled to a judgment as a matter of law.

The standards for reviewing summary judgments on appeal are well-settled. Summary judgments are proper in virtually any civil case that can be resolved on the basis of legal issues alone. *Fruge v. Doe*, 952 S.W.2d 408, 410 (Tenn.1997)...They are not, however, appropriate when genuine disputes regarding material facts exist. Tenn.R.Civ.P. 56.04. Thus, a summary judgment should be granted only when the undisputed facts, and the inferences reasonably drawn from the undisputed facts, support one conclusion--that the party seeking the summary judgment is entitled to a judgment as a matter of law. *Staples v. CBL & Assocs., Inc.*, 15 S.W.3d 83, 88 (Tenn.2000)...

Summary judgments enjoy no presumption of correctness on appeal. *Penley v. Honda Motor Co.*, 31 S.W.3d 181, 183 (Tenn.2000... Accordingly, appellate courts must make a fresh determination that the requirements of Tenn.R.Civ.P. 56 have been satisfied. *Hunter v. Brown*, 955 S.W.2d 49, 50-51 (Tenn.1997).... We must consider the evidence in the light most favorable to the non-moving party, and we must resolve all inferences in the non-moving party's favor. *Terry v. Niblack*, 979 S.W.2d 583, 585 (Tenn.1998)... When reviewing the evidence, we must determine first whether factual disputes exist. If a factual dispute exists, we must then determine whether the fact is material to the claim or defense upon which the summary judgment is predicated and whether the disputed fact creates a genuine issue for trial. *Byrd v. Hall*, 847 S.W.2d at 214.

(continued)

Ms. Green asserts that the trial court erred by granting Dr. Sacks's motion for summary judgment because she presented "sufficient evidence [of] ... fraudulent conduct" to toll the running of the statute of repose in Tenn.Code Ann. § 29-26-116(a)(3). While we do not find any evidence of fraudulent conduct on the part of Dr. Sacks, we have determined that he is not entitled to a summary judgment because Ms. Green's evidence creates a jury question regarding whether he should have advised Ms. Green postoperatively of the unanticipated placement of the Angelchik.

Ever since the enactment of the Medical Malpractice Review Board and Claims Act in 1975, all medical malpractice claims have been governed by a one-year statute of limitations and a three-year statute of repose. With regard to the statute of repose, Tenn.Code Ann. § 29-26-116(a)(3) states:

> In no event shall any such action be brought more than three (3) years after the date on which the negligent act or omission occurred except where there is fraudulent concealment on the part of the defendant, in which case the action shall be commenced within one (1) year after discovery that the cause of action exists.

The purpose of this provision is to address the perceived medical malpractice insurance crisis by placing an absolute three-year limit upon the time within which a medical malpractice action may be brought. *Cronin v. Howe,* 906 S.W.2d 910, 913 (Tenn.1995).

The statute of repose begins to run from the date the allegedly negligent act or omission occurred. The running of the time within which a suit must be filed cannot be tolled except as provided in the statute itself or in another statute that specifically references the particular statute of repose. *Penley v. Honda Motor Co.,* 31 S.W.3d at 184-85. The only current statutory basis for tolling Tenn.Code Ann. § 29-26-116(a)(3)'s three-year statute of repose is "fraudulent concealment on the part of the defendant." Once a defendant makes out a prima facie defense that the three-year period in Tenn.Code Ann. § 29-26-116(a)(3) has elapsed, the burden of proof shifts to the plaintiff to demonstrate that he or she is entitled to take advantage of the statute's tolling provision. *Benton v. Snyder,* 825 S.W.2d 409, 414 (Tenn.1992).

The courts' understanding of the sorts of conduct that amount to "fraudulent concealment" for the purpose of tolling the running of a statute of limitations or a statute of repose has evolved over time. For many years, the courts permitted "fraudulent concealment" tolling only when the physician had actual knowledge of the wrong done and concealed it from the patient. *Housh v. Morris,* 818 S.W.2d 39, 43 (Tenn.Ct.App.1991); *Ray v. Scheibert,* 484 S.W.2d 63, 72 (Tenn.Ct.App.1972); *Clinard v. Pennington,* 59 Tenn.App. 128, 139, 438 S.W.2d 748, 753 (1968). In 1992, the Tennessee Supreme Court signaled that "fraudulent concealment" included more than concealing that a wrong had been done. Invoking the confidential nature of the relationship between a physician and his or her patient, the Court held that "fraudulent concealment" could also occur when the physician fails to disclose information that he or she has a duty to disclose. *Benton v. Snyder,* 825 S.W.2d at 414. While the court did not directly describe the type of information that physicians were expected to disclose, it stated that "[k]nowledge on the part of the physician of the facts giving rise to a cause of action is an essential element of fraudulent concealment." *Benton v. Snyder,* 825 S.W.2d at 414.

In 1998, the Tennessee Supreme Court returned to the question of the elements of the "fraudulent concealment" exception to the medical malpractice statute of repose. The court stated that in all medical malpractice cases, persons desiring to rely upon the fraudulent concealment exception to Tenn.Code Ann. § 29-26-116(a)(3) must establish that "(1) the health care provider took affirmative action to conceal the wrongdoing or remained silent and failed to disclose material facts despite a duty to do so, (2) the plaintiff could not have discovered the wrong despite exercising reasonable care and diligence, (3) the health care provider knew of the facts giving rise to the cause of action, and (4) a concealment, which may consist of the defendant withholding material information, making use of some device to mislead the plaintiff, or simply remaining silent and failing to disclose

(continued)

material facts where there was a duty to speak." *Shadrick v. Coker*, 963 S.W.2d 726, 736 (Tenn.1998).

There is no reasonable dispute that Ms. Green could not have discovered the information regarding the placement of the Angelchik on her own without being told by Dr. Sacks or another physician. It is also undisputed that Dr. Sacks knew where he had placed the Angelchik and that he never informed Ms. Green about where he had placed the device or why he had placed it in that location. Thus, the dispositive question in this case is whether Dr. Sacks affirmatively acted to conceal wrongdoing or failed to disclose material facts to Ms. Green despite a duty to do so.

For the purposes of this opinion, we readily concede that there is no evidence in the record that Dr. Sacks knew or suspected that he might have made a mistake when he placed the Angelchik prosthesis around Ms Green's stomach. Thus, to create a jury issue regarding "fraudulent concealment," Ms. Green must demonstrate that she will be able to prove that Dr. Sacks had a duty to inform Ms. Green, following the surgery, that he had placed the Angelchik around her stomach rather than at the gastroesophageal junction. Conversely, to be entitled to a summary judgment, Dr. Sacks must demonstrate that Ms. Green will be unable to establish this essential element of her case and, therefore, that he is entitled to a judgment as a matter of law.

Whether a particular defendant owes a duty of care to a particular plaintiff is a question that must be decided by the court as a matter of law. *Staples v. CBL & Assocs., Inc.*, 15 S.W.3d at 89; *Rice v. Sabir*, 979 S.W.2d 305, 309 (Tenn.1998); *Dillard v. Vanderbilt University*, 970 S.W.2d 958, 960 (Tenn.Ct.App.1998). Physicians have a confidential relationship with their patients. Because of the trust that patients repose in their physicians, patients rely implicitly, not only on what their physicians tell them, but also on their belief that their physicians will not leave anything of importance unsaid. Accordingly, the Tennessee Supreme Court has determined that physicians have a heightened duty to disclose material medical facts to their patients. *Shadrick v. Coker*, 963 S.W.2d at 735; *Benton v. Snyder*, 825 S.W.2d at 414. The questions that remain to be answered are (1) what sorts of facts should be deemed to be material enough to require disclosure and (2) how should the question of materiality be decided.

The sorts of facts that require disclosure to a patient involve matters that are not already known by the patient or that are not within the realm of common experience. To be material, these facts must involve the patient's medical condition and must consist of the sort of information that a reasonable person in the patient's position would want to know in order to understand and to make decisions regarding medical matters. *Arato v. Avedon*, 11 Cal.Rptr.2d 169, 175-76 (Ct.App.1992); *Nixdorf v. Hicken*, 612 P.2d 348, 354 (Utah 1980); *Brown v. Dibbell*, 227 Wis.2d 28, 595 N.W.2d 358, 366 (1999); Marjorie M. Schultz, *From Informed Consent to Patient Choice: A New Protected Interest*, 95 Yale L.J. 219, 283-84 (1985).

It is neither improper nor altogether uncommon to vary a procedure in some substantial way from that discussed with the patient beforehand during the consent process. A number of courts, including this court, have held that in this circumstance, a physician has a duty to inform the patient that he or she varied the procedure and that the failure to provide this information was sufficient to create a jury issue on fraudulent concealment. *Hall v. DeSaussure*, 41 Tenn.App. 572, 582-83, 297 S.W.2d 81, 86 (1956); *see also Roberts v. Francis*, 128 F.3d 647, 649 (8th Cir.1997); *Hershley v. Brown*, 655 S.W.2d 671, 677 (Mo.Ct.App.1983). Conversely, other courts have held that there is no fraudulent concealment when a physician informs a patient postoperatively that he varied the procedure. *Wheeler v. Schmid Labs., Inc.*, 451 N.W.2d 133, 139 (N.D.1990).

That leaves for determination how should the question about whether particular information is material be decided. Decisions regarding the scope and parameters of a physician's duty to disclose material information must be guided, at least in part, by the medical profession. For a physician's failure to disclose information to constitute fraudulent concealment for the purpose of tolling the statute of repose, the failure to disclose should also be, in the words of Tenn.Code Ann.§ 29-26-115(a)(1), below the "recognized standard of acceptable professional practice in the profession and specialty thereof." Making this determination

(continued)

calls for expert medical testimony consistent with Tenn.CodeAnn.§ 29-26-115(b).

A relatively recent case involving the use of teflon pledgets to support lung sutures makes this point. A surgeon used teflon pledgets to support his sutures following the removal of his patient's right lung but did not tell the patient after the surgery that he had used these pledgets. When the patient died nine years later from respiratory insufficiency caused, in part, by the teflon pledgets, her estate filed a medical malpractice action against the physician. When the physician asserted that the suit was barred by the statute of repose in Tenn.Code Ann. § 29-26-116(a)(3), the estate responded that the physician had fraudulently concealed the cause of action by failing to inform his patient that he had used the teflon pledgets. In affirming the summary judgment for the physician, this court pointed to the surgeon's uncontradicted testimony "that it was not the standard of care in the community to discuss with a patient after surgery a particular instrument or device used in surgery, like pledgets." *Burris v. Ikard,* 798 S.W.2d 246, 249 (Tenn.Ct.App.1990). Had the surgeon's opinion regarding his postoperative disclosures to his patient been contradicted by opposing expert testimony, the summary judgment would not have been warranted.

Keeping in mind the pivotal role of expert testimony in establishing the scope of a physician's duty, we must examine the record to determine whether it contains competent evidence regarding Dr. Sacks's duty to inform Ms. Green about the placement of the Angelchik prosthesis. Dr. Sacks testified in his February 4, 1994 deposition that he did not inform Ms. Green postoperatively about his decision to place the Angelchik below the gastroesophageal junction. He explained:

> I don't think Ms. Green would have had the vaguest idea what I was talking about if I even tried to explain that to her, and ... had I done that, I think it would have created further problems for Mrs. Green in terms of her trying to understand what I was saying and mis-construing what I was saying. So I felt that in the best interests of my patient and in my relationship with my patient it was best not to advise her of anything because I had no plans at that time to do anything differently.

He also explained that he did not inform any of Ms. Green's family members about the procedure because he did not see any of them after the procedure and because Ms. Green had not authorized him to discuss her medical condition with anyone else. In a May 16, 1994 affidavit, Dr. Sacks also asserted that "[a]t all times in my care and treatment of Ms. Green, I conformed to the recognized standard of acceptable surgical practice in this community." Reading these statements together, Dr. Sacks testified that he did not owe a duty to Ms. Green to inform her postoperatively that he had placed the Angelchik prosthesis below the gastroesophageal junction, a location different from the location he had discussed with her when he had obtained her consent to perform the surgery.

To oppose Dr. Sacks's summary judgment motion, Ms. Green presented the testimony of Martin T. Evans, a practicing surgeon from Virginia who was clearly qualified to give an expert opinion pursuant to Tenn.Code Ann. § 29- 26-115(b). Dr. Evans was extremely critical of the Angelchik prosthesis, stating that "[t]he majority of surgeons avoided the use of this device altogether due to the extreme complications associated with its use that had been documented in medical journals and periodicals prior to September 1988." He also stated that "I cannot find any basis to justify placement of an Angelchik device around the mid-portion of the stomach." Turning to Dr. Sacks's obligation to inform Ms. Green about the actual placement of the Angelchik prosthesis, Dr. Evans testified that "Dr. Sacks had a medical obligation to inform the patient of this improper placement and obtain consent for the continued application of the device in its then location." Dr. Evans also testified that "[b]y failing to inform Mrs. Green that the device was inserted in the improper location, Dr. Sacks deviated from the generally medically accepted standards for proper disclosure of risks associated with medical care."

Dr. Sacks's testimony and Dr. Evan's testimony regarding Dr. Sacks's duty to inform Ms. Green about the placement of the Angelchik prosthesis is diametrically opposed. A summary judgment should not be granted when there exists a genuine dispute regarding the material facts. Dr. Sacks's decision to place the

(continued)

Angelchik around Ms. Green's stomach rather than at the gastroesophageal junction was more than a "gory detail" or matter of technique because it arguably affected the Angelchik's efficacy to stop the reflux that was causing Ms. Green such discomfort. Thus, the trial court should not have granted Dr. Sacks a summary judgment based on his statute of repose defense. The conflict between the testimony of Dr. Sacks and Dr. Evans with regard to Dr. Sacks's obligation to inform Ms. Green about the actual placement of the Angelchik prosthesis created a jury question on the "fraudulent concealment" exception to the statute of repose.

Ms. Green also asserts that the trial court erred by concluding that her claim against Dr. Sacks is time-barred under the one-year statute of limitations in Tenn.Code Ann. § 29-26-116(a)(1), (2). She insists that her suit was timely because it was filed within one year after she discovered that she had suffered an injury as a result of Dr. Sacks's wrongful conduct. We agree.

In 1974, the Tennessee Supreme Court adopted the discovery rule for determining when the statute of limitations begins to run in medical malpractice actions. *Teeters v. Currey,* 518 S.W.2d 512, 515 (Tenn.1974). The Tennessee General Assembly later codified the discovery rule in the Medical Malpractice Review Board and Claims Act in 1975, and the rule can now be found in Tenn.Code Ann. § 29-26-116(a)(2). The purpose of the rule is to "alleviate the intolerable result" of barring a patient's medical malpractice claim before the patient knows or should have known that the claim exists. *Foster v. Harris,* 633 S.W.2d 304, 305 (Tenn.1982).

Under the discovery rule, the medical malpractice statute of limitations begins to run when the patient discovers, or reasonably should have discovered (1) the occasion, the manner, and the means by which a breach of duty that caused his or her injuries occurred and (2) the identity of the person who caused the injury. *Stanbury v. Bacardi,* 953 S.W.2d 671, 677 (Tenn.1997); *Roe v. Jefferson,* 875 S.W.2d 653, 656 (Tenn.1994); *Foster v. Harris,* 633 S.W.2d at 305. However, the discovery rule does not permit a patient to delay filing suit until he or she becomes aware of all the injurious consequences of the alleged negligence. *Shadrick v. Coker,* 963 S.W.2d at 733. Thus, the statute of limitations will begin running when the patient becomes aware of facts that would put a reasonable person on notice that he or she has sustained an injury as a result of a tortious act of a health care provider. *Shadrick v. Coker,* 963 S.W.2d at 733-34; *Roe v. Jefferson,* 875 S.W.2d at 657; *Hathaway v. Middle Tenn. Anesthesiology, P.C.,* 724 S.W.2d 355, 359 (Tenn.Ct.App.1986).

Dr. Sacks's statute of limitations argument is not without some irony. On one hand, he asserts that his treatment of Ms. Green was consistent with the "recognized standard of acceptable surgical practice in this community." On the other hand, he asserts that Ms. Green, whom he describes as "of limited intelligence ... often ... unable to make associations," should have known or suspected "within two or three days after the surgery" that he had done something wrong. He bases this argument on Ms. Green's state of mind following the surgery. Specifically, Ms. Green explained in her deposition that "I kn[e]w there was something, you know, unusual, that didn't feel right, but that's all I can explain, you know." While she attributed her discomfort to the surgery, she added, "I didn't have the knowledge what was going on. I knew I was sick." Ms. Green complained to Dr. Sacks "several times [that] something [is] wrong here, I don't feel right." These statements prompted Dr. Sacks to assure Ms. Green that she would be "all right in a few days." According to Ms. Green, the "few days" lasted almost one month, but she eventually began to feel better.

Ms. Green's complaints of postoperative pain are not evidence that she knew that she had been injured or that she knew of the tortious origin of her injury. She knew that Dr. Sacks had implanted the Angelchik prosthesis in her abdomen but she could not see or feel precisely where it was located in her body. She did not correlate the location of the Angelchik to her discomfort but rather explained that she felt like she was "choking" and "almost busting" inside. For all she knew, this discomfort was part of her body's adjustment to the presence of a foreign object. She had no reason to be alarmed or suspicious, especially when Dr. Sacks assured her that her pain would eventually subside and when her postoperative pain eventually did decrease. Thus, unlike the patient in *Stanbury v. Bacardi* who could plainly see the botched surgery on her feet soon

(continued)

after surgery, Ms. Green had no factual basis, two or three days following her surgery, for knowing or discovering that Dr. Sacks had inserted the Angelchik prosthesis in a negligent manner.

Receiving advice from another health care professional is not the only way for a patient to discover that he or she has been injured. *Stanbury v. Bacardi,* 953 S.W.2d at 678. For discovery to take place, it is only necessary that the patient become aware of facts that would lead a reasonable person to grasp the manner and means by which the injury occurred. Merely experiencing pain and sickness following surgery does not necessarily signal that an injury has occurred or the manner or means by which the injury was caused. We find that Ms. Green did not reasonably discover the manner and means of her injury until June 1992 when the physicians at Vanderbilt University Medical Center told her that the Angelchik was around her stomach, not at the gastroesophageal junction. Accordingly, by the express terms of Tenn.Code Ann. § 29-26-116(a)(3), Ms. Green's May 1993 medical malpractice complaint was timely filed.

We reverse the summary judgment and remand the case to the trial court for further proceedings consistent with this opinion. We tax the costs of this appeal to Eugene I. Sacks for which execution, if necessary, may issue.

ASSIGNMENT 6.1

In the following situations, explain when the statute of limitations would begin and end assuming the following statutory language applies:

"An action alleging medical malpractice shall be commenced within one year of the alleged wrongful conduct or the reasonable discovery of the basis for a cause of action by plaintiff whichever is later. In no event shall an action be commenced beyond a period of five years from the act complained of."

Assume also that the doctrines of fraudulent concealment and continued treatment are recognized by the jurisdiction. No statutory limitation extension are given to minors or incompetents.

1. On January 1, 1998, Suzanne delivered a baby girl. On March 1, 1999, the baby was formally diagnosed with mild cerebral palsy. Suzanne's pediatrician stated that the condition was more than likely the result of an event during the delivery. Prior to this Suzanne had no reason to suspect her child was less than within normal ranges of development.

2. On May 9, 1996, George suffered a heart attack and underwent open heart bypass surgery. He suffered complications after surgery and was taken back to the operating room on May 15. At that time, the doctors discovered a place where the sutures connecting the bypass artery to the heart were not fully sewn and the area was leaking. It was corrected at that time. George was never fully informed by the physician as to the reason for the second surgery. He also never asked why he required additional surgery. However, for insurance purposes a few years later he requested a copy of his past medical records and received them on June 20, 2001.

(continued)

3. Max was a freshman in college and on September 29, 1999, he suffered an injury to his knee during a football game. He was taken to the hospital and the knee was operated on the morning of September 30, 1999. He did not progress well and his physician told him that with this particular type of injury additional surgery would be needed to reach the maximum result. On January 3, 2000, Max underwent an additional surgery. After this surgery, he progressed very well. Max re-injured his knee April 5, 2002. He lived in another city at this time and requested his medical records from the prior surgery. His new physician informed him that the second surgery had been to correct errors made during the first surgery by a surgical resident in training.

4. Mary received treatment on June 25, 1998, by a chiropractor for a back ailment. Her chiropractic doctor told her that a six-month course of treatment would be necessary to achieve correction of her problem. She continued the treatment for exactly six months. Finally, on February 10, 1999, she felt no better and actually had additional symptoms. She sought the advice of another chiropractor. Within three visits her back ailment was relieved, including the symptoms developed during the prior treatment. Her last visit with the second chiropractor was on March 31, 1999. She suspects incompetence on the part of the initial chiropractor.

5. On September 21, 2000, Lisa began treatment for depression with a clinical psychologist. The doctor was well known for unconventional treatments that often produced success. Lisa had been seeing the doctor one to two times per week for nearly a year with moderate improvement but she still had episodes of suicidal thoughts. On August 15, 2001, the doctor told her that it might help to realize the inappropriateness of the suicidal thoughts by acting out some of the harmless but necessary preliminary steps of these thoughts when they came about. On August 29, 2001, Lisa climbed onto the roof of her apartment building and stood at the edge as the doctor had indicated she should when having suicidal thoughts. A friend was with her at the time and Lisa explained she did not really want to die but wanted to stop thinking she wanted to commit suicide in stressful times such as that day had been. It was a very windy day and Lisa lost her balance and fell to her death in front of her friend.

CASES INVOLVING INJURY TO MINORS AND THOSE LEGALLY INCOMPETENT

Until this point, the discussion has been confined to pure issues of statutory limitation, especially how they are affected by the discovery rule. The question raised in these cases is most often regarding when the injury occurred or should have been identified by the plaintiff as it relates to protecting the defendant from liability unlimited by time. However, another aspect of the statute of limitation issue deals with plaintiffs who, at the time of injury, are not in a position to protect their own rights. This significant factor has evolved in recent years and involves cases of those who are minors or legally incompetent at the time of injury. Historically, statutes of limitation were tolled until the age of majority or legal emancipation was reached, or the condition causing mental or legal incompetence was removed. But, as another consequence of the rapid increase in the number of medical malpractice cases, this too has been modified in a majority of jurisdictions.

In the past, in situations involving minors, the statute of limitation would not begin to run until the time the child became a legally emancipated adult through operation of law such as by court order or legally recognized marriage, or when the child reached the legal age of adulthood.[1] Thus, an action for malpractice might not be brought for a period of 20 years or more from the time the cause of action first accrued. Even if the physician was aware that his or her malfeasance had caused an injury, it would be a tremendous burden to present a viable defense two decades after the fact. For this reason, the vast majority of jurisdictions have established limits in recent years on medical malpractice actions brought by minors. It is important to note that even in jurisdictions with shortened limitations of actions in medical malpractice cases brought by parties injured as minors, that statute and consequent limitation may not apply to all providers and in all types of cases. As always, the evaluation of a claim for malpractice must show whether a medical malpractice statute is in place within the jurisdiction and whether it applies to the particulars of the case.

In jurisdictions that have not adopted shortened statutory limitations in malpractice actions for minors, health care providers may be at risk for the duration of the patient's **minority** and the additional statute of limitation period as it first begins to run when minority ends. As such the providers are obligated to maintain their patient records at least until the statutory period of limitations ends after the minor patients have reached majority. In the past, this was a huge expense given the volume of patient records on paper. This problem has been somewhat reduced with the advance of technology in electronic record keeping, but the cost of transferring paper documents, as well as creating and maintaining electronic records, is still substantial. As a risk management measure it is necessary to properly maintain the records of patients.

Supreme Court of Arkansas.

Jay Michael RALEY
v.
Dr. Charles WAGNER.
Oct. 11, 2001.

RAY THORNTON, Justice.

In his first point on appeal, appellant contends that the trial court erred in granting appellee's motion for summary judgment. Specifically, appellant argues that his claim was not barred by the Medical Malpractice Act's two-year statute of limitations. We outlined the applicable law surrounding our review of a granting of summary judgment in *Shelton v. Fiser*, 340 Ark. 89, 8 S.W.3d 557 (2000). We explained:

> The law is well settled that summary judgment is to be granted by a trial court only when it is clear that there are no genuine issues of material fact to be litigated, and the party is entitled to judgment as a matter of law. Once the moving party has established a prima facie entitlement to summary judgment, the opposing party must meet proof with proof and demonstrate the existence of a material issue of fact. On appellate review, this court determines if summary judgment was appropriate based on whether the evidentiary items presented by the moving party in support of the motion leave a material fact unanswered. This court views the evidence in a light most favorable to the party against whom the motion was filed, resolving all doubts and inferences against the moving party. Our review focuses not only on the pleadings, but also on the affidavits and other documents filed by the parties.

Id. (citing *Adams v. Arthur*, 333 Ark. 53, 969 S.W.2d 598) (internal citations omitted).

Remaining mindful of our standard of review for summary-judgment cases, we must determine whether there was a genuine issue of fact in dispute. Specifically, we must determine whether appellant's claims were barred by the two-year statute of limitations applicable to the Arkansas Medical Malpractice Act. Appellant first argues that pursuant to section four of Act 709 of 1979, codified as Ark.Code Ann

(continued)

§ 16-114-203 (1987), his claims were not barred. Arkansas Code Annotated section 16-114-203 (1987) provides:
> (a) All actions for medical injury shall be commenced within two (2) years after the cause of action accrues.
> (b) The date of the accrual of the cause of action shall be the date of the wrongful act complained of, and no other time. However, where the action is based upon the discovery of a foreign object in the body of the injured person which is not discovered and could not reasonably have been discovered within such two-year period, the action may be commenced within one (1) year from the date of discovery or the date the foreign object reasonably should have been discovered, whichever is earlier.
> (c) A minor under the age of eighteen (18) years at the time of the act, omission, or failure complained of, shall in any event have until his nineteenth birthday in which to commence an action.
> (d) Any person who had been adjudicated incompetent at the time of the act, omission, or failure complained of, shall have until one (1) year after that disability is removed in which to commence an action.

Id. Appellee responds by contending that this statute was repealed by Act 997 of 1991. Act 997 provides as follows:
> Be it enacted by the General Assembly of the State of Arkansas:
> SECTION 1. Ark.Code Ann. § 16-114-203 is amended to read as follows:
> "16-114-203. *Statute of limitations.*
> (a) Except as otherwise provided in this section, all actions for medical injury shall be commenced within two (2) years after the cause of action accrues.
> (b) The date of the accrual of the cause of action shall be the date of the wrongful act complained of and no other time. However, where the action is based upon the discovery of a foreign object in the body of the injured person which is not discovered and could not reasonably have been discovered within such two-year period, the action may be commenced within one (1) year from the date of discovery or the date the foreign object reasonably should have been discovered, whichever is earlier.
> (c) Except as otherwise provided in the subsection (d) of this section, if at the time at which the cause of action for medical injuries occurring from obstetrical care shall or with reasonable diligence might have first been known or discovered, the person to whom such claim has accrued shall be nine (9) years of age or younger, then such minor or the person claiming through such minor may notwithstanding that the period of time limited pursuant to subsection (a) of this section shall have expired, commence action on such claim at any time within two (2) years next after the time at which the minor shall have reached his ninth birthday, or shall have died, whichever shall have first occurred.
> (d) If, at the time at which the cause of action for medical injuries occurring from obstetrical care shall or with reasonable diligence might have been first known or discovered, the person to whom such claim has accrued shall be a minor without a parent or legal guardian, then such minor or the person claiming through such minor may, notwithstanding that the period of time limited *239 pursuant to subsection (a) of this section shall have expired, commence action on such claim at any time within two (2) years next after the time at which the minor shall have a parent or legal guardian or shall have died, whichever shall have first occurred; provided, however, that in no event shall the period of limitations begin to run prior to such minor's ninth birthday unless such minor shall have died.
> (e) Any person who had been adjudicated incompetent at the time of the act, omission, or failure complained of, shall have until one (1) year after that disability is removed in which to commence an action."

*

> SECTION 4. All laws and parts of laws in conflict with this Act are hereby repealed.

Id.

(continued)

We must determine whether the statute of limitations provisions of Act 709 were repealed and replaced by Act 997 of 1991. A basic rule of statutory construction is to give effect to the intent of the legislature. *Ford v. Keith*, 338 Ark. 487, 996 S.W.2d 20 (1999). Where the language of a statute is plain and unambiguous, we determine legislative intent from the ordinary meaning of the language used. *Id.*

In order to determine the intent of the General Assembly, we first review the language of Act 709 in comparison to the language of Act 997. We note that in many respects the Acts are similar. First, section four of Act 709 of 1979 provides an all-inclusive two-year statute of limitations. Specifically, the Act states "all actions for medical injury shall be commenced within two (2) years after the cause of action accrues." The language in Act 997 of 1991 is somewhat similar to Act 709. However, the General Assembly added an additional phrase in Act 997. Specifically, Act 997 states "*except as otherwise provided in this section,* all actions for medical injury shall be commenced within two (2) years after the cause of action accrues." (emphasis added). Next, Act 709 of 1979 and Act 997 of 1991 each provide an exception to the two-year statute of limitations for the discovery of foreign objects. Then, Act 709 of 1979 and Act 997 of 1991 each provide an exception to the two-year statute of limitations for specified minors. However, the savings statute for all minors with medical malpractice claims allowing the claims to be brought until the minor's nineteenth birthday, included in Act 709 is not included in Act 997 of 1991. Act 997 replaced that exception with a narrow, specific exception for minors with medical malpractice claims for medical injuries occurring from *obstetrical care.* Finally, both Act 709 of 1979 and Act 997 of 1991 each provide an exception to the two-year statute of limitations for persons adjudicated incompetent.

Both Act 997 of 1991 and section four of Act 709 of 1979 were complete statements of the statute of limitations applicable to medical injuries. We conclude that by enacting Act 997 of 1991 the General Assembly expressed its intention that the statute of limitations provisions found in Act 709 of 1979, codified as Ark.Code Ann. § 16-114-203 (1987), were replaced by Act 997 of 1991's adoption of a new and complete section of Ark.Code Ann. § 16-114-203. We note that the language in Act 997 which states "*except as otherwise provided in this section,* all actions for medical injury shall be commenced within two (2) years after the cause of action accrues," clearly demonstrates the legislative intent that Ark.Code Ann. § 16-114-203, as amended and enacted by Act 997, replaces the provisions of Ark.Code Ann. § 16-114-203 (1987) derived from Act 709 of 1979. The General Assembly further expressed its intent to repeal the statute of limitations provisions found in Act 709 of 1979 by including within Act 997 of 1991 the following language: "all laws and parts of laws in conflict with this Act are hereby repealed." Because Act 997 of 1991 repealed the statute of limitations provisions set out in Act 709 of 1979, and because appellant does not have a medical injury arising from obstetrical care, we hold that appellant was required to bring his claim within two years from the time the cause of action accrued.

Appellant next argues that because he is a minor, the statute of limitations applicable to his action is found at Ark.Code Ann. § 16-56-116 (1987). We have previously addressed this issue. Specifically, in *Shelton, supra,* we were asked to determine whether the general statute of limitations found in Ark.Code Ann. § 16-56-116, or the specific two-year statute of limitations found in the Arkansas Medical Malpractice Act, applied to a minor's medical malpractice claim. *Id.* Noting that a general statute must yield when there is a specific statute involving the particular issue, we held that the statute of limitations applicable to a minor in a malpractice case was the specific two-year statute of limitations found in the Medical Malpractice Act and not the general savings statute for claims brought by minors found at Ark.Code. Ann. § 16-56-116. *Id.* Applying our holding in *Shelton* to the case now before us, we conclude that appellant's argument must fail.

In his second point on appeal, appellant argues that the two-year statute of limitations found in the Arkansas Medical Malpractice Act is unconstitutional. Specifically, appellant argues that the statute of limitations found in the Arkansas Medical Malpractice Act violates the equal protection and due process clauses

(continued)

of the United States Constitution and the Arkansas Constitution. Appellant argues that there is no rational basis for treating minors with medical injuries differently than minors with other tort injuries. Specifically, he contends that there is no rational basis for applying the two-year statute of limitations set forth in the Medical Malpractice Act to minors with medical malpractice claims and applying the general savings statute to minors with other tort actions.

Appellee responds to appellant's contention by arguing that there is a rational basis for applying a different statute of limitations to minors with medical malpractice actions. Appellee argues that the General Assembly intended to control health care costs through its enactment of the Arkansas Medical Malpractice Act. Appellee contends that health care costs are controlled by encouraging individuals to bring their medical malpractice claims within two years and that health care costs are further controlled by applying the two-year statute of limitations to minors with medical malpractice claims. Appellee cites the following language from Act 709 of 1979 as articulating the legislature's intentions. Act 709 of 1979 states in relevant part:

SECTION 11. Emergency Clause. It is hereby found, determined and declared by the General Assembly that the threat of legal actions for medical injury have resulted in increased rates for malpractice insurance which in turn causes and contributes to an increase in health care costs placing a heavy burden on those who can least afford such increases and that the threat of such actions contributes to expensive medical procedures to be performed by physicians and others which otherwise would not be considered necessary and that this Act should be given effect immediately to help control the spiraling cost of health care. Therefore, an emergency is hereby declared to exist, and this Act being necessary for the immediate preservation of the public peace, health and safety shall be in full force and effect from and after its passage and approval. *Id.*

After reviewing the emergency clause, we hold that there is a rational basis for applying the two-year statute of limitations to minor plaintiffs in medical malpractice actions while allowing minor plaintiffs in other tort actions until their twenty-first birthday to bring forward a claim. We conclude that the rational basis for applying the shorter statute of limitations to the minors with the medical malpractice actions is to control health care cost paid by the people of Arkansas. The trial court found that the Arkansas Medical Malpractice Act is constitutional, and we cannot say that this finding was erroneous. *See Gay v. Rabon*, 280 Ark. 5, 652 S.W.2d 836 (1983) (holding that every act carries a strong presumption of constitutionality). Having found no reversible errors, we affirm the trial court.
Affirmed.

Finally, the statutes of limitation have long been considerate of those who suffer from a severe mental disability that prevents them from acting in their own best interest. Whether a lack of competence exists is based on a number of factors, but is always focused on the particular aspects of a specific plaintiff's condition. These individuals receive greater protection than virtually all other plaintiffs in terms of protecting their rights. The reason is quite clear. Competent adults have a responsibility to inquire about their own health care and conditions and must use reasonable diligence to discover irregularities. While minors may or may not be in a position to act on their own behalf in legal matters, there is typically an adult or adults who are responsible to act on behalf of the minor until such time as they are competent. However, individuals suffering from a lack of **mental competence** may or may not have a legal guardian who is in a position to protect the best interests of the one who suffers incompetence. As a result, the legislatures and courts have generally extended greater latitude to such individuals. Indeed, in many jurisdictions the otherwise limited statutes of limitation in medical malpractice cases continue to be extended for those suffering a lack of mental competence until such time as the disability designation is removed.

Because the condition of mental incapacity often receives a wider margin than other conditions for purposes of calculating the statute of limitations, the courts tend to employ a multifaceted approach to the consideration of whether the statute should be tolled. Rather than a standardized rule, such as whether the person has been declared legally incompetent, a number of factors are often considered collectively. Some of these may include the following:

- Whether there has been an adjudication of incompetence;
- Whether there has been a governmental finding of incompetence such as through an application for Social Security Disability benefits;
- Whether qualified medical professionals have rendered an opinion of incompetence on the part of their patient;
- Whether there is evidence of a weakened mental state sufficient to establish that a person is not in a position to appreciate and assert his or her own legal rights.

As can be seen from the sampling of considerations above, it is not always necessary to demonstrate that an individual is totally devoid of mental ability. The core question asks whether the individual has the ability to understand the nature of his or her actions and the actions of others as they impact one's well being as well as the ability to assert and act in the best interest of one's own legal rights. If the answer to this question is negative and the case falls in a jurisdiction that tolls the statute of limitations for those lacking mental competence, then it is likely that the statute of limitations will be suspended from running until the disability designation has been removed.

CASE

265 Wis.2d 169, 665 N.W.2d 353, 2003 WI 120

Supreme Court of Wisconsin.

Sheri J. STORM, Tiffany J. Storm, by her guardian ad litem, William Smoler, and Justin S. Storm, by his guardian ad litem, William Smoler, Plaintiffs- et.al.
Appellants,
v.
LEGION INSURANCE COMPANY, Kenneth C. Olson, M.D., Joanne Cooper, Cooper Resource Center, Inc. and Wisconsin Patients Compensation Fund, Defendants-Respondents, et. al.
Decided July 18, 2003.

...The facts are taken from the summary judgment record. On January 22, 1990, Sheri Storm began receiving psychiatric treatment from Kenneth Olson, M.D. Doctor Olson provided periodic inpatient and outpatient treatment to Storm after that date. In early 1991, Dr. Olson diagnosed Storm as suffering from a multiple personality disorder, which is referred to in the psychiatric nomenclature as a dissociative identity disorder.

(continued)

The last day that Storm received treatment from Dr. Olson was August 3, 1992, at which time Olson moved his practice out of Wisconsin. Four days later, Storm applied for Supplemental Security Income (SSI) benefits related to her mental disability, for which she was eventually deemed eligible, retroactive to the date of her application. After August 3, Storm also received treatment from a social worker named Valerie Hamilton at the same offices where Dr. Olson had treated Storm. Hamilton had previously assisted Dr. Olson with some of Storm's treatment. The last session between Storm and Hamilton occurred on September 9, 1992. Shortly after Storm discontinued her visits to Hamilton, she briefly received treatment from two other mental health care providers, neither of whom is a subject of this action.

Near the end of 1992, Storm began receiving psychological treatment at the Cooper Resource Center (the CRC). On January 22, 1993, Dr. Joann Cooper, Ph.D., a psychologist who owns the CRC, evaluated Storm and diagnosed her as possessing a multiple personality disorder. In February 1993 Dr. Marcelo Castillo, a physician and the alleged medical director of the CRC at the time, allegedly admitted Storm for inpatient psychiatric treatment to be performed by Dr. Cooper. After Storm was discharged in March 1993, Cooper continued to treat Storm for her disorder on an outpatient basis until September 24, 1993. This was Storm's last day of any relevant involvement with the CRC and Doctors Cooper and Castillo.

On September 9, 1997, Storm filed a medical malpractice suit alleging, among other instances of malpractice, that Doctors Olson and Cooper negligently treated her by using hypnosis to recover memories of childhood sexual abuse that were later found to be untrue. According to Storm, these false memories formed the basis of a multiple personality disorder and caused her suffering. The complaint also named the CRC and Legion Insurance Company, Dr. Olson's professional liability insurer, as defendants. On June 14, 2000, while the case was still undergoing discovery, Storm filed an amended complaint naming Dr. Castillo as an additional defendant. Storm sought a variety of damages alleged to have resulted from the negligent care or supervision of the defendants.

11 Doctors Olson and Castillo each filed a motion for summary judgment in the fall of 2000, asserting that Storm's action was untimely filed under Wis. Stat. § 893.55(1). Section 893.55(1) prohibits the commencement of a medical malpractice action more than three years from the date of injury or one year from the date of discovery of an injury, whichever is later, but, with respect to discovery, an action may not be filed more than five years from the date of the act or omission giving rise to the alleged injury. Wis. Stat. § 893.55(1). Doctor Olson asserted that Storm was required to commence her action against him by either August 3, 1995, or, assuming that Storm did not discover her injury until on or after August 3, 1996, by August 3, 1997. Similarly, Dr. Castillo claimed that Storm had until either September 24, 1996, or September 24, 1998, to bring her claim against him.

Storm argued that the statute of repose in § 893.55(1)(b) applies only to the discovery rule of accrual in paragraph (b) and is inapplicable to the injury rule of accrual in paragraph (a), upon which she relies. She also contended that Wisconsin's disability tolling statute, § 893.16, applies to actions brought under § 893.55(1)(a) and that she was "mentally ill" at *179 the time her causes of action accrued. Therefore, adding the five-year maximum tolling period provided under § 893.16 for someone with a mental illness to the three-year limitations period in § 893.55(1)(a), Storm reasoned that she had until August 3, 2000, to bring her claim against Dr. Olson and until September 24, 2001, to bring suit against Dr. Castillo.

On February 15, 2001, the circuit court granted the defendants' summary judgment motions, determining that § 893.16 does not apply to medical malpractice actions and that Storm failed to commence her suit within either the three-year statute of limitation in § 893.55(1)(a) or the five-year statute of repose in § 893.55(1)(b). By a written judgment dated April 30, 2001, the court dismissed all claims against Dr. Olson, Legion Insurance, and Dr. Castillo. Storm appealed this decision and the court of appeals requested certification, which we granted.

(continued)

... Storm's medical malpractice claims are procedurally governed in large part by Chapter 655, while the time limitations for bringing her claims are circumscribed by § 893.55. To assess the appropriateness of the circuit court's grant of summary judgment, we are required to interpret § 893.55(1) and its interplay, if any, with § 893.16, which is the limitations tolling provision for persons under a disability, including the disability of mental illness. The fundamental goal of our statutory interpretation is to discern the intent of the legislature in drafting these provisions. *Landis v. Physicians Ins. Co. of Wis., Inc.,* 2001 WI 86, ¶ 14, 245 Wis.2d 1, 628 N.W.2d 893.

The parties' arguments on appeal track those made before the circuit court, as discussed above. Therefore, our inquiry requires four primary determinations.

First, we address whether the statute of repose in § 893.55(1)(b) applies to all medical malpractice actions, including those brought under § 893.55(1)(a), thereby barring a medical malpractice action from commencing more than five years after the last act or omission giving rise to the claim. Second, we look to whether the disability tolling statute, § 893.16, applies to the periods of limitation in § 893.55. Third, if § 893.16 does toll a limitations period for medical malpractice, we must define "mental illness" under the statute and the standard by which a court determines if a plaintiff is mentally ill and qualifies under the tolling provision. Finally, we address Dr. Castillo's argument that, however the foregoing matters are decided, Storm's disability ceased as a matter of law when she retained or utilized legal counsel.

A. Scope of the Statute of Repose in Wis. Stat. § 893.55(1)(b)

The time limitations for filing medical malpractice actions are provided in subsection (1) of § 893.55, which reads:

(1) Except as provided by subs. (2) and (3), an action to recover damages for injury arising from any treatment or operation performed by, or from any omission by, a person who is a health care provider, regardless of the theory on which the action is based, shall be commenced within the later of:

(a) Three years from the date of the injury, or

(b) One year from the date the injury was discovered or, in the exercise of reasonable diligence should have been discovered, except that an action may not be commenced under this paragraph more than 5 years from the date of the act or omission.

The parties dispute the preclusive effect of the five-year statute of repose in paragraph (b). In particular, Doctors Olson and Castillo contend that the repose period absolutely required Storm to file her action against Dr. Olson no later than August 3, 1997, and against Dr. Castillo no later than September 24, 1998 (five years, respectively, after each doctor ended his involvement with Storm).

We conclude under a plain reading of § 893.55(1)(b) that the five-year repose period applies only to actions brought pursuant to the discovery rule in paragraph (b). Paragraph (b) is an alternative limitations period. It permits a claimant, irrespective of the three-year limitations period for injury accrual in § 893.55(1)(a), to file a medical malpractice action up to "one year from the date the injury was discovered or, in the exercise of reasonable diligence should have been discovered." It then creates an exception, which states that "an action may not be commenced *under this paragraph* more than 5 years from the date of the act or omission." Wis. Stat. § 893.55(1)(b) (emphasis added). The term "paragraph" governs the scope of this five-year period of repose, which, as we have previously held, serves to bar medical malpractice actions even if a claimant has yet to discover a latent injury. *See Aicher v. Wis. Patients Comp. Fund,* 2000 WI 98, ¶ ¶ 26, 47, 237 Wis.2d 99, 613 N.W.2d 849.

... As we stated in *Czapinski v. St. Francis Hosp.,* 2000 WI 80, 236 Wis.2d 316, 613 N.W.2d 120, "A court will not ordinarily engage in statutory construction unless a statute is ambiguous. 'When a statute is plain and unambiguous, interpretation is unnecessary and intentions cannot be imputed to the legislature except those to be gathered from the terms of the statute itself.' " *Id.,* (citing and quoting *Harris v. Kelley,* 70 Wis.2d 242, 249, 234 N.W.2d 628 (1975)).

(continued)

The preceding interpretation of § 893.55(1) was signaled by this court in *Paul v. Skemp,* 242 Wis.2d 507, 625 N.W.2d 860. In *Paul,* we recognized the potential conflict between the periods of limitation and period of repose located in § 893.55(1), observing that "[t]he plain language of Wis. Stat. § 893.55(1) does not indicate whether the five-year statute of repose in § 893.55(1)(b) applies to actions governed by the injury rule of accrual in § 893.55(1)(a)." *Id.,* The court surmised that the statute of repose did not limit the injury rule of accrual and that:

> a medical malpractice action might be able to be timely filed more than five years after the act or omission under the injury rule of accrual where, for example, the injury occurs more than two years after the negligent act or omission and the action is filed within three years from the injury.

The *Paul* court ultimately decided the issue presented in that case on other grounds, determining that the actionable injury was not the physician's faulty diagnosis but instead was the date of the patient's death. *Id.,* While *Paul* did not settle the scope of the repose period in § 893.55(1)(b), its reasoning on this matter conforms with the understanding that we presently adopt.

Because the five-year statute of repose in § 893.55(1)(b) does not affect a plaintiff's ability to bring a claim under § 893.55(1)(a), Storm can rely solely upon § 893.55(1)(a) in determining the effective limitation periods within which she needed to bring her claims.

... Wisconsin Stat. § 893.16 permits a period of limitation in Chapter 893 to be extended for an additional five years if a claimant is mentally ill at the time a cause of action accrues. Wis. Stat. § 893.16(1), (3). Subsection (1) of § 893.16 provides in full:

> If a person entitled to bring an action is, at the time the cause of action accrues, either under the age of 18 years, except for actions against health care providers; or mentally ill, the action may be commenced within 2 years after the disability ceases, except that where the disability is due to mental illness, the period of limitation prescribed in this chapter may not be extended for more than 5 years.

Storm asserts that she was mentally ill at the time her causes of action accrued and, further, that she continued to be mentally ill until she filed her claims against all the defendants in this action. Therefore, she maintains, the time for her to file suit under § 893.55(1)(a) was extended up to five additional years by application of § 893.16. If this view is correct, Storm had three years from her injury to bring her action under § 893.55(1)(a), plus, by operation of § 893.16(1), an additional five years to bring her claims. As a result, she would have eight years from the date of any alleged injury to bring her action. This would mean she had until August 3, 2000 to file her action against Dr. Olson and September 24, 2001, to bring her claims against Dr. Castillo. Storm brought her action against Dr. Olson on September 9, 1997, and impleaded Dr. Castillo in this action on June 14, 2000--both events occurring less than eight years from when she contends the last negligent act or omission was undertaken by each of these defendants.

In determining whether §893.16 applies to any of the limitation periods in §893.55, we first observe the absence of any language in either statute that precludes them from operating in concert. To the contrary, language in §893.16 and in §893.56--which is a companion limitations statute to § 893.55--strongly indicates that they are meant to apply in tandem.

When the legislature revised and recreated Chapter 893 in 1979, the newly created disability tolling statute was expected to subject all limitation periods in the chapter to its provisions. This intention is manifested by the declaration that its tolling provision will affect the "period of limitation prescribed *in this chapter* " affecting a plaintiff's claim. Wis. Stat. §893.16(1) (emphasis added). Of course, "this chapter" is Chapter 893, where § 893.55 is located. This observation is especially important, because subsection (5) of §893.16 explicitly exempts certain limitations periods located within Chapter 893 from its tolling requirements. Subsection (5) reads, in its relevant portions:

> This section applies only to statutes in this chapter limiting the time for commencement of an action or assertion of a defense or counterclaim except it does not apply to: ....

(continued)

(b) Extend the time limited by s. 893.33 [actions concerning real estate], 893.41 [breach of contract to marry], 893.59 [damage to highway or railway grade], 893.62 [usury], 893.73 to 893.76 [certain actions against governments], 893.77(3) [municipal power district bonds], 893.86 [recovery of legal fees paid for indigents] or 893.91 [actions related to forest fires] or subch. VIII for commencement of an action or assertion of a defense or counterclaim[.]

As part of the overall structure of this statute, subsection (5) demonstrates that the legislature understood exactly how to enumerate those limitation periods in Chapter 893 that would not be affected by § 893.16. Section 893.55 is not one of those listed.

Moreover, when the legislature enacts a new statute, it is presumed to know the new statute's relationship with existing and contemporaneously created statutory provisions, especially those directly affecting the statute. *City of Milwaukee v. Kilgore,* 193 Wis.2d 168, 183-84, 532 N.W.2d 690 (1995). A disability tolling statute substantively equivalent to current § 893.16 existed at the time the legislature created §§ 893.55 and 893.56 Therefore, it is difficult to conceive how the legislature, fully aware of § 893.16's general applicability, would not have undertaken some overt action to exempt § 893.55 from the disability tolling provision, if it so intended.

The legislature has indicated an express intent to curtail the application of § 893.16 to medical malpractice actions with respect to minors. Section 893.16 excludes children under the age of 18 that are bringing actions against health care providers from the tolling provisions of the statute. Wis. Stat. § 893.16(1). The reason for this exclusion is that there is a specific statute for medical malpractice actions by minors. Wis. Stat. § 893.56. The grammatical structure of subsection (1) makes clear that any exception "for actions against health care providers" *does not* apply to the disability of mental illness. If such a result had been intended, it could have been easily accomplished. The exception for claims by minors against health care providers was added when § 893.56 was created. See Ch. 390, Laws of 1977. Hence, the exception for minors in § 893.16(1) creates symmetry between these two statutes--a correlation entirely absent between §§ 893.16 and 893.55.

Wisconsin Stat. § 893.56 provides insight for another reason. Its language demonstrates how the legislature contemplated that the disability tolling provisions of § 893.16(1) generally apply to medical malpractice claims. The immediate predecessor to section 893.56 was added in 1978, three years after Chapter 655 was created. See Ch. 37, Laws of 1975, & Ch. 390, Laws of 1977. The new statute was premised on a legislative finding that the number of suits and damages arising from medical malpractice actions commenced by minor claimants had "increased tremendously" and needed to be restrained. See § 1(a), ch. 390, Laws of 1977; *see also Aicher,* 237 Wis.2d 99, ¶ 22, 613 N.W.2d 849. Prior to this change, time limitations for medical malpractice suits brought on behalf of minors were governed by Wis. Stat. § 893.33 (1977), the relevant predecessor to § 893.16, which allowed claims until children were one year beyond the age of majority. See Wis. Stat. § 893.33(3) (1977).

Section 893.56 was created to *decrease* the time otherwise available to minors for bringing medical malpractice actions. However, the statute specifically exempts minors suffering under a disability by reason of mental illness from this new limitation. If § 893.16 did not, and does not, apply to medical malpractice cases, there would be no reason to create § 893.56 for purposes of limiting the time in which minors could bring an action and little reason to include the language regarding insanity. Moreover, if § 893.16 does not apply to claims against health care providers governed by §§ 893.55 and 893.56, then minors under the age of 10 who *are* insane would be governed by some unknown limitations period. This whole statutory context reveals that, for one specific class of people who are accorded filing extensions because of their "disability," namely, minors--the legislature consciously incorporated a provision that modified the tolling provision when they file medical malpractice actions. THE same cannot be said about the class of people disabled by mental illness.

Despite the foregoing analysis, Dr. Olson asserts that Chapter 655 exclusively governs medical malpractice claims and, therefore, § 893.16 must have no applicability. We believe that Dr. Olson overstates the

(continued)

exclusivity of Chapter 655 in the context of the disability tolling statute. Chapter 655 is not exclusive in the sense that it is a *comprehensive* set of procedural rules for medical malpractice claims. Numerous statutes, including civil procedure and discovery statutes, that are not located in Chapter 655 apply to claims brought for medical malpractice. *See Hoffman v. Memorial Hosp. of Iowa County,* 196 Wis.2d 505, 513-14, 538 N.W.2d 627 (Ct.App.1995). As one example, rules governing the service of a summons under Wis. Stat. § 801.02 apply to medical malpractice tort claims as they do to other civil actions In addition, the limitations periods in § 893.55(1)-(3) are nowhere mentioned or expressly incorporated by reference in Chapter 655. Section 893.55 supplements the procedures prescribed by Chapter 655.

The cases that Dr. Olson cites to support his exclusivity argument deal with issues of damages, which are matters that Chapter 655 and § 893.55 have expressly addressed by modifying the common law or other statutory law. For example, in *Rineck v. Johnson,* 155 Wis.2d 659, 456 N.W.2d 336 (1990), we stated that Chapter 655 "*modif[ies]* general civil law in instances where [it] speak[s] to a given subject." *Rineck,* 155 Wis.2d at 665, 456 N.W.2d 336. The court noted that Chapter 655 "expressly delineates the damages limitation imposed in medical malpractice actions," *id.,* superseding the more-restrictive limits found in Wisconsin's general wrongful death statute. *Rineck* stands for the proposition that if general statutory provisions *conflict with* Chapter 655, the latter will trump the general statute. Neither § 893.55 nor Chapter 655 includes any *tolling* provision that conflicts with § 893.16.

The defendants contend that the two exceptions to the limitation periods in § 893.55(1), namely, subsections (2) and (3of § 893.55] denote that the legislature did not intend to provide any additional exceptions, including those for persons disabled by mental illness. We do not find this contention persuasive. First, the exceptions granted in subsections (2) and (3) plainly relate to actions taken by a health care provider that obfuscate the availability of a claim. They have no relation to a patient's mental capacity to understand rights and file an action. They operate to extend the discovery rule in § 893.55(1)(b), not as tolling provisions.

Second, the legislature chose to place the periods of limitation for medical malpractice actions in Chapter 893, not in Chapter 655. It made this placement without expressing any intent that the tolling statute in § 893.16, which is written to apply to *all* periods of limitation in Chapter 893 unless expressly excluded by § 893.16(5), not apply to § 893.55

In sum, we conclude that the legislature intended for § 893.16 to toll the period of limitations in § 893.55(1)(a) for medical malpractice actions involving qualified claimants. Therefore, if Storm qualifies for a disability under § 893.16, she may extend the three-year limitations period up to five additional years.

In applying § 893.16 to medical malpractice actions, we must interpret the meaning of "mental illness" in § 893.16. The term is not defined in § 893.16 or anywhere else in Chapter 893 and, since it is capable of being understood by reasonably well-informed persons in more than one way, it is ambiguous. *See Landis,* 245 Wis.2d 1, ¶ 15, 628 N.W.2d 893. Therefore, the court must "ascertain the legislative intent from the language of the statute in relation to a number of extrinsic factors including the legislative object intended to be accomplished." *Reyes v. Greatway Ins. Co.,* 227 Wis.2d 357, 365, 597 N.W.2d 687 (1999) (citing *Kelley Co., Inc. v. Marquardt,* 172 Wis.2d 234, 248, 493 N.W.2d 68 (1992), and *Terry v. Mongin Ins. Agency,* 105 Wis.2d 575, 584, 314 N.W.2d 349 (1982)).

Storm suggests that "mental illness" in § 893.16(1) merely requires a diagnosis that a claimant suffers from a clinically recognized mental illness. She suggests that, since the other two disabilities to which § 893.16 has recently applied--imprisonment and minority (under 18 years of age)--do not require any functional incapacity to qualify under the statute, her undisputed clinical diagnosis of having a multiple personality disorder should mean that she is mentally ill under § 893.16.

We disagree that a professional diagnosis of a clinically recognized mental illness is sufficient to establish a mental illness for purposes of § 893.16. In other contexts in which a person's insanity affects legal rights and

(continued)

responsibilities, such as the insanity defense in a criminal case, the standard rule is that insanity is a legal term, not a medical standard. While we do not adopt the standard for insanity found in these other contexts, we agree that a statutory term requires a legal standard that may not be equivalent to a medical diagnosis. Likewise, the receipt of SSI benefits based on mental disability, which Storm has been qualified to receive since August 7, 1992, is not sufficient to prove mental illness under § 893.16. The disbursement of SSI benefits to someone who claims a mental impairment is based on whether the person is unable to engage in substantial gainful activity, including employment, for an extended period of time. *See* 42 U.S.C. § 1382c(a)(3)(A)-(B) (2000). It does not require that a person be unable to understand and act upon his or her legal rights. In fact, a person's act of applying for SSI benefits may be an indication that the person understands his or her legal rights.

We must therefore search for the meaning of the term "mental illness" through its common understanding and usage, along with the context and purpose of § 893.16. We note at the outset that, in 1998, the legislature replaced the terms "insanity" and "insane" with "mental illness" and "mentally ill" in § 893.16.1997 Wis. Act 133, § 37. However, we do not see that any substantive change was intended or accomplished by this revision. Therefore, for the purpose of interpreting § 893.16, we take these terms to be synonymous.

... Wisconsin statutes define insanity and mental illness in several places. Even though the statutory contexts in which these definitions occur are unrelated to §893.16, they provide some insight. The common denominator in these varying definitions of mental illness entails an evaluation or assessment of an individual's ability to function and to comprehend his or her actions. These definitions also reinforce the notion when "mental illness" is used in the statutes, it is a legal term of art not a medical standard.

If we combine these general, definitional understandings of insanity and mental illness with the legislative purpose of § 893.16, it is apparent that a mental illness under § 893.16 implicates a functional incapacitation. The definitions speak of a person's inability to function at an ordinary level of conduct in civil society. Meanwhile, § 893.16 serves to extend limitation periods for persons that have an actual or legal incapacity to bring a claim while they are under the disability recognized by the statute. *See Scott v. First State Ins. Co.*, 155 Wis.2d 608, 615, 456 N.W.2d 152 (1990); *Korth v. Am. Family Ins. Co* 115 Wis.2d 326, 332, 340 N.W.2d 494 (1983). It follows, therefore, that the disability must relate to one's inability to bring suit.

We hold, for purposes of § 893.16(1)'s tolling provision, that a "mental illness" is a mental condition that renders a person functionally unable to understand or appreciate the situation giving rise to the legal claim so that the person can assert legal rights or functionally unable to understand legal rights and appreciate the need to assert them. Each of the elements of this standard requires comment.

"Mental illness" under the statute is a seriously disabling mental condition. The condition may overlap developmental disability, but it is not congruent with developmental disability. *See* Wis. Stat. § 880.01(2). In addition, because "insanity" has been defined since statehood to include "idiots," the statute may include a person of such low intelligence and comprehension that the person is unable to appreciate and protect his or her interests. However, an impaired ability to assert legal rights resulting from aging is not sufficient to toll a statute of limitations; not because senility is always less incapacitating than mental illness, but because, historically, senility has not been equated with "insanity" or "mental illness." *Cf. Fiandaca v. Niehaus* 570 S.W.2d 714, 717 (Mo.Ct.App.1978) ("That a person is old, infirm, has a weakened mind, impaired mental capacities and is subject to influence and domination by her children does not establish that she is insane.").

A person is functionally unable to appreciate the situation giving rise to the legal claim when the person is unable to make a rational assessment of his or her own circumstances. If a person does not realize that he or she is delusional or mentally unstable or does not understand and appreciate that he or she has been wronged, the person cannot be expected to protect his or her interests. A person that is mentally ill may have a basic grasp of lawyers, lawsuits, and the legal process but not recognize that his or her own situation requires the invocation of legal rights.

(continued)

A person that is functionally unable to understand or appreciate the situation at issue will probably be unable to relate the situation to the need to assert legal rights. On the other hand, a person that is functionally unable to understand his or her legal rights may realize that something is amiss but be unable to relate the problem to a remedy in the law or be unable to reach out for assistance to assert legal rights. In short, the person's mental condition leads to an inability to bring suit.

The standard for mental illness that we articulate today is consistent with *Burnham v. Mitchell,* 34 Wis. 117, 135 (1874), which after more than 125 years is still the most relevant Wisconsin decision interpreting "insanity" for purposes of Wisconsin's disability tolling statute. *Burnham* involved a suit brought by the administrator of an estate to recover an amount due on a promissory note unpaid by a debtor of the decedent. *Id.* at 119. The debtor raised a statute of limitations defense. The estate replied that Wis. Stat. ch. 138, § 29 (1858), the progenitor of § 893.16, provided an extended time in which to file the claim because of the decedent's "insanity." The parties disputed the degree of "insanity" required for tolling to occur, with the debtor advocating a total loss of understanding and the estate arguing that the decedent need not have had a total deprivation of mind but rather an insufficient mental ability to know what he was doing and the nature of the act done. *Id.* at 120-21. The trial court granted an instruction along the lines advanced by the estate. *Id.* at 127.

In answering "what constitutes insanity within the sprit and meaning" of the tolling provision, *id.* at 134, the *Burnham* court approved the less-restrictive instruction given to the jury. *Id.* at 136. Our court approved inquiry into whether a person had become so enfeebled and disordered by disease that the person did not act rationally, did not recognize the obvious and ordinary relation of things, but acted without such understanding or from delusion or insane impulse. *Id.* at 135. The court added, "when the capacity to do a certain act is in issue, the question is whether or not the alleged insane person had sufficient mental ability to know what he was doing, and the nature of the act done." *Id.* If he did not, then the limitations statute was tolled during his insanity, which in Burnham's case ultimately lasted until his death. *Id.* at 137. In reaching this conclusion, the court alluded to an equivalency between the mental capacity requirements demanded by law to execute a will, to enter into a contract, or to otherwise transact business. *Id.* at 136-37.

Surprisingly, no Wisconsin appellate cases since *Burnham* appear to have addressed the issue of what degree of mental illness or insanity is required for someone to benefit from Wisconsin's disability tolling statute. We believe that, on balance, *Burnham* accurately described the nature of a mental illness that is required to toll limitations periods, and its holding that a total deprivation of mind is not required remains fully valid. The standard we describe above is an effort to restate and contemporize our understanding of *Burnham* in the context of the modern disability tolling statute.

... Having defined "mental illness" under Wis. Stat. § 893.16, we conclude that summary judgment on this question is inappropriate at the present time. This factual issue was not addressed by the circuit court, nor was it otherwise adequately developed in the record before this court. It is an issue yet to be decided by the fact-finder. Specifically, a functional analysis of Storm's illness must be undertaken to determine whether she was mentally ill under the meaning of § 893.16(1). In addition, any disability that qualifies under this standard must have existed when her cause of action accrued against each defendant. Wis. Stat. § 893. 16(3). Finally, she must also have remained mentally ill until at least two years before she filed each of her claims against each of the defendants. *See* Wis. Stat. § 893.16(1).

Regardless of how the foregoing issues are resolved, Dr. Castillo contends that Storm's disability ceased, as a matter of law, when she obtained legal counsel in April 1997 or no later than when she filed her initial complaint on September 9, 1997. The initial complaint failed to name Dr. Castillo. Doctor Castillo was not added as a defendant in the complaint until June 14, 2000. If Dr. Castillo's view were accepted, then § 893.16(1) required Storm to file her claims against Dr. Castillo within two years of September 9, 1997, at the latest, which she failed to do.

(continued)

Doctor Castillo's argument is premised on the notion that Storm had the necessary mental capacity to understand her legal rights as of the time that she hired an attorney to represent her and to investigate her claims. He suggests that allowing Storm's action to be deemed timely against him would be contrary to the purpose of § 893.16 and would be inequitable. Storm contends that while a mentally ill person's act of contacting an attorney to investigate a lawsuit may trigger a "discovery" after which a claim must be brought within a specified time, *see Awve v. Physicians Ins. Co. of Wis., Inc* 181 Wis.2d 815, 824, 512 N.W.2d 216 (Ct.App.1994), such as under § 893.55(1)(b), it does not alter a plaintiff's mental illness for purposes of § 893.16.

We conclude that the retention of legal counsel does not *automatically* cause a plaintiff's mental illness, as we have defined it, to cease for purposes of § 893.16. This would hold true even if the retained counsel filed some cause of action on behalf of the mentally ill client. However, we also conclude that such legal consultation and filing are probative of a plaintiff's mental health and functional ability to appreciate and act upon his or her legal rights.

We reject Dr. Castillo's bright-line rule on this issue for several reasons. First, the legislature has determined that mentally ill persons may extend the time within which to file their causes of action to a maximum of five additional years, so long as the disability continues. While the overarching purpose of § 893.16 is to ensure that rights are not lost because of a person's inability to comprehend or assert a claim, *Scott*, 155 Wis.2d at 615, 456 N.W.2d 152;*Korth*, 115 Wis.2d at 332, 340 N.W.2d 494, and the hiring of legal counsel evinces a degree of legal wherewithal, a mentally ill person may acquire legal representation through means unrelated to an ability to appreciate or act upon his or her rights. We can envision instances in which a client's mental illness could significantly hinder his or her ability to assist retained counsel in timely filing a claim or naming all defendants.

Second, under Dr. Castillo's view, the retention of an attorney would cause a mentally ill person to lose the ability to raise claims at an earlier time than if counsel had not been retained. It is not sound policy to devise a rule whereby newly retained legal counsel for a mentally ill person must rush to review *all* possible claims held by the disabled plaintiff--no matter how distant in time or distant in subject matter the claims are from the claims inspiring the attorney's retention--simply to avoid being cut off. Although the facts of this case involve a claim closely related to those for which counsel was hired, Dr. Castillo's proffered rule would not be limited to such a circumstance.

... Overall, an attorney's appreciation of legal rights and competency in bringing legal claims cannot be applied vicariously to a mentally ill client for purposes of timely filing actions. There may be situations in which a mentally ill plaintiff is unable to assist his or her attorney in the same manner as a sane personTherefore, absent anything in the tolling statute to the contrary, we do not find that the retention of legal counsel by itself ends a person's mental illness under § 893.16 as a matter of law.

Even if the retention of counsel does not mark the end of the disability, Dr. Castillo maintains that Storm's disability must have ceased in this case when her legal counsel filed an action on her behalf. He argues that when Storm's counsel filed suit against the other defendants in this action on September 9, 1997, she faced no impediment in asserting her legal rights and that she had all the information necessary to pursue additional claims against Dr. Castillo. We agree that, under these circumstances, any fears that newly retained legal counsel will be obligated to review *all* legal claims of the mentally ill person they represent are diminished. In this case, the claims that Storm could be deemed "capable" of advancing against Dr. Castillo *were directly related to* the reason that counsel was retained.

However, the filing of a lawsuit in behalf of a mentally ill person does not invariably establish a plaintiff's capacity to understand and act upon his or her legal rights. Nor is such a finding appropriate as a matter of law in this case. Rather, we believe that when an attorney acts on a plaintiff's behalf, as in filing a lawsuit, such an occurrence serves as one of the many possible indicia that the plaintiff's actual mental state is sufficient to appreciate the availability of her legal rights and her means of legal recourse. *See generally*

(continued)

Bestwina v. Village Bank, 235 Mont. 329, 767 P.2d 338, 340 (1989) ("Retention of counsel is evidence, although not conclusive, of a person's legal capacity for purposes of tolling the statute of limitations.") (citing cases). It is for the trier of fact to determine if, under the circumstances of each case, such activity does or does not exhibit the requisite level of mental health.

Therefore, as part of our remand to determine whether Storm possessed a mental illness that made her unable to understand and act upon her legal rights, her activity regarding the hiring and use of legal counsel may serve as evidence of her mental capabilities, but it will not alone be dispositive.

Based on the foregoing reasons, we conclude that the five-year statute of repose in Wis. Stat. § 893.55(1)(b) does not apply to the injury accrual rule in § 893.55(1)(a). In addition, the tolling provision in § 893.16 may operate to extend the time for filing a medical malpractice action beyond the three-year period in paragraph (a), provided that a factual finding is made that the person was mentally ill at the time her causes of action accrued. This finding of "mental illness" requires that the person possess a mental condition that renders her functionally unable to understand or appreciate the situation giving rise to the legal claim so that she can assert legal rights or functionally unable to understand legal rights and appreciate the need to assert them. We also hold that retention of legal counsel by a mentally ill person does not, as a matter of law, cause that person's mental illness to cease for purposes of § 893.16.

Applying these principles, we reverse the circuit court's grant of summary judgment and dismissal of Dr. Olson, Legion Insurance, and Dr. Castillo from this action. We remand this action to the circuit court for factual determinations regarding Sheri Storm's mental health on the dates relevant to her use of Wis. Stat. § 893.16. If Storm was mentally ill at the time her causes of action accrued against each defendant, and if her illness did not cease at a time more than two years before she filed a claim against any of the individual defendants, then Storm timely filed her claims alleging medical malpractice against Doctors Olson and Castillo.

The judgment of the circuit court is reversed and the cause is remanded.

APPLICATION 6.3

Brooke was 21 years old and had just started her senior year in college when she was shot and raped and her entire family was murdered in their home during a robbery. She was the only survivor and had no living relatives. During initial treatment for her injuries and during transport the ambulance attendants committed alleged malpractice. Immediately after the incident and her release from the hospital she was transferred to a mental health facility where she remained in a catatonic state for more than two years. Slowly she began to interact with others but still frequently had episodes best described as hysterical outbursts whenever she encountered the slightest stress. She eventually recovered and was discharged from the mental health facility. Approximately three years after the incident she sought legal counsel regarding the malpractice claim. A case was filed. However, the statute of limitations for medical malpractice in the jurisdiction was two years. In this situation, it is very likely that Brooke would be considered mentally incompetent, at the very least, for the period she was catatonic. Beyond that, all the factors of her recovery would need to be considered before it could be established when her disability designation was removed and the statute of limitations began to run.

ASSIGNMENT 6.2

In the following situations, explain when the statute of limitations expired assuming the following statutory language applies:

"An action alleging medical malpractice shall be commenced within one year of the alleged wrongful conduct or the reasonable discovery of the basis for a cause of action by plaintiff, whichever is later. In no event shall an action be commenced beyond a period of five years from the act complained of."

Assume also that the doctrines of fraudulent concealment and continued treatment are recognized by the jurisdiction. With respect to minors, the following statutory language applies:

"A minor entitled to make an allegation of medical malpractice shall bring such action within two years of the occurrence giving rise to the allegation of malpractice or by the minor's thirteenth birthday, whichever is later.

1. On his birthday, July 21, 2001, 9-year-old Mathias was riding his new bike when he was struck by a car. During treatment of his injuries the doctors set his broken leg. The fracture did not heal properly and Mathias is now crippled. It was apparent when the cast was removed at a doctor's appointment on September 25, 2001, that there was an improper healing.

2. Josie was 14 years old when she began to receive counseling from a licensed psychologist. On March 1, 2002, while still 14, Josie became pregnant and confided this information to the psychologist who recommended she undergo an abortion and not tell her parents of her situation. Following these instructions, Josie obtained an abortion from an unlicensed individual and suffered serious physical complications resulting in her inability to ever bear children. Josie and her parents intend to sue the psychologist.

3. Lark is 11 years old. On January 10, 2000, she suffers a back injury during a gymnastics class. The parent of another student is a chiropractor and offers to assist Lark. The chiropractor is manipulating Lark's back when her legs go numb. She is later found to have suffered a spinal cord injury and is paralyzed from the shoulders down. Lark wishes to sue the chiropractor who treated her during the gymnastics class.

4. Boyd is swinging upside down by his knees on a playground jungle gym when he falls to the ground. When he strikes the ground he bites through his tongue. His mother contacts their family physician who instructs her that the tongue will heal on its own just as quickly as if it were sutured. She does not bring Boyd to the hospital or the doctor's office. Ten days later Boyd has a foul odor coming from his mouth, which indicates a sign of infection. She takes him to the hospital where it is discovered the infection is so far advanced, a large of part of Boyd's tongue must be removed. The initial injury and phone call to the doctor occurred on May 29, 2003, when Boyd was 10 years old. His birthday is June 2. Boyd wishes to sue the doctor whom his mother called on the day of the accident.

5. On August 1, 2003, 10-year-old Mikala goes to see a dentist for a routine cleaning. The dentist states that Mikala's two front teeth are her baby teeth and should be removed to encourage the adult teeth to come in. He pulls the teeth without first taking X rays. Approximately nine months later on May 9, 2004, Mikala returns to the dentist because the permanent teeth have not yet begun to come in. At this time he does X rays and finds that no permanent teeth have ever developed in this location. Mikala wants to sue the dentist for removing her only front teeth without first completing X rays to determine that other teeth were present.

> **Problem 6.1**
>
> Complete 6.1 of the Comprehensive Problem in Appendix A.

CHAPTER SUMMARY

Limitation of actions statutes can put an end to even the most warranted action for medical malpractice. The rationale behind all statutes of limitation is the same. Defendants should not be subject to indefinite and unknown risk of liability while evidence deteriorates to the point that the other party has an unfair advantage. The dramatic increase in professional liability insurance as the result—at least in part—from the increase in medical malpractice suits has caused a number of states to employ statutory measures to bring the situation under control. With regard to limitation of actions, the response of legislatures has been to severely curtail the window of opportunity for plaintiffs to discover and pursue cases of medical malpractice. From the perspective of the legislatures, plaintiffs have a certain amount of responsibility to ascertain in a timely manner if their legal rights have been compromised. The exception to this rule, of course, is when there is evidence the defendants deliberately concealed information from the plaintiffs which would have reasonably led to the discovery of the malpractice.

An additional consideration of the legislatures in placing limitations on the time frame for bringing suit deals with those who are not in a position to protect their own best interests. With respect to minors, many jurisdictions have enacted statutes of limitation in such cases, but they are often longer than those allowed for adults. The rationale is that even though injuries to children who are still in developing stages may not be as readily visible as in adults, the adults are responsible for the children and should protect their rights as they would their own as soon as injuries are reasonably discernible. Other states have left the original theory intact with respect to minors, and the time for their cause of action does not begin to run until they have reached majority through age or emancipation.

Last, the question of mental incompetence is one that has largely been left alone by legislatures. Unlike minors who generally have an adult who is legally responsible for their care and protection of their rights, this is not always the case with those who are mentally incompetent to act in their own best interest regardless of age. Consequently, in most jurisdictions it is still the law that those who provide health care to individuals who have strong evidence of mental incompetence are at risk for malpractice actions until such time as competence in the individual is restored.

Two key points to keep in mind with respect to statutes of limitations: Do malpractice laws apply to the circumstance? If so, determine if there are special statutory limitation of action provisions in place within the jurisdiction. What are the applicable statutes of limitation if malpractice laws do not apply? Finally, consider whether any special circumstances exist, including, but not limited to, fraudulent concealment by the provider, minority of the plaintiff, and lack of mental competence. Any of these can affect the limitation period.

Key Terms

discovery rule
fraudulent concealment
mental competence
minority
limitation of actions

End Notes

[1]Piselli v. 75th Street Medical, 808 A.2d 508 (Md 2002).

 For additional resources, go to http://www.westlegalstudies.com.

CHAPTER 7

Investigation of the Claim by the Potential Plaintiff

CHAPTER OBJECTIVES

When you complete this chapter, you should be able to:

- Determine the legal causal relationship between the alleged malpractice and injury
- Prepare a comprehensive plan to identify, locate and contact relevant witnesses
- Conduct a proper witness interview
- Evaluate the general liability of a claim of medical malpractice

ESTABLISHING THE CAUSE OF THE INJURY

Claims of medical malpractice originate with a perceived injury. Typically, in the case of a plaintiff, a client will seek legal counsel to determine whether there is a viable case. From a defense perspective, an incident may be acknowledged by the health care provider. It is then reported to the appropriate insurance or risk management officer to consider the potential for litigation. Regardless of the side from which the case is approached, the first step is to determine the complete nature and extent of the alleged injury. The next step is to establish whether the cause of the injury is the result of professional malfeasance or simply a less-than-desired result by the patient, but one which was a disclosed risk and which falls within the normal parameters of medical care, treatment, or services. The last step, as a practical matter, is to establish whether the injury is significant enough to warrant the expense of litigation and support the likelihood of a judgment that would result in compensation to the plaintiff.

From the plaintiff's side, the preliminary **investigation** into a claim of medical malpractice requires an extensive interview with the client. It is important to gather as much information as possible at this stage in order to facilitate a thorough examination of the claim and collection of the information necessary to properly evaluate the viability of a legal action. A key consideration in all legal actions is the cost of litigation. Many more cases are evaluated than ever filed, which emphasizes the importance of conducting the investigation and evaluation of a claim of alleged malpractice as efficiently as possible. For the plaintiff's counsel and support staff, this requires obtaining sufficient initial information from the client to fully explore the claim. Ultimately, the evaluation by either side will determine whether there is adequate evidence to support each element of the cause of action that must be proven in order to prevail at a trial. The goal from the outset is to gather all information, both positive and adverse, that is pertinent to the final burden of proof.

> **APPLICATION 7.1**
>
> Mark comes to a local attorney and claims that a physician treating Mark after a motorcycle accident committed malpractice. Mark alleges that the doctor performed surgery on Mark's broken leg and, as a result of the surgery, he now walks with a pronounced limp. An extensive interview with Mark reveals that he had broken the same leg previously. It also comes out during the interview that Mark had to have his cast replaced because it was damaged from his walking on it despite the doctor's instructions that he use crutches and keep the leg elevated for the first three weeks after surgery.
>
> This additional information does not negate malpractice by the physician. However, it does send up an alert that there may be additional issues such as a preexisting condition and Mark's own contributory negligence that may play a role in a claim of malpractice.

What follows is a sample interview questionnaire for an initial meeting with a medical malpractice client. It collects the information necessary to open a case file for the client, basic background and contact information, and a variety of questions designed to elicit information that may be relevant to a claim of malpractice. A key component is to obtain identifying information about anyone who might later serve as a witness or defendant. It is always important to remember when using forms such as these that the forms are merely guides and tools to control the flow of the interview and investigation. But equally important is the ability and willingness of the researcher, whether a paralegal, attorney, legal investigator or risk manager, to expand on questions that develop information relevant to the case. The parties being interviewed should always be clearly reminded that an essential part of the process is to be as accurate and complete as possible when answering questions. Without total candor, it is impossible to make an accurate assessment of the viability of the claim.

Following the initial gathering of information and the identity of persons who may have relevant knowledge, the investigation begins in earnest. This is a different component of the litigation process from discovery. Discovery is the exchange of information between parties and their witnesses following commencement of the formal lawsuit or statutory proceedings in a jurisdiction with a medical malpractice statute that affects discovery. During discovery, the parties comply with court rules of procedure and respond to requests for access to information about the evidence of the case. More about this will be discussed in the chapter that addresses the discovery process. The investigation process begins as a tool to assist the plaintiff or defendant in evaluating the claim, prior to any formal initiation of a claim of medical malpractice.

During investigation, a party, or their representative, collects as much information as available about the case. It is important that the investigation be as complete and accurate as possible. For example, a mistake as simple as a lawsuit that is brought against a provider identifying the provider by a commonly known name, such as a shortened name or nickname, rather than the true legal name of the provider in legal documents can cause the complaint or petition to be dismissed almost immediately. In most cases this error can be corrected and the case refiled, but it can result in a delay of the progression of the case. If many such avoidable mistakes are made, the time frame of the case and expense to both parties can rapidly increase. Exhibit 7.1 is a limited sample of questions that might be asked during an initial interview.

Exhibit 7.1   Client Interview Checklist

SAMPLE CLIENT INTERVIEW
CLIENT INTERVIEW
MEDICAL MALPRACTICE

(attach additional sheets where necessary to obtain complete information)
Plaintiff's full legal name _____
Current mailing address (and residence if different) _____
E-mail address _____
Phone numbers: home _____; work _____; cellular/pager _____
Best times to reach plaintiff _____
Alternate name/phone contact _____
Social Security number _____ Age ____ Date of Birth _____
Educational background _____
Employment history (occupation, employer prior 10 years) _____
Marital status _____ Full Name of Spouse _____
Name, age, date of birth of dependents _____

General health history and status _____

Insurance coverage current and at time of incident (company and policy number)

Reason plaintiff believes that a claim may exist against defendant

Whether any health care provider has advised plaintiff that any errors occurred in the course of medical treatment (name, professional occupation, address, date)

Whether plaintiff has previously consulted any other attorneys regarding this matter (name, date, recommendations, status of attorney/client relationship) _____
Plaintiff's prior claims and total litigation history (parties; nature of case, date, jurisdiction, attorney; outcome)

Plaintiff's preinjury general health condition and complaints immediately prior to injury _____

Health care providers for 10 years prior to injury (name, address, dates/nature of treatment or consultation ____

Hospitalizations for 10 years prior to injury (name, address, dates/nature of treatment) _____

Any other ongoing treatment for any other condition for 10 years prior to injury _____

Activities, if any, in which plaintiff was limited prior to injury, and reason for limitation _____

(continued)

Exhibit 7.1, continued

History of employment related to injuries or physical limitations _____

Any physical examinations for any reason within last 10 years (e.g. insurance, employment) (date, reason, examiner) _____

Manner in which plaintiff's injury occurred:
When and where did plaintiff first seek medical treatment from provider for condition that resulted in injury _____

Description of testing and treatment for condition prior to injury _____

Was plaintiff compliant with all instructions by provider _____
When and how was plaintiff first aware of injury _____

Description of what occurred to cause injury _____

Is this description from plaintiff's own memory or an account supplied to plaintiff by others. If not plaintiff's own recollection, name sources of that information _____

Witnesses to incident causing injury (name/description of all persons with knowledge) _____

Explanations given by by provider to plaintiff regarding injury _____

Once aware of injury by provider, did plaintiff report or discuss with provider or others, and if so, when and to whom _____
Testing and treatment description, dates and identity of providers with whom plaintiff has treated or consulted as a result of injury _____

Complaints plaintiff reported to each provider with whom plaintiff has consulted regarding injury _____

Medical expenses incurred (name, address, dates of service, amounts) _____

Future treatment anticipated _____

"Before and after" self-description:

Plaintiff's description of charges attributable to injury [note that the list below is representative, but not exhaustive, of questions that may be asked of a plaintiff]. For each, provide description in plaintiff's words, approximate dates, and extent (e.g., mild, moderate, severe, incapacitating)

(continued)

Exhibit 7.1, continued

Increased/Diminished (state which with a + or -):
-- Fatigue
-- Memory
-- Disinhibition
-- Frustration level
-- Pain/swelling/stiffness (specify)
-- Other
-- Ability to perform routine tasks (e.g., work, leisure, housekeeping, hobbies)
-- pain
-- Depression
-- Emotional outbursts
-- Sexual interest/ability
-- Attention; ability to concentrate
-- Comprehension
-- Mobility
-- Change in employment performance (documented)
-- Scarring/disfigurement/change in appearance

Documents from plaintiff:
(Obtain necessary written releases for the following documents plaintiff does not possess):

Written statements from defendant relevant to incident causing plaintiff's injury
Copies of plaintiff's medical records and treatment-related medical bills, or authorizations to obtain such records
Employment/school records
Experts' reports, if any, describing defendant's deviation from standard of care and extent of plaintiff's damages

MEDICAL EXPENSES
For each of the following, state the amount paid, who was paid, and who paid the bill (obtain copies if not in plaintiff's possession):
.. Doctors _____
.. Hospitals _____
.. Nurses _____
.. Medicines _____
.. Surgical apparatus _____
.. Ambulance _____
..Assistive Devices (crutches, cane, special equipment) _____

LOSS OF EARNINGS, GENERALLY (if applicable)
1. Name of employer at time of accident? _____
2. Describe duties. _____
3. Length of time employed there? _____
4. Education and possibility of advancement? _____
5. Amount of wages? _____
6. When did you return to work? _____
7. Duration of absence from work? _____

(continued)

Exhibit 7.1, continued

8. Total loss of wages. _____
9. Were wages paid during absence? _____
10. Did you receive worker's compensation benefits? Sick benefits? Unemployment insurance? _____
_____
11. Was substitute hired? Who? _____
12. Employment since accident? _____
13. Present duties. _____
14. Present wages. Amount of income reported for tax purposes? _____
_____

LOSS OF EARNINGS, IF OWN BUSINESS OR PROFESSION
1. Duties? _____
2. Amount of time devoted to business? _____
3. Reasonable value of service? _____
4. Length of time absent from business due to accident? _____
5. Cost of hiring substitute? _____
6. Average income? _____

IDENTIFICATION OF ALL PERSONS CONNECTED TO THE INJURY IN A PROFESSIONAL CAPACITY

During the initial client interview, information may be obtained regarding the identity of the actual provider who was in charge of providing treatment. However, there are frequently many other individuals involved in the care of the patient who have relevant knowledge with respect to the details of the client's case, as well as the provider's general abilities, credentials, and professional history.

Once it is determined there is a meritorious case and legal proceedings have begun, the discovery process is a valuable tool to glean the identity and extent of knowledge of all relevant witnesses. Prior to this, many of these individuals can, at the very least, be identified through proper investigation. It is important to obtain as many names and addresses of all family, friends, and professional contacts of the plaintiff who might have any knowledge regarding the case. These people may be co-workers who've observed the effects of a plaintiff's injury, a family member or friend who observed a plaintiff's care and treatment by medical staff, or anyone else with pertinent information. Often these are the most supportive and friendly witnesses to the plaintiff and they may have observed or heard things the plaintiff did not. Any friends or family members who were present around the time of, or following, the injury may be able to further identify health care professionals connected with the plaintiff's care. This might include other professionals, support staff, even clerical personnel in some cases. Regarding the provider, all records should be scoured for reference to individuals connected to the provider or the plaintiff who might have relevant information.

Exhibit 7.2   Investigative Data Collection

INVESTIGATIVE DATA COLLECTION

Objective	Method/Source
General Facts	Client Interview
Specific Facts	Client/Witness Interviews Medical/Provider Records 　Healthcare 　Incident Reports 　Equipment Maintenance
Witness Identity	Client/Witness Interview Medical/Provider Records 　Healthcare 　Incident Reports 　Equipment Maintenance Insurance/Billing Records
Evidence to Support Allegations	Client/Witness Interview Medical/Provider Records 　Healthcare 　Incident Reports 　Equipment Maintenance Insurance/Billing Records

After potential witnesses and defendants have been identified by the plaintiff, other sources of information should be explored. This can be accomplished through the review of patient records and any documentation the patient may have from the provider that includes reference to others (appointment cards, signatures or initials on billing documents, receipts, etc.). A check by the plaintiff of government records regarding the business organization may provide the proper designation of the business and possibly a registered agent to whom legal documents should be directed. These avenues will be discussed in greater detail later. At this early stage, the goal is to obtain identifying information from as many individuals as possible connected to the case.

Below is a list of possible resources to consult when attempting to identify individuals who may be potential defendants or witnesses, and a basic description of the common content for each.

- medical records
- records for patient from primary health care provider in the case

- records from all other health care providers independent of the primary who provided services at time of injury or following
- laboratory records
- testing records (e.g., X rays, CT scans, MRI reports)
- rehabilitation records (e.g., physical or occupational therapy)
- pharmaceutical records
- billing records
- insurance records, including but not limited to, explanation of benefits statements provided by insurance regarding payment.

Whether the information is provided by plaintiff, family or friends or through medical records, the same basic information should be initially collected for each potential witness:

- name
- job title or occupation
- address
- phone number
- relationship to plaintiff/case including a brief description of involvement/knowledge including dates.

In the case of a combination of several circumstances coming together to create a case for malpractice, each of the providers involved is a potential defendant. It is important to identify all defendants when the proceedings begin. Attempting to add defendants once a case has begun can raise a variety of procedural issues that could result in dismissal. Failure to include a defendant who played a critical role could jeopardize the case against other defendants if it is determined they were individually not the proximate cause of the injury.

In many cases, even the most prominent provider in a chain of staff members may not be the proper party to name as a defendant. A provider may be part of a corporation, partnership or other business organization that, for legal purposes, acts as the actual entity providing services. In that instance, it may be necessary to identify and name the business organization as the defendant in addition to the individual provider.

During the identification of health care professionals connected to a claim of alleged malpractice, those who are identified fall into either the category of potential defendant or potential witness. In today's scene of complicated medical treatment and procedures, it is likely that a patient will be in contact with any number of health care providers. While all may have information to contribute, a defendant bears responsibility and, potentially, legal liability for the plaintiff's injuries. Thus the distinction of witness or defendant is an important one. As a general rule, individuals are only responsible for their own negligence. In a simple case the same may be true in a lawsuit based on medical malpractice. But for injuries that occur during delivery of professional services, it is also quite common to base liability on the responsibility for the acts of employees or agents who are ultimately under the primary provider's direction or control.

Stated in simple terms, the legal theory of respondeat superior imposes liability on a principal for the tortious acts of an agent or employee who is acting within the scope of their employment at the time the alleged injury is caused. In the case of a business organization, the entity as a whole may be responsible for the acts of the providers even if they also jointly own the entity. In other circumstances, an organization or provider may be accountable for the acts of a subordinate employee. Many early cases of malpractice were brought against hospitals for the acts of physicians and their staff members if the injury occurred within the confines of the hospital. However, medical facilities were quick to respond by clearly establishing all non-regular employees as independent contractors through contractual agreements and stated policies. As independent contractors, the providers are not under the actual control of the facility and as such are responsible for their own actions. But, even contracts and stated policies will not prevent the theory of respondeat superior from being applied if the actual evidence demonstrates that the provider did not exercise independent judgment in the delivery of services and instead, carried out the direction of the facility staff.

Once the potential witnesses and defendants are identified, it is necessary to establish their role in producing the injury, and their place in the organization of providers. After this is accomplished, it can be determined who are the most appropriate parties to be named as defendants in the action. The remaining individuals can be considered as witnesses either for the plaintiff's case or the defense.

INTERVIEWING POTENTIAL WITNESSES

Once individuals with relevant knowledge have been identified, the next step is to begin developing evidence that will eventually support the case. Regardless of whether the witness is consulted by the plaintiff or defense, the primary objective remains the same: to determine the exact nature and extent of the witnesses' knowledge, and evaluate their credibility in the event they are needed to provide sworn testimony. For reasons of efficiency, cost control, witness availability, and to avoid the argument that a witness was "coached" regarding their testimony, it is important to follow certain basic guidelines when interviewing a witness. Following some basic and simple steps can result in an effective and complete interview.

There are several schools of thought regarding the proper physical environment for interviewing legal witnesses. Entire books have been authored on the interview process and setting. Some would argue an arrangement establishing an atmosphere of authority or "turf" is important. Others argue that a friendly and open area assures open dialogue. Wherever the interview takes place, the atmosphere should encourage open and forthright communication and be free from distractions or interruption. As a general rule, but especially in the event an employee of a potential defendant is being interviewed, be aware that the individual may be less inhibited somewhere other than the usual workplace where they may perceive a sense or a pressure from superiors to respond in a specific way, or only communicate positive information about their employer's position. Public places should generally be avoided as interview locations because they do not communicate a sense that the information is confidential and thus may inhibit witnesses from full disclosure.

Once the location for the interview is established, other preparatory steps should be taken. The interviewer should always be prepared for the specific type of interview planned. It is important to have a working knowledge of the facts of the case as they exist thus far. As a result, it is important to review whatever documents and notes have been prepared in the file to this point. It is also important, under the circumstances, to obtain as much background information about the interviewee as possible. While in most cases it is probably not necessary or cost effective to hire a private investigator to prepare a report on the interviewee, it can be helpful to make note of whatever historical information is readily available about the witness prior to the interview.

APPLICATION 7.2

Brenda is the client in a medical malpractice case against a local hospital. During her initial client interview, she identified Marianne Newsly as one of several nurses who attended Brenda during her hospitalization. The notes from Brenda's interview indicate "very friendly" by Marianne's name. Prior to asking Marianne for an interview, Brenda is contacted and asked why she described Marianne in particular as "very friendly." Brenda discloses that Marianne had shared with Brenda her plans to quit at the hospital and accept another job because she could no longer put up with some of the practices at the hospital which she felt endangered patients.

This information would be extraordinarily useful to an interviewer in exploring Marianne's knowledge of unsafe hospital practices and other potential witnesses willing to testify about them.

In addition to reviewing the file and gathering information about the witness, there are also additional preparatory steps to be taken. In order to conduct a thorough interview in an efficient manner, it is necessary to properly prepare the subjects of discussion. Prior to the interview of a witness, an outline of the subject matter should be arranged. The outline should set out language that can be used to guide the entire interview in a logical progression. This will help ensure that all of the important areas are addressed and the potential testimony of the witness is fully developed and revealed.

While an outline is essential to guide the overall tone and depth of the interview, specific questions are also a helpful tool to keep the interview on track and create opportunity for further questions based on the answers received. A list of preliminary questions for each subject area of the interview will help ensure a complete result.

In summary, the preparatory stage for the interview encompasses the following:

- Determine the best physical setting and arrangement for the particular interview;
- Review the case file including any relevant documents, notes, prior interviews, etc.;
- Gather available information about the witness to be interviewed;
- Prepare a complete outline of the subject areas to be addressed and arrange them in a logical sequence;
- Compose several questions for each of the subject areas within the outline to assist in developing further questions during the interview.

Once all of the preparations are complete, a successful interview process can begin. Certain key elements create an atmosphere that will define the outcome of the interview. As mentioned earlier, the setting should, of course, be determined prior to the interview. A witness who arrives for an interview and is shuffled from place to place or asked to wait while space can be created in a cluttered office will likely have a negative first impression. This can start the interview process with the idea that the witness is unimportant and possibly even an afterthought. If this interviewee's testimony is considered valuable and necessary to contribute to the case, and the interview is warranted, creating a proper and inviting setting for the interview process will provide the incentive for the witness to be helpful.

Once the witness is seated in the appropriate setting, the interview itself can begin. First and foremost, a professional attitude by the interviewer should always be maintained. This includes the appearance of the interviewer as well as the general tone of the interview. A slovenly or unkempt appearance of the interviewer or their office space sends a strong unspoken message. It is essential that the tone of the interview be one that establishes the interviewer as a consummate professional who is confident and in control of the situation. This should be balanced with genuine interest and respect for the witness. The language and questions of the interviewer should remain at a professional level without being condescending, authoritative, or judgmental. The average individual has very little contact with the legal system over a lifetime. This is combined with the often negative treatment to witnesses in the media (such as courtroom dramas on television). It is understandable that many people are nervous, even uncomfortable, when speaking with legal professionals. The more that can be done to assuage any fears or concerns, the more likely the witness is to fully disclose the information that is sought. A key objective is to reassure the witness that he or she is attending an interview and not an interrogation.

In the process of the discourse, it is extremely important that the interviewer communicate only details about the case that are necessary for the interview. The goal is to find out what the witness knows or can confirm rather than to provide them with information. The risk is that a witness who is given information may then assimilate it into his or her own recollection. Even though this is something that can occur in a totally innocent and unconscious manner, it is possible for a skilled cross-examiner to totally discredit such a witness's entire testimony under oath as having been coached. Also, discussion of the specifics of interviews with other witnesses or defendants should be avoided. It is important to get the independent observations of every witness rather than to supply them with information that might alter their own testimony. Providing information or discussing the facts of another person's recollections would leave the witness's credibility regarding his or her own personal recollection of the facts of the case open to question. It is perfectly acceptable to review with the witness certain nonprivileged documents pertaining to the case to gain a different view, but avoid disclosing evidence or the opinions of others regarding the facts of the case.

To open the interview, it is often helpful to gather some basic personal information in a friendly and nonthreatening manner. This "small talk" approach can be used to convey interest in the witness and what he or she has to offer. A fundamental quality of human nature is that people like to be liked. Asking non-invasive questions can be a way to make him or her feel more comfortable and prepared for more involved questions. Examples of such preliminary questions may be to inquire in a relaxed manner about the individual's employment background including educational level, types of jobs they've held, where they are from, etc. Even a reluctance by the witness to discuss such basic matters has value because it conveys a potential reluctance to discuss more important issues in the case which could translate into difficulty as a witness in a deposition or on the stand at a trial. Consideration of this portion of the interview can give a great deal of insight into how well the witness would likely fare in a testimonial situation subject to the stresses of a courtroom and/or cross-examination.

APPLICATION 7.3

Margaret is a kindergarten teacher. She also volunteers at a local hospital during the summer. She was volunteering at the hospital on June 18, 2003. When she went into a patient's room to deliver flowers, she found the alarm sounding on some medical equipment. She found the patient had died and immediately went in search of medical personnel. She found the nurses in the lounge celebrating the birthday of a co-worker. The

(continued)

> nurse's station had been unattended for several minutes when the alarm would have registered. A malpractice case has been filed by the deceased patient's family and Margaret is the key witness.
>
> At the initial interview, the paralegal asks Margaret for her name and place of employment. Approximately 10 minutes later the paralegal regains control of the interview. In the interim, despite several attempts by the paralegal to interrupt, Margaret has detailed her entire educational and teaching background as well as a thorough description of her current class of students. This type of individual could prove to be devastating on the witness stand. The key to a good witness is one who answers the questions asked but who doesn't over-communicate. Extremely talkative witnesses can often be led by a skilled examiner to reach conclusions under oath that the witness may not necessarily have intended to disclose. Thus, while this part of the interview had nothing to do with the case, it disclosed information that is certainly relevant to the possible effectiveness of the witness in legal proceedings.

An important point is that once litigation has begun it is generally not permissible to contact witnesses, agents or employees of the opposing party or the opposing party themselves directly. Rather, all communication must go through the counsel for that party. However, prior to litigation, if an individual is willing to discuss matters that are not of a confidential nature, or if the party holding the privilege of confidentiality (usually the patient) consents, it is acceptable to contact them. One should be well aware that, typically, individuals are not going to willingly open themselves to an interview with what might be considered a potential opposing party in a lawsuit. This is especially true when the individual is the defendant's employee, or a potential defendant themselves. If the interview is obtained, the task of the interviewer to gain a full disclosure is a substantial one.

The in-depth segment of the initial witness interview must be conducted in a manner to glean the most information, positive and adverse, as both are necessary to make an accurate assessment of the case. Generally, questions can be asked in one of two ways: open or closed. The open-ended question is also often referred to in legal settings as a "direct" question. These questions seek a narrative answer based on the respondent's own sources of information. Frequently, open or **direct questions** include words such as "what," "how," or "why." These questions seek more than the confirmation or negation of a specific fact. A direct line of questioning explores the knowledge of the respondent without attempting to suggest answers or bring the respondent to a particular conclusion. The key to a direct line of questioning is that it is objective and seeks to obtain independent information from another source. Below are some examples of open or direct questions.

- What is your recollection of the person claiming injury as a patient in general?
- What are your basic job duties on an ordinary day?
- Do you recall what, if anything, was out of the ordinary in the basic routine on the day the injury allegedly occurred?

The other type of questioning is known as "closed" or "leading." **Leading questions** are the opposite of direct questions. Subjective in nature, leading questions suggest a specific, or at least a narrow, selection of answers to the respondent. In the legal arena, most individuals are familiar with leading questions in the setting of a cross-examination. The leading question typically requires the respondent to confirm or deny a statement without opportunity to expand upon or explain the reasons that underlie their answer. As a rule, the initial witness interview could not be farther from cross-examination in its scope and purpose. In some instances, leading questions can be used to control the flow of the interview or confirm basic information that is already known to the interviewer. Below are some examples of leading questions that might be used in a witness interview.

- Is your address 234 South 9th Street?
- Were you employed during January of 2004 by the Zylon Avenue Clinic?
- Were you working at the Zylon Avenue Clinic on Friday, January 2, 2004?

While the way questions are framed can be important to the tone of the interview and the amount, as well as type, of information obtained, the actual questions asked produce the results. The exact questions to ask vary as much as the possible scenarios for the case of malpractice. Many reference sources exist to provide questions often used in interviews and depositions for very specific factual circumstances. In the illustration that follows are some of the more generic interview questions often covered in medical malpractice witness interviews. Beyond the generic interview questions, certain questions regarding the specifics of the case should be prepared to consider it from the witness's full recollection as much as possible. When preparing questions as well as during the interview, do not allow preconceptions about the matter prevent learning all the witness knows. Also, while questions should be asked to keep the interview flowing, have the witness explain in their own words everything he or she knows or has heard about the matter. Carefully separate personal knowledge from hearsay and speculation about what the witness presumes happened, but for which they have no personal knowledge. The sample witness interview checklist in Exhibit 7.3 demonstrates how the witness interview varies from the plaintiff interview.

Exhibit 7.3   Sample Interview Questionnaire

Sample Witness Interview Checklist
Name_____ Phone: Home_____Alternate_____
Address _____
Employer/Position_____ _____
Alternate name/address/phone number of person who can reach witness
_____   _____   _____
Witness Relationship to plaintiff/defendant_____
Narrative of witness regarding connection to, and knowledge of, incident
_____
_____
_____
_____

(continued)

Exhibit 7.3, continued

Specific times, dates, events of importance: (Specify whether based on personal knowledge, conclusion, communication from another, and if so, who).
_____
_____
_____

Review any nonprivileged documents or items of evidence, e.g. photos, for which that witness may be able to add clarification, or which may yield additional information from the witness. For each item determine the following:
   1. *Ability to identify the document/exhibit*
   2. *Prior knowledge of the document/exhibit*
   3. *Explanation of the document/exhibit in witness's own terms.*
*Item*_____
   Witness
*Identification/Recollection/Explanation/Opinion*_____
_____

Witness opinion regarding strong and weak facts of each side of case
_____
_____

Individuals witness thinks may have additional information regarding incident/case
_____
_____

Who, if anyone, has contacted witness or discussed matter in any way with witness? (Provide name, date of contact, nature of communication)
_____
_____

Has witness provided any form of recorded (video, audio, written) statement to any party regarding incident including notations in medical records? (If so, when, to whom, does witness have copy? If not, witness can and should request any written statement other than another's medical records and obtain.)

Does the witness have any anticipation that he or she may be absent from the jurisdiction for an extended period of time in the future (moving, military service, etc)? If so, would witness be willing to provide a written notarized statement or deposition of their recollections?
_____

Witness should be encouraged to contact with any further recollections or if they are contacted by anyone else regarding the case.
Witness should be counseled they are under no obligation, absent a subpeona, to discuss matter with anyone.
Request permission to contact for further discussion if any new information regarding the case is developed with which witness may have connection.

ASSIGNMENT 7.1

Consider Application 7.3, and prepare a list of specific questions to ask the witness, Margaret.

Another important element of witness interviews is objective observations about the witness as a potential trial witness. Just as important as the information a witness may contribute in the form of evidence is how effectively the information is delivered to the judge and/or jury. As mentioned previously, the willingness to communicate is significant. Additional observations about a witness include a variety of characteristics that impact the actual testimony. However, this is something that can be manipulated to some extent by the manner in which questions are asked.

One item to consider when evaluating a witness is his or her ability to communicate to the average juror. Is the witness articulate? Does he or she speak at a language level that is approximately the same as the typical person? Individuals who have a limited vocabulary, or, on the contrary, who speak in highly technical terms, often do not make a positive impression regardless of the importance of their information.

Another consideration is the credibility of the witness. Is the witness confident regarding what they claim to have as personal knowledge about the case? Is that information complete or is it disjointed and missing several critical facts? Is the knowledge based on personal experience or on information received second hand from other sources (e.g., rumor or gossip)? Is there anything about the witness that might influence their testimony? For example, a witness who was a former employee of the defendant health care provider might have left on unfavorable terms and his or her testimony could be portrayed as an attempt to retaliate against the provider. The bottom line is to determine if there are any extraneous facts about the witness or his or her testimony that could cause it to be brought under suspicion as sincere, believable, and true.

Attention must be paid to how the witness presents him or herself physically. Jurors do not expect witnesses to be dressed in the latest and most expensive fashions, however, witnesses who do not present themselves in a clean and well-kept manner may be given less credibility than other witnesses. While this is certainly an improper basis for determining the truthfulness of one's testimony, it is human nature and widely accepted that personal impressions affect the opinions of jurors. It is also important to observe the physical demeanor of the witness. Does he or she sit still, make good eye contact, speak at an appropriate level, and avoid extensive gesturing? The body language of a speaker can send all sorts of unspoken messages to the recipient about the credibility of the information being communicated. Witnesses who constantly look down or away, who fidget in their seat or with objects at hand, who have a nervous laughter at inappropriate times such as during questioning, and who make constant and extreme gestures may be interpreted as less than forthright or honest.

While this discussion is far from exhaustive, it is meant to provide some insight. One of the most crucial parts of evaluating a medical malpractice case lies in the witness interview. Unlike most documentary evidence, witnesses are subject to change and frequently challenged by the opposition. Their physical appearance, demeanor, and communication skills all may affect the true nature and acceptance of the evidence only they can deliver. Even though the evidence is subject to varied circumstances that may affect how it is interpreted, testimonial evidence is quite often the strongest element in the case. Consequently, proper initial interview and evaluation of the client (plaintiff or defendant) and potential witnesses can offer a great deal of information about the likelihood of a successful petition or defense and suggest any steps that might be necessary to assist the witness in presenting effective testimony.

OBTAINING NECESSARY EVIDENCE

After the initial facts have been obtained and corroborated by the client and witnesses, it is time to start considering the possible causes of action that could be alleged in support of a claim of malpractice. Each cause of action, whether it is negligence, products liability, breach of contract, or some other form of civil action, has a specific list of elements that must be proven to prevail in a lawsuit. Additionally, most medical malpractice statutes have certain requirements that must be satisfied. This drives the continued investigation which has the objective to collect the supporting evidence for the elements of the causes of action and any statutory prerequisites. Investigation includes collecting any relevant testimonial, documentary, and tangible evidence. While this is a procedure that continues throughout the litigation process, the initial steps are often the most fruitful and have the greatest evidentiary impact on the case.

An important next step is to obtain any publicly available information about the specific case, about the particular type of malpractice case, or the client's injuries. Sources may include newspapers, magazines, scientific or technical journals, trade associations, government agencies, libraries, universities, or businesses. Another possible source in a type of case that is unusual or new to plaintiff's counsel or paralegal is contact with other legal professionals, including attorneys with similar cases who may be located through bar associations, periodical articles, case reports, or word of mouth.

In addition to public records, there are a number of potential sources for documentation regarding the specific client. These generally require a written consent for release signed by the injured party or his/her representative and a formal written request to the party holding the documentation. Some of the more typical records requested are described in Exhibit 7.4 below.

Exhibit 7.4 Chart of Common Records in Medical Malpractice

Record	*Content*
Facility Medical Record	Documentation of all treatments, procedures, care, observations, evaluations, contact with medical professionals including nurse's notes, primary care provider notes, consultations, diagnostic testing results, therapuetic treatments (e.g., physical/respiratory therapy), prescribed treatments while in the facility and upon discharge
Medical/Occupational Evaluations of Injury or Condition	Detailed observations and results of testing to support diagnosis, conclusions, and recommendations of health care professionals
Medical Bill	Care, treatment, and service provided, date of service, provider code representing type of care, treatment, services provided for insurance billing purposes

(continued)

Exhibit 7.4, continued

Explanation of Benefits (E.O.B.)	Statement from insurer to patient detailing care, treatment, services billed, and their disposition for payment
Laboratory/Pathology/Radiological Report	Results and evaluations from diagnostic testing
Operative Note	Physician summary of all significant events during an operative medical procedure
History & Physical (H&P)	Provider summary and current evaluation of basic physical condition and all past significant health-related events
Incident Report	Detailed documentation of event that resulted in injury and/or was not within parameters of normal policies and procedures
Medical Devices/Equipment Documents	Inspections, maintenance records, purchase or repair orders, or any other documentation related to the item
Photographic and Tangible Evidence	Photographs of the injury, site, and actual physical items such as medical devices, products, packaging or equipment

The following examples in Exhibit 7.5 are partial excerpts of sample records similar to those that might be encountered in the development of evidence. While not exhaustive, the samples below provide a view of how various records are constructed.

Exhibit 7.5   Sample Medical Records

1. History and Physical
   Note for Mary Janes 12/1/2004 Chart # 04-837

   CHIEF COMPLAINT - *Female, age 34/6 months presents for initial obstetrical examination. Patient assessment is that she is in early stages of 2nd trimester.*
   Last menstrual cycle: 8/3/04

(continued)

Exhibit 7.5, continued

Menses Onset 14 years old. Regular intervals 28 days. Duration 4-6 days. No complications. No reported history of gynecological infection, disease process, procedures.
Last Pap Smear 4/21/04 Results Normal
Contraception: Patient uses none
Previous Pregnancies: Patient admits 1 prior pregnancy at age 17, ending in spontaneous miscarriage in approximately 6th week, 1987. Patient reports there were no other complications and was under medical care prior to and following event.

Allergies: None
Medications: None
Past Medical History: Unremarkable
Past Surgical History: Tonsillectomy 1984.
Social History: Patient denies tobacco, illegal drug use, STD history, admits mild social use of alcohol, but denies alcohol use in past 90 days.
Family History: Patient admits a family history of breast cancer associated with mother (deceased from same).
Review of Systems: Neurological: (+) unremarkable, Respiratory: (+) unremarkable, Psychiatric: (+) admits to feelings of anxiety associated with pregnancy, Cardiovascular: (-) cardiovascular problems or chest symptoms, Genitourinary (-) decreased libido, (-) vaginal dryness, (-) vaginal bleedings. Patient assess diet "fairly balanced."

Physical Exam : BP standing: 126/80 Resp: 21 HR; 76 Temp: 98.9 Height 5'5" Weight 146 lbs. Pre-Gravid weight 132 lbs.
Patient is a 34 year old female who appears in no apparent distress, well developed, well nourished, and with good attention to hygiene and body habitus.
Mood and Affect appear normal and appropriate to situation. ....

....
<u>2. Emergency Department Medical Record</u>

PATIENT NAME: *John Doe 18*   *Patient:No. Stat 18*
MEDICAL RECORD: *STAT 18*   *Sex: Male*
Date of Birth: __/__/__   *Race: Caucasion*
Arrival Date: 08/25/04   *Age: _____*
Arrival Time: 2315   *Arrival by: Med Evac Helicopter*
Discharge Time: Admit to ICU 0045   *Physician: Smart*
Nursing Triage: L. Smith

CHIEF COMPLAINT
Fully developed adult male presented with multiple trauma.
Arrival Information: Triage Time: 2316, Mode of Arrival: MEH, Mental Status on

(continued)

Exhibit 7.5, continued

arrival: Unconscious and unresponsive. Pre-Hospital Course/Treatment = IV Solution, Oxygen 10 L by mask, immobilized on backboard, C-collar in place

Timing/Duration of Injury: Abrupt, Time of occurrence appox. 2225
Context: MVA- Patient unrestrained passenger, ejected from vehicle.
Modifying Factors: Patient on IV fluids .9% Sodium Chloride, 2 oL
Quality/Description: Acute
Severity: Critical
Location: Skull = right side; right arm; right leg, Abdomen = all quadrants.

Vital Signs
BP: 100/60   Pulse 110   Resp 26   Temp 97.1   Pulse Ox 96%
Weight: 190 lbs.   Height 5'9"-6'
COURSE OF TREATMENT ...

....

2. INVOICE

```
                                                              FINAL
                                                              PAGE 1
BILL DATE 8/XX/
                    PATIENT BILL DETAIL TRANSACTIONS
                                                              ADMISSION
PATIENT 6406919- 5          GUARANTOR 2103490                 DATE 8/25/

                                                              DISCHARGE
                                                              DATE 8/XX/
```

DATE OF SERVICE	DATE OF POSTING	CHARGE NUMBER	DESCRIPTION/BILL CODE		QUANTITY	EXTENDED PRICE
		380 ***	EMERGENCY SERVICES			
8/25/	8/25/	3801000	EMERGENCY ROOM, CODE	450	1	38.80
			(380) DEPARTMENT TOTAL		1	38.80
		390 ***	PROFESSIONAL SERVICES			
8/25/	8/25/	3909282	ER MD EXAM #2	981	1	62.05
			(390) DEPARTMENT TOTAL		1	62.05
		440 ***	RADIOLOGY - GENERAL			
8/25/	8/25/	4402010	SPINE ENTIRE	320	1	153.65
8/25/	8/25/	4402040	CERVICAL SPINE AP/LAT	320	1	50.45
8/25/	8/25/	4403010	SCAPULA	320	1	51.50
8/25/	8/25/	4403030	SHOULDER - 3 VIEWS	320	1	58.15
			(440) DEPARTMENT TOTAL		4	313.75
			PATIENT TOTAL		6	414.60

(continued)

INVESTIGATION OF THE CLAIM BY THE POTENTIAL PLAINTIFF

Exhibit 7.5, continued

Diagnostics®

10406

Page 1
Laboratory Invoice
For services not included in your physician's bill.
Invoice Number 2886597135
Lab Code

Important Notice
THIS BILL IS FOR LAB WORK REFERRED TO US BY YOUR DOCTOR.

LABORATORY SERVICE	CPT CODE / DATE RECEIVED	AMOUNT
CYTO AUTO THIN LAYER PREP	88142	$66.15

Patient Name
Date of Service
Amount Due
Payment Due Date $66.15
Responsible Party
Requested by:
Invoice Date

PATIENT AMOUNT DUE	$66.15

ICD-9 Codes: V76.2
Tax ID # 38-2084239
Services Performed by: DIAGNOSTICS

If you have Medicare, Railroad Medicare or Medicaid as your primary or secondary insurance, please send us the information - see reverse side

For billing inquiries or to pay by phone:
Please have your invoice available for reference.
Weekdays 8AM - 6PM
1-800-555-1234
Fax: 1-800-555-4321
Or visit our website at
www.labinvoice.com
Se Habla Español 9AM - 6PM Tiempo del Este

The CPT codes provided are based on AMA guidelines and without regard to specific payor requirements.

▼ Please fold and tear payment coupon along perforation and remit with payment in the envelope provided ▼

Diagnostics®

Payment Coupon

Please make check payable to: Diagnostics. Please include invoice number on your check. Diagnostics also accepts MasterCard, Visa & American Express. Please complete credit card information on reverse or visit our website at www.labinvoice.com

Amount Due	$66.15	
Payment Due Date		
Invoice Number 2886597135		Lab Code STL
Patient Name		
Amount Enclosed		

MAIL PAYMENTS ONLY TO: **DIAGNOSTICS INCORPORATED**

☐ Check here if address has changed. Indicate change on back.
Diagnostics reserves the right to assign this receivable to any of its affiliates.

(continued)

Exhibit 7.5, continued

3. EXPLANATION OF BENEFITS

886489   816239

EXPLANATION OF BENEFITS

Please Retain for Future Reference
Date printed: 05/07/04
Page 1 of 1

THIS IS NOT A BILL

QUESTIONS? Contact Us
Or write to the address shown above

Notes:
To reduce the number of informational Explanation of Benefits mailings you receive, we are consolidating when possible a greater number of statements for your household into one envelope.

Claim Activity for (*Spouse*)
Member:
Group Name:

Member ID: Please refer to ID Card
Group Number: 31-002 B

DATE AND TYPE OF SERVE	SUBMITTED CHARGES	NEGOTIATED AMOUNT	NOT PAYABLE BY PLAN	SEE REMARKS	YOUR COPAY	YOUR DEDUCTIBLE	AMOUNT REMAINING	PAID AT	PLAN PAYS	YOUR SHARE OF AMOUNT REMAINING	Total Patient Responsibility
J 04/29/04											
Fillings	120.00		15.00	1		$5.00	70.00	80%	56.00	14.00	64.00
Fluoride Application	22.00		22.00	2							22.00
Cleaning	55.00		3.00	1			52.00	100%	52.00		3.00
Oral Exam	28.00						28.00	100%	28.00		
	A	**B**	**C**		**D**	**E**	**F**		**G**	**H**	**I**
Column Totals	225.00		40.00			35.00	150.00		136.00	14.00	89.00

	J	May Bill you: C + D + E + H=	**$89.00** I

Remarks:
1 - Your plan provides benefits for covered expenses at the plan's recognized percentile level of charges received by Aetna for the same service. If there is additional information that should be brought to our attention, please let us know.
2 - Under the terms of your plan, this service is covered only when performed on a dependent child. Please refer to your plan booklet for details.

Plan Summary for 01/01/04 - 12/31/04

Description			
Individual Limits	**Annual Limit**	**Year To Date**	**Remainder**
Dental In Network Calendar Year	$1,000.00	$136.00	$864.00
Dental Out of Network Calendar Year	$1,000.00	$136.00	$864.00
Individual Lifetime Maximums	**Limit**	**Used**	
Dental In Network Orthodontia	$1,000.00	$0.00	
Dental Out of Network Orthodontia	$1,000.00	$0.00	

Payment Summary:
Send To: J
Date Sent:
Amount: $136.00

EVALUATION OF THE VIABILITY OF THE CLAIM

Once the preliminary investigative steps have been taken, it is possible to better consider the viability of the plaintiff's claim and whether it is advisable to proceed with litigation of a case of medical malpractice. To do this, the facts and evidence previously gathered must be considered from several perspectives: actual evidence of compensable injury as the proximate result of professional malpractice; if legislation is in place that affects the potential outcome of the case in terms of a successful verdict and/or damage award; and the plaintiff's contribution in a material way to his or her own injury or consequent damages. Any of these questions can have a vital impact on the decision of whether a case should be legally pursued.

Generally as an Act of Malfeasance

Not every medical procedure or treatment results in professional malpractice. If it did, the public as a whole would avoid medical care—choosing the illness rather than the cure. In a very small percentage of cases, however, an unexpected and less than desirable result may occur. When this happens, the cause must be considered objectively. A patient unhappy with the outcome of his or her medical care is not enough to substantiate a malpractice claim. There must be evidence that the result is outside the parameters of normally expected results. Certain results, that while less than ideal, are within the range of risks associated with the type of care, which assumes that the patient was properly informed of those risks and consented to the care after such information was provided.

APPLICATION 7.4

Crystal wished to have plastic surgery to alter her body shape. During the course of the preliminary examination, the doctor noticed two distinct and quite noticeable raised scars. Upon questioning, Crystal explained they were the result of stitches she received after an accident. The doctor explained that there was the possibility she could scar in this manner again with any additional incisions such as through the performance of plastic surgery, despite his best efforts to conceal them. This discussion was noted in Crystal's chart and on her pre-operative paperwork. She also initialed it. Crystal, believing the plastic surgeon would have better skill at dealing with her scars, went through with the surgery. A few months later she came to an attorney and complained that the plastic surgeon had left her disfigured with scars. In fact, she had numerous noticeable scars at the sites of her surgery. Investigation revealed that Crystal had been informed of the risk due to her own tendency to scar and that she had proceeded in spite of the risk. After consulting with another plastic surgeon who found no evidence of malfeasance under the circumstances, the attorney declined to represent Crystal.

In this case, it is not enough that Crystal was unhappy with her result. At no time did her physician indicate to her that he could achieve a result without scarring. Rather, even though he was a plastic surgeon who specialized in such matters, he specifically pointed out that she had a tendency to naturally produce an abundance of scar tissue and he could not prevent this.

It is often advisable to obtain at least a preliminary assessment of the case by an objective medical professional. Preferably, the professional will have a similar background, training and practical experience to that of the one whose actions are in question. This type of individual would be more likely to have information about the standard practices common to the medical community where the injury allegedly took place. It is true that the general rule today is to apply a national as opposed to the former locality rule regarding the standard of care. But, for practical purposes, in some instances a jury may be more likely to give some consideration as to how things are done in their own community. And, at this stage, all aspects of the likely successfulness of a claim should be taken into account.

In a case based on breach of contract, where the potential defendant failed to meet the agreed-upon terms of medical care, treatment or services, both legal and medical evaluations of the claim should be made. First, the elements of contract must be established along with evidence of breach. Second, it must be determined whether the agreement, or failure to meet its terms, were the product of malpractice by the medical professional. If the determination is made that there is in fact evidence of professional malfeasance, either through tort or contract principles, there are still additional factors to consider before the decision can be made to proceed with litigation.

Legislation That Might Affect Recovery

In earlier chapters there was discussion about the consistently increasing number of state and federal statutes that affect the delivery of health care. These statutes should be viewed not only in terms of laws that limit or deny some claims of malpractice. Granted, they are the ones most often discussed in the media. However, there is an equal, if not greater, area of growth in legislation and regulation to protect the patient population. In the proper circumstances, these can be effective tools to the plaintiff in litigating a case of alleged malpractice by a plaintiff.

With regard to laws enacted to better control the claims of medical malpractice in the court system, there are a number of approaches that various jurisdictions have taken. As mentioned earlier in the text, these may include pre-approval or certification of claims by state appointed panels, affidavits of experts that there is evidence to support a claim of malpractice, special procedural rules for litigation of malpractice cases, limitations on general or noneconomic damage recoveries, and others. Because the laws are in a state of rapid change at this time, it is important that the most currently enacted, amended, and even pending statutes be consulted for the particular jurisdiction in which a case is intended for litigation. Several basic steps should be taken prior to commencing any case involving medical malpractice.

- Identify all currently effective legislation and regulations that might affect the case. This includes pending legislation/regulations that might take effect prior to filing.
- Resolve any and all necessary preliminary steps that must be accomplished prior to the actual institution of a case in the courts.
- Address any limitation of actions issues that might affect the case due to statutory provisions that shorten or change the standard limitation of actions statute in a civil case.
- Determine any procedural requirements that must be satisfied in addition to the standard procedures for filing a civil case (e.g., attaching a panel certification or expert affidavit, etc.).
- Prepare a timeline for completing all necessary steps according to statutory requirements that can be accomplished within the applicable statute of limitations.
- Take into account any statutory limitations on damage recovery when preparing petition and other documents necessary to begin litigation.

As Affected by Comparative Negligence of the Plaintiff

Finally, one of the less pleasant aspects of preparing litigation for the plaintiff's side is to consider, and present to the plaintiff, how his or her own conduct may have a detrimental effect on the case. Nevertheless, there is often conduct that can be pointed to by the defense which can be attributed to exacerbating the negative aspects of the plaintiff's condition. Studies have shown that in many cases where a plaintiff is already in financial straights, and even perhaps without health insurance, there is an increased likelihood of poor patient compliance with prescribed treatment or therapy. This action may be through no intention on the part of the plaintiff, but the defense may point this out as a contributing factor for which the health care professional should not be held accountable.

APPLICATION 7.5

Scott was a construction worker without steady employment or health insurance. On January 12, 2004, he went to a union hall and secured a one-day job with a small general contracting company to help with some cement work. During the day, Scott twisted his knee. After several days it continued to worsen and he sought medical care. He was advised he needed immediate knee surgery. The doctor advised Scott to stay off the leg as much as possible and to schedule the surgery with the front desk at the office for sometime in the next two days. Scott tried scheduling the surgery through the doctor's office. Because he had no health insurance, he was required to make a $1,000 deposit before the hospital would allow the office to schedule the surgery. Scott left and said he'd be back as soon as possible. He continued to work and favored the knee as much as he could. It was approximately two months before he had the money to make the deposit. When the surgery was performed, Scott's knee injury had been worsened by the continued use to the point it could not be fully repaired and he will always suffer a noticeable limp. Scott wants to sue his doctor for failing to prescribe proper treatment or therapy during the time he was unable to afford the surgery. However, Scott's failure to have the surgery immediately as prescribed and/or obtain additional care from his doctor until such time as he could have the surgery could be construed as a significant contributing factor to his own condition.

ASSIGNMENT 7.2

Prepare a comprehensive checklist to address each of the necessary steps in the consideration of a case of alleged malpractice for possible litigation.

Problem 7.1

Complete 7.1 of the Comprehensive Problem in Appendix A.

CHAPTER SUMMARY

From the perspective of the plaintiff, there are a number of issues to address when a client presents a potential claim of medical malpractice. It must be established whether or not the claim is supported by a legal cause of action and whether or not the evidence is available to support each of the legal elements ranging from professional malfeasance to compensable damage. The initial investigation requires a thorough assessment of the evidence that will be necessary, a comprehensive interview of the client and potential witnesses, collecting relevant information for the particular type of case, particular defendants, and consideration of any role the plaintiff may have played in contributing to the injuries.

A key element of early investigation is the witness interview. When conducting interviews it is important to create an atmosphere conducive to open communication. The interviewer should avoid providing the witnesses with any more information than necessary in order to establish the actual content of the witness's own personal knowledge. While leading questions can be used to guide the flow and direction of the interview, direct questions are more productive in terms of eliciting independent recollections.

Procedural concerns must also be addressed in terms of applicability of statutes, limitation of action, and any other issues that are specific to the case. Once this information has been amassed, it is necessary to consider it as a whole and make a determination of the likelihood of success of an action.

Key Terms	
investigation	leading questions
direct questions	

For additional resources, go to http://www.westlegalstudies.com.

8 CHAPTER

Investigation of the Potential Claim by the Defendant

CHAPTER OBJECTIVES

When you complete this chapter, you should be able to:

- Discuss the differences between plaintiff and defense perspective when evaluating potential claim of malpractice
- List methods and sources to identify potential witnesses
- Discuss the importance of various documents used to evaluate claim

ESTABLISHING THE CAUSE OF THE INJURY

In many respects, the initial steps taken by those evaluating a potential malpractice claim from the perspective of the defense are similar to those evaluating a plaintiff's claim. Theoretically, the task should actually be an easier one because the defendants often have access to information not readily available to plaintiffs. For instance, injuries often occur on the business premises of the defendant and many of the most active roles are played by the defendant and defendant's employees. Because the claim involves the delivery of health care, treatment, and services to the plaintiff by defendant, the defendant typically has extensive records with respect to the plaintiff's injuries. If this is the situation, what could be the problem? One part of the answer is that the plaintiff may have friends or relatives as witnesses of whom the defense is not even aware. Also, if the provider–patient relationship has ended, the defense cannot know the extent or current effects of the injuries. Finally, even though individuals who played a critical role may ultimately be the defendants themselves, they may not be anxious to expose their own misconduct or professional shortcomings. As for those who are employees of possible defendants rather than owners, those relationships present another set of issues. Individuals may change their employment and with it, possibly, their loyalty. Others who remain employed may be fearful that full disclosure would jeopardize their employment and thus be less than forthright, such as in Application 8.1.

APPLICATION 8.1

Jared was a certified nursing assistant in a long-term-care facility that specialized in treating Alzheimer's patients. One particular patient was Mr. Winker. He was in advanced stages of Alzheimer's. He had to be hand-fed pureed foods. But, he had a habit of regularly spitting the food back onto the health care worker who was feeding him. On one occasion Jared was feeding Mr. Winker, who spat his food directly into Jared's face. Angry, Jared started shoveling the food into Mr. Winker's mouth. Mr. Winker began choking, aspirated the food, and died soon thereafter. At the time Mr. Winker began choking, Jared noticed a visitor in the doorway. Jared was unsure if the visitor had witnessed his actions. Nevertheless, Jared filed a report with the nursing home that stated Mr. Winker had spontaneously started choking and despite all attempts to save him, had expired.

In this case, the employee withheld important information. Without further knowledge by the employer from another source, they have no way of knowing that the entire incident may have been witnessed by a friend of the deceased, and that the facts are somewhat different from those stated by the employee.

There are also those cases of medical malpractice when the defendant or risk manager is unaware an incident has even occurred until such time as they receive legal notice from the plaintiff. Or, there may be knowledge of the occurrence but the initial perception is that it was purely accidental or noninjurious. Regardless of how the potential defendant becomes aware of the possibility of a medical malpractice claim, the investigation and evaluation of the claim must still be completed and should be as comprehensive as possible. Whether the investigation is completed by a risk manager, representative of the defendant's insurance, or legal professional retained to represent the defendant, the process is essentially the same.

One of the first objectives of the investigation is to determine how the injury occurred. This can be accomplished through a combination of steps that, when considered together, can give a clear view of whether the claim of malpractice and subsequent injury is supported by professional malfeasance. To determine how the injury occurred, it is necessary to thoroughly interview all those who the defense is aware of and who potentially have information about the case. Additional factors to consider include all of the physical evidence such as the scene of the occurrence and any instruments, tools, or equipment involved. A comprehensive evaluation of any documentation of the incident is also important.

IDENTIFICATION AND INTERVIEW OF ALL PERSONS CONNECTED TO THE INJURY

In this respect the individual responsible for investigating a possible claim of malpractice from the side of the defense has a distinct advantage over a plaintiff in most cases. All records are readily available and there is free access to gather information from the existing staff who are potential defendants and witnesses. Nevertheless, the basic background work must be done in order to properly identify all those involved and obtain the relevant information.

The first step in opening an investigation and evaluation of a medical malpractice incident or claim is to collect the basic facts of the circumstances surrounding the incident and identify all those with any knowledge about what precipitated the incident, how it occurred, and what followed. A good place to start is to open a file with a preliminary investigation checklist. Completing this document allows the individual evaluating the claim to focus on the areas to develop in the investigation. An example of a preliminary checklist is included in Exhibit 8.1.

Exhibit 8.1 Risk Management Preliminary Investigation Checklist

PRELIMINARY INVESTIGATION CHECKLIST
Risk Management Preliminary Investigation Checklist

    Patient/Claimant
Name_____
Address_____
Primary Care Provider (name, address, professional license/registration #)_____
_____

Insurance Co. & Policy #_____ Billed?_____
Cause for Investigation:
In-house incident notification_____ Legal Action _____ Patient complaint _____
Notification by Attorney for claimant_____ Other_____

    Incident
Dates of Treatment_____ Provider:_____
Summary of condition prior to treatment_____
Treatment plan_____
Treatment outcome_____
Incident location_____
Incident time and date:_____
Summary of circumstances relevant to claim _____
_____
_____
_____
_____

Identity of all parties present at time of incident or with knowledge relevant to incident—name, relationship to incident, status (e.g., physician, nurse, family member, friend, etc.)
_____
_____
_____
_____

Notification to Professional Liability Insurers:
Date of Notice _____ Contact Person at Insurer_____

    Medical Records
Record Number_____

(continued)

Exhibit 8.1, continued

Requests for Record (name, date of request, date of compliance)

_____ _____ _____
_____ _____ _____
_____ _____ _____
_____ _____ _____

Missing dictation_____
Missing signatures_____
Missing authorizations_____
Identity of all persons referenced in records not previously listed
_____
_____
_____

Other relevant medical records (e.g., test, laboratory, radiological films, etc.). Identify and date of record.
_____
_____
_____
_____
_____
_____

Areas of significance or concern regarding potential liability
_____
_____
_____
_____
_____
_____
_____

Persons to interview re incident/patient (name, contact resource)
_____
_____
_____
_____
_____
_____
_____

With a preliminary investigation checklist completed, the real investigation can begin in earnest. First, it is important to follow through with the identification of those with relevant knowledge of all circumstances surrounding the case. This includes not only the key player(s) at the time the injury occurred, but also those who had prior contact or later contact with the plaintiff, or others who may be involved as witnesses due to their presence even though they had no direct role.

If an incident report was filed at the time of the occurrence, individuals involved may be identified in the report. A review of personnel records should disclose all those who were in and around the plaintiff while in the defendant's employ. While most often the health care professionals come to mind, do not discount the contributions other employees might be able to make. Consider all staff members, including the housekeeping staff in a hospital situation and the billing clerk or receptionist in a private office or clinic. Anyone with whom the plaintiff, or witnesses friendly to the plaintiff, had contact are important to at least rule out as potential witnesses. The failure to do so could be disastrous. The following example in Application 8.2 is based on an actual occurrence.

APPLICATION 8.2

Jolene was to undergo a routine orthopedic surgery at a major hospital. She had been admitted to the hospital following an accident the day before. She was in no immediate danger that would warrant emergency surgery. On the day of her surgery, the nurse assigned to Jolene records a fairly high temperature in the chart. This goes unnoticed by the anesthesiologist and surgeon who are running well behind schedule. Ordinarily, a patient would not be taken to surgery for a nonemergency while suffering from an active infection and high fever. As the result of her condition, Jolene suffers serious complications during the surgery and subsequently dies. A case of malpractice is brought against the surgeon and anesthesiologist. During trial the case seems to be favoring the defense position that the incident was an unfortunate incident but within the normal range of risk of surgery and general anesthesia. Midway through the trial a former employee of the hospital sees an article about the case in the newspaper. He contacts the plaintiff's counsel and informs them that he recalls the incident very well because he was cleaning the floors on the night after the patient died and overheard two surgeons discuss the need to change Jolene's chart to reflect a normal temperature. He thought the conduct did not sound ethical but didn't understand the significance at the time, did not report it, and no one ever asked him about the case.

The witness was brought into the courtroom to testify. The defense objected to the late notice of the witness. The plaintiff's counsel explained to the judge the nature of the testimony and how they came to know of the witness. The judge required the original medical records be brought into his chambers where both sides could view them. A brief examination demonstrated that the original chart had clearly been physically altered with respect to the patient's temperature chart on the day of the surgery. During discovery the plaintiff's counsel had received rather poor quality copies of the records that masked the alteration. Rather than risk this information being given to the jury, the defense immediately settled the case for a sum substantially more than any previous settlement offers.

While not all cases are as sensational as this, and certainly not all defendants or witnesses withhold information, it does demonstrate the need to be comprehensive in identifying all those who could possibly have relevant knowledge. In the example above, a thorough investigation would have benefited the defendants in more than one way. First, the witness could have been interviewed while still employed, making him less likely to bombshell the defense at trial. Second, if the altered record had already occurred by the time of the interview, it could be dealt with immediately. When something as clearly wrong as this occurs, an early settlement saves both sides a great deal of time and expense in the litigation process.

An advantage to early discovery and reporting of incidents that occur in the delivery of health care, treatment, and services is the access to witnesses for both sides. As mentioned before, once litigation has begun, they can only be reached through counsel and in prescribed methods discussed later in the text. However, if litigation has not been initiated, it is entirely acceptable for those investigating from the viewpoint of potential defendants to contact and interview anyone of whom they are aware to have knowledge. This even includes the plaintiff if they have not yet retained legal counsel.

The interview process for the defense is very similar to that for the plaintiff. The objective is the same: To obtain all relevant information from individuals with personal knowledge of the circumstances of the case. This includes the incident and any precipitating factors or subsequent events that impact a finding of fault on the part of the defendant, contribution to injury by the plaintiff, and the extent of injury.

It is important to create an atmosphere conducive to open communication by the witness and to stress the importance of full and honest disclosure. It is commonly agreed upon by legal professionals that one of the greatest hurdles in dealing with witnesses is that everyone likes to be liked. As a result, they do not always provide full and accurate information if they feel it may place them in a negative light, even though they are communicating with their own legal representative. This behavior is even more prominent when dealing with an individual who is not only a witness or a potential defendant, but who is employed by the primary defendant. The risk of losing one's job is significant and must be considered when attempting to place the interviewee at ease and encourage an open dialogue and when evaluating the comments made by the interviewee.

As with interviews by those representing a plaintiff, the physical location and arrangement should be conducive to open communication. Depending on the circumstances of the case and the seriousness of the allegations and the injuries, the interview might be more productive in a location away from the defendant's premises. For example, a hospital employee called into the risk management office of the hospital in a case involving the death of a patient may be very intimidated. Regardless of the location, or even the physical arrangement of the room, the demeanor of the interviewer should be professional and objective. It is important that the interviewee not sense an accusatory tone if open dialogue is to occur.

The questions to ask when interviewing a potential witness or defendant from the perspective of the defense are essentially the same as for those of the plaintiff's side of the case. Cases are phrased in either leading or narrative terms. The decision of which to use is determined by the type and amount of information the interviewer wishes to elicit. While the plaintiff most often has access to friendly witnesses who are willing to share what personal knowledge they have of the incident, defense witnesses have additional information that, as mentioned, they may or may not be anxious to disclose. Some of the areas to explore in the initial witness interview with an employee or potential defendant may include the following:

- professional background (education and training);
- status of licensure, registration, or certification and the accrediting entity;
- current personal statistics (contact methods, address, social security, etc.);
- history of professional employment;
- any relevant professional disciplinary/criminal background;
- immediate supervisor (if any) at the time of the incident;
- knowledge of any established incident reporting procedures and whether they were complied within the present case;
- knowledge of the incident.

> **ASSIGNMENT 8.1**
>
> Consider the following true-fact situation and prepare a list of specific questions to be used when interviewing the nurse.
>
> Nineteen-year-old Sasha is visiting a friend in the hospital. She is approached by a volunteer who is seeking donors for the blood bank. Sasha agrees to donate blood and goes to the hospital lab. The hospital is quite large and a special area is set up for blood donors. Sasha arrives just as the shift of nurses is changing. She is not asked to complete any forms or answer any questions. Rather, she is immediately escorted to an area where she is placed in a chair and the blood draw is begun. The nurse tells her to squeeze her fist periodically and informs Sasha she will return. The nurse then attends to several other donors. Sasha suffers from anorexia and has not eaten in more than two days. Before the nurse returns to check on her, Sasha faints and collapses in the chair. She slides to the floor and strikes her head along the way. She suffers a laceration to her scalp that requires 22 stitches.

Once all of the individuals with potential relevant knowledge have been identified and interviewed, consideration can be given to those who are most likely to be named defendants in a case of medical malpractice. If the case is based on the delivery of health care, treatment, or services, rather than another collateral occurrence, such as a slip and fall on the premises, the potential defendants are generally going to be confined to health care professionals and facilities. Once these individuals have been separated from the other employees of the defendant, an evaluation should be conducted of the role of each as a member of the professional staff and with respect to their level of participation in the circumstances that produced the injury.

Earlier discussions of the theory of respondeat superior have addressed the legal doctrine that holds principals and employers responsible for the acts of agents and employees who are within the scope of their employment at the time injury occurs to a third party. In this case, that third party would be the patient. Legal professionals for the defense are well aware of two primary considerations taken into account by plaintiff's lawyers when determining who will be the named defendants. These considerations deal with the number of defendants named and the resources of those defendants. The first approach is sometimes referred to as a "shotgun." The idea is to name as many defendants as possible in the hopes that recovery will be achieved against at least one or some of them. This is often applied when there are numerous individuals connected with an injury, such as in a case of alleged medical malpractice where several health care professionals are involved in a patient's care.

In a case where there is the possibility for a large number of individuals to be named as defendants, the conduct of each must be evaluated based on their individual and collective role in the case. Also to be considered is the position of the professional in the employment chain. The facts must be taken into account for each individual and may be different in every case. But the questions are essentially the same: What were the critical factors in producing the circumstances that caused the injury? Was the health care professional acting based on independent judgment or within the scope of an employment relationship under the direction of another? If the answers to these questions indicate an individual played a significant role and exercised independent judgment, there is a good possibility he or she will be named as a defendant. Again, the defense should keep in mind that the plaintiff's goal is to go after every viable defendant.

A second method used by plaintiffs in searching out potential defendants in any kind of case seeking compensation is known as the "**deep pocket**." This also must be considered by the investigator when evaluating those most likely to be named as defendants. An accepted principle in tort law is that it does no good to gain a monetary judgment against one incapable of satisfying that judgment. It is just as important to find a defendant with adequate resources or "deep pockets" as it is to prove liability. From a defense perspective, identifying potential defendants is impacted by the availability of financial resources of those health care professionals involved in the case. This often causes a claim of respondeat superior against more heavily insured health care professionals than might otherwise be alleged.

APPLICATION 8.3

Dr. G is a pediatrician in a small community. She has malpractice insurance coverage in an amount commensurate with the statutory limit of malpractice judgments, which is $3,000,000. An incident occurs when a nurse (uninsured) in the employ of Dr. G undertakes to provide treatment to a child on a very busy day in the clinic. The child is quite ill and Dr. G has left the office for a few moments. In an attempt to get caught up with the number of patients still to be seen, the nurse goes ahead with what she assumes Dr. G would ordinarily order and administers penicillin to the child. The nurse does not check the chart, which clearly states the child is allergic to penicillin. The child goes into anaphylactic shock, is unable to breathe for several minutes, and suffers extensive brain damage.

The claim could be made that the nurse acted independently and caused the injury. Thus, any judgment against her as an individual would be satisfied by what personal assets she might have available. However, if a successful claim can be made that the nurse's conduct was something that occurred as part of her employment, then Dr. G might be held accountable, thus making the doctor's malpractice insurance available to satisfy a judgment.

At first glance the deep pocket theory may seem a somewhat calculated and cold attempt by plaintiff's counsel to obtain more money from defendants with insurance who may not even be personally responsible for causing an injury. However, the absence of overt conduct on the part of the defendant does not relieve them of responsibility for the actions of a subordinate in appropriate circumstances. The plaintiff's counsel is retained to obtain the most compensation possible for his or her client who was allegedly injured as a direct result of the malpractice by the provider. In the application above the doctor has no greater role than to employ the nurse who administered the medicine without the doctor asking her to do so. The clients are the child and parents who entrusted the care of their child to the doctor and her staff. Those parents and the child are faced with a lifetime of dealing with the brain injury and the costs that go along with it. As with any type of litigation, the situation is seldom, if ever, single-sided. An effective investigator considers the case from both sides whenever collecting information, and, ultimately, it is left to the judge and jury to properly sort out the real facts, apply the law properly, and award damages if they are warranted. The objective at this point in an investigation is not to sort out culpability, but to determine those most likely to be named defendants and those likely to be called as witnesses with the greatest accuracy possible by considering all aspects of the case and possible strategies of the opposition.

DOCUMENTARY EVIDENCE

Fortunately, the delivery of health care is a field that depends on comprehensive documentation. Most of those documents are created by, and in the possession of, those who are typically on the defense. Also, because the case is brought against health care providers, there is often ready access to other providers for consultation. The investigator for the potential defendants in a case of alleged malpractice often has an advantage with regard to accessibility of evidence, but not all information is at the disposal of the defense. In fact, there are situations where some documentary evidence is more accessible to the plaintiff. The goal at this stage of preliminary investigation is to obtain all available documentary information and properly consider its impact on a case of malpractice.

At first glance, obtaining medical records relevant to the plaintiff's injury may seem to be the easiest of all possible tasks, especially because the records within the defendant's possession are usually readily accessible. However, very often in the case of significant injuries, the plaintiff will seek treatment from other providers besides the defendant. The plaintiff may also have had medical care prior to the injury that is relevant to the extent of injury claimed as the result of malpractice. These may or may not be within the reach of the investigator. It is important to note that, as discussed early in the text, the federal and state legislatures and administrative agencies have quite heavily protected the privacy of patients with respect to medical records. It has also been quite clearly established that the content of the physical records is owned by the patient and not the provider. Thus, one provider cannot simply hand over records to another, or even discuss the content of those records without the express permission of the plaintiff. As with witnesses, once litigation has commenced, medical records must be obtained through discovery from the plaintiff. Prior to that, the investigator acting on behalf of potential defendants can only consider those records within the defendant's control or those which a plaintiff might supply consent for willingly. In an adversarial situation it would not be likely that someone considering filing a legal action would be open to the idea of turning over evidence to the same party they intend to sue. However, in the interest of early settlement, the issue is one that should at least be explored in appropriate circumstances.

What should the investigator and his or her team be focusing on in the available medical records? In cases of medical malpractice, the medical record is often a key element of the case presented by both parties. Even if the record does not provide a report of the alleged incident that caused injury, it may still provide a great deal of information regarding the patient and individuals from whom the patient received professional services. It is essential that the records be reviewed by someone with a working knowledge of their general content, and resources to decipher the many abbreviations and symbols frequently used. It is not at all uncommon for legal professionals emeshed in litigation to hire individuals with both a medical and legal background (e.g., nurse, paralegal), to review medical records for indications of error or irregularity. Even prior to litigation, the available records of when the investigation began can provide a great deal of information about the case. Below are some important points for the investigator to consider when examining medical records:

- identity of all individuals noted in the record;
- evidence of any corrections, alterations, and additions to the record;
- reference to any additional records that may have been created by other health care professionals (e.g., another department within a health care facility);
- any and all notations that occurred on or about the time of the alleged injury;
- subsequent notations that reference the alleged injury or any effects thereof;
- any contributory conduct by the plaintiff (e.g., noncompliance with medical instructions).

Whether the record is one from an independent health care practitioner, health care facility, or one functioning as an independent contractor within the facility (e.g., a respiratory therapist within a hospital), all records pertaining to the patient should be reviewed as soon as they become accessible. When reviewing the records it is of equal importance to examine what went right as it is to examine what went wrong. All reports regarding the patient's condition should be evaluated with respect to matters falling within or without normal ranges. For example, a lab report on a blood analysis will typically provide various levels of chemicals, enzymes, and other components found in the blood. The report will often state the specific patient's levels along with an accepted range of high and low values considered to be within a normal range.

It is important to identify any values near to or outside the normal ranges. If parameters are not given with the report, they should be obtained for comparison. Also look to see whether the values falling near to or outside normal ranges were addressed by health care professionals in the report or in other records.

Finally, and perhaps most important to consider: Are there any notes or reports specifically directed to the incident that are the basis for the alleged malpractice? While it is entirely possible no such document exists, when it does, it can be a key element of the case. Depending on the content, such a report can be used by the plaintiff to demonstrate knowledge of the malfeasance, or by the defendant to demonstrate proper response to an unexpected occurrence. It is important also to remember that recently it has become a requirement for all facilities accredited by JCAHO to inform patients in writing of any unanticipated event during the course of delivery of health care, treatment, or services. Such a document should also be in the patient files. Failure to provide this document to the patient could result in disciplinary action by the JCAHO or as a negative piece of evidence against the defense in a medical malpractice action.

In addition to the above, consider nonmedical documents that pertain to the delivery of professional services to the plaintiff. These include billing statements, insurance documents, and correspondence. Billing documents will, no doubt, be used by the plaintiff in establishing the extent of financial injury; therefore, they should be examined. In some instances the bills are in error, services are charged and not delivered, or vice versa. Insurance documents can also be relevant. When an insurer considers a claim for payment they will usually issue an "Explanation of Benefits," commonly referred to as an "EOB." As explained earlier in the text, insurance companies often negotiate payments of much less than what is charged by the provider. Typically, insurance is not to be considered or even mentioned at trial. Thus, the plaintiff's duty is to present the original bills for services as evidence of the extent of that component of damage. The defense can, however, without making reference to the insurance, demonstrate the actual amount accepted as payment for services. This may seem like a trivial item, but in cases of even minor surgical treatment the amounts billed and accepted as payment can differ by tens of thousands of dollars. This is evidenced in Application 8.4.

APPLICATION 8.4

Ben suffered a broken rib in an accident. The emergency room doctor determined Ben had a punctured lung resulting from the broken rib. Part of his emergency medical treatment at the hospital was a commonly performed, but invasive, procedure to reinflate his lung. Ben was released from the hospital two days after his accident. He later contracted a serious bacterial infection and was hospitalized for an additional 10 days. Ben distinctly recalled watching the doctor in the busy emergency room treat another patient on a nearby bed and then undertake Ben's treatment without washing his hands or even changing his gloves. During litigation it was discovered that the doctor found Ben's lung had not actually been punctured. It was also discovered that the other patient treated by the doctor suffered from exactly the same bacterial infection contracted by Ben. Ben sued the hospital and the doctor for malpractice.

The billing for the initial two days in the hospital and the procedures in the emergency room was $12,500. The second hospitalization was $35,000. However, the contract between the hospital and insurance company resulted in an actual payment of $14,250 for all charges. In litigation of a case of this type, a plaintiff might well submit the original bills as evidence. In response, the defendant could show that the actual charges accepted as full payment was $33,250 less than the plaintiff

(continued)

alleged. Care must usually be taken not to discuss the presence of insurance, and in this case the defense would need to be careful not to create the impression that they lowered the bill as an implicit admission of fault.

MEDICAL DEVICES AND EQUIPMENT

There are two different issues with respect to the role of medical devices and equipment in medical malpractice cases. One involves a defect in the device or equipment. The other involves the actual use of the device or equipment. Obviously, if the device or equipment is flawed either in design or manufacture, an action based in products liability may be brought against those in the chain of commerce from creation to delivery of the product. However, this is not usually considered part of the medical malpractice action. It would most often be brought as a civil case founded on products liability principles, but if a health care professional knew or should have known of the flaw and proceeded to use the product, a medical malpractice case may ensue as well. In the second situation, when the product is not defective but is used in an inappropriate manner by the health care professional, and even though the key elements of the case involve medical equipment or devices, the liability is claimed based on the improper use by the health care professional in the delivery of services.

In the first situation, as soon as the risk management team or legal investigator become aware of a possible product defect, the research trail must begin. The first step is to determine if the flaw in the equipment or device was previously known by members of the profession or the manufacturer. This requires contact with the manufacturer, distributor, and researching publications that have information regarding the product. These publications range from newspapers, to Internet news sources, professional medical publications, and even legal publications for other cases involving the product. It is important to realize that the plaintiff is probably conducting the very same research. If it can be established that the defect was previously discovered and information about the defect published, it will be more difficult to defend on the basis that the professional did not know or should have known of the defect as demonstrated in Application 8.5.

APPLICATION 8.5

Katrina was employed as a nurse on a hospital surgical team. Part of her routine duties was to inspect any tools and products to be used in surgery. She is also required to review any correspondence from the risk management department and manufacturers regarding the products used. On one occasion, after a week-long vacation, she is scheduled as part of the surgical team early in the morning on her first day back. She plans to go over her mail later in the day. She is unaware that her mail contains a correspondence requesting the immediate cessation of use of a particular product used with patients under general anesthesia. In the surgical case that morning, complications arise and the patient dies. Ultimately, it is discovered that the product to be discontinued was the same product that resulted in the patient's death.

In this case, proper investigation by the defense and full disclosure by staff would allow a clearer evaluation of the potential liability if it could be shown at a trial by plaintiff that the health care professionals should have known the product was unsafe and used it anyway.

In the second situation, the investigation proceeds much the same way as any other malpractice action, but product flaws or defects should also be ruled out at this time. In addition to the ordinary steps of investigation, the individual(s) who allegedly committed the malpractice should be reviewed quite thoroughly with respect to their knowledge, training, and skill in the use of the item of equipment or device which was alleged to have been improperly used. See Application 8.6.

APPLICATION 8.6

Mark was a longtime patient of his family physician who had a large practice in an urban community. He was injured during a softball game and was concerned he'd broken his ankle. He went to his family physician's office where an X ray was taken by the technician on staff. The technician was the niece of the physician, who employed her. She had been unable to obtain employment anywhere else locally due to the fact that she had only the minimum acceptable grades to graduate from the training program she'd attended and no references or recommendations to support her. In this instance, she positioned the foot and leg improperly during the X ray. The X ray did not reveal a fracture at the juncture of the foot and leg. As a result Mark's leg was not properly treated. Ultimately, he sought the advice of another physician who advised surgery to correct the problems as the result of leaving the fracture untreated.

Proper use of the x-ray equipment would have revealed the fracture; however, the marginal skills of the technician resulted in the physician's failure to properly diagnose the injury. A plaintiff might allege respondeat superior on the part of the physician as well as independent responsibility of the physician for failing to recognize the X ray was not sufficient to make a proper diagnosis.

PHOTOGRAPHIC AND TANGIBLE EVIDENCE

One additional step that should be completed in the preliminary investigation of the case is the evaluation and, possibly, creation of photographic and tangible evidence that may be used in litigation. Photographic evidence consists of photos, video, or any other pictorial documentation relevant to the incident. This may include pictures of the site where the incident occurred, injuries, etc. Tangible evidence includes those physical items other than documents and photographic evidence. Examples of such items might be medical equipment or devices. While popular media such as television and movies often portray testimony as the most powerful evidence, in reality that is not always the case. Consider the following example based on an actual case scenario.

APPLICATION 8.7

Margie was a 48-year-old woman hospitalized for removal of her gallbladder. A few hours after surgery she was found lying on the floor of her room. She alleged that she had rolled over in her sleep and fallen from the bed where the side rail had been left down by a nurse after Margie was returned to her room following surgery. Margie

(continued)

complained of severe back pain. Ultimately, she filed suit against the hospital claiming malpractice. Among her allegations were the claims that she was completely and totally disabled from her injury and unable to work in any capacity. During the investigation of the case, a legal investigator observed and videotaped Margie carrying two buckets (one full of cleaning supplies and another full of water). She then positioned a ladder alongside her house and proceeded to carry the two buckets up the ladder and began cleaning the windows on the exterior of her two-story home.

In this case, it would be quite beneficial to the defense to have this information as early on as possible for purposes of dismissing the claims of the plaintiff and avoiding costly litigation.

While not every case develops such dramatic evidence as in Application 8.6 above (based on an actual case), the objective from the defense perspective is the same. It is important to consider the validity of all aspects of the claim by a plaintiff from allegations of liability to the true nature of the injuries claimed. The earlier the information, both positive and adverse, is ascertained, the more likely the case can be concluded with a minimum of cost to both sides.

EXPERT OPINIONS

A final consideration in the evaluation of a medical malpractice claim is the presentation of **expert opinions**. These consist of documented statements by health care professionals who have reviewed the available information in the case and rendered a formal opinion as to whether malfeasance has occurred. Essentially, the expert gives a statement based on professional expertise, education, and training as to whether the health care provider deviated from the customary and accepted practices of their profession to the extent it could have caused injury. Expert opinions are of paramount importance in medical malpractice cases. In several states they are required by statute for a case to succeed. The logic behind this is that the average layperson may not have sufficient knowledge of how a health care professional should conduct him or herself in a given situation, especially where decisions involving treatment are concerned. Thus, the judge and jury are entitled to consider the opinion of other health care professionals. As a result, one of the early steps in investigation of a medical malpractice claim is to seek out the opinion of a medical health care professional. Typically, the expert will consider all information available concerning the claim and then issue a written statement, sometimes in the form of a sworn affidavit, if necessary, that states whether in his or her professional opinion the health care professional(s) involved deviated from the accepted standard of care in the delivery of health care, treatment, and services. While not controlling, this type of information tends to be very influential with juries and thus is extremely important in the consideration of the viability of a case. Keep in mind that the opposition is very likely seeking the same type of evidence and will very possibly have a contradictory expert opinion. At that point, it boils down to which side has the most credible opinion, making the selection of the proper expert in a case a crucial part of the investigative process.

EVALUATION OF THE VIABILITY OF THE CLAIM

From the perspective of the defense, it is extremely important for the party evaluating the viability of the claim to remain objective. When viewing the case from the viewpoint of the plaintiff it is from one who believes they have been injured. In the case of the defense, it is necessary to consider whether one's conduct was so below the standards of the profession as to constitute malpractice. Even if someone is in the position of a risk manager employed by a potential defendant, it is important to consider the case in terms of legal and professional standards and put personal feelings and loyalties aside.

To properly evaluate the viability of the claim, the following questions must be answered:

- Were any regulatory, statutory, certification, or licenser provisions violated?
- Were the actions of the potential defendant(s) subject to the theory of respondeat superior?
- What are the qualifications and credibility of the potential defendant(s) as a health care professional?
- Was the incident witnessed by individuals who are objective, partial to the defense, or partial to the plaintiff?
- Was the incident identified and documented at the time of the occurrence?
- To what extent were the plaintiff's alleged injuries the direct and proximate result of the potential defendant(s) conduct?
- What evidence is available to support or refute a claim of malpractice?
- What are the strengths and weaknesses of the available expert opinion?

An extremely important consideration in the summary evaluation of a potential claim of malpractice is whether any applicable medical malpractice statutes will apply to the procedure or outcome of the case. From the perspective of the defense, it is necessary to be prepared to compel the plaintiff to comply with any statutory pre-litigation requirements and to be ready to deal with any requirements on the part of the defense. In most cases, malpractice legislation has a greater impact on the plaintiff, but a diligent defense has won many cases of alleged medical malpractice on procedural points. For example, as discussed in earlier chapters, the discovery rule in many states has been severely limited in malpractice cases and can be a way to avoid litigation almost from the outset if a defendant can establish that the time for bringing the claim has passed. As a result, it is just as important to consider the statutory requirements as the actual basis for liability.

Court of Appeals of Michigan.

Muriel SILLS and Thomas Sills, Plaintiffs-Appellant,
v.
OAKLAND GENERAL HOSPITAL, Howard S. Glazer, D.O., Dennis Kelly, D.O., Simon Simonian, D.O., and Harold P. Finkel, D.O., Defendants-Appellees.

Decided Nov. 26, 1996, at 9:40 a.m.

(continued)

In 1987, forty-one-year-old plaintiff Muriel Sills, who had a twenty-year history of back trauma and back surgeries, complained of back pain and difficulty walking. Defendant Dr. Howard Glazer admitted plaintiff to defendant Oakland General Hospital on July 16, 1987. That same day, defendant Dr. Dennis Kelly evaluated plaintiff and ordered the administration of Solu-Medrol, a steroid. One potential side effect of the use of steroids is necrosis. From July 16 through July 28, plaintiff received varying doses of the steroid. During this time, defendants Dr. Simon Simonian and Dr. Harold Finkel each provided a consultation. On July 30, 1987, plaintiff discharged herself from Oakland General Hospital because she was dissatisfied with her progress. She continued to see defendant Glazer.

In 1991, plaintiff complained to Glazer of pain and swelling in her legs and knees. In May, 1993, Glazer ordered an x-ray of plaintiff's right knee. Glazer told plaintiff that in his opinion she had arthritis. In October 1993, Kelly ordered a Magnetic Resonance Imaging (MRI) of plaintiff's right knee. The MRI revealed osteonecrosis (a change in bone and cartilage), which can be caused by steroid use. Doctors eventually replaced plaintiff's right knee.

In her March 1994 suit, plaintiff alleged in part that in 1987 defendants failed to provide the proper diagnosis, improperly ordered extremely high doses of steroids, and neglected to warn her of the risks of steroids. The circuit court granted summary disposition for defendants, ruling that plaintiff's action was untimely under the statute of limitation, M.C.L. § 600.5838a(2); M.S.A. § 27A.5838(1)(2). The court also ruled that defendants' conduct did not meet the fraudulent conduct standard under M.C.L. § 600.5838a(2)(a); M.S.A. § 27A.5838(1)(2)(a). Plaintiff appeals.

Plaintiff first argues that defendants did not assert as an affirmative defense the statute of repose upon which they rely on appeal. Plaintiff contends that, because the Legislature has recognized a distinction between a statute of limitation and a statute of repose, defendants should have referenced the statute as one of repose rather than limitation.

Defendants moved for summary disposition under MCR 2.116(C)(7); such a motion asserts that the cause of action is statutorily barred. *Witherspoon v. Guilford,* 203 Mich.App. 240, 243, 511 N.W.2d 720 (1994). When reviewing a motion under MCR 2.117(C)(7), this Court must accept the plaintiff's well-pleaded allegations as true and construe them in the plaintiff's favor. If the facts are not in dispute, whether the statute bars the claim is a question of law for the court. *Witherspoon,* at 243, 511 N.W.2d 720. We review questions of law under the de novo standard. *Rapistan Corp. v. Michaels,* 203 Mich.App. 301, 306, 511 N.W.2d 918 (1994).

M.C.L. § 600.5838a(2); M.S.A. § 27A.5838(1)(2) provides in part:

> Except as otherwise provided in this subsection, an action involving a claim based on medical malpractice may be commenced at any time within the applicable period prescribed in section 5805 or sections 5851 to 5856, or within 6 months after the plaintiff discovers or should have discovered the existence of the claim, whichever is later. However, except as otherwise provided in section 5851(7) or (8), the claim shall not be commenced later than 6 years after the date of the act or omission that is the basis for the claim. The burden of proving that the plaintiff, as a result of physical discomfort, appearance, condition, or otherwise, neither discovered nor should have discovered the existence of the claim at least 6 months before the expiration of the period otherwise applicable to the claim is on the plaintiff. A medical malpractice action that is not commenced within the time prescribed by this subsection is barred.

Plaintiff contends that M.C.L. § 600.5838a(2); M.S.A. § 27A.5838(1)(2) is a statute of repose, not limitation. A statute of repose prevents a cause of action from ever accruing when the injury is sustained after the designated statutory period has elapsed. *O'Brien v. Hazelet & Erdal,* 410 Mich. 1, 15, 299 N.W.2d 336 (1980).

(continued)

A statute of limitation, however, prescribes the time limits in which a party may bring an action that has already accrued. *Id.; Smith v. Quality Const. Co.*, 200 Mich.App. 297, 300-301, 503 N.W.2d 753 (1993). Here, M.C.L. § 600.5838a(2); M.S.A. § 27A.5838(1)(2) serves both functions: it prescribes the time limit in which a plaintiff who is injured within the statutory period must bring suit and also prevents a plaintiff from bringing suit if she sustained an injury outside the statutory period. Because the statute is both a statute of limitations and a statute of repose, defendants **352 were not obliged to refer specifically to their defense as a statute of repose.

Moreover, plaintiff claims that her injury occurred in 1987, when defendants treated her with steroids during her hospitalization. M.C.L. § 600.5838a(2); M.S.A. § 27A.5838(1)(2) bars her cause of action because plaintiff brought suit outside the statutory period after sustaining injury. M.C.L. § 600.5838a(2); M.S.A. § 27A.5838(1)(2) thus acted as a statute of limitation in this case. Defendants raised the statute of limitation as an affirmative defense. Plaintiff's argument that defendants did not refer to M.C.L. § 600.5838a(2); M.S.A. § 27A.5838(1)(2) as a statute of repose is thus immaterial here. Likewise, plaintiff's claim that defendants did not give her sufficient notice of their statutory defense is without merit. Defendants properly asserted the statute as an affirmative defense. MCR 2.111(F)(3)(a).

Plaintiff next attacks the circuit court's finding that defendants did not engage in fraudulent conduct. Plaintiff asserts that defendants prevented her from discovering the existence of her claim by failing to inform her of the risk of steroids. Plaintiff adds that Glazer misrepresented her condition by diagnosing arthritis rather than necrosis.

M.C.L. § 600.5838a(2)(a); M.S.A. § 27A.5838(1)(2)(a) provides that the limitation period does not apply "[i]f discovery of the existence of the claim was prevented by the fraudulent conduct of the health care professional against whom the claim is made ... or of the health facility against whom the claim is made...." Thus, if plaintiff demonstrates that defendants displayed fraudulent conduct, her claim survives the statutory limitation period.

This Court has not yet interpreted "fraudulent conduct" as it is used in M.C.L. § 600.5838a(2)(a); M.S.A. § 27A.5838(1)(2). To define fraudulent conduct, we look to cases involving the limitation period and fraudulent concealment under M.C.L. § 600.5855; M.S.A. § 27A.5855. Courts consider together statutes that have the same general purpose when ascertaining the intent of the Legislature. *In re Miller Estate*, 359 Mich. 167, 172, 101 N.W.2d 381 (1960). Additionally, statutes that affect similar policies should be interpreted in a like manner. *Swantek v. Automobile Club of Michigan Ins. Group*, 118 Mich.App. 807, 810, 325 N.W.2d 588 (1982).

Under M.C.L. § 600.5855; M.S.A. § 27A.5855, the statute of limitation is tolled when a party conceals the fact that the plaintiff has a cause of action. *Smith v. Sinai Hosp. of Detroit,* 152 Mich.App. 716, 727, 394 N.W.2d 82 (1986). The plaintiff must plead in the complaint the acts or misrepresentations that comprised the fraudulent concealment. *In re Farris Estate*, 160 Mich.App. 14, 18, 408 N.W.2d 92 (1987). The plaintiff must prove that the defendant committed affirmative acts or misrepresentations that were designed to prevent subsequent discovery. Mere silence is insufficient. *Buszek v. Harper Hosp.*, 116 Mich.App. 650, 654, 323 N.W.2d 330 (1982).

In her complaint, plaintiff did not claim that defendants affirmatively acted or made misrepresentations to prevent her from discovering the alleged malpractice. Although plaintiff claimed that defendants failed to inform her of the risks of steroids, that allegation was part of her general claim of malpractice, not a claim of fraud. While Glazer may have misdiagnosed plaintiff's condition, plaintiff did not show that he acted fraudulently to conceal her potential cause of action. A misdiagnosis is not an affirmative act to conceal a claim. Plaintiff has not sufficiently asserted that defendants committed fraudulent conduct so as to toll the statute of limitation.

Plaintiff next asserts that she did not discover, nor should she have discovered, the existence of her claim at least six months before the limitation period expired. Plaintiff contends that the six-year limitation for discovery of her malpractice claim thus should not apply. M.C.L. § 600.5838a(2); M.S.A. § 27A.5838(1)(2)

(continued)

provides in part that the action must be commenced within six months after the plaintiff discovers or should have discovered the existence of the claim but no later than six years after the date of the act or omission that is the basis for the claim. Our Supreme Court has noted that the above statute sets a limit for discovery of a medical malpractice claim at six years from the date of the act or omission that is the basis of the claim. *Chase v. Sabin*, 445 Mich. 190, 201-202 n. 16, 516 N.W.2d 60 (1994). Plaintiff has not met her burden of showing why the six-year limitation should not apply.

Finally, plaintiff contends that the statute violates her due process and equal protection rights. We review the constitutionality of a statute, which is a question of law, under the de novo standard. *Monroe Beverage Co., Inc. v. Stroh Brewery Co.*, 211 Mich.App. 286, 295, 535 N.W.2d 253 (1995); *In re Lafayette Towers*, 200 Mich.App. 269, 273, 503 N.W.2d 740 (1993).

In *O'Brien, supra*, our Supreme Court addressed whether a six-year period of limitation, M.C.L. § 600.5839; M.S.A. § 27A.5839, violated the plaintiff's due process and equal protection rights. Although the statute in that case applied to actions against architects, engineers, contractors, and land surveyors, the Court's analysis equally is applicable. Under *O'Brien*, to determine whether a statute violates due process, we ask whether it bears a reasonable relation to a permissible legislative objective. *O'Brien*, at 13, 299 N.W.2d 336.

Statutes of limitation are designed to encourage the rapid recovery of damages, to penalize plaintiffs who have not been assiduous in pursuing their claims, to afford security against stale demands when the circumstances would be unfavorable to a just examination and decision, to relieve defendants of the prolonged threat of litigation, to prevent plaintiffs from asserting fraudulent claims, and to remedy the general inconvenience resulting from delay in asserting a legal right that is practicable to assert. *Lemmerman v. Fealk*, 449 Mich. 56, 65, 534 N.W.2d 695 (1995). Because the statute at issue bears a reasonable relationship to the noted legislative purposes, it does not violate plaintiff's right to due process.

The Legislature has the power to determine that a particular cause of action cannot arise unless it accrues within a specified period. *O'Brien*, at 15, 299 N.W.2d 336. Courts should uphold statutes of limitation unless the consequences are so harsh and unreasonable that they effectively divest a plaintiff of the court access intended by the grant of the substantive right. *Bissell v. Kommareddi*, 202 Mich.App. 578, 581, 509 N.W.2d 542 (1993). The statute here is not so harsh and unreasonable that it effectively denies a plaintiff access to the courts.

Likewise, to decide whether a statute violates equal protection, courts must determine whether the classification is rationally related to a legitimate governmental interest. *O'Brien*, at 13, 299 N.W.2d 336. In *Bissell, supra*, this Court addressed equal protection in the context of M.C.L. § 600.5851(7); M.S.A. § 27A.5851(7), which provides in part that a medical malpractice claim that accrues to a person older than thirteen is subject to the limitation period in M.C.L. § 600.5838a(2); M.S.A.§ 27A.5838(1)(2). This Court held that the state unquestionably has a legitimate interest in securing adequate and affordable healthcare for its residents. Additionally, this Court stated that it could reasonably assume that a decrease in exposure to malpractice claims would encourage healthcare providers to remain in this state. *Bissell*, at 579-581, 509 N.W.2d 542. Likewise, in this case, Michigan has a legitimate interest in supporting affordable and adequate healthcare for its residents. Setting an upper limit for the period within which a plaintiff may bring medical malpractice decreases doctors' exposure to malpractice claims. The classification is rationally related to those interests. Affirmed.

Finally, the case must be considered from the perspective of whether the plaintiff has contributed in any way to his or her own injury or damage. This was discussed early in the text in terms of contributory or comparative negligence standards. Consider whether the plaintiff suffered from any pre-existing conditions that were exacerbated rather than created by the defendant's conduct. Also, was the patient in compliance with all prescribed care, treatment, and services prior to and following injury? Has the plaintiff's conduct in any way failed to mitigate the damage or repair it? These considerations all affect issues of liability and damage and must be taken into account when determining whether the potential defendant is likely to be found responsible for the plaintiff's injuries and damage as the result of malpractice.

Problem 8.1

Complete 8.1 of the Comprehensive Problem in Appendix A.

CHAPTER SUMMARY

As can be seen from the discussion in this chapter, there are many issues to be addressed from the viewpoint of the defense that are distinct from those of the plaintiff when evaluating a potential case of medical malpractice. While the defense may have increased access to some evidence, there may also be severely limited access to information that the defendant may be unaware of. Another pitfall is the possible unwillingness of individuals to admit wrongdoing to superiors because of the threat of ramifications to their own employment, licensure, or certification. Nevertheless, it is necessary to gather and compile information, including a thorough investigation of the known facts of the case, proper witness interviewing techniques, consideration of available documentary and tangible evidence, the role of the plaintiff, and the effects of applicable regulations and legislation. If all these steps are properly completed, they can provide a well-founded evaluation of the viability of a medical malpractice claim against the potential defendant(s).

Key Terms	
deep pocket	expert opinion

For additional resources, go to http://www.westlegalstudies.com.

9 CHAPTER
The Pretrial Stages of a Malpractice Claim

CHAPTER OBJECTIVES
When you complete this chapter, you should be able to:

- Explain the reasons why it is necessary to fully research medical malpractice legislation prior to filing suit
- Discuss the basic procedures for commencement of suit
- Distinguish the various types of pleadings and pretrial motions
- Define a prima facie case
- Describe the various elements of discovery
- Discuss alternative dispute resolution and settlement

STATUTORY CONSIDERATIONS

The commencement of a medical malpractice action is quite different from other civil actions in many jurisdictions. Earlier discussions in this book have explored the various attempts by jurisdictions to deal with the increasing number of malpractice actions and their often sizable judgments in cases where the plaintiff prevails. Many of these statutes have incorporated preliminary steps designed to reduce the number of claims that are frivolous or those that, at best, have doubtfully sufficient evidence to support a claim of medical malpractice. Some of the more common statutory schemes leading to this end include panels that review potential suits; the option for a preliminary arbitration of the claim, or required review of the claim; and affidavit or certification by an expert witness who finds the potential for a meritorious case. The following illustration, Exhibit 9.1, provides a sample of statutory excerpts of preliminary provisions applied in some jurisdictions to medical malpractice cases.

Once it has been determined that any statutory prerequisites are properly satisfied, the plaintiff may move forward with the commencement of suit. At this point, the case takes on many of the aspects of a traditional lawsuit in terms of framing the initial pleadings and commencement.

Exhibit 9.1 Sample Statutory Language

Neb.Rev.St. § 44-2840

NEBRASKA REVISED STATUTES OF 1943
CHAPTER 44. INSURANCE
ARTICLE 28. NEBRASKA HOSPITAL-MEDICAL LIABILITY ACT

§ 44-2840. Medical review panels; review claims; procedure; waiver.

(1) Provision is hereby made for the establishment of medical review panels to review all malpractice claims against health care providers covered by the Nebraska Hospital-Medical Liability Act in advance of filing such actions.

(2) No action against a health care provider may be commenced in any court of this state before the claimant's proposed complaint has been presented to a medical review panel established pursuant to section 44-2841 and an opinion has been rendered by the panel.

(3) The proceedings for action by the medical review panel shall be initiated by the patient or his or her representative by notice in writing with copy of a proposed complaint served upon the director personally or by registered or certified mail. Such notice shall designate the claimant's choice of the physician to serve on the panel, claimant's suggestion of an attorney to serve, and the court where the action shall be filed, if necessary.

(4) The claimant may affirmatively waive his or her right to a panel review, and in such case the claimant may proceed to file his or her action directly in court. If the claimant waives the panel review, the claimant shall serve a copy of the complaint upon the director personally or by registered or certified mail at the time the action is filed in court.

Source: Laws 1976, LB 434, § 40; Laws 1984, LB 692, § 16; Laws 2002, LB 876, § 75; Laws 2003, LB 146, § 5. Effective date August 31, 2003.

West's F.S.A. § 766.203

West's Florida Statutes Annotated
Title XLV. Torts
Medical Malpractice and Related Matters

766.203. Presuit investigation of medical negligence claims and defenses by prospective parties

IN;1**(1) Application of presuit investigation.**—Presuit investigation of medical negligence claims and defenses pursuant to this section and - shall apply to all medical negligence claims and defenses. This shall include:
(a) Rights of action under and defenses thereto.
(b) Rights of action involving the state or its agencies or subdivisions, or the officers, employees, or agents thereof, pursuant to and defenses thereto.

IN;3**(2) Presuit investigation by claimant.**—Prior to issuing notification of intent to initiate medical negligence litigation pursuant to, the claimant shall conduct an investigation to ascertain that there are reasonable grounds to believe that:
(a) Any named defendant in the litigation was negligent in the care or treatment of the claimant; and
(b) Such negligence resulted in injury to the claimant.

Corroboration of reasonable grounds to initiate medical negligence litigation shall be provided by the claimant's submission of a verified written medical expert opinion from a medical expert as defined in, at the time the

(continued)

Exhibit 9.1, continued

notice of intent to initiate litigation is mailed, which statement shall corroborate reasonable grounds to support the claim of medical negligence.

IN;4**(3) Presuit investigation by prospective defendant.**—Prior to issuing its response to the claimant's notice of intent to initiate litigation, during the time period for response authorized pursuant to, the prospective defendant or the defendant's insurer or self-insurer shall conduct an investigation as provided in to ascertain whether there are reasonable grounds to believe that:

(a) The defendant was negligent in the care or treatment of the claimant; and

(b) Such negligence resulted in injury to the claimant.

Corroboration of lack of reasonable grounds for medical negligence litigation shall be provided with any response rejecting the claim by the defendant's submission of a verified written medical expert opinion from a medical expert as defined in, at the time the response rejecting the claim is mailed, which statement shall corroborate reasonable grounds for lack of negligent injury sufficient to support the response denying negligent injury.

IN;5**(4) Presuit medical expert opinion.**—The medical expert opinions required by this section are subject to discovery. The opinions shall specify whether any previous opinion by the same medical expert has been disqualified and if so the name of the court and the case number in which the ruling was issued.

COMMENCEMENT OF THE SUIT

The case actually begins its process through the court system with what is known as commencement. This stage begins when the legal documents are filed with the courts and copies, along with proper notice of the suit, are given to the defendant. The first legal document of substance, as opposed to procedural forms, is the **complaint** or **petition**. An action is filed by the plaintiff, who presents the complaint or petition along with the proper procedural forms and filing fees to the clerk of the court. Traditionally, there were two types of courts and, in turn, two types of opening pleadings. A complaint sought monetary damages and a petition sought some sort of equitable relief (conduct demanded by fairness) such as the distribution of assets or some other sort of specific court-ordered action by the defendant for the benefit of the plaintiff. In recent years, the terms complaint and petition have both come to represent the opening pleading for either type of lawsuit in some jurisdictions as the authority of many courts has become blended regarding their ability to determine matters of equity and law. Some courts still distinguish actions at equity from actions at law (e.g., an action for an order of dissolution of marriage versus an action for compensatory damages). Today the proper choice of terminology is usually guided by the custom of the court where the case is filed rather than the type of relief sought. The key is to consult the procedural rules of the jurisdiction and specifically of the court where the case is intended to be filed to obtain the proper form.

Once the form is established, it is necessary to prepare the appropriate documents to commence the lawsuit. Typically this will include the complaint or petition and necessary paperwork to properly notify the defense of the action. In medical malpractice cases, there may be additional statutory requirements with respect to how a complaint is formed or information that must be included. However, because of the numerous potential variations among jurisdictions, the discussion here will be confined to the traditional principles that support a proper complaint.

PLEADINGS AND PRETRIAL MOTIONS

Once the complaint has been properly filed, proper notice of the suit must be provided to the defendant. The facts of the case and state requirements regarding preliminary steps in medical malpractice cases are open to the public, allowing the defense to be aware of the impending litigation. Nevertheless, a defendant in a medical malpractice case is generally entitled to the same procedural benefits as any other civil defendant, including proper notice of the exact nature of the claim against the defendant and all legal theories—known as causes of action—that are advanced by the plaintiff. Consider the following example in Exhibit 9.2.

Exhibit 9.2 Complaint

**IN THE DISTRICT COURT
COUNTY OF NEWVILLE
STATE OF ILINCH**

**Estate of Jorge Jones (deceased) ;
Jeanette Jones,
Marcus Jones (a minor) by and through his next friend
Jeanette Jones,**

v.   Case No. 04-1106

Michie A. Xwander, M.D.

COMPLAINT

**COUNT I
NEGLIGENCE**

Now comes the **Estate of George Jones (deceased)**, hereinafter referred to as "decedent," by and through its legal representative hereinafter referred to as "plaintiff," and for Count I of its cause of action against Defendant Michie A. Xwander, M.D. hereinafter referred to as "defendant" states as follows:

1. This court has jurisdiction over this matter by virtue of the following facts:

    a) Decedent, at the time this cause of action accrued was domiciled within the city of Newville, county of Newville, Ilinch;

    b) Defendant's primary place of business is within the City of Newville, County of Newville, Ilinch;

    c) all circumstances giving rise to this cause of action occurred within the geographical boundaries of Newville, Ilinch.

(continued)

Exhibit 9.2, continued

   d) Plaintiff is the duly appointed legal representative of the Estate of the decedent per order of the Newville District court dated April 1, 2003.

   2. Defendant has continuously operated a medical practice, specializing in adult internal medicine, at 1006 Diamond Drive, South City, County of Newville, State of Ilinch since on or about May 30, 2000.

   3. On or about October 11, 2000, the decedent, a 62-year-old male, established himself as a patient of defendant's medical practice.

   4. On or about March 1, 2002, decedent was seen by defendant in her medical practice at which time the defendant diagnosed the decedent as having common flu after decedent provided complaints of intermittent nausea, dizziness, periodic fevers, and chronic headache for a period of several weeks prior.

   5. On or about March 1, 2002, defendant prescribed an antibiotic medication for a period of five days and further prescribed rest. Defendant conducted no diagnostic tests at this time and the physical exam consisted only of listening to plaintiff's lungs with the assistance of a stethoscope.

   6. Defendant saw decedent as a patient on three subsequent occasions, specifically March 28, 2002, April 15, 2002, and May 8, 2002. On each occasion the decedent complained of the same symptoms as on the March 1, 2002.

   7. On each of the visits to defendant, aforementioned in paragraph 6 of this complaint, the defendant's diagnosis and prescribed treatment remained the same. On none of these visits did defendant conduct or prescribe diagnostic testing including, but not limited to, taking plaintiff's blood pressure.

   8. On or about June 15, 2002, the decedent lost consciousness at work and was transported by ambulance to Saints of Mercy hospital in Newville.

   9. Diagnostic X rays revealed a large tumor in the brain of the decedent which was later found to be an advanced form of cancer.

   10. Further diagnostic tests found the tumor had progressed to a stage of growth so as to be inoperable and unresponsive to treatment.

   11. On or about August 2, 2002, decedent died as a result of the brain tumor.

   12. That defendant, as decedent's primary care physician owed a direct duty toward the decedent to act with reasonable skill for decedent's medical care and treatment.

   13. That defendant breached said duty on multiple occasions when she failed to conduct any investigative procedures or tests with respect to decedent's symptoms.

(continued)

Exhibit 9.2, continued

14. That the form of cancer from which decedent suffered was highly treatable and operable if diagnosed in a timely fashion.

15. That defendant's breach of duty was the direct and proximate cause of the undiagnosed progression of decedent's cancer to a point where it was no longer operable or treatable.

16. As a direct and proximate result of defendant's negligent conduct, decedent suffered greatly and ultimately died on or about August 2, 2002.

WHEREFORE, plaintiff prays judgment in its favor and against the defendant in an amount in excess of Eight Million dollars and such other and necessary relief as the court deems necessary and proper.

COUNT I I
NEGLIGENCE

Now comes the Jeannette Jones and Marcus Jones, a minor by and through his next friend Jeannette Jones, hereinafter referred to as "plaintiffs," and for Count II of their cause of action against defendant Michie A. Xwander, M.D. hereinafter referred to as "defendant" states as follows:

1. Plaintiffs repeat and incorporate by reference Paragraphs 1-16 of Count I of this complaint.

2. During his lifetime, decedent provided income, comfort, and support for himself and members of his family.

3. As a result of defendant's negligence, the decedent's family no longer has the benefits of his income, comfort, and support.

WHEREFORE, plaintiff prays judgment in its favor and against the defendant in an amount in excess of Eight Million dollars and such other and necessary relief as the court deems necessary and proper.

_____

Attorney For Plaintiff

License #_____

A summons is a formal legal notice of a lawsuit. It is issued to the defendant in the lawsuit, and is usually accompanied by a copy of the complaint that has been filed with the court. The method of giving this notice of the suit is prescribed by procedural law. A summons indicates how long a party has to respond to the allegations of the complaint. Methods of service include personal delivery to the defendant or an allowable representative; publication of the information in a newspaper where the defendant is known to have last resided; and other methods, permitted in some jurisdictions, such as notice by registered mail.

Whatever method used, it must be one permitted by law and one that is reasonably believed to be the best method by which to provide the defendant with notice of the claim. If the defendant does not respond to the complaint within the allotted time period, the court will accept everything alleged in the complaint as true and grant a decision in favor of the plaintiff. This is known as a default judgment.

A defendant has a variety of alternatives when responding to the complaint. While the title of the document may vary somewhat among jurisdictions, the options are basically the same and include the following:

- challenge to the method and timeliness of service of process;
- challenge to the procedural form and content of the complaint;
- request for additional information prior to a response;
- response to the allegations of the complaint.

When a challenge is made to the method or timeliness of service of process it is typically referred to as a "Motion to Quash." There are many types of motions used throughout the litigation process. The common denominator is that a Motion is a formal request for an order of court on a particular issue. In the Motion to Quash, the defendant alleges that there is a defect in the preparation or execution of the summons. It may be something such as an inappropriate identification of a defendant (e.g., incorrect name); publication in a remotely used newspaper when the defendant was openly conducting business at a public location (i.e., personal service would have been more appropriate), or failure to use proper diligence. There was a time when some plaintiffs would use a tactic of filing a suit prior to the expiration of statute of limitations but then hold off pursuing notification to the defendant for strategic reasons. However, this has been largely disapproved of by the courts and the failure to properly and timely attempt service can result in the case being dismissed for lack of due diligence. The following Motion to Quash demonstrates one method used to accomplish this (see Exhibit 9.3).

Exhibit 9.3 Motion to Quash

IN THE DISTRICT COURT
COUNTY OF NEWVILLE
STATE OF ILINCH

Estate of Jorge Jones (deceased);
Jeanette Jones,
Marcus Jones (a minor) by and through his next friend
Jeanette Jones,
Plaintiffs
v.

Case No. 04-1106

Michie A. Xwander, M.D.
Defendant

(continued)

Exhibit 9.3, continued

MOTION TO QUASH

Now comes the Defendant, by and through her attorneys and serves notice to the Plaintiff Marcus Jones, in the above-captioned cause that she will move this court on the 6th day of March, 2005, for an order quashing service on the defendant in the above-styled case on that basis that service was improperly completed by delivery to an unknown minor visitor at defendant's residence during a large gathering of children at defendant's residence and as such, defendant was not properly or timely notified of the action instituted against her.

Respectfully Submitted,

Another option of a defendant in response to a complaint is a Motion to Dismiss or Demurrer. This type of motion at this stage of the proceedings is used to seek dismissal of the complaint itself. The grounds may be that the motion does not satisfy procedural requirements—ranging from statute of limitations to the form of the document itself. The motion may also be based on a failure to state sufficient information to support the elements of a legally recognized cause of action. In some jurisdictions, only the barest facts need be stated to establish a complaint. In others, the elements and reference to supporting evidence for each cause of action or legal theory advanced must be stated with some specificity. It is important—from the perspective of both the plaintiff and the defendant—to be familiar with the requirements not only of the statutory requirements but also the local rules of the court where the case is filed with respect to the appropriate content of complaints.

If a motion to dismiss or demurrer is granted on grounds other than expiration of the statute of limitations, it is then typical for a plaintiff to be permitted to amend (correct) and refile the complaint within a given period of time. Such a dismissal is considered to be "without prejudice," as the case is still allowed to proceed once defects have been cured. See Exhibit 9.4.

Exhibit 9.4 Motion to Dismiss

**IN THE DISTRICT COURT
COUNTY OF NEWVILLE
STATE OF ILINCH**

**Estate of Jorge Jones (deceased) ;
Jeanette Jones,
Marcus Jones (a minor) by and through his next friend
Jeanette Jones,
Plaintiffs**

(continued)

Exhibit 9.4, continued

v.   Case No. 04-1106

Michie A. Xwander, M.D.
Defendant

MOTION TO DISMISS

Comes now the Defendant in the above-entitled action, by and through her attorney, pursuant to Rules of Court and moves this court that the above-entitled action be dismissed on the ground that it appears on the face of the complaint that this court has no jurisdiction of the subject matter of the action in that the allegations of said complaint fail to state a cause of action upon which relief can be granted pursuant to the requirements of applicable statutory law, specifically the medical malpractice limitation statute, Ilinch Rev. Stat. 40-3451.

WHEREFORE, the defendant prays the Complaint of Plaintiffs be dismissed with prejudice and the plaintiffs be ordered to pay appropriate costs to the defendant, costs of court, and such other necessary and further relief as the court deems necessary and appropriate.

Respectfully Submitted,
Defendant

_____

When a defendant requests additional information from a plaintiff prior to a response to the complaint, it may be known as a "Motion for a Bill of Particulars" or a "Motion to Make More Definite and Certain." See Exhibit 9.5. This document essentially states that the plaintiff failed to include sufficient information in the complaint to permit the defendant to fully understand the nature of the claim and that more information is needed before a response can be properly prepared. In this type of motion the defendant seeks a court order that compels the plaintiff to further clarify or provide additional information before the defendant is required to respond. If the motion is denied, the defendant is generally ordered to answer the complaint as filed.

After any issues with respect to the complaint and service of process are resolved, the defense is in the position of responding to the allegations of the complaint. See Exhibit 9.6 on page 301. Again, jurisdictional practices vary. In some courts, the defendant is permitted to make an "answer" or "response" as a blanket admission or denial of the allegations. In others, however, the defense responds to each allegation of the complaint. The response may be framed in one of three ways. The defendant may admit the allegation—this is common with basic information, such as the identity and location of the parties and jurisdiction of the court, assuming it is uncontested. Second, the defense may deny the allegation, which is commonly the case with respect to claims of wrongdoing by the defendant. Third, the defense may opt to neither admit nor deny until such time as more specific information is available. Once the response has been filed, the parties can begin discovery and the process of litigation.

Exhibit 9.5 Motion to Make More Definite and Certain

**IN THE DISTRICT COURT
COUNTY OF NEWVILLE
STATE OF ILINCH**

**Estate of Jorge Jones (deceased) ;
Jeanette Jones,
Marcus Jones (a minor) by and through his next friend
Jeanette Jones,**

v.   Case No. 04-1106

Michie A. Xwander, M.D.

MOTION TO MAKE MORE DEFINITE AND CERTAIN

Now comes the Defendant, by and through her attorneys and serves notice to the Plaintiff Marcus Jones, in the above-captioned cause that she will move this court on the 6th day of March, 2005, for an order requiring said plaintiff to more fully and completely state the facts supporting the alleged causes of action and damages complained of.

Respectfully Submitted,

_____
Attorney for Defendant
License # _____

In addition to the answers provided to the specific allegations of the complaint, a defendant may also advance an affirmative defense. An affirmative defense is based on the proposition that, regardless of the validity of the allegations of fault, there is an applicable legal theory that would prevent the plaintiff from recovering against the defendant. In situations where an affirmative defense is advanced by the defendant, if the elements of the particular defense are proven, the question of whether the defendant committed malpractice becomes moot. The affirmative defense does not require a balance of the defendant and plaintiff's actions or that the plaintiff sufficiently establishes a prima facie case. In effect, it prevents prosecution of the plaintiff's claim for the purpose of establishing damages. There are a number of affirmative defenses applicable to various types of tort cases, but they typically involve some act or omission on the part of the plaintiff either in sustaining the injury or in legal proceedings that overshadow the conduct of the defendant. Examples of affirmative defenses often advanced in medical malpractice cases include application of a Good Samaritan doctrine recognized in the jurisdiction; pre-existing conditions that would have produced the same result in plaintiff regardless of defendant's conduct; limitation of actions, assumption of risk (with knowledge and appreciation of the danger), sovereign immunity, and so forth.

Exhibit 9.6 Answer

**IN THE DISTRICT COURT
COUNTY OF NEWVILLE
STATE OF ILINCH**

**Estate of Jorge Jones (deceased) ;
Jeanette Jones,
Marcus Jones (a minor) by and through his next friend
Jeanette Jones,
Plaintiffs
v.**

Case No. 04-1106

**Michie A. Xwander, M.D.
Defendant**

ANSWER

Now comes the Defendant, by and through her attorneys and for her answer to plaintiff's complaint, in the above-captioned cause states as follows:

  1. Defendant stipulates to the jurisdiction of this court and supporting facts thereof stated in the plaintiff's complaint.

  2. Defendant wholly denies each and every allegation within plaintiff's complaint as to negligence and/or any other form of malfeasance which would support plaintiff's cause of action.

  3. Defendant denies that any alleged damage on the part of plaintiffs is in any way the proximate result of any conduct by the defendant.

WHEREFORE, the defendant respectfully requests that the above-styled cause of action be determined in the favor of the defendant and that costs be assessed to plaintiff and such other further and necessary relief as the court deems necessary and proper.

Respectfully Submitted,

THE DISCOVERY PROCESS PRIMARY OBJECTIVE: A PRIMA FACIE CASE OR NOT?

During the period prior to trial or settlement, procedural rules guide the parties in their preparations for the ultimate conclusion of the dispute. The most significant event during this time is the **discovery** process. At this stage, the parties further develop their respective investigations and exchange information in accordance with procedural rules and, when necessary, court supervision. Discovery serves a dual purpose. First, it allows the parties to determine what evidence exists on both sides and judge whether there is sufficient supportive evidence of a prima facie case. Second, it enables both parties to negotiate intelligently toward settlement. So, what is a prima facie case in a medical malpractice lawsuit?

In any kind of tort action, a **prima facie** case consists of evidence to support each allegation of the tort claimed by the plaintiff to have been committed by the defendant. For example, in a case of simple negligence, the prima facie case would include evidence that 1) demonstrates the defendant owed a duty toward the plaintiff; 2) shows what a reasonable person (by legal definition) would have done under like circumstances; 3) the defendant failed to act in a manner consistent with what the reasonable person would do under like circumstances; 4) the conduct of the defendant was the proximate cause of compensable damage to the plaintiff. Each tort consists of specific elements that must be established by evidence of a prima facie case in order for the plaintiff to prevail. In a medical malpractice case, a variety of torts may be claimed against a defendant. A prima facie case of each must be shown in order for each particular cause of action to result in a positive outcome for the plaintiff. However, in addition to traditional legal principles, the medical malpractice plaintiff must also take into account any statutory requirements that have been imposed on cases based in allegations of medical malpractice. For example, in many states, a case of medical malpractice cannot succeed without evidence consisting of an expert opinion. This is in contrast to a case of ordinary negligence which may or may not include expert opinion evidence based on whether it is warranted by the facts of the case.

It is not an overstatement that an expert witness can be the single greatest factor in whether a case of medical malpractice is successful. Since both parties will typically have expert witnesses that offer contradictory testimony as to whether malpractice has occurred, it often boils down to which expert testimony is the most credible. While the facts of the case are obviously important, also highly relevant are the qualifications of the expert who interprets these facts. There are a number of considerations when choosing an expert.

Some physicians are well known for their expertise in a subject and have developed the skills to communicate effectively in a legal setting. The potential problem with such an expert is that he or she may be perceived as a "hired gun" who will say whatever the hiring party in the case requests. This situation can be overcome if the expert is, in fact, a recognized authority on the specific subject area of the case. Another difficulty is that any expert is subject to the full scope of the discovery rules applicable to the parties, and not only the expert's opinion is considered. The opposition will seek to locate any relevant and material information that might discredit the expert, including a thorough examination of the professional education, training, licensure, malpractice and ethical history, and any other useful information. Consider the following example, based on a real-life scenario, in Application 9.1.

APPLICATION 9.1

Dr. S was an orthopedic surgeon well known in the relatively small community where he practiced. He was the doctor to whom most local patients went when back surgery was considered necessary. In a lawsuit where a patient had been injured in a car accident and another local doctor, Dr. X, had allegedly negligently performed unnecessary

(continued)

> back surgery, Dr. S was hired as the patient's expert witness in the ensuing lawsuit against his original physician, Dr. X. During the suit, the attorneys for Dr. X took the deposition of expert witness Dr. S. A selection of the questions to Dr. S follows:
>
> Question: Dr. S, isn't it true that prior to coming to this community to establish your practice 10 years ago, you were in practice in the community of Smithville, in the state of L?
>
> Answer: Yes. My wife's family was here and we moved so our children were nearer their grandparents.
>
> Question: Dr. S, isn't it also true that you left that community after your privileges were suspended for performing excessive and unnecessary surgery at both of the hospitals where you were on staff?
>
> Answer: I explained why I left that community.
>
> Question: Dr. S, were your privileges at hospitals A and B suspended?
>
> Answer: Yes.
>
> Question: Dr. S, were your privileges suspended for performing excessive and unnecessary surgery?
>
> Answer: That was the reason stated but I did not agree.
>
> Question: Dr. S, what would you consider the real reason for the suspension?
>
> Answer: They feared my excellence.

In the example above, the doctor chosen as an expert had a background that was relevant and testimony that would be detrimental to the plaintiff's case. The failure to carefully consider the background of this expert was a costly mistake. The only real alternative was to locate another expert and start over. Because highly qualified expert witnesses can add significant costs to medical malpractice litigation, it is important that they be fully evaluated before they are retained as the expert and disclosed to the opposition.

The primary objective during the continued investigation and discovery process is to locate any and all evidence that refutes the claims of the opposition. This is accomplished by challenging credentials, qualifications, and standards of conduct of the opposing party; identifying weaknesses in the evidence such as credibility of expert witnesses or eye witnesses; and determining any contributory or comparative fault on the part of the plaintiff with respect to either producing the injury or mitigating the damage. With an understanding of the goal in mind, the discovery process can be used in the most effective manner. There are a variety of choices in discovery to obtain information about the evidence possessed by the opposing party. They range from document requests to actual interviews of the opposing party and witnesses. Each of these methods is explained in the discussion that follows. Some jurisdictions do not mandate periodic updates of the information, therefore, a discovery calendar in the file should contain periodic reminders for discovery update requests, including immediately prior to trial. Do you recall the example in Chapter 8 of the video tape showing the allegedly disabled plaintiff doing strenuous physical activity? If this tape had not been recorded until shortly before trial and no update for discovery was mandated or requested, it could pose a tremendous and damaging surprise to the plaintiff's case during trial.

Today, many jurisdictions have adopted rules establishing discovery schedules. This requires each party to complete their discovery of evidence from the opposition within a set time frame. Scheduling has have evolved largely as one more attempt to quickly move the large volume of cases through the judicial system and to prevent parties from dragging out discovery in an attempt to allow evidence to grow stale or even disappear. Even in jurisdictions that do not impose discovery schedules, statutory rules of procedure establish time limits within which many of the various types of discovery are to be completed once they have been submitted by the opposing party. Failure to comply with time limits or reasonably cooperate can result in a Motion to Compel seeking an order of court for immediate compliance and/or cooperation. Ultimately, a Motion for Sanctions may be granted if a court finds that a party is deliberately attempting to thwart the discovery process. If granted, sanctions may range from monetary awards to dismissal of a party's pleadings leaving them no basis to proceed in the case.

Interrogatories

These written questions are submitted to the opposing party (not witnesses) in the case. The party who receives them must answer them within a specified time frame. Generally, they are answered in writing and under oath. A party may object to answering those questions that are irrelevant, immaterial, in violation of the attorney-client privilege, or in violation of some other procedural or evidentiary rule. When an objection is raised, the judge will determine whether the party must answer the questions. Many jurisdictions limit the number of interrogatories and subparts that may be sent to the opposition. Because this information is typically one of the first methods of discovery used and provides a basis to guide additional areas of discovery, the questions should be carefully framed to glean the most information. The following exhibits are examples of some more common medical malpractice interrogatories.

Exhibit 9.7   Plaintiff to Defendant Interrogatories

**IN THE DISTRICT COURT
COUNTY OF NEWVILLE
STATE OF ILINCH**

**Estate of Jorge Jones (deceased) ;
Jeanette Jones,
Marcus Jones (a minor) by and through his next friend
Jeanette Jones,
Plaintiffs
v.**

Case No. 04-1106

**Michie A. Xwander, M.D.
Defendant**

Interrogatories

Plaintiff to Defendant

(continued)

Exhibit 9.7, continued

*note: The following interrogatories are not intended to be exhaustive. Rather, they are a sample of typical subject areas of questions in a malpractice case and are to be used for illustrative purposes only.

Educational History

Name, address, years of attendance, degree or certification earned at all post-secondary schools attended.

All practical training including internships, residency, fellowship and other post-graduate experiences stating identity of training entity, location, start and end dates, and completed programs of study.

Board-certification, including dates of all certification attempts, whether attempts were successful, organization granting certification if successful.

All professional licenses and certifications held, states where licensed, and whether licensing was obtained by examination or by reciprocity.

All hospital affiliations and whether privileges are general or limited and the extent of any limitations.

All professional organizations of which the defendant is a member, date membership commenced, and offices held.

Any teaching positions held, names of institutions, beginning and ending dates of positions, courses and subjects taught.

Any professional publications written, co-authored or contributed, dates, names, and titles of publications including specific title with which defendant is associated.

Each policy of defendant's insurance coverage potentially applicable to the plaintiff's claims, including primary and excess malpractice coverage. Provide identity of all insurance carriers, policy number and monetary limits of coverage.

Any professional disciplinary proceedings in which defendant's conduct was subject by any state or municipal disciplinary board or organization granting defendant certification, including the nature of the proceedings, action taken, reasons, dates, results of action including fines, temporary suspension of license, and revocation of license or other disciplinary measures.

All civil malpractice and related verdicts or judgments won against the defendant.

All lawsuits in which defendant has been named a defendant, including jurisdiction, case number, type of case, and how resolved.

(continued)

Exhibit 9.7, continued

A complete listing of all medical and scientific reference books, journals, or other publications published, updated, or supplemented within immediately preceding five years that are maintained by the defendant, including the author, title, date of copyright, and dates of supplements or updates as applicable, and publisher of each.

Any medical and scientific reference books, journals, or other publications consulted by the defendant prior to, or subsequent to, the plaintiff's treatment, including reason for consultation.

The names, addresses, specialties, and qualifications of each expert expected to testify on behalf of the defendant at trial, and the substance of the expected testimony of each expert witness.

The names, addresses, and titles, if any, of all nonexpert witnesses expected to testify on behalf of the defendant at trial, and the substance of the expected testimony of each witness.

The names addresses, affiliation to defendant, if any, and title, if any, of all persons known by defendant or his or her representatives to have knowledge relevant to the plaintiff, plaintiff's injuries, delivery of health care services to the plaintiff by defendant, or any other information relevant to the conduct of plaintiff or defendant with respect to the plaintiff's injuries.

Exhibit 9.8 Defendant to Plaintiff Interrogatories

IN THE DISTRICT COURT
COUNTY OF NEWVILLE
STATE OF ILINCH

Estate of Jorge Jones (deceased) ;
Jeanette Jones,
Marcus Jones (a minor) by and through his next friend
Jeanette Jones,
Plaintiffs
v.   Case No. 04-1106

Michie A. Xwander, M.D.
Defendant

Describe in detail, how the alleged occurrences happened, giving all events, in detail in the order in which they occurred, which have any relevance on the cause and manner of the alleged occurrences.

(continued)

Exhibit 9.8, continued

Identify to the best knowledge of plaintiff or plaintiff's counsel, any agent or employee of the defendant with relevant knowledge of the allegations against defendant, plaintiff's injuries, or other information relevant to this case. State the name, summary of knowledge or involvement, and the current title, occupation, current or last known residential and business address of each such person.

Describe in detail all aspects of the defendant's employee's or agent's professional medical relationship with the plaintiff, indicating the date of commencement, the nature and extent of any medical relationship prior to the alleged occurrences, and the date and circumstances of the discharge of the plaintiff.

Disclose fully the particulars under which any agent or employee of the defendant came into contact with the plaintiff with regard to the problem for which any agent or employee of the defendant was attending the plaintiff relevant to plaintiff's injuries. State the date and time of day and identify the agent or employee of the defendant involved stating name, current or last known residence and business address, and occupation or profession.

State in detail the nature of all physical examination, treatment, or other health care services that were delivered by any agent or employee of the defendant performed on the plaintiff relevant to plaintiff's injuries, as well as plaintiff's complaints of conduct of defendant, defendant's agents or employees.

Describe in detail the substance of all conversations between any agent or employee of the defendant and the plaintiff at the time any agent or employee of the defendant agreed to care for the plaintiff for the problems for which any agent or employee of the defendant was treating the plaintiff and which are relevant to the allegations against plaintiff and/or plaintiff's alleged injuries, stating the date and time of each such conversation and identifying all agents and employees of the defendant involved in each such conversation stating name, last known residence and business address, and occupation or profession.

Describe in detail the course of the plaintiff's treatment by defendant or defendant's agents or employees for all conditions relevant to plaintiff's alleged injuries.

Request for Production

Another discovery method commonly employed early in the process is the Request for Production. This may also be referred to as a Request for Production of Documents. Unlike the Interrogatory which seeks factual information known by the plaintiff, the Request for Production seeks documentary evidence. This method of discovery is a key tool in the medical malpractice case. It enables each party access to all of the documentation relevant to the case (other than attorney-generated documents such as notes) that is in the possession of the other party. Because medical care is so heavily dependent on documentation for continuity of care, billing, and insurance purposes, the medical malpractice case or defense can benefit tremendously from this method of discovery.

The Request for Production can be used to obtain any form of documentary evidence. This includes not only paper reports and notes, but also photographs, video, and any other form of recorded information. It should be noted, however, that only the information requested need be produced. As a result, it is essential to be broadly descriptive when stating the types of information sought. The following is an example of a Request for Production in a medical malpractice case.

Exhibit 9.9 Motion to Produce

**IN THE DISTRICT COURT
COUNTY OF NEWVILLE
STATE OF ILINCH**

**Estate of Jorge Jones (deceased);
Jeanette Jones,
Marcus Jones (a minor) by and through his next friend
Jeanette Jones,**

v.   Case No. 04-1106

Michie A. Xwander, M.D.

MOTION TO PRODUCE

Now comes plaintiffs and, pursuant to the Rules of Court, requests that the defendant produce the following documents and materials within 45 days at the offices of plaintiff's counsel of Swartz & Swartz, 10 Marshall Street, Boston, Massachusetts, for inspection and photocopying:

1. All insurance policies which operate to insure the defendant for claims of professional negligence or other conduct as alleged in the plaintiff's Complaint.

2. Any and all insurance policies which operate to insure the defendant for claims of professional negligence as alleged in the plaintiff's Complaint and which operate to provide insurance coverage in excess of the insurance policies described in paragraph No. 1 of this Request.

3. Copies of the defendant's complete records concerning the plaintiff, including but not limited to the following: care and treatment, billing, complaints by the plaintiff, and referral to and consultation with other physicians.

4. Copies of any and all correspondence sent to the defendant by the plaintiff.

5. Copies of any and all correspondence sent to the plaintiff by the defendant.

6. Copies of any and all notations or other documentation of any research or discussions with other health care professionals in regard to plaintiff or plaintiff's medical condition.

The plaintiff,

By her attorney,

_____

Depositions

This type of discovery is used not only for parties to the suit, but witnesses as well. It provides the opportunity for each side in the case to determine the exact nature of the testimonial evidence, ascertain the extent of knowledge, and identify areas that need further investigation. The rules for depositions vary somewhat among jurisdictions. But there are essentially three types. The first is the discovery deposition where the opposing party is allowed to ask a broad array of questions. The second is the evidentiary deposition where the party who has named the individual as their witness asks questions as if they were at trial. The opposition can then ask questions in a cross-examination that are generally limited to the scope of the questions asked on direct exam. Finally, some jurisdictions offer a blended version where the scope is quite broad but both sides may examine the witness. In addition to using the deposition to assess the witnesses for the opposition, depositions can also be used to impeach the witness if his or her testimony changes at trial since depositions and trial testimony are both usually given under oath.

From a practical standpoint, depositions are generally taken at a prescribed place and time (often the office of legal counsel). There is generally a court reporter present who administers the oath and then transcribes the testimony. An increasingly common practice is the videotaped deposition. This method is beneficial because it provides the opportunity not only to review the content of the testimony given, but also the tone, demeanor, and general appearance of the witness. If a party objects to a question posed during the deposition, objections are made and ruled upon later by a judge. If the judge rules the individual must answer, then the deposition is usually supplemented in writing unless the questions are so numerous it would be best to depose the witness again. The following is an example of deposition questions that might be asked in a medical malpractice case.

Exhibit 9.10 Sample Deposition Questions

SAMPLE DEPOSITION QUESTIONS

Medical Expert Witness

Background and Qualifications

    Full name, professional address
    Current nature of practice and expertise
    Education
        Graduate degrees (Area of specialty, school, years of attendance)
        Undergraduate degrees (major, school, years of attendance)
        Field of specialization (specialty, location, and years of training)
    Board certifications
    Clinical experience in addition to any described above
    Hospital affiliations
    Psychiatric facility affiliations
    Teaching credentials and expertise
    Medical and scientific books and articles published

(continued)

Exhibit 9.10, continued

    Prior expert testimony given on behalf of plaintiffs or defendants in medical malpractice cases including number of times testified, number of times hired by plaintiff/defense respectively
    Purpose of Expert's Opinion Testimony
    Nature of testimony in the present case and professional opinion on the following:
        Standard of care
        Duties of care
        Malpractice act
        Breach
        Causation
        Damages
        Affirmative defenses

Knowledge of Facts of the Case
    Physical examination performed on patient - findings and conclusions

    Studied patient's medical and hospital records pertaining to diagnosis and treatment - findings and conclusions

    Studied patient's diagnostic test results, pathology report - findings and conclusions

    Studied patient's deposition testimony or any other recorded statements - findings and conclusions

    Studied deposition testimony of defendant's other medical and scientific experts - findings and conclusions

    Studied defendant's deposition testimony

    Discussed facts with defendant

Knowledge of Standard of Care, Breach, Causation

    On what is familiarity with standard of care based? (e.g., same locality of practice, medically documented standard in relevant textbooks and journals, etc.)

    Summarization of findings and conclusions

    Does the witness have any professional opinion as to standard of care owed by defendant regarding harm, and if so what is it?

    Does the witness have any professional opinion regarding the duty of care owed by defendant regarding the injuries allegedly suffered by the plaintiff and if so what is it?

(continued)

Exhibit 9.10, continued

> Whether expert agrees or disagrees with plaintiff's theory of standard of care and duties owed by defendant in subject area of harm, and basis for agreement or disagreement
>
> Opinion as to whether defendant comported with prevailing and accepted standard of care in subject area of harm, and basis for opinion
>
> Does the witness have a professional opinion as to whether defendant was in compliance and acting in accordance with prevailing and accepted duties of care in the delivery of professional services to the plaintiff, and what is the basis for the opinion
>
> Does the witness have a professional opinion with regard to whether the defendant breached the prevailing and accepted standard of care in the delivery of professional services to the plaintiff, and what is the basis for the opinion
>
> Does the witness have a professional opinion with regard to whether defendant breached prevailing and accepted duties in the delivery of professional services to the plaintiff, and what is the basis for the opinion
>
> Does the witness have a professional opinion with regard to whether defendant's alleged breach of prevailing and accepted standard of care in the delivery of professional services to the plaintiff was the proximate cause of plaintiff's injury, and what is the basis for the opinion
>
> Does the witness have a professional opinion with regard to whether the defendant's alleged breach of prevailing and accepted duties of care was the proximate cause of the plaintiff's injury, and what is the basis for the opinion
>
> Does the witness have a professional opinion with regard to the cause(s) of plaintiff's injury, and what is the basis for the opinion
>
> Does the witness have a professional opinion with regard to the actual nature and extent of injury and damage alleged by plaintiff, and what is the basis for the opinion

Physical Evidence Examinations and Inspections

In the medical malpractice case, physical evidence is an integral part of the lawsuit. The condition of the plaintiff and any alleged injuries are the basis for the entire suit. Because it is alleged to have been caused by professional malfeasance, an examination by another health care professional to render an opinion regarding the validity and extent of the claimed injury is entirely reasonable. Additionally, if the claim involves some item or items of medical equipment or device, it is also appropriate that the opposition have the opportunity to examine the items and to have them examined by an expert of their choosing to render an opinion on whether the item was flawed, defective, altered, or used improperly.

When physical evidence is owned or controlled by another party to the suit, the discovering party may file a Request for Inspection. This type of discovery allows a party to inspect, photograph, measure, and evaluate a particular item or place. If the party wants custody of an item or wants to subject the item to any procedures that might affect its validity, court approval may be required. Otherwise, in most cases, plaintiffs and defendants are entitled to reasonable inspection of items that may be produced as evidence at trial.

A party may request a physical or mental examination of an opposing party if such examination is relevant to the lawsuit. In a case alleging medical malpractice, the defendant is usually allowed to select a physician or other health care professional of their choosing to examine the plaintiff and give an opinion as to the nature and extent of any injuries. While the examination may be thorough with respect to the injuries alleged, a court may also enforce limits on the extent and nature of examinations or admissibility if it goes beyond what is relevant to the case at hand. For example, a plaintiff alleging an orthopedic injury would not generally be compelled to submit to a mental exam without additional circumstances making the mental condition of the plaintiff relevant to the case. The following are examples of both a Motion to Inspect and Motion for Examination in a medical malpractice case.

Exhibit 9.11   Motion to Inspect

IN THE DISTRICT COURT
COUNTY OF NEWVILLE
STATE OF ILINCH

Estate of Jorge Jones (deceased) ;
Jeanette Jones,
Marcus Jones (a minor) by and through his next friend
Jeanette Jones,
Plaintiffs
v.   Case No. 04-1106

Michie A. Xwander, M.D.
Defendant

MOTION TO INSPECT

Comes now the plaintiffs by and through counsel and pursuant to the Rules of Court requests that defendant provide access to the following location for inspection and generation of documentary evidence via recording methods, including, but not limited to, video, photographic, digital, and auditory methods, at the hour of 8 o'clock a.m., in the office of defendant at 1006 Diamond Drive, South City, County of Newville, State of Ilinch.

The above-described documents, objects, and real estate are relevant to the subject matter of the above-captioned action.

Respectfully Submitted,

Plaintiff

_____

Exhibit 9.12   Motion to Compel

**IN THE DISTRICT COURT
COUNTY OF NEWVILLE
STATE OF ILINCH**

**Estate of Jorge Jones (deceased) ;
Jeanette Jones,
Marcus Jones (a minor) by and through his next friend
Jeanette Jones,
Plaintiffs
v.**   Case No. 04-1106

**Michie A. Xwander, M.D.
Defendant**

MOTION TO COMPEL

Now comes the defendant by and through her attorneys and move this court for an Order to Compel the plaintiffs to respond to the Interrogatories submitted by defendant and in support thereof states as follows:

1. Pursuant to the applicable Rules of Court the defendant submitted Interrogatories to the plaintiff in the above-styled cause of action on or about August 25, 2004.

2. Applicable Rules of Court prescribe that Response to Interrogatories should be delivered no later than 45 days from the date upon which they were duly submitted.

3. Plaintiff has failed to submit any Response to the Interrogatories despite two written requests by defendant for compliance on or about October 15, and October 30, respectively.

4. Said response to Interrogatories are now two months beyond the date prescribed by the rules of court.

WHEREFORE, defendant requests that the plaintiffs be ordered to respond to the aforementioned interrogatories within seven days of the Order of court, and failure to do so result in striking the plaintiff's pleadings and dismissing the case with prejudice.

Respectfully Submitted,

Defendant

_____

Exhibit 9.13 Motion for Examination

IN THE DISTRICT COURT
COUNTY OF NEWVILLE
STATE OF ILINCH

Estate of Jorge Jones (deceased) ;
Jeanette Jones,
Marcus Jones (a minor) by and through his next friend
Jeanette Jones,
Plaintiffs
v.   Case No. 04-1106

Michie A. Xwander, M.D.
Defendant

MOTION FOR PHYSICAL EXAM

Defendant by and through her attorney, respectfully represents unto the court that:

1. She is the defendant in the above-captioned action, which is an action for damages for personal injuries alleged to have been sustained by the plaintiff on December 28, 2002, in the office of defendant in Newville City, Newville, County, State of Texas, by reason of the alleged professional negligence of petitioner.

2. The action has been set for trial on December 12, 2005.

3. The physical condition of the plaintiff is in controversy in this action, and the nature and extent of disability now allegedly suffered by plaintiff as the direct result of the alleged injuries is an important issue in this action.

4. Defendant is without information as to the extent and nature of plaintiff's injuries and has no means of acquiring such information except by an independent medical examination, which information is necessary to enable the defendant to prepare for the trial of this action.

5. Defendant suggests that Dr. Orlando Fornia, whose office is located at 7912 Nottaway, Newville, Texas, is a physician who has had considerable experience in the care, treatment and evaluation of injuries and disabilities such as are alleged to have been sustained by plaintiff, and he is a suitable person to conduct the examination.

6. If Dr. Fornia is permitted to make such examination, he will, within 30 days after the completion of the examination, deliver or mail to the plaintiff's attorney a duplicate original of his written report of the examination,

(continued)

Exhibit 9.13, continued

setting out his findings, results of all tests made, his diagnosis and conclusions, and a duplicate original of all corrections, supplements or additions to the report.

7. Defendant will pay the fee of the examining physician and will pay to the plaintiff compensation for any loss of earnings incurred by plaintiff and will advance such reasonable expenses as plaintiff may incur in complying with such order as the court may enter requiring plaintiff to submit to a physical examination.

WHEREFORE, defendant prays the court for an order requiring plaintiff to be and appear at the office of said physician for the purpose of submitting to a physical examination by the physician, and for such other relief as the court deems necessary and proper.

Respectfully Submitted,
Defendant

_____

As the discovery process progresses and the case moves toward trial, it is possible that certain procedural steps will be taken by one or both parties to accelerate the outcome of the case. The first instance generally deals with specific information identified that causes irreparable damage to one party's position. It is known as a Motion or Request to Admit Genuineness. The second is an attempt to resolve the situation with finality and without the presentation of evidence at a trial. This is accomplished through a Motion for Summary Judgment. Both may occur independently or in conjunction with each other.

The Motion or Request to Admit Genuineness is used if a party discovers information through discovery or independent investigation and the information is so crucial that if proven, it could ruin the other party's case. Although this type of motion is not usually considered an official form of discovery, it is directly linked to the evidentiary information identified in the pre-trial stages when discovery normally occurs. The document asks that the opposing party review the facts or documents and either admit or deny the truthfulness and validity of the content. If the truthfulness is admitted or verified, the party who filed the motion may seek an early end to the lawsuit with a Motion for Summary Judgment in their favor and against the opposing party. The procedure and effects of this type of motion are discussed below. Usually a Motion or Request to Admit Genuineness is not submitted unless the evidence directly contradicts the core basis of the other party's case. Because most parties believe their case and have at least some evidence to support it, these motions are not seen in the majority of lawsuits. But, consider the example in Chapter 8, of the surprise witness. In that situation an individual employed in the housekeeping department overheard two health care professionals conspiring to cover up an act of malpractice. If this individual had approached the plaintiff's counsel before trial, it would have likely resulted in an affidavit of the proposed testimony being sent along with a Motion to Admit Genuineness of Facts to the Defense. See Exhibit 9.14.

Exhibit 9.14 Motion to Admit Genuineness

**IN THE DISTRICT COURT
COUNTY OF NEWVILLE
STATE OF ILINCH**

**Estate of Jorge Jones (deceased);
Jeanette Jones,
Marcus Jones (a minor) by and through his next friend
Jeanette Jones,**

v.   Case No. 04-1106

Michie A. Xwander, M.D.

MOTION TO ADMIT GENUINENESS OF FACTS

Now comes the plaintiff by and through her counsel and, pursuant to Rules of Court, calls upon the defendant to admit or deny the truth of the following statements within 45 days, for the purpose of this litigation only:

1. The defendant is a physician duly licensed to practice medicine in the State of Ilinch.

2. The defendant is board certified in the specialty of internal medicine in the State of Ilinch.

3. On or about March 1, 2002, and continuing through May 8, 2002, the defendant had an office for the practice of internal medicine at _____, _____, _____.

4. On or about March 1, 2002, and continuing through May 8, 2002, decedent Jorge Jones was an established patient of the defendant.

5. On or about March 1, 2002, and continuing through May 8, 2002, the defendant was a physician and surgeon skilled and experienced in internal medicine.

6. On or before March 1, 2002, and continuing through May 8, 2002, the defendant had represented herself to decedent Jorge Jones as being skilled and experienced in the care and treatment of patients who suffered from symptoms such as those exhibited by the decedent Jorge Jones.

7. On or before March 1, 2002, and continuing through May 8, 2002, the defendant knew that plaintiff had suffered increasingly from the same general symptoms for a period of months despite her prescribed treatment.

(continued)

Exhibit 9.14, continued

8. On or before March 1, 2002, and continuing through May 8, 2002, the defendant did not prescribe diagnostic testing; perform diagnostic testing; recommend diagnostic testing; or refer plaintiff to another physician for consultation and/or diagnostic testing.

9. Based on the medical standards as practiced by physicians and surgeons of the same medical specialty as the defendant on or about March 1, 2002, and continuing through May 8, 2002, it was acceptable medical practice at that time:

   a. to perform diagnostic testing relevant to decedent Jorge Jones' symptoms complained of at each office visit;

   b. to prescribe diagnostic testing relevant to decedent Jorge Jones' symptoms;

   c. to recommend diagnostic testing for decedent Jorge Jones' symptoms;

   d. to refer a patient for further consultation and/or diagnostic testing relevant to symptoms such as those exhibited by decedent Jorge Jones.

10. On or before March 1, 2002, and continuing through May 8, 2002, it was known to the defendant that persons who had continuing symptoms such as those exhibited by plaintiff may suffer from an underlying disease process that could only be definitively identified through diagnostic procedures.

Respectfully submitted,

The Plaintiff,

By her Attorney,

_____

Motion for Summary Judgment

This is a Motion that is not routinely filed and one that is even more rarely granted because of the severity of its effect. The basis for the motion is that the evidence is so overwhelmingly in favor of one party that no reasonable judge or jury could find in favor of the other party if a trial were held. Consequently, the party seeking the motion contends that there is no basis for a trial and the case should be determined without trial and in favor of the requesting party. The Motion for Summary Judgment is one of the most serious motions that can be filed in any lawsuit. It asks that the judge make a final decision on the issues of the suit without a trial. The decision is made solely on the basis of the evidence that exists at the time of the motion. The effect of such a motion is that the judge removes the case from the hands of the jury before it ever reaches them. Because our system of government places so much importance on the jury system, this is a very serious step for any judge to take.

When a Motion for Summary Judgment is sought, the judge must make a serious evaluation of the evidence. If the evidence is so strongly in favor of a party that a jury could only reasonably reach one decision and there is no substantial question left to be determined regarding the facts that occurred, a Motion for Summary Judgment may be granted. However, if there is any way that the jurors could reach a different conclusion as to whose version of the story is more probable, a Motion for Summary Judgment must be denied, and the case must be left to the trier of fact.

Because the effect of a successful Motion for Summary Judgment is that there will be no trial in the case, such a motion must be filed before trial begins. Beyond that, when or if the motion is filed is up to the moving party. Usually, a Motion for Summary Judgment will not be filed unless there is evidence so strong that the opposing party's case is effectively defeated by overwhelming evidence. In most cases, each side has evidence that would tend to prove or disprove the case. Consequently, Motions for Summary Judgment are filed less often than other types of motions and are rarely granted.

If a Motion for Summary Judgment by a defendant is granted, the case is dismissed with prejudice. This means that the lawsuit brought by the plaintiff will be dismissed and can never be brought again. No amendments to the complaint can be made at this point, and the issue between the parties is permanently settled. If a Motion for Summary Judgment by a plaintiff is granted, the defendant is not entitled to a trial to present evidence in defense to the plaintiff's claims. If the plaintiff asked for a specific dollar amount of damages in the complaint, the defendant is automatically judged liable and must pay the plaintiff an appropriate amount. Sometimes the amount of damages specified in the complaint is deemed appropriate. In others, a limited trial is held to determine exactly how much the defendant should pay.

ARBITRATION, MEDIATION, AND SETTLEMENT CONSIDERATIONS

Statistically, the vast majority of lawsuits never reach trial. In addition to suits filed, many others reach a settlement or end prior to suit being initiated in the courts. Of the enormous number of cases that are started and litigated to some extent in the courts without reaching trial, there are a variety of possible outcomes. In this chapter, discovery has been discussed as the second stage of litigation. While evidence is typically collected with the intent that it will be necessary at trial, another obvious benefit is to educate both parties about the strengths and weaknesses of their respective cases. This in turn allows a more informed decision with regard to the appropriateness of electing an alternative to trial.

The most traditional alternative is when the parties negotiate and reach a compromise or settlement. In that situation, the defense usually pays a specified amount to the plaintiff in exchange for an agreement not to pursue the action and, in turn, there is no required admission or legal finding of culpability on the part of the named defendants. Even if a defendant is confident in their ability to win at trial, this must be balanced against the costs of litigation. And in some instances, the wiser choice may be to settle.

Other alternatives to trial and settlement have gained favor in the courts in recent years. They are **mediation** and **arbitration**. These methods are also referred to as Alternative Dispute Resolution. In mediation, an objective third party who is specially educated in legal matters acts as a facilitator. Each side presents their case and the mediator assists the parties in resolving the legal issues between them. The mediator does not issue a verdict or any sort of binding decision. Rather, the mediator is neutral and hopefully leads the parties toward a settlement of their issues.

Arbitration is significantly different from mediation in several respects. While it is also an alternative to the traditional costly and time-consuming process of litigation, an arbitrator may—in certain instances—issue a binding decision with respect to the outcome of the case. This, however, generally requires the consent of all parties concerned. Most often a party will not agree to a binding determination by a single arbitrator in lieu of a full jury, but it is an alternative that can greatly reduce the time and expense of litigation.

Alternative dispute resolution via mediation conferences and arbitration are largely favored among the jurisdictions. The approaches vary from state to state and there is no clear majority as to the most appropriate option. Some states require mediation conferences prior to, or as part of, the litigation process. Some states allow the parties to submit their cases to an arbitrator for a nonbinding decision. Many jurisdictions allow the parties to pursue alternative dispute resolution for binding results if the parties agree that the outcome will be adhered to.

A popular alternative is the medical legal review panel. While it goes by a variety of names and the effects of the outcome vary among jurisdictions, many states do require potential claims of medical malpractice to first be submitted to such a panel for consideration. The panel is typically comprised of both health care professionals (usually physicians) and legal professionals (usually lawyers or judges) who review the case. Their findings as to liability and, in some states, damages provide the parties with an objective view of how the case is likely to be perceived in litigation. In many states the findings of the panel are admissible at trial. In some states if the panel makes a finding of no liability, the plaintiff must post a bond to offset costs of the defense in the event the ultimate trial verdict also finds no liability. These panels came about, much like mediation and arbitration, as methods to resolve legal issues that have the potential to result in great expense to the parties and time on the dockets of the courts.

Finally, throughout the litigation process is the continuing possibility of settlement. In fact, alternative dispute resolution developed in response to a growing need for communication between parties regarding concluding a case without the time and expense of full-blown litigation, trial, and appeals. Even before alternative dispute resolution, the majority of cases reached settlement and that has only been enhanced. But how does one know when settlement is appropriate? It comes down to evaluating a number of variables on both sides.

Settlement attempts may begin at any time. In reality, many claims are settled shortly after the injury occurs and without legal intervention. Others are settled as the investigation and discovery progress and both parties become more and more aware of the strengths and weaknesses of the case. There may be numerous attempts at settlement as the case moves forward and cases even settle in the midst of trials or even at the appellate stage. Ultimately, there has to be a confluence of the parties. They must reach a compromise whereby it is in the best interest of both to walk away on agreed terms. As mentioned above, a defendant may be secure in his or her ability to prove innocence. However, other considerations include the cost of litigation, the risk of losing, the potential costs of an appeal, and the public notoriety often associated with such cases. All of these may give the defendant incentive to settle the case. Similarly, the plaintiff may believe the case is full of merit and a large judgment is almost a certainty. But the one thing that must always be remembered in the law is that there are no guarantees. Juries may see things from a different perspective. A judge may rule certain evidence crucial to the plaintiff's case as inadmissible for any number of reasons. And the time and expense necessary to carry a case through the entire litigation process and potential appeals can rapidly deplete a judgment. As a result, it may be in the best interest of the plaintiff to settle the case for a lesser amount and avoid the potential pitfalls just described.

Typically, as the case develops, one of the parties will submit a proposal to the other outlining their view of the strengths and weaknesses of the case and a proposed settlement amount. The opposition will counter and the negotiation process begins. Some settlements are obtained fairly quickly while others stall and start throughout the litigation process. For this reason, some jurisdictions order mediation settlement conferences whereby an objective third party attempts to facilitate an agreement both parties can adopt.

> **Problem 9.1**
>
> Complete 9.1 of the Comprehensive Problem in Appendix A.

CHAPTER SUMMARY

In any lawsuit, the pretrial process can be long and complicated. This is emphasized even more in the medical malpractice cases because many malpractice statutes directly impact the procedural requirements of litigation. As discussed throughout the text, such statutes range from affecting statute of limitation, to preliminary affidavits or panel review, to the necessity for expert opinions. Once any applicable statutes have been incorporated into the early stages of litigation, the case proceeds much like other civil cases.

Discovery includes the court supervised exchange of information among the parties. The rationale is that the more informed the parties are with respect to both sides of the case, the more likely they can reach a settlement and/or dismissal, avoiding the time and expense of a trial. Discovery includes opportunities to examine parties and witnesses for the opposition, inspect documentary and tangible evidence, and generally evaluate the strengths and weaknesses of the opposing case.

A relatively recent but important development in civil law and especially malpractice has been the evolution and increasingly widespread acceptance of arbitration and mediation as methods of alternative dispute resolution. These methods allow the input of objective third parties and assist those involved in litigation with reaching possible settlement or conclusion of the case without full litigation. However, when attempts at settlement or alternative dispute resolution do not bring the litigation to an end, the pretrial process of discovery and continued investigation prepares the parties for the presentation of their evidence to a judge and/or jury for an ultimate conclusion.

Key Terms	
complaint	prima facie (case)
petition	mediation
discovery	arbitration

For additional resources, go to http://www.westlegalstudies.com.

CHAPTER 10

The Medical Malpractice Trial

CHAPTER OBJECTIVES

When you complete this chapter, you should be able to:

- Explain the process of voir dire
- Describe the elements of presenting a case in chief
- Discuss the objectives of the case of the defense
- Prepare a flowchart of the stages of a trial

VOIR DIRE—SELECTING A JURY IN A MEDICAL MALPRACTICE CASE

The first stage of trial is generally the **voir dire**. During this stage, the jury that will hear the evidence of the case is selected. In what is known as a bench trial, the trier of fact is the judge. But, if the case is to be determined by a jury, a fair and impartial jury must be selected. In cases involving medical malpractice, voir dire can be exceptionally difficult because the defendant is often well known by the community and frequently has many public and personal connections.

Voir dire begins with a large pool of potential jurors who are brought into a group. The attorneys for the parties—and sometimes the judge—ask each potential juror a number of questions, the goal of which is to determine whether a potential juror has any biases regarding the parties, attorneys, or circumstances of the case. The jurors may be asked to take an oath to be honest in their responses. At the very least, the importance of being forthright is expressed to them. If an attorney believes that a potential juror has a particular bias that would influence the decision in the case, the attorney has the right to challenge the juror's right to sit on the jury at trial.

An attorney can exercise two types of challenges with regard to potential jurors: peremptory challenges and challenges for cause. Each party to a lawsuit may use a specified number of peremptory challenges, which vary in number from state to state. An attorney exercising a peremptory challenge does not have to give a reason. The peremptory challenge gives the party an absolute right to have the challenged juror removed from the jury. The only exception is if the removal is based on a person's status within a federally protected class, such as race.

In a challenge for cause, an attorney asks that a juror be excused on the basis of a particular prejudice that was evident from the juror's answers to the questions previously asked. In challenge for cause, the opposing party can object to the challenge. Usually the objection will state that the prospective juror did not exhibit a bias so strong that the juror could not fairly consider the case. The judge considers the challenge, any objections, and the statements of the juror and then renders a decision as to whether the juror will be excused.

When the required number of jurors has been reached, voir dire is ended. Traditionally, juries are composed of 12 persons and one or two alternates. Some states also have petit juries, usually juries of fewer people. Petit juries may be utilized in cases that are less serious but still warrant the right to a trial by a jury of one's peers under state or federal law. Some states do not allow jury trials in very minor cases, such as traffic violations, where loss of liberty is not at stake.

In the medical malpractice trial, it is especially important to have appropriate questions to pose to the jury pool. Both parties want to know which jurors, if any, are current or past patients of the defendant. If so, the nature of the relationship and the attitude of the juror toward the defendant should be explored. Even if a juror is not a past or present patient, it is also important to identify all potential jurors who have knowledge of the plaintiff, defendant, the case, and any impressions that have been formed. Often, well-known individuals who are sued may be seen by the media as noteworthy and, as a result, medical malpractice cases may be more publicized. Even if the case has not generated widespread media attention, news of this type of case may have a reached a broader segment of the population through word of mouth than a case involving private individuals. Once an impression has been formed, it may be quite difficult for a juror to overcome personal impressions despite valid evidence. Thus, identifying any individual with knowledge of the case, regardless of its foundation, is extremely important.

There is no majority rule with respect to voir dire in medical malpractice cases. Many states do have procedural rules that establish fundamental bases for excluding jurors based on special relationships to the parties in various types of lawsuits. But, for the most part, it is necessary to clearly establish the bias or potential for bias of a prospective juror during voir dire.

2003 WL 3095693 (KyApp2003)

Court of Appeals of Kentucky.

Charlene D. McCARTY, Individually and as Administratrix of the Estate of Charles Christopher Dylan McCarty, and Shannon McCarty, Appellants
v.
Kurt JAENICKE, M.D. and Ashland Women's Care, P.S.C., Appellees.

Dec. 31, 2003.

BUCKINGHAM, Judge.

(continued)

The issue in this case is whether the trial court erred in refusing to strike two jurors for cause in a trial in a medical negligence case even though the jurors were patients of the defendant doctor. We conclude the court erred and thus reverse and remand for a new trial.

Charlene McCarty's pregnancy ended at approximately 37 weeks with the stillbirth of an infant male, Charles Christopher Dylan McCarty. Dr. Kurt Jaenicke was McCarty's obstetrician, and McCarty filed a civil complaint in the Boyd Circuit Court against Dr. Jaenicke and his group, Ashland Women's Care, P.S.C. McCarty filed the complaint individually and as administratrix of the infant male's estate, and her husband, Shannon McCarty, joined as a plaintiff in the suit. The complaint alleged negligence by Dr. Jaenicke in his care and treatment of McCarty.

The case was tried by a jury in the Boyd Circuit Court in May 2002. By a 9-3 vote, the jury returned a verdict in favor of Dr. Jaenicke and his group. This appeal followed.

During the voir dire proceedings, two of the prospective jurors, Nancy Kiger and Bonnie Prince, related that Dr. Jaenicke was their doctor. Juror Kiger stated several times that she would be uncomfortable if she were on the jury and it were to render a verdict against Dr. Jaenicke, but Juror Prince stated that "[i]t wouldn't make any difference to [her]." Juror Kiger also stated that all her family considered Dr. Jaenicke to be their doctor and that Dr. Jaenicke was also the doctor for all her female co-workers. Further, Juror Kiger stated that her niece had given birth to a baby the day before the trial began and that a nurse midwife employed by Dr. Jaenicke's group had delivered the child. In response to questions by the trial judge, both jurors indicated that they could evaluate the evidence and render a verdict against Dr. Jaenicke as if he were not their doctor in the event the evidence warranted such.

McCarty's attorney moved the court to strike Juror Kiger for cause, but the court gave Dr. Jaenicke's attorney an opportunity to attempt to rehabilitate the juror. Juror Kiger and Juror Prince then responded to questions in a manner indicating that they could evaluate the evidence and render a verdict in a fair and impartial manner. At the conclusion of questioning by Dr. Jaenicke's attorney, one of McCarty's attorneys moved the court to strike all jurors that were patients of Dr. Jaenicke. He argued that "to require the Plaintiff to prove a case against a physician where the physician's own patients are sitting on the jury is a burden we don't believe we're capable of meeting. If these were clients of the lawyer they certainly wouldn't be sitting on the jury." The court denied the motion, and McCarty used all her peremptory challenges, two of which were used to strike Juror Kiger and Juror Prince.

Whether or not a juror should be stricken for cause is within the discretion of the trial court, and this court will not reverse the trial court's determination unless it abused its discretion or was clearly erroneous. *Commonwealth v. Lewis*, Ky., 903 S.W.2d 524, 527 (1995). "Irrespective of the answers given on voir dire, the court should presume the likelihood of prejudice on the part of the prospective juror because the potential juror has such a close relationship, be it familial, financial or situational, with any of the parties, counsel, victims or witnesses." *Ward v. Commonwealth*, Ky., 695 S.W.2d 404, 407 (1985), *quoting Commonwealth v. Stamm*, 286 Pa.Super. 409, 429 A.2d 4, 7 (1981). Once such a close relationship is established, the court must grant a request that the juror be stricken for cause. *Id.* This close relationship test applies to civil cases as well as criminal cases. *See Davenport v. Ephraim McDowell Mem'l Hosp., Inc.*, Ky.App., 769 S.W.2d 56, 60 (1988).

Furthermore, the court in the *Ward* case noted that the juror should be stricken for cause once the close relationship is established "without regard to protestations of lack of bias." *Id.* In *Montgomery v. Commonwealth*, Ky., 819 S.W.2d 713 (1991), the Kentucky Supreme Court addressed the propriety of attempting to rehabilitate jurors who should be considered biased by asking whether they can put aside their personal knowledge, relationships, and opinions and decide the case solely on the evidence presented by the

(continued)

court and the court's instructions. In the following strong language, the court condemned the practice of allowing the rehabilitation of a biased juror by such means:

The message from this decision to the trial court is the "magic question" does not provide a device to "rehabilitate" a juror who should be considered disqualified by his personal knowledge or his past experience, or his attitude as expressed on voir dire. We declare the concept of "rehabilitation" is a *misnomer* in the context of choosing qualified jurors and direct trial judges to remove it from their thinking and strike it from their lexicon. *Id.* at 718.

Kentucky cases do not directly address the specific issue of whether a juror must be stricken for cause in the trial of a medical negligence action because the juror is currently a patient of the defendant doctor. However, several cases guide us in our conclusion that the trial court erred in not striking the two jurors for cause in this case.

Altman v. Allen, Ky., 850 S.W.2d 44 (1992), involved facts somewhat similar to those herein. The *Altman* case was a medical negligence action filed against two obstetricians, at least one of whom was retired, as a result of the treatment of an infant following his premature birth. During voir dire the trial court refused to strike three prospective jurors for cause even though they were former patients of the defendant doctors. A panel of this court reversed the verdict and judgment in favor of the doctors and remanded the case for a new trial on the ground that the trial court had abused its discretion in not excusing the jurors. However, our supreme court reversed this court and reinstated the trial court's judgment in favor of the doctors. *Id.* at 46. The court held that there was no evidence that a close relationship between the jurors and doctors had been established. *Id.* Further, the court stated in dicta that "[n]o court should speculate so as to presume a special bond between a woman and her obstetrician." *Id.* The court also noted that there was no current or continuing professional relationship between any of the jurors or members of their family with either of the doctors. *Id.*

Several other cases have relevance to this issue. In *Mackey v. Greenview Hosp., Inc.,* Ky.App., 587 S.W.2d 249 (1979), this court affirmed the trial court's denial of a plaintiff's motion to strike three prospective jurors for cause in a medical negligence case even though each juror revealed a prior professional relationship with one or more of the defendant doctors. *Id.* at 253. Like the *Altman* case, the court in the *Mackey* case specifically noted that "[t]here was no current or continuing professional relationship between any of the jurors or members of their immediate family and any of the physicians involved in the case." *Id.*

In *Riddle v. Commonwealth*, Ky.App., 864 S.W.2d 308 (1993), this court reversed a criminal conviction where several prospective jurors had been represented by the prosecutors in the past and stated that they would seek their representation in the future. *Id.* at 312. The court first noted that the prior attorney-client relationship did not automatically cause a juror to be excused for cause under a presumed bias theory. *Id.* at 310. The court cited the *Altman* case to support that conclusion. However, the court further stated that the trial court abused its discretion in not striking the jurors for cause because each challenged juror stated that he or she would seek a future attorney-client relationship with the prosecutors. *Id.* at 311. Likewise, in *Fugate v. Commonwealth*, Ky., 993 S.W.2d 931 (1999), the Kentucky Supreme Court agreed with this court's conclusion in the *Riddle* case "that a trial court is required to disqualify for cause prospective jurors who had a prior professional relationship with a prosecuting attorney and [/or] ... profess[ed] that they would seek such a relationship in the future." *Fugate*, 993 S.W.2d at 938.

McCarty urges this court to establish a rule holding that it is reversible error for a trial court to refuse to strike for cause jurors who are current patients of defendant obstetricians. On the other hand, Dr. Jaenicke argues that Kentucky has not adopted such a rule and notes the language in the *Altman* case that "[n]o court should speculate so as to presume a special bond between a woman and her obstetrician." 850 S.W.2d at 46. Both parties have cited cases from other jurisdictions in an attempt to support their arguments.

In the *Altman* case the Kentucky Supreme Court indicated that it would not favor such a bright line or per se rule. It refused to presume a special bond between a woman and her obstetrician, and it also stated that

(continued)

a presumption of bias in situations involving psychiatrists, psychologists, clergy, and other counsel-type relationships with patients or clients would also be unwarranted. *Id.* Nevertheless, the supreme court appeared to approve such a rule in the *Fugate* case when it approved this court's decision in the *Riddle* case and held that it was reversible error not to excuse a juror for cause when the juror had been represented by the prosecutor in the past and stated that he or she might use him again in the future. *Fugate,* 993 S.W.2d at 938-39. In other words, in Kentucky there appears to be a bright line or per se rule that persons who are represented by an attorney in the case or who have been represented by the attorney in the past and might hire him or her again in the future should be stricken for cause at the request of a party or else reversible error will result.

In the case *sub judice,* we conclude that Juror Kiger should have been stricken for cause and that it was reversible error not to do so. Juror Kiger stated that she was currently a patient of Dr. Jaenicke's, that "my family all goes to him," that "all the girls I work with go too," and that she would be uncomfortable sitting on the jury and possibly returning a verdict against the doctor. Under these circumstances we believe Juror Kiger should have been presumed prejudiced or biased to the extent that rehabilitation as a prospective juror should have been out of the question. *Montgomery,* 819 S.W.2d at 718.

Whether Juror Prince should have been stricken for cause by the trial court is more problematic. While Juror Prince stated she was currently a patient of Dr. Jaenicke, she consistently answered questions in a manner indicating that she could evaluate the evidence and render a verdict in a fair and impartial manner. The question we must face in regard to this juror is whether she should have been presumed prejudiced or biased by virtue of her current relationship with Dr. Jaenicke to the extent that she should have been stricken for cause despite well-intentioned rehabilitation efforts.

Direction given by our supreme court in earlier cases persuades us that it was error for the trial court not to strike Juror Prince for cause. The *Altman* case is distinguishable because the jurors who were not stricken in that case were *former* patients of the defendant obstetricians. In fact, the *Altman* court noted that it would follow the *Mackey* case where there was no current or continuing professional relationship between the jurors and the doctors rather than the *Davenport* case where the relationship between the jurors and the parties was a current one. 850 S.W.2d at 45-46. Furthermore, in the *Fugate* case our supreme court emphasized that the failure of the trial court to strike the prospective juror was reversible error because the juror stated that he would seek to employ the prosecutor in the future. 993 S.W.2d at 938.

We are well aware that it is generally within the discretion of the trial court as to whether a juror should be stricken for cause. *Lewis, supra.* However, that discretion is not unbridled, and the trial court abuses its discretion when it fails to strike jurors who have a "close relationship" with a party, counsel, victim, or witness. *Montgomery, supra.* It simply does not make sense that a prospective female juror could be found to be unbiased and fit to serve as a juror in a trial against her obstetrician with whom she has a current ongoing doctor-patient relationship. It is no more logical to assume that such a juror would be fit to serve than it would be to assume that a prospective juror could serve on a jury in a case where his attorney was one of the attorneys in the case. *See Riddle* and *Fugate, supra.* While we do not go so far as to say that our supreme court's dicta in the *Altman* case that there is no "special bond between a woman and her obstetrician" is "incredibly naive" or "ignores reality" as asserted by Justice Leibson in his dissent in that case, we do hold that the failure of the trial court to strike the two jurors who had a current doctor/patient relationship with the defendant doctor in this case warrants a new trial.

The judgment of the Boyd Circuit Court is reversed, and this case is remanded for a new trial.
ALL CONCUR.

Following the completion of voir dire, preliminary motions for the trial are made. This allows the parties to submit various requests to the court that will affect the proceedings. One of the more common motions typically made by each party is the Motion to Dismiss. Very early in litigation a Motion to Dismiss may be made in response to alleged defects in the initial complaint. Once the case reaches the trial stage, it is common for each party to file a Motion to Dismiss on the basis that the accumulated evidence in the case is not sufficient to support the plaintiff's case or, alternatively, the defense. These motions are often made at the beginning of the case and then again by the opposing party at the conclusion of the other party's presentation of evidence. These motions are seldom granted because if the case of either party was that strong, it is likely that settlement or dismissal would have occurred previously. Nevertheless, these motions have long been a part of standard trial practice and give the court the opportunity to rule in situations where settlement could not be achieved.

Another common motion that is typically filed prior to the beginning of trial is the Motion in Limine. This may also be known as the motion to exclude or limit. This motion is generally filed in one of two situations. The first is when one party is in possession of evidence that is so graphic it could cause an emotional rather than logical reaction by the jury. Such motions can be filed for any type of evidence that might produce such a reaction. This includes videography, photographs, and even graphic testimony. The second situation is when evidence is so complex that it cannot be considered appropriately with the other evidence by a jury and would tend to mislead or confuse the jury in its consideration of the case. Motions in Limine are usually filed in conjunction with a thorough description of alternative evidence that will properly inform the jury without the risk of confusion or outrage.

CASE

700 So2d. 1340
Supreme Court of Alabama.

Dr. Thomas R. DEMPSEY
v.
James PHELPS and Cynthia Phelps, as Guardians of a Minor, James Phelps, Jr.

Rehearing Denied Aug. 15, 1997.

KENNEDY, Justice.

A jury's verdict is presumed correct and will not be disturbed unless it is plainly erroneous or manifestly unjust. *Crown Life Insurance Co. v. Smith,* 657 So.2d 821 (Ala.1994). In addition, a judgment based upon a jury verdict and sustained by the denial of a postjudgment motion for a new trial will not be reversed unless it is plainly and palpably wrong. *National Security Ins. Co. v. Donaldson,* 664 So.2d 871 (Ala.1995). Because the jury returned a verdict for the Phelpses, any disputed questions of fact must be resolved in their favor, and we must presume that the jury drew from the facts any reasonable inferences necessary to support its verdict. *State Farm Auto. Ins. Co. v. Morris,* 612 So.2d 440, 443 (Ala.1993). In short, in reviewing a judgment based upon a jury verdict, this Court must review the record in a light most favorable to the appellee. *Liberty National Life Ins. Co. v. McAllister,* 675 So.2d 1292 (Ala.1995).

(continued)

The facts of this case were thoroughly set forth in our opinion on the first appeal of this case. For the reader's convenience, the following facts are recited here as excerpted from that opinion:

"James, Jr., was born with spina bifida. It was eventually also determined that his right foot was a clubfoot. The foot condition worsened as the child grew older, and it required corrective surgery when he was two years old.

"Dr. Dempsey performed the foot surgery on June 30, 1987, and James, Jr., was released from the hospital the following day. The child's right foot was enclosed in a cast that extended the full length of his leg. On July 2, the Phelpses noted that the toes of the child's right foot had turned a dark red; the toes continued to darken in color until on Saturday, July 4, the Phelpses noted that the big toe on that foot had a dark purple color and that the second and third toes were lighter purple. They also noted that the child had a slight fever. The Phelpses attempted to contact Dr. Dempsey that day through his answering service, but were unable to. The child's condition worsened and on July 5 they again attempted to contact Dr. Dempsey through his answering service; they were instructed to bring the child to Dr. Dempsey's office the next morning.

"On July 6, the child's condition had worsened, his big toe was nearly black, and the second and third toes were dark purple. Dr. Dempsey cut a small hole in the cast to observe the condition of the foot and concluded that the child had 'cast blisters' on the foot. The child's condition worsened the next day, July 7; his fever persisted, his toes were darker, and pus was draining from his foot. Although Mrs. Phelps returned the child to Dr. Dempsey, the doctor simply informed her that the cast blisters had broken and were draining. Mrs. Phelps returned James, Jr., to Dr. Dempsey on July 8. He instructed her to take the child to his pediatrician to be evaluated for an ear or respiratory infection.

"On July 9, Mrs. Phelps took James, Jr., to Dr. Van Chunn, his pediatrician. Dr. Chunn noted the child's fever and the blackened color of all his toes; he prescribed an antibiotic, even though he found no ear or respiratory infection. He also sent James, Jr., for an X-ray of his right foot. Mrs. Phelps returned James, Jr., to Dr. Chunn on July 10. Dr. Chunn advised her that the child's condition had to be caused by something occurring beneath the cast, but that the X-ray did not show the foot well enough to indicate the cause, and instructed her to return the child to Dr. Dempsey.

"On the morning of July 11, the condition of the child's foot had worsened and the big toe was completely black. Mrs. Phelps telephoned Dr. Dempsey and informed him that she and her husband were taking James, Jr., to the emergency room at Springhill Memorial Hospital. Dr. Dempsey met the Phelpses at the hospital and, at the insistence of Mr. Phelps, removed the cast from the child's foot and leg. Dr. Dempsey had informed them that removing the cast could upset the surgical procedure that had been performed to correct the child's clubfoot condition. Removal of the cast revealed that the foot was swollen and blackened and was draining pus. Dr. Dempsey bandaged the foot and told the Phelpses to bring James, Jr., to his office the next morning.

"On the morning of July 12, Dr. Dempsey cleaned and rebandaged the child's foot and gave them an antibiotic used to treat skin infections. He told the Phelpses that James, Jr., had some dead skin and instructed them to clean and bandage his foot several times daily. During the following week, the child's fever decreased, but the condition of his foot did not improve.

"On July 17, the child's fever returned and, on July 18, his parents took him to the Mobile Infirmary emergency room, where they were met by Dr. Chunn. Dr. Chunn admitted James, Jr., and put him on an intravenous antibiotic. He also ordered a test of a culture from the surgical wound on the child's foot; that test was positive for staphylococcus bacteria. Over the next several days, the child's condition improved somewhat and, on July 24, Dr. Dempsey discharged him from the hospital and placed him on the same antibiotic he had prescribed earlier.

(continued)

"On August 1, Mrs. Phelps discovered a great deal of 'black stuff' while changing *1344 the bandages on the child's foot. She took him to Dr. Dempsey, who informed her that the child needed to see a plastic surgeon. James, Jr., was admitted to the Mobile Infirmary on August 3, and the dead tissue on his right foot, including the big toe, was amputated."

656 So.2d at 377-79.

Initially, Dr. Dempsey argues that the trial court erred in allowing the Phelpses' expert witness, Dr. Frank Catinella, to testify regarding the standard of care allegedly breached in this case. He maintains that Dr. Catinella was not a "similarly situated health care provider" as required for medical liability standard-of-care testimony pursuant to Ala Code 1975, § 6- 5-548, and this Court's interpretation of that statute in *Medlin v. Crosby*, 583 So.2d 1290 (Ala.1991). In *Medlin,* this Court established a framework under § 6-5-548 for determining whether an expert witness is qualified to testify in a medical malpractice case. Pursuant to *Medlin,* the trial court must answer the following questions before determining whether as to the defendant an expert witness is "similarly situated":

"(1) What is the standard of care alleged to have been breached? (2) Is the defendant 'health care provider' a specialist in the discipline or school of practice of the standard of care that the court has previously determined is alleged to have been breached? (3) Does the proffered expert witness qualify as a 'similarly situated health care provider' under the subsection determined in the second step to apply."

583 So.2d at 1293.

As to question (1), Dempsey maintains that the standard of care alleged to be breached here is that of an orthopedic surgeon providing care for a child after clubfoot surgery. Dempsey argues that Dr. Catinella, who is a board-certified cardiovascular thoracic surgeon, was not qualified to testify as to this standard of care. However, we agree with the trial court that this case concerned "a vascular matter, not an orthopedic matter"--in other words, that the Phelpses' claims regarded Dr. Dempsey's alleged failure to properly treat the child's foot during the post-surgery phase for the circulatory and vascular problems that developed after the surgery and casting of the foot. These problems are not isolated to this type of surgery, and they do not concern the orthopedic surgery performed by Dr. Dempsey; they concern the treatment of the infection after the surgery that resulted in the loss of his foot. The standard of care allegedly breached was that of a health care provider treating a patient for post-surgical vascular problems and infection, which are not specific to orthopedic surgery.

Dr. Dempsey is, without question, a specialist in orthopedic surgery. He is a board-certified orthopedic surgeon, and since 1980 he has been licensed to practice medicine in Alabama. However, he is not a specialist in treating vascular problems resulting from surgery; it was in regard to treating those problems that the alleged breach of the standard of care occurred. "[F]or purposes of determining whether a 'health care provider' is a 'specialist,' ... the trial court should look to whether the defendant 'health care provider' is board certified in the specialty or discipline or school of practice that covers the area of the alleged breach." *Medlin,* supra, at 1294.

Because Dr. Dempsey was not a "specialist" in the area of the alleged breach, we must determine whether Dr. Catinella, as the Phelpses' expert witness, was a "similarly situated health care provider" under § 6-5- 548(b). That section states:

"[A] 'similarly situated health care provider' is one who:

"(1) Is licensed by the appropriate regulatory board or agency of this or some other state; and

"(2) Is trained and experienced in the same discipline or school of practice; and

"(3) Has practiced in the same discipline or school of practice during the year preceding the date that the alleged breach of the standard of care occurred."

(continued)

Dr. Catinella is board-certified in the areas of general surgery and cardiovascular and thoracic surgery. Because of this certification. Dr. Catinella is permitted to practice vascular surgery. After his internship at Northshore University Hospital in Chicago and his residency in New York University Medical Center, Dr. Catinella completed a three-year fellowship in cardiovascular, vascular, and thoracic surgery at Rush-Presbyterian St. Luke Medical Center in Chicago. He has specialized in cardiovascular and thoracic surgery and has published medical studies in numerous journals. Dr. Catinella is consulted by other surgeons regarding the treatment of post-surgical infections relating to a loss of blood flow to the body area affected by the surgery.

Dr. Catinella was at least as qualified as Dr. Dempsey in the field of the alleged breach in this case, and we conclude that he is a "similarly situated health care provider" as that term is defined in § 6-5-548(b). In holding that Dr. Catinella could testify as to the standard of care in this case, the trial court correctly relied upon this Court's holding in *Olsen v. Rich,* 657 So.2d 875 (Ala.1995). Like the witness in *Olsen,* Dr. Dempsey, although he was a specialist in his own surgical practice, was not a specialist in the area of the alleged breach---the treatment of vascular injury. Therefore, the trial court did not err in allowing Dr. Catinella to testify regarding Dr. Dempsey's alleged breach of the standard of care. As this Court noted in *Rodgers v. Adams,* 657 So.2d 838 (Ala.1995), the experience and training of an expert witness and that of a defendant medical provider are not required to be exactly the same:

"The Medical Liability Act does not require that the defendant health care provider and the expert witness have identical training, experience, or types of practice, or even the same specialties. To be 'similarly situated,' an expert witness must be able to testify about the standard of care alleged to have been breached in the procedure that is involved in the case."

657 So.2d at 842.

Dr. Dempsey next maintains that the trial court erred in excluding evidence of the child's Social Security records, as well as photographs from medical articles authored by his expert witness Dr. David Hootnick. The Social Security records indicated that, shortly after the child was born, the Phelpses applied for him to be classified by the Social Security Administration as 100% disabled. The Social Security Administration evaluated the child's spina bifida condition and determined that he was 100% disabled. Dr. Dempsey maintains that the Social Security records would have helped him to cross-examine the Phelpses regarding their statements that the child was not "abnormal" before he lost a portion of his foot.

The photographs in question showed tissue injury suffered by other patients following surgery similar to that undergone by the Phelpses' child. The photographs, which were portions of Dr. Hootnick's articles, were not admitted into evidence, although the text of the articles was read into evidence by Dr. Hootnick. Dr. Hootnick meticulously testified regarding several cases of postsurgery tissue loss that were described in the articles.

Before trial, the court granted the Phelpses' motion in limine regarding the Social Security evidence. The Phelpses maintained that the evidence would prejudice the jury. Their motion stated:

"[James, Jr.,] was born with spina bifida. He was declared totally disabled by Social Security not based on any limitations that this condition placed on him, but rather on this condition's existence alone so that his impoverished family could obtain state medical care for him. Thus the evidence would mislead the jury concerning [the child's] condition [and] would unfairly prejudice his claim."

The trial court excluded the photographs during the trial, stating in part that the prejudice the photographs would cause outweighed their probative value.

Whether to exclude evidence because of its potential to prejudice the jury is within the sound discretion of the trial court. See C. Gamble, *McElroy's Alabama Evidence* § 21.01(6) (5th ed.1996). A trial court may exclude evidence, even if it is relevant, if it would serve little or no purpose other than to arouse prejudice in the jury. *Ayres v. Lakeshore Community Hospital,* 689 So.2d 39 (Ala.1997), citing C. Gamble, *McElroy's Alabama Evidence* § 21.01(4) (5th ed.1996). As the Phelpses note, there was no evidence regarding the

(continued)

factors used by the Social Security Administration in determining the child's disability. Assuming, without deciding, that the Social Security records regarding the child's spina bifida were relevant evidence, we conclude that the trial court did not abuse its discretion in prohibiting this evidence, which clearly held a strong potential for prejudice under the circumstances of this action.

We also find no abuse of discretion in the trial court's exclusion of the photographs from the jury. Dr. Hootnick was allowed to testify thoroughly concerning the cases dealt with in his articles, and he compared those cases to the surgery and postoperative vascular problems of the Phelpses' child. In these circumstances, the photographs could conceivably have been excluded as cumulative evidence. See C. Gamble, *McElroy's Alabama Evidence* § 10.07 (5th ed.1996). However, in light of the graphic nature of the photographs and the fact that the cases pictured in the photographs had already been described in detail by Dr. Hootnick, the trial court certainly did not abuse its wide discretion in finding the photographs to be more prejudicial than probative. See C. Gamble, *McElroy's Alabama Evidence* § 21.01(6) (5th ed.1996). Contrary to Dr. Dempsey's contention that the photographs of the Phelpses' child also should have been excluded, those photographs "depicted the location and severity" of the injury this child sustained; the trial court did not abuse its discretion in admitting them. *Olympia Spa v. Johnson,* 547 So.2d 80, 83 (Ala.1989) ("The trial judge is vested with discretion not only in his determination as to the preliminary proofs offered to identify the photograph or to prove that the photograph is an accurate representation ..., but also in his determination of whether the picture will aid the jury or tend to confuse or prejudice it.").

Dr. Dempsey next argues that the trial court erred in submitting the issue of wantonness and punitive damages to the jury. As noted above, the jury awarded a total of $270,000 in damages to the Phelpses. The jury classified the award as $125,000 for punitive damages; $20,000 for past compensatory damages; and $125,000 for future compensatory damages. Dr. Dempsey maintains that the Phelpses submitted "only evidence ... that there was a difference of opinion about the care [the child] should have received after his clubfoot surgery was performed," and that there was no evidence to demonstrate the wantonness required for an award of punitive damages. He also contends that if the award is not set aside, then the punitive damages award should be remitted.

Wantonness occurs where a person intends to injure another; it also occurs where one acts, or fails to act, with a knowledge and consciousness that his action or failure to act will likely result in injury to another. *Wright v. Terry,* 646 So.2d 11 (Ala.1994); *Lynn Strickland Sales & Service, Inc. v. Aero-Lane Fabricators, Inc.,* 510 So.2d 142 (Ala.1987); *Sington v. Birmingham Ry., Light & Power Co.,* 200 Ala. 282, 76 So. 48 (1917). The Phelpses presented evidence from which a jury could have found that Dr. Dempsey failed to properly examine the child in regard to the infection after the surgery. Dr. Dempsey told Mrs. Phelps to bring the child back to his office in one month following the surgery, even though he knew that children with spina bifida are at risk for postoperative wound healing infection. Mrs. Phelps testified as to Dr. Dempsey's treatment after he cut back a small part of the top of the child's cast to inspect his foot on July 6, 1987:

"A. On the top of the foot all the toes were purple and blue and red on the side some. And the top of the foot had kind of a mushy looking place on it that it was draining. It had some drainage on it there and it was--a little black around the edges and it was red. It was just real inflamed looking.

"Q. Did James have any other symptoms on the 6th of July?

"A. He had fever and he had diarrhea. He wouldn't eat.

"....

"Q. What information did Dr. Dempsey give you about James's foot?

"A. He told me that it was relatively common, that he saw it a lot, that it was cast blisters and that ... I had nothing to worry about. He said to take him home and not to worry about it, that everything would be fine. To come back in about a week or so....

(continued)

"Q. Did Dr. Dempsey take James's temperature?

"A. No, he did nothing else. The only thing that he did that day was cut back on the cast some and talk to me. And he didn't do anything else.

"....

"Q. Did he recommend any kind of treatment for the fever?

"A. No.... On the 7th he was having more diarrhea, he was still running fever, and I just couldn't get him to eat and I was so afraid he was going to dehydrate. So I took him back down to Dr. Dempsey's office and he wouldn't even see us.

"I sat out there and argued with the nurse for a while and then he came to the door and took us right inside the hall. And he looked at it and he said it's the same thing I told you yesterday, it has cast blisters and he dismissed us.... [James, Jr.,] still had the fever, the diarrhea, the toes were swollen and he had some drainage. It was starting to smell.

"Q. On the 7th did Dr. Dempsey take James's temperature?

"A. No.... On the 8th I went back to Dr. Dempsey's office. [James, Jr.,] was still running a fever, still had the diarrhea. I was just--I was starting to panic. I took him back to Dr. Dempsey's office and he just seemed angry that I was there and he looked at his foot again and he told me, he said there's nothing wrong with this foot, it has some cast blisters and if he's having these problems that you keep explaining you take him to the pediatrician ... maybe he's got an ear infection....

"Q. On the 8th of July did Dr. Dempsey take James's temperature?

"A. No.

"Q. Did Dr. Dempsey check James's ears?

"A. No.

"Q. Did Dr. Dempsey check James's throat?

"A. No.

"Q. Did Dr. Dempsey listen to his lungs?

"A. No.

"Q. Did Dr. Dempsey take a culture of James' foot on the 8th?

"A. No."

After the child had visited his pediatrician, Mr. Phelps took the child back to Dr. Dempsey, on July 11. At Mr. Phelps's insistence, Dr. Dempsey removed the front of the cast and cleaned the foot and wrapped it, but he did not prescribe antibiotics until the next day. At that time the foot was, according to Mrs. Phelps, "swollen" and "the smell was horrible, undescribable" and "it was black on his foot and it was purple and dark red and it had all kinds of pus and drainage." Mrs. Phelps stated that Dr. Dempsey told her and her husband that he "didn't think it was necessary" to remove the cast. The Phelpses produced expert testimony indicating that the child should have been hospitalized on July 12 for evaluation of his vascular infection.

The evidence set out above--merely a sample of the graphic testimony found in the record--combined with the rest of the Phelpses' evidence, including the testimony of the Phelpses' experts, was such that the jury could have properly inferred that Dr. Dempsey acted wantonly in treating the child's infection. Therefore, the jury could properly award the Phelpses punitive damages. Moreover, the trial court did not err in refusing to remit the $125,000 punitive damages award. The trial court has much discretion in determining whether to grant a new trial and, in that regard, whether to require a remittitur; that discretion was not abused here. See *Fields v. Parker,* 361 So.2d 356 (Ala.1978); *Crown Life Insurance Co. v. Smith,* 657 So.2d 821 (Ala.1994).

Dr. Dempsey next contends that the trial court erred in submitting to the jury a charge regarding future damages, as well as a charge stating that the child's preexisting condition did not excuse negligence or

(continued)

wantonness on Dr. Dempsey's part. However, the Phelpses submitted expert testimony indicating that the child could later need an artificial foot or lower leg because there is now "nothing on the inner side" of his foot, and that, therefore, his entire foot might have to be amputated. The trial court did not err in charging the jury regarding future damages. In addition, the charge concerning the child's preexisting condition was a correct statement of the law--a defendant is responsible for the probable consequences of his actions, regardless of the preexisting condition of the plaintiff. See *Britton v. Doehring*, 286 Ala. 498, 506, 242 So.2d 666, 673 (1970) (" 'once the element of injury proximately caused by the [defendant] is introduced, it is traditional that the defendant take the plaintiff as he finds him' ") (quoting *Lipscomb v. Diamiani*, 226 A.2d 914 (Del.Super.1967)). See also *Prescott v. Martin*, 331 So.2d 240 (Ala.1976) (holding no error where trial court informed a jury that it could base an award on all damage proximately resulting from the defendant's actions, even if the plaintiff's injuries were more serious because of her preexisting condition).

Dr. Dempsey next argues that the trial court erred in striking Juror A from the jury during the trial. A was a teacher at a school affiliated with Dr. Dempsey's church, and Dr. Dempsey's daughter attends that school. During a break in the trial, Mrs. Phelps overheard a conversation in a restroom in which another juror said to A, "I am surprised that they left you on the jury." The Phelpses moved to strike A, and the trial court held a private interview with A. The trial court stated that A felt that she did not want to serve any further on the jury and that she could not give either side a fair and impartial trial. A was then questioned by the attorneys for both the Phelpses and Dr. Dempsey. A stated that some friends of Dr. Dempsey were present during the trial and that those friends were the parents of A 's daughter's best friend. She stated that "she would rather not sit on this trial," but stated that she "thought" she could make a fair decision. Although during the voir dire examination the Phelpses knew of A 's employment at the church school, they were unaware of Dr. Dempsey's connections with the church until he testified at trial.

The trial court has broad discretion in sustaining or denying a challenge for cause, and its ruling in that regard will not be reversed unless it was plainly erroneous. *Boykin v. Keebler*, 648 So.2d 550 (Ala.1994); *Roberts v. Hutchins*, 613 So.2d 348 (Ala.1993). The trial court took proper steps in questioning A about her involvement with Dr. Dempsey's church and then allowing the attorneys for both sides to question her. We must conclude that the trial court did not abuse its discretion in granting the Phelpses' motion to strike A from the jury because of A 's connections with the church school, particularly when we consider those connections along with her acquaintance with Dr. Dempsey's friends and her equivocal statements about whether she could fairly decide the case.

Dr. Dempsey next argues that the trial court abused its discretion in granting the Phelpses' motion in limine in regard to several experts Dr. Dempsey planned to call as witnesses, and in denying his motion for a continuance after the trial court granted that motion in limine.

The motion was made in response to Dr. Dempsey's supplemental response to the Phelpses' interrogatories; that response listed several new witnesses to be called and expanded the testimony of other witnesses that had been previously listed. Dr. Dempsey's attorneys stated that they had had problems obtaining medical records from the Phelpses' attorneys and had only recently received certain arteriogram films of the child. After the trial court had conducted an extensive hearing on the morning the trial began, it granted the motion in limine and denied the motion for a continuance. The trial court stated:

"THE COURT: I grant the motion in limine. And I knew this was coming and I don't want to put this up here for the jury later.

"DEFENSE COUNSEL: Your Honor, can I make a motion, though, to move for a continuance? Your Honor, because--

"THE COURT: This is nothing more than gamesmanship.

*1349 "DEFENSE COUNSEL: Your Honor, it--

(continued)

"THE COURT: And, you know, you've got another motion claiming that he didn't give you something and you've been complaining consistently that, you know, you haven't been getting this and you haven't been getting that and it is just simply two-faced for you to come in here when you've had records since at least the 16th of February and say, you know--
"DEFENSE COUNSEL: Well, Your Honor, can--
"THE COURT:--'I didn't give them to him because of something that's just totally irrelevant.'
"DEFENSE COUNSEL: Your Honor, well, could we move for a continuance? Your Honor, we cannot--
"THE COURT: The motion for a continuance is denied.
"....
"DEFENSE COUNSEL: Your Honor, we cannot--Your Honor, I don't understand what you're--
"THE COURT: Well, it's real simple and I'll put it in the record. You have had these scans, by your own admission, for over a month, since at least the 16th of February. And for reasons known only to you, and they may be perfectly valid reasons to you, I don't impute anybody's motivations here, you chose not to disclose the names of thirteen doctors until approximately one week before trial."

Our review of the record indicates that the trial court did not abuse its discretion in granting the Phelpses' motion in limine concerning these experts and in denying Dr. Dempsey's motion for a continuance.

For the foregoing reasons, the judgment of the trial court is affirmed.
AFFIRMED.

OPENING STATEMENTS—DON'T LET YOUR MOUTH WRITE A CHECK YOUR EVIDENCE CAN'T CASH

Following voir dire, the final jury is sworn in, pretrial motions are made and ruled upon, and the proceedings of trial actually begin. The first step in most trials is the **opening statement** and cases involving medical malpractice are no different. Usually, the party who has the burden of proof—the plaintiff—makes the first opening statement. The responding party—the defendant—has the option of making an opening statement at this time or of waiting until the presentation of his or her evidence. Opening statements are not to be argumentative. They are to serve as an opportunity for the attorneys to outline their evidence to the jury. Legal conclusions, arguments, and pleas for verdicts are inappropriate at this time. Opening statements are not evidence. Rather, they serve as an outline of the evidence to be presented.

A common misconception about opening statements is that they are wildly inflammatory against the opposition, as portrayed in popular media. In reality, the purpose of the opening statement is to lay the foundation for the actual case to be presented and to briefly introduce the evidence that is anticipated by both parties. In the medical malpractice case, this may include a description of the burden of proof that must be met, such as the basic elements of negligence, and how the parties intend to prove or refute the existence of the elements in the case. Counsel for each party will usually confine opening statements to reveal just enough information to interest the jury, provide them with some basic insights about the nature of the case, and hopefully make some initial impressions about their respective clients. There is a fine line to navigate in presenting the opening statement because any attempt to be overtly argumentative is likely to produce objections of misconduct by the other side, which in turn could have a negative impact on the impression of the jury. Indeed, the opening statement requires perhaps the greatest amount of finesse in the trial in terms of presenting information and guiding the jury toward the desired outcome. One pitfall of the opening statement phase is to make assertions about the evidence that are not supported during the trial. Therefore, the opening statements should be closely linked to the actual evidence that a party expects to present. The key is threefold: use the opening statement to explain what the evidence will be, present the evidence, and close by summarizing what verdict the weight of the evidence supports. The failure of any one of these key elements can result in the failure of an otherwise valid case or defense.

THE PRESENTATION OF EVIDENCE

Case in Chief—The Prima Facie Case

Earlier discussion emphasized the importance of collecting sufficient evidence during investigation and discovery to support a prima facie case. That is to say, there should be credible evidence sufficient to establish each legal element of the cause of action alleged, such as medical malpractice by virtue of negligence. The presentation of the evidence to support the prima facie case necessary to win the lawsuit begins during the case in chief.

The case in chief is the stage of a trial during which the party with the burden of proof presents evidence to support its claim. The burden of proof previously mentioned refers to the party who must convince the jury of his or her case in order to win the suit. In a civil case, the burden of proof is generally on the plaintiff, who claims injury or damage due to the defendant's fault. The party with the burden usually presents evidence first. The standard burden of proof in most medical malpractice cases to prove one's claim by a preponderance of the evidence is the same as in most civil cases. Unlike the standard criminal cases where fault for the alleged wrongdoing or crime must be proven beyond any reasonable doubt, in these cases the burden is much lighter. The party who does not have the burden of proof needs only to present enough evidence in opposition to prevent the burden (minimum level of evidence) from being met.

APPLICATION 10.1

Joe is the plaintiff in a case of alleged medical malpractice. He is suing Dr. Herman for failure to properly diagnose and treat hypertension (high blood pressure). At trial, Joe presented evidence of four scheduled appointments to Dr. Herman complaining of severe headaches and feeling generally unwell over a period of several months. Dr. Herman diagnosed Joe's condition as chronic migraine headaches. Approximately two months after Joe's last appointment with Dr. Herman, Joe suffered a massive stroke that was attributed to hypertension. In response, Dr. Herman presented expert testimony that showed the symptoms noted in Joe's medical charts were consistent with migraine headaches. Dr. Herman's charts on Joe also included his medical records from a previous physician who had diagnosed Joe with chronic

(continued)

> migraines over a period of some 10 years. Dr. Herman also presented evidence that showed a strong history of strokes in Joe's family, and that Joe had significant contributing risk factors including obesity and a history of heavy smoking. Dr. Herman's chart showed he had warned Joe of the risk factors for stroke and the need to reduce his weight and stop smoking.
>
> In a case such as this, where the burden is a preponderance, the jury must consider all of the evidence and determine whether it is more likely than not that the failure to diagnose and medically treat hypertension was the cause of Joe's stroke. If they do not find failure, then the burden has been met. However, if the jury finds that the evidence shows the failure to treat hypertension was a breach of the duty by Dr. Herman toward Joe, and that it failed to meet the standard of care by other similarly situated physicians, and perhaps most important, that it was the proximate cause of Joe's stroke, then Joe would have met the burden of proof.

If a prima facie case is not established, the claims of the complaint have not been proven by the minimum legal standard. At this point, the party responding to the claims can make a Motion for a Directed Verdict, which requests the court to instruct the jury that there is no need to present a defense because the allegation of the complaint has not been proven. If the motion is granted, the judge directs the jury to render a verdict against the party with the burden of proof.

Most parties with the burden of proof attempt to establish a much stronger case than one that is merely prima facie. The evidence presented must withstand contradictory evidence presented by the defense and still prevail as the most likely explanation of the circumstances that created the dispute. Realistically, a prima facie case is usually not enough to win the case.

With respect to the presentation of evidence, it can come in several forms. The most dramatic evidence portrayed in popular media is often by the witness. But other types of evidence can be just as powerful. A party may present testimonial evidence, documentary evidence ranging from paper to digital recordings and images, and tangible evidence consisting of physical items. It does not matter how much evidence is presented but how it collectively supports the case or defense.

The gathering and introduction of evidence is subject to a number of rules specific to the type or content of the evidence, but the evidentiary rules of relevance and materiality apply to all evidence presented at trial. These rules serve the purpose of ensuring that the evidence presented to support a claim or defense are both fair and proper, and contribute to the determination by the judge and/or jury. In order to be included in the trial, evidence must be 1) relevant; 2) material; and 3) meet the requirements of any more specific applicable evidentiary rules.

So how does one know if the evidence obtained during the discovery and investigation of a medical malpractice case is relevant and material? Relevant evidence is that which tends to establish some basic element of the dispute as truthful or unfounded. Both sides in a lawsuit are allowed to introduce evidence that will prove their version of the story is the most accurate depiction of what occurred. Material evidence is considered necessary to a fair and informed determination of the dispute, but the same information from 20 different witnesses may not be material, nor would evidence that is extremely graphic be considered material. If the graphic images are so unsettling that they prevent emotional impartiality of a jury, an alternative form of evidence may be required.

APPLICATION 10.2

Julia is having a cesarean delivery of her first child. The plan was to use an epidural anesthetic so that she felt no pain below the rib cage in order to be alert and awake during the birth of the baby. Her husband planned to stand in the room and videotape as the birth occurred. Everything was in place and surgery began. Immediately, Julia began to express concern and pain. As the doctor progressed with the incision Julia became hysterical. The procedure was stopped and it was discovered the epidural was improperly administered and she was not anesthetized below the ribs as thought. Rather she felt the entire incision as it was made. During the attempted surgery, Julia's husband did videotape the entire process including the incision and discovery of what had gone wrong. A lawsuit was brought against the anesthesiologist for negligence as well as the obstetrician on the basis he negligently failed to test the area for adequate anesthesia before beginning the surgery. The anesthesiologist settled out of court. The obstetrician went to trial on the basis that it was not part of his duty, but rather that of the anesthesiologist, to establish proper anesthesia.

The position of the defense would be that the videotape is quite obviously immaterial on the basis a jury could never remain impartial after witnessing the videotape with respect to the actual duty of the obstetrician. The defense would likely claim a verbal description by witnesses who were present could be just as effective in establishing what occurred. The plaintiff's side would argue that the experience was horrific and a jury needs to see the video to fully appreciate what took place. A judge would have to determine if there was other available evidence that would be as effective as the video but less inflammatory. If none exists, then the judge must determine if a jury could remain objective and properly consider all of the evidence of both sides after watching the video.

As with interviews, the testimony of witnesses consists of two types of questioning. The witness called on behalf of a party's case is questioned by the indirect method. This involves primarily open questions that allow for narrative answers. Only the most basic information can be obtained through direct or leading questions. Witnesses called who are openly in support of the opposition, and witnesses who are questioned by the opposing party during cross-examination, may be asked leading questions.

Very effective tools in cross-examination during medical malpractice trials are the statements, medical records, and depositions accumulated during investigation and discovery. Unlike many other types of lawsuits, medical malpractice cases usually involve heavily documented circumstances. Additionally, witness statements and depositions are widely used to record individual memories of the events surrounding the case. If a witness changes his or her version of what occurred in any way, these statements and depositions can be used to assist the witness with his or her recollection or to discredit ("impeach") the witness. However, this requires an extensive knowledge of the contents of the medical records and depositions and a system of indexing and organization that allows the attorney access to particular facts of a particular record—quite literally—within a moment's notice.

Another element of testimonial evidence that is present in only some civil cases, but necessary in most medical malpractice cases, is the statement of the expert opinion. As discussed, many jurisdictions require either a pre-litigation review of the case by an expert or, at the very least, testimony by an expert at trial. It is essential that the expert be well qualified for the particular type of case and reside within the particular jurisdiction where the case is tried. In addition, the expert witness should be someone who communicates effectively to a jury in terms of explaining information in layman's terms, appearance, and demeanor. All of these aspects can impact the weight a jury will give to the content of the testimony when two or more experts express conflicting opinions.

The evidence, whether testimonial, documentary, or tangible, must cumulatively support each of the facts alleged in the complaint and support the elements of the cause of action on which the lawsuit is based. This establishes the prima facie case. If a prima facie case is not established, the claims of the complaint have not been adequately proven. At this point, the party responding to the claims can make a Motion for a Directed Verdict, which requests the court to instruct the jury that there is no need to present a defense because the allegations of the complaint have not been established by a preponderance of evidence. If the motion is granted, the judge directs the jury to render a verdict against the party with the burden of proof.

The Defense

After the plaintiff has presented all of the evidence and made a prima facie case, that party will rest. At this point, the responding party will present the evidence in support of the defense. If the defense did not make an opening statement at the beginning of the trial, the opportunity is available to make one at this time. The opening statement is followed by the presentation of the defendant's evidence.

In the presentation of evidence, the defendant has no initial burden to meet. Rather, a burden occurs only if the plaintiff establishes a prima facie case. At this point, the burden shifts, and the defendant must present enough evidence in response to the plaintiff's evidence to create a question in the minds of the jury that the plaintiff's version is not the most likely and accurate version of the facts.

After the defendant has concluded the presentation of evidence, the plaintiff may request permission to reopen his or her case. This may be allowed when the plaintiff has additional evidence that will respond in a direct way to specific evidence introduced by the defendant. The plaintiff is permitted to respond only to the evidence of the defendant and not to merely supplement the previously introduced case in chief. If the plaintiff is allowed to introduce additional evidence, the defendant may then be permitted to introduce rebuttal evidence.

THE CLOSING, DELIBERATION, AND VERDICT

After both parties have concluded the presentation of evidence, the attorneys for the plaintiff and defendant are each allowed the opportunity to make a summation, also known as a **closing argument**. In some jurisdictions, the party who speaks first may be permitted a brief period to rebut the arguments of the party who speaks second. During closing arguments, each side summarizes all of the evidence and attempts to persuade the jury of the most plausible explanation for the course of events that led to the lawsuit. It is at this juncture that the attorneys use their best advocacy skills and persuasive tactics to convince the jury in favor of their client.

In recent years, the intense media coverage surrounding the surge in malpractice litigation and judgments is an additional hurdle the plaintiff's attorney must overcome. The attorney has the burden of establishing the client's case by a preponderance of evidence, and must also present the case in such a way as to overcome any underlying bias or concerns of the jury with regard to the effects of making a significant damage award. Unlike other types of cases where the jury is not allowed to consider whether either of the parties has the benefit of applicable insurance, it is difficult to escape the fact that the average juror knows full well of a) the existence of malpractice insurance and b) the fact that the media has given wide coverage to the allegations that some physicians are leaving their practices and communities in response to rising malpractice insurance rates as the result of large awards in malpractice cases. Even though this may not be proper information for consideration by a jury, it is a reality and the attorneys must determine how, if at all, to approach it during summation while somehow connecting it to the evidence.

After the closing arguments, the judge will read the instructions to the jury. These instructions explain the law that applies to the case as well as the burden of proof. They also indicate what the jury is allowed to consider as evidence when making their decision. The judge may also offer cautionary instructions with respect to disregarding information that may have been presented at trial and then overruled, and any outside influences such as those discussed in this chapter. The jury is then sequestered for deliberations; that is, the jurors are secluded from outside influences while they meet and attempt to reach a decision. Some courts will allow the jurors to take evidence such as documents and photographs into the jury room during their deliberation. In many jurisdictions, the verdict of the jury must be unanimous in favor of one party. If a jury needs more than one day to reach a verdict, the judge will determine whether the jurors can return home for the night or whether they must be sequestered in a hotel during those times when they are not deliberating but before a verdict is reached.

When the jury returns with a verdict, the verdict is read to the parties. If a party requests, the judge may poll the jury. When the jury is polled, the judge asks each juror whether the verdict represents his or her opinion in the case. This is used as a safeguard to assist the court in discovering situations where jurors have been influenced or even coerced by other members of the jury to change their vote in order to reach a specific verdict. If the judge discovers that a juror does not actually support and believe in the verdict, the verdict may be set aside. The effect would be the same as a hung jury, a situation when the jurors return without a verdict. In a civil suit, a jury that cannot reach a decision regarding the likelihood of truth of the plaintiff's case indicates that the burden of proof has not been met, and the decision prevails.

Counsel, witnesses, parties, or anyone connected in any way with the lawsuit is allowed contact with jurors throughout the pretrial and trial stages. After trial this restriction may be dropped. In jurisdictions where juror information is not protected by the courts, it is not unusual for jurors to be contacted and interviewed by the counsel for the parties with respect to how the decision was reached. Any sort of misconduct among jurors that is discovered by either party may be the basis for a post-trial motion or appeal. Each jurisdiction has its own standards with regard to what constitutes juror misconduct sufficient to warrant a new trial. One of the more common grounds is that the jurors reached their determination by considering information other than that provided as evidence at trial. This has been a heavily litigated issue in medical malpractice cases where there have been allegations that jurors obtained independent medical information from health care professionals in their family circle or through acquaintances. If such information or other evidence of juror misconduct is substantial, and there is evidence it was shared with the other jurors, and if that evidence influenced the verdict, there may well be grounds to set aside the verdict.

POST-TRIAL PROCEEDINGS

In the event a party believes there has been an improper verdict on the basis that something occurred during the trial process—for example juror misconduct—that prevented the legally correct result, they can file a Motion for a New Trial. Other errors might include the wrongful exclusion of certain evidence, improper testimony by a witness, or a procedural error. Anything a party can point to that had a significant impact on the case and that the party can convince the judge was irregular or inappropriate can serve as the basis for a Motion for New Trial.

An alternative to the Motion for New Trial is a Motion for Judgment Notwithstanding the verdict (Non Obstante Verdicto). This request is made after the verdict has been delivered by the jury and a party contends the jury misconstrued the evidence and reached a result that is in conflict with the totality of the evidence. If the motion is granted, the judge will substitute his or her own verdict for the verdict of the jury. Because this usurps the jury's function to interpret the evidence, it is a motion that is very rarely granted.

Appellate procedure is largely governed by the appellate system of each jurisdiction. The appellate court generally reviews only what has occurred procedurally in the lower court. It will not usually consider the actual evidence in the context that it should determine the innocence or culpability of the parties. Again, that is a jury function and is typically respected as such. The review of the appellate court may encompass what took place before, during, or after the trial. It may consider all evidence that was offered and whether it was properly admitted or excluded. Appellate court decisions are usually confined to the issue of whether or not an error was made in the trial court. Further, the error must be serious enough to warrant intervention by the appellate court. Consequently an appellate court will not exchange its opinion of right or wrong, guilt or innocence for that of the judge and jury. It will only consider whether the result was based on a fair presentation of the case according to the requirements of substantive and procedural law.

The appeals process is started by notice served from the appealing party to the other parties, the appellate, and the trial court. The appealing party is typically referred to as the appellant and the opposing party is referred to as the appellee.

Once notice has been properly given, several events must occur. The order and time limits for these events may vary somewhat by jurisdiction. Generally, the appellant is responsible for having the trial court records of the case history and trial prepared and forwarded to the appellate court. These often include a detailed transcript of everything said on the record by all those present at the trial.

In addition to submitting the court records, both parties may submit appellate briefs. These are detailed explanations of the progression of the case, opinions about the alleged irregularities, and any supporting legal standards such as cases, statutes, procedural rules, and administrative rules and regulations. In many appellate cases, the courts permit attorneys for the parties to present short oral arguments outlining the briefs. At this stage, each attorney presents the brief and answers questions by the appellate court about their content. The court may ask the attorneys to explain why they think a particular point of law is applicable to the present case. In addition, the attorneys may respond to the points raised in the brief of their adversaries.

The appellate court will consider the case and render a written opinion. The court may affirm (approve) the proceedings of the lower court or it may reverse the lower court and remand the case to the trial court with an order for new or different proceedings to be conducted. Occasionally, the appellate court will hold that the lower court erred to the point that the proceedings should not even have been conducted. In such situations, the case is dismissed entirely.

The illustration that follows is a flowchart of the steps in a civil suit. See Exhibit 10.1. It outlines the procedure discussed in the chapter regarding the litigation process. One significant point to note is that settlement can occur, quite literally, at any stage. The vast majority of cases are settled before the trial ever begins, but settlement can occur during the trial or even after a verdict is rendered. For example, if a party thinks he or she has a strong case but the witnesses are very ineffective, the first party may approach the opposing party mid-trial for a settlement conference. It is rare that a party is absolutely certain of a win and thus a reasonable settlement may appeal to both sides even though trial has begun. With regard to cases in which a verdict has been rendered, what possible reason could a prevailing party have to settle? It is quite simple. The appellate process is costly in terms of legal expenses and is very time consuming. Even though the party receiving a judgment and damage award wins (and a modest rate of interest usually runs from the date of the verdict), it is not yet money in the bank. Because appeals can remain undecided for years, a party may be inclined to consider a post-trial settlement and accept a cash settlement rather than waiting and risking an overturned verdict.

Exhibit 10.1 Chart of Stages of Trial

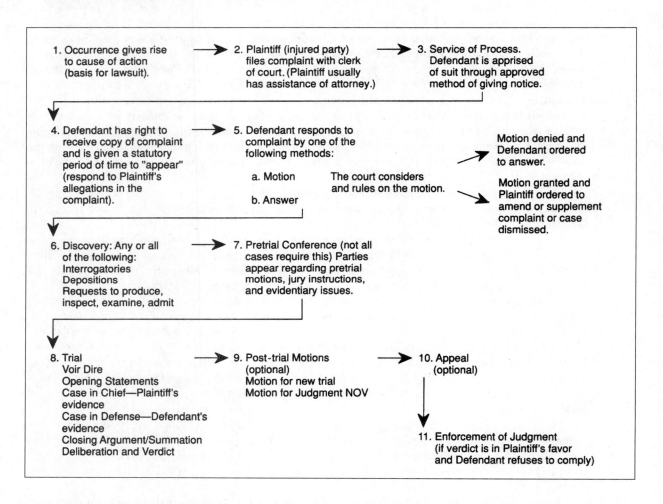

Problem 10.1

Complete 10.1 of the Comprehensive Problem in Appendix A.

CHAPTER SUMMARY

When all attempts at resolving the issues between parties engaged in litigation fail, the final alternative is to take the case before an objective judge or jury for resolution. This is also true of medical malpractice lawsuits. However, the jury selection process known as voir dire can be quite complicated due to the fact that the defendant(s) may have public and private ties to the community and potentially the jury pool as well. These connections must be discovered and evaluated if a fair result is to be achieved. Once jury selection is complete, the trial can begin in earnest. In the opening statements, the parties typically provide a road map of sorts outlining what they expect the evidence in the case to be. This is followed by the actual presentation of that evidence in the form of testimony, documentation, and tangible exhibits. Each party has the opportunity to present his or her side or version of what occurred. The plaintiff has the burden of proving a prima facie case that is established as superior over the defendant by a preponderance. After all evidence is presented, each party is permitted to make a closing argument. Following this, the case is submitted to the jury for deliberation.

In the event a party is dissatisfied with the outcome and feels it was due to some irregularity at trial, such as wrongfully introduced or excluded evidence or some other error, an appeal may be taken. The appellate court will determine whether or not the trial court exceeded its authority and, if so, whether this caused an improper result in the case. However, it should be kept in mind that throughout the trial and even post-trial proceedings, settlement is still an option if the parties can reach an accord.

Key Terms

voir dire	closing argument
opening statement	

For additional resources, go to http://www.westlegalstudies.com.

APPENDIX A

COMPREHENSIVE ASSIGNMENT

Below is a detailed set of facts. These facts will be used for the comprehensive problem assignment at the conclusion of each chapter. Complete the comprehensive problem assignment at the conclusion of each chapter.

Facts

In the spring of 2001, Sue Smith began experiencing heartburn and nausea. Her family doctor made a diagnosis of gallstones. The family doctor recommended Sue have her gallbladder removed surgically. Sue then contacted Dr. Sears, a general surgeon. This same surgeon had operated on Sue approximately five years earlier to repair a bowel obstruction. On June 3, 2001, Dr. Sears operated on Sue to remove her gallbladder laparoscopically. This procedure involved several incisions, each less than one inch, around the abdomen. The various incisions accommodated the various instruments and a small camera that allowed the surgical team to view the inside of the abdomen and to dissect and remove Sue's gallbladder. Sue's doctor informed her she would be home within 48 hours and back to work within an additional three days.

Dr. Sears removed the gallbladder. He also removed several areas of adhesion (excessive scar tissue) on the bowel. During this part of the procedure, Dr. Sears performed a small bowel resection. A nurse on the operating staff noticed through the visual on the camera that Dr. Sears had perforated a small area of the bowel with an instrument shortly before he performed the bowel resection of the same portion of the bowel. She commented on this to Dr. Jenkins, an associate of Dr. Sears. There were four other staff members in the operating room during surgery. When questioned by Dr. Jenkins, none recalled seeing Dr. Sears perforate the bowel. The notes of the doctor with regard to the surgery did not mention the perforation of the bowel. It did state however that the area of the bowel was resected due to a small bowel obstruction.

After surgery, Sue developed a serious infection involving fevers, a purulent yellow and white discharge from the incision, and on June 9, a foul-smelling green discharge. On this date, another member of Dr. Sears practice, Dr. Jenkins, was on call. Upon examining the nurse's findings, Dr. Jenkins returned Sue to surgery. Dr. Jenkins found a large amount of bowel that had leaked through perforations in the bowel and spread throughout the abdomen causing a massive infection. Dr. Jenkins resected a large area of the bowel and cleaned the abdomen as much as possible in a three-hour surgery.

Following surgery, Sue was placed in intensive care in critical condition for a period of three days. One day after being returned to a regular room, Sue developed pneumonia and once again was placed in intensive care. She was eventually discharged from the hospital on July 6. Two additional surgeries were required to correct the conditions caused by the infection and perforated bowel. Additionally, Sue was treated by a pulmonologist and received respiratory therapy for a period of six months due to conditions caused by the severe pneumonia she had developed while in the hospital.

At no time was Sue informed that a nurse claimed to have seen Dr. Sears perforate Sue's bowel. Further, Sue is unaware of the nurse's comment at all. Dr. Sears informed Sue that she was just one of those unfortunate people for whom those outside risks of complication occurred and that it is something that sometimes "just happens" in medicine. On August 1, 2004 Sue contacted another physician for consultation because of her ongoing problems. This physician, Dr. Tootau, stated his opinion that Sue was the victim of gross malpractice. Sue immediately contacted an attorney and along with the information above, brought the following information with her to the initial meeting:

Medical Bills (doctor, hospital, prescription, outpatient therapy)	$347,516
Lost Wages	$14,400

Pain & suffering

Disfigurement

Shortness of breath and lung pain causing inability to engage in even moderately strenuous sports or other physical activity

Predisposition to pancreatitis (three episodes in 2002; four episodes in 2003, all requiring hospitalization one to four days)

Inability to engage in normal marriage relationship resulting in divorce

Additionally, Sue claimed to have seen Dr. Sears in a local restaurant recently where she observed him order four alcoholic drinks in a period of less than 90 minutes. She also claims her brother Marty smelled alcohol on Dr. Sears breath when he came out of surgery to report Sue's condition to the family.

The attorney is familiar with Dr. Sears and is aware that he lost privileges at a different hospital two years prior to Sue's surgery as a result of staff smelling alcohol on his breath and an appearance of impairment. However, the attorney also knows that another member of his firm has seen Dr. Sears many times at Alcoholics Anonymous® meetings.

Assignments

Chapter 1. Assignment 1.

Consider the facts of the case and answer the following questions:
What evidence, if any, is presented to support the following causes of action:

a. Negligence
b. Negligence based upon res ipsa loquitur
c. Respondeat superior of the medical group of which Dr. Sears is a member
d. Battery
e. Strict liability
f. Breach of contract

Chapter 2. Assignment 1.

What is the possible relevance of a medical malpractice statute to this case?
What is the relevance of the professional licensure, certification and, hospital privileges at this and other hospitals of Dr. Sears in this case?

Chapter 3. Assignment 1.

Specify each type of injury that could be claimed in this case and could possibly obtain legal recovery. (Do not necessarily limit yourself to the information presented in the facts if it can be reasonably deduced from the knowledge obtained thusfar and warrant further investigation.)

Chapter 4. Assignment 1.

What procedures should have been in place to notify the risk management department of all aspects of the series of events involving Sue as they occurred?

Does Dr. Jenkins have any immunity from liability based on the Good Samaritan doctrine?

Chapter 5. Assignment 1.

Identify the information that would be necessary for the plaintiff to obtain with regard to the defendant's professional liability insurance.

Identify the information that would be necessary for the defendant to obtain with regard to the plaintiff's health insurance.

Chapter 6. Assignment 1.

What is the date that Sue's cause of action arose for purposes of statutes of limitation?

How would this date change, at all, if at the time of the initial surgery, Sue was 15 years and one day old?

Chapter 7. Assignment 1.

Prepare a list of questions for the in-depth interview of Sue by her own attorney's staff (don't forget to address the issue of possible comparative negligence).

Prepare a list of individuals to identify specifically by name who may have been employed by the hospital and have knowledge of this case.

Prepare a list of specific questions to ask the nurse (assuming she will grant an interview) who alleged to have witnessed Dr. Sears perforate Sue's bowel.

Prepare a list of documents to request from the hospital and Dr. Sears.

Chapter 8. Assignment 1.

Assume the risk management department was wholly unaware of the incident involving Sue until the request for medical records by Sue's attorney was flagged by the medical records department and forwarded to risk management.

Prepare a checklist investigation sheet of steps to take in a preliminary evaluation of the hospitalization as the risk management department assesses why the attorney would want the records and what possible hospital involvement there was, if any.

Chapter 9. Assignment 1.

Draft the following documents:

Complaint

Motion to Dismiss by defendant on the basis that Dr. Sears was improperly identified in the complaint as his actual legal name is Searsansurai.

Discovery Outline of Information sought by the plaintiff and the method of discovery best suited to obtain that information.

Discovery Outline of Information sought by the defendant and the method of discovery best suited to obtain that information.

Chapter 10. Assignment 1.

Prepare a list of questions to ask the jury on voir dire by each party.

Prepare a list of items that should be brought up in the opening statement. For each item, prepare a nonargumentive statement to present that item of information.

Prepare an outline of each element necessary for the prima facie case and what evidence should be presented to establish that element.

Prepare an outline of each element necessary to rebut the prima facie case and what evidence should be presented to establish that element.

GLOSSARY

A

alternative health care methods of providing care, treatment, and services for matters related to personal health and methods that fall outside the traditional medical forms of treatment.

arbitration a type of alternative dispute resolution where an agreed upon neutral party or parties helps make decision and decision is binding.

B

board certified a physician who successfully completes an additional and voluntary certification program to establish a high degree of competence in a particular area of speciality.

breach of contract when a party to an otherwise enforceable contract allegedly fails to provide the consideration in accordance with the agreed upon terms.

C

claims made policy insurance which covers all claims made within a given period of time.

closing argument the stage of trial when each of the parties summarizes the evidence presented and attempts to persuade the trier of fact as to the verdict they feel the evidence best supports.

complaint the initial pleading which serves to formally commence litigation.

confidentiality the obligation to keep private that information disclosed as the result of a professional relationship.

continuing medical education (CME) education designed for the licensed health care professional to keep abreast of developments and changes in the delivery of health care, treatment, and services.

contract an agreement by two or more people to do, or not do, something for a legal purpose that they are not otherwise obligated to do. Necessary elements to create a contract include an offer, acceptance, and legal consideration (promise of performance) of value by each party.

criminal conduct those actions which are considered injurious to the public good and therefore punishable by criminal prosecution and penalities such as fines, imprisonment, community service. These may be in addition to personal civil actions by the injured party.

D

deep pocket the theory that legal actions be brought against the party who can be held legally responsible and who has the greatest ability to satisfy a monetary judgment.

direct question questions in which the answer is not implied and the interviewee is free to form his or her own answer.

discovery the pretrial process for court-supervised exchange of evidence between parties to suit.

discovery rule the applicable statute of limitations begins to run from the date of the injury or the date when the injured party should have reasonably discovered the injury was due to malfeasance.

E

ethics a standard of conduct which is expected by the majority based on accepted moral standards and honest social standards.

expert opinion one who, through acquired knowledge, education or experience, has gained knowledge of a particular subject so that he or she could present an informed opinion that would not be possible without that specific adequate knowledge, education, or experience.

F

fraudulent concealment affirmative steps to conceal information or perpetrate a deception to prevent another from awareness of possible injury and/or legal rights.

G

Good Samaritan rule the legal theory that one should not be held accountable for malfeasance when delivering voluntary assistance in an emergency situation.

H

HIPAA Health Insurance Portability and Accountability Act.

I

informed consent when one agrees to medical care, treatment or services after receiving information regarding all significant associated risks.

intentional tort an act or omission which one knows or should know is substantially certain to produce injury to another.

investigation collection of information and evidence available to a party without the assistance or cooperation of the opposing party.

J

JCAHO Joint Commission on Accreditation of Health Organizations

L

leading question a question in which the answer is implied (e.g., yes/no).

limitation of actions statutorily controlled period of time from the date of the occurrence/injury in which legal action may be instituted.

locality rule legal theory that a professional should be held to a standard of care consistent with that practiced by other like professionals in a similarly situated community.

M

managed care insurance policy of insurance in which the insurer has the right to determine, to a certain extent, the medical provider and care received by the insured patient.

mediation technique for a professionally trained and agreed upon mediator to help parties work out a mutually agreeable resolution.

mental competence one who is considered legally able to appreciate the quality and effects of his or her actions.

minority one who has not reached the legal age of emancipation and as a result is considered unable to protect his or her own legal rights.

N

negligence commission or omission of an act which a person exercising ordinary care would or would not do under similar circumstances, which causes compensable injury to one who should have been forseeably affected by the act or omission.

O

occurrence policy insurance which provides coverage for all occurrences giving rise to a legal claim within a given period of time.

opening statement The initial stage of trial in which the parties outline the evidence they intend to present and the conclusion they seek.

P

petition see complaint.

prima facie case "On Its Face"—the minimum required amount of proof /evidence to prevail in litigation.

privilege legally protected confidentiality of specific types of communications (e.g., doctor-patient). The privilege belongs to the individual who would be at risk for injury through disclosure.

professional liability insurance insurance obtained by a licensed professional against potential claims of professional malfeasance.

R

res ipsa loquitur "the thing speaks for itself." The rule used in cases where there is insufficient evidence of proximate cause, but it can be established that 1) the occurrence was one that would not ordinarily occur in the absence of negligence, 2) the plaintiff was not responsible for contributory negligence, and 3) the injury producing instrument was within the exclusive control of the defendant.

residency/internship period of specialized training following completion of medical degree program of study.

respondeat superior theory that an employer/principal may be liable for the actions of an employee/agent committed while acting within the scope of employment.

risk management process by which steps are taken to monitor, prevent, and manage potential matters at risk for litigation.

S

specialist one who holds him/herself out as having advanced specialized knowledge in a particular subject area.

strict liability legal theory principle that one who benefits from an activity that is ultrahazardous to others, and from which no protection is available in the event the activity escapes control, may be liable for any resulting property damage or physical injuries.

T

tail coverage policy of insurance obtained to address claims arising from a prior period of insurance which is no longer in effect.

V

voir dire stage of trial in which potential jurors are examined and a final jury is selected.

INDEX

A

abandonment, 26, 28, 67–70
Acquired Immune Deficiency Syndrome (AIDS), personal information and, 138–140
Advocat, Inc. v. Sauer, 114–120
Aetna Health Inc. v. Davila, 198–206
affirmative defense, 300–301
AIDS. *See* Acquired Immune Deficiency Syndrome
alternative care, cases involving, 120–122
Alternative Dispute Resolution, 318–319
Americans with Disabilities Act, 60
answer, make an, 299, 301
appeals process, 339
appearance of witness, 262
appellate briefs, 339
appellate procedure, 339
appropriation, 27
arbitration, 318–320
assault, 27, 29
assumption of risk, 301
audit, 61

B

background check, 70
Barker v. St. Barnabas Hospital, 111–112
battery, 27, 29–30
bench trial, 321
bill. *See* medical bill
Bing v. Thunig, 101–105
board-certified, 53, 58
Bowman v. Woods, 46
breach of confidentiality, 27, 30
breach of contract, 37, 270
breach of duty, 7
burden of proof, 333, 334, 337–338

Burks v. St. Joseph's Hospital, 189–197
businessowner's liability insurance, 186
but-for test, 5, 7

C

cap, 57
care
 duty of, 4
 injuries from, 63
 standard of, 4, 51
case in chief, 334–337
cases
 against health care facilities, 99–100
  clinics offering outpatient services, 111–113
  hospitals, 100–110
  long-term care facilities, 113–120
 against physicians, 84–93
 involving independent providers, 95–99
 involving non-physician medical professionals, 93–95
 involving non-traditional and alternative care, 120–122
 resulting from defective products/equipment, 122–130
causes of action, 294
CDC. *See* Center for Disease Control
Center for Disease Control (CDC), 67, 133
certification of providers and facilities, 59–61, 154
challenge for cause, 321–322
challenges
 for cause, 321–322
 peremptory, 321–322
Charell v. Gonzalez, 121–122
charitable immunity, 100–106
charitable organizations, 100–106
Chin, Estate of, v. St. Barnabas Medical Center, 123–130

chiropractors
 cases involving, 95–99
 malpractice statutes and, 54
civil liability for professional malfeasance, history of
 contractual liability, 37–38
 intentional torts, 25–28
  abandonment, 28
  assault, 29
  battery, 29–30
  miscellaneous torts, 30–31
  strict liability, 32–37
 law of negligence, development of, 2
  negligence as concept, 3
  negligence, elements of, 3–8
claim, investigation by plaintiff
 establish cause of injury, 248–253
 evaluate viability of claim, 269–271
 identify professional persons connected to injury, 253–256
 interview potential witnesses, 256–262
 obtain necessary evidence, 263–268
claim, pretrial stages of
 arbitration, mediation, settlement considerations, 318–320
 discovery process primary objective, 302–304
  depositions, 309–311
  interrogatories, 304–307
  motion for summary judgment, 317–318
  physical evidence examinations and inspections, 311–317
  request for production, 307–308
 pleadings and pretrial motions, 294–301
 statutory considerations, 291–293
 suit, commencement of, 293
claims, role of insurance in
 patient insurance, 187–206
 professional liability insurance, 177–187

349

claim, viability of, 269
   act of malfeasance, 269–270
   by defendant, 285–290
   comparative negligence of plaintiff, 271
   legislation affecting recovery, 270
claims made policy, 179
client interview checklist, 250
clinics offering outpatient services, cases against, 111–113
closed questions, 259
closing arguments, 337–338
"coached" witness, 256
Commonwealth v. Thompson, 40, 41–45
communicate, ability of witness to, 262
comparative negligence of plaintiff, 271
compensatory damage, 47
complaint, 293, 294–296
comprehensive assignment, 342
   by chapter, 343–345
   facts, 342–343
confidentiality, 133, 138–151
constructive knowledge, 40, 47
continuing medical education, 154
contract, breach of, 270
contracts, 37
contractual liability, 37–38
correspondence (nonmedical documents), 282
court records, 339
covered entity, 66
credibility of witness, 262
criminal conduct, 79–83
crisis, malpractice, 186
cross-examination, 336

D

damage, 8
deep pocket, 279
defamation, 30
defendant, 255
   number named, 279
   resources of, 279
defendant, investigation of claim
   documentary evidence, 280–283
   establish cause of injury, 273–274
   evaluate viability of claim, 285–290
   expert opinions, 285
   identify and interview persons connected to injury, 274–280
   medical devices and equipment, 283–284
   photographic and tangible evidence, 284–285
defense and presentation of evidence, 337
deliberate conduct, 106–109
deliberation, 337–338
Dempsey v. Kennedy, 326–333
dentists
   cases involving, 95–99
   malpractice statutes and, 54
depositions, 309–311
direct questions, 259, 336
disclosure of information
   confidentiality and patient privilege, 138–151
   ethical duties, 64–67
   informed consent, 133–138
disclosure of injury
   discovery rule, 210–230
   injury to minors and legally incompetent, 230–245
disclosure of unexpected outcomes, 221
discovery process
   in claim by plaintiff, 249
   primary objective, 302–304
     depositions, 309–311
     interrogatories, 304–307
     motion for summary judgment, 317–318
     physical evidence examinations and inspections, 311–317
     request for production, 307–308
discovery rule, 210–230
discovery schedule, 304
documentary evidence, 280–283, 307, 335–337
documentation, risk management issues, 151–153
documents
   medical devices/equipment, 264
   nonmedical, 282
Doe v. Chand, 143–151
duty of care, 3

E

education, continuing, 59
education, proof of, 59
emergency medical personnel, 54
emergency situation, 155–163
EOB. *See* Explanation of Benefits
equipment
   cases resulting from defective, 122–130
   devices documents, 264, 283–284
ethics, 64
ethical duties, violation of, 64–78
evidence
   court-ordered delivery of, 11
   documentary, 280–283, 307, 335–337
   material, 335
   obtain necessary, 263–268
   photographic and tangible, 264, 284–285, 335–337
   physical — examinations and inspections, 311–317
   presentation of
     case in chief, 334–337
     defense, 337
   publicly available, 263
   relevant, 335
   testimonial, 335–337
evidentiary rules of relevance and materiality, 335
expert opinions, 285, 302–303, 336–337
Explanation of Benefits (EOB), 264, 282

F

facility medical records, 263
facility safety, risk management issues, 164–175
false light, 27, 31
fellowships, 53
Fox v. Ethicon Endo-Surgical, Inc., 212–221
fraudulent concealment, 221

G

Gates v. Fleischer, 52
Gonzalez v. Paradise Valley Hospital, 106–109
good faith, 180
Good Samaritan rule
   affirmative defense, 300
   emergency medical personnel and, 54
   risk management issues, 155–163
Graham v. Gautier, 47

Green v. Sacks, 223–229
gross negligence, 54

H

H&P. *See* History & Physical
health care facilities, cases against, 99–100
   clinics offering outpatient services, 111–113
   hospitals, 100–110
   long-term care facilities, 113–120
health care facility
   licensure of, 59–61
   risk management issues, 164–175
health care industry, risk management issues
   confidentiality and patient privilege, 138–151
   documentation, 151–153
   facility safety, 164–175
   Good Samaritan doctrine, 155–163
   informed consent, 133–138
   provider qualifications and compliance with standards, 153–155
   — as part of delivery of health care, 132–133
health care provider, definition of, 54
health care provider, licensure of, 59–61
health care providers, mass exodus of, 186
Health Insurance Portability and Accountability Act (HIPAA), 65–67, 139–140
Hegarty, Estate of, v. Beauchaine, 12–23
HIPAA. *See* Health Insurance Portability and Accountability Act
History & Physical (H&P), 264
HIV, personal information and, 138–140
home health care professional, 54
homeopathic practitioner, 46
hospitals, cases against, 100–110
hung jury, 338

I

immunity, 155–163. *See also* charitable immunity
impeach the witness, 336
inappropriate contact, 70–78
incident report, 264, 277
incompetent (legally), injury to, 230–245

independent contractors, 256
informed consent
   risk management issues, 133–138
   sample document, 136–137
injury, disclosure of. *See* disclosure of injury
injury, establish cause of
   defendant, 273–274
   plaintiff, 248–253
injury from
   care/treatment/services, 63
   professional misconduct, 79–83
   violation of ethical duties, 64–78
injury, identify professional persons connected to, 253–256
injury, medical/occupational evaluations of, 263
injury to minors and legally incompetent, 230–245
instructions to jury, 338
insurance. *See* patient insurance; professional liability insurance
insurance documents, 282
insurance, role in medical malpractice claims
   patient insurance, 187–206
   professional liability insurance, 177–187
insurance company
   audits by, 61
   medical malpractice claims and, 177–207
intentional torts, 25–28
   abandonment, 28
   assault, 29
   battery, 29–30
   miscellaneous torts, 30–31
   strict liability, 32–37
internship, 53
interrogatories, 304–307
interview
   client checklist, 250
   persons connected to injury, 274–280
   questionnaire, 249, 260
   types of questions, 259
   witness, 255, 256–262
investigation checklist, preliminary, 274
investigation process of claim by defendant
   documentary evidence, 280–283
   establish cause of injury, 273–274
   evaluate viability of claim, 285–290
   expert opinions, 285

   identify and interview persons connected to injury, 274–280
   medical devices and equipment, 283–284
   photographic and tangible evidence, 284–285
investigation process of claim by plaintiff
   establish cause of injury, 248–253
   evaluate viability of claim, 269–271
   identify professional persons connected to injury, 253–256
   interview potential witnesses, 256–262
   obtain necessary evidence, 263–268
investigative data collection, 254

J

JCAHO. *See* Joint Commission on Accreditation of Healthcare Organizations
Johnson Foundation, Robert Wood, 2
Joint Commission on Accreditation of Healthcare Organizations (JCAHO), 99–100, 133, 221, 282
jury
   instructions to, 338
   misconduct, 338
   polled, 338
   selecting a, 321–333
   sequestered, 338

L

laboratory report, 264
leading questions, 259, 336
legal counsel, personal, 180
legally incompetent, injury to, 230–245
legislation affecting recovery, 270
legislative movement in medical malpractice, 55–58
Lewis v. Capalbo, 68–70
licensure of providers and facilities, 46–47, 59–61, 154
limitation of action, 246, 301
limitations on monetary recovery, 57, 106
litigation. *See* medical malpractice law and litigation
litigation explosion, 55
locality rule, 52–53
long-term care facilities, cases against, 113–120

M

malfeasance, act of, 269–270
malfeasance, history of civil liability for
  contractual liability, 37–38
  intentional torts, 25–28
    abandonment, 28
    assault, 29
    battery, 29–30
    miscellaneous torts, 30–31
    strict liability, 32–37
  law of negligence, development of, 2
    negligence as concept, 3
    negligence, elements of, 3–8
  res ipsa loquitur, use of, 9–11
  respondeat superior in cases of negligence, 11–25
malpractice insurance, 56
managed care, 197–206
material evidence, 335
McCarty v. Jaenicke, 322–325
mediation, 318–320
medical bill, 263, 282
medical devices documents, 264, 283–284
medical legal review panel, 319
medical malpractice civil law, 46
medical malpractice law, development of
  early cases, 40–51
  legislative movement, 55–58
  licensure and certification of providers and facilities, 59–61
  refinement of theories and principles, 51–55
medical malpractice law and litigation
  cases against health care facilities, 99–100
    clinics offering outpatient services, 111–113
    hospitals, 100–110
    long-term care facilities, 113–120
  cases against physicians, 84–93
  cases involving independent providers, 95–99
  cases involving non-physician medical professionals, 93–95
  cases involving non-traditional and alternative care, 120–122
  cases resulting from defective products/equipment, 122–130
  cost of, 248
  injuries from care/treatment/services, 63
  injuries from professional misconduct, 79–83
  injuries from violation of ethical duties, 64–78
Medical Mutual Liability Insurance Society of Maryland V. Azzato, 79–83
medical/occupational evaluations of injury or condition, 263
medical records, 263
  obtaining, 281
  sample, 264
Medicaid, 134
Medicare, 60, 134, 189
mental competence, 234
Methodist Hospital of Indiana, Inc. v. Rioux, 166–167
minority, patient's, 231
minors, injury to, 230–245
misappropriation, 31
misconduct. *See* professional misconduct
Monahan v. Devinny, 45–46
monetary recovery, limitations on, 57
moral obligation, 222
Motion for a Bill of Particulars, 299–300
Motion for a Directed Verdict, 335, 337
Motion for a New Trial, 338
Motion for Examination, 312, 314–315
Motion for Judgment Notwithstanding, 338–339
Motion for Sanctions, 304
Motion for Summary Judgment, 315, 317–318
Motion in Limine, 326
Motion to Admit Genuineness, 316–317
Motion to Compel, 304
Motion to Demurrer, 298
Motion to Dismiss, 298–300, 326
Motion to Exclude, 326
Motion to Inspect, 312–313
Motion to Limit, 326
Motion to Make More Definite and Certain, 299–300
Motion to Produce, 307–308
Motion to Quash, 297–298

N

negligence, 106–109
  comparative — of plaintiff, 271
  law of, 2
  negligence as concept, 3
  negligence, elements of, 3–8
Non Obstante Verdicto, 338–339
noneconomic damages, 57
non-physician medical professionals
  cases involving, 93–95
  cases involving independent —, 95–99
non-traditional care, cases involving, 120–122
Notice of Privacy Practices, 66
nurses, 54

O

objective observation, 262
Occupational Safety and Health Administration (OSHA), 133
occurrence policy, 178–179
open-ended questions, 259, 336
opening statements, 333–334
operative note, 264
optometrists, cases involving, 95–99
oral arguments, 339
OSHA. *See* Occupational Safety and Health Administration
outpatient services, cases against, 111–113

P

pain and suffering conditions
  cases involving long-term care facilities, 114
  limited damages on, 57
Parker v. Mercy General Health Partners, 5–6
pathology report, 264
patient abandonment. *See* abandonment
patient confidentiality, 64–67
patient education materials, 134
patient information, disclosure of, 64–67
patient insurance, 187–206
patient privilege, 138–151
patient records, proper documentation of, 151–153, 231
Patient Self Determination Act, 134
Patient's Bill of Rights, 113
patient's minority, 231
peer review, 154–155

peremptory challenge, 321–322
petit juries, 322
petition, 293
pharmacists
   cases involving, 95–99
   malpractice statutes and, 54
PHI. *See* private health information
photographic evidence, 264, 284–285
physical evidence examinations and inspections, 311–317
physicians, cases against, 84–93
plaintiff, comparative negligence of, 271
plaintiff, investigation of claim
   establish cause of injury, 248–253
   evaluate viability of claim, 269–271
   identify professional persons connected to injury, 253–256
   interview potential witnesses, 256–262
   obtain necessary evidence, 263–263
pleadings, 294–301
podiatrists, 54
poll the jury, 338
post-trial proceedings, 338–340
pre-existing conditions and affirmative defense, 300–301
premises liability insurance, 186
pretrial motions, 294–301
pretrial stages of claim
   arbitration, mediation, settlement considerations, 318–320
   discovery process primary objective, 302–304
      depositions, 309–311
      interrogatories, 304–307
      motion for summary judgment, 317–318
      physical evidence examinations and inspections, 311–317
      request for production, 307–308
   pleadings and pretrial motions, 294–301
   statutory considerations, 291–293
   suit, commencement of, 293
prima facie, 302–304, 334–337
principles, refinement of, 51–55
privacy issues, 64–67
privacy policy, 138–142
   sample, 140–142
private company audits, 61
private health information (PHI), 65–66

proactive risk management approach, 153–155, 175
products, cases resulting from defective. *See* products liability claims
products liability claims, 122–130
professional liability insurance, 177–187
   claims made policy, 179
   occurrence policy, 178–179
   tail coverage, 179
professional misconduct, injuries from, 79–83
professional persons connected to injury, 253–256, 274–280
provider qualifications and compliance with standards, 153–155
proximate cause, 4–9
psychologists, cases involving, 95–99
public records, 263
public trust, standards for, 40
publicly available evidence, 263
punitive damages, 58

Q

questionnaire, interview, 249, 260
questions
   closed, 259
   direct, 259, 336
   leading, 259, 336
   open-ended, 259, 336

R

radiological report, 264
Raley v. Wagner, 231–234
recovery for damages, 57
recovery, legislation affecting, 270
relevant evidence, 335
report (laboratory/pathology/radiological), 264
Request for Inspection, 311–312
Request for Production (of Documents), 307–308
Request to Admit Genuineness, 315
res ipsa loquitur, use of, 5, 9–11
residency, 53
respondeat superior, 71
   in cases of negligence, 11–25
   legal theory of, 255

response, make a, 299, 301
review boards, 154–155
risk management issues
   confidentiality and patient privilege, 138–151
   documentation, 151–153
   facility safety, 164–175
   Good Samaritan doctrine, 155–163
   informed consent, 133–138
   provider qualifications and compliance with standards, 153–155
   — as part of delivery of health care, 132–133
risk management preliminary investigation checklist, 275
R.W. v. Schrein, 72–78

S

Saucedo v. Winger, 180–185
sequester, 338
settlement considerations, 318–320, 339
sexual misconduct, 70–78
shotgun approach, 279
Sills v. Oakland General Hospital, 286–289
Smothers v. Hanks, 3, 47–51
Social Security Disability benefits, 235
sovereign immunity, 301
specialist, 84
standard of care
   cases against
      health care facilities, 99
      independent non-physician provider, 96
      physicians, 84–94
   compliance with —, 153–155
   negligence, fundamental element of, 4
statute of limitations, 209, 211
Statutes of Repose, 211
statutory considerations, 291–293
statutory language, 292–293
statutory limits, 179
statutory privilege, 221
Storm v. Legion Insurance Company, 235–244
strict liability, 32–37
subordinate medical personnel, 92–93
substantial factor analysis, 7
suit, commencement of, 293

summons, 296
survey, 61

T

tail coverage, 179
tangible evidence, 264, 284–285, 335–337
Tempchin v. Sampson, 97–99
testimonial evidence, 335–337
theories, refinement of, 51–55
tolling, 211
tort law, 209
training, proof of, 59
treatment
    injuries from, 63
    method of, 40
trial
    chart of stages, 340
    closing, deliberation, verdict, 337–338
    opening statements, 333–334
    post-trial proceedings, 338–340
    presentation of evidence
        case in chief, 334–337
        defense, 337
    selecting a jury, 321–333

V

Velazquez v. Jiminez, 155–162
verdict, 337–338
Veterans Administration, 66
voir dire, 321

W

Wilkinson v. Duff, 32, 33–37
willful misconduct, 54

Winona Memorial Foundation of Indianapolis v. Lomax, 167–175
witness
    ability to communicate, 262
    appearance, 262
    coaching, 256
    credibility, 262
    impeach a, 336
    interview potential, 255, 256–262
    questioning, types of, 336
        direct, 336
        indirect method, 336

Z

Zaverl v. Hanley, 84–92